CW01530156

BRITISH
BY-ELECTIONS

BRITISH
BY-ELECTIONS
1769–2025

THE 88 BY-ELECTION CAMPAIGNS
THAT SHAPED OUR POLITICS

IAIN DALE

Biteback Publishing

First published in Great Britain in 2025 by
Biteback Publishing Ltd, London
Selection and editorial apparatus copyright © Iain Dale 2025
Copyright in the individual essays resides with the named authors

Iain Dale has asserted his right under the Copyright, Designs and Patents Act 1988
to be identified as the editor of this work.

All rights reserved. No part of this publication may be reproduced, stored in a retrieval system or
transmitted, in any form or by any means, without the publisher's prior permission in writing.

This book is sold subject to the condition that it shall not, by way of trade or otherwise, be lent,
resold, hired out or otherwise circulated without the publisher's prior consent in any form of
binding or cover other than that in which it is published and without a similar condition,
including this condition, being imposed on the subsequent purchaser.

Every reasonable effort has been made to trace copyright holders of material reproduced in this book,
but if any have been inadvertently overlooked the publisher would be glad to hear from them.

ISBN 978-1-78590-978-8

10 9 8 7 6 5 4 3 2 1

A CIP catalogue record for this book is available from the British Library.

Set in Adobe Garamond Pro

Printed and bound in Great Britain by
CPI Group (UK) Ltd, Croydon CR0 4YY

FSC
www.fsc.org
MIX
Paper | Supporting
responsible forestry
FSC® C013604

In memory of my old friend and sparring partner Alex Salmond

'There is not a safe Tory seat in the country.'
– Victorious Liberal candidate Eric Lubbock after the
Orpington by-election in March 1962

'The straight choice.'
– Liberal campaign slogan used against gay Labour candidate
Peter Tatchell in the 1983 Bermondsey by-election

'It's not the voting that's democracy; it's the counting.'
– Tom Stoppard

*'A politician thinks of the next election. A statesman,
of the next generation.'*
– James Freeman Clarke

*'Elections belong to the people. It's their decision. If they decide to turn
their back on the fire and burn their behinds, then they
will just have to sit on their blisters.'*
– Abraham Lincoln

*'One of the penalties for refusing to participate in politics is that
you end up being governed by your inferiors.'*
– Plato

CONTENTS

PREFACE

IAIN DALE

Parliamentary by-elections are far from a unique British institution, yet there is something unique about the way we conduct them in this country. They often seem to take on a far greater political significance than, in retrospect, they really have. At the time, they can appear to break the mould of British politics, signify the seemingly terminal decline of a particular political party or signal the end of a premiership. Some by-elections take on iconic status and are remembered several decades after they take place. Others quickly disappear into the depths of our memories, rarely to be thought about ever again.

The one thing they all have in common is they each tell a story. Whether they occur because of the death of the sitting Member of Parliament, the corruption of an MP or simply the fact that the MP has had enough, there's always a human tale to tell.

By-elections often attract celebrity candidates and therefore the media spotlight falls on a constituency that has maybe never hit the headlines before.

There's rarely a dull by-election, as these pages will testify to.

When I published *British General Election Campaigns 1830–2019*, a book on famous by-elections seemed the obvious follow-up. But were there really enough to warrant it? I sat down to compile a list off the top of my head and got to fifty without any trouble at all. In the end, after consulting experts and the general reader through social media, I came up with a list of 130, which I then had to whittle down. When I announced the list of seventy-five, there were howls of outrage that I hadn't included x or y by-election, which is why the number I eventually settled on was a rather awkward eighty-eight. I suppose I could have just picked by-elections from the twentieth and twenty-first centuries, but then we would have missed out the fascinating tales from by-elections going back to the eighteenth century. So here we are. Eighty-eight by-elections, and eighty-eight unique stories of political tragedy, triumph, success and failure.

By-elections have taken place for centuries, but few took on great significance until the Great Reform Act of 1832, which abolished rotten boroughs and constituencies which had only a dozen voters. Since then, the electoral franchise has grown, in stages, to include every adult over the age of eighteen, with a further extension to sixteen- and seventeen-year-olds under discussion.

Some by-elections are more interesting than others. If a challenger party is doing well in the polls, for almost whatever reason, the media will be far more interested than if it is just a contest between the established parties. Sometimes parties decide not to field a candidate in a particular by-election and urge their supporters to vote for another one. Occasionally, as in Clacton in 2014, an MP will cross the floor and join another party and seek the endorsement of their voters in a by-election.

In wartime, it is usual for by-elections to be uncontested, so if an MP dies, the party he or she belongs to stands a new candidate unopposed. This, of course, doesn't prevent minor parties from standing. The same thing can, but doesn't always, happen after a terror attack. In 1990, after Ian Gow was murdered by an IRA car bomb, the Liberal Democrats overturned a massive majority to win the seat of Eastbourne. Yet when Jo Cox and Sir David Amess were murdered, the main parties did not contest the ensuing by-election, although in each there was a plethora of minor candidates.

Up until 1926, by-elections were held more frequently because all ministers, upon being appointed to office, had to get the endorsement of their electorates.

You will find some fascinating facts in the statistics section. The swing from one party to another is perhaps the most important statistic to emerge from any by-election. Not once has there ever been a swing of more than 50 per cent. Only four times since 1945 has there been a swing of more than 40 per cent. In 2024, George Galloway won Rochdale from Labour for the Workers Party with a swing of 41.8

per cent. In 1973, sitting Labour MP Dick Taverne resigned his Lincoln seat and then won it back under the Democratic Labour banner with a 43 per cent swing. The second highest swing occurred in 2014 in Clacton when, as mentioned, Douglas Carswell defected from the Conservatives to UKIP and retained it with a 44.1 per cent swing. The biggest by-election swing of all time occurred in perhaps one of the most notorious by-elections ever, in Bermondsey in 1983, when the Liberals, in the shape of Simon Hughes, took the seat from Labour with a swing of 44.2 per cent.

It is, of course, the norm for a governing party to suffer in by-elections. Invariably, they will be suffering mid-term popularity blues. In only ten by-elections since the Second World War has there been a swing in favour of the governing party, the largest being in Hartlepool in 2019 when there was a 16 per cent swing from Labour to Conservative.

There is a lot of talk about safe seats and so-called 'impregnable majorities'. Nowadays, there is no such thing. If you look at the list of the biggest majorities overturned in a by-election since 1945, the top three have occurred in the past ten years. In 2016, Lib Dem Sarah Olney overturned the Conservative Zac Goldsmith's 23,015 majority by 1,672 votes. She lost the seat at the 2017 general election, then won it back in 2019. The second biggest majority to fall to the Lib Dems was in Tiverton & Honiton. Richard Foord vanquished a Tory majority of 24,230 and won with a majority of 6,144. But the biggest overall majority to be eliminated was 24,664 – achieved by Nadine Dorries in Mid Bedfordshire in the 2019 general election. She resigned her seat in solidarity with Boris Johnson and it was lost to Labour's Alistair Strathern in the by-election, where he triumphed with a majority of 1,192.

Small majorities in by-elections are far from the norm. Only Alan Beith, in Berwick-upon-Tweed in 1973 for the Liberals, and Tory Fred Silvester in Walthamstow West in 1967 have won with double-figure majorities – fifty-seven and sixty-two, respectively. The smallest majority was achieved by Reform UK's Sarah Pochin in Runcorn on 1 May 2025. In addition, only forty-four by-elections since 1945 have resulted in a three-figure majority – i.e. less than 1,000.

Turnout in by-elections is another subject which obsesses electoral geeks. Normally, turnout is far lower than in general elections, although there are exceptions to this. The biggest came in 1935, when Malcolm MacDonald retained Ross & Cromarty for National Labour with a 14 per cent swing. On reflection, this by-election should have been included in this book. It was also notable for Randolph Churchill coming within a whisker of losing his deposit. The second biggest increase in turnout came in Torrington in 1958 when the Liberals gained their first seat in a by-election since 1929. Mark Bonham Carter prevailed with a tiny majority of 219. Turnout increased by 11.4 per cent to 80.6 per cent.

Low turnouts occur when the voters don't see the need for a by-election. Manchester Central gets the medal for the lowest turnout in a by-election, when only 18.2 per cent of the voters could be bothered to go to the ballot box in 2012. Since 1945, there have been seventeen by-elections with a turnout of under 30 per cent. Interestingly, of these seventeen, twelve have taken place since 2000.

Of course, by-elections represent a brilliant opportunity for fringe candidates or independents to show their wares. This means that there are usually more candidates in by-elections than in general elections. Most of them will not retain their deposits, but they don't care. The most candidates to stand in a by-election was twenty-six, in 2008 at the Haltemprice & Howden by-election, which David Davis had caused by resigning his seat over the issue of civil liberties. In second place was Newbury in 1993, where nineteen candidates stood. David Rendel toppled the Conservatives.

Unless you are a serial candidate like William (Bill) Boaks or Screaming Lord Sutch from the Official Monster Raving Loony Party, there are very few people who contest more than one by-election. Among well-known politicians, Tony Benn holds the record for most fought – since 1945 – with four, in Bristol South East in 1950, 1961 and 1963 and Chesterfield in 1984. Roy Jenkins and Betty Boothroyd each fought three by-elections. Prior to that, Winston Churchill had fought five by-elections – Oldham in 1899, Manchester North West in 1908, Dundee in 1908, Dundee in 1917 and Westminster Abbey in 1924. The former and latter contests both feature in this book. Arthur Henderson not only fought five by-elections in Barnard Castle, Widnes, Newcastle upon Tyne East, Burnley and Clay Cross – he was victorious in all of them.

Bill Boaks fought nineteen by-elections in various guises, most commonly railing against the Common Market. Of the nineteen, Beaconsfield in 1982, which also saw Tony Blair fighting as the Labour candidate, scored his highest vote – all of ninety-nine! He was a mere amateur compared to Screaming Lord Sutch, who fought thirty-four by-elections between 1963 and 1997. He achieved his best result in Rotherham in 1994, gaining 1,114 votes in the contest won by Labour's Denis MacShane, who himself was to cause a by-election in 2012. This was the ninth by-election in Rotherham in 120 years. Sutch's successor as the leader of the Official Monster Raving Loony Party, Alan 'Howling Laud' Hope, has so far fought twenty-one by-elections.

Fighting a by-election always used to be a good way for defeated MPs to find their way back into Parliament. However, nowadays, this happens rather less frequently. In the twenty-first century, it has only been achieved on three occasions, once by the DUP MP William McCrea and twice by George Galloway. Over the same period, a total of nine ex-MPs stood in by-elections but failed to be elected.

Since 1945, only six by-election victors have served fewer than 100 days in Parliament before defeat in a general election or death. They are Bobby Sands (Fermanagh & South Tyrone, 1981 – twenty-five), Michael Carr (Bootle, 1990 – fifty-seven), Oswald O'Brien (Darlington, 1983 – seventy-seven), George Galloway (Rochdale, 2024 – ninety-one), Margo MacDonald (Govan, 1973 – ninety-two), Jane Dodds (Brecon & Radnorshire, 2019 – ninety-nine).

In 2023, there was a lot of comment on the age of the winner of the 2023 Selby & Ainsty by-election, Keir Mather. He was a mere twenty-five years old, although looked younger. However, the youngest ever by-election winner was Esmond Harmsworth, who won the Isle of Thanet in 1919 at the age of twenty-one years and 170 days. The youngest ever woman was Bernadette Devlin, who won Mid Ulster in 1969 at the age of twenty-one years and 359 days. The oldest by-election winner was the Conservative John Benbow, who won Dudley in 1844 at the age of seventy-five or seventy-six.

The first woman to be elected in a by-election was Nancy Astor, who succeeded her husband at the 1919 Plymouth Sutton contest. She became the first woman to take her seat in the House of Commons.

The first woman to actually gain a seat in a by-election was Susan Lawrence, who won the East Ham North by-election in 1926, having previously sat for the same seat between 1923 and 1924.

The first ethnic minority candidate to be elected in a by-election was Ashok Kumar, who succeeded Tory MP Richard Holt in the 1991 Langbaurgh by-election. It wasn't until 2007 that all three major parties fielded ethnic minority candidates in a by-election, in Ealing Southall.

There have only been four full calendar years in history without a single by-election – 1992, 1998, 2010 and 2020. The longest period since the Second World War with no by-election was 645 days, between 1 August 2019 and 6 May 2021.

General elections and by-elections are usually held on a Thursday. The last by-election not held on a Thursday was the Hamilton contest in 1978. Why? Because that evening, Scotland's opening World Cup match was taking place, so the by-election was held on the Wednesday.

Due to an administrative error, the 1973 Manchester Exchange by-election was held on Wednesday 27 June 1973. In 1965, the Saffron Walden by-election, held to elect a successor to R. A. Butler, was held on Tuesday 23 March, and on the following day, David Steel was elected at the Roxburgh, Selkirk & Peebles contest. Up until the mid-1960s, it was common to hold by-elections on any day of the week (other than Sunday).

On rare occasions, a scheduled by-election may be overtaken by the calling of a general election and the dissolution of Parliament. In these cases, the by-election is cancelled, or in official language, countermanded. This has only happened three times since the First World War – Warwick & Leamington in 1923, London University in 1924 and Manchester Gorton in 2017.

There are many causes of a by-election, the most common being the death of the sitting MP. But since 1918, there have been six by-elections due to the MP being assassinated.

In 1922, Conservative MP Sir Henry Wilson was shot dead outside his home by the IRA. In November 1981, the Rev. Robert Bradford was shot by the IRA. Three years later, Sir Anthony Berry was killed in the IRA Brighton Bomb attack. In 1990, Conservative MP Ian Gow was killed at his home by an IRA car bomb. In 2016, Labour

MP Jo Cox was killed by a white nationalist, and in 2022, Sir David Amess was stabbed to death at his constituency surgery. The only one of those where the incumbent party did not win the ensuing by-election was in Eastbourne in 1990, when the Liberal Democrats beat the Conservatives.

Since 1932, there have been ten by-elections caused by the MP's suicide. The last was Gordon McMaster, the MP for Paisley, in July 1997.

Since 1933, twenty-three MPs have caused by-elections due to accidental death, many of them in car crashes.

In 2015, Parliament passed a law, the Recall of MPs Act, which allowed voters to petition for the 'recall' of an MP. So far, this has happened on four occasions. In 2017, Fiona Onasanya, Labour MP for Peterborough, was convicted for perverting the course of justice. A recall petition succeeded in 2019. In the same year, Brecon & Radnorshire was declared vacant after Conservative MP Chris Davies filed inaccurate expenses claims. In 2024, Peter Bone was recalled after accusations of bullying and sexual misconduct.

Since 1926, twenty-nine by-elections have been caused following a scandal involving the incumbent MP. More than half of these (sixteen) have occurred since the year 2000.

On only five occasions have there been by-elections caused by the previous result being declared void. The last occasion was in 2011, in Oldham & Saddleworth, because the winner of the seat in the 2010 general election was found guilty of knowingly making false statements about a rival candidate. In 1997, in Winchester, the general election was declared null and void because ballot papers which had not received the official mark would have affected the result, if counted. This is covered in detail later in this book.

There have also been nine by-elections which have been held after the sitting Member was disqualified. The last time this happened was in 1961, when Tony Benn had inherited a seat from his father in the House of Lords.

On only one occasion has a by-election been provoked by an MP being declared of unsound mind. That happened to Charles Leach, Liberal MP for Colne Valley, in 1916.

During the Second World War, there were twenty by-elections

caused by MPs dying while on active service, two more than in the First World War.

There was no scientific way of choosing which by-elections to include in this book. I did take advice, but in the end the selection is mine and mine alone. The best bit about editing a book like this is matching authors to their subjects. It's like doing a jigsaw. As you will see, some of the contributors are well known in the fields of media, politics or academia. There are also several who are totally unknown but are people I am delighted to have given a chance to show what they can do. There are a number of young contributors who are under the age of thirty, all of whom have written quality essays on a par with those who have been around the block a bit.

Each of the contributors have been asked to adhere so far as is possible to a style guide, and I am delighted by the way they have done so. Some of the contributors, like Andrew Marr, reported on the by-election they wrote about at the time; others, like John Barnes, have or have had a relationship to the constituency they have written about.

Inevitably, there will be one or two errors in a text of 250,000 words. The team at Biteback and I have done our best to catch everything, but if you do spot an error, please do let me know at info@iaindale.com.

If you enjoy the book as much as I hope and think you will, please do share the book's details on your social media, because the best way of marketing it is by word of mouth.

Iain Dale
Tunbridge Wells
March 2025

MIDDLESEX

13 APRIL 1769
MINISTRY GAIN

ROBIN EAGLES

Result: John Wilkes (Whig), 1,143, 79.2 per cent; Henry Lawes Luttrell (Tory), 296, 20.5 per cent (elected); William Whitaker (Rockingham Whigs), 5, 0.3 per cent; David Roache (Independent), 0, 0.0 per cent
Size of majority: 847
Swing: N/A
Name of previous MP and party: John Wilkes (Whig)
Reason for by-election: Expulsion from the House of Commons
Result at previous general election: John Wilkes (Whig), 1,297, 42.2 per cent (elected); George Cooke (Tory), 827, 28.3 per cent (elected); William Beauchamp Proctor (Whig), 802, 27.4 per cent
Date by-election called: 17 March 1769
Date by-election took place: 13 April 1769
Size of total electorate: 3,500
Total number of votes cast: 1,444
Turnout: 41.3 per cent

By the spring of 1769, the government was thoroughly fed up with John Wilkes. Ever since he had returned from exile in France to participate in the 1768 general election, the controversial former MP for Aylesbury, journalist and convicted felon had thrown a veritable toolbox of spanners into the works. Eighteenth-century elections were often raucous affairs and Wilkes was far from the first person to seek to overturn a result, but he presented a whole new type of challenge to an administration ill-prepared to deal with someone so willing to test limits to their extremes.

As a consequence, few elections caused as much of a stir in the period as that for Middlesex in 1769. At the general election, Wilkes had caught the government on the hop by standing first for London and then, when unsuccessful there, for the notoriously impossible-to-control county of Middlesex. Populated as it was with numbers of small tradesmen and artisans, Middlesex was not a place where either the government or any particular aristocratic interest could ever call the shots. Wilkes understood this and, bolstered by a broad range of support, was able to create a movement which left the two sitting Members, William Beauchamp Proctor and George Cooke, fighting for their places. Where London had proved difficult, Middlesex was the perfect location for someone like Wilkes, and he had emerged at the end of that contest at the head of the poll.

Britain in the 1760s was undergoing significant political upset. The state of the economy was weak, prompting numerous groups to go on strike, among them coalheavers and sailors. Minor disputes and pro-tests frequently morphed into more general rioting and disorder. Not everyone was committed to a particular cause, but plenty were happy to take advantage of circumstances to take to the streets and indulge in some more or less harmless forms of protest. After the dominance first of Sir Robert Walpole and then of the Pelhams (Henry Pelham and his brother, Thomas, Duke of Newcastle) under George II, there had also been significant instability at the top of government. Indeed, by the time the 1769 by-election was called, George III was on his sixth Prime Minister (the Duke of Grafton).

It was into this unstable environment that Wilkes, the ultimate eighteenth-century lord of misrule, sidled in, peddling a variety of causes, though all of them based on the very broad theme of 'liberty'. Just how unstable things were in Middlesex is shown by the fact that the April 1769 by-election was the fourth the voters of the county had been required to respond to since the general election at the end of March the previous year. It was the third involving Wilkes, the other one being caused by the death of George Cooke, who had been re-placed in December 1768 by Wilkes's lawyer, John Glynn. Wilkes's return at the general election had shocked the political establishment and resulted in his expulsion from the Commons in January 1769. In February and again in March, he stood for re-election unchallenged but each time was declared ineligible by the Commons. The king took a close interest in the results and received detailed reports from Lord North telling him what was happening in Parliament. By the time of the third by-election in April, patience had worn thoroughly thin with Wilkes's constant re-elections and the administration had determined on finding someone willing to stand against him.

The timing of the April by-election was very much driven by the need to achieve a resolution to the preposterous stand-off between Commons and electors, who were determined to return Wilkes whatever Parliament might say to the contrary. Indeed, it might be said that by the time of the final by-election, Wilkes had effectively already won. After his initial election in 1768, he had surrendered himself to the courts and been sentenced to twenty-two months in prison. Fighting the campaigns from his cell, he had been able to cast himself as a martyr and from prison oversaw the beginning of a movement that would outlive this particular election – and in many ways outlive him too. For the administration, they hoped one way or another to bring to an end the disruption Wilkes represented, hoping that ejecting him from the Commons would deprive him of the oxygen his campaign required. It had precisely the opposite effect.

Alongside the two main candidates, Wilkes and Luttrell, a ministry supporter in Parliament who had taken the Chiltern Hundreds so that he might be free to take Wilkes on, there were two others. Little is known about one of them, Daniel Roache, who seems to have opted not to appear on the day. The other, William Whitaker, risked humiliation and struggled to gain any support at all.

Possibly the most striking feature of this campaign, though, was the absence of the principal candidate: Wilkes. Missing candidates at polls were not entirely unusual in the period. Pitt the Elder did not bother to turn up to his election at Bath in 1757 and there are several examples of MPs being elected while overseas. The future Prime Minister Lord Shelburne, for example, was elected an MP while serving with the army on the Continent.

Wilkes's absence was somewhat more unusual, though. He was not there because he was in jail, serving out his sentence for his earlier convictions for libel and pornography. This did not mean, of course, that there were not plenty of his supporters in attendance. One of the key features of all Wilkite elections was the superb organisational ability of both Wilkes himself and his associates. Carriages and boats were laid on to convey voters from the far reaches of Middlesex – a sprawling county reaching from Berkshire in the west to Essex in the east, Hertfordshire in the north to Surrey in the south – to the polling place at Brentford. Detailed advice was spread through the newspapers telling prospective voters where to gather and which routes to avoid, to minimise the risks of violence between the various sets of supporters. On arrival at Brentford, each was to be given a blue cockade, the Wilkite colour, and placards inscribed with popular slogans, such as 'Wilkes and Liberty'. In spite of the establishment's concerns about the disorder that followed Wilkes everywhere, he and his lieutenants were eager to ensure that their voters were well disciplined and knew how and when to appear to the best advantage.

Wilkes's people may have been well drilled but, for the most part, Luttrell was able to rely on a better class of voter. Among those polling for him were at least seven knights or baronets, along with two Irish peers. There were fellow MPs – Martin Bladen Hawke, son and heir of the naval hero Admiral (Lord) Hawke, who had himself been elected to Parliament in the 1768 general election; George Augustus Selwyn, MP for Gloucester; and Sir Roger Newdigate, 5th Baronet, the long-standing MP for Oxford University. There were also higher-class artisans, like Frederick Kuhff, a confectioner on the Haymarket, who counted the king among his clientele.

No titled voters backed Wilkes, but he was able to draw on a broad base of smaller tradesmen and artisans, like Silvanus Odell, who seems to have been a butcher originally from Bedfordshire, along with a smattering of professional types and established men in the City of London. These included Liscombe Price, an attorney, and respectable tradesmen, like Isaiah Fleureau, a cutler of Huguenot descent operating on the Haymarket. It is not clear whether the Edward Gibbons from Marylebone polling for Wilkes was the same as Edward Gibbon, the historian and future MP, whom Wilkes certainly knew well from his days as a militia officer, or indeed Gibbon's father, also Edward, himself a former MP. John Horn of Brentford was almost certainly the Brentford curate John Horne (later Horne Tooke), at that point one of Wilkes's most important adjutants but later a fierce rival.

The result demonstrated clearly to the ministry — and the authorities in the Commons — that the populous county of Middlesex would not take a hint and that for as long as Wilkes continued to stand, they would vote for him. However, having finally found someone willing to stand against him, the establishment was in no mood to accept the outcome. Two days after the poll, the Commons took the result into consideration and voted to overturn it, Wilkes being deemed, once again, ineligible. His votes were considered void, and Luttrell was seated as the candidate with the highest number of legitimate votes. It was not just in Parliament and Middlesex itself that the election had an impact. In the City of London, where Wilkes was already developing a powerful interest, things began to run against the supporters of government, and in June one of Wilkes's voters and close supporters, John Sawbridge, MP for Hythe and a future Lord Mayor of London, was elected sheriff on a Wilkite ticket.

The true victor of the campaign was, of course, Wilkes. Just before the election, a new organisation had been founded: the Society of Gentlemen Supporters of the Bill of Rights (SSBR). While its major function was as a subscription organisation intended to settle Wilkes's debts, it also had an important role as a campaigning political outfit. Wilkesism rapidly became about a great deal more than Wilkes himself and at the 1774 general election, several candidates stood on SSBR tickets, espousing a shared set of aspirations for reforming the franchise.

Having chosen to appear as the government's champion against Wilkes, Luttrell never really recovered his reputation. He had shown a very personal animus against Wilkes prior to standing for Middlesex, and he was to find his victory came at considerable personal cost. For months after the election, he was *persona non grata* both within and outside Parliament, Horace Walpole recording that he 'did not dare to appear in the streets or scarce quit his lodgings'. There were even petty legal actions, such as one by a coffeehouse keeper, who sued one of Luttrell's servants to recover a debt of £16.19s for a breakfast she had provided to Luttrell's supporters. By 1771, he had had enough and attempted to resign the seat but was not allowed to do so. Subsequently, he even suggested that Wilkes should be given the seat after all, but that was also ignored. For the final two years of the parliament, he largely based himself in Ireland. Nevertheless, this was not the end for Luttrell in Parliament. In 1774, he stood for his previous seat of Bossiney, being returned on the local grandee's interest. He then represented two more seats, Plympton Erle and Ludgershall, during the remainder of his long career, which only ended with his death in 1821 – having outlived his rival by nearly a quarter of a century.

The decision to sit Luttrell rather than Wilkes was of huge significance. It emphasised the Commons' insistence that they maintained the right to adjudicate on who should be seated in Parliament rather than the electorate itself. In resolving to void all of Wilkes's 1,143 votes, it was argued that it was as if those casting them had each chosen to spoil their ballots. For Wilkes, the whole affair represented another stage on his journey to dominating popular politics. He had caused a furore back in 1763 with his newspaper, *The North Briton*; now, he showed the authorities how effectively he was able to harness the power of the crowd. What was to come was the development of a new force based on the SSBR and Wilkes's successful move into the City of London. He would ultimately secure election as Lord Mayor, the same year as his eventual return to the Commons in the 1774 general election. Ironically, all of this eventually outstripped Wilkes himself. Circumstances would later persuade him to transform himself once more into a far more respectable sort of public figure, ending his days as an elder statesman and noted patron of the arts. But the movement he had inspired would continue to grow, helping to inform the later radical movements of the 1790s and early 1800s.

Robin Eagles *is the editor of the House of Lords 1660–1832 section at the History of Parliament and the author of* Champion of English Freedom: The Life of John Wilkes, MP and Lord Mayor of London *(Amberley, 2024).*

2

COUNTY CLARE

---

5 JULY 1828
IRISH CATHOLIC GAIN FROM TORY

RICHARD A. GAUNT

Result: Daniel O'Connell (Irish Catholic), 2,057, 67.69 per cent; William Vesey Fitzgerald (Tory), 982, 32.31 per cent
Size of majority: 1,075
Swing: N/A
Name of previous MP and party: William Vesey Fitzgerald (Tory)
Reason for by-election: Promotion to ministerial office
Result at previous general election: William Vesey Fitzgerald (Tory) and Lucius O'Brien (Tory) both elected unopposed
Date by-election called: 12 June 1828
Date by-election took place: 1–5 July 1828
Size of total electorate: 8,557
Total number of votes cast: 3,039
Turnout: 35.5 per cent

The County Clare by-election of July 1828 remains unique in the history of UK parliamentary by-elections. While it acted, like many such contests, to expose differences within the government of the day on a controversial and long-standing issue, the result of the election led directly to a major constitutional change – the granting of Catholic emancipation (the right for Catholics to sit as MPs) – in April 1829. This outcome not only represented a government U-turn of the first order but generated divisions among its traditional supporters which contributed to its subsequent downfall in November 1830.

In January 1828, the Duke of Wellington became Prime Minister of a

Tory administration which attempted to maintain the delicate balancing act of its predecessors since 1812. Emancipation remained an 'open' question, which ministers could support or resist individually, while the government remained uncommitted, though in effect opposed, to its passage through Parliament. The 1820s had witnessed growing support for emancipation within the House of Commons, although 'No Popery' sentiment remained widespread among the population at large. Buoyed in part by the success of the anti-slavery movement, the Catholic Association was established in Ireland in 1823 to step up the campaign for emancipation. It was efficiently organised and run, not least because of the enthusiastic participation of the Catholic clergy. Such was its effectiveness as an organisation, that Lord Liverpool's Tory government banned it between 1825 and 1828. Ministers were particularly worried by the association's use of the 'Catholic Rent', a membership subscription which was charged at a minimum rate of a farthing a week. The rent was paid by people from every social class and every religious denomination to fund the association's activities in support of emancipation; during 1828 alone, it brought in some £23,000.

As the Catholic Association resumed its legal status, during 1828, events at Westminster provided it with a major opportunity for embarrassing Wellington's government. The resignation of several pro-Catholic ministers in May 1828 necessitated a Cabinet reshuffle in which William Vesey Fitzgerald became president of the Board of Trade. Under the Succession to the Crown Act of 1707, promotion to an 'office of profit under the crown' required the candidate to put themselves forward for re-election. Consequently, Fitzgerald had to fight a by-election at County Clare, which he had represented since 1818. Fitzgerald was a popular constituency MP with landlords and tenants alike and was supportive of emancipation. The Catholic Association had already pledged itself in January 1828 to oppose any government candidate when the occasion arose and, after several alternatives were considered, Daniel O'Connell, the leader of the association, agreed to contest the seat.

O'Connell had risen from relatively prosperous Catholic roots in County Kerry to become an accomplished lawyer and a political leader of wit, skill and daring. He had plagued successive Tory governments with his oratory and impudence, consciously modelling himself on Simón Bolívar, 'The Liberator' of Spain's former South American colonies during the 1820s. O'Connell seemed the obvious candidate to take on Fitzgerald but remained conscious of his opponent's popularity and pro-emancipation sentiments and aware of the influence which local landlords exerted over their tenantry, who enjoyed the right to vote as forty-shilling freeholders.

In order to differentiate himself from Fitzgerald and appeal beyond the electorate of County Clare to Ireland itself, O'Connell issued an election address which struck the partisan and sectarian tone that was to hallmark the contest. Fulminating against Fitzgerald as a false friend to Catholics ('If he be sincerely our friend, let him vote for me'), he pledged himself not only to removing the hated oaths required of MPs (oaths which denied 'the sacrifice of the mass, and the invocation of the blessed Virgin Mary, and other saints') but also to a 'Radical REFORM in the representative system' and the redistribution of the surplus wealth of the established church in Ireland. He was bold enough to propose the repeal of the Acts of Union between Great Britain and Ireland, which had come into force in 1801, but, when the address was subsequently published as an election leaflet and distributed in its thousands, this clause was omitted.

O'Connell's election platform ranged far beyond the achievement of emancipation, though this was clearly the centrepiece of his campaign. It proved discomfiting not only to Protestant Irish supporters of emancipation, who were alienated by its naked sectarianism, but to landlords and members of the gentry, who rallied to Fitzgerald as a bulwark against the social and political revolution which O'Connell held out to them.

By contrast, O'Connell mustered vocal support from the Catholic priesthood. Some 150 priests were involved in O'Connell's election campaign at County Clare, with prominent support offered by Reverend James Warren Doyle (Bishop of Kildare), Father Tom Maguire of Leitrim and Father John Murphy of Corofin. Murphy proved particularly adept at persuading various contingents of tenantry – marched to the poll in feudal style by their landlords in order to vote for Fitzgerald – to cast them off and vote for O'Connell instead. In an age of open voting, it took especial courage for tenants to defy the wishes of their landlords, on pain of eviction, but defy them they did, heartened by the knowledge that this was a Catholic tenant revolt on a massive scale.

The contest took place at the Court House in the county town of Ennis. In a sharp contrast with the bacchanalian excesses illustrated in William Hogarth's famous eighteenth-century election scenes, sobriety prevailed throughout the town. The Catholic Association had issued general orders against the distribution of spirits and against any sort of (alcohol-fuelled) disturbance. As Robert Peel, the Home Secretary and Leader of the House of Commons, subsequently observed to Sir Walter Scott, 'I wish you had been present at the Clare election, for no pen but yours could have done justice to that fearful exhibition of sobered and desperate enthusiasm.' The prevailing tone of temperance among the electorate did not prevent O'Connell and his supporters using Mrs Carmody's tavern as their unofficial campaign headquarters – their liquid enjoyments interrupted only by Father Murphy's stern intonations against allowing the 'wolf ... on the walk' (alcoholism) to take root among them.

Fitzgerald was proposed at the election by an influential local land-lord, Sir Edward O'Brien, and seconded by Francis Gore, a lawyer whose forebears included a nail maker – a fact which was treated with derision by O'Connell and his principal supporters, Charles James Patrick O'Gorman Mahon (who nominated him) and the Protestant liberal Thomas Steele (who seconded him). Fitzgerald made a widely appreciated speech to the assembled crowd, culminating with an af-fecting peroration in which he shed tears for his ailing father, who had opposed the Acts of Union. O'Connell retorted with a characteristic put-down, offering the barbed comment that he had 'never shed tears in public' – a statement which served to diminish any sentiment in favour of his opponent.

In common with pre-reform election contests, the poll extended across several days. Polling of O'Connell's supporters was initially delayed by enforcing the requirement (usually waived by mutual agreement) for every Catholic voter to formally declare their loyalty by obtaining a magistrate's certificate to that effect. Magistrates proved unusually reluctant to sit, in order to take and certify the oath, until

O'Connell found a sympathetic magistrate who dealt with cases in batches.

Such was the celebrity which surrounded the contest, and especially O'Connell, that the population of Ennis, which was around 12,000 in normal times, swelled to some 30,000 people – comprising electors, campaigners and their relatives, including their wives and children. O'Connell's campaign supplied them with vouchers to spend on provisions in local shops and taverns: some 650 payments, totalling nearly £7,000, were made. This was financed by a successful fundraising campaign spearheaded by Patrick Vincent Fitzpatrick and by the resources of the Catholic Association buoyed by the restoration of the Catholic Rent. At the start of the contest, O'Connell had been voted election expenses of £5,000; this sum was later raised to £8,000 – a testament to the seriousness with which the contest was treated by the association.

Realising general expectations, O'Connell triumphed in the by-election with 2,057 votes to Fitzgerald's 982, securing two-thirds of all votes cast in the contest. About 300 additional votes for O'Connell were disqualified on technical grounds. It was the wholesale revolt of the forty-shilling freeholders, powerfully assisted by the promptings of the Catholic clergy, 'wot won it' for him. As the defeated Fitzgerald observed, in writing to Peel after the result:

> All the great interests broke down and the desertion has been universal. Such a scene as we have had! Such a tremendous prospect as it opens to us! ... The conduct of the priests has passed all that you could picture to yourself! ... It was a hopeless contest from the first! Everything was against me ... I do not understand how I have not been beaten by a greater majority.

At the opening of the new session of Parliament on 5 February 1829, Peel introduced a Catholic Relief Bill in the House of Commons, encompassing the effective realisation of Catholic emancipation. The seven months which elapsed between O'Connell's spectacular by-election victory and the government's momentous U-turn had been spent in concerted attempts by Wellington to convince first Peel, then his Cabinet, then King George IV, to embrace the measure – however reluctantly – while the tone of public sentiment on the subject became progressively more heated. Throughout this period, O'Connell remained the elected, though unseated, MP for County Clare. When the time came to test his position with the House of Commons, O'Connell refused to take the existing oaths, the House refused to concede and he was forced to fight a fresh by-election for County Clare, in expectation of returning to Parliament after emancipation had passed. O'Connell was subsequently re-elected for County Clare, without opposition, on 30 July 1829.

Nor did O'Connell succeed in preventing the suppression of the Catholic Association and the disfranchisement of the Irish forty-shilling freeholders – measures which the government insisted on introducing, as corollaries to emancipation, in the hope of fending off perpetual agitation and potential electoral anarchy. O'Connell had initially resisted disfranchisement, given his indebtedness to the freeholder vote in Clare. However, with the prize of emancipation within reach, he accepted the measures as necessary overtures to try and calm Protestant anxieties.

For the Wellington government, the granting of emancipation was a wholly unexpected and unlooked-for achievement, given the Protestant complexion of the Cabinet after May 1828 and the long-proclaimed opposition to the measure of its leading members, especially Peel. Above all others, it placed a question mark over his reputation for political consistency, which was never expunged and which subsequent events (notably the repeal of the Corn Laws in 1846) only served to reinforce. More immediately, the passage of emancipation, in the face of significant anti-Popery feeling in the country, converted some (though by no means all) of the government's Ultra-Tory supporters to embrace the cause of parliamentary reform, for they were convinced that emancipation had only been passed because of the influence which ministers had brought to bear through its electoral resources and government patronage. William Gladstone, though a supporter of emancipation, later observed that a reformed parliament would never have passed the measure. Such was the level of resentment at the government's 'betrayal' of its Protestant heartland, after April 1829, that the ministry could never be sure of its political standing during the remainder of its time in office. Assailed on all sides and faced with growing demands for parliamentary reform, it resigned office in November 1830, ending the long period of Tory rule which had begun in 1807 and paving the way for a decade of Whig reforms, commencing with the 'Great' Reform Act of 1832.

Dr Richard A. Gaunt is an associate professor in history at the University of Nottingham. An expert in British political history c.1780–1850, he is the co-editor of the journal Parliamentary History *and co-editor of the Royal Historical Society's* Camden Series.

3

PRESTON

17 DECEMBER 1830
RADICAL GAIN FROM WHIG

GORDON PENTLAND

Result: Henry Hunt (Radical), 3,730, 52.37 per cent; Edward George Geoffrey Smith Stanley (Whig), 3,392, 47.63 per cent
Size of majority: 338
Swing: N/A
Name of previous MP and party: Edward George Geoffrey Smith Stanley (Whig)
Reason for by-election: Promotion to ministerial office
Result at previous general election: Edward George Geoffrey Smith Stanley (Whig), 2,996; John Wood (Radical), 2,386, 35.67 per cent; Henry Hunt (Radical), 1,308, 19.55 per cent
Date by-election called: 22 November 1830
Date by-election took place: 17 December 1830
Size of total electorate: N/A
Total number of votes cast: 7,122
Turnout: N/A

The sitting MP for Preston, the 31-year-old Edward Smith Stanley, was appointed as Chief Secretary for Ireland on 29 November 1830. Re-election to his parliamentary seat – normally a formality – must have been low down on his list of concerns. As a member of Earl Grey's new government, which had supplanted the Duke of Wellington's ministry, he and his colleagues faced a country in crisis. Stubborn and widespread material distress was accompanied by increasingly fraught demands for retrenchment and for parliamentary reform to end misgovernment.

The whole European scene was once again reeling from revolution emanating from Paris. The agricultural counties of southern England were in the midst of one of the most violent periods in their history. The so-called Swing Rising was named for the mythical figure of Captain Swing, who led nocturnal bands of labourers to burn ricks, destroy machinery and threaten farmers and landowners.

The estates of Stanley's own family, the Earls of Derby, were relatively untouched by the rising, being concentrated in the north of the country rather than the heartland of Captain Swing in the south. But the very explicit challenge to rank and to the norms of English life were certainly sufficient to worry this conscientious young aristocrat. To cap it all, Ireland, his proposed ministerial posting, seemed again to be on the brink of rising. The immense campaign for Catholic civil liberties in the 1820s, helmed by Daniel O'Connell, had given way to demands for the repeal of the union of Great Britain and Ireland. There was widespread and frequently violent opposition to the payment of tithes to uphold the established Protestant Church of Ireland in a nation whose people largely rejected its teachings.

The vast majority of ministerial by-elections were uncontroversial. They nevertheless had considerable potential to generate high-profile upsets until their final abolition in 1926. This had been demonstrated powerfully and recently in O'Connell's victory in County Clare in the summer of 1828. And Stanley's challenger, Henry 'Orator' Hunt, was cut from very similar cloth to the Great Liberator himself. Indeed, the two had become closer and closer allies over the previous year. Hunt was the archetype of the English gentlemanly radical. He came from Wiltshire gentry farming stock and experienced a personal and political midlife crisis in his thirties. His abandonment of his own wife for his friend's earned him exclusion from polite society and the enduring hostility of the uxorious William Cobbett. His conversion from a committed loyalism in the 1800s to an equally zealous radicalism completed his transformation.

Hunt was most celebrated or notorious (depending on one's politics) as a pioneering and flamboyant leader of popular radicalism in the years after the end of the Napoleonic Wars. In particular, he was the central protagonist in the infamous Peterloo Massacre of August

1819. Hunt was the headline speaker at the crowded meeting on St Peter's Fields, when the Manchester magistrates had attempted to effect his arrest for holding a seditious assembly. The unarmed crowds were charged by the yeomanry, leaving the ground carpeted with the dead and horribly wounded. It was the defining event of Hunt's life and would shape the remainder of his career.

Standing over six-feet tall, with a stentorian voice and his trademark white hat, Hunt was an imposing and formidable opponent. He had a knack for salesmanship which fitted him to compete in the political marketplace. Following his stint in 'Ilchester Bastille', Hunt had moved into a range of commercial endeavours, through which he still flew the flag for radical political reform. His breakfast powder, manufactured from roasted corn, provided workers with an alternative to tea and coffee that pointedly did not put tax revenues into the hands of a corrupt and illegitimate government. His 'matchless shoe blacking' was an endless source of satires and snooty put-downs against him during the by-election and beyond. But it was also a vehicle for his political message and bottles of it were stamped with the slogan 'Equal Laws, Equal Rights, Annual Parliaments, Universal Suffrage, and the Ballot'. In a nutshell, this was his platform for the by-election at Preston.

Hunt had considerable form as a disruptor of parliamentary elections. In the 1810s, he had contested elections in Bristol, standing as an independent champion of the people and putting the feet of moderate Whig reformers to the fire. He also had form in Preston and, indeed, with the Stanleys themselves. The 13th Earl of Derby (father of Hunt's rival at Preston) had offered a measured and unpopular defence of the Manchester authorities in the aftermath of the massacre. Before his trial at York in 1820, Hunt had unsuccessfully contested the Preston seat 'in the people's cause' at the general election occasioned by the death of George III. He took another unsuccessful run at it a decade later at the general election caused by George IV's laudanum-soaked demise. He had electrified that contest. Stanley, a noted and clever parliamentary orator, clearly lacked any kind of a popular street touch. Even Whig fixers thought that Hunt might have won in the summer, had it not been for the large quantities of ale distributed in Stanley's interest.

A great deal had occurred since that summer contest to make the

December by-election an altogether different prospect. Prior to the fall of Wellington's government in November 1830, Hunt had been lecturing to large audiences at the Rotunda, the new London radical venue just south of the river. On especially packed occasions, his own nearby blacking factory could accommodate overspill meetings. Letters to the Home Office in the autumn and winter accused Hunt of, once again, heading a radical conspiracy to overthrow the government. His business trips around the inflamed counties adjacent to London raised fears of him leading gangs of agricultural labourers and joining up with the London mob.

This fraught context meant that, by the time of the by-election in December, there had been a significant uptick in both radical commitment and organisational capacity. In the general election over the summer, parliamentary reform had competed as one among a number of live issues which included colonial slavery, the pervasive material distress and the future of the East India Company. By December, reform was the issue that subsumed all others. Hunt's supporters in Preston pushed the kind of radical version of reform championed by him at and since Peterloo in 1819. Universal manhood suffrage, annual parliaments and vote by secret ballot – three of the Chartists' later famed 'six points' – were its key features. His local champions took a powerful new form in the shape of political unions, bodies created explicitly to campaign for reform.

The government of which Stanley was a part was pledged to bring in a measure of parliamentary reform. Therein lay Stanley's confidence of renewed success at Preston. There was widespread suspicion, however, that the Grey ministry's offering would be a meagre one, a shallow tinkering with a few seats rather than the kind of bold and sweeping change that was required. It was straightforward enough, therefore, to paint Stanley as part of a moderate and self-interested aristocratic clique. He fit the bill in many respects. The ballot, for example, was seen as the working man's only protection against influence and intimidation from his betters. It provided a litmus test of someone's seriousness as a reformer. Stanley was a vocal opponent.

These by-election arguments surfaced much wider issues that would come to characterise the crisis around reform and stretch into the following decade and beyond. One was the nature of representation itself. Stanley, in his point-blank refusal to pledge himself to measures demanded by constituents, upheld the classic position laid out by Edmund Burke in the 1770s. MPs, while bound to serve their constituents, were nevertheless members of a deliberative assembly. They went to Westminster unshackled by promises and free to debate and then to legislate in the national interest. The pledging in which Hunt and other radicals indulged enshrined a radically different principle. MPs were delegates, the embodiment of the people's will in Parliament.

Preston itself enjoyed an unusually broad franchise for the time, vested in 'the inhabitants at large'. In practice, this almost meant manhood suffrage, a working version of the right Hunt would ideally extend to all men. This also ensured that the MPs returned for the borough could claim a certain degree of popular legitimacy. And it brought the challenge of engaging with and mobilising a large and unruly electorate. Such an effort required candidates to observe the customary expectations of the constituency. Nightly addresses and substantial 'treating' – which was the unreformed system's euphemism for the liberal distribution of free booze – were part and parcel of these. An electorate numbering in the thousands also required organisation via a series of street captains – men who would get voters to the pubs but also crucially get them out of the pubs again to vote.

After days of polling, Hunt was substantially ahead of Stanley. Unsurprisingly, accusations of corruption came thick and fast. Though he ultimately conceded, Stanley blamed his defeat on the incompetence of the mayor and returning officer, Nicholas Grimshaw, who had failed to suppress the fraudulent voting and 'system of outrage' which had marred the contest. These sour grapes continued, even after Stanley had secured a snug berth at the king's discretion for the rotten borough of Windsor. One of Stanley's allies sneeringly reported on the chairing of Hunt as the successful candidate at Preston, attended by '6,000 or 7,000 of the *canaille*'. *The Times* put Hunt's crowd at 45,000. Hunt was jubilant and made arrangements for 3,730 commemorative medals to be minted for his electors. These bore the inscription: 'The Time is Come. Triumph of Principle.' The example in the British Museum's collections has a small hole drilled in it, an almost certain sign that it was worn proudly by its elector-owner during subsequent meetings and marches.

Given the gravity of the issues at stake during the contest and the turbulent politics of the time, Hunt's election, just like O'Connell's in 1828, attracted considerable attention. After his triumph in Preston, Hunt tried to make the most of the by-election as a lightning rod for issues he held dear. He toured Manchester, Blackburn, Oldham, Bolton and the great up-and-coming nerve centre of radicalism at Birmingham, drawing crowds in the thousands and calling for radical reform and an inquiry into the Peterloo Massacre. At the site of Peterloo itself, his supporters proposed to arrange for Hunt a triumphal entry into London. This took place in early January, with 10,000 joining Hunt around the Painted Red Lion Inn in Islington. From there, they marched with Hunt and his matchless blacking van around the city and over Westminster Bridge to Hunt's residence on Stanford Street. Hunt positioned himself explicitly as a kind of English O'Connell. What the latter had done for poor Catholics, he would do for poor Englishmen. The two would act together on many issues and formed the vanguard of a new and often unruly radical presence in the House of Commons.

In Parliament, Hunt was in something of an uncomfortable position. He reluctantly supported the Grey government's reform measure with his votes but bitterly opposed it in his speeches. It was, for him and for many of his constituents, simply not radical enough. Worse still, the £10 franchise qualification the legislation planned to bring in would, in time, disfranchise exactly the kinds of voters who had elected Hunt to his seat at Preston. From that perspective, legislation that went down in history when it passed as the 'Great' Reform Act could be presented as a step away from democracy, rather than a tentative one towards it.

Hunt never stopped denouncing the reform as a clever but dishonest ploy by those in power to keep it. He found plenty to confirm this in the first reformed election in the remapped Preston constituency in December 1832. Hunt finished third behind Tory Peter Hesketh-Fleetwood and his friend Henry Smith Stanley, the younger brother of Edward, his vanquished opponent from two years before. As for

Edward Stanley himself, his eloquence assisted the passage of reform in Parliament before he moved gradually in the 1830s into the Conservative Party. He went on as Lord Stanley and then the Earl of Derby to be the longest-serving party leader in modern times and three times Prime Minister. He nursed throughout this glittering career a distrust of demotic and demagogic popular politics. His bruising encounter with Hunt in 1830 cannot have helped.

Gordon Pentland is a professor of history at Monash University. He is currently writing The Reform Crisis, 1830–1832.

4

MANCHESTER

26 NOVEMBER 1867
LIBERAL HOLD

PETER KELLNER

Result: Jacob Bright (Liberal), 8,260, 53.6 per cent; John Bennett (Conservative), 6,499, 42.2 per cent; Mitchell Henry (Liberal), 642, 4.2 per cent
Size of majority: 1,761
Swing: N/A
Name of previous MP and party: Edward James (Liberal)
Reason for by-election: Death of incumbent
Result at previous general election: Thomas Beazley (Liberal), 7,909, 64.8 per cent (elected); Edward James (Liberal), 6,698, 54.9 per cent (elected); Jacob Bright (Liberal), 5,562, 45.6 per cent; Abel Heywood (Liberal), 4,252, 34.8 per cent
Date by-election called: 19 November 1867
Date by-election took place: 26 November 1867
Size of total electorate: 21,542
Total number of votes cast: 15,401
Turnout: 71.5 per cent

On 26 November 1867, an apparently routine by-election gave British politics an accidental heroine, a key event in the story of women's suffrage and a bitter constitutional argument that was finally settled six decades later.

The contest, for one of Manchester's two seats, followed the death of Edward James, a Liberal MP. Jacob Bright had been one of four Liberal candidates at the previous election in 1865 for this two-seat constituency and had come third. This time he was one of two Liberals competing to fill the vacancy. Like his better-known brother, John Bright, Jacob was a committed reformer. The other Liberal was Mitchell Henry, who belonged to the party's less radical, Whig, faction. Unlike three years earlier, the Conservatives fielded a candidate, John Bennett. *The Times* said he 'has probably been brought out by the Conservatives because of his moderate principles, and no doubt he will get many votes from moderate Liberals'. The stage was thus set for a contest between one radical and, by the standards of the time, two moderates.

One of Bright's radical causes was women's suffrage. In October 1865, he and Ursula, his wife, supported the establishment of the Manchester Committee for the Enfranchisement of Women. At the time, the city could claim to be the centre of the suffrage movement – and, indeed, the heart of progressive causes generally, not least via the pages of the *Manchester Guardian*.

In those days, just 8 per cent of adults had the vote: men who owned or leased enough property. The occupant of 25 Ludlow Street ran a small crockery shop and met the property qualification – and so was added to the electoral register as elector no. 12326, possibly by a local Liberal activist keen to ensure that as many likely supporters as possible had the vote. What the local registrar failed to notice was that the shop owner was a woman, Mrs Lily Maxwell. (Her husband had died some years earlier. The law then deemed that the property of married women belonged to their husband. As Lily was a widow, the shop was hers.)

The suffrage movement's local leader was Lydia Becker, a scientist who worked from time to time with Charles Darwin. On behalf of Bright, Becker contacted Maxwell to encourage her to use her unexpected right. Maxwell replied: 'If I'd 20 votes I would give them all to Jacob Bright.'

Yet this seemed not to be something that Bright chose to talk about openly during his campaign. On the day before the election, at the meeting to confirm the nomination of the three candidates, Bright made no mention of women's suffrage; though he did argue for other radical reforms, including the secret ballot at elections. Contemporary reports gave no sign of the drama that would soon unfold. Indeed, one journalist reported that 'it is not often that we have had less of a feeling or enthusiasm than has been manifested in the present contest'. It did, however, judge that Bright 'has had the advantage of a better and more complete organisation of committees and canvassers than his opponents. He addresses two meetings sometimes, and at others three meetings per day.'

On election day, Maxwell and Becker marched together from one of Bright's committee rooms to the polling station, Chorlton Town Hall. According to the *Daily News* – journalists had been tipped off in advance – they were accompanied by 'a large number of persons, including members of [Bright's] All Saints ward committee, and were much cheered as they passed to and from the poll'. Inside the polling station, Maxwell announced not only her presence but her vote. (Secret ballots did not come until 1872.) Amid the commotion, the polling clerk decided that, as Maxwell's name was on the register, he had to allow her vote. The *Yorkshire Post* criticised him for this, arguing that he should have rejected Maxwell's vote 'as he would have ignored that of a child 10 years old'.

A small insight into the world of Victorian by-elections before the secret ballot was provided by *The Times*, which recorded the voting tally hour by hour. At 9 a.m., Bright led Bennett by 1,716 to 917. His lead grew steadily through the day. When voting ended at 4 p.m., Bright, the radical, had secured more votes than his two moderate rivals combined. He had won 8,260 votes (53.6 per cent). Bennett came second, with 6,499 (42.2 per cent). Henry trailed a distant third. In his victory speech, Bright singled out Maxwell, praising her as 'a hardworking honest person who pays her rates as you do, and therefore if any person should possess a vote, it is precisely such as she'.

The ripples from the by-election quickly started to spread. An editorial in *The Times* on 29 November demonstrated a habit it has perfected over two centuries of justifying its reactionary beliefs with apparently progressive principles:

The ladies constitute, in every sense, more than one-half of the British nation; but, nevertheless, in violation of every principle of numerical and logical proportion, they have not vote in the election of the national representatives … A woman of Manchester, more enterprising than the rest of her sex, resolved to assert her natural rights, and actually recorded her vote for a member of parliament. The event ought to create a thrill of admiration in every female heart. It is like one of those sudden and unexpected strokes which have sometimes aroused oppressed classes to a sense of their powers and their rights.

Having bathed the cause of equality in sunlight, *The Times* then summoned the storm clouds:

[Women] ought, it is said, to have a vote because of their great social influence. But what if to obtain a vote would be to sacrifice their social influence? They have now more influence of a certain kind than men have; but if they obtain the influence of men, they cannot expect to retain the influence of women. Nature, it may be thought, has established a fair distribution of power between the two sexes. Women are potent in one sphere, and men in another; and, if they are conscious of the domestic sway they already exercise, they will not imperil it by challenging dominion in a field in which they would be less secure.

We may safely assume that this view of the best interests of women was written by a man.

More significantly, supporters of women's suffrage followed up news of Maxwell's vote with a nationwide campaign. Because the law supposed that husbands owned everything and wives nothing – the law that led Mr Bumble, in Charles Dickens's *Oliver Twist*, to declare that 'if the law supposes that, the law is an ass' – few women met the property qualification. But the campaign argued that the few female ratepayers who did qualify should have the vote.

The task of drawing up voting registers was handled by local overseers. Many continued to keep women off their registers – but not all. In twenty-one towns and boroughs from Southwark to Aberdeen, the names of more than 10,000 women were added to the draft lists – more than half of them in Manchester. These were referred to revising barristers, most of whom struck off the names of women. Some women who lost the vote at this stage appealed against the decision. Now things started to get nasty. Revising barristers persuaded courts in Leeds and Batley to fine the women for 'making a frivolous claim'.

As the 1868 general election approached, there were two groups of women relevant to this story: those who had been struck off and who continued their fight; and those whose names had not been challenged by revising barristers and who remained on their local register.

The legal battle over the first group came to a head in a test case in November 1868 in the Court of Common Pleas, before the Lord Chief Justice. It was known as *Chorlton v. Lings*. Thomas Chorlton was the legal adviser to the Manchester Society for Women's Suffrage; he put the cases of Mary Abbot and Philippine Kyllman, two of the names that an overseer had included on the register only for them to be removed by Mr Lings, the revising barrister.

At the heart of Chorlton's case was the Interpretation Act, passed in 1850 with the aim of 'shortening the language used in Parliament'. It stated that 'unless expressly provided to the contrary', masculine words in legislation are 'deemed and taken to include female'. Chorlton's barrister, John Coleridge, argued that this should apply to the right to vote.

Lings retorted that women had, indeed, been 'expressly' denied the vote. Only the previous year, Parliament had passed the 1867 Reform Act, which had lowered the property hurdle for having the vote. During the course of the debate, John Stuart Mill – the philosopher, champion of women's rights and, at the time, MP – proposed an amendment designed to make explicit the right of women to have the vote. He wanted the word 'man' to be replaced by 'person' throughout the Bill. (Hansard recorded that one of his opponents was a fellow Liberal, Guildford Onslow, who told MPs he had 'asked two young ladies in the lobby how they would vote, supposing they possessed the franchise; and their reply was that they would give their vote to the man who would give them the best pair of diamond earrings'.) By 196 votes to seventy-three, MPs sided with Onslow. They decided 'that the word "man" stand part of the Clause'.

That decision was good enough for the court. It found unanimously for Lings. One of the judges, Sir James Shaw Willes, explained the court's broader thinking on the matter:

Women are under a legal incapacity to vote at elections. What was the cause of it, it is not necessary to go into: but, admitting that fickleness of judgement and liability to influence have sometimes been suggested as the ground of exclusion, I must protest against its being supposed to arise in this country from any under-rating of the sex either in point of intellect or worth. That would be quite inconsistent with one of the glories of our civilisation – the respect and honour in which women are held. This is not a mere fancy of my own, but it will be found in Selden [a seventeenth-century expert in ancient constitutional rights], in the discussion of the origin of the exclusion of women from judicial and like public functions, where the author gives preference to this reason, that the exemption was founded upon motives of decorum, and was a privilege of that sex.

That judgment was handed down on 9 November. Voting started in that year's general election just eight days later. The court ruling applied to all the women whose place on the register had been challenged by revising barristers. While it would apply to future registers, those women whose names had NOT been challenged were still able to vote this time. Around 230 women were estimated to have remained on the register. The suffrage movement identified eighty-one women who succeeded in voting in Kent, Dublin and the Manchester area. The full number across the United Kingdom was clearly greater.

Some of those women helped to secure Jacob Bright's re-election. However, Mill lost his seat, and Jacob Bright became the leading advocate of the suffrage movement in Parliament. In 1870, he introduced a Bill 'to remove the Electoral Disabilities of women'. In his speech to MPs on 4 May 1870, he gave his answer to Sir James Shaw Willes:

I confess I am surprised when I am told that women, as a class, are unfit for the franchise; women who are the subjects of a female Sovereign, are engaged in many literary pursuits; who are at the head of educational establishments; who are managing factories and farms, and controlling thousands of businesses throughout this country …

I have also been told that women should not be political, or, in other words, that it is the duty of women to be politically ignorant. I might as well be told that grass should not be green; and, no doubt, if you sufficiently excluded air and light and moisture it would no longer be so ... To tell me that women should not be political is to tell me that they should have no care for the future of their children, no interest in the greatness and progress of their country.

Then, and again in the following year, Bright was defeated. William Gladstone, the Liberal Prime Minister and a reformer on many issues, opposed Bright, arguing that to give women the vote in parliamentary elections would be 'a practical evil of an intolerable character'. However, Gladstone's premiership did see the passing of the 1869 Municipal Franchise Act, which gave women the right to vote in local elections on the same terms as men, only for a court ruling in 1872 to restrict this right to single women and widows. A single woman who met the property qualification would lose the vote when she got married.

Bright lost his seat in the 1874 general election, only to regain it in 1876. Apart from another brief spell out of Parliament in the mid-1880s, he remained an MP until he retired in 1895. Parliament did not give women the vote in parliamentary elections until 1918, when it was granted to women over thirty. Not until 1928 did women finally get the vote on the same terms as men.

As for the *Chorlton v. Lings* court ruling, it remained an accepted precedent for limiting women's rights until 1930. That year, the Privy Council met to consider its application to 'The Famous Five', five Canadian women who had been denied the right to sit as Senators. The issue came to the Privy Council in London, as the British Empire's final court of appeal. Lord Sankey, the Labour Lord Chancellor, presided over the hearing.

Opponents of the women cited *Chorlton v. Lings* to assert that, without specific legal permission, by 'neither the common law nor the constitution from the beginning of the common law until now can a woman be entitled to exercise any public functions'.

Sankey and his fellow judges found for 'The Famous Five'. Sankey ruled:

The exclusion of women from all public offices is a relic of days more barbarous than ours, but it must be remembered that the necessity of the times often forced on man customs which in later years were not necessary … Customs are apt to develop into traditions which are stronger than law and remain unchallenged long after the reason for them has disappeared.

Finally, the constitutional cause sparked by Lily Maxwell's by-election vote had triumphed. The 63-year journey from 25 Ludlow Street to the Privy Council was complete.

Peter Kellner *is a journalist (*Sunday Times, New Statesman, Inde-*pendent* and others), *political analyst (*BBC* Newsnight* and election results programmes) and former pollster (YouGov). He received a Special Recognition Award from the Political Studies Association in 2011. His grandmother was a suffragette.*

5

COLCHESTER

LUKE BLAXILL

Result: Alexander Learmonth (Conservative), 1,363, 61.5 per cent; Sir Henry Storks (Liberal), 853, 38.5 per cent
Size of majority: 510
Swing: 15 per cent from Liberal to Conservative
Name of previous MP and party: John Gurdon Rebow (Liberal)
Reason for by-election: Death of incumbent
Result at previous general election: John Gurdon Rebow (Liberal), 1,467, 27.2 per cent; William Brewer (Liberal), 1,417, 26.3 per cent; Edward Karslake (Conservative), 1,284, 23.8 per cent; Alexander Learmonth (Conservative), 1,217, 22.6 per cent
Date by-election called: 27 October 1870
Date by-election took place: 3 November 1870
Size of total electorate: 3,145
Total number of votes cast: 2,216
Turnout: 70.5 per cent

The Colchester by-election of 1870 is historically notable because it was successfully hijacked by a national pressure group. The Ladies' National Association for the Repeal of the Contagious Diseases Acts, led by the Christian feminist social reformer Josephine Butler, sought to engineer the defeat of the Liberal candidate, Sir Henry Storks, to protest against the Acts. Crucially, Butler's campaign not only succeeded electorally but her association's intervention at Colchester was seen as a telling factor in the establishment of a Royal Commission to investigate the Acts' effectiveness and their eventual repeal. This contest thus set a precedent for by-elections to become mini-referendums on topical issues where pressure groups could funnel their limited resources into a single constituency and 'send a message' to governments.

The Contagious Diseases Acts were a quintessentially Victorian series of public health measures passed in 1864 and extended in 1866 and 1869. They granted local police and medical authorities powers to detain and inspect prostitutes suspected of carrying venereal infections. They were controversial from the outset. On the one hand, they angered conscientious moralists because they obliquely sanctioned prostitution by giving licence to men to indulge without risk. They also dismayed feminists because women were obliged to undertake humiliating inspections (Butler called them 'medical rape') to be deemed suitable instruments for satisfying male desire. On the other hand, supporters pointed to the Acts' track record. They had dramatically reduced the number of women visibly soliciting, validating the conception of prostitution as a problem that could be marginalised and 'cleaned up' by medical and police authorities.

Colchester, an ancient market town of Essex, became the focus for this agitation for several reasons. First, its large barracks meant the demand for prostitution was high, and the consequent collapse of visible soliciting in vice-afflicted neighbourhoods after the Acts' extension was particularly striking. Second was the candidature of Storks. As well as an accomplished military and colonial administrator who Gladstone wanted in the Commons, Storks was seen by repealers as a leading advocate of the Acts which he had ruthlessly implemented during his tenure as Governor of Malta. Butler's league hoped that Storks's defeat, whether to their own candidate or to a Conservative without such an offensive stance on the Acts, would advance the cause of repeal.

This by-election was fought in 1870 during Gladstone's first premiership, a ministry widely recognised by posterity to have been among the most successful reforming governments of the nineteenth century. Among other achievements, it instituted a large school building programme, disestablished the Irish Church and established meritocratic appointment in the army, judiciary and civil service.

The Colchester contest, caused by the death of its senior member

John Gurdon Rebow, was fought during a brief interregnum between two major democratic reforms: after the Second Reform Act of 1867 (which enfranchised most working-class men in boroughs) but before the Secret Ballot Act of 1872. During this period, electoral culture was evolving swiftly, moving unevenly and haltingly towards modernisation and the principles of mass democracy. First, political parties had become more partisan and highly organised; for instance, Conservative Central Office had been established just seven months earlier. Second, both parties were led by celebrity national leaders in Gladstone and Benjamin Disraeli. Third, urban electorates had grown significantly (Colchester, for example, had 3,145 voters), making public speeches almost mandatory as campaign tools. On the other hand, substantial elements of old Dickensian 'Eatanswill' electoral culture remained: the raucousness of the hustings, bribery and treating (greatly facilitated by the absence of secret voting) and violence. This latter element was particularly in evidence in this election, with hired roughs, bludgeon men and 'lambs' breaking up meetings and even assaulting candidates.

From 1832 to 1885, Colchester was a double-member borough with lively, competitive council politics. Chartism had a modest presence in the 1830s and 1840s; the Colchester Working Men's Association, founded in 1838, promoted only moderate radicalism. The town was characterised by its large barracks, strong agricultural interest and substantial Nonconformist population. The first two features tended to benefit the Conservatives, and the latter the Liberals, but the borough was one of relatively few where the Tories had been in ascendency since the Great Reform Act. The town had been strongly protectionist before Rebow successfully captured one of its seats for the Liberals in 1857. His staunch advocacy of free trade and opposition to the Corn Laws brought meaningful electoral competition to the town and (in the judgement of a local Liberal) 'through him, Colchester learned to take an interest in national politics, and to know the difference between a Tory and a Liberal'. In 1868, the expanded electorate returned a second Liberal, Dr William Brewer, and the borough seemed to have switched party allegiance. However, Rebow's death in 1870 created political opportunities: for the Liberals, to get Storks into Parliament after a local selection row had forced his withdrawal at Newark in April; for the

Conservatives, to capitalise on recent by-election gains at Shrewsbury and West Surrey. Their candidate was Colonel Alexander Learmonth of Edinburgh and the 17th Lancers who had stood unsuccessfully for the borough in 1868. Like Storks, Learmonth was a soldier and a 'carpet bagger' from outside the town. But unlike his uncompromising Liberal opponent, the colonel was a congenial figure whose instinct was to avoid polarising stances on controversial issues. It should be noted that while (as *The Times* highlighted earlier that year) by-elections 'on the whole favour whichever party may be in Opposition', the modern 'mid-term blues' phenomenon of governments doing badly did not exist, and the Liberals had successfully held and indeed gained seats earlier that same year. Thus, both sides felt they stood a good chance.

The contest would have been quite straightforward but for the intervention of a third candidate, Dr John Baxter Langley, who was on the 'ultra radical' wing of the Liberal Party and was vice-president of the Reform League. He was persuaded by Butler at short notice to contest Colchester as a second unofficial Liberal candidate. Both Butler and Langley were devout Christians who no doubt shared the view of *The Shield* (the journal of the National Association for the Repeal of the Contagious Diseases Acts) that Colchester was 'a town of low morals' where the Acts 'had given the appearance of propriety' that amounted only to 'whitening the outside of a sepulchre'. Butler and Langley hoped that sufficient dissenting or conscientious Liberal voters who shared their disdain for the Acts would vote for them and split Storks's vote, and thus 'render his return impossible'. Langley was in poor health when he arrived in Colchester by train just nine days before the poll, whereupon he was launched immediately into a violent public meeting.

As was not unusual for contemporary by-elections, the campaign was short: it opened on 19 October immediately after Rebow's funeral, with the poll held just fifteen days later on 3 November. The most striking facet of Storks's and Learmonth's campaigns was that both men studiously avoided mentioning the Contagious Diseases Acts or the candidature of Langley. Learmonth – no doubt aware of the convenient consequences of the Liberal split to the Conservative cause – treated Storks with the utmost courtesy. Campaigns in this period tended to encourage personal clashes: the hustings brought both candidates together head-to-head, and campaigns consisted of daily meetings where it was de rigueur to rebut what the other side had said. Despite this, Learmonth refused to be drawn and praised Storks as 'a well-known and well-respected Englishman who had served his country'. He confined criticisms to policy, emphasising the operational shortcomings of the Education Act and particularly the deleterious effects of the Gladstone government's 'reduc[tion] of the army to a mere skeleton in order to make a good budget' and its dismissal of dockyard workers. Normally, a challenging candidate attempting to gain a seat would be more aggressive, but Learmonth realised that the three-cornered race had stacked the odds in his favour and did not want to rock the boat. Learmonth's campaign was smooth and his meetings free of much disruption. He clearly enjoyed the local party's united support and was able to mitigate his reputation as a weak orator with assistance from guest speakers on the platform in the form of James Round, the first-class cricketer and current MP for North Essex, and the former Colchester member Edward Karslake. At the hustings, Learmonth's supporters comfortably outnumbered (and outcheered) those of Storks, and carriages on polling day flying Conservative blue reportedly outnumbered those flying Liberal yellow by more than three to one.

There is more to say about Langley's brief campaign. He pledged in his address to 'rescue my party from the obloquy which would attain to it if it sent to Parliament one of the principal supporters of the most immoral and unjust legislation which has disgraced the civilisation of Europe'. Initially, he wrote strong public letters to Storks demanding he relent on his uncompromising advocacy of the Contagious Diseases Acts but received only 'evasive and conditional replies'. He held only two public meetings, complaining of great difficulty in securing the town's main venues, owing to his opponents having quiet words with their proprietors to ensure they shut their doors on him. Langley eventually secured the theatre and caught the train up from London. It was a trap. The vast majority of the audience that packed the stalls were roughs, reportedly hired by Storks's agent, and the meeting swiftly descended into disaster. After declaring that 'I have come here at the wish of a quarter of a million women of this country', Langley proceeded to criticise Storks and was immediately pelted with his opponents' election address attached to various missiles, including rotten apples, mud and walnuts. After a burlesque dancer led the crowd in storming the stage, Langley was 'struck by a bag of flour in the neck which burst upon him … ludicrously streaming down his black coat and waistcoat'. He was unable to proceed and was forced to flee the meeting. He tried once more a few days later after employing twenty sandwich board men to walk the streets with pleas of 'fair play for Langley'. Unfortunately, his second attempt was equally disastrous, and after loftily comparing his campaign to the efforts of 'apostles from the early ages to Christianise the world', roughs armed with weapons stormed his platform and threw chairs at him, once again forcing his retreat and inflicting injuries which required bandages.

Butler herself also came to Colchester to assist Langley alongside numerous female volunteers. Butler – whose favourite phrase was 'God and one woman make a majority' – planned to make speeches to local women who in turn might persuade their husbands, brothers and sons to vote against Storks. However, if Butler expected to be given a polite hearing befitting of a lady, she was mistaken. She recounted that after taking a room in a Tory hotel, the innkeeper informed her that a large crowd of Storks's supporters as well as 'scoundrels and brothel keepers' had assembled outside the building and had threatened to burn it down if she did not vacate. Assisted by fellow female activists Mrs King and Mrs Hampson, she disguised herself as 'a poor woman' and was smuggled out of a back door before sheltering in the basement of a friendly Methodist grocer 'amongst his bacon, soap, and candles' until the mob had dispersed.

For his part, Storks reciprocated his Conservative opponents' courtesy, calling Learmonth a 'gallant colonel' and 'a gentleman of very good character'. He confined his platform remarks to a robust espousal of Gladstonian principles of efficiency regarding the cuts to the standing army and dockyard workers, commenting that it was 'bad economy to keep up a larger army than was absolutely necessary' and that 'the colonial policy of the government had been framed with a view of lightening the taxpayer's burden'. He also gently mocked Disraeli's rather limp opposition to many of Gladstone's measures by observing that the Conservatives had 'caught the Liberals bathing and put on their clothes'. He entirely refrained from mentioning his published opinion on the Contagious Diseases Acts (where he had written that 'prostitution is a necessity') and on only one occasion obliquely referred to Langley and Butler's campaign as 'an opposition which I call unfair, unmanly, and un-English'. A Liberal newspaper was less restrained, however, and, after Langley's disastrous attempts to speak, mocked the repealers for having 'taken up the notion that the good people of Colchester were wild about a certain question … they have found them calm and indifferent or contended on the point' before acerbically remarking that 'all the sobriety of Mr Langley and all the eloquence of Mrs Butler have not been able to raise them beyond the display of a capital popular joke'. Another newspaper writing in support of Storks described Langley's views as 'repugnant' and mocked Butler for addressing an audience of 'about 50 women from the lower class of life'. While Storks's campaign experienced nothing like the disruption of Langley's, he was not given as easy a ride as Learmonth. In one meeting, Brewer and some other leading town Liberals sustained mild injuries from hired roughs at the public hall. Storks himself also suffered significant musical heckling with drunken songs featuring the lyrics 'Poor old Storks' and 'We'll hang old Storks by a sour apple tree'. Most worryingly, a handbill of uncertain origin reprised a poem likening Storks to an avian stork, which concluded:

> And the women of Colchester, Stork, King Stork!
> Will rival their sisters of Newark, King Stork,
> When they know who's come down
> To give laws to the town,
> Where Boadicea once fought, King Stork!
> Contagious Diseases are bad, King Stork;
> But Tyranny's worse than disease, King Stork:
> So off to your bugs,
> And your own native frogs,
> For we won't be swallowed by you, King Stork!

On the day before polling, Langley took the dramatic decision to withdraw his candidature with a 'farewell address'. His reason, which he shared with *The Shield*, was to sound 'a clap of thunder on their opponents' by appealing to sympathetic town Liberals to abstain in protest not just against the Acts but on account of the manner 'Storks' ruffians' had caused him and his female canvassers to be 'hounded in the most hideous manner'. Langley estimated that they had weakened Storks to the tune of 600 votes. When the result was declared, Storks had indeed been thrashed by Learmonth by more than 500. While it was not customary for turnout in by-elections in this period to be lower than general elections, only 70.5 per cent of electors on the register had voted (down from 90.7 per cent in 1868). The Liberals had been decimated by mass abstentions. Butler received a telegram at Liverpool to confirm the news which read simply: '[The Bird] shot dead.'

Despite Langley's ignominious campaign, the repealers' succeeded beyond their wildest dreams. Storks's tactic of strategic silence on the Contagious Diseases issue and the violent disruption of his opponents' campaign had spectacularly backfired. Characteristically, Langley and Butler interpreted the result as a moral epiphany by a sizeable segment of the towns' Liberals. While no doubt minded to exaggerate their own campaign's effectiveness, there seems no doubt that judicious application of targeted pressure to this marginal seat proved decisive. Langley boasted to *The Shield* that 'we may have the courage to feel that we can beat them at anytime, anywhere, no matter how eminent the candidate they put forward … It has sounded the death knell for the Contagious Diseases Acts.' The result was an important factor in prompting Gladstone's government to rethink its policy on the issue. 'When popular feeling is excited,' the premier reflected in December, 'due allowances for executive difficulties are refused.' More substantially, Henry Bruce, the Home Secretary, set up a Royal Commission to examine the Acts in 1871. An unnamed Liberal MP told Butler: 'Your manifesto has shaken us very badly in the House of Commons … We know how to manage any other opposition in the House or in the country, but this is very awkward for us – the revolt of women.'

Learmonth, the fortunate beneficiary of Liberal internal strife, went on to represent Colchester for a decade until losing in 1880. The shrewd pragmatism he displayed in the by-election did not extend to his personal life, and his extravagant London lifestyle caused his bankruptcy in 1887 a month before his death. Storks won a subsequent lower-key by-election at Ripon a year later, and while he was only an MP for three years, he provided telling assistance to Edward Cardwell in his ambitious reforms at the War Office. Langley, meanwhile, repeated his tactic of acting as a 'kingmaker candidate' at two subsequent elections but was later found guilty of conspiracy to defraud in his capacity as chairman of the Artisans, Labourers and General Dwellings Company and was sentenced to eighteen months' hard labour. Butler continued to lead her association to interventions at other by-elections (including at Pontefract, Burnley and Wigan), and eventually the Acts were suspended in 1883 and repealed in 1886. Butler herself described Colchester as 'a turning point in the history of our crusade' and continued to be involved in more general campaigns against prostitution throughout the British Empire, ultimately drawing praise as a brave feminist social reformer who developed new methods of political agitation. This became perhaps the lasting political legacy of the Colchester contest. In the years that followed, numerous campaigning groups agitating for a cause – including temperance reformers, trade unionists, pacifists and suffragists – increasingly recognised the parliamentary by-election as a powerful tool for applying targeted political pressure.

Luke Blaxill is a lecturer in British history at Hertford College, University of Oxford. He is an expert on British electoral history, as demonstrated in his recent open-access article on campaign violence in Past & Present. *His book* The War of Words: The Language of British Elections, 1880–1914 *was published in 2020 by the Royal Historical Society.*

6

NORTHAMPTON

21 FEBRUARY 1884
LIBERAL HOLD

SIMON BARROW

Result: Charles Bradlaugh (Liberal), 4,032, 52.4 per cent; Henry Charles Richards (Conservative), 3,664, 47.6 per cent
Size of majority: 368
Swing: N/A
Name of previous MP and party: Charles Bradlaugh (Liberal)
Reason for by-election: Bradlaugh's refusal to swear a religious Oath of Allegiance
Result at previous general election: Charles Bradlaugh (Liberal), 4,000, 27.7 per cent; Henry Labouchère (Liberal), 3,842, 26.6 per cent; Charles Isham (Conservative), 3,366, 23.3 per cent; Pickering Phipps (Conservative), 3,248, 22.4 per cent
Date by-election called: N/A
Date by-election took place: 21 February 1884
Size of total electorate: 8,886
Total number of votes cast: 7,696
Turnout: 86.6 per cent

Northampton has a unique place in British electoral history as the town that helped change the law on parliamentary oaths for good. The reform took place after a protracted, colourful drama involving political activist, atheist and founder of the National Secular Society (NSS) Charles Bradlaugh, who wished simply to affirm his allegiance to Parliament rather than taking a specifically religious oath. The by-election that took place in the constituency on a damp Thursday, 21 February 1884, proved a pivotal moment in this saga, which was only finally settled by law in 1888.

In the meantime, Bradlaugh, who had first been elected as a Liberal MP for Northampton in the 1880 general election, following defeats in 1868 and 1874, found himself needing to navigate – successfully, as it turned out – three by-elections. The last of these was the decisive 1884 one. He was then returned to Westminster twice more, at general elections in 1885 and 1886, before inadvertently creating yet another by-election in 1891, following his untimely death in London, aged fifty-seven, on 30 January that year.

The drama began in 1880, when the Liberals scored a stunning electoral success against Disraeli, securing a majority which brought Gladstone back to power after his retirement in 1874. The general election, which also featured the return of sixty-five Irish Nationalists, was seen primarily as a sign of public dissatisfaction with Disraeli's imperialist policies. But the new government had barely taken its seats in the House of Commons before the Bradlaugh controversy exploded into the headlines. As well as Home Rule for Ireland, the new, radical member for Northampton advocated three causes which caused particular uproar in Victorian society: birth control, republicanism and atheism.

It was the last which proved to be the eye of the storm. On 3 May 1880, Bradlaugh came to the table of the House of Commons. He carried a letter to the Speaker, 'begging respectfully to claim to be allowed to affirm', instead of taking the religious Oath of Allegiance. He cited the Evidence Amendment Acts of 1869 and 1870 in his defence. A Select Committee was called to evaluate the matter and voted against Bradlaugh being able to affirm. His attempts to take the oath illegally led to a short imprisonment under Big Ben in the Clock Tower at one point, and he finally forfeited his seat in Parliament once he cast a vote in early 1881. He was re-elected in the by-election of 12 April 1881, with the loss of ninety votes and a slight swing against him. His continuing refusal to take a religious oath led to Bradlaugh's expulsion from Parliament once more. He was returned again in the by-election of 4 March 1882.

This sets the scene for the 1884 by-election. It took place nearly two

years after the previous one, due to continued wrangling and disputa-
tion over the oath, during which time Bradlaugh was unable to represent his constituents in the House. Its specific context was one in
which, despite support from Gladstone's government, the Affirmation
Bill was defeated by just three votes in 1883, having taken a considerable time to reach Parliament. The opposition had been able to disrupt
government business and thwart Bradlaugh's attempts to take his seat
for four years by this stage, despite several appearances to plead his case
at the Bar of the House and (at that stage) two successful by-elections.

A major focus of the campaign Bradlaugh fought in the 1884
by-election, as in the previous ones, was around free speech and democratic representation. His opponents, meanwhile, characterised him
as an irresponsible and subversive proponent of blasphemy, sedition
and obscenity. He was a threat to good order and the well-being and
propriety of society at large, they contended. The odds seemed stacked
against the doughty campaigner by virtue (as it was seen then) of opposition to his cause not just from the Conservatives – bar a couple of
minor rebels – but from the Archbishop of Canterbury, Edward White
Benson, and other senior figures from both the Church of England
and the Roman Catholic Church.

There was growing Nonconformist consciousness, but many who
shared that spirit feared speaking out in public because of the possible
deleterious consequences for their reputations and livelihoods. Meanwhile, ecclesiastics sought to portray the situation as a confrontation
between ordinary God-fearing folk and the onslaught of godless hea-
thenism. Benson had succeeded Archibald Campbell Tait, who had also
been unsympathetic, a year before the 1884 by-election. The tension
continued to build when, in 1883, Bradlaugh took his seat and voted
in the Commons three times. He was fined £1,500 for casting votes
illegally. Another Bill which would have allowed him to affirm was defeated in Parliament, and the stage was set for the 1884 by-election.

Among the many ancillary confrontations which re-emerged in the
course of the 1884 campaign was Bradlaugh's recent close association
with Annie Besant, the socialist, freethinker, freemason and women's
rights advocate. In particular, they together republished a pamphlet on
birth control by Charles Knowlton entitled *The Fruits of Philosophy*.

As a result, they were prosecuted on grounds of obscenity. Bradlaugh and Besant received an unfavourable trial and lost the case. They were sentenced to six months in prison. However, they escaped penalty on a technicality at the Court of Appeal. This definitely brought increased support to the National Secular Society, which stood firmly against religious exception and privilege. But it also produced counter-pressure on Liberals who might otherwise have been instinctually Nonconformist.

After a notable general election victory and two previous by-election wins, Bradlaugh's critics hoped that the good voters of Northampton (8,361 of them were registered at this time) would be fed up with what they described as the radical candidate's 'antics'. This proved not to be the case. Interest remained high. Turnout in 1884 was 86.6 per cent, an estimated increase of 1.3 per cent from 1882, with 525 more electors being entitled to vote.

In 1881 and 1882, Bradlaugh's majority over his then Conservative opponent Edward Corbett had been 132 and 108 votes, respectively. In 1884, he was up against the Conservative candidate Henry Charles Richards, a skilled barrister, a high church Anglican and a leading member of the Church Defence Society. The choice, on those grounds, was clear. This time Northampton voters gave Bradlaugh a 368 majority on 52.4 per cent of votes cast. That was the largest margin and percentage in any of the by-elections he fought, the previous two being 51 per cent (1881) and 50.7 per cent (1882), respectively. These may not be huge margins, but they demonstrate an entrenched level of support which deepened in affection and intensity from 1880 onwards.

The Reuters cable report of the 1884 result was, as ever, a masterclass in understatement, given the degree of controversy around the man, the issues and the campaign. 'The election of a member of Parliament for Northampton, which was necessary owing to Mr Bradlaugh's recent resignation, took place yesterday, when Mr Bradlaugh was again elected, the majority of votes recorded in his favour being larger than on any previous occasion,' it noted in a European telegram on 22 February 1884, misdated as 20 February. Opponents of the dogged Liberal were less sanguine, but their frustration had by now been well schooled.

The National Secular Society, which in the late 1880s could claim over 100 branches in England, Australia, India and New Zealand, stood firmly behind its founder. Bradlaugh had helped set up the NSS in 1866, nearly two decades before the 1884 by-election, and the controversies he occasioned undoubtedly assisted its growth, even if some were unhappy with his opposition to socialism. The connection with the socialist Besant helped with that.

Other factors conditioning the 1884 poll outcome were the particular circumstances surrounding both the constituency and the Liberal Party locally. Northampton returned two members from 1880 onwards, when Bradlaugh was selected as the junior candidate. His senior was Henry Labouchère, a writer and theatre owner whose liberalism did not extend to homosexuality. Today, he is best remembered for an amendment which for the first time outlawed all male homosexual activity across the United Kingdom. He was also ferocious in pursuit of the prosecution of Oscar Wilde and bemoaned the fact that the prison sentence which broke him was 'too short'. Nevertheless, he was seen as a radical in other respects, backed Home Rule like Bradlaugh and sought co-operation in Parliament with Irish Nationalists.

There are mixed views as to the relationship between the two men. Although it seems he was an agnostic, Labouchère provided a counterpoint to Bradlaugh in the 1884 campaign, as he had previously, when he described himself mischievously as 'the Christian member for Northampton'. The pairing proved electorally successful, although Labouchère always secured a few more votes than his counterpart. It is likely that the combination contributed to Bradlaugh's success by assuaging more nervous voters. They also helped to sort out some levels of disorganisation within the Northampton party, and they built enduring support by championing local as well as 'national' concerns.

One other feature of the 1884 by-election campaign was that, although Home Rule was not necessarily a major issue for voters, it did feature. As a result, in the succeeding 1886 general election, there was one Conservative candidate and one 'Liberal Unionist', Richard Turner, who tried to make the Irish question a larger concern and attract votes away from Labouchère and Bradlaugh. This proved unsuccessful, although with 23.7 per cent of the poll, he undoubtedly made an impact, even though the two official Liberal Party candidates were returned once more, albeit with a reduced combined share of the vote.

What this demonstrates, among other things, is that the commit-ment to the Liberals evident in Northampton throughout the 1880s, and perhaps especially to high-profile and pungent characters, re-mained strong. With Bradlaugh re-elected once more in 1884, he again tried to affirm and take his seat. He also sought once more, as he had in the past, to vote three times. He was later fined for having done so. But the political ground had clearly shifted. A further attempt by Brad-laugh to affirm rather than take a religiously grounded oath, in January 1886, was finally accepted by the Speaker, Sir Arthur Wellesley Peel. At last, Bradlaugh was allowed to sit and vote legitimately in Parliament.

This was not quite the end of the 'Bradlaugh affair', however. Po-litical turmoil had resulted in general elections being called in both 1885 and 1886. Although a breakthrough for him personally became possible as a result of the actions of Peel, probably influenced by the clear evidence that the voters of Northampton were not about to be swayed into ditching the determined Liberal rebel, the law remained unchanged. So Bradlaugh's ability to take his seat and participate in the regular business of Parliament remained the exception rather than the rule. His doing so also risked prosecution under the Parliamentary Oaths Act. By this time, however, opposition to affirming had been seriously eroded by the indefatigability of its proponents.

Finally, in 1888, Charles Bradlaugh and his allies secured passage for a new Oaths Act. This was one which enshrined into law the right of affirmation for members of both Houses. It also extended and clarified the law as it related to witnesses in civil and criminal trials. That was important, because the Evidence Amendment Acts of 1869 and 1870 had proved unsatisfactory in this respect, whatever their other merits in providing relief to many who would otherwise have been put at a disadvantage.

In truth, it is insufficient to claim that this success was down to the February 1884 Northampton by-election. It was clearly part of a cumulative process, rather than one single event in electoral politics. Nevertheless, it was the 1884 poll which helped to tip the scales deci-sively, not just for Bradlaugh but for the campaign to equalise the law for religious and non-religious adherents alike. This is one of the most significant reforms in parliamentary history. The determined people of

Northampton definitely played their part in entrenching a parliamentary rebel who came to emblemise the case for an important change.

Simon Barrow *is a writer, commentator and former director of the beliefs, ethics and politics think-tank Ekklesia. He has authored and edited many books and articles, including* Britain Needs Change: The Politics of Hope and Labour's Challenge, *with Gerry Hassan (Biteback, 2024).*

7

MID-LANARK

BARONESS BRYAN

Result: John Philipps (Liberal), 3,847, 52.1 per cent; William Bousfield (Conservative), 2,917, 39.5 per cent; Keir Hardie (Independent Labour), 617, 8.4 per cent
Size of majority: 930
Swing: N/A
Name of previous MP and party: Stephen Mason (Liberal)
Reason for by-election: Resignation of incumbent
Result at previous general election: Stephen Mason (Liberal), 3,779, 56.5 per cent; James Shand-Harvey (Liberal Unionist), 2,909, 43.5 per cent
Date by-election called: March 1888
Date by-election took place: 27 April 1888
Size of total electorate: 9,143
Total number of votes cast: 7,381
Turnout: 80.7 per cent

On paper, this by-election may not look that interesting. The Liberals held the seat. The Independent Labour candidate received barely 600 votes. Not a lot to see here.

The opposite is true. It came at a critical point in British politics, and the participants and onlookers recognised its significance at the time. There were four elements at play: there was an ongoing crisis in the Liberal Party with splits between the Whigs and more radical Liberals; Irish Home Rule was in the balance; in Scotland, the Crofters' Party had made significant gains, but wider land reform remained an electoral issue; and the demand for working-class representation was beginning to get traction, but the debate around how to achieve it was unresolved. All these tensions came together in this one by-election.

The struggles over who controlled the Liberal Party had been rumbling on for decades before the 1888 Mid-Lanark by-election. This was mostly played out in England, with Joseph Chamberlain leading the challenge against the established leadership.

The Liberal Party in Scotland was separately organised from the English and Welsh Party. In both, there was a battle for power between the landed aristocracy and the new generation representing middle-class voters, but the specific issues in Scotland were to do with land reform and disestablishing the Church of Scotland.

The old Whigs, who had for generations controlled the party, continued to hold sway through Liberal associations. The constitution and rules in Scotland restricted the party's role to 'giving information and advice at elections' and 'not in any way to interfere with the independent action of the various Liberal Associations from which it is formed'.

The more radical elements wanted a party membership organisation that could directly influence party policy. A members' council was established, but although it could pass policy resolutions, the executive simply ignored them.

Despite Gladstone being a Scottish MP, he was busy fighting on many fronts in London and left the Scottish Liberal Party in the hands of Lord Rosebery, one of the many Scottish Liberal aristocrats. The breakdown in party unity in Scotland caused serious concern when rival Liberal candidates began contesting the same seat. The members looked to Gladstone to support their demands on disestablishment of the Church of Scotland, but he eventually decreed that it must be placed 'at the end of a long vista' and that it would not be a commitment in the general election.

The Liberal Association's earlier decision not to interfere in local associations contributed to the chaos of the 1885 general election as across Britain twenty-seven constituencies had rival Liberal candidates with eleven independent Liberals and four Crofters' Party candidates winning seats. Gladstone was only able to form a government with the support of the Irish Party. This laid the ground for a new split in the party on his commitment to Irish Home Rule.

To gain the support of the Irish Party, Gladstone introduced the Government of Ireland Bill of 1886, known as the 'First Home Rule Bill'. The limited Home Rule on offer was still too much for Liberal Unionists and contributed to an even bigger split in the Scottish Party. The traditional Whig Scottish Liberal Association withdrew its support from Gladstone and those who had opposed his earlier stance on disestablishment became his most loyal supporters.

The Bill was defeated, resulting in a second general election, just seven months into Gladstone's premiership. Liberal Unionists defected and formed a pact with the Conservatives. In Mid-Lanark in 1886, it was a Liberal Unionist candidate who unsuccessfully stood against the Liberals, but elsewhere the Liberals were heavily defeated, losing 127 MPs to the Tories and Liberal Unionists.

Irish politics had become intimately linked to the success of the Liberal Party. This was particularly so in the towns and cities with large Irish populations.

The famine in Ireland had resulted in huge levels of migration. In 1847 alone, over 50,000 Irish migrants arrived in Glasgow. They joined an already destitute population where jobs were hard to find and precarious.

When work became available in Lanarkshire, many Irish families moved eastwards, where men and boys found work as miners, navvies and general labourers. They were mainly from Donegal and Ulster in the north of Ireland and were mostly Catholic. They established their own organisations and as the Irish Home Rule movement developed, many became politically affiliated to Irish political organisations.

The two most influential leaders from Ireland were Charles Stewart Parnell and Michael Davitt. Davitt came from extreme poverty and was known for his radical politics. Parnell came from a wealthy Anglo-Irish family and intended to win support from landowners. Although from very different backgrounds and politics, they both, ultimately, put the cause of Home Rule above other political issues.

Davitt was a frequent visitor to Scotland and became associated with the crofters' struggles in the Highlands and Islands. In central Scotland, he urged the Irish immigrant population to integrate into the politics of their adopted country. While he favoured the establishment of a Labour Party, he joined Parnell in encouraging Irish voters to support the Liberals in the 1886 general election.

The land issue was a further source of difference within the Liberal Party, with the Duke of Argyll and other Whig landowners opposing more rights for their tenants. Despite this, the Gladstone government passed the Crofters' Holdings Act of 1886.

Support for land reform in Scotland was not exclusive to the Highland Land League and its political wing, the Crofters' Party. As the Crofters' Act was limited to just seven 'crofting counties', it left large parts of Scotland still demanding land reform. The issue was taken up by socialist groups and many Liberals. The Scottish Land Restoration League was founded in Glasgow in 1884 and the Edinburgh-based Scottish Land and Labour League followed a year later. The radical Liberal MP Robert Cunninghame Graham campaigned to end the mineral royalties paid to landowners such as the Duke of Hamilton whose ancestral home was in the Mid-Lanark constituency.

Politics during the nineteenth century was largely a hobby for the wealthy. Sons waiting to enter the House of Lords at the death of their fathers could spend time in the House of Commons. It was very much a gentlemen's club which met around the other annual activities of the landed gentry. It would often not meet at all between the summer and January.

MPs were not paid, so it was necessary to have an income from another source. Laws on bribery and corruption were ineffective, particularly in rural areas, where the landlord and the MP could be one and the same person.

During the nineteenth century, more working-class men were able to vote. But the widening of the franchise didn't result in a widening of political choice. As Gilbert and Sullivan put it in *Iolanthe* in 1882:

> I often think it's comical,
> How Nature always does contrive
> That every boy and every gal
> That's born into the world alive
> Is either a little Liberal
> Or else a little Conservative!

The Labour Representation League, formed in 1869 by John Stuart Mill with the support of the Trades Union Congress (TUC), tried to change this, but it made little progress and was subsumed into the Liberal Party. Meanwhile, under Gladstone's leadership, a split occurred between the Whigs, who opposed any challenge to their control of the party and strongly objected to having working-class Members of Parliament, and those who thought they could incorporate a small number of TUC-supported candidates, as long as they were carefully chosen.

The Liberal Party continued to benefit from working men's votes, but in the 1880 election, only three candidates could be said to represent their needs, and even that was questionable. Henry Broadhurst was Secretary of the TUC, but he was far from radical. Indeed, he spent much of his time battling with Keir Hardie and others over issues such as the importance of the eight-hour day, a key demand of the workers' movement, and whether there was any need for independent labour representation.

In 1887, Keir Hardie attended his first TUC Congress. In his debut speech, he attacked Henry Broadhurst MP on the grounds that he had supported a Liberal candidate who employed sweated labour. This lone intervention by Hardie was his earliest salvo in a campaign for working-class representation that eventually resulted in the formation of the Labour Party.

Keir Hardie was a socialist and a member of the Liberal Party. He wanted to test the Liberal Party's commitment to make space for working-class candidates. Mid-Lanark seemed particularly auspicious as it had a sizable working-class electorate and Hardie was born in Lanarkshire and had worked as a miner and trade union organiser there. He also had the support of local Liberal Party members. The Liberal member for North West Lanarkshire was Robert Cunninghame Graham, considered to be the first socialist in Parliament. He encouraged Hardie to run for the seat.

Hardie applied to the Mid-Lanark Liberal Association describing himself as 'a Radical of a somewhat advanced type'. His address to the miners of Mid-Lanark claimed that a vote for Hardie would be 'a vote for Gladstone, Parnell and you'. The TUC had recently established the Labour Electoral Association, which committed £400 towards Hardie's campaign.

The support of local members, however, was not enough. He needed the support of the Liberal Association, but it decided to select an English candidate with no local connections, from one of the elite Liberal families based in Wiltshire. It is probable that Cunninghame Graham and Hardie had anticipated rejection and already had plans for launching an independent Labour Party, so that if Hardie was not selected for the Liberal Party, he would stand as a Labour candidate.

Hardie had been assured by his supporters that he could count on the 3,500 Irish votes. With that and the backing of important trade union figures such as Tom Mann from Manchester, he could win the seat.

His campaign poster tried to appeal to all his target voters. It listed: Home Rule, democratic government, justice to labour, no monopoly, no landlordism, temperance reform, healthy homes, fair rents, the eight-hour day and work for the unemployed.

The London leadership of the Liberal Party had real concerns that Hardie's support among Liberal voters would split their vote, so they offered him a safe seat at the next general election with a salary of £300 a year if he would step down in Mid-Lanark. When he turned this down, the Labour Electoral Association withdrew its earlier commitment to financial support.

He then lost the backing of the Irish voters as Parnell and the Irish National League encouraged support for the Liberal candidate as the best means of keeping influence with Gladstone. An article in the *Glasgow Catholic Observer* said that 'Home Rule had to come first before the interests of the workmen'.

Hardie had hoped to receive strong support from land reform campaigners, but he had never involved himself with either land reform or the crofters' movement as all his efforts had been in industrial trade union organisation.

Furthermore, some trade unionists were concerned about where Hardie's funding was coming from; he was damaged by consistent rumours that he was receiving money from the Tories. His appointment of Tom Mann as his campaign manager, rather than help his prestige, upset local socialists who did not think it was necessary to bring in someone from England. The high hopes with which he started evaporated as the campaign progressed.

After the result was declared, he celebrated the support of the 'gallant

600' who had voted for him. He must have been disappointed that he could not win in such ideal conditions. As it turned out, it was to be the one and only time he fought a seat in Scotland.

In the immediate aftermath of the by-election, Hardie and Cunninghame Graham formed the Scottish Labour Party and Hardie went on to help found the Independent Labour Party, a British-wide movement in 1893. He continued to campaign for the TUC to back a labour party and was eventually successful in 1900 with the formation of the Labour Representation Committee, the forerunner of the Labour Party, which was founded in 1906.

Although he lost in Mid-Lanark, he was making a name for himself elsewhere and was selected as a candidate in the London seat West Ham South, which he won in 1892. He lost the seat at the following election and described his time in the House of Commons 'as a place which I remember with a haunting horror'. In 1900, however, he was elected in Merthyr Tydfil, which he held until his death in 1915.

Hardie was greatly admired by leading socialists including James Connolly, Jean Jaurès, Eugene Debs, Eleanor Marx, Friedrich Engels and Sylvia Pankhurst. He was loved by working men, women and children. He was the first leader of the Parliamentary Labour Party, but his main role was as an agitator. He died aged fifty-nine, worn out by decades of campaigning and opposition to the First World War.

The successful candidate, John Wynford Philipps, was the eldest son of a baronet. He served as the MP for Mid-Lanark for six years before resigning and later becoming the MP for Pembrokeshire in Wales, which was something of a family seat. Ironically, this made him a Welsh MP at the same time as Keir Hardie was MP for Merthyr Tydfil.

For a while at least, Westminster housed both the victor and defeated candidates from the 1888 Mid-Lanark by-election, one representing the entrenched privilege of the British class system and the other committed to its demise. Only one of these names is remembered, that of Keir Hardie.

Baroness Bryan is president of the Keir Hardie Society and has edited books on his life and work. In 2025, she edited a book marking the fiftieth anniversary of the Red Paper on Scotland titled: Keep Left: Red Paper on Scotland 2025. *She was appointed a Labour peer by Jeremy Corbyn.*

8

OLDHAM

6 JULY 1899
LIBERAL GAIN FROM CONSERVATIVES

ALEX PUFFETTE

Result: Alfred Emmott (Liberal), 12,976, 26.7 per cent (elected); Walter Runciman (Liberal), 12,770, 26.2 per cent (elected); Winston Churchill (Conservative), 11,477, 23.6 per cent; James Mawdsley (Conservative), 11,449, 23.5 per cent

Size of majority: Majority for Emmott: 1,499; majority for Runciman: 1,293

Swing: 2.4 per cent from Conservative to Liberal (Emmott); 1.8 per cent from Conservative to Liberal (Runciman)

Name of previous MPs and party: Robert Ascroft (Conservative); James Oswald (Conservative)

Reason for by-election: Oswald's resignation due to ill health and then Ascroft's death

Result at previous general election: Robert Ascroft (Conservative), 13,085, 26.3 per cent (elected); James Oswald (Conservative), 12,465, 25.0 per cent (elected); Adam Lee (Liberal), 12,249, 24.6 per cent; John Tomlinson Hibbert (Liberal), 12,092, 24.2 per cent

Date by-election called: 27 June 1899

Date by-election took place: 6 July 1899

Size of total electorate: 28,476

Total number of votes cast: Approx. 24,550

Turnout: 86.2 per cent

The Greatest Briton put himself at the mercy of the electorate for the first time in Oldham in July 1899. Winston Churchill would contest over twenty elections during a political career that spanned six decades, but this first contest was seminal.

Not least because Churchill lost, which ended up being an unintended masterstroke. Had he won, the 24-year-old would almost certainly have never served as a journalist in the Second Boer War, where he escaped capture in a scene reminiscent of *Indiana Jones* involving a freight train and a coal mine, which turned him into a national hero. The incredible publicity that this posting brought him did far more for the tale of Churchill than victory in Oldham in 1899 ever would. Nevertheless, this contest greatly shaped the political animal that Churchill was and, therefore, arguably in the history of British by-elections, is among the most consequential.

Oldham was meant to be a rather straightforward affair. It was a true Conservative/Liberal marginal, in what was then Lancashire, and as a multi-member constituency had two MPs, both Conservative in early 1899. So, when James Oswald, one of the two incumbents, decided that it would be in his and the party's interests to stand down after suffering from a bout of ill health, the other MP, Robert Ascroft, quickly approached Churchill to stand as Oswald's replacement. The son of former Chancellor Lord Randolph Churchill was well known to harbour political ambitions, which combined with the weight that the Churchill name carried, and the youngster's successful career as a journalist and writer, left Winston Churchill as a competitive candidate. The Conservative ticket had been drafted, with the energetic Churchill, supported by the locally popular Ascroft, primed to take on the Liberals.

However, only a few weeks later, Ascroft died, and so another by-election was needed. Lord Salisbury's Conservative government, and Conservative Central Office, feared defeat in both elections and to mitigate the damage decided to call a double by-election, meaning that both Oldham MPs would be elected on the same day. From the beginning, optimism was not a word that would be associated with Lord Salisbury's attitude to his candidates' chances.

The political reality for the Conservatives at the time was stark. Some Prime Ministers are masters of foreign policy, others roam the domain of domestic affairs, and in 1899 the Conservatives were being led by a

Prime Minister who was squarely in the former category. Unlike the 1900 khaki election a year later, the by-election in Oldham was not to be fought on Britain's place in the world and the policies implemented beyond its borders. Churchill was aware that he was effectively being sent as a lamb to the slaughter but decided that 'any political fight in any circumstances seemed to me better than no fight at all'.

Churchill would be one of the Conservative combatants, but a second was to be found. The local Conservatives and Liberals both had an initial idea to only stand a candidate each, which would lead to each party gaining one MP. As it would today, this suggestion provoked outrage from local activists on both sides. As a result, rather perceptively, to run with a through-and-through member of the establishment, the Conservative Party picked a trade unionist, who claimed he would be, in effect, a Conservative–Independent Labour candidate. James Mawdsley had started working in a cotton mill before he turned ten, and as an adult had been a part of the Trades Union Congress, becoming chairman four years before the by-election. The newspapers found the pairing incredulous, with Churchill, who was raised in a palace, and Mawdsley, a factory, being labelled as 'The Scion and the Socialist'.

To take on 'The Scion and the Socialist', the Liberals picked Alfred Emmott and Walter Runciman, perhaps as close to an ideal Liberal election pairing as could be found at the time – Emmott was local *and rich* and Runciman was young *and rich*. As the leading cotton spinner in the town, a former mayor and with a wife who was active in the local community, Emmott had exactly the sort of local connections that serve candidates well. Runciman, on the other hand, was a 29-year-old energetic campaigner whose father had founded a successful shipping company. Helpfully, for Runciman, just like Emmott, his wife was also keen to play a role in his political career, joining her husband at events and campaigning sessions. Pamela Plowden, the first love of Churchill, however, refused to come to support her partner. The Conservatives already had a mountain to climb, but the Liberals were keen to ensure that there was no chance that The Scion nor The Socialist made it to the summit.

The scale of his opponents' wealth alarmed Churchill and, given the importance of finance to a political campaign, he was right to be perturbed. Churchill rallied against what he perceived as double standards:

> The poor Trade Unionist friend and I would have had very great difficulty in finding £500 between us, yet we were accused of representing the vested interests of society, while our opponents, who were certainly good for a quarter of a million, claimed to champion in generous fashion the causes of the poor and needy.

Across the eighty-eight by-elections covered in this book, there are themes that emerge. Some campaigns become referendums on the government, others a temperature check on particular political issues, and some insurgencies by radical candidates. In Oldham, the campaign ultimately came down to one issue – the Clerical Tithes Bill. This legislation, which was being proposed by the Conservative government, stipulated that local tax rates would be used to help fund the Church of England clergy and church schools, which were not greatly strapped for cash in the eyes of the populace. As the only Anglican candidate, Churchill was being aimed at to take the brunt of the blame for the Bill from the Oldham electorate. An electorate which contained a significant chunk of Nonconformists, who dissented from the Church of England, and as a result were particularly unhappy with the Bill and the fact that it meant that their taxes would fund the very church they dissented from. With the candidates being forced to subscribe to the party line on the Bill, the Conservative campaign was not in a strong position going into the by-election.

'The Liberal candidates present their compliments and respectfully solicit your vote and influence,' read the Liberal leaflets in Oldham. These leaflets formed part of the strong campaign that the Liberals fought, which showed Emmott and Runciman as two safe pairs of hands, compared to the incredibly baby-faced Churchill and, to some, scraggly Mawdsley. Churchill wrote to his mother during the campaign conceding that Emmott and Runciman were far better at 'placarding and pushing their propaganda' than he was, which perhaps makes it sound simply that the Liberals were just the superior campaigners.

On occasion, the combatants went for the jugular. Runciman

accused Churchill of having spent the previous years 'swashbuckling' round the world, referring to Churchill's military service. Churchill retorted with rage: 'A Lancashire regiment was up the Nile! Was that swashbuckling? Mr Runciman, of course, has not had the same experience as the Queen's Own Lancashire Fusiliers.' Churchill knew, however, that these broadsides would do little to change the outcome, as in reality the Conservative government had made their candidates' task almost impossible.

In another attempt to counter the unpopularity of his party and halt the Liberal swing, Churchill gave speech after speech during the campaign, with up to eight speaking engagements per day. His campaign launch was attended by 2,500, with subsequent speeches attracting 1,000 at peak. The sheer scale of his orations caused one of his tonsils to become inflamed. Merely in his twenties, Churchill was a remarkable public speaker, but to escape the dire hand that the Conservative government had dealt, it would take more than an impressive turn of phrase.

Mere days before voters in Oldham were due to go to the polls, at a Methodist school no less, Churchill reversed his stance on the central issue of the campaign. Declaring that the Conservative Clerical Tithes Bill was a mistake and that if elected he would vote against it, Churchill undertook a screeching U-turn that represented a desperate final roll of the dice to stop the march of the Liberals. While the audience gathering to hear Churchill speak roared, outside the hall the attempt entirely backfired. Voters who were unhappy with the Bill were going to vote Liberal anyway, and all Churchill did was enrage his base, who already were struggling to be enthused by 'The Scion and the Socialist' ticket. Days prior, the Conservative MP for nearby Stockport had defected to the Liberals over the Bill and so the central Conservative Party did not take well to another betrayal by one of its high-profile members. Arthur Balfour, soon to be Prime Minister, said of Churchill's change of heart: 'I thought he was a young man of promise, but it appears he is a young man of promises.' Churchill later reflected that if you do not defend your party in its darkest hour, there is little point defending it at all. No doubt those that lead modern political parties feel that this is a lesson that some modern by-election candidates could also learn.

Less than three weeks after Ascroft had suddenly died, polling day arrived, and the Conservative campaign was treated to a much-needed high-profile campaign visit. Lady Randolph Churchill arrived dressed head to toe in blue to support her eldest son. Another reinforcement was due, in the form of a car that a friend lent Churchill. Unfortunately, the car broke down before it even reached the Lancashire town, perhaps a portent of the result that was to come for the Conservatives.

As the people of Oldham, minus all the women and the disenfranchised men, headed to the secret ballot – which had only been introduced three decades before, with voters then having to declare their choice of candidate openly – it became clear that as Churchill had realised during the campaign, the Conservatives were in a difficult position. Both campaigns transported voters to the polling station by car, something still done in British elections to this day. The Conservatives managed to ferry more people, but no amount of ground campaigning by Churchill and Mawdsley could change the result.

After the Liberal victory was declared, in a scene still seen today, the Conservatives headed to the local Conservative club to drown their sorrows. Churchill, in typical fashion, wrote that he was left with 'those feelings of deflation which a bottle of Champagne or even soda-water represents when it has been half emptied and left uncorked for a night'. While in hindsight losing greatly benefited Churchill, he certainly did not feel that at the time.

'Everyone threw the blame on me,' wrote Churchill. The Conservative establishment blamed him for allowing Mawdsley, the antithesis of what they, unwisely, believed a Tory should be, to run with him. Others suggested that Churchill's youth caused the defeat, ignoring the fact that youthful Runciman had prevailed. Arthur Balfour, taking a different tone to his reprimand for Churchill's U-turn, wrote to console along with helpfully summarising the reason why the youngster's chances of victory were slim to begin with:

The employers dislike the compensation bill; the doctors dislike the vaccination bill; the general public dislike the clergy, so the rating [Clerical Tithes] bill is unpopular: the clergy resented your repudiation of the bill: the Orangemen are sulky and refuse to be conciliated even by the promise to vote for the Liverpool proposals. Of course, those benefited by our measures are not grateful, while those who suppose themselves to be injured resent them. Truly unpromising conditions under which to fight a Lancashire seat!

It is clear that for Churchill in 1899, Oldham was the perfect storm.

Churchill's biographer, Roy Jenkins, fairly concluded that the future Prime Minister 'neither distinguished nor disgraced himself' in the contest. A fair characterisation, given that Churchill reversed his views on the paramount issue of the campaign, the Clerical Tithes Bill, abandoning his party as a result. While his packed schedule of speaking engagements perhaps should be a benchmark for those that seek election even today, in reality, they were futile and always would be. To Churchill, by-elections 'are even worse than ordinary elections because all the cranks and faddists of the country ... fasten upon the wretched candidate' – perhaps the living by-election candidates featured in later chapters feel exactly the same.

Excerpts from the 'Ditties of the Day' section of the *Westminster Budget* newspaper, widely circulated at the time, summarise the contest in Oldham in 1899 well and rather humorously:

> The Scion and the Socialist were standing hand in hand; They wept like anything to see the Liberals sweep the land. 'If Oldham only puts us in they said that would be grand!' ...
>
> The Scion and the Socialist stood for a week or so. And then they took a Tory line, Conveniently low: and all the little voters stood and listened in a row ...
>
> 'O Voters,' said the Socialist. 'Shall you be giving us your votes?' But answer comes there none – and this is scarcely odd, because they're Liberals every one.

Runciman and Emmott both went on to serve in Cabinet, the former joining in 1908 and the latter in 1914. The Runciman Report was drafted by its namesake in 1938, which marked a key step towards the Munich Agreement and the wider appeasement of Nazi Germany. The fate of 'The Scion and the Socialist', on the other hand, is very much a tale of two halves. The Socialist, Mawdsley, died a few years later after breaking his china bath due to his sizeable weight and succumbing to the injuries this caused. The Scion, however, was not to be left deflated. Prior to standing in the election, Churchill consulted a palm reader, who relayed to him that she had a very positive reading for his future, and Churchill was no doubt keen to still make that a reality. Fresh from escaping having been captured in South Africa, where he had been a war correspondent reporting on the Second Boer War, in the 1900 'khaki election', Churchill defeated Walter Runciman to become the new MP for Oldham.

A blue plaque remains on the Oldham Town Hall to commemorate where Churchill gave his first speech as a Member of Parliament. A year prior at the by-election count, the victorious Runciman had sauntered out of the very same town hall, turned to the defeated 24-year-old Conservative and said, 'Don't worry, I don't think this is the last the country has heard of either of us.' Certainly in the case of Winston Churchill, the man who would go on to save Britain, that was to be the understatement of the century.

Alex Puffette is a recent philosophy, politics and economics graduate. He is Iain Dale's researcher and wrote the chapter on Napoleon Bonaparte in The Dictators *(Hodder & Stoughton, 2024). He wrote his first book aged sixteen and stood in his first election aged nineteen.*

9

BARNARD CASTLE

24 JULY 1903
LABOUR REPRESENTATION COMMITTEE GAIN

DAVID LAWS

Result: Arthur Henderson (Labour Representation Committee), 3,370, 35.4 per cent; William Vane (Conservative/Unionist), 3,323, 35.0 per cent; Hubert Beaumont (Liberal), 2,809, 29.6 per cent
Size of majority: 47
Swing: N/A
Name of previous MP and party: Joseph Pease (Liberal)
Reason for by-election: Death of incumbent
Result at previous general election: Joseph Pease (Liberal), 5,036 votes, 58.7 per cent; William Vane (Unionist), 3,545 votes, 41.3 per cent
Date by-election called: 6 July 1903
Date by-election took place: 24 July 1903
Size of total electorate: 11,226
Total number of votes cast: 9,502
Turnout: 84.6 per cent

Between January 1900 and the outbreak of the First World War, there was a veritable tsunami of by-elections – 274, or over one and a half on average each month.

Of these, the Barnard Castle by-election of July 1903 stands out as one of the most historically significant. Though it made no difference to the balance of forces in the Commons, this was the first by-election in which the Labour Party (then the Labour Representation Committee) was to win a seat against both Liberal and Conservative/Unionist opponents. It helped reinforce the case for an anti-Unionist Lib–Lab pact, which led on to the establishment of a Labour bridgehead in Parliament which would eventually be used to assault the Liberal Party.

Liberal leaders, including the Chief Whip, were content for Labour to win the by-election. And during the campaign, the chairman of the Northern Liberal Association angrily complained to the *Daily News* that Liberal leaders had 'cheerfully cast Barnard Castle to the wolves in the hope perhaps of keeping them from their own doors'. He cautioned that the Liberals were in danger of 'nursing into life a serpent which would sting their party to death'.

At Barnard Castle, the Liberal leadership conspired to deliver Labour its fifth MP and assisted in placing into Parliament the man who would become Labour's first ever Cabinet minister and serve three spells as its party leader. What explains this extraordinary behaviour?

In 1903, the Liberals were only three years away from winning a landslide general election, inflicting on the Unionists their worst ever defeat (until 2024).

But the Liberals were feeling neither confident nor strong. The Unionists had beaten them in the last four general elections, and they had enjoyed only two brief spells in office since 1885. The party was split over Home Rule. It was struggling to raise money. And in the 1900 election, it fielded a feeble 402 candidates for 670 seats.

Although Labour had won only two seats in the 1900 general election, the party was now growing – particularly in the north. By 1902, its affiliated membership, backed by the trade unions, exceeded 700,000. And in this year, the party began to receive union political levies to help fund electioneering – a crucial development.

In August 1902, the LRC won its third seat in a by-election at Clitheroe, after the Liberals decided not to field a candidate. By now, the Liberal leadership was talking to the LRC about a potential pact in certain seats.

North-east England was still, however, a Liberal stronghold, and the few working-class MPs being elected were 'Lib–Labs', accepting the Liberal whip. In 1900, the LRC stood a candidate only in Sunderland, but in February 1903, it decided to target four seats in the region – including Barnard Castle. The north-east Liberals became aware of this – and the Liberal industrialists who dominated the party in the region were deeply suspicious of the LRC.

By March 1903, the Liberal Chief Whip at Westminster, Herbert Gladstone, was secretly briefing his party leader, Henry Campbell-Bannerman, that there were no 'material points of difference' in the policies of the LRC and Liberals and that a national deal was possible to give a number of Labour candidates 'an open field against a common enemy'.

On 13 March 1903, Gladstone sent Campbell-Bannerman a memorandum, summarising his very talks with Ramsay MacDonald, Secretary of the Labour Representation Committee. As well as setting out the principles behind a possible seats deal, he identified around thirty-five seats where the Liberals might consider giving Labour an unchallenged run.

The memorandum listed around fifty named seats – divided into clusters based on their likelihood of deals being done. Twenty-three seats were described as 'where there is no difficulty'. The reason for their inclusion looks fairly obvious. None had Liberal MPs. Some had not even fielded Liberals in 1900. Many had already been contested by the LRC or Lib–Labs, without Liberal involvement. And in the two member seats, one Liberal and one LRC candidate could be fielded.

Next was a list of five seats considered 'adjustable' – including Leicester, a two-member seat, where Ramsay MacDonald would stand and win in 1906. This was followed by a list of five, described as 'claimed by LRC and difficult', including Sheffield, Rochdale and Jarrow. It is not difficult to see why these seats were 'difficult'. Three were already Liberal and in another the second-placed Liberal was well ahead of an LRC candidate.

Below this was a list of six seats classified as 'available alternatives'. The rationale for these seats looks to be based on one obvious characteristic – they were seats held by the Conservatives/Unionists and in most cases for the best part of twenty years. Only one seat failed to fit that pattern. That seat was Barnard Castle – a held Liberal seat and one that had been Liberal for decades. Including this seat on the list was not going to be popular with the local party, unless it was willing to embrace the LRC candidate as a natural ally.

At the end of the Gladstone memorandum, it was noted that local Liberal associations would still determine whether to field candidates or not – 'but the Liberal Council will use every legitimate effort to secure this open field and to maintain it for authorised and responsible Labour candidates'.

Two days before the memorandum was sent, on 11 March 1903, there had been a by-election at Woolwich in London. The Unionists had held the seat continuously since its creation – in 1895 by a huge 10,519 majority and in 1900 unopposed. But this time, Will Crooks, a well-known trade unionist, local politician and LRC member, stood against the Unionists, without Liberal competition, and won easily – securing over 60 per cent of the vote.

It looked to Liberal leaders as if co-operation with the LRC was both desirable and necessary. In some seats, like Woolwich (on Gladstone's list as a seat where 'there is no difficulty'), Labour might be able to win in areas in which the Liberals had failed to break through. In others, avoiding a Lib–Lab contest might remove the risk of Unionists triumphing because of a split 'progressive' vote.

If Woolwich was the perfect seat for Lib–Lab co-operation, Barnard Castle was the constituency on the MacDonald/Gladstone list that might prove most tricky. And now, barely three months later, the seat's Liberal MP, Sir Joseph Pease, who had been MP since 1885, died on his seventy-fifth birthday, on 23 June 1903.

Pease had a gold-standard CV for a Liberal of this era. His father was a Quaker industrialist who had served as Durham's MP. He was a prominent north-east businessman, with interests in coal, mills, manufacturing and the family's own bank. He was a Justice of the Peace, a deputy lieutenant, the president of the Peace Society and a campaigner against the opium trade.

As for Barnard Castle, it had been a Liberal seat in every year since its creation in 1885, while the Liberals had also finished in first place in the predecessor seat of South Durham in every election since the seat was established in 1832.

In 1903, Barnard Castle was regarded as a safe Liberal seat – in which the party would often bank 65 per cent or 70 per cent of the vote. The LRC had never put up a candidate there. But this time they would field one – and his background could not be more different from that of the silver-spooned Sir Joseph.

Arthur Henderson was born in Glasgow – his mother a domestic servant, his father a textile worker who died when he was only ten. The Hendersons moved to the north-east of England, where young Arthur started his employment at the Robert Stephenson and Sons' Foundry – aged just twelve. By the 1890s, Henderson was a trade unionist of moderate disposition, and in 1895 he applied to be the Liberal candidate in Newcastle. He was, however, rejected, as had been other future Labour leaders – Keir Hardie and Ramsay MacDonald. Some Liberal associations favoured wealthy candidates, who would be able to help shoulder the heavy election costs. Others may have been sniffy about adopting working-class members. It was to be a disastrous missed opportunity for the Liberals. Many workers and trade unionists now concluded that they needed their own party.

In 1900, Henderson was one of the 129 founder delegates who voted to establish the LRC, and by 1903 he was treasurer. Henderson was now also the Liberal agent in the Barnard Castle seat, working for Sir Joseph Pease, and funded by him. On 7 February 1903, Pease informed his constituency association that he would not stand again at the next general election. The Liberals began to mull who might be their next candidate. The Northern Liberal Federation had already had talks with the Durham Miners Federation about seats in which Lib–Lab candidates might stand. Barnard Castle was not one of these.

In late 1902, Pease – perhaps deciding he no longer needed to fund campaigning work – informed Henderson that the funding for his role as agent would end on 31 December. Not wishing to immediately lose their agent, the Liberal Association agreed to pay Henderson's salary until 31 March 1903.

But Henderson was no longer planning to play second fiddle to the Liberal aristocracy of the region. On 1 April 1903, the day after he lost his paid post, he was adopted as the seat's LRC candidate.

Many Liberals felt that he would be a good MP. But others were angry. They were not keen to have a member of another political grouping forced on them. And they were furious that Henderson seemed to have arranged to become the LRC candidate while still being the paid Liberal agent. Samuel Storey, chair of the Northern Liberal Federation, was particularly unhappy.

With the death of Pease, the issue of Lib–Lab strategy in the seat was very pressing. Could the Liberals and the LRC unite behind one candidate? They could not.

The LRC was committed to fielding Henderson. He was supported by a notable minority of local Liberals, and Barnard Castle seemed to be a seat which the national Liberal leadership were willing to concede to Labour. Herbert Gladstone, close to signing off the seats deal with MacDonald, preferred the Liberals not to field a candidate.

But that was not the way the majority of Liberals in the north-east saw the matter. Why should they concede a 'safe' Liberal seat to another party, whose candidate had seemingly betrayed them? It was a good question.

On 6 July, just two weeks after Pease's death, the election writ was moved. Election day would be Friday 24 July. And there would be a three-way battle.

But Gladstone was even now arranging low-key support for Henderson – infuriating the local association. His failure to support his own candidate was even more striking when one considers the man's exemplary credentials. For the Liberals chose the 39-year-old Hubert Beaumont – third son of Wentworth Blackett Beaumont, who was later to become 1st Baron Allendale, a Liberal politician, landowner and industrialist who had been in Parliament for a thumping thirty-nine years. Hubert's brother was also a serving Liberal MP. Hubert was, then, part of the Liberal elite – educated at Eton and Oxford, he had already stood in two general elections, without success. When he was selected for Barnard Castle, he must initially have been confident of victory. After the seventy-one years of Liberal table-topping local success, surely he was a shoo-in?

But he and his major backer – Samuel Storey – were aware that Henderson's intervention was a serious threat. Storey was another affluent Liberal businessman, active in north-east politics, who had served as MP for Sunderland from 1881 to 1895. He was also a newspaper owner – having helped establish the *Sunderland Echo* in 1873 and added other titles to his group thereafter.

Storey was a man of strong political opinions – advocating Home Rule even before it was Liberal policy and championing tariff reform which was deeply unpopular with his party colleagues.

As the campaign commenced in early July, Beaumont and Storey concentrated their fire on Henderson. Storey now fired off a string of open letters to Henderson, seeking to dissuade Liberals from backing him.

On 6 July, the *Sunderland Daily Echo* was loyally reporting the first such letter which stated that Beaumont was offering to stand down – if Henderson would promise to 'act in Parliament with the Liberal Party' and reserve his freedom to vote as he wished on 'labour questions'. Beaumont and Storey knew that these were not guarantees that Henderson could give.

The *Echo* reported a second Storey letter on 8 July. This stated that most Liberal associations in the north-east were opposed to backing an LRC candidate, while angrily noting that 'certain officials in London' were ignoring this local sentiment.

On 10 July, the *Echo* reported on further Lib–Lab squabbling. Beaumont had set out another public challenge to Henderson and had again offered to stand down if Henderson would promise to support local Lib–Lab candidates in future elections, take the Liberal whip and promise that he would be free from any LRC pressure to take a common line on 'labour questions'.

By 15 July, the *Echo* was reporting Storey's third public letter to Henderson. This time things were getting more heated – Storey was drawing attention to Henderson's supposed bad faith in arranging to be the LRC candidate while also serving as the Liberal agent.

Storey and Beaumont took up these themes in their frequent public speeches. They contrasted the situation in Barnard Castle with that in Woolwich – where there was an agreement by all the 'radical forces' to unite behind the LRC candidate.

Emotions were running high and a week before polling day, the *Echo* was reporting that legal proceedings had been issued by Henderson because of allegations in Liberal election leaflets.

Labour was already fighting back, and on 17 July the radical LRC MP Keir Hardie wrote an open letter of his own to Beaumont, claiming that Beaumont had met him in the House of Commons and sought to become a Labour candidate. The letter also raised the issue of Beaumont's views on the sensitive issue of tariffs – claiming Beaumont was supporting Storey's pro-tariff views. Hardie claimed that Beaumont was 'Mr Storey's protégé' and that Henderson was the only true free trade candidate in the election.

In May 1903, Joseph Chamberlain had publicly launched his campaign for tariffs and 'imperial preference'. The issue was hugely politically divisive, not least because it raised the possibility of additional taxes on food. Chamberlain split the Unionists but largely united Labour and the Liberals against tariffs.

But Storey was in favour of tariffs. He felt so strongly that by October, he would resign as chairman of the Northern Liberal Association to become a tariff reformer — and in January 1910, he would be elected MP in Sunderland as an Independent Tariff Reform candidate.

Storey's views were a problem for Beaumont. He didn't want to offend his political patron but could not afford to upset the majority of local Liberals. So, in the election address which he issued on 2 July, he advocated a carefully contrived compromise. In this, he asserted that he was a 'Free Trader, opposed to food taxation', but also that he 'favoured an inquiry [into tariffs] and would consider with an unbiased mind any concrete fiscal proposals made by the government'. Later in the campaign, he claimed that he supported an open inquiry — believing it would 'strengthen the cause of Free Trade'. It was a fully fledged 'fudgerama', which must have upset many and convinced few.

And Beaumont's position on free trade was dangerously vague in an election where tariffs were a big issue. On 15 July, the *New Daily Chronicle* reported that 'Imperial Tariff League agents are becoming increasingly aggressive' in their campaigning and were holding a mass public meeting in Barnard Castle Music Hall that night.

Meanwhile, all the candidates were dashing around the constituency, speaking at large numbers of public meetings — the staple of election campaigns of the time.

On 20 July, Beaumont addressed twenty meetings in a day. On Wednesday 22 July, fighting for every vote, he met with farmers in the Market Place in Barnard Castle. According to the *Sheffield Daily Telegraph*, 'several questions on agricultural matters were satisfactorily answered'.

Normally, the national parties would arrange strong support for their candidates. In other by-elections this year, Herbert Gladstone sent ten to twelve Liberal MPs to speak in support. And the national parties often funded huge leaflet campaigns.

The Unionists did their best to support their candidate, Colonel Vane, who benefited from many visits from prominent Unionist MPs. The LRC did its best for Henderson. But Beaumont received scant central support. Not a single prominent Liberal MP came to back him.

Instead, he had to make do with the occasional supportive letter to local newspapers. On 20 July, the *Echo* published one such missive from a Liberal MP bemoaning the lack of party loyalty to Beaumont from 'those trying to wreck and ruin the Liberal Party'. It cannot have been of much help.

By the end of the campaign, it was clear the outcome was close.

Polling day was Friday 24 July. The day was hot and dry – the best of English summer weather. Agricultural workers were allowed to vote early, to get swiftly back to work. The party election machines were in full gear. Eight motor cars provided by Liberal supporters were driven up from London. Colonel Vane had nine such cars at his disposal, but they turned out to be a mixed blessing. The highways were dry and dusty, and drivers and passengers complained of the 'large clouds of limestone powder with which they are assailed'. While driving around the thirty-five polling stations, Vane's car suffered a puncture, which took three hours to fix. He arrived at Barnard Castle at 4 p.m. in a foul mood, complaining of 'injury to his eyes by dust'.

The polling stations were packed. In the 1900 election, almost 8,600 had voted – a turnout of 77.7 per cent. This time, with three candidates and a furious fight to the finish, turnout surged to just over 9,500 voters – 84.6 per cent, the highest recorded in the constituency.

The count took place at the Witham Memorial Hall on Saturday 25 July. It was soon clear that many Liberal voters had deserted. Barnard Castle, Liberal 'for ever', had experienced a political earthquake. At just after 2 p.m., the Sheriff of Durham, Mr Hogg, announced the result. The Conservative candidate, William Vane, a 43-year-old colonel, had seen his vote fall a little to 3,323, despite a rise in the turnout. This was no big surprise, given Unionist political weakness at the time.

But it was the Liberals who suffered the big electoral caning. Their 5,036 votes (58.7 per cent) of 1900 plunged to just 2,809 (29.6 per cent). They had fallen from first place to third.

It was the LRC's Arthur Henderson who was the beneficiary of this Liberal collapse – he polled 3,370 votes, to secure a narrow majority of forty-seven.

Henderson walked to the window of the Witham Memorial Hall, to address the crowd gathered below. The *Manchester Evening News* reported 'loud cheers, intermingled with groans'. Henderson proclaimed that it had been a 'workers fight' and noted that the Liberals and Labour now needed to work together 'as they had done at Woolwich'.

Henderson's new colleagues were overjoyed. The LRC MP Richard Bell wrote congratulating him on 'the greatest Labour victory of all'.

The newspapers were not slow to draw wider conclusions. The *Western Daily Press* saw it as a big defeat for Chamberlain's tariff plan. The *Daily Chronicle* concluded that it was now obvious that the Liberals and Labour needed to do a deal. The *Morning Post* warned that the Liberals had to more actively embrace the concerns of workers and realise that 'united the Liberals and Labour stand, divided they fall'.

For the Liberals and Labour, there seemed to be a powerful message. Even in seats that looked solidly Liberal, where they were heavily dependent on working-class support, this might now easily switch away to the LRC. By 1914, this would be even clearer. In the eighteen three-way by-elections between 1903 and 1914, where Labour had not previously stood, the average Unionist vote rose by 0.6 per cent, while the average Liberal vote fell by 18.8 per cent. These were not simply anti-government swings. Even when the Unionists were in power, third-party interventions were now much more damaging to the Liberals.

It followed that if both parties competed head-to-head, they might easily let the Unionists come through the middle and win. Since 1832, no Unionist had ever topped the poll in Barnard Castle – but this time Colonel Vane was just forty-eight votes from victory.

For Herbert Gladstone, this appeared to make his deal with the LRC even more important. It could protect Liberal seats and allow both parties to launch a tactical pincer movement against the Unionists.

Just six weeks after the by-election, on 6 September, Gladstone concluded his deal with Ramsay MacDonald. Its effects would be evident in the general election of 1906, when the Unionists suffered their worst ever defeat. They fell from 402 seats in 1900 to just 156, despite securing 43.4 per cent of the vote. Gladstone's political secretary wrote to him to conclude of the pact: 'Was there ever such a justification of a policy by results?'

Other Liberals continued to believe that their party had delivered short-term success at huge long-term risk.

In July 1903, Storey, still chairman of the Northern Liberal Association, had warned that 'the effect of surrendering to this new party will be the destruction of organised liberalism here in the North'. And nineteen of the twenty-three presidents of Liberal associations in the region had made clear their opposition to future deals.

Barnard Castle had highlighted for the Liberals and Labour the opportunities, and the risks, from co-operation. Could the Liberals contain and manage Labour? Or would Labour consolidate its bridgehead and then break out into Liberal territory? A decade after the by-election, the answer to that question was not clear. It would take the First World War and its political consequences to answer it.

David Laws was Liberal Democrat MP for Yeovil from 2001 to 2015 and was a Minister in the Cameron–Clegg Coalition. He has written a number of books on politics, of which his latest is Serpents, Goats and Turkeys *(Biteback, 2024), a history of Liberal–Labour relations since 1903.*

10

NORWICH

---

15 JANUARY 1904
LIBERAL GAIN FROM CONSERVATIVES

DUNCAN BRACK

Result: Louis Tillett (Liberal), 8,576, 48.3 per cent; Ernest Wild (Conservative/Unionist), 6,756, 38.0 per cent; George Roberts (Independent Labour), 2,440, 13.7 per cent
Size of majority: 1,820
Swing: N/A
Name of previous MP and party: Harry Bullard (Conservative/Unionist)
Reason for by-election: Death of incumbent
Result at previous general election: Samuel Hoare (Conservative/Unionist) and Harry Bullard (Conservative/Unionist) both elected unopposed
Date by-election called: 8 January 1904
Date by-election took place: 15 January 1904
Size of total electorate: 19,725
Total number of votes cast: 17,772
Turnout: 90.1 per cent

The Norwich by-election of January 1904 is not nearly as well known as the subject of the previous chapter, the Barnard Castle by-election of July 1903. It is worthy of inclusion here, however, because it was far more representative of the political temper of the times. A Liberal gain from the Unionists, in a seat which had not even been contested at the previous election, was proven to be the first of fourteen Liberal by-election gains over the following twenty-one months that accompanied the disintegration of the Unionist government, culminating in the Liberal landslide victory in the general election of 1906. It well illustrates the key political debates of the time, over free trade versus protection and over religion in education. And since the Liberals beat both a Labour as well as a Unionist candidate, the by-election played an important part in cementing the Gladstone–MacDonald pact, proving to the Labour Representation Committee (LRC) that their ability to win seats against the Liberals was highly limited, an outcome which had not been clear following Barnard Castle.

On 26 December 1903, Sir Harry Bullard, one of the two Unionist MPs for Norwich, died of a heart attack at the age of sixty-two. The head of the city's largest brewing firm, Bullard was a popular and well-respected local politician 'who lived in a glow of hearty amiability', as *The Scotsman* put it; he had represented the same ward on the city council for thirty-six years and had served as mayor three times. He had first been elected to Parliament in 1885 but had been unseated for electoral malpractice (an activity for which Norwich had something of a reputation) and did not stand again until 1895, when he was elected together with his Unionist colleague Sir Samuel Hoare (father of the future Conservative Foreign Secretary, of Hoare–Laval pact fame). This was the first occasion since 1838 on which the Liberals had not won either one or both of Norwich's two seats; since 1871, the Liberal Jeremiah Colman, the mustard manufacturer, had been elected, usually alongside one Conservative, occasionally with a second Liberal. Colman stood down in 1895, his seat was lost and such was the disarray of the Liberal Party in the following election that Bullard and Hoare were re-elected unopposed, the two Norwich seats being among the 264 (out of 670) that the Liberals did not fight in 1900.

Bullard's death was not unexpected; a diabetic, he had been seriously ill for well over a year. His funeral and a public memorial service both took place on 30 December. The local Conservative Party met the same day and decided to offer the candidacy to Ernest Wild, a locally born 35-year-old barrister, judge of the ancient Norwich Guildhall Court of Record and son of the leader of the Conservatives on Norwich Town Council. Wild had made his name defending the accused in the Peasenhall murder case (in which two successive juries had been unable to reach a verdict; Wild's client is one of the few people in English history to have been tried for murder and to have no verdict ever returned). He was well known in Norwich and had probably already been identified as the likely candidate during Bullard's long illness.

The same expectation of a by-election – or possibly a general election, given the government's increasing disarray – had meant that both the Liberals and the Independent Labour Party (ILP) had already selected candidates. The Liberal was Louis Tillett, aged thirty-eight, a local solicitor, grandson of Jacob Henry Tillett (Mayor of Norwich 1875–76 and Liberal MP for Norwich 1880–85) and leader of the Liberals on Norwich Town Council. 'He is stated to be an advanced political thinker, an orator of considerable power, and one who has done good local work,' observed the *Derby Daily Telegraph*. George Roberts, the ILP candidate, was another local man, originally a compositor and now in charge of the printing works of Messrs Colman; thirty-five years old, he had been president of the Norwich and District Trades and Labour Council.

Whether the two opponents of the Unionists would both stand, however, was not immediately clear. Roberts had been selected to fight the seat in February 1903, when ILP leader Keir Hardie had visited Norwich, in the expectation that he would run together with one Liberal for the two-member seat, an arrangement formalised in the Gladstone–MacDonald pact agreed in September of that year (see previous chapter). Norwich, with no sitting Liberal MPs or even candidates from the previous election, and with two seats, offering each party a candidate, was included in Liberal Chief Whip Herbert Gladstone's list of seats for which there was expected to be no difficulty in organising the pact. There was even a local precedent for Liberal–Labour co-operation, when in 1890 Tillett had won his first seat on Norwich Council in harness with a working-man candidate in a two-member ward.

Although the Liberals were confident of winning the by-election in a straight contest with the Unionists, the intervention of the ILP threatened to split the anti-Unionist vote. As the Liberal-supporting *Westminster Gazette* put it on 28 December: 'We trust that the Progressives will lose no time in agreeing to the candidature of whichever of these two candidates is most likely to win at a by-election.' *The Observer* agreed: 'It would be a scandal if the differences between the Liberal and the Labour parties at Norwich could not be accommodated, which would give a reasonable chance of a Free Trade victory.' On 2 January, the local Free Church Council, the voice of the Nonconformist churches, attempted to persuade Roberts not to stand.

But Roberts refused to stand down, believing, as the ILP newspaper the *Labour Leader* put it, that 'a clear fight on independent Labour lines will be of permanent advantage to the cause of Socialism and Labour, not only in the city but in the eastern counties generally'. Norwich had a history of electing Labour councillors, sometimes against Liberal as well as Conservative opponents, and undoubtedly there was support for the views expressed by a letter-writer to the *Westminster Gazette*: 'Why not play the game? The Labour Party has as good a right to put forward a candidate as either the Liberal or Conservative. Its ideals are as much opposed to Liberalism (Manchester School) as Conservatism.' Labour-supporting newspapers argued that it was Tillett who should stand down, pointing out that Roberts had been selected before him; Hardie thought that the Liberals would give way in the face of the ILP's determination to stand.

But the Barnard Castle result had stiffened the Liberals' backbone. As *The Scotsman*'s correspondent wrote on 2 January:

> There is, however, also a feeling among the Radicals that a stiff front should be shown to the Labour party. Any effort at conciliation must, it is thought, be preceded by a stand-up fight. If the Whips were to show weakness, as they did in connection with Barnard Castle, they would, I am informed, be thrown over by the local committees at Norwich and Gateshead [another pending by-election].

Most Liberals wanted to co-operate with the LRC, but there were limits, and by defeating Labour candidates in three-cornered fights, they aimed to strengthen their negotiating position for the general election. Having failed to convince the LRC's Secretary Ramsay MacDonald to persuade Roberts not to stand – and it was not clear whether the LRC could have enforced its will on the ILP anyway – Jesse Herbert, the Liberal Party's chief agent, privately expressed the wish that Roberts would get 'such a beating as [would] teach the LRC a deserved lesson'.

Accordingly, all three candidates began their campaigns on Monday 4 January. Two main issues dominated. The first was tariff reform, the proposal put forward the previous year by Joseph Chamberlain, the leader of the Liberal Unionist wing of the Unionist coalition, to increase import duties, including – possibly – on basic foodstuffs. Chamberlain's aims were twofold. He wanted to raise revenue for the ambitious social programmes, such as old-age pensions, that he had long supported, but which had been prevented by his Conservative coalition partners' opposition to raising other taxes, together with the need to meet the costs of the South African war of 1900–02. He also wished to bind Britain's colonies more firmly to the mother country by trading with them at preferential rates ('imperial preference'); strengthening the empire, he believed, was the only way in which a small island like Britain could hope to compete with other great powers such as Russia, Germany or the United States. In May 1903, Chamberlain called for an inquiry into the fiscal system; his Conservative allies established the Tariff Reform League – and triggered civil war in the Conservative Party.

Arthur Balfour, the Prime Minister, had no strong views on the issue but could see the electoral dangers of food taxes and attempted to find a compromise position to hold his party together. He so badly mishandled discussions in Cabinet, however, that both his free trade-supporting ministers and Chamberlain resigned, followed later by the Duke of Devonshire, the former Liberal Unionist leader, who remained faithful to his Liberal free trade inheritance. As Chamberlain's campaign gathered force, Unionist free trade MPs came under increasing pressure; in the middle of the Norwich campaign, the papers carried the news of Oldham Conservatives declaring a lack of confidence in their free trade-supporting MP, one Winston Churchill. (Five months later, Churchill crossed the floor to join the Liberal Party; eight other Unionist free trade MPs eventually followed.)

The divisions within the Conservative Party were reflected in Norwich, where the other MP, Sir Samuel Hoare, had been a member of the executive of the tariff reform-opposing Unionist Free Food League, though he had retired from that position by the time of the by-election, while Ernest Wild was a full-blown Chamberlainite. Hoare loyally supported Wild's campaign, though the Liberal-leaning papers enjoyed reminding their readers of his declaration 'to have been a life-long Free Trader' a few weeks before. The Tariff Reform League and the Free Trade Union opened offices next door to each other in Norwich marketplace and, according to the *Daily News*, 'lively scenes take place there'. Liberal election propaganda made plentiful use of two loaves: the 'big loaf' under free trade versus the 'little loaf' that would follow protection – 'the lie of the loaves', as the tariff reform-supporting *Daily Express* characterised it.

The other main issue in the by-election was education. Balfour's Education Act of 1902 had rationalised the provision of elementary education, in the process abolishing the school boards established in 1870 which had ensured that board schools, funded from local rates, were to provide only non-denominational religious teaching (which meant in practice learning the Bible and a few hymns), to avoid Nonconformist ratepayers subsidising Anglican education. The ratepayer funding for Anglican schools that the Balfour Act introduced outraged Nonconformists (for most people at this time, religious questions were more politically salient than class divisions). The Free Churches established a National Passive Resistance Committee to co-ordinate non-payment of rates, and the Nonconformist churches' alignment with Liberalism was strongly reinforced, after Liberal MPs almost unanimously opposed the Act. Norwich itself was a stronghold of Nonconformity, and on 7 January the Norwich Protestant Electoral Council, the Church Association and the National Protestant League jointly declared their support for Tillett. The local Church of England Temperance Society, on the other hand, came out for Wild, calling on 'every communicant, every Church teacher, every choir man, every man who wants to save his country from godless socialism and pagan childhood [to] vote for Mr Ernest Wild' – a puzzling stance, given Wild's support for the drink trade.

Wild's election address was firmly in support of tariff reform and imperial preference; he denounced the system of 'dumping' the products of foreign countries in England. Tillett's much more detailed address demonstrated his position on the radical wing of the Liberal Party.

He accused the government of incompetence over the conduct of the South African War, army reform and the Education Act and strongly opposed any suggestion of protection, whether from Chamberlain or Balfour. He advocated an equitable scheme of old-age pensions, the amendment of trade union law (in the wake of court decisions which had eroded trade union rights), a housing Act, the taxation of land values and the graduation of income tax. Since most of this was entirely in line with the LRC's position, the ILP candidate, Roberts, devoted considerable time to criticising the Liberals, denouncing the division between the older parties as fictitious. He highlighted the low wages, bad housing and irregular employment suffered by working men and argued for state ownership of land, mines and the railways. 'Free Trade has enabled us to accumulate national wealth,' claimed his manifesto. 'A labour policy must now supplement Free Trade to enable us to distribute that wealth equitably.'

Yet although Roberts was supported by some of the LRC's leaders, including David Shackleton, who had won the Clitheroe by-election in 1902, in the absence of Liberal opposition, others, such as Will Crooks, who had won the Woolwich by-election in 1903, also in co-operation with the Liberals, stayed away, viewing the ILP's intervention as unwise. On 8 January, it was reported that a manifesto was about to be issued by a number of local Labour and socialist leaders, including several councillors and trade union officials, calling for a vote for Tillett as the candidate best placed to beat the Unionist, thereby laying the groundwork for a successful joint candidacy at the next election. Tillett himself made the same case in meetings with factory workers and trade union members and received a warm reception. Liberal posters and leaflets emphasised again and again how a vote for Roberts 'was a vote for the Tory candidate and Joe'. Also on 8 January, the Free Church Councils called for a vote for Tillett. The day before, the Liberal campaign was boosted by news of the by-election victory in Ashburton, in Devon, where the Liberal candidate held the seat with an increased majority in the face of a strong challenge by a popular local Conservative, who was, however, a Chamberlainite.

The writ for the by-election was finally moved on Friday 8 January, with the deadline for nominations on Tuesday 12th and polling day set for Friday 15th. Given the brevity of the campaign, all three parties threw themselves into frantic activity. The *Daily News* reported:

> The Liberal organisation is very good. The work is being done in the sixteen wards which make up the city from sixteen separate centres … The Tory organisation is excellent, large sums of money having been lavished upon it for years … The hoardings show a great predominance of blue and white, the Liberal colours. In numbers of private houses Mr Tillett's portrait is displayed, and 'The Daily News' leaflets showing the German and English loaf are also displayed by many Norwich enthusiasts.

Large numbers of Liberal MPs visited Norwich in support of the campaign, led by Augustine Birrell, who was later to become a Cabinet minister in the Liberal government, and election agents from nearby constituencies were brought in to help.

No fewer than fourteen Unionist meetings were held in the final week, featuring many Unionist MPs. At one of them, two days before the poll, Wild read out supportive telegrams from the Unionist leaders: 'You ask for watchwords; I suggest union and fiscal reform' from Balfour; and 'My watchwords are more employment for the masses, and closer union for the Empire' from Chamberlain. The pace of the campaign took its toll of both main candidates: Wild fainted at the end of one hard day's electioneering, and Tillett had to give up speaking for a time, such was the strain on his throat. No Liberal meeting was held on the eve of poll, however, to ensure that Liberal activists were not distracted from the preparations for polling day. In contrast, the *Liberal Agent* reported, 'the Tories had two mass meetings, crowded and Wildly enthusiastic (no pun intended) and it was wonderful what an amount of cocksuredness it put into them'.

The campaign was in general conducted in good temper, the main exception being the disorderliness which occurred at meetings organised by the Tariff Reform League. At the largest of these, an audience of 2,500 experienced, as the *Westminster Gazette* described it, 'perfect pandemonium'. Liberal literature and placards were displayed around the hall. Apart from the chair, a local vicar, speakers were treated with derision and shouted down; the league's secretary's attempt to use a megaphone 'was met with excited loud laughter and dissent, and shouts of "Take that trumpet off!" … General confusion followed, and the meeting was brought to an abrupt ending by the singing of the National Anthem.' However, the singers' 'vocal powers were drowned by shouts of dissent against Chamberlain and cheering for the Liberal candidate. Subsequently Mr Morgan, of the Free Trade Union, addressed an open-air meeting, and was enthusiastically received.'

Polling day dawned bright and cold, and at first voting was slow but picked up strongly at lunchtime. Newspapers reported on the enormous number of motor cars in use, at the time an innovation; unsurprisingly, most of them were used to ferry Conservative voters. 'In the heart of the City Mr Wild's favours predominated,' reported the *Western Times*, 'but in the working class districts Mr Tillett was apparently the most popular. Mr Roberts' candidature was not approved by the general body of Trades Unionists.'

The result was announced after midnight: a majority of 1,820 for Tillett over Wild, with Roberts in a distant third place. The result exceeded Liberal hopes. 'Splendid!' declared the *Western Times*, 'Protection Utterly Routed at Norwich. Enormous Majority of Free Trade Votes.' All the newspapers, regardless of their own position, regarded the result as a clear blow against protection, pointing out that the combined free trade vote was more than 4,000 ahead of the Unionists' vote. More than one commented on the irony that the result coincided with the first meeting of a commission of fifty-nine businessmen established by Chamberlain to examine his proposals for tariff reform. While 'the Tory Party has been swept off its feet by Mr Chamberlain's agitation', concluded the *Westminster Gazette*, 'the public is not so dense as to mistake the trend of events'. The cause of free trade was to deliver another thirteen by-election gains for the Liberals – the next of which, at Ayr Burghs, just two weeks later – and sweep them to an electoral landslide victory in 1906.

The other outcome of the Norwich by-election was to cement the Gladstone–MacDonald pact. Roberts blamed his defeat on 'subtle misrepresentations' by the Liberals, but the truth was that many Labour voters – Liberal agents estimated about half of the potential Labour vote – recognised that Tillett was better placed to win the seat. Furthermore, Tillett was an orthodox advanced Liberal, a clear supporter of free trade – unlike the Liberal candidate at Barnard Castle – and a radical on matters of social reform. On all the major issues of the day, there was very little reason for Labour voters to dislike him and plenty of reasons to support him, including paving the way for a joint candidacy with Roberts at the general election. If Labour insisted on fighting further by-elections against Liberal opposition, all they could hope to do was damage Liberal chances (Liberals won the Ayr Burghs by-election on 29 January by only forty-four votes; a Labour intervention would have saved the seat for the Unionists). Accordingly, Labour candidates refrained from standing in any further by-elections before the 1906 election (with the sole exception of North East Lanarkshire, in August 1904, where the candidate of the Scottish Workers' Representation Committee, which was not part of the LRC, came third), and the pact operated smoothly, delivering scores of Liberal and Labour seats in 1906.

This included Norwich, where Tillett and Roberts were elected together. Wild was again the defeated Unionist candidate but was eventually elected to Parliament, for West Ham, in 1918. Roberts held his Norwich seat until 1923, served as a minister in Lloyd George's coalition government from 1916 to 1920 and shifted steadily rightwards, finally losing Norwich to Labour in 1923 as a Conservative. Tillett stood down in 1910, but the Liberals held the seat, with the brief exception of 1923–24, until 1945. He died in 1929 at the age of sixty-four; he was described as 'widely-loved' in the local paper's obituary, with 'the streets lined with hatless and reverent spectators'.

Duncan Brack *is the editor of the* Journal of Liberal History. *He has also co-edited, with Iain Dale, a series of collections of political counterfactuals, the most recent of which is* Prime Minister Priti … *and other things that never happened (Biteback, 2021). Professionally, he is an independent environmental policy analyst and adviser.*

11

COLNE VALLEY

GERARD HETHERINGTON

Result: Victor Grayson (Independent Socialist), 3,648, 35.2 per cent; Philip Bright (Liberal), 3,495, 33.7 per cent; Granville Wheler (Conservative), 3,227, 31.1 per cent
Size of majority: 153
Swing: N/A
Name of previous MP and party: James Kitson (Liberal)
Reason for by-election: Elevation to the House of Lords
Result at previous general election: James Kitson (Liberal) elected unopposed
Date by-election called: 28 June 1907
Date by-election took place: 18 July 1907
Size of total electorate: 11,771
Total number of votes cast: 10,370
Turnout: 88.1 per cent

Colne Valley has a unique place in UK by-election history. It is the only constituency where a by-election has been held following the disqualification of the sitting Member of Parliament under the Lunacy (Vacating of Seats) Act of 1886. The Liberal MP Reverend Dr Charles Leach, who won the seat in the general election of 1910, went on to serve as an army chaplain during the First World War. His experiences visiting the wounded in hospital resulted in a mental breakdown which led to his disqualification from Parliament, with a by-election held in 1916.

Yet this unique event was not the most notable by-election in the seat. That distinction goes to the contest in July 1907 when Leach's immediate predecessor, Victor Grayson (the man Leach was to defeat in 1910), took the seat from the Liberals only eighteen months after the Liberal landslide of 1906 in what has been described as an electoral earthquake which has resonated down the generations.

Grayson was a charismatic figure and a gifted orator. Aged only twenty-five at the time of his election, he has been hailed as Britain's only true socialist Member of Parliament. He remains a figure of reverence on the left, with his story given a twist of mystery by his disappearance some years after leaving Parliament.

The Colne Valley constituency is set mainly on West Yorkshire moorland but in the early twentieth century extended into what is now Greater Manchester. At that time, it housed twenty or so small mill towns and villages which produced cotton and woollen cloth of the highest quality. The area was far from impoverished and in some senses an unlikely breeding ground for socialism, but there was something of a radical tradition in the community which had felt the impact of the Luddites and the Chartist movement in the first half of the nineteenth century.

Since its creation in 1885, the constituency had returned a Liberal MP. The emerging Labour movement was active in the area in the 1890s, with Colne Valley electing the first Labour county councillor in England in 1891. The local Labour movement persuaded the leading trade unionist Tom Mann to stand for Parliament in the constituency in 1895. Despite this background of organising in Colne Valley in the 1890s, Labour did not field a candidate in either 1900 or 1906, preferring to concentrate its resources in nearby Huddersfield and Bradford.

Although the Liberals had won a huge landslide in 1906, Labour had done better than expected, winning twenty-nine seats. Many Labour figures in Colne Valley regretted that the movement had not contested the seat and were determined to contest it in the widely expected by-election.

Sir James Kitson, an industrialist and locomotive builder, had been Liberal MP for Colne Valley since 1892 and in the 1906 general election had been elected unopposed. Aged seventy and well connected to senior figures in the Liberal Party, Kitson was widely expected to be raised to the peerage.

Members of Parliament did not receive a salary until 1911. Until then, Labour could afford to support only a small number of candidates for Parliament who were reliant on financial support from the wider Labour movement, particularly the trade unions.

The process for selecting Labour candidates for Parliament was complicated, reflecting the movement's complex organisational structures involving the Independent Labour Party, the Labour Representative Committee, the Fabian Society and the trade unions. The unions guarded their interest jealously and tended to have their own preferred type of candidate.

It was against this background that the local Labour organisation, the Colne Valley Labour League (CVLL), sought approval from the party authorities to have Victor Grayson as their candidate. The fact that such an endorsement was not forthcoming remains the subject of debate and dispute to the present day.

Grayson was not a local man. Born in Liverpool as the seventh son of a carpenter, he served an apprenticeship in engineering before beginning training as a minister in the Unitarian Church. Leaving aside his church studies to preach the gospel of socialism, he became a well-known speaker and activist, building a political hinterland across the north of England.

Grayson first came to attention in the Colne Valley when he stood in for a speaker at a rally in Huddersfield Town Hall in December 1905. His speech established him as a serious politician. The audience, which included members of the CVLL, left greatly impressed. Grayson was then invited to speak at local meetings across the Colne Valley, where his brand of ethical socialism was well received. Grayson cultivated the constituency. He made many visits and held well-attended meetings across the Colne Valley well before the by-election was called.

He was keen to be the official Labour candidate and wrote to the Labour leader Keir Hardie in April 1906 to seek his advice. Hardie proved to be evasive and never actually replied to the letter.

The reasons Hardie and the Labour hierarchy did not endorse Grayson's candidacy were partly procedural. Colne Valley was unable to meet the requirement to convene a properly constituted local Labour Representative Committee with local union representatives. With its smaller mills and factories and workers who generally enjoyed better wages and conditions than elsewhere, Colne Valley was not fertile ground for organising by trade unions. Also, many Labour figures and trade union leaders felt that candidates should be established figures with a track record in the movement. Some in the union movement preferred to deal with the Liberals and, in some areas, there were tacit agreements that Labour would not field a candidate against a Liberal opponent.

Against this background, Grayson appeared to be something of an upstart. There was resentment of his youth and flair and his lack of political experience and, in some quarters, concern about his fondness for drink and rumours about his sexuality.

The Colne Valley Labour League persevered with its own local process, which concluded in January 1907 with Grayson defeating three trade union-supported candidates (all of whom went on to become MPs elsewhere). However, this recommendation of Grayson was not accepted by the party at national level.

The issue was still unresolved in June when Sir James Kitson announced his resignation from Parliament on his ennoblement as Baron Airedale. Lacking endorsement from the Labour authorities, Grayson was obliged to stand as an Independent Socialist.

While the Liberal government was flailing, unable to deliver on its contradictory election promises of social reform and reducing taxes, it was widely expected that the Liberals would hold Colne Valley with ease. The group of Labour MPs made little impact and were regarded as too close to the Liberals for many in the Labour movement.

Grayson opposed the gradualist approach of leading Labour figures of the time such as Hardie and MacDonald. His message to the voters in Colne Valley was uncompromisingly socialist. His election address began: 'I am appealing to you as one of your own class. I want emancipation from the wage-slavery of capitalism.'

After a false start, the Liberals selected Philip Bright, son of the free trade radical John Bright. The party expected to win partly by trading on the reputation of Bright's father. However, Grayson's campaign made much of the fact that John Bright had opposed the Ten Hours Act. The younger Bright was a poor speaker who failed to establish any rapport with the voters. His appearances became less frequent as the campaign progressed. The Liberal slogan 'Beware of Socialist Bosh' failed to cut through.

The Conservatives were caught out when the by-election was called and scrambled to select Granville Wheler, a barrister from Castleford. Wheler was a supporter of imperial preference and a vehement opponent of socialism, which he equated with atheism, republicanism and the road to tyranny. The Liberal and Conservative candidates engaged in a rather sterile dialogue about the merits of free trade and tariffs far removed from the everyday concerns of the voters of the Colne Valley.

Grayson's opponents and the press stressed the fact that he was not an official Labour candidate but an extremist. However, the lack of official endorsement in some ways worked to Grayson's advantage. Activists who did not care for Hardie or MacDonald turned out in great numbers to support Grayson.

Without official backing, Grayson's campaign had to be funded by appealing directly to local supporters who contributed small amounts, selling jewellery and watches to support the cause, although Grayson received financial support from at least one mill owner, France Littlewood.

Grayson generated enthusiasm wherever he went in the valley. He was an inspirational speaker who frequently employed biblical imagery. His campaign drew the support of around forty local clergymen. While all three candidates drew large crowds, Grayson's audiences ran into thousands. He addressed large outdoor meetings, often from the back of a wagon.

Alongside his socialist message, Grayson was an enthusiastic supporter of votes for women. Large numbers of women attended his meetings, where he was on occasion supported by Emmeline and Christabel Pankhurst. One of Grayson's celebrity supporters, the Countess of Warwick, loaned her distinctive red motor car to the campaign.

The poll was held on Thursday 18 July. At the count, the following day at Slaithwaite Town Hall, there was mounting excitement as the bundles of votes for Grayson grew. The result was a sensation: Victor

Grayson 3,648, Philip Bright 3,495 and Granville Wheler 3,227. A majority for Grayson of 153. The turnout was 88.1 per cent.

There was jubilation among the crowd at the town hall, with Grayson carried shoulder-high through the streets to make his victory speech at the Dartmouth Arms, where he said, 'We have proclaimed our socialism on every platform.' The *Daily Express* reported that 'the red flag waves over Colne Valley today'. Other newspapers predicted rather prematurely that Grayson's victory represented a watershed in British politics.

Although little further was heard of Philip Bright, Granville Wheler went on to serve as MP for Faversham from 1910 until his death in 1927.

Grayson did not thrive in Parliament. Although introduced to the Commons by leading Labour figures Philip Snowden and J. R. Clynes, he refused to sign the Labour constitution. He was not enamoured of the club atmosphere of the House of Commons and frequently interrupted debates to raise the plight of the unemployed.

He was suspended from the Chamber on several occasions and began to attend the Commons less frequently, his drinking becoming a serious problem. He failed to hold Colne Valley in the general election of 1910 and lost his deposit in Kennington in the second general election of that year.

Grayson's post-parliamentary career is one of adventure and mystery. Unlike many on the left, Grayson became an enthusiastic supporter of the First World War. He travelled with his actress wife to Australia and New Zealand, where he wrote newspaper articles in support of the war. After being challenged at a public meeting to demonstrate his commitment, he joined the New Zealand Expedition Force. He endured the horrors of Passchendaele, where he was wounded.

On returning to England with no obvious source of income other than occasional journalism and speeches, Grayson maintained an expensive apartment in London and enjoyed a lavish lifestyle. His path crossed with the notorious Maundy Gregory, who sold honours on behalf of Prime Minister Lloyd George. It has been claimed that Grayson was extorting someone over the sale of honours or that he was himself was being extorted. Grayson disappeared in 1920 when two men collected him from his London apartment, although there was speculation about sightings of Grayson as late as the 1940s.

Grayson's true significance lies in his sensational by-election victory. The victory did not prove to be the harbinger of the socialist uprising and was more of an extreme version of a protest vote against an increasingly unpopular government. However, his victory was also a triumph for local political organisation against national party machinery.

Grayson occupies a unique place in Labour history and his memory lives on, particularly in the Colne Valley where the Victor Grayson Society meets monthly.

Gerard Hetherington *is a former senior civil servant. He lived in the Colne Valley constituency for over twenty years.*

12

MANCHESTER NORTH WEST

24 APRIL 1908
CONSERVATIVE GAIN FROM LIBERAL

PIPPA CATTERALL

Result: William Joynson-Hicks (Conservative), 5,417, 50.7 per cent; Winston Churchill (Liberal), 4,988, 46.7 per cent; Dan Irving (Social Democratic Federation), 276, 2.6 per cent
Size of majority: 429
Swing: 8.2 per cent from Liberal to Conservative
Name of previous MP and party: Winston Churchill (Liberal)
Reason for by-election: Promotion to ministerial office
Result at previous general election: Winston Churchill (Liberal), 5,659, 56.2 per cent; William Joynson-Hicks (Conservative), 4,398, 43.8 per cent
Date by-election called: 15 April 1908
Date by-election took place: 24 April 1908
Size of total electorate: 11,914
Total number of votes cast: 10,681
Turnout: 89.7 per cent

The writ moving the Manchester North West by-election was received by the city's Lord Mayor on the morning of 15 April 1908. Polling day was set for Friday 24 April. With the interposition of Easter weekend, when there would supposedly be a party truce, that only allowed seven days for campaigning (five including Passover). Yet the political forces in the division had been mobilising for this contest almost since the moment the Tory MP turned Liberal free trader, Winston

Churchill, had seized this seat from his former party in the 1906 general election.

In contrast, the Tories had won all but one of Manchester's seats in the 1900 khaki election. The sole Liberal in Manchester North only hung on by twenty-six votes over William Joynson-Hicks, while Sir William Houldsworth retained unopposed the Manchester North West seat he had held since it was created in 1885. Subsequently, however, the launch of Joseph Chamberlain's campaign for tariff reform in 1903 had sown dissension in Conservative ranks and nowhere more so than in Manchester, often described as the 'citadel of free trade'. This made Manchester the natural home for the headquarters of the Unionist-dominated Free Trade League (FTL). With Houldsworth standing down and aided by Unionist free trader defections, Churchill secured an impressive majority of 1,241 in 1906.

The new MP seemed destined for swift elevation in the Liberal ministry formed by Sir Henry Campbell-Bannerman in December 1905. There was regular speculation as to when this would occur, accompanied by anticipatory political activity. Yet those spoiling for a rematch of the 1906 contest in which Churchill defeated Houldsworth's replacement, Joynson-Hicks, had to wait until an ailing Campbell-Bannerman – who died during the by-election campaign – resigned the premiership on 3 April 1908. Speculation rose to fever-pitch on news that Churchill was detained in London on 11 April. The following day, he was appointed president of the Board of Trade and consequently ceased to be an MP and needed to seek re-election.

In the letter he then issued to his electorate, Churchill complained of the 'antiquated and anomalous … technicality which renders a contest possible'. This technicality was Clause 25 of the Succession Act of 1707, which required holders of offices of profit under the Crown to seek re-election. As Churchill noted, opposing the return of ministers in such contests was unusual and, in his case, would vexatiously 'delay and hamper the work of a great Department charged with important and complex legislation of a purely non-party character'. The Unionist leader, Arthur Balfour, had hinted towards the end of the previous parliament that he supported repeal of this provision. Nonetheless,

Churchill continued: 'I welcome this opportunity … The constituency which gave the signal for the free trade triumph of 1906, will not now consent to obey the dismal trumpet of retreat.'

In an era in which by-elections were keenly fought battlegrounds for varied special interests, one of the first groups to respond was the suffragists. Although they had often disrupted Churchill's meetings in the past, with all the candidates in favour of their cause, they indicated that they would not do so on this occasion. Nonetheless, the replacement of the sympathetic Campbell-Bannerman as Prime Minister with the rigidly hostile Asquith led them to note that 'defeat at by-elections is the only possible way of bringing Mr Asquith to reason and saving the honour of the Liberal party before it is too late'. The Manchester and Salford Women's Trade Council was also dissatisfied with Churchill's support for attempts to control the employment of barmaids. The newly formed Barmaids' Political Defence League joined suffragists in actively campaigning against him during the by-election.

Suitably qualified women attained the vote at municipal elections in 1907, but the parliamentary vote remained a male preserve. This difference in the franchise explains the lack of contemporary attention paid to results in the seven wards that comprised the constituency. Only one of these, Cheetham, was considered mixed. Most of the 503 additions to the constituency register since 1906 were in Cheetham because of new better-quality housing for the upper working classes.

Four wards were dominated by mercantile and manufacturing interests, though the number of plural voters enfranchised by virtue of their business properties had declined as partnerships were converted into joint stock companies. In consequence, many Unionist free traders, including Tootal Broadhurst, their leader, no longer had a vote in the constituency. In any case, in municipal contests in which national issues like free trade mattered little, only the wealthy Nonconformists of Oxford ward consistently elected Liberals. Although Churchill sought to appeal to the retailers of Collegiate Church during the campaign, they were solidly Tory. So were the other business wards.

Liberal prospects were also limited in the two impoverished 'slum' wards. A Tory preference for keeping rents low, as opposed to expensive slum clearance schemes, appealed to these voters. This was supplemented by a defence of Englishness and working-class leisure in a city in which brewing interests remained robustly aligned with Toryism. The brewers' enthusiasm for Joynson-Hicks might have been muted by his position as an officer of the Church of England Temperance Society, but in 1908 they could unite with him in opposing the Liberals' Licensing Bill. The Tory candidate characterised this as a confiscatory measure likely to do little to promote sobriety. He was also careful to focus his criticisms as much as possible on the failure of the legislation to deal with drinking clubs. Although the Liberals issued a pamphlet on 15 April alleging that Joynson-Hicks's evidence to the Royal Commission on Licensing in 1898 suggested that he was then in favour of an even more drastic curtailment of licences than now proposed, Tory claims that this had been taken out of context blunted this attack.

Joynson-Hicks similarly condemned the Liberals' education policy as confiscatory appropriation of the voluntary schools created by various religious denominations. He had long been prominent in campaigns for the defence of religious education. As he pointed out in his election address at the start of the by-election, Lancashire was the heartland of the voluntary school and the Liberals' Education Bill 'violated the consciences of churchmen, Roman Catholics, and Jews, and many devout Nonconformists'. Churchill, in contrast, argued that 'schools maintained by public funds must be amenable to public control. State paid teachers as Civil Servants cannot be subjected to religious tests' but that this did not preclude special provision for religious groups. Liberal arguments that such arrangements were already commonplace within the empire, however, did little to dent the cultural conservatism that was the basis of Tory success in the slum wards of Manchester.

It was not just opposition to the Licensing and Education Bills that helped Joynson-Hicks to mobilise his vote, though he initially focused on these issues. Although born in Kent, he also made much of his local connections after his 1898 marriage into the Joynson family of Bowdon, not least through the addition to his surname. Initially, he made less of tariff reform and resisted Churchill's efforts to make the election about free trade. Instead, Joynson-Hicks insisted that the issue was the record of the Liberal government overall, appealing to patriotic imperialist sentiment by attacking Churchill's role in conciliating Boers in South Africa during his recent under-secretaryship at the Colonial Office. This was a tricky line to pursue given Churchill's eventually successful libel action against the prominent local Liberal Unionist John Saxon-Mills over his allegations in the Conservative-supporting *Manchester Courier* about Churchill's conduct when a prisoner of war during the South African War. Nonetheless, imperial matters, including claims that the Liberals had failed to tackle the Chinese slavery in the Transvaal they had emphasised so much in 1906, initially featured prominently in Joynson-Hicks's campaign.

He was helped by a contemporaneous trade slump and rise in unemployment. This prompted Joynson-Hicks to attack the Liberals' Eight Hours (Mines) Bill as detrimental to business and an attack on free trade. Meanwhile, from the left, the by-election featured protests about unemployment which sometimes spilled over into window-smashing. During the campaign, four members of the Marxian Social Democratic Federation were sentenced to twelve months' imprisonment for criminal damage.

These circumstances produced an unpropitious economic backdrop against which the governing party could defend free trade, despite Churchill pointing out that unemployment in protectionist Germany was currently higher. When the new Chancellor of the Exchequer, David Lloyd George, broke the precedent that Cabinet ministers did not campaign in by-elections to come to his native city to speak on Churchill's behalf, he faced heckling about the voting down of Labour's Right-to-Work Bill the previous month. In these circumstances, Churchill's promise that the Liberals would, unlike the Tories in 1895, deliver social reforms like old-age pensions cut little ice.

With the Tory vote seemingly firm and two experienced and popular candidates packing out their many meetings to overflowing, press coverage of the campaign was dominated by speculation as to whether the electoral coalition that had delivered Churchill victory in 1906 could be maintained. Attention focused on three groups. Of these, the Jews were numerically the smallest. Concentrated in Cheetham, there were an estimated 800 or so Jewish electors (6.7 per cent) in a constituency containing 11,914 registered voters. The Jewish vote was widely considered to have been solid for Churchill in 1906 and he certainly spent

much of the by-election courting their continuing support. His promises over abolition of naturalisation fees and criticism of the Aliens Act
of 1905 won over a Jewish deputation. Churchill's letter to the deputation also emphasised that he had already provided for immigrant
homes in the Port of London Bill he inherited from Lloyd George,
his predecessor at the Board of Trade. Additionally, he had instructed immigration officers 'that in all cases in which immigrants coming
from the parts of the Continent which were at present in a disturbed
condition alleged that they were flying from religious or political perse-
cution, the benefit of the doubt, where any existed, should be given to
the immigrant'. On the eve of poll, the Liberals were able to read out
at their meetings in Jewish areas a letter of endorsement from Rev. Dr
Moses Gaster, Chief Rabbi of the Spanish and Portuguese Jews.

Both Churchill and Joynson-Hicks had spoken at non-party meetings in Manchester in 1905 calling for amendment of the legislation.
After the Aliens Bill was passed, however, Joynson-Hicks's defence of
this Tory legislation led to him being depicted in propaganda as antisemitic. So did his remark that he would not pander to the Jewish vote,
which he explained at a meeting in Cheetham Town Hall on 20 April
merely meant that he regarded Manchester's Jews as being as English as
any Gentile. That same day, a Jewish deputation came away impressed,
while the Tory-supporting president of the Manchester Congregation
of Portuguese and Spanish Jews, David Garson, was vocal on Joynson-
Hicks's behalf. Nonetheless, the main threat to Churchill's hold on
Jewish votes was felt to come from a different quarter.

Unlike in 1906, there was a third candidate. Honouring the Lib–
Lab pact which had delivered them two seats in the city in 1906, the
local Labour Representation Committee (LRC) had declined to field a
candidate. However, the Social Democratic Federation, which had ten
branches in the city, was unaffiliated to the LRC. It invited Dan Irving
from nearby Burnley to stand. Their rivals in the Independent Labour
Party were instructed not to support Irving. The local party executive
nonetheless did so, despite H. G. Wells urging his fellow socialists to
vote for Churchill. That the Social Democratic Federation held their
annual conference in Manchester over Easter was also felt to have given
them a canvassing boost. The party had a small Jewish branch in the

constituency, in which Irving's brother was active, while Irving's campaign was the only one to produce posters in Yiddish.

An even more significant section of the electorate were the estimated 900-plus Irish voters (7.5 per cent) in the division. This figure was arrived at partly through using the number of Catholics, though it was also admitted that these included a small number of old Lancashire recusant families who would almost certainly vote for Joynson-Hicks. Nor was it certain all the Irish Catholics would vote Liberal. Joynson-Hicks closed his remarks in Cheetham on 20 April by pointing to the numerous private meetings Churchill was having in his efforts to secure their votes.

One problem was the attitude of the Irish Parliamentary Party to the Liberals' Irish Council Bill of 1907. Although their leader, John Redmond, had initially welcomed this as a step towards Home Rule, the party rejected it, leading to the Bill's withdrawal. On 30 March 1908, Redmond instead moved a Home Rule motion in the Commons. Even though Asquith had voted for this, Redmond followed this up with a speech in Dublin on 16 April 1908 that called for Irishmen in England to compel the newly formed ministry to make Home Rule a key issue at the next general election, noting it was therefore impossible to ask Irishmen to support Churchill in Manchester North West. The Liberals could draw some comfort from supportive pieces on the same day in the *Manchester Catholic Herald* and the *Catholic Times*. These argued that Liberal victory might help to win concessions from the government in the Manchester roundtable conference seeking a resolution of the education question due to commence on 22 April. Nonetheless, Redmond had undoubtedly complicated Churchill's chances. This was not least because, until the Liberal position on Home Rule was clarified, priestly concern over religious education was instead to the fore. Divisions in the local branches of the United Irish League (UIL) became apparent. Although the UIL managed to prevent a clear statement of policy being distributed after Mass on Easter Sunday (19 April), a manifesto was issued by Catholic clergy the following day urging 'unflinching opposition' to Churchill and a solid vote for Joynson-Hicks. The local Catholic teachers' guild also later warned that the Liberals' education policy was 'turning old allies into snipers on its flank'. The Manchester Protestant League's retaliatory endorsement of Churchill was probably less significant.

The issue took another twist on 21 April, the day the three candidates were formally nominated. Liberal negotiations with the UIL resulted in the latter issuing a statement that

> as they have elicited a declaration from the Prime Minister that Home Rule in the sense of Mr Redmond's resolution will be put by the Government before the electors at the General Election, and as Mr Churchill's personal pledges are on the whole satisfactory, they call upon the Irish Nationalists to vote for him.

Churchill gave a speech in similar vein. The UIL president, T. P. O'Connor, weighed in, speaking at several meetings to support Churchill, while the local Catholic Federation urged votes for Joynson-Hicks. Irving's committed support for Home Rule does not seem to have helped him much and it is not clear that the UIL's endorsement of Churchill helped him that much either. Contemporary pundits estimated that the religious education issue secured most of the Irish votes for the Tories.

The final group of voters whose support was felt to be key to Churchill in this by-election were the uncertain numbers of Unionist free traders. The only prominent local Unionist free trader to openly support Joynson-Hicks, E. L. Oliver, tried to help his candidate's cause by suggesting he was 'a Free Trader at heart'. Certainly, the Tariff Reform League initially regarded Joynson-Hicks with suspicion. Its executive unanimously resolved on 12 March 1908 'that unless Joynson-Hicks … would unreservedly accept Balfour's Birmingham programme, we would run a Tariff Reform candidate'. Despite Lloyd George accusing him of shilly-shallying on the issue, Joynson-Hicks was indeed careful to stress his loyalty to Balfour's line throughout the contest. As a co-founder in 1906 of the Unionist Propaganda Club under the presidency of Joseph Chamberlain, his real position ought never to have been in doubt. Yet initially, he was understandably keen to soft-pedal on tariff reform.

Churchill had spoken in January 1908 to great applause at an enormous rally in the Free Trade Hall at which he scoffed at the twenty Tariff Reform League vans roaming Lancashire armed with gramophones. This meeting was organised and chaired by Unionist free traders. This did not stop some of them trying unavailingly to persuade Broadhurst to stand as Tory candidate. They simultaneously reached out to Joynson-Hicks, trying to secure the Unionist nomination for one of their number. Local brewing interests similarly pressed for a compromise. However, the Tory Chief Whip, Sir Alexander Acland-Hood, feared that such a deal would reopen the recent dissensions in the party. It was emphasised to Joynson-Hicks that he had to follow the official line and Percival Hughes was dispatched from Central Office to ensure he did so.

Caution at stirring up Unionist free trader opposition was apparent in the decision to refuse offers from Balfour and the prominent tariff reform MP Harry Chaplin to speak on Joynson-Hicks's behalf. The Unionist free trader Lord Robert Cecil even refused to join Joynson-Hicks on a platform to speak about religious education. Nonetheless, by 15 April, it was reported that 'some Unionists [think] … Joynson-Hicks would have been better advised to put tariff reform in the forefront of his programme rather than to reserve the question as a measure for the next general election', not least considering the depressed trade in Manchester.

Churchill clearly thought tariff reform was the Tories' weak spot, likely to benefit the wealthy not the Exchequer, and enjoyed the endorsement of the FTL. Joynson-Hicks retorted that the latter were an association of millionaires. Towards the end of the campaign, he took a stronger line against those who voted against their party despite disagreeing with it only on one issue. This prompted the FTL to respond defensively on the eve of the poll. They declared that mistakes on education and licensing can be repaired, but 'handicap us with import duties on the materials used in our industries and in the food consumed by our people, and we must inevitably lose much of our commerce and reduce many of our workers to idleness and starvation'. Yet the empty seats at their closing meetings, during an election marked by packed gatherings, suggested that Unionist free traders were wavering.

One Tory who did speak for Joynson-Hicks was H. C. Gooch, the victor in the recent Peckham by-election, while Balfour sent a letter of support in response to Lloyd George's visit. In Peckham, the Navy League had been an important factor, but Joynson-Hicks's attempts to make defence policy an issue had little resonance in this contest. The media may have been more significant in Manchester North West. Certainly, the Tories made extensive use of gramophones and cine-matographs. As he admitted at a meeting at Strangeways Labour Hall, Churchill seems to have been more exercised by the interventions of the *Daily Mail*. Its owner, Lord Northcliffe, had also bought the failing *Manchester Courier* in 1904 to support Unionist propaganda in the city. Although the *Courier* added over 10,000 to its circulation during the by-election, it was the *Mail* that had more impact. It was distributed for free and, as the *Liberal Magazine* subsequently complained, 'its contents ... became almost every day a mere anti-Churchill poster'. This was literally the case, as Manchester was placarded with *Mail* hoardings proclaiming slogans like 'Radical Record – Dear Bread, Dear Sugar, Dear Coal and a Hundred Pounds a Week for Churchill'. These culminated with: 'If Churchill is beaten, will he change his party again?'

Despite Churchill's outward confidence, being beaten seemed likely throughout the campaign, though on 15 April the bookmakers shortened the odds on him succeeding to four to three against. Churchill's prospects did not look brighter when polling day opened with a snowstorm. At the time, a higher turnout was generally felt to favour the Liberals. Despite the weather, the turnout nonetheless increased from the already high 87.9 per cent of 1906 to 89.7 per cent. This was a tribute to the extraordinary efforts of all parties. As *The Times*' special correspondent put it: 'Every hour, nay, every minute of the day is occupied with conferences, deputations, meetings and speeches – the candidates, their committees, and agents endeavouring to rival each other in feats of endurance.' Even Irving was able to pack 3,000 into the Free Trade Hall for his meeting on 19 April, though this audience, as at the myriad others throughout the campaign, was no doubt swollen by women and folk from outside the constituency. Buoyed by his campaign's momentum, Irving apparently claimed: 'If I cannot poll a thousand votes in a working-class constituency like North-West Manchester, I will eat my hat.' Whether he did is unknown, but in the event, he only secured just over a quarter of that figure. His poll suffered a classic third-party squeeze consequential on the fierce fight between Liberals and Tories.

Manchester awoke on 25 April to the news that Churchill was out. There was a swing of 8.2 per cent resulting from an increase in the Tory vote of 1,019 and a Liberal decline of 671, with Joynson-Hicks home by 429. In his acceptance speech, the victor attributed his triumph to the Education, Licensing and Eight Hours Bills and Home Rule. He also paid tribute to those Unionist free traders 'who frankly declared that upon the fiscal question they did not agree with my views' but voted for him 'to put a nail in the coffin of this miserable Government'. That a former Unionist free trader, Sir George Kemp, was able to recapture the seat for the Liberals in 1910 suggests Joynson-Hicks's diagnosis was probably correct.

This did not stop tariff reformers who had never strayed near Manchester crowing over this victory and claiming without a shred of evidence that the majority would have been bigger if Joynson-Hicks had been a whole-hogger. Churchill's own words throughout the campaign nonetheless suggested that his defeat was, as the *Montreal Witness* put it, 'a great triumph for the tariff reformers'. Reactions in French, German and Austrian newspapers demonstrated that this closely followed by-election was seen both at home and abroad as a step towards protectionism and a major blow to the Liberal administration.

Churchill told the Manchester Reform Club that the one blemish of the election was the influence of the Harmsworth press. Privately, he primarily attributed his defeat to the Catholic priesthood. With Home Rule back in the Liberal programme and the Education Bill dropped, Kemp was to benefit from a much more solid Irish vote in 1910. Meanwhile, Joynson-Hicks wished Churchill a swift return to Parliament and the defeated candidate set off to Dundee to secure it.

One immediate significance of the result was that it marked the start of Joynson-Hicks's parliamentary career, which culminated when he sat together with Churchill in the Conservative Cabinet of 1924–29. The effectiveness of Joynson-Hicks's campaign also prompted Lloyd George to come to the aid of his successor, breaking the unwritten rule that Cabinet ministers did not campaign in by-elections. Notwithstanding the immediate interpretations offered at home and abroad, its significance in the struggle over tariff reform is easily overstated. It was probably more important in wresting a pledge to introduce Home Rule out of Asquith in an abortive attempt to save Churchill's seat. Acland-Hood emphasised that the result indicated that none of the Liberals' gains of 1906 were now safe. Lord Wolmer later claimed that this led to a change in the attitude of the Liberal government to its parliamentary opponents. He made those remarks in a debate in 1919 about removing the requirement of ministers to stand for re-election. That the 1908 Manchester North West by-election regularly featured in such debates until this change was achieved by a Private Members' Bill in 1926 was yet another of its legacies.

Pippa Catterall is a professor of history and policy at the University of Westminster. She has published extensively on British political history and is currently researching a monograph on Prime Ministers and public policy.

13

NORTH EAST DERBYSHIRE

20 MAY 1914
CONSERVATIVE GAIN FROM LABOUR

GORDON MARSDEN

Result: G. R. Harland Bowden (Conservative), 6,469, 39.7 per cent; John Houfton (Liberal), 6,155, 37.8 per cent; James Martin (Labour), 3,669, 22.5 per cent
Size of majority: 314
Swing: 14.9 per cent from Labour to Conservative
Name of previous MP and party: W. E. Harvey (Liberal; Labour; Liberal)
Reason for by-election: Death of incumbent
Result of previous general election: W. E. Harvey (Labour), 7,838, 56.3 per cent; Josiah Court (Conservative), 6,088, 43.7 per cent
Date by-election called: N/A
Date by-election took place: 20 May 1914
Size of total electorate: N/A
Total number of votes cast: 16,293
Turnout: N/A

Edwardian Britain was a frenzied place, breezing into the twentieth century, bursting with exciting new inventions – motor cars, aeroplanes, silent films, wireless telegrams and the press becoming more available to ordinary people.

A world fizzing with controversies, over gender, equalities, class, women, sexuality and politics, along with the ethics of eugenics – hotly contested. Britain and its empire saw growing tensions in Europe, arms races and colonial wars, which were more poignant by the fact that the monarchs of Britain, Germany and Russia were blood cousins via Queen Victoria.

What has this to do with a by-election in North East Derbyshire in May 1914?

Plenty. The 1906 general election landslide, sweeping the Liberals into government, had faded. Prime Minister Asquith now had to balance factions – making Lloyd George and Churchill ministers to satisfy 'New Liberalism' radicals but also powerful Whig grandees in the countryside (including Derbyshire), influential Nonconformists, MPs and activists.

However, Asquith had to take a back seat on the redistribution of wealth (higher rates on supertax, unearned income and land tax to fund old-age pensions and social welfare initiatives) when the Lords – with a huge Tory majority – systematically tried to block them. Lloyd George's 'People's Budget' in 1909 was controversial and an unholy alliance with the press baron Viscount Northcliffe (whose *Daily Mail* exercised vast influence over popular opinion and relentlessly attacked the government, along with the aristocracy) protesting against the Budget. General elections in 1910 that were meant to settle the issue left the Liberals as a minority government, but the Parliament Act of 1911 finally passed, removing the powers of the Lords to veto money bills.

By the time the MP for North East Derbyshire, W. E. Harvey, died of pneumonia on 28 April 1914, the Liberal government was mired in crisis. Their Irish Home Rule Bill provoked half a million Ulster Protestant Unionists to sign a covenant in September 1912 to defy Home Rule and, with Ulster Volunteers and Irish Volunteers, pile up weapons and threaten civil war. Finally, the government had to face widespread industrial unrest, including the miners' strike of 1912, fearing trade unions were becoming closer to the Labour Party in matters not just confined to industrial disputes. This would be a key factor in the North East Derbyshire by-election, where miners made up about 40 per cent of the electorate.

Derbyshire had a long history of coal mining – major exploitation did not take off until the nineteenth century, but by 1914 coal mining in Chesterfield, Clay Cross, Bolsover and elsewhere was a crucial contributor to the economy and defence. Attempts by miners to form a union early in the nineteenth century were abortive, but in 1880 the Derbyshire Miners' Association was founded. In 1889, the Miners' Federation of Great Britain (MFGB) came into existence. These two bodies were to be critical actors in the by-election.

The first working-class representatives in Parliament became known as 'Lib–Lab' MPs – with mining officials Thomas Burt and Alexander Macdonald elected in 1874. Lib–Labs accepted the Liberal whip while utilising their experience to speak freely on labour issues. About half of the Lib–Lab MPs were miners before entering Parliament. Gladstone in 1891 called for more Lib–Lab MPs, but local Liberal committees failed to select more working-class candidates or finance them.

Spooked by Labour's five MPs in the 1900 general election and more in subsequent by-elections, Herbert Gladstone signed a secret agreement in 1903 with Ramsay MacDonald, secretary to the Labour Party. The Liberals agreed not to contest fifty seats where Labour was in pole position and in the 1906 general election, twenty-nine Labour candidates became MPs, twenty-four of them unopposed by the Liberals. Disengagement from the Liberal Party accelerated when the twenty-nine MPs formed a Parliamentary Labour Party, prompting some trade unions, including the miners, to affiliate with the Labour Party.

The historian Robert Taylor, writing in the *Liberal News*, says: 'Trade union finances were always crucial for the funding of Labour's national machine and constituency parties … Trade union officials and activists made up the bulk of the party's rank and file … The Liberal party found it increasingly difficult to accommodate the force of an emerging self-confidence.'

But the road to independence for Labour via the trade unions was tortuous and thorny.

Taylor says that 'Liberalism's ethical appeal to many respectable, prudent and thrifty working class male voters up to the outbreak of the Great War should not be neglected' and though after 1906 union activists started to join a Labour Party in pursuit of power, 'such a transition had hardly begun to take place among their rank and file before 1914, let alone the wider working classes'. All these tensions crystallised over affiliation by the Miners' Federation of Great Britain to the Labour Party.

In 1906, the MFGB held a national ballot of miners on whether to affiliate with the LRC, but the proposal was defeated by 101,714 to 92,222. After the vote, the federation's president Enoch Edwards – just elected to Parliament as the Lib–Lab MP for Hanley – told their conference 'the question like all others will ripen'.

A second ballot was held in 1908. This time, the MFGB did affiliate with the Labour Party by 213,137 votes to 168,446. MPs or would-be MPs sponsored by unions would now be asked to join the Labour group in Parliament. This was a significant event – the MFGB was by far the largest trade union in the country, with its estimated membership of 600,000. Most did – but a number of Lib–Labs remained ambiguous about taking the Labour ticket.

The years between 1908 and 1914 were deeply frustrating for Labour. Radical 'New Liberalism' began to steal Labour's clothes. Lloyd George's Budget, the attack on the Lords, old-age pensions, social reform and the Trade Disputes Act were all welcomed by the unions. The two 1910 general elections were bitterly disappointing – in any contest against both Liberal and Unionist candidates, Labour did badly. Labour MPs had to rely on Liberal associations giving them a free pass so not to split the anti-Tory vote (twenty-seven of the forty-two Labour MPs were elected in straight fights with Tories).

To make matters worse, two by-elections came up in predominantly mining constituencies where Labour MPs had died – Enoch Edwards, the Hanley Lib–Lab MP, who died suddenly in June 1912, and the Chesterfield MP James Haslam, who died in July 1913. He had been the secretary of the Derbyshire Miners' Association and since 1906 was a Lib–Lab MP. He then took the Labour whip and was re-elected in both 1910 elections without facing a Liberal opponent.

Neither of these by-elections turned out well for Labour. The new Labour candidate Samuel Finney in Hanley, unlike Enoch Edwards, had no sympathies with the Liberal Party, so the local Liberal association put up Robert Outhwaite, a radical Liberal politician. He was elected as Hanley's MP with 6,647 votes over the Tories' 5,993, with Labour a poor third with 1,694.

Chesterfield was another matter. When Haslam died in July 1913, the Derbyshire Miners' Association nominated one of their officials, Barnet Kenyon, who held Lib–Lab sympathies. When the Liberal candidate pulled out, Kenyon agreed to be adopted by the Liberals as well. After much intrigue on Kenyon's part, a local meeting of trade unionists and socialists nominated a London docker, John Scurr, to contest Chesterfield. Kenyon won as a Liberal with more than 2,000 votes over the Tory candidate, Edward Christie; Scurr only amassed a paltry 583 votes.

As 1914 came, Ramsay MacDonald was increasingly worried about Labour's position vis-à-vis the Liberals. In his 1942 memoir, the veteran pacifist Fenner Brockway, at that time in his twenties and editor of the *Labour Leader*, records just how nervous MacDonald was:

> Early in the spring of 1914 I had an appointment with Keir Hardie at the House of Commons. He was white and looked worried. 'Fenner, something has just happened which I could never have believed. MacDonald has suggested to the Parliamentary Executive that we make an alliance with the Liberal Party at the General Election.' He turned to me: 'Laddie, we must kill this plan at the Independent Labour Party (ILP) Conference. Do what you can.'

The ILP meeting was held in April. By the end of the month, MacDonald had even more cause to be shaky when the death of W. E. Harvey, MP for North East Derbyshire, was announced. He was the third Lib–Lab mining MP to die in the Midlands in two years. For MacDonald, it meant a difficult by-election in Derbyshire and tricky negotiations with the miners just when the party in London was hardening over candidates taking the Labour whip.

Harvey had been cut from the same cloth as Haslam in Chesterfield and Edwards in Hanley. All three had worked in the mines from their teens, then afterwards as officials both in their local associations and the Miners' Federation. Harvey had held office in both. He, like the other Lib–Lab MPs, helped more working men into local politics for the Liberals and was strongly opposed to socialism.

Harvey was the Liberal candidate in the 1907 North East Derbyshire by-election, which he won. As an MP, he held the Liberal whip and as an active trade unionist, followed instructions from the Derbyshire miners – including joining the Labour Party (reluctantly). He had been re-elected under Labour colours in a straight fight with the Tory candidate in the 1910 general elections, when Liberals not wishing to split the vote supported Harvey instead.

Harvey was very unhappy about how Labour treated Barnet Kenyon when he won as a Lib–Lab in the 1913 Chesterfield by-election. He resigned the Labour whip, taking the Liberal whip in March 1914, just before his death. We will see how his legacy muddied the Lib–Lab waters for the voters.

Harvey's death doubtlessly shook the Derbyshire Miners' Association, but with about a third of the electorate directly involved in the mining industry, and the seat effectively in the association's gift, they probably thought swift action would put them in pole position for the coming by-election. If so, it turned out to be a disastrous course to follow.

First of all, their executive took the unusual action of appointing their own election agent, Bertram Mather, rather than approaching the local Liberal agent. Then they looked for their candidate. The front-runners were their president, James Martin, and their chief secretary, Frank Hall.

The consensus suggested Hall would get the nomination – Mather was a Labour man and Hall agreed to sign up to the Labour Party. Martin, on the other hand, was on the local Liberal executive and a sub-agent – and the local Liberal association had been willing to adopt Martin as their candidate, hoping a Lib–Lab candidate would beat the Tory.

But when the mining lodges met, they overturned the executive's preference for Hall and voted to nominate Martin. Mather met with the Labour Party which insisted Martin had to sign up to the party. Under pressure, Martin agreed to stand as a Labour Party candidate. The local Liberals had warned that if Martin decided to run for Labour, they would adopt their own candidate, so now they invited John Houfton, the managing director of the Bolsover Colliery, to be their candidate.

What the good voters of North East Derbyshire made of these

shenanigans cannot be known. They only knew their MP Harvey had died suddenly, had worked as a man and a boy in the mines and was active in the constituency as a trade unionist, serving them for seven years as a Labour MP, just before his death.

But if the voters were in the dark, the local papers soon began to fill them in on the by-election. In the 1860s, taxes on existing newspapers had been slashed, and a cheap postal system enabled papers to be carried mainly by train – sometimes three times a day in Edwardian Derbyshire.

Technological innovations carried news quickly by telegraph and enabled local newspapers to be sold cheaply with hordes of advertisements – appealing to a lower middle class and in Derbyshire an increasingly literate working class. (My grandfather Fred Marsden, whose father was a bootmaker in Bakewell, got a medal for being one of the top Derbyshire scholars leaving school at fourteen in 1900 – which I still have.)

All these changes were fuelled by the 'New Journalism' – the *Daily Telegraph* being followed by the *Daily Mail*, the *Daily Mirror*, the *Daily Herald* and others between 1890 and 1914. The intense interest in politics in the same period encouraged local papers follow suit. Their characteristics spilled over into regional and local newspapers. Pages of advertisements highlighted the new consumerism – health remedies and small ads for readers who wanted to enjoy the new 'Bank Holidays' including in the Peak District, in Buxton's and Matlock's spas and in the Dales.

They appeared cheek by jowl with pages on politics and featured speedy reporting (the Press Association, founded in 1868, enabled swift news input into the provincial newspapers) with brisk writing and often aggressive interviews from young journalists eager to make their mark.

A clutch of local papers – the *Derbyshire Times*, the *Derbyshire Courier*, the *Derby and Chesterfield Reporter*, the *Derby Daily Telegraph* and the *Eckington, Woodhouse and Staveley Express* followed the North East Derbyshire by-election closely. Their reports are crucial in understanding how the campaign progressed and its outcome in a 'short and sharp' election.

From the start, the Derbyshire Miners' Association was on the back foot with the local newspapers for their precipitant haste for the by-election. The miners' hasty appointment of Mather as their own election agent went against the elaborate Edwardian culture of paying respect – with its intricate rites of mourning, dress code and the etiquette of the funeral which all classes observed, especially when it concerned the sudden death of their MP. The press duly pilloried the miners for ignoring it and set the tone:

> The miners have taken this step with their eyes wide open, so eager were they to get in the first blow, that they were positively indecent, attempted to seduce the Liberal sub-agents, and failing completely, at once appointed a new Election Agent of their own in Mr Bertram Mather on Thursday of last week, two days before Mr Harvey's funeral took place.

Others took up the cry:

> The Derbyshire Miners' Association in deciding to run their President Mr James Martin of Staveley on the Labour ticket have done their best to hand North-East Derbyshire to the Tories. It is a course of action which could not possibly have been taken in the lifetime of Mr Haslam and Mr Harvey, both of whom during the whole of their political life were the staunchest opponents of 'split'.

A second wave of criticism then came, attacking the association for muddling the procedure and dividing the anti-Tory forces:

> Owing to the Derbyshire Miners' Association, who have persisted in running a candidate on the 'Labour ticket', there will be a three cornered fight in the North East Derbyshire by-election … Every effort was made by the Liberals, and in particular Sir Arthur Markham MP, to get the Miners' Association to decide upon a candidate who would represent both Liberals and Labour. These attempts at conciliation have met with no response – after a vote of the miners' lodges, the Association adopted Mr James Martin, their President, as their candidate on 'the Labour Ticket'.

In a move to pressurise the miners, the paper then published in full Markham's open letter to the Derbyshire Miners' Council. Markham was the Liberal MP for Mansfield, renowned for his technical skills in the coalfields – and had been close to Harvey and Haslam.

To modern eyes, it seems a verbose and pompous letter but maybe not to Edwardian readers. Markham challenged the miners on both moral and practical grounds, 'having chaired both Harvey and Haslam campaigns in previous elections and as a friend to Labour in Derbyshire'.

> Gentlemen, I am most anxious that the progressive forces in the division should not be broken and divided; it would indeed be a calamity if, immediately following the death of our dear friend [Harvey], the two forces of progress should be at war … Derbyshire has now been for many years the stronghold of Liberalism, yet the Liberal party are to be asked that a candidate [Martin] whose views they may be in full sympathy with, is not to address them from their own platform.
>
> Within the ranks of Liberalism there is room for men of all thoughts … but the decision of the Labour Party in London to have a Labour candidate was arrived at by a few extreme men whose views were repugnant both to the late Mr Harvey and to the late Mr Haslam, and I firmly believe that the Derbyshire miners as a body likewise share the same view.

The paper applauded Markham and said: 'What was the reply to his conciliatory letter to the Miners' Council? It was a total rejection of the offer of co-operation and the ordering of a lodge vote.' Under a subheading 'Why not a Ballot', they continued: 'These questions, let us remember, were submitted to a lodge vote, and not to a ballot of the Association. Why? Simply because a ballot would not have suited the extremists. A ballot would have revealed that a very large majority of the miners are Liberals and not Socialists.'

The press then speculated that the nominee would be Frank Hall. But a press release came from the Miners' Council:

> We desire to express our appreciation of Mr Frank Hall's service to our

Association, and learn with pleasure that at this juncture he deems it the better course to remain at his post at the head office, and we are pleased to note the magnanimity which characterises his withdrawal in favour of the candidate for North East Derbyshire Division.

Stalin would have been proud of this explanation. Was there arm-twisting on Hall? Was Hall already fearing a split vote that would let the Tory in? What we do know is that he, Mr Martin, and the agent Mr Mather travelled immediately down to London where, the papers reported, 'at a meeting of the Miners' Federation, Mr Hall having addressed the Federation on the situation, it was agreed to endorse the candidate'.

What we do know – again from the papers – is that the Emergency Committee of the Labour Party agreed the endorsement, with the big guns of the party, Ramsay MacDonald and Arthur Henderson, deputed to be official speakers, and that Arthur Peters, the national agent, was to proceed at once to Derbyshire.

Meanwhile, the Liberal executive called a meeting in Chesterfield to adopt John Houfton. The papers reported that 'there was a large and representative attendance from all parts of the constituency' and that 'a deputation was received from the Derbyshire Miners' Association' who 'reported the decision of their association with regard to nominating Mr Martin and then withdrew'. (Later, the Liberals, in a press release, scolded both the miners and the Labour Party for refusing 'the public co-operation'.)

Meanwhile, Martin, wanting to get off the back foot, gave an interview designed to clarify his position. He declared: 'In all essential things I am a Liberal, but as the Derbyshire Miners' Association is connected with the Miners' Federation of Great Britain, I, as President of the County Association, can take no other stand than to support the Labour principles of the Miners' Federation.'

If Martin thought this showed him in a philosophical light, he was sorely mistaken. The interview was a disaster. The sarcastic heading the sub-editor put up – 'What Mr Martin's Candidature Means/Where Is His Liberalism?' – was a prelude for scathing attacks on his judgement and being a turncoat, reminding its readers that:

we do not forget that Mr Martin is one of those who stood by Mr Barnet Kenyon when he declined to be bound by the Labour ticket, presided at his meetings and rejoiced that Mr Kenyon had won. It will not do for him to reiterate his Liberalism. He knows that having adopted the Labour ticket, he would be bound to abide by the constitution of the Labour Party. He would be, if elected, merely a delegate to carry out the policy of the Socialist party who control the Labour Party in London. It is clear that Mr Martin is out to try and run with the Socialist and the Liberal, and it won't do.

The final paragraph put the knife in: 'We cannot see Mr Martin's candidature doing anything else than bringing in the danger of handing the seat over to the Tory candidate.'

While the local press was shredding James Martin, they also turned their attention to the Liberal candidate, John Houfton, and the Conservative candidate, Harland Bowden.

Under the headline 'Promise of a Keen Fight', the papers turned first to the Liberals:

The Liberals, although handicapped by the death of their highly esteemed election agent Mr S. E. Short, have everything ready and the agency will be in the hands of his brother. Mr Houfton will not be adopted until the Liberal Council this afternoon, but the whole organisation so far is working with perfect smoothness.

The other parties got shorter shrift: 'The Tory agent, MD Blackham, has his headquarters at Staveley, and Bertram Mather, Mr Martin's agent, is making Chesterfield his centre.'

Meanwhile, the love-in with the Liberals in the local papers continued, and the pen portrait that John Houfton was given amounted to hagiography:

Mr Houfton has always taken a deep interest in the social welfare of working men. His father worked at the coal face, and he himself served in all the grades in the mine, until now he occupies his present position as managing director of the Bolsover Colliery – a position won by sheer doggedness and determination. No man knows the needs and regulations for safety of a mining community better than he does.

Seeing the fratricidal contest between Labour and the Liberals, Harland Bowden, the Tory candidate, must have had a spring in his step. Already attacked as a carpetbagger (though he was a mechanical engineer, installing colliery plant), the press covered his adoption with a list of local worthies – to give Bowden confidence – and excerpts from his speech.

Bowden wisely avoided wading into local issues and ticked off a list of national Tory concerns – Home Rule for Ireland and resistance from Ulster, Lloyd George's radical Budget and the National Insurance Bill. He said he would demand at Westminster the threat to Ulster be removed and made a big pitch for tariff reform, 'making the foreigner pay his fair dues with the British working man and the prosperity of Great Britain and the Empire'.

Bowden had a leaden dig at Lloyd George – 'The only things of which we are sure of under a Radical government are death and taxes.' He promised to associate himself with industrial life in Derbyshire and serve not just one part but the whole of it (a jab at his opponents for just concentrating on miners).

In the Edwardian era, there was a revival of single-issue groups, on the back of intense interest in politics. By-elections were ideal venues for them to show off their wares – and North East Derbyshire with its small market towns was ideal. The local papers reported their activities:

The Free Trade Union have shown the greatest enterprise, and up to <u>Thursday midday</u> had distributed 60,000 leaflets to the electors. The National League for Opposing Women Suffrage has opened committee rooms in the Market Place, Bolsover and are taking an active part in the present by-election. They are adopting a strictly non-party attitude and leaflets are already being distributed in large numbers. Eckington is receiving a considerable amount of attention for the Suffragettes.

Suffragette activity was fairly common in Derbyshire before 1914. At the 1910 Ilkeston by-election, Mrs Pankhurst spoke at a suffragette meeting at Heanor Town Hall – 'The hall was densely packed, with hundreds of people stood outside trying to get in.'

In the campaign's last week, a piece entitled 'Ill Feeling between Liberals and Socialists' remarked that 'a strong element of bitterness has entered into the campaign':

> Neither side can claim much credit for the attitude adopted to its former ally, for whilst Mr Martin yesterday declared with emphasis that he would prefer any Labour elector who would not vote for him should support Major Bowden rather than Mr Houfton, the Liberals have sent round with their poll card a leaflet, titled 'The Houfton Herald', telling electors under the heading 'The Record of Socialist Wreckers', giving a list of the results of three-cornered contests from 1911 to 1914, with the comment 'The Socialists have forced twenty-three contests. They have won none and handed over seven seats to the Tories. Will you allow North East Derbyshire Liberalism to be sacrificed on the Socialist altar?'

On eve of poll, 19 May, the *Manchester Evening News* summed up the field of battle: 'Whilst the division of the Progressive vote is a big factor in the Tory candidate's chances, there is no falling off in the efforts of the Liberal and the Labour parties to prevent the division from being represented, for the first time in its history, by a Conservative.'

The edition also carried the text of a telegram sent to Houfton by Lloyd George, the Liberal Chancellor. His message opened bluntly: 'I deplore the division in the Progressive forces in North East Derbyshire. It is only reactionaries who rejoice in it or who profit by it.'

Under the headline 'Why I Should Win', when asked by the reporter what the secret of his success was, the Tory candidate, Harland Bowden, replied: 'Honesty of purpose' and then rolled off his list of Tory policies. His agent was more crisp: 'If the Labour candidate can poll 3,000 votes, the seat will be won by the Conservatives.'

His agent was right. When the result was announced, with a heavy turnout of 84.2 per cent of the electorate (16,293), the brash Harland Bowden just edged it with 6,469 for the Conservatives with a majority of 314 over John Houfton for the Liberals, who polled 6,155. The ill-fated James Martin came third, with 3,669 votes.

How are we to interpret this result from 110 years ago? Clearly, there was no lack of enthusiasm from the voters, as the turnout shows. Bowden said he won because of his opposition to the National Insurance Act and Home Rule in Ireland – but overplayed both. Some working men might have moved their votes to the Tories but hardly enough. 'It was the split wot done it.'

I think that in the campaign – and the by-election caused by the sudden death of Harvey, who had been to all intents and purposes a Lib–Lab MP – his death hung heavily in the air. Nervousness – with the PLP and Ramsay MacDonald down in London and shared with the Derbyshire Miners' Association – led to hasty decisions being baked in. Being egged on by the local press made it easier for would-be Derbyshire miner voters to lose confidence in Labour.

Heavy press bias in favour of the Liberals was relentless. The Labour candidate, James Martin, was a haunted man, torn between his obedience to friends and the association and his lifelong links to the Liberals. He made a number of gaffes which the press duly leaped on, while the Liberals' 'Houfton Herald' tightened the screw further on 'London Socialists'.

The three candidates had a melancholy afterlife in politics. James Martin, now over seventy, in poor health and scarred by the by-election, left his union posts in 1917, and Derbyshire, lived out his final years in a nursing home in Sheffield.

Harland Bowden went to the Great War commanding a battalion on the Western Front. He held his seat during the war but found himself estranged from the local Conservative association. In October 1919, he was awarded £125 in damages for libel against its vice-chairman. Twice in the general elections of 1918 and 1924 he lost defending the seat and three years later, in 1927, he died suddenly, aged fifty-four.

John Houfton did stand again for Parliament – in 1922 but not in Derbyshire, nor for the Liberal Party, but as a Coalition Unionist winning a seat in Nottingham East. He was then defeated at the 1923 general election by the Liberal candidate but then knighted shortly before his death in November 1929.

What was the short-term significance of the North East Derbyshire by-election? Ramsay MacDonald brooding over another Labour seat lost. The Derbyshire miners left to lick their wounds after the Labour ticket fiasco. And another shallow Tory MP to irritate a Liberal minority government.

But the clock was ticking for war – and those unstable central and Balkan states. Three months after the by-election in Derbyshire, the Great War broke out, and the world of politics, work, gender, society and trade unions in Great Britain was utterly changed.

Gordon Marsden is the co-founder of the Steering Group at the Right to Learn and a trustee of the History of Parliament Trust. He has an honorary doctorate from the Open University. He was a former shadow Minister for Higher and Further Education and Skills and MP for Blackpool South 1997–2019. He wrote the Aneurin Bevan chapter in Eminent Parliamentarians *(Biteback, 2012).*

14

MERTHYR TYDFIL

25 NOVEMBER 1915
INDEPENDENT LABOUR GAIN

SIR VERNON BOGDANOR

Result: Charles Stanton (Independent Labour), 10,286, 63 per cent; James Winstone (Labour), 6,080, 37 per cent
Size of majority: 4,206
Swing: N/A
Name of previous MP and party: Keir Hardie (Labour)
Reason for by-election: Death of incumbent
Result at previous general election: Edgar Jones (Liberal), 12,258, 42 per cent; Keir Hardie (Labour), 11.507, 40 per cent; John Henry Watts (Liberal Unionist), 5,277, 18 per cent
Date by-election called: 15 November 1915
Date by-election took place: 25 November 1915
Size of total electorate: 24,740
Total number of votes cast: 16,366
Turnout: 68 per cent

The Merthyr Tydfil by-election of 1915 appeared to show that a seemingly radical mining constituency was more supportive of the war than many had imagined, more supportive indeed than many of the leaders of the working class. For this reason, the outcome of the by-election was, *The Times* believed, 'one of the most significant events that have occurred at home since the beginning of the war' and a 'decisive numerical test of the strength of patriotism in Great Britain at the very point where it was thought to be weakest'. The by-election helped clear the way for conscription and created the atmosphere in which, just over a year later, Lloyd George was to become Prime Minister with a mandate for total victory against Germany. It is no surprise that the future Prime Minister was, according to his secretary and mistress, Frances Stevenson, jubilant at the outcome in Merthyr Tydfil.

Merthyr Tydfil, also known as Merthyr Boroughs, was a two-member constituency created in 1885, dominated by miners. In 1900, Keir Hardie, founder of the Labour Party and himself a former miner, had been elected, thanks to a split in the Liberal Party, as the country's first Labour MP. He continued in harness with a Liberal until the First World War which Hardie, a Christian Socialist and pacifist, together with just three other Labour MPs, refused to support.

It was, however, soon clear that Hardie's anti-war views were not those of his constituents. A meeting which he addressed on 6 August 1914, just two days after Britain had declared war on Germany, was broken up by protesters and Hardie was forced to withdraw under police escort. He was later to declare grandiloquently that he now understood how Christ had felt at Gethsemane.

In September 1915, Hardie died – of a broken heart, so his supporters alleged. That necessitated a by-election. The wartime electoral truce meant that Labour could be expected to enjoy an unopposed return in the constituency, as had occurred in four previous by-elections in Wales since the outbreak of war.

By tradition, the South Wales Miners' Federation had the right of nominating the Labour candidate. The first two miners' ballots put Charles Stanton, a miners' agent, ahead, but he was defeated on the final ballot by the establishment candidate, James Winstone, as a result of vote transfers from losing candidates. Winstone was a Baptist lay preacher who had just become president of the South Wales Miners' Federation and had been a Labour councillor since 1906. His nomination was duly approved by the Miners' Federation, the local Labour Representation Committee and Labour's national executive. In accordance with the wartime truce, Arthur Henderson, leader of the party and president of the Board of Education in Asquith's coalition government, called for Winstone to be given an unopposed return.

By contrast with Keir Hardie, Winstone supported the war, addressing recruiting meetings and calling on men to volunteer, as his two sons had done. But in accordance with Labour Party and trade union policy, Winstone was hostile to conscription, opposition to which had been recently confirmed at a TUC conference at which some delegates had called for a general strike were it to be enacted.

But Winstone had an Achilles heel. He was a member of the Independent Labour Party – the ILP – a left-wing component of the Labour Party. At that time, Labour was a federal organisation. There were few constituency parties and few individual members. Most of its members joined through an affiliated organisation, primarily a trade union, but also a socialist organisation of which the ILP was the most prominent. The ILP opposed Labour's support for the war and refused to assist with recruiting – although some of its members did in fact assist. Even though Winstone rejected the ILP's anti-war policy, he remained a member and was incautious enough to ask ILP leaders such as Ramsay MacDonald to speak in his support.

The Conservative and Liberal parties adhered to the wartime electoral truce and did not put up a candidate to oppose Winstone. But Charles Stanton, the defeated candidate in the Miners' Federation ballots, declared that he would stand as 'Independent Labour'. Merthyr Tydfil became only the second constituency outside Ireland to be contested since the outbreak of war – the first having been Glasgow Central in July 1915, when an independent Conservative challenging the official Conservative candidate had secured just 266 votes.

Charles Stanton had enjoyed a chequered political career. He had begun on the far left, claiming that Keir Hardie was insufficiently militant. In 1893, at the age of twenty-one, he had been accused of firing at the police during a miners' strike. Convicted of illegally possessing firearms, he had been sentenced to six months in prison. He had fought East Glamorganshire unsuccessfully in December 1910 as a Labour candidate, when he had been regarded as too extreme by the miners, many of whom remained attached to the Liberal Party.

In 1914, Stanton came out as a strong supporter of the war. He resigned from the ILP and helped to break up Keir Hardie's 6 August meeting. He also resigned his position as a miners' agent, claiming that there was a 'pro-German' element in the union and declaring that 'although a Socialist, I was a Britisher'.

In his campaign, Stanton insisted that a victory for Winstone would also be a victory for the ILP. It would therefore 'be a message of discouragement to our soldiers in the field' and so would please 'the Hun'. His election agent declared the contest to be one 'between everything they understood as British and the ILP'. The appeal of an anti-war party such as the ILP had never been strong and was undermined in 1915 by the first German gas attack at Ypres in April; the sinking of the liner *Lusitania* in May, with the loss of over 1,000 passengers; and in October, just one month before the by-election, the execution by Germany of nurse Edith Cavell for helping Allied soldiers escape from Belgium to the Netherlands, from where they could return to Britain or France to resume the fight.

Stanton's election agent urged voters to send 'a message of encouragement to the boys in the trenches and not one of joy to Germany of which Mr Ramsay MacDonald was such a professed friend'. The voters did indeed send such a message. Although Winstone enjoyed the support of the trade unions and the Labour Party, this did not help him. Stanton received considerable unofficial support, despite the party truce, from Conservatives and Liberals and was triumphantly returned by a majority of almost two to one. He had won despite not enjoying the support of any minister, political party or organised interest group such as the TUC or the miners' union. He had financed his own campaign and it was said that he had been forced to sell furniture to pay his election expenses, although in fact he had enjoyed secret finance from the Conservatives.

The *Manchester Guardian*, as *The Guardian* then was, declared that 'Mr Stanton's huge majority exceeds the wildest dreams of his supporters'. Stanton himself interpreted the result as 'a message of good cheer to the boys in the trenches and certainly a setback to the pro-German section'. *The Times* welcomed the victory of 'an independent and patriotic Labour candidate as a protest against the anti-recruiting and pacific policy of the Independent Labour Party'. The *Western Mail* drew the lesson that 'the working men of Merthyr Boroughs are not, in fact, as Socialistic in their views as the associations of the late Mr Keir Hardie with the constituency may have led many to believe'. Not only did it appear that ILP leaders such as Ramsay MacDonald were out of touch with those whom they claimed to represent – but even the pro-war leaders of the Labour Party, such as Arthur Henderson, seemed to have underestimated the intense patriotism of working-class voters.

The by-election seemed to provide a mandate for conscription. Stanton had not explicitly advocated it but had indicated that he would accept it if the voluntary system failed to secure sufficient recruits – the position of most of the ministers in the Asquith coalition government. Lloyd George, however, was jubilant, even though the candidate whom the government supported, a government of which he was a member, had been defeated. For Lloyd George, like Stanton, favoured conscription. Winstone, by contrast, was against conscription in principle, and Stanton was denounced for being willing to consider it.

Looking at the result soberly, although few did so at the time, the outcome was perhaps not quite as remarkable as it appeared. Winstone's percentage of the vote, after all, was only slightly lower than that secured by Hardie in December 1910; while Stanton's vote was not much higher than the combined Liberal/Conservative percentage in that general election.

Still, in politics, immediate impressions often count for more than psephological realities. The outcome of the by-election appeared to undermine the argument of Labour ministers such as Henderson that conscription, because it bore most heavily on the working class, would undermine national unity and generate class conflict. It seemed to show that working-class hostility to conscription was far weaker than ministers had feared; and it paved the way for the Asquith government's first Conscription Bill, introduced in January 1916.

By the time of the 1918 general election, the Merthyr Tydfil constituency had been divided into two single-member constituencies – Merthyr and Aberdare. Merthyr was won by Sir Edgar Jones, the pro-war Liberal MP, standing as a Lloyd George coalition Liberal, with Conservative support. Winstone was once again the defeated candidate and made no further attempt to enter Parliament.

In Aberdare, Stanton, who had sat in the Commons as an Independent, stood for the National Democratic Party (NDP). This was a new and short-lived patriotic party formed to support the Lloyd George coalition government after the armistice. The NDP was given the 'coupon' by Lloyd George, which meant that its candidates would not face Conservative or coalition Liberal opposition. Labour, which had left the coalition at the time of the armistice, fought the election as an independent party. Rather foolishly, it put up against Stanton one Rev. T. E. Nicholas, a pacifist who, at his first election meeting, was asked whether he would shake hands with a German. He replied, 'Yes, why not?' Stanton won even more convincingly than in 1915. But Stanton, so it was said, could have defeated even St John the Baptist in the feverish atmosphere of a 'khaki election', fought so soon after the end of the war.

In the next general election, in 1922, Stanton stood as a coalition Liberal supporter of Lloyd George. But by then, the atmosphere was far less frenetic than at the time of the armistice. Class and party ties were reasserting themselves. A reunited Labour Party had recovered its self-assurance and divisions between the pro- and anti-war factions appeared to have been healed. Stanton, moreover, was accused of lax attendance in the Commons. Unsurprisingly, he was defeated by Labour, which was to hold both Aberdare and Merthyr Tydfil constituencies continuously, with just one short interval, from 1922. Labour votes in Aberdare and Merthyr Tydfil constituencies as in other Welsh mining valley constituencies were, it has been said, weighed rather than counted! Between 1950 and 1972, Merthyr was to be represented by an avowed pacifist, S. O. Davies, a far cry from Stanton. As for Stanton himself, he joined the temporarily reunited Liberal Party in 1928 but never returned to the Commons.

Despite the leftist complexion of Merthyr after 1922, there is nevertheless some evidence that its working-class constituents retain that patriotic fervour which had propelled Stanton to victory in 1915. In 2024, nearly 110 years after the by-election, Nigel Farage was to launch his Reform UK manifesto, *Contract with You*, in Merthyr Tydfil – the constituency not only of Keir Hardie and S. O. Davies but also of Charles Stanton, whose ghost perhaps still stalks the valleys.

Sir Vernon Bogdanor *is a professor of government at King's College London and was for many years a professor of government at Oxford. His books include* The Strange Survival of Liberal Britain *(Biteback, 2022) and* Making the Weather: Six who Changed Post War Britain *(Haus Publishing, 2024).*

15

EAST CLARE

10 JULY 1917
SINN FÉIN GAIN FROM IRISH
PARLIAMENTARY PARTY

RICHARD S. GRAYSON

Result: Éamon de Valera (Sinn Féin), 5,010, 71.1 per cent; Patrick Lynch (Irish Parliamentary), 2,035, 28.9 per cent
Size of majority: 2,975
Swing: N/A
Name of previous MP and party: William Hoey Kearney Redmond (Irish Parliamentary)
Reason for by-election: Death of incumbent
Result at previous general election: William Hoey Kearney Redmond (Irish Parliamentary) elected unopposed
Date by-election called: 19 June 1917
Date by-election took place: 10 July 1917
Size of total electorate: 9,130
Total number of votes cast: 7,045
Turnout: 77.2 per cent

East Clare ought to have been an easy win for the Irish Parliamentary Party (IPP). The party dominated Irish politics from the 1880s, winning seventy-three of Ireland's 103 parliamentary seats in December 1910. The IPP also dominated East Clare. It won every election from the seat's creation in 1885, and after 'Willie' Redmond won in 1892 and 1895, he held it at the next four elections (1900, 1906 and twice in 1910) uncontested.

121

The circumstances of the by-election ought also to have created sympathy for any IPP candidate, since Willie Redmond died of wounds while serving as a major in the British Army at the Battle of Messines. German brutality in Belgium was a central element of the Irish nationalist case for enlistment, and Willie Redmond was one of five IPP MPs to enlist. They did so at the behest of Willie's brother, John, the leader of the IPP, who saw Ireland's support for Britain against Germany as a fight for 'small nations'. At fifty-six, there was no need for him to go into battle with the men he commanded in the 6th Royal Irish Regiment, but he had bravely chosen to do so.

The roots of East Clare's turn against the IPP are found in the Easter Rising. From 24 to 29 April 1916, Irish republicans attempted a revolution in Dublin only to be surrounded and flushed out by British forces, leaving parts of the city centre in ruins. W. B. Yeats wrote that the Rising saw Ireland 'changed utterly', but that was not evident immediately. In the days and weeks after the Rising, its leaders were deeply unpopular with many Dubliners who saw the Rising as a stab in the back for the Irish war effort. Some arrested rebels were spat at by locals as they were led away.

However, when the British executed sixteen of the Rising's leaders, opinion started to change. Home Rule (devolution for Ireland within the UK) had been passed in September 1914, but implementation was immediately suspended for the duration of the war. Willie Redmond articulated frustration over the delay when he spoke in the House of Commons on 7 March 1917 while home on leave. He reminded MPs that 'the great, generous heart of the Irish race beats in sympathy with the Allies' cause' but that the Irish were still 'a people denied justice, a people with many admitted grievances' and that 'Ireland is the only portion of the Empire now fighting which is not self-governing'.

Such frustration did not affect electoral results for nearly a year after the Rising. The IPP safely held West Cork in a November 1916 by-election, partly because there was no obvious alternative with the leaders of the Rising either executed or in prison. Moreover, although Sinn Féin became in 1917 the standard-bearers of republicanism, its leaders had not taken part in the Rising and they were not in 1916 a republican party (instead supporting a shared monarchy with Britain). They also had an abstentionist policy, which then meant not taking seats in Westminster and also generally not standing in Westminster elections.

A sign of possible change was the North Roscommon by-election of February 1917, won by Count George Plunkett. He was not then a member of Sinn Féin but was supported by key party figures and described as the 'Sinn Féin candidate'. Plunkett won convincingly with 56 per cent of the vote. Further change came in May 1917 in South Longford when Sinn Féin's Joseph McGuinness – at the time held in Lewes Prison – won by just thirty-seven votes over the IPP. By then, Sinn Féin leaders had realised – just as they would again during the 1981 Hunger Strike – that putting a prisoner on a ballot paper might apply pressure on the British government. Posters for McGuinness appealed 'Put him in to get him out', and the British government did carry out a mass release of republican prisoners in mid-June.

News of Redmond's death at Messines broke in newspapers from Saturday 9 June, and tributes were paid in the Commons on Monday 11th. The writ for the by-election was not moved until 19 June, with the campaign already under way. Among the prisoners released was Éamon de Valera, the most prominent leader of the Rising not to be executed. He was wary about standing in elections, but his prominence in the Rising made him an obvious choice. At a Sinn Féin meeting of 200 people, representing a broad range of republican opinion (including sixty priests), in Ennis, County Clare, on Thursday 14 June, de Valera's name was up against candidates including the president of Sinn Féin, Arthur Griffith, but won unanimous nomination. Released from prison a few days after this selection, de Valera was able to campaign in a way that McGuinness could not do in South Longford, which immediately raised his profile as a candidate.

The IPP candidate, Patrick Lynch, a barrister, was a prominent County Clare man. Selected for the IPP on Sunday 17 June, he was described by the *Irish Examiner* as someone who could 'advocate eloquently the cause of Ireland' in Parliament, reminding voters that a Sinn Féin MP would not attend Westminster. In these early stages of the campaign, Lynch wore the mantle of tributes to Willie Redmond. On 17 June, around 2,000 – including Lynch – took part in a procession in Ennis, with speeches emphasising that Redmond 'had so gallantly fallen fighting for the freedom of Ireland'. However, an immediate problem for Lynch was that his legal career allowed Sinn Féin to portray him as a prosecutor for the British. One poster showed de Valera in a heroic pose in military uniform in the dock, while Lynch stood near a British judge who was writing out a death sentence.

Rival public meetings on Saturday 23 June outlined the campaign messages. Speaking in Ennis, with a slogan of 'Justice for Ireland', de Valera argued that 'every vote given now for Mr Lynch was a vote given for conscription', suggesting that the IPP could in the future support extending conscription from Britain to Ireland. De Valera argued that instead of sending representatives to Westminster, Ireland should independently send them to a future peace conference. He also stressed that Sinn Féin was not anti-clerical, saying that the party 'regarded their first duty as to God and their second to their country'. He often appeared with priests at this and other meetings and rebutted arguments that republicans had been murderers during the Rising by asking how could they be when 'in the rebellion 1,200 of them stood up against 40,000 military'?

Lynch's contrasting message at Tulla appealed to the traditions of Charles Stewart Parnell and the long 'patriotic' record of the IPP in Parliament. He said that mistakes had been made by his party 'for it was only human nature to do so; but were they [the voters] going to crucify the Party or fling it to the wolves?' He also argued that MPs needed to attend Parliament so as not 'to allow the land and industries of Ireland to be taxed out of existence'. Lynch's early tone was mild and almost pleading for understanding of practicalities. However, at later meetings, IPP criticism of Sinn Féin was intensified as they sensed the possibility of defeat. One speaker characterised de Valera's platform as a 'policy of revolution, chaos and bloodshed'. Later IPP arguments, seen in the *Freeman's Journal*, a newspaper closely allied to the party, portrayed Sinn Féin's policy of 'total separation from Great Britain' as dependent on Britain being defeated in the war or at least the war reaching a crisis point, which was not in Ireland's interests. They also sought to deflect blame for the non-implementation of Home Rule away from the IPP and onto the British government.

Both sides canvassed extensively. They hurled insults at each other saying that their opponent's supporters had applied for jobs in the British establishment. Campaign events were spectacles, with black and green flags flying for the IPP and Sinn Féin displaying the green, white and orange tricolour. Both parties were linked to legal paramilitary groups, so IPP rallies were attended by National Volunteers in uniform, and Irish Volunteers supported Sinn Féin. Motor cars were widely used by campaigners and remarked upon in the newspapers. Extra police were drafted into East Clare due to fears of violence, which were partly justified. Shots were fired at a car of de Valera's supporters in Broadford, and windows broken at the Sinn Féin headquarters. In Ennis, police baton-charged a Sinn Féin crowd which had got out of hand.

During the campaign, de Valera gave some appearances of moving towards an electoral rather than a military strategy. In his book *Judging Dev* (2007), Diarmaid Ferriter points to de Valera saying, 'Every vote you give now is as good as the crack of a rifle in proclaiming your desire for freedom.' However, as Ferriter also points out, this did not prevent de Valera using 'threatening language' and he cites de Valera saying during the campaign, 'If you cannot get arms, get that old useful weapon at close quarters – the seven foot pike.' He was also pictured wearing an Irish Volunteers uniform. Such comments lead inevitably to comparisons with much later Sinn Féin strategy and the words of Danny Morrison at Sinn Féin's *ard fheis* (conference) in 1981: 'Will anyone here object if, with a ballot paper in this hand, and an Armalite in this hand, we take power in Ireland?'

Counting of the votes began in Ennis at 9 a.m. on Wednesday 11 July. Accompanying Lynch and de Valera were their agents, J. B. Lynch and H. O'Brien Moran, respectively, both solicitors. When de Valera's majority of nearly 3,000 was announced in the afternoon, the *Irish Independent* called it 'the most remarkable and surprising election result of recent times in Ireland'. The newspaper was nationalist but opposed both the IPP and Sinn Féin. It offered no praise for Sinn Féin but described the result as a rejection of the IPP for 'their weakness, their blundering, and inefficiency'. The *Freeman's Journal* was devastated. It said that in North Roscommon and South Longford, local and short-term matters led to IPP defeats. However, in East Clare, 'the people were invited to vote for an Irish Republic and total separation from England, and five out of every seven of the electors in a most exhaustive poll responded to the call'. The blame, it said, rested with the British government, for using force after the Rising and denying 'the prompt grant of liberty' by not implementing Home Rule. In his victory speech, de Valera said, 'England has her answer' that 'the Nationalists of Ireland wanted … absolute independence'. He hailed the result as 'a monument to the glorious men of Easter Week'. He was, though, one by-election winner who would never take his seat, rejecting the authority of the British Parliament.

East Clare was a turning point partly because the scale of the victory showed the potential breadth of Sinn Féin's appeal. They had not merely beaten the IPP but done so handsomely. Moreover, as Michael Laffan argued in *The Resurrection of Ireland: The Sinn Féin Party, 1916–1923* (1999), it changed the way people in Sinn Féin looked at themselves. Previously, they had often 'suspected or disapproved of each other', but victory gave them 'a sense of cohesion and common purpose'. Simultaneously, as Diarmaid Ferriter argues, de Valera's win meant that people increasingly saw 'him as a statesman with a strategy'. This solidified the leadership position he had from his role in the Rising. De Valera emerged as, in the words of Charles Townshend in *The Republic: The Fight for Irish Independence* (2013), 'an adept navigator of Sinn Féin's diverse ideological currents'. He could now take a pivotal role in moving Sinn Féin to a republican position, while still being able to draw in strands of thought from across nationalism in a broad movement. Finally, an immediate practical change, as David Fitzpatrick pointed to in *Politics and Irish Life* (1977), was that Sinn Féin had learned how to campaign. Groups of former prisoners canvassed, while local Sinn Féin clubs and the Irish Volunteers gained practical knowledge on getting the vote out which would be invaluable in later elections.

A month after East Clare, Sinn Féin again took an IPP seat, this time in Kilkenny City with two-thirds of the vote. But there were then three convincing IPP holds in 1918 before another Sinn Féin gain: South Armagh (February), Waterford City (March) and East Tyrone (April). In Tullamore in mid-April, Sinn Féin won unopposed after the death of an Independent Nationalist MP. Not until June 1918 did Sinn Féin win a contest with a big margin: East Cavan, with 60 per cent of the vote. What had changed following the IPP's brief rally in early 1918? Simply, the British government tried to introduce conscription in Ireland in April. That led to a joint campaign by the IPP, Sinn Féin and the Catholic Church, with the IPP not standing in Tullamore in the early stages of that. It also caused a radicalisation of nationalist opinion, with people once more deciding, as they had at East Clare in July 1917, that the IPP was not delivering for Ireland and another path should be taken.

There were no more Irish by-elections during the war, but the swing from IPP to Sinn Féin was confirmed in the December 1918 general election. Sinn Féin took seventy-three seats and the IPP fell to just six from the seventy-four they had won previously (and the Unionists took the remaining twenty-two, up from seventeen). Symbolically, Patrick Lynch joined Sinn Féin within a year of his defeat in East Clare and later became Attorney General of the Irish Free State (appointed by his former opponent, de Valera). Sinn Féin's general election success provided the party with a rationale for setting up an Irish parliament, Dáil Éireann, in January 1919, while the Irish Republican Army launched its war against British rule using the same 'mandate' argument. The Irish War of Independence was fought until the Truce of July 1921, which led to the Anglo-Irish Treaty in December 1921 and the creation of the Irish Free State.

Throughout this period, the victor of East Clare was de facto leader of the Irish Republic, first as President of the Dáil and then as President of the Republic. Though de Valera resigned as President after the Dáil ratified the Anglo-Irish Treaty in early 1922, only Michael Collins could rival his prominence in politics in the new Irish Free State. Collins's murder during the Civil War perhaps made it inevitable – and certainly very likely – that at some point de Valera would again lead his country, and he did so again either as President or Taoiseach from 1932 with only short interruptions until 1973.

Would de Valera's career have developed as it did had he not won in East Clare? Perhaps if he had not, Arthur Griffith might have become a more prominent figure having won in East Cavan, though Griffith died in 1922. We can be clear that East Clare was the first electoral victory by the central figure of Irish politics for the next six decades.

It also showed for the first time – unlike earlier Sinn Féin victories – quite how much opinion could shift from the seemingly dominant IPP to the new insurgent force. That alone paved the way for what would happen in late 1918, by which point Ireland truly was 'changed utterly'.

Professor Richard S. Grayson *is the Head of the School of Education, Humanities and Languages at Oxford Brookes University. He has published widely on Ireland's First World War and the Irish Revolution.*

16

SPEN VALLEY

20 DECEMBER 1919
LABOUR GAIN FROM COALITION LIBERAL

ROGER GOUGH

Result: Tom Myers (Labour), 11,962, 39.4 per cent; John Simon (Independent Liberal), 10,244, 33.8 per cent; Bryan Fairfax (Coalition Liberal), 8,134, 26.8 per cent
Size of majority: 1,718
Swing: 11.9 per cent from Coalition Liberal to Labour
Name of previous MP and party: Thomas Whittaker (Liberal/Coalition Liberal)
Reason for by-election: Death of incumbent
Result at previous general election: Thomas Whittaker (Coalition Liberal), 10,664, 55.6 per cent; Tom Myers (Labour), 8,508, 44.4 per cent
Date by-election called: 2 December 1919
Date by-election took place: 20 December 1919 (result declared 3 January 1920)
Size of total electorate: 39,667
Total number of votes cast: 30,340
Turnout: 76.5 per cent

Opening his groundbreaking book *The Impact of Labour*, Maurice Cowling remarked: '"Resistance to socialism" first became a possible programme when Labour won the Spen Valley by-election held in December 1919. In this story, Spen Valley was crucial. From Spen Valley onwards, the Labour Party was the major problem.'

If Spen Valley gave a boost to Labour, it was also an important staging post in the deepening split in the Liberal Party. Nonetheless, Labour's victory would be reversed at the subsequent general election. One of the candidates would over the next two decades have a notable national political career; but he was not the by-election winner.

Created in 1885, the Spen Valley constituency in the West Riding of Yorkshire sat between Huddersfield to the south-west, Leeds and Bradford to the north and Wakefield to the east. The biggest towns were Liversedge, Cleckheaton, Mirfield (which had come into the constituency through boundary changes for the 1918 general election), Heckmondwike and Birstall. It had a strong history of the woollen industry, along with some mining, engineering and agricultural employment. It was also chapel-going Nonconformist country – Heckmondwike was described as 'the Canterbury of Congregationalism' – and the temperance lobby had historically had a grip on the Liberal nomination. It had held firm to the Liberals even in years of strong Conservative performance such as 1886 and 1895.

Yet while grey-bearded Nonconformists were still a visible presence at Liberal meetings, by 1918 the vast expansion of the electorate to previously disenfranchised men and women, the addition of mining areas such as Gildersome and the rise of Labour were changing the basis of electoral contests.

From 1892 onwards, Spen Valley was represented by the Liberal MP, businessman and former newspaper editor Sir Thomas Whittaker. At the 1918 general election, Whittaker was returned as a Coalition Liberal (a supporter of Lloyd George and his continuation of the wartime coalition) in a two-horse race with a majority of 2,156 over Labour's Tom Myers. A by-election was triggered when Whittaker died suddenly on 9 November 1919.

Labour once more put forward Tom Myers as their candidate. Forty-seven years old, Myers had been born in Mirfield and had been a coal miner and factory worker, including a lengthy spell in a glass bottle works in nearby Thornhill. He had advanced through local government, where he was known for his interest in housing issues, the trade union movement and co-operative societies; before the election, he was the manager of the Health Insurance Department of the Dewsbury Co-operative Society. He had nursed the constituency since his defeat in 1918, and Labour went into the by-election with some confidence.

The calculation for the local Liberals was much more complex, reflecting the split that went back to Lloyd George's supplanting of Asquith as Prime Minister in December 1916. At the general election two years later, Liberals who supported the coalition (such as Whittaker) were endorsed by the 'coupon' whereas opposition Liberal MPs were challenged and most, including Asquith, were defeated.

Whittaker had kept the Spen Valley Liberals in support of the coalition through the force of his 'trenchant' personality and the prestige of a long-serving MP. Even so, in the months before he died, discontent was surfacing with local party notables challenging him over 'the [political] company he had been keeping' (i.e. Lloyd George). Initially, there still seemed to be some possibility of a Coalition Liberal candidate in Lieutenant Colonel A. L. Mowat, son of a former Liberal association president; however, he declined because of business commitments.

The 'Wee Frees' in the party, eager to challenge the coalition, were reinforced by a visit from Geoffrey Howard, a national party manager. Rumours circulated that Asquith, who had strong local roots, might stand. On 14 November, the day of Whittaker's funeral, the party leader in the Commons, Sir Donald Maclean, gave a speech in Bradford suggesting that Asquith 'would at no distant time be back in [the] Commons'.

Saturday 15 November saw three vital local meetings. The local Liberal executive held a three-hour meeting in Cleckheaton, at which it was decided – reportedly on a thirty-two to twenty-two vote – to establish a selection committee to find a candidate who would support Maclean (in other words, to oppose the coalition). The Conservative Party executive responded that, in the absence of a Coalition Liberal, they would put forward a candidate of their own. Meanwhile, at Heckmondwike, Labour formally adopted Tom Myers. A three-way contest was inevitable.

However, Asquith did not wish to contest the seat and the local Liberal executive extended an invitation to Sir John Simon. On Saturday afternoon (22 November), at a well-attended meeting in Cleckheaton – 'women as well as men', a newspaper noted – Simon presented his 'statement of [Liberal] political faith' and was adopted unanimously.

Simon, a year younger than Myers, had been the Liberal MP for Walthamstow in 1906–18 and had served in the Cabinet as Attorney General and Home Secretary, resigning in protest at the imposition of conscription in January 1916. His legal and academic careers had been stellar, the more impressive since he came from a relatively modest background of provincial Nonconformism; but his analytical and forensic qualities were not complemented by personal warmth, decisiveness or political judgement. He was often disliked and his motives distrusted, sometimes unfairly.

Lloyd George viewed Simon's return to Parliament as the worst possible outcome: 'It will be a disagreeable and disconcerting fact', he told his mistress Frances Stevenson, 'and will take a great deal to get over for it will undoubtedly weaken my influence.' He later told a Conservative official: 'I don't care who wins if that blighter is last.' He would get some, but not all, of what he wanted.

There was more to this than personal animus. If there were a Conservative–Liberal battle, it would symbolise a return to traditional party politics and undermine the coalition. The Coalition Liberal Chief Whip, Freddie Guest, had visited the area; he had met local Conservatives, but there were also Liberals who held to the coalition. On the evening of Wednesday 26 November, reports identified Colonel Bryan Fairfax as a candidate and he was formally adopted at the weekend.

Fairfax, scion of a celebrated Yorkshire family, had a distinguished military career in China, South Africa and India, where he had also been a first-class cricketer. He had rejoined the army for the war and had suffered a gas attack in the Somme offensive (to which the loss of his voice in the closing days of the campaign was attributed). He was self-consciously a political novice and presented himself as a strong admirer of Lloyd George. His difficulty was to make up for lost time.

The writ was moved on 2 December, and nominations closed on the 11th. The candidates undertook an intensive schedule of evening public meetings while 'lunch-hour meetings' were an opportunity to address factory workers. There were specific initiatives to attract the relative novelty of the women's vote, including female speakers (Simon's outgoing Irish wife was seen as an asset in this regard) and 'cottage meetings' in villages with a female audience.

Myers had early campaign momentum, boosted by endorsements from unions, co-operative societies and groups linked to the local Irish community. The co-operative society endorsements proved internally controversial, even more so when when some of the societies' vehicles were pressed into service on election day. Simon, lawyerly and measured but persistent and energetic, proved successful in energising the Liberal base, and his campaign showed growing confidence. Fairfax took some of the local Liberal leaders who were aligned with the coalition but found himself organisationally very reliant on the Conservatives, including both the agent and the association chairman.

The parties brought a selection of big guns to the constituency, including Ramsay MacDonald in support of 'his old friend' Myers, Sir Donald Maclean for Simon and the Prime Minister's wife, Margaret Lloyd George, for Fairfax. The coalition campaign also added a touch of spiky star quality with the visit of the first female MP, Nancy Astor.

The crises of the post-war world and the coalition's record were at the heart of the campaign. Myers 'hammered' nationalisation of the mines, the country's financial situation (he advocated a capital levy to address this), the operation of trusts (cartels) and the war in Ireland. He also urged an expansion of educational opportunity ('democratisation of education').

Simon's platform was a strong restatement of Liberalism; he advocated free trade and critiqued government extravagance, while wishing to move away from the restrictions (and coalition arrangements) of war. Like Myers, he was deeply critical of intervention in Russia and coercion in Ireland. He supported a level of co-operation in industrial relations and took a careful middle position on mine nationalisation and capital taxation.

Fairfax's theme was 'that this was not the time to revert to party strife' and that Lloyd George should be supported in addressing dangerous international crises. He was the least polished of the candidates and the least comfortable in addressing policy questions, prompting Simon's jibe that 'I have no quarrel with him or his opinions. My quarrel is with his want of opinions.'

Cutting across these policy debates and adding a harder edge to the election campaign were two other questions: the divisions in the Liberal Party and the candidates' war records.

The Liberal split played out locally and then reflected back to national politics and media. Asquith's letter on 5 December 'to a Yorkshire correspondent' attacked the coalition's record and contrasted Simon, as the choice of the local Liberal Party with 'a candidate labelled a "Coalition Liberal" whose campaign is being conducted by the local Tory organisation'. Asquith later spoke of a 'pitiless vendetta' against Simon by the coalition, while Simon insisted: 'I am not going to tie myself up as a tame puppy dog of the Coalition Government.'

Local decision-making, the Liberals argued, had been crushed by what Maclean called 'the dictation of a caucus in Downing Street'. Among Liberal MPs, unease over Spen Valley combined with concern over the Anti-Dumping Bill as an abandonment of free trade principles, though an effort to raise the by-election issue was squashed by Guest. The Coalition Liberals hit back, Lloyd George dripping with contempt for his predecessor while the MP for Huddersfield, Sir Charles Sykes, attacked Simon as a 'discredited politician' with a 'streak of yellow'.

Myers, meanwhile, came under fire for his lack of war service. He was believed to have pacifist views but simply stated: 'So far as I was concerned, [the war] went on its own way, and I took no part in it in any shape or form.' On the eve of poll, Fairfax was excoriating: 'I do not believe that the people of Spen Valley have any use for a man who has declared, without apology or regret, that he took no part in the nation's struggle for its existence and its liberty.'

Simon was attacked over his opposition to conscription in 1916. Fairfax argued that such an error of judgement on an existential question effectively disqualified him, while Lloyd George referred to 'Sir John Simon, who opposed measures which were ... essential to winning the war.'

There was more. In *John Bull*, Horatio Bottomley (allegedly primed by Guest) claimed that Simon had given a legal opinion in 1914 denying that the country had an obligation to Belgium, while others insinuated that his wartime service as a staff officer to Sir Douglas Haig had been 'mere camouflage'. Simon denounced this 'poison gas from the Coalition munition factory', asking for and securing a testimonial from Haig. Churchill (Secretary of War and an ardent coalitionist) intervened to redouble the attack on Simon, while Fairfax added: 'If Sir

John Simon feels that he needs a coupon of this sort he is welcome to it.' At its close, the contest was turning very bitter.

Saturday 20 December was 'a perfect voting day' until it turned rainy later on. Turnout was high (76.5 per cent, compared with 50.2 per cent just a year earlier), many people wore party rosettes and colours while cars crisscrossed the eighty square miles of the constituency. And then, a fortnight's wait.

At 2 p.m. on Saturday 3 January, the acting deputy returning officer, J. H. Linfield, declared the result on the steps of Cleckheaton Town Hall in front of a crowd of around 6,000:

- Tom Myers (Labour) 11,962 (39.4 per cent)
- Sir John Simon (Independent Liberal) 10,244 (33.8 per cent)
- Colonel Brian Fairfax (Coalition Liberal) 8,134 (26.8 per cent)

After the formal speeches, Myers was carried shoulder-high to the Trades Hall. *The Red Flag* was sung and he declared that 'Spen Valley today has made history', adding that there would be fewer three-cornered fights in future 'and we shall have the vested interests of the country on one side and the great democracy of the country on the other'.

Simon told his supporters that 'the heart of Liberalism was still sound and strong' and pointedly highlighted the low level of support for the coalition. Fairfax was greeted warmly by his supporters, but they expressed frustration at the delay in selecting a candidate and anger at the Liberals who had abandoned the support they had given to Whittaker and the coalition.

The result buoyed Labour, reinforcing their standing as a political force, even if it was arguably a lucky outcome achieved on a relatively low share of the vote. Others emphasised the setback for the coalition. *The Times*, admittedly hostile to the government, described it as 'a political event of great significance' and for the government 'a humiliation that cannot be explained away'. Yet its greater significance was to highlight and deepen the split in the Liberal Party, an implication masked by Simon's strong performance.

Myers' victory did not last. At the 1922 general election, there was no split among Liberals, although this time there was a Conservative candidate. The switch in vote shares was modest, but it was enough to result in a Liberal majority of 787. Myers fought the seat again in 1923 and 1924, but Simon's majority rose with each contest.

Tom Myers returned to local government, serving as the Mayor of Dewsbury in 1940–41. He died on 21 December 1949, almost exactly thirty years after the by-election.

After 1923, Simon did not face a Conservative opponent in Spen Valley and became increasingly aligned with that party. As a National Liberal, he held a succession of high offices, but his reputation as one of the 'Guilty Men' of the 1930s dragged down his standing, as did his unappealing personality. Harold Nicolson recalled his repulsion on having his arm grabbed by him. 'God, what a toad and a worm Simon is!' Simon died in 1954.

Spen Valley was recaptured by Labour in 1945, but the constituency was abolished in 1950. It was in Birstall that Jo Cox, the MP for one of the successor seats, Batley & Spen, was fatally attacked during the 2016 European referendum campaign. At the 2024 general election, the Spen Valley constituency was restored with very similar boundaries to those of 1919, and Jo Cox's sister, Kim Leadbeater, was returned as its Labour Member of Parliament.

Roger Gough was the leader of Kent County Council 2019–25. He is the author of A Good Comrade: János Kádár, Communism and Hungary *(I. B. Tauris, 2006) and (with Andrew Tyrie and Stuart McCracken)* Account Rendered: Extraordinary Rendition and Britain's Role *(Biteback, 2011).*

17

PAISLEY

20 FEBRUARY 1920
LIBERAL HOLD

HUGH GAULT

Result: H. H. Asquith (Liberal), 14,736, 48.4 per cent; John Biggar (Labour/Co-operative), 11,902, 39.1 per cent; James MacKean (Conservative), 3,795, 12.5 per cent
Size of majority: 2,834
Swing: 4.4 per cent from Labour/Co-operative to Liberal
Name of previous MP and party: John McCallum (Liberal)
Reason for by-election: Death of incumbent
Result at previous general election: John McCallum (Liberal), 7,542, 34.0 per cent; John Biggar (Co-operative), 7,436, 33.5 per cent; John Taylor (National Democratic), 7,201, 32.5 per cent
Date by-election called: N/A
Date by-election took place: 12 February 1920
Size of total electorate: 39,218
Total number of votes cast: 30,433
Turnout: 77.6 per cent

After more than thirty years as the MP for East Fife, Asquith was defeated there in the 1918 coupon election. Under pressure to be re-elected, Asquith waited until January 1920 before he allowed his name to be put forward in Paisley on the death of the sitting Liberal MP. The Paisley Liberals faced the dilemma of finding a local candidate who would combine the Liberal and Unionist votes against Labour or, if they nominated Asquith, guaranteeing that the by-election would be a three-cornered contest. Unable to decide, the Liberal executive turned it over to the association as a whole, who narrowly came down in Asquith's favour. Labour were the favourites in the by-election, not least because they had secured the Irish vote. Yet with the support of Unionist newspapers and the collapse of the Unionist vote, Asquith came top of the poll, the irony of an anti-coalition candidate being returned by a coalition vote being noted. As in East Fife, however, Asquith neglected the constituency and by 1924 had alienated many of his previous supporters in Paisley.

In the December 1918 coupon general election immediately after the First World War, the Lloyd George coalition returned 485 MPs out of 707, comprising 338 Conservatives, 137 Liberals and ten Labour (standing as the National Democratic Party). There were 149 opposition MPs, among whom were the 'Wee Free' Liberals reduced to twenty-six, as well as seventy-three Sinn Féin MPs who did not take their seats. Asquith, the man Lloyd George had replaced as Prime Minister in 1916, lost his seat in East Fife after more than thirty years as its MP, comprehensively defeated by 2,000 votes by the Unionist Alexander Sprot. Sprot's candidacy had not been endorsed with the coupon for even the coalition thought Asquith should be in the House of Commons, yet the *Morning Post*, a Conservative newspaper, described his defeat as 'an independent demonstration [that] was one of the healthiest and most salutary things ever done in politics'.

Sir Donald Maclean stood in for Asquith as leader of the Liberals in the Commons, but this was not a situation that could continue indefinitely. Maclean's position was equivocal for it was questioned whether he spoke as the Liberal authority or whether Asquith retained the final say, and it was thought that in any case the House of Commons 'lost prestige for the lack of an Opposition able to stand boldly up to the government' in the absence of Asquith. Inevitably, Asquith was under pressure to find another seat or relinquish the Liberal leadership, and though he must have missed the House he had been in since 1886, he did not rush to return. The Liberals won three of the first six by-elections in 1919, all at the coalition government's expense, but failed to win any of the other fourteen. There was no obvious way back for Asquith who had found the last three years bruising but itched to challenge Lloyd George directly in the Commons.

The first Liberal seat to become vacant was in the industrial constituency of Paisley, where the sitting MP Sir John McCallum died in January 1920. He had been in indifferent health for the previous six months, a heart condition restricting his political workload for much of that time, but under the impression that he was recovering had aggravated matters in early January. The immediate cause of his death on 10 January was recorded as a cerebral thrombosis five days earlier.

McCallum had held the seat since 1906, but his majority had declined in the three subsequent elections and in 1918 he had been within 106 votes of losing to the Co-operative Party candidate John Biggar, contesting the seat for the first time. The vote had split three ways in 1918 with little more than 300 votes separating McCallum from the National Democratic candidate who came third. Whereas McCallum was a soap manufacturer well known in the town, Biggar was not a Paisley local. According to an interview he gave to *Forward*, the radical weekly newspaper then edited by Tom Johnston (a future Secretary of State for Scotland), Biggar was a member of the Milngavie branch of the Independent Labour Party and had been a member since the party was formed. He was a Labour representative on Glasgow Education Authority, having previously been on the Glasgow School Board, and would take the Labour whip if elected – as did the only existing Co-operative MP in Parliament. Biggar expected to be the automatic progressive candidate in the by-election, arguing that a 'representative committee has been formed of all the progressive bodies in the town' in his support. However, this belied the tensions between the ILP and the Labour Party so that, while the ILP had held their Scottish Divisional conference in Paisley the day McCallum died, with nearly 75 per cent of the 200 delegates voting to continue the alliance with Labour and thus maintain the appearance of a united front, other Socialists did not entirely approve of Biggar and were discussing a fortnight later whether he was sufficiently radical or whether they should run an additional candidate. This subtext to the by-election would remain for some time and must have affected Biggar's campaign. Despite his claims in the *Forward* interview, he was standing on this occasion as a Labour/Co-operative Party candidate.

Paisley was far from a safe Liberal seat, if such there be anywhere by that point, but within days of McCallum's death the *Paisley Daily Express* was alive to the possibility of Asquith being parachuted in:

> London correspondents who don't properly understand the position in Paisley continue to harp on the Asquith string … All this seems to arise from the old-time tradition that this Burgh was a safe Liberal seat. But the circumstances are now changed, for both the old constitutional parties have to reckon with Labour, which is powerful and well-organised.

The evidence for this was not hard to find. The population of 87,000 included a large Irish community of 2,500, and while McCallum had received official endorsement from the United Irish League in 1918, this had been contentious and was expected to transfer to Biggar. In addition, more than 15,000 (nearly 40 per cent) of the electorate of 39,000 were women who had voted for the first time in 1918 and, while their voting intentions could not be guaranteed, were just as likely to vote for Biggar as any other candidate. Given the composition of the constituency, Biggar was the clear favourite next time. Furthermore, were Asquith to stand, another factor would come into play for, as the *Paisley Daily Express* report continued, 'the advent of Mr Asquith we know without doubt would precipitate a triangular fight, for the Unionists would certainly bring forward a candidate to oppose him'.

Yet the newspaper was also aware that Paisley Liberals would be honoured to have an ex-premier standing. They would have to weigh this against the possibility of defeat in what was now a marginal seat, one that they had come close to losing in 1918. The dilemma was whether Asquith would bolster the Liberal campaign or weaken it.

Asquith may have had similar doubts himself, but such were the other pressures that he could not keep havering in the hope of a solid Liberal seat falling into his lap. Consequently, despite his reservations, Asquith let the local Liberals know that he was prepared to be nominated 'if a substantially-supported invitation' from the local Liberal association was forthcoming. The Liberal executive, however, were acutely aware of the real dilemma they faced. This was similar to that posed by the *Paisley Daily Express* but carried with it further subtleties for the executive: if Asquith was adopted, 'a triangular contest ... [was] inevitable', for while the coalition Liberals might defer to him, the Unionists were determined 'not to let him have a straight fight with Labour'; on the other hand, rejecting Asquith was tantamount to giving up their existence as independent Liberals, throwing in their lot with the coalition and perhaps consigning the Liberal Party to history. An Edinburgh advocate J. C. Watson and J. Clark from the local Coats combine were considered, but the executive proved unwilling, or at any rate unable, to prefer them over Asquith even should they stand as a 'Coalition candidate uniting the Liberal and Unionist vote'. Consequently, the matter was turned over to the Liberal association to resolve what might have been an 'epoch-making decision'. On 21 January, less than a fortnight after McCallum's death, it was Asquith who the association selected by ninety-three votes to seventy-five over the local man. The invitation to Asquith that followed was unanimous, thereby more than meeting Asquith's demand for substantial support and omitting the information that the association had been within nine votes of a dead heat.

Although the *Westminster Gazette* thought the Unionists might still stand aside for Asquith, the local Paisley intelligence proved more accurate: they had been prepared to leave the field free for a local candidate shared with the Liberals for they judged this the best means of defeating Labour, but the Unionists were not inclined to do so for Asquith. However, 'finding a local man who would meet their requirements' was not straightforward. Another Clark from the prominent textile family had first been approached but had declined, as had another local who refused to stand against Asquith. It looked, therefore, that they might have to go outside Paisley to find a coalition representative, with their meeting on 23 January initially appointing a search committee to find someone. But rather than delay matters further, one of the Unionists attending the meeting, J. A. D. MacKean, a member of the Paisley Corporation, treasurer of the Burgh and starch manufacturer, agreed to be nominated. As the *Paisley and Renfrewshire Gazette* would later put it in MacKean's obituary, 'so keen was [he] that the principles of the coalition government should have a spokesman' that he put himself forward, stepping 'into the breach to maintain the cause'.

According to *The Times*, this was a local decision, neither supported nationally nor forbidden. Although J. B. Firth described it as a blunder in his article for *Fortnightly Review* after the by-election, the *Westminster Gazette* was clear that it was a calculated risk rather than one based on principle: 'The Paisley Unionists will rather risk the election of a Labour candidate than stand aside for a straight contest between Liberalism and Labour. Their party always has profited by three-cornered contests and it will continue to seek such profit.'

As MacKean explained to the *Morning Post*, he was standing as a Unionist only because the Liberals had not selected a coalition candidate who could have beaten Labour. The *Morning Post* claimed MacKean was 'likely to receive the support not only of Unionists, but also of Liberals who are enthusiastic for Mr Lloyd George, and think the time has not yet arrived for breaking up the Coalition. Mr MacKean is one of the strongest candidates that his side could put into the field.'

Even allowing for the hyperbole of the last sentence, it was apparent that the stakes were high once Asquith had received the Liberal nomination. MacKean had been comprehensively defeated on the one previous occasion he had contested Paisley, but the *Morning Post* had printed a leading article the day before excoriating Asquith for his responsibility for the war, an allegation that MacKean would repeat throughout the campaign. The *Morning Post* article judged Asquith 'complacently oblivious of the danger which nearly overwhelmed him and his country' and concluded that, rather than standing in Paisley, he should be defending 'charges of bringing the country to the verge of ruin by the neglect of the most ordinary precautions'.

MacKean had joined the Unionists in 1886 when the Liberals split over Irish Home Rule and Asquith's advocacy of home rule would have been one of the most potent reasons why the Unionists felt unable to give him a clear run. Another was that Asquith was believed to be out to smash the coalition. But MacKean had baggage of his own, having criticised the coalition for extravagant spending in 1919 but now claiming to support them. Furthermore, he gave the Asquith campaign 'many openings', not least in preferring personal animosity to argument. This would have confused his potential supporters as the prospect of another Socialist candidate must have alarmed Biggar's.

Although this latter candidacy failed to materialise in 1920, it was indicative of the local division between the Labour and Co-operative parties as to who had the right to be nominated in the seat and to what end. In the meantime, Biggar's claims to be an 'out and out Socialist' were ridiculed while his supporters complained that 'the Socialists [would] simply [be] making a present of the seat' to Asquith if they were to put up another candidate. Such disputes must have proved a bonus for Asquith, not least in turning off the non-political electors of Paisley who might incline towards national reputation in the absence of any more tangible evidence. Nor was Asquith weighed down by his local record as he had been in East Fife.

Yet only on nomination day did it finally become clear that there would be no fourth candidate and that the election would be contested by Asquith, proposed by McCallum's widow and seconded by a Paisley draper, the Glasgow-based Biggar, nominated by two Paisley men, and the local man MacKean, nominated by William Hodge Coats and John Robertson, both substantial Paisley manufacturers. All three could hardly have signalled their appeals more transparently, with Asquith the continuity and sympathy candidate, and both he and Biggar doing their best to redress their out-of-Burgh background.

One of the cartoonist David Low's first assignments in Britain was to cover the by-election for *The Star*. Not long off the boat from Australia, Low was appalled by the poverty he found: 'There was nothing like this in the Dominions. I had never seen real poverty and degradation before ... I was filled with rage and disgust ... at the blind stupidity that allowed such things to be.'

Early twentieth-century Paisley is often thought of mainly as a textiles town, but at the end of the nineteenth century the bulk of the town's workforce was employed in five shipyards, thirteen marine and general engineering works, twelve chemical and soap factories and in fireclay and food firms. The economy was, therefore, more broad-based, with textile manufacturers co-existing alongside shipbuilders and engineering in particular. Indeed, it was the poor quality of much of the housing that was as notable, with 50 per cent of houses overcrowded in 1919. Evidence to the Royal Commission on housing in Scotland that year concluded that at least another 1,500 houses were required, for more than 3,000 houses had been identified as overcrowded by housing inspectors.

The Star, like the *Daily News*, the newspaper that Low thought he would be joining, was generally Liberal but friendly to Labour, and Low is clear that in this instance he would have voted for the latter.

A key characteristic of the by-election was that Biggar, standing on a joint Labour/Co-op Party ticket, was endorsed during the campaign by nine men who had previously sat on the Liberal benches, including Bertie Lees-Smith, Charles Trevelyan, Josiah Wedgwood and Arthur Ponsonby. That they had transferred their allegiance to Labour indicated to the electorate that they had moved on from the Liberalism that Asquith represented, while Asquith, aware that he had to challenge this implication directly, claimed in a speech on 5 February that during the First World War it was these Liberal defectors who had given the impression the nation was divided, whereas responsible Labour leaders (such as Arthur Henderson, J. H. Thomas and J. R. Clynes) had shown it to be united. The ex-Liberals had, therefore, compounded a lack of patriotism with an absence of principle. In the speech, entitled 'Replies to his critics', Asquith derided the Labour manifesto claim 'that it is unlikely that Mr Asquith will ever lead the British people into new paths of democracy', accusations of 'secret treaties', such as that with Italy which had seen it fighting alongside Britain, France and Russia, and the assertion that nobody was 'more profoundly distrusted … in Ireland'. Asquith doubted this last could be remotely true given the time he had devoted to Irish self-government.

In an interview for the *Daily News* at the start of the campaign, Biggar stated that any prospect of Liberal–Labour rapprochement was illusory. As Firth put it, Labour 'despises Liberalism as a creed outworn'. Ponsonby, for example, had declared that 'if Liberals were present in a Labour administration they would destroy all prospect of the social reconstruction and international reconciliation in which Labour believed'. He had even gone so far as to argue 'Better a Tory government than a Liberal–Labour' one. However, as the *Paisley and Renfrewshire Gazette* commented: 'If speech-making does it, Labour should win the day; but, fortunately, there are other deciding factors in an election, and none more potent than the silent elector who troubles little with political meetings and is a bit of a problem to the canvassers. Watch their votes.'

Initially, Biggar had a head start with his first meeting for 3,000 people on 20 January at the town hall. The following week, the Paisley Trades and Labour Council asked him to augment his factory gate meetings with one for night shift workers on Sunday 1 February. Other Biggar meetings were addressed by Labour notables such as Ramsay MacDonald (then in the middle of four years out of Parliament having been defeated in Leicester West in 1918), the trades union leader Robert Smillie and the Labour MP who had campaigned for women's suffrage, Frederick Pethick-Lawrence. G. B. Shaw and Beatrice Webb were among the leading Fabians who opposed Asquith, while Tom Myers, who had won Spen Valley for Labour in a by-election the previous December, defeating the Liberal Sir John Simon in the process, gave a 'stirring indictment' of Asquith when he spoke in Glasgow at the end of January. 'The great failure of Liberalism', he argued, 'was that it could not apply principles of individualism to the economics of Collectivism', with Asquith condemned for not opposing conscription and for being premier when the suffragettes were force-fed. Biggar argued for nationalisation of the mines, railways and land, the latter a cause that Lloyd George had come close to espousing some years previously, and against the continuing intervention of foreign troops in Russia. His chances may have been hampered, though, by the by-election co-inciding with a strike at a local Co-operative boot factory.

By 25 January, Asquith was based nine miles away at the Central Station Hotel in Glasgow with his wife, daughter and secretary, and between then and the by-election on 12 February, Asquith held four or five meetings each day, with sixteen of his major speeches (one each day apart from the two Sundays) collected together in book form and published later that year. Even in print, they manage to convey Asquith's charm and his powerful hustings performance, with his final speech the day before the poll concluding with the injunction: 'Be true to Liberalism and I will be true to Paisley.' According to Catriona Macdonald in her 2000 book *The Radical Thread*, this book would come to dominate Liberal policy throughout the 1920s. Asquith had the help of Glasgow University students with canvassing, an effective strategy, for as the *Paisley Daily Express* noted, 'the streets [were] littered with paper [indicating] the extent to which electioneering literature is being circulated'.

Asquith's election agent was an experienced local solicitor and his friend Sir Donald Maclean spoke for him early in the campaign, but otherwise Asquith's campaign received only limited assistance from elsewhere.

The election would turn on a number of issues that could be seen as indicative of their time. Firstly, the campaign was fought by male candidates but the women's vote would be pivotal. Asquith was in a particularly difficult position in this regard for he had long opposed women's suffrage. He confronted this head on, opening his speech on 31 January:

> That women have come in such numbers to hear what I have to say is not only an indication of their keen political interest, but, so far as I personally am concerned, is perhaps an act of political generosity; for undoubtedly, as you will remember, there was a time, now a very remote time, in which I did not see my way to join those who were in favour of giving women the vote.

Asquith added that the war had changed his mind and that women should now be enfranchised on the same basis as men (i.e. at the same age – which did eventually happen in 1928). Some have questioned Asquith's sincerity, but his mea culpa might not have been sufficient in any case had his daughter Violet Bonham Carter not proved a huge campaigning asset in winning over the women's vote. She had in effect generated this aspect of the campaign herself, aware that 'the women's vote is the dark horse & that Labour is stealing a march on us every hour'. Such was the Unionist alarm at Violet Bonham Carter's impact that Nancy Astor was called in to help MacKean.

Secondly, Asquith was himself close to seventy years old and MacKean three years older. Biggar in his mid-forties must have appeared almost youthful by comparison, though while this would have the advantages of energy could also enable his opponents to portray him as callow and inexperienced. Violet Bonham Carter was aware that age might be considered a factor in her father's case, raising it herself – taking it 'tightly by the throat', as she put it – when Asquith was introduced to the Liberal association on 28 January.

This was overlaid by Biggar and MacKean questioning whether they would be better placed to represent Paisley's interests while Asquith's focus might be on his national political rehabilitation. Asquith himself admitted that he didn't know the affairs of Paisley, and that he didn't have 'intimate acquaintance' even with those of Scotland, but he argued that he should be elected 'because I am qualified to represent you on all those larger and wider questions of general legislation'. Only by electing him could the country be saved from the 'imminent, formidable, financial dangers which confront it ... and which are the real ... obstacles to ... true social reform'. As further evidence that Asquith was the continuity candidate with the right values, three of Gladstone's sons appeared on his behalf, as did his own son Brigadier Asquith DSO.

A variant of the age issue was Biggar and MacKean damning Asquith as living in the past while they were focused on the present. Biggar described him as 'behind the times' and MacKean judged him a Rip Van Winkle who had failed to keep up with change. In an article headed 'Paisley Uber Alles', *Forward* described Asquith as 'a mumbling of the old bones', continuing: 'He belongs to a type that is becoming extinct, which the times have passed by.' It added: 'Paisley is asked to choose Mr Asquith on the strength of his past; it is all he has got.'

Asquith's political longevity, therefore, might act in his favour if he could convince the Paisley voters that he understood their concerns, but it might equally count against him if he expected them to defer to his judgement. He argued that he had never betrayed the faith or trust of the Liberal Party's supporters and the electors of Paisley should therefore have confidence in him. He held another meeting for women on 7 February while individual speeches focused on, for example, industrial issues, housing and Ireland (on which he had always been a home ruler). Asquith used the latter speech to advocate Dominion status for Ireland, a stance that would appeal to the Irish in Paisley even if the coalition government thought it insanity, while also distancing him from the Unionist MacKean. The United Irish League now supported Labour, and Asquith 'resented and denounced what he saw as the Irish defection'. *Forward* countered by asking: 'What are [Asquith's] pledges worth?', arguing that the Irish should 'Vote Straight and Vote for Labour'.

Asquith attacked the government over several of its policies (not least that of 'trying to grind Germany into the dust' over reparations), an electoral strategy designed to capture the moderate Tory vote as well as secure the Liberal one. The editor of the Liberal *Daily News*, A. G. Gardiner, went so far as to claim that he expected an Asquith victory to demonstrate the 'national resentment against that criminal hoax', the last general election.

The *Paisley and Renfrewshire Gazette* indicated its preference by invariably discussing the MacKean campaign first, followed by Asquith's and then Biggar's. On 7 February, it considered how each candidate dealt with hecklers at their meetings, with MacKean praised for his humour that came straight to the point, while it judged Asquith as 'cool and collected' and deprecated Biggar for being too blunt. In case this did not differentiate MacKean and Asquith sufficiently, another article on the same page commented that 'a single hearing of the prosaic, professional politician known as [Asquith] has been an almost sensational disillusionment ... revealing abilities of a kind that refrigerate enthusiasm'.

The newspaper noted that the contrast with MacKean was very marked, a judgement it repeated in MacKean's obituary in 1932 when it described him as 'in his element [with hecklers] for he had a gift of ready repartee'.

For her part, Violet Bonham Carter described the overall campaign as

the strangest and most memorable experience of my life. I can only describe it as a nightmare with streaks of ecstasy ... I spoke once or twice every day the whole time we were there – & the blaze of publicity we lived in prevented one ever repeating a sentence ... The Paisley people were wonderful material to work upon – an extraordinary combination of cool heads & warm hearts.

There was a two-week delay between the poll on 12 February and the count, with Asquith decamping to London as soon as the polls closed and only returning to Paisley for the count. Yet if Stephen Koss was clear why Asquith chose Paisley, it might still be questioned why Paisley chose Asquith, for that was the outcome, which on a vastly increased turnout (77.6 per cent compared to 57.6 per cent in 1918) saw the Liberal vote almost double to 14,736 with Asquith's majority 2,834 over Biggar, whose vote had itself increased by nearly 4,500 to 11,902 in little over a year. The corollary was that the third-party vote collapsed, an outcome that Asquith had predicted, and MacKean lost his deposit. Macdonald concludes that this was 'a conscious statement in favour of "pre-war" principles in a post-war world'. Alternatively, it might be suspected that MacKean's campaign foundered on the Irish and worker votes and, while Biggar was more popular with these groups, Asquith's campaign had been sufficiently canny to appeal to Unionist and Conservative voters who sought to keep Labour out. *Forward* had predicted after the polls closed that Biggar's election would depend on whether the Tory vote 'slumped' to Asquith. In addition, Asquith's speeches and reputation had done just enough to convince women voters that he was the most likely to secure reform, a perspective that Violet Bonham Carter's initiative and hard work reinforced.

The *Paisley and Renfrewshire Gazette* expressed surprise that their preferred candidate MacKean had come such a 'poor third' but not at the overall result. MacKean agreed that some voters had deserted him, voting for Asquith to keep Labour out, with many rushing to do so on the final day, while some who had voted for the coalition and Lloyd George in the aftermath of the First World War had reconsidered, transferring their allegiance to Asquith in the by-election. Biggar's explanation was that 'the capitalists had united to keep Labour out' and that 'so far as the workers are concerned there is no difference between the Liberal and Tory candidates'. Tellingly, however, 'in this election the Liberal has been chosen because he is the abler to defend that policy [maintaining the privileges of landlordism and capitalism]'. *Forward* added in its March post-mortems Ramsay MacDonald's view that Asquith had won on an anti-Labour combination, together with the conviction that as a former leader, he 'should be returned to the House of Commons'.

The newspaper's immediate conclusion was that 'the Paisley election furnishes another example that political principle does not count for much when there are other and more plausible considerations thrown into the election'.

Three weeks later, the *Paisley and Renfrewshire Gazette* added Lloyd George's view that there was 'absolutely no doubt that thousands of Unionist and Coalition Liberals had swung round at the last moment in order to keep Labour out', and Asquith had in effect received the coupon from six Unionist peers who supported him (including Northcliffe and Robert Cecil). Lloyd George argued that Asquith was wrong to say he had won because he 'sold the pure unadulterated milk of Liberalism. It was not so.' Rather, the peers had judged Asquith the most 'distinguished defender of the fabric of society', and their support, together with that of Unionist Glasgow newspapers which wanted to defeat the Socialists, was enough – drawing votes from MacKean in the process. *Forward* also remarked on the irony that though Asquith had stood as anti-coalition, 'he was in reality returned by a Coalition vote'.

According to Firth, 'before Paisley [Asquith] stood in danger of total eclipse ... a spent force and [people were saying] that his day was done'. The result enabled Asquith to 'rehabilitate himself; but [could] he restore the Liberal Party?' The answer proved to be a resounding 'no'. As G. R. Searle puts it, 'disillusion with Asquith's tired performances soon set in' – performances that, with the single exception of his condemnation in October 1920 of the Black and Tan reprisals in Ireland, lacked any fight or fire. By mid-1922, Harold Laski recorded that he was 'generally recognised as hopeless', but Asquith's great personal charm, together with the lack of any obvious alternative as Liberal leader, kept him in place. In November 1923, the Asquithian and Lloyd George wings of the Liberal Party came back together, but Lloyd George was no more trusted than before and it was assumed he would join up with the Conservatives again as soon as he could. Meanwhile, a remote Asquith rarely appeared in Parliament and left much of the hard work of leadership to his friend Maclean.

Asquith went on to win the next two elections in Paisley in 1922 (when there was an ILP landslide in neighbouring Glasgow) and 1923 before losing the seat to Labour in 1924, an election in which Labour lost seats nationally, but the Liberals were trounced, reduced from 159 to forty seats overall. In Paisley, 'a group of leading businessmen [had] ... publicly [withdrawn] their support for Asquith and United Free Church clergymen were said to be abandoning the Liberal Party in vast numbers'.

That this should prove the outcome was in many ways inevitable. Asquith had been a poor local MP in East Fife, speaking in the constituency only three times in three years between May 1915 and May 1918 and judged to have 'neglected the seat to the point of contempt' after being ousted as Prime Minister at the end of 1916. Stuart R. Ball describes him as 'a politician out of his depth ... arrogant, with an excessive assurance of his own indispensability'. Defeat at Paisley would have consigned Asquith to an indefinite period out of Parliament – perhaps for ever, for there was no safe seat that was going to be found for him as an alternative. But it was not apparent that his attitude and approach as a constituency MP had been altered by defeat in East Fife and if he had failed to learn the lessons, why should he treat Paisley any differently? Asquith had exerted himself to win the campaign, but there was little evidence that he would put much energy into nurturing the constituency.

Asquith visited Paisley in May and December 1920 and addressed a rally at the town hall in July 1921. After that, however, he seems to have reverted to type. The Liberal association minute book records that he sent his apologies for the AGMs in March 1923 and 1924, adding on the latter occasion that he hoped to 'see them face to face shortly'. He did not and in June 1924 sent his private secretary to answer questions on his behalf. His tacit support for the short-lived Labour government of 1924 had provoked at least one member of the executive to resign, arguing that 'the Liberal Party in the House of Commons was more concerned with tactics than with principles'. In other words, the electors had been hoodwinked. A win in the 1924 general election in Paisley might have been beyond Asquith's abilities in any case, but his neglect of the constituency had not helped. Gardiner, no longer the editor of the Liberal *Daily News* but still a Liberal himself, described this as 'the final and humiliating blow ... which ended [Asquith's] career in the House of which he had been the most illustrious figure'.

Asquith had been in Parliament for nearly forty years, but his contemporaries included Gladstone, Balfour, Baldwin and Lloyd George, so he may have been one 'illustrious figure' but certainly not the most. Like these colleagues, Asquith came back from the wilderness of being defeated as premier, and unlike them, he also had to contend with electoral defeat. However, he no longer had the energy or determination to make the most of his comeback. As Firth put it, Asquith should 'beware the omen of the Paisley shawl which was always designed to be the comfort of declining years'. The Paisley by-election proved a false dawn for Asquith and the Liberal Party, and the town itself, which required a physical rehabilitation (of its housing, for example), could do little but mark time politically.

Hugh Gault *is an independent writer and historian. His most recent book is* Labour, Lancashire and the 1924 Government *(2024). The original version of this article appeared in the* Journal of Liberal History *(2020), where it was illustrated with some of the cartoons David Low published during the Paisley campaign.*

18

WOOLWICH EAST

2 MARCH 1921
CONSERVATIVE/UNIONIST GAIN FROM LABOUR

NAN SLOANE

Result: Robert Gee (Conservative/Unionist), 13,724, 51.3 per cent; Ramsay MacDonald (Labour), 13,041, 48.7 per cent
Size of majority: 683
Swing: N/A
Name of previous MP and party: Will Crooks (Labour)
Reason for by-election: Resignation due to ill health
Result at previous general election: Will Crooks (Labour), elected unopposed
Date by-election called: 16 February 1921
Date by-election took place: 2 March 1921
Size of total electorate: N/A
Total number of votes cast: 26,805
Turnout: 78.5 per cent

In February 1921, the Labour MP for Woolwich East, Will Crooks, resigned from Parliament. He had held the Woolwich seat almost continuously since 1903, and in the general election held only weeks after Armistice Day in 1918, he had been re-elected unopposed. Crooks was an active and lifelong trade unionist who had risen to prominence through his role in the famous London Dock Strike of 1889. By early 1921, however, he was sixty-eight years old and suffering from serious illness. His resignation, though inevitable, inadvertently opened the door to what became one of the most deeply unpleasant by-election campaigns of the early post-war period.

The 1918 election had, predictably, resulted in a massive majority for David Lloyd George's national coalition consisting of the Conservative and Unionist Party together with the larger portion of the fragmented Liberal Party. The Labour Party, which had withdrawn from the coalition government at the end of the war, had slightly increased its number of seats but had not done as well as hoped. Many Labour candidates had opposed the war, and almost all of these were defeated. This included several of the party's leading lights, not least of whom was Ramsay MacDonald, who had been an MP since 1906 and, before the war, had effectively been the party's leader. MacDonald was a charismatic and skilful politician, as well as one of the great public orators of the age, and the Parliamentary Labour Party knew itself to be the poorer for his absence. Woolwich East seemed to offer a real opportunity to get him back onto the national stage.

However, MacDonald was also a highly controversial figure, mainly because of his dogged opposition to the war. In 1914, he had resigned his leadership role rather than support a conflict he believed to be unnecessary, wrong and the result of secret diplomacy between elites. The Labour Party, however, had officially supported the war, though many individual members had agreed with MacDonald. Since this was a time when it was still possible for MPs to oppose their own party's policy, MacDonald, though relegated to the back benches, remained a Labour MP. The new chairman, Arthur Henderson, joined Lloyd George's War Cabinet in 1915, while MacDonald and a substantial part of the left in the party continued to campaign for peace.

If the Labour Party and the trade unions were able, albeit not always very happily, to tolerate MacDonald's dissent, the same was not true of the wider public. For many people, opposition to a war in which their husbands, sons and brothers were actively fighting and dying seemed outrageous. MacDonald became the focus for an outpouring of hatred which pursued him well beyond the war's end, and although in 1921 he was still a hero for the political left, he was also a villain for the right and particularly for the right-wing press, which loathed him with real and enduring venom.

By the time Will Crooks resigned, however, Labour was determined to get MacDonald back into Parliament, and Woolwich East seemed as good an opportunity as any to do it. But if Labour thought they would get an easy ride or that MacDonald would be welcomed or forgiven for his wartime record, they could not have been more wrong.

There was obviously no question of the Conservatives leaving the seat uncontested again, and they chose their candidate with care. Captain Robert Gee was a decorated war veteran, a man whose outstanding bravery under fire had brought him the ultimate accolade of the Victoria Cross. He was not, however, a stereotypical upper-class career soldier but a working-class orphan with a long military career in the lower ranks behind him before he was commissioned as an officer in 1915. In 1918, he had stood unsuccessfully as a candidate for a small anti-pacifist socialist party before accepting an invitation to stand as the Conservative candidate in Woolwich.

In the event, Gee's selection was almost a stroke of genius. He enabled the Conservative Party to frame the election as a choice between patriotism and pacifism, courage and cowardice, loyalty and betrayal. The Woolwich Arsenal was still a major employer of local labour and there was strong pro-war sentiment in large parts of the electorate. Wounds – both physical and psychological – from the war remained raw, and many people detested anything and anyone appearing to be pro-German. The candidates offered to them represented two diametrically opposed views of the war and its aftermath, a choice complicated by growing unemployment, a challenging economic situation and the intervention of a bombastic populist MP and newspaper proprietor.

Horatio Bottomley was the Independent MP for Hackney South and a newspaper proprietor. He was a gifted but completely unscrupulous man with a talent for propaganda who used his newspaper and his political platform to promote extreme nationalism and xenophobia. Like both MacDonald and Gee, he had working-class origins, and in the course of a career of mixed fortunes he had, among many other things, made a great deal of money, been prosecuted for fraud and acquitted, been elected to Parliament, been declared bankrupt and then been ejected from the House of Commons as a consequence. Since his return to Parliament in 1918, he had positioned himself as 'the unofficial prime minister' ready to pounce on any weakening of the government's stance on foreigners, immigration or German reparations.

His activities during the war had brought him to real national prominence as a patriot. He had used his considerable oratorical skills to whip up support – both moral and financial – for the war effort, using his newspaper to attack anyone who opposed the war, disagreed with him or simply had a German-sounding name. Into the first two categories fell Ramsay MacDonald, and Bottomley had become obsessed with trying to get him prosecuted for treason. In 1915, he had obtained a copy of MacDonald's birth certificate and published it in his proto-tabloid paper *John Bull*, thus making MacDonald's illegitimacy public. At a time when illegitimacy was regarded as a stain on the child as well as the mother, this was not only deeply humiliating but also enabled Bottomley to question MacDonald's fitness for public office. The prospect of his old enemy re-entering Parliament enraged him, and he immediately applied both his mind and his considerable resources to preventing it.

By 1921, his star was on the wane, but he was still very popular and the by-election offered him an excellent opportunity to continue to persecute MacDonald. This he did by supporting Gee's campaign but also by taking steps of his own. Anyone passing through Cannon Street Station, for instance, might have been mildly surprised to find themselves confronted by large placards demanding 'A Traitor for Parliament?' while at Woolwich they would have found trams plastered with the same question. Canvassers were primed to repeat the slur as often as possible and given that the Woolwich Arsenal was still the largest employer in the area, there was plenty of fertile ground on which it could germinate, particularly since people familiar with Bottomley's crusade during the war were often already hostile to the Labour candidate.

The Conservative campaign, however, did not just depend on Bottomley's populist style. The party could also mobilise the Primrose League, a women's organisation which, since 1883, had been fundraising and campaigning for Conservative candidates. It had a large and electorally experienced membership and many of these ladies now descended on Woolwich to help with the ground campaign. They were almost as unscrupulous as Bottomley in their allegations about

MacDonald. He was described as a threat to society, a revolutionary atheist who wanted to destroy marriage. The allegation that he was a traitor was repeated on doorstep after doorstep, but this time by well-dressed and well-spoken women who were a far cry from Bottomley's wild oratory. Labour canvassers found this onslaught very difficult to rebut and were inevitably driven onto the negative ground of their opponents.

In common with many other places whose industries had done well out of the war, Woolwich's local economy was already in decline, and despite the Conservative propaganda there were plenty of unemployed men and former soldiers who remained loyal Labour supporters. But MacDonald and his campaign wanted to talk about jobs and the price of food, and although he was one of the great orators of the day and could attract large audiences, he found it hard to be heard above the torrent of Conservative allegations.

Nor were Bottomley and the Conservative Party the only ones keen to see MacDonald defeated. The Communist Party, formed the previous year, had a deep loathing of the Labour Party and although they did not field a candidate, they roundly attacked both it and MacDonald. Labour was accused of standing for 'capitalism and all its manifestations' and MacDonald of wanting to crush the workers with 'the spiked club of the exploiters'. Given the anti-MacDonald narrative that he was a communist in disguise and would happily murder people in their beds, the Communist Party intervention should have been more of a help than a hindrance, but in fact it only contributed to the general sense that neither Labour nor its candidate could be trusted and the electoral effect was to fray the Labour vote from the left just as the Conservative attacks ate into it from the right.

A week before polling day, the whole campaign finally boiled over into a violent confrontation. Thousands of angry Labour supporters gathered in the streets outside a venue where Bottomley and Gee were due to hold a public meeting, and the crowd grew progressively more threatening. Bottomley's car was surrounded and he had to be rescued by the police. Later, Gee was attacked, according to press reports, by 'a virago of a woman' who hit him with a chair leg. His injuries were not serious, but they did exacerbate a war wound and his campaign was not slow to point out yet again the contrast between the heroic soldier and the cowardly pacifist – a pacifist who nevertheless seemed to be bringing in vicious thugs to disrupt the election and intimidate voters. MacDonald and the Labour Party hotly denied this, but the denial was hard to prove and, undoubtedly without MacDonald's consent though equally certainly with his knowledge, the final days of the campaign were imbued with a degree of overt violence stemming from Labour supporters.

On polling day, there was extensive doorstep organisation by both sides and, perhaps as a result, the outcome was narrower than might have been anticipated. Robert Gee won by less than 700 votes on a turnout of over 78 per cent. Given that the seat had previously been regarded as something of a Labour stronghold, this was a notable Conservative victory, although, as is often the case with by-election victories, it proved more ephemeral than might have been hoped. Gee managed to hang on to the seat only until the general election of 1922, when it returned to Labour with a majority of nearly 4,000. After that, it remained a more-or-less safe Labour seat until its abolition in 1983.

Robert Gee himself re-entered Parliament in 1924 as the MP for Bosworth in his home county of Leicestershire, but in 1927 he abandoned politics and emigrated to Western Australia, where he lived until his death in 1960.

In 1922, Horatio Bottomley's luck ran out. He was prosecuted for embezzling funds from a war bonds scheme he had set up in 1919, and by the time MacDonald was returned to Parliament later that year, Bottomley was serving a seven-year prison sentence. What he thought as he sat in his prison cell and heard of MacDonald becoming the first Labour Prime Minister in 1924 we do not know. After his release, he tried to restore his reputation and career but failed, and he died in 1933, bankrupt again and forgotten.

In the end, the 1921 Woolwich East by-election had very little significance except that of the moment, but some aspects of it did cast a long shadow. In 1931, Ramsay MacDonald, once the fêted hero of the left, entered a National government with the Conservative Party, thus finally acquiring the reputation for treachery with which Bottomley had so long tried to destroy him and which, until very recently, almost entirely defined his place in Labour history.

Nan Sloane *is a Labour historian writing about left-wing and radical movements with particular reference to women's involvement in them. Her books include* The Women in the Room: Labour's Forgotten History *(I. B. Tauris, 2018) and* Uncontrollable Women: Radicals, Reformers and Revolutionaries *(I. B. Tauris, 2022).*

19

CARDIGANSHIRE

18 FEBRUARY 1921
NATIONAL LIBERAL HOLD

RUSSELL DEACON

Result: Ernest Evans (National Liberal), 14,111, 57.3 per cent; William Llewelyn Williams (Liberal), 10,521, 42.7 per cent

Size of majority: 3,590

Swing: N/A

Name of previous MP and party: Matthew Vaughan-Davies (Coalition Liberal)

Reason for by-election: Elevation to the House of Lords

Result at previous general election: Matthew Vaughan-Davies (Coalition Liberal) elected unopposed

Date by-election called: 1 February 1921

Date by-election took place: 18 February 1921

Size of total electorate: 30,751

Total number of votes cast: 24,631

Turnout: 80.1 per cent

In current UK politics, the political parties have factions within them that can almost make them feel like different political parties. In the United States, they call this 'Big Tent' politics, including all of the different wings of your party under one roof or label. In 1916, however, for the Liberal Party, the factions were unable to be contained within one party. The replacement of the Liberal wartime Prime Minister Herbert Asquith by the dynamic Liberal force that was David Lloyd George at the head of a new coalition government split the Liberal Party into two different camps. This Liberal split and its successor splits would last on and off for a generation and the legacy of those splits even longer in some constituencies, such as Cardiganshire, in west Wales.

Cardiganshire, now known as Ceredigion, was mainly a rural coastal constituency and county, with three main urban centres – Cardigan, Lampeter and Aberystwyth. The latter two were also university towns, for whose graduates there was also the opportunity to vote for the University of Wales seat that covered the whole of Wales. This was called plural voting and it nearly always benefited the Liberals. While the University of Wales seat nearly exclusively returned Liberals, Cardiganshire could also go down as one of the UK's most constantly Liberal constituencies. Between 1880 and 1992, the seat was held by a Liberal of one sort or another for all but eight years (Labour between 1966 and 1974). This was over 100 years of Liberal dominance in a period when the Liberal MPs in the UK fell down to just five.

In fact, so Liberal was Cardiganshire that on 18 February 1921 at the Cardiganshire by-election, only two candidates stood and both were different types of Liberals – National Liberal (coalition government) and Liberal (opposition). So how did this unique factional Welsh election occur?

The story starts back in 1918 when the sitting Liberal MP Matthew Vaughan-Davies received the coalition government 'coupon' as endorsement and consequently stood unopposed, taking the seat as he had done at every election since 1895. Vaughan-Davies not only supported the Lloyd George coalition government, as did most Welsh Liberal MPs, but as an octogenarian, he had some national prominence by being the oldest Member of the House (of Commons) between 1918 and 1921. With a reputation as 'the silent backbencher', he had such a long and undistinguished career that the local Liberal association were not that unhappy with the speculation that he was seeking to retire and Liberalism could lift itself from the moribund state it now found itself in.

It was not only the Cardiganshire Liberal Association that was looking forward to Vaughan-Davies announcing his retirement. Back in 1917, William Llewelyn Williams, the Liberal and anti-Lloyd George coalition Liberal MP for Carmarthen Boroughs, wrote to Cardiganshire Liberals to say his seat was being 'wiped out' (most of the borough seats were being combined with rural ones into single constituencies) and he had heard there were 'prospects of a Liberal vacancy in Cardiganshire', with a potential Vaughan-Davies retirement. Cardiganshire was a constituency Llewelyn Williams had first tried for in 1895 but had lost out to the same Vaughan-Davies he was now hoping would soon retire. In 1918, however, there wasn't a vacancy and, in the event, Llewelyn Williams did not stand in this 'coupon election' for any parliamentary seat in Wales or elsewhere. He did not forget Cardiganshire, however, and kept his eye very much on prospective parliamentary developments there.

Llewelyn Williams's non-parliamentary background was both as a newspaper editor and barrister/recorder, something which was not uncommon in Liberal parliamentarian career paths. In fact, across their history, Welsh Liberal MPs' backgrounds were more often than not legally based, resulting in many Welsh MP/QCs or MP/KCs emanating from the various London Bar associations to represent Welsh constituencies. As well as being an MP/KC, Williams was also a Welsh Nationalist/Congregationalist (the latter being a Nonconformist Christian sect) committed to the disestablishment of the church in Wales and the Welsh nationalist Cymru Fydd movement.

Williams had closely allied himself with Lloyd George on many issues until 1916 when he, like a number of MPs close to Lloyd George, developed an intense hostility towards him and his style of leadership and backed the then Liberal leader and Prime Minister Henry Herbert Asquith in the Liberal Party split. This political move would result in him seeking to defeat the Liberal Nationalists led by his former ally some five years later, while himself residing in Asquith's Liberal Party (also known as Asquithians).

The incumbent Cardiganshire MP Vaughan-Davies had expected a peerage prior to the 1918 election as a loyal supporter of Lloyd George. He was now a man in his late seventies who felt he had served his parliamentary time in the Lower House but ennoblement was still not forthcoming, so he carried on his representation in the Commons. Then in early 1921, at eighty years of age, Vaughan-Davies was finally elevated to the peerage as Baron Ystwyth. This appointment, however, was not entirely due to his twenty-six years' parliamentary service nor his role as chair of the Welsh Parliamentary Party. The primary reason for his elevation was actually that a parliamentary vacancy was needed to ensure that the Lloyd George loyalist, none other than his own private secretary, Captain Ernest Evans, a local Cardiganshire man, Welsh speaker and another KC, was desired in a supportive MP's role by the Prime Minister. A suitable vacancy, therefore, was required, which Vaughan-Davies's elevation gracefully facilitated.

As we noted earlier, in 1921 across the UK, the Liberal Party was split in two: coalition Lloyd George Liberals (Collies) and Liberals (Asquithian). In Wales, as opposed to the wider UK, the Collies still dominated the political scene. As proof of this, the Welsh Liberal National Council was the only Liberal national council which was run by the Collies. The coalition government was backed by the overwhelming number of Welsh Liberal MPs and constituency associations and led by Lloyd George's key ally, Viscount St Davids. It was the Welsh Liberal National Council that supported Ernest Evans's candidature by forty-three votes to five. In turn, the anti-coalition Liberals had established their own Welsh Liberal Federation that endorsed one of their own council members, the aforementioned William Llewelyn Williams. This same split during the election now divided not only the Liberals of Cardiganshire but also the wider electorate there.

As the previous 1918 general election in this seat had been unopposed, this was the first chance for women to vote in the seat since their enfranchisement, although at this stage in history, it was only if they were aged over thirty. The Labour Party did not field a candidate because firstly they were still not well enough established in the seat and secondly it was felt their supporters would back any leftward-leaning anti-coalition candidate, for which Llewelyn Williams now fitted the bill, boosting future Liberal chances against their own.

When the campaign was going at full throttle, there were up to 100 coalition government organisers plus local campaigners in the seat seeking to promote Evans. In addition, many voters in the constituency were also Lloyd George diehards, but against these were those Liberals who disliked the coalition government's record and the diluting of the Liberal brand with their traditional Conservative foe. Voters were also influenced by which brand of Nonconformist religious fervour they branded themselves. These religious voting influences depended on where the voter went to chapel on a Sunday. Thus, they could be influenced by Lloyd George's, Evans's and Llewelyn Williams's Nonconformist backgrounds (Baptist, Methodist and Congregationalist) and put their cross next to them on the ballot accordingly. Although, the issue of the disestablishment of the Church of England, which had distinguished politics in Wales from elsewhere for several generations, had by this time finally been resolved by the Welsh Church Act of 1914. This had the effect of moving the campaign issues themselves onto the issue of 'tariff reform', in essence to what extent should there be full free trade. Asquithian Liberals were for free trade, with the Collies less so.

As well as the influence of differing types of Nonconformist religion on the vote, in Cardiganshire the Liberal voters were also split down urban and rural lines (urban being more coalition and rural more Asquithian). These splits also resulted in Cardiganshire getting two different Liberal associations. In Aberystwyth, there were two different Liberal clubs in the same street. There was even a split between the county newspapers – with the *Cambrian News* supporting Evans and the *Welsh Gazette* supporting Llewelyn Williams.

There were plenty of national Liberal figures from both factions who came to speak and campaign in the by-election. At this time in history, party leaders did not campaign themselves in by-elections, but this did not stop their own family members acting as proxies. In this by-election campaign, both Lloyd George through his wife Margaret and Asquith through his daughter Violet Bonham Carter made sure that the voters knew exactly what the two Liberal leaders believed and desired from this election and how the Cardiganshire electorate should vote.

In the event, turnout was more than 80 per cent – for Cardiganshire, near a record high. Overall, 14,111 votes were cast for Evans and 10,521 for Llewelyn Williams, giving Evans a majority of 3,590 votes. At the count, Llewelyn Williams announced he would be standing at the next election once more, but in the event, he died of double pneumonia on 22 April 1922 aged just fifty-five, which meant that he would never get to be an MP again.

Less than two years after the by-election, a general election was called for November 1922, after the downfall of Lloyd George's coalition government. In this next Cardiganshire electoral contest, Evans beat another Liberal (Asquithian) candidate – Rhys Hopkin Morris – in another two-way contest. Just over a year from this, however, the new Liberal-free Conservative government called another general election. This time, the Conservatives put up a candidate and it was not solely a Liberal vs Liberal contest. The Lloyd George Liberal Evans lost the seat to Asquithian Hopkin Morris by 46.9 per cent to Evans's 27.7 per cent.

Evans wouldn't contest the seat again but instead moved to the University of Wales seat in the 1924 general election, which he held until 1942 when he was appointed a county judge. In the 1924 general election, Evans's only opponent was a Labour candidate, and he'd never again face a Liberal opponent of any description in the University of Wales seat. Hopkin Morris, always a strong anti-Lloyd George Liberal, left Parliament to become a London metropolitan magistrate in 1932, which was not compatible with being an MP as it was an 'office of profit under the Crown'. He returned to Parliament in 1945, winning the neighbouring constituency of Carmarthen, in the only Labour loss of that year's landslide election. He was regarded in the House of Commons as the last representative of Gladstonian liberalism and not aligned with the newer social liberals, who had been shaped by his nemesis, the recently deceased David Lloyd George. Hopkin Morris's death in 1956 ironically now resulted in his nemesis's daughter Megan Lloyd George returning as an MP to the House of Commons, this time in support of an even more socialist agenda as a Labour MP.

When we look back at the Cardiganshire by-election, although in many ways it could be said to have been shaped by a bygone era of issues and politics that have long since vanished, it also had some important lessons for future politics. These were on:

- *Technology in order to 'Get out the vote'*: It showed the benefits of technology. The Collies were able to mobilise 250 vehicles on polling day against the Liberals' fifty. These enabled them to get more rural voters to the polls – 'Getting out the vote!' It indicated that those who made the most use of technology could get out the most supporters!

- *Tactical voting*: It illustrated tactical voting in that the 7,000 Conservative voters in the seat backed the Collies to defeat the opposition Liberals (Asquithians). Something which led Llewelyn Williams to declare that this was the first Tory victory since 1874 in Cardiganshire. As an indication of the importance of this Tory vote supporting the Liberals, in the eleven parliamentary Cardiganshire elections that followed between 1923 and 1959, they only contested the seat three times, so their supporters got lots of practice at voting Liberal and giving the party a boost.
- *One-party dominance*: It foreshadowed one-party dominance in Wales, where the seat could only be won by a different faction of the same party. This dominance would pass from Liberal to Labour within a generation across most of Wales. Labour would then experience this later on in Welsh constituencies, for instance in Merthyr Tydfil in 1970 with the Independent (former Labour) MP S. O. Davies winning the seat, with Labour coming second. It would be repeated again in Blaenau Gwent when former Labour 'Independents' won the seat in elections in 2005 and again in 2006.
- *Rural/urban divide*: The by-election highlighted the differing voting habits of rural and urban voters. The urban population tended to support the government's candidate Evans, whereas the rural population supported Llewelyn Williams. In Wales and England, rural and urban seats continue in most elections to still support different parties.

Although the Liberal hegemony of Welsh politics passed into history more than a century ago, the Liberal (Democrat) brand still stays at it strongest in Mid Wales seats, such as the former Cardiganshire, but with nowhere near the absolute dominance it enjoyed in this 1921 by-election.

***Professor Russell Deacon** is a visiting professor of politics and history at the University of South Wales specialising in Welsh, history, devolution and governance. He authored* The Government and Politics of Wales *(Edinburgh University Press, 2018), a key text on Welsh politics, and has published extensively on British and Welsh political history.*

20

NEWPORT

18 OCTOBER 1922
UNIONIST GAIN FROM LIBERAL

STEPHEN WILLIAMS

Result: Reginald Clarry (Unionist), 13,515, 40.0 per cent; William Bowen (Labour), 11,425, 33.8 per cent; William Lyndon Moore (Liberal), 8,841, 26.2 per cent
Size of majority: 2,090
Swing: N/A
Name of previous MP and party: Lewis Haslam (Coalition Liberal)
Reason for by-election: Death of incumbent
Result at previous general election: Lewis Haslam (Coalition Liberal), 14,080, 56.4 per cent; William Bowen (Labour), 10,234, 41.0 per cent; Bertie Pardoe-Thomas (Independent Democrat), 647, 2.6 per cent
Date by-election called: 19 September 1922
Date by-election took place: 18 October 1922
Size of total electorate: 42,645
Total number of votes cast: 33,781
Turnout: 79.2 per cent

'The most politically significant by-election in British history'
– WELSH ACADEMY ENCYCLOPAEDIA OF WALES

'The only British by-election which brought down a government'
– HISTORIAN JOHN RAMSDEN

*'One of the most exciting boomerangs in the long
history of English political strategy'*
– DAILY EXPRESS OWNER LORD BEAVERBROOK

The third of these startling claims was made by one of the significant players in national events in October 1922, commenting years later on how the electoral gamble of Tory leader Austen Chamberlain had backfired, spectacularly.

The Newport by-election took place during an international crisis. The result was awaited eagerly in Westminster and Fleet Street. The fate of Prime Minister David Lloyd George and his coalition government depended on the result. Chamberlain needed to regain the confidence of his MPs. Labour expected another by-election gain, furthering momentum towards breaking out of third-party status. The irony of Newport is that the voters were not concerned mainly with national and international issues. In their minds, pub opening hours ranked ahead of the future of Constantinople. Two of the candidates avoided association with their national leaders. Newport was a by-election where 'all politics is local' applied, but the result had national implications for all the main parliamentary groupings.

Newport's population and economic fortunes had soared in the nineteenth century as it became the premier port for the export of Welsh iron and coal, until overtaken by Cardiff. Migration into the Glamorgan and Monmouthshire Valleys was mainly from rural Wales. Newport's migrants came from further afield, by rail from England and by ship from Ireland. By 1922, half of Newport's population had been born outside the town and it had Wales's largest concentration of Roman Catholics. It was a most un-Welsh town.

Newport's demographics had come to the fore in 1896 when the South Wales Liberal Federation (SWLF) met in the town. The leader of the SWLF was Newport resident David Alfred Thomas, one of the most powerful coal owners and MP for Merthyr Tydfil. The main debates were about church disestablishment, stronger links with the north Wales federation and the incorporation of the soft nationalist group, Cymru Fydd, roughly translated as Young Wales.

Enter Lloyd George, the emerging leader of radical Welsh liberalism, voice of Nonconformity, temperance and champion of home rule for Wales. D. A. Thomas was determined to see him off his turf. Lloyd George was howled down and then denied a second speech when he asked for a right of reply. He wrote home complaining that the meeting had been 'packed with Newport Englishmen'.

Newport was kinder to Lloyd George the following year, when he was admitted to the Gorsedd of the Bards at the national Eisteddfod. By then, Lloyd George was switching his political focus away from Welsh affairs. He became the most famous critic of the Boer War, establishing him as a rising star on the national stage.

Jump forward a quarter century. Lloyd George is the 'man who won the war', in his sixth year as Prime Minister, arguably the most famous man in the world. His place at the pinnacle of British politics and global esteem was precarious; in the autumn of 1922, he had few remaining political allies. He had alienated much of the Liberal Party, split in two since he supplanted Asquith as Prime Minister in December 1916.

Bitterness deepened in 1918 as Liberal MPs loyal to Asquith had coalition-supporting Tory opponents endorsed by Lloyd George and the then Conservative Leader Bonar Law. Asquith quipped, 'Candidates were ticketed and political coupons distributed.'

The 'coupon election' of December 1918 was a triumph for the coalition, but the Asquithians shrank to just thirty-six MPs, with the man himself also defeated at East Fife. Lloyd George led a faction of 127 coalition Liberals, outnumbered by 379 Tories. Asquith returned to the Commons at the Paisley by-election in February 1920, in no mood for Liberal reconciliation.

The Cabinet had a majority of Conservatives, led since 1921 by Austen Chamberlain, due to Bonar Law's illness. They were broadly loyal to Lloyd George, wanting the coalition to continue beyond 1922 as the political vehicle most likely to resist the rising challenge of the Labour Party. Many Tory junior ministers and backbenchers disagreed. They felt trapped inside a coalition that had served its purpose of winning the war and securing the peace. Lloyd George was a man many had hated for twenty years; he had served his purpose and was dispensable.

The shine had also gone off Lloyd George among Liberals. The post-war boom had turned to economic depression, with numerous strikes. The coalition promised the 'land fit for heroes', but worsening public finances had led by 1922 to the 'Geddes Axe' of expenditure cuts. The brutal tactics used by the 'Black and Tan' police auxiliaries to suppress the IRA had horrified liberal opinion. The high priests of Welsh liberalism, Nonconformist ministers and academics at the University of Wales condemned Lloyd George. Although he settled the Irish question in 1921, it was too late to salvage his reputation.

Lenin, a contender for most famous man in 1922, said, 'There are decades where nothing happens; and there are weeks where decades happen.' September and October 1922 were indeed eventful, at home and abroad. Lloyd George had been one of the framers of the post-war peace settlements, redrawing the maps of Europe and the Middle East. Turkish nationalists rejected the Treaty of Sevres that had been signed by the Ottoman Sultan's representatives. On 9 September 1922, Kemal Atatürk entered the Anatolian coastal city of Smyrna (İzmir), threatening the majority Greek population. Atatürk's next aim was to cross the Dardanelles to capture Constantinople. A British garrison at Chanak stood in his way.

Lloyd George acted fast to halt Atatürk, backed by Austen Chamberlain, Lord Birkenhead and also Churchill, his fellow Liberal. The Dominion Prime Ministers were telegrammed, asking for urgent military aid. New Zealand and Newfoundland responded enthusiastically. Billy Hughes, the Welsh-born Prime Minister of Australia, was reluctant to return to the scene of Gallipoli. The Canadian Prime Minister William Lyon Mackenzie King baulked at the implication that Canada should automatically follow Britain's lead. Canada's ruffled sensibilities were presumably not lost on the Canadian-born Bonar Law. He had become increasingly disenchanted by his successor Chamberlain's clinging to the coalition and Lloyd George.

During this international crisis, the coalition Liberal MP for Newport died suddenly on 12 September. A political butterfly wing had flapped. Lewis Haslam had served Newport since the 1906 Liberal landslide. A wealthy cotton weaver from Bolton, he had neither Newport nor Welsh credentials. His support for temperance had not endeared him to Newport residents, a more bibulous population than much of Wales.

The seat won by Haslam in 1906 was Monmouth Boroughs, created by the Act of Union of 1536 that gave each Welsh county two MPs plus another for a grouping of boroughs. Monmouth Boroughs were Monmouth, Usk and Newport. One of Haslam's predecessors was Benjamin Hall, the minister whose name is commemorated in Parliament's clock tower.

By 1906, about 90 per cent of the electorate was in Newport. The Representation of the People Act of 1918 gave Newport its own MP with a much-expanded electorate of men over twenty-one (plus younger war veterans) and women aged thirty. Haslam, a supporter of Lloyd George, received the coalition coupon and held the new seat against a strong Labour challenge from William Bowen, a postal workers union official.

During the war, the opening hours of public houses were reduced. In 1921, a new Licensing Act was proposed, generating huge interest in Newport. Gladstonian legislation in 1881 had closed Welsh pubs on Sundays. It was the first law since 1543 to treat Wales separately to England, but crucially, Monmouthshire's MPs had carved out an exemption for their less Nonconformist and temperance-orientated county. Lloyd George removed this exemption in the 1921 Bill, supported by Haslam. The Bill was opposed by Haslam's Tory neighbour, Leolin Forestier-Walker, speaking in the Commons about protest disturbances in Newport.

Local Tories decided that they would oppose Haslam at the next election, even if the coalition continued. On 26 July 1922, 300 members selected Reginald Clarry as the Unionist candidate for the next general election. Clarry was a Cardiff engineering graduate from Derby who'd risen fast to be the young managing director of the Steel and Tin Plate Works in Swansea. He'd spent the war as an adviser to the Ministry of Munitions.

In London, Lloyd George and his close colleagues were preparing to call a snap general election. Prior to Parliament's summer recess on 4 August, there had been growing opposition among Tory MPs to the continuance of the coalition. On 20 July, junior ministers had warned Chamberlain of Lloyd George's unpopularity, demanding their own leader. On the eve of recess, attitudes hardened when they felt that they had been patronised and dismissed in a meeting with Lord Birkenhead.

Chequers had been given to the nation the previous year as a country retreat for Prime Ministers. Lloyd George's Cabinet met there on 17

September 1922 and agreed to call an election as soon as Chamberlain could get the agreement of a meeting of MPs, to be held before the National Union of Conservative Associations could wrest the initiative. Chamberlain faced opposition from union chairman Sir George Younger, warning him that the party would be split in two. The Chief Whip, Leslie Wilson, alerted Chamberlain that 184 constituencies, Newport included, had selected candidates to run independently of any national endorsement.

Campaigning had begun in Newport, oblivious to private discussions in Westminster. Clarry had the vocal support of local publicans. Bowen was reselected for Labour on 14 September, without waiting for Haslam's funeral. With a net gain of thirteen seats from the coalition since 1918, Newport was a key test for Labour. The *Express* reported that the campaign was 'an endless procession' of Labour frontbenchers arriving in Newport to support Bowen. Among them were James R. Clynes, the Commons party leader, one of his predecessors (and a successor) Arthur Henderson and the future ministers Margaret Bondfield and Ernest Bevin. Bowen was well connected in London, living there since 1919 as the general secretary of the postmen's union.

Newport Liberals were in a bind. The Welsh Liberal Federation was the only federation not under Asquith's control, but Newport members included Asquith supporters. A potential Asquithian candidate was Reginald McKenna, the former Monmouthshire MP and Chancellor, who declined in favour of his lucrative directorship of Midland Bank.

Another refusal came from businesswoman Margaret Haigh Thomas, who had been refused entry to the House of Lords on succeeding her father D. A. Thomas as Viscountess Rhondda in 1918. Her candidacy would have ignited the campaign, given her family's local prominence and her fame as an imprisoned suffragette and a survivor of the *Lusitania* sinking. Lady Rhondda finally got her Newport recognition with a statue unveiled in 2024.

The Liberal chosen on 27 September was William Lyndon Moore, a solicitor and the Newport coroner. He was a 'Liberal without a prefix or suffix' but protested that he was not 'Mr Facing Both Ways, I keep my face in one direction and that is the direction in which Liberal progress marches'.

Moore's selection meant that neither the Liberal nor the Tory candidates clearly supported the coalition. Ministers did not campaign in the seat. Notable by her absence was Dame Margaret Lloyd George, who campaigned nationwide for her husband and had spoken sixty times in the 1921 Cardigan by-election. Moore's campaign was undermined by local weaknesses. Seven of the nine wards had no active Liberal branches and the party had not fought a vigorous campaign against Newport Tories since 1910.

In a town full of Irishmen, Clarry campaigned hard on beer and Lloyd George's handling of Irish partition. He held his meeting in the town's theatres, hotels and six Tory clubs. Bowen and Moore played into his hands by holding their meetings in the temperance hall.

Some of the by-election tactics used by the candidates and their supporters in the local press would be familiar today. The Tory *Western Mail* warned not 'to waste votes on Mr Lyndon Moore'. The *South Wales Argus* countered that 'there was no hope for Clarry ... Conservatives are out of the running'. Labour published canvass returns showing them ahead with 45 per cent of the vote. In election week, attention shifted to the local economy as a miners' strike in Ebbw Vale led to the coal export wagons lying empty in Newport, probably undermining Labour.

Chamberlain believed Labour would win Newport. Moreover, it was the result he wanted, to prove that Labour would gain ground if the coalition ended. He stabbed Clarry in the back by instructing Central Office to do the bare minimum so that the party could 'point to the moral when the election is over and the seat was lost'.

Newport was Chamberlain's big electoral gamble. He set the date of the MPs' meeting at the Carlton Club for 11 a.m. on Thursday 19 October, when the result would be known. When Newport's mayor declared the victory of Clarry at 2 a.m., Chamberlain's gambit blew up in his face.

The night before, Lord Beaverbrook, owner of the *Express* and close friend of his fellow Canadian Bonar Law, had helped persuade him to attend the meeting and speak against Chamberlain. Law had grown increasingly concerned about Lloyd George's Chanak brinkmanship, risking a return to war. On 7 October, he had written to *The Times*, saying that Britain could not act alone 'as the world's policeman'. Beaverbrook ran the story in the *Express*. On 11 October, a pact was signed at Mudanya and war was averted. The crisis had turned more Tory MPs against Lloyd George and several went to Newport to help Clarry over the line.

The news of Law's attendance at the crucial Tory meeting was carried in the morning papers, with *The Times* London edition also carrying an editorial about the lessons of Newport, 'a vindication of those Conservatives ... who have been so determined to preserve their individuality ... Newport will be hailed as the emancipation of the party'. The result was a great disappointment for Labour – 'The significance of Newport lies in the heavy defeat of Labour expectations.'

Any waverers among Conservative MPs gathered at the Carlton Club now had evidence that their party had nothing to fear from three-way contests and might even prosper. The writing was already on the wall for Chamberlain and the coalition once Bonar Law decided to join the insurrection. The then lower-profile Stanley Baldwin famously warned the meeting that the 'dynamic force' of Lloyd George was 'a terrible thing' and because of it the 'Liberal Party has been smashed to pieces ... and it is my firm opinion that in time the same would happen to our party'. The killer blow was landed by Bonar Law, warning that the party faced a split as damaging as that under Peel if it did not fight the next election as an independent party. Chamberlain lost the vote 187 to eighty-seven and his leadership ended.

Lloyd George resigned at 4 p.m. that day and the king sent for Bonar Law, who called a general election. It was assumed widely that Lloyd George would one day return to office, but that prospect never materialised. Labour overtook the combined forces of the Liberals, who have remained the third party ever since. Clarry held Newport (with a short blip between 1929 and 1931) until 1945. Bowen was elected at Crewe in 1929 but defeated in 1931. Moore returned to the law and led the Liberals on Newport Council.

October 1922 was a pivotal moment in British politics. Lloyd George was toppled and within two years the country had settled into a long hegemony of Conservative versus Labour elections, won mostly by Conservatives. Lloyd George and his government had stood on a precipice on 19 October. Newport alone did not blow him over the edge, but it did stiffen the resolve of Tory MPs to rebel and once Bonar Law joined them, the long age of Liberal-led governments was over. Over the space of a quarter century, events in Newport had first averted Lloyd George's attention to British national issues and then helped terminate his premiership.

Stephen Williams grew up in Glamorgan and is a history graduate of Bristol University. He was Bristol West's Liberal Democrat MP from 2005 to 2015 and spoke for the party on public health, higher education and the Treasury, before becoming Minister for Communities during the coalition. In 2024, he returned to office as a Bristol councillor.

21

MITCHAM

3 MARCH 1923
LABOUR GAIN FROM CONSERVATIVES

LEWIS BASTON

Result: James Chuter Ede (Labour), 8,029, 38.0 per cent; Arthur Griffith-Boscawen (Conservative), 7,196, 34.1 per cent; Ernest Brown (Liberal), 3,214, 15.2 per cent; John Catterall (Independent Conservative), 2,684, 12.7 per cent
Size of majority: 833
Swing: 34.5 per cent from Conservative to Labour
Name of previous MP and party: Thomas Cato Worsfold (Conservative)
Reason for by-election: Resignation
Result at previous general election: Thomas Cato Worsfold (Conservative), 10,934, 65.0 per cent; A. E. Bennetts (Liberal), 5,898, 35.0 per cent
Date by-election called: 13 February 1923
Date by-election took place: 3 March 1923
Size of total electorate: 31,927
Total number of votes cast: 21,123
Turnout: 66.2 per cent

The Mitcham by-election of March 1923 was important for several reasons. It was the first Labour victory in a suburban constituency and therefore a major step towards the party's status as a national force. It saw a major innovation in election campaigning with Labour's technique of the mass canvass, and it was an underappreciated skirmish in the decade-long battle between the press barons and the Conservative leadership. It killed off the political ambitions of one minister but elevated those of a future Prime Minister and a long-serving future Home Secretary. Mitcham also influenced housing policy for generations.

The Mitcham by-election took place shortly after the November 1922 general election, which had resulted in a comfortable majority for the Conservatives after a period of political upheaval and cross-party coalition. Paradoxically, while the Conservatives were not overwhelmingly popular, there seemed to be no real prospect from the 1922 results of anyone displacing them any time soon. Labour had consolidated their position as the main opposition party, but with only 142 MPs and representation largely confined to heavy industrial constituencies, they were not yet looking like an alternative government. The Liberals were still suffering from the effects of the Asquith–Lloyd George split and the ex-coalition National Liberals were the main losers from the election. While the Liberals made a public spectacle of their divisions, there were also strains on the Conservative side. In forming the government, Bonar Law had to do without the services of many coalitionists who had recently been in leading positions; Winston Churchill, then a Liberal coalitionist, called the Tory government formed in October 1922 the 'Second Eleven' because of all the talent that refused to serve or was overlooked.

The cross-currents of public opinion meant that there were an unusual number of ministers who lost their seats even as their party was winning a majority in the 1922 election. The first by-election of the parliament, Portsmouth South in December 1922, was called to get the government Chief Whip back in the Commons. There were three other seatless ministers who stayed on in office while seats were found for them, most prominently the Health Secretary Sir Arthur Griffith-Boscawen. Boscawen was a long-serving Conservative politician first elected in 1892 but whose membership of the Commons was frequently interrupted by electoral defeat. By 1923, he had a reputation as an electoral Jonah. He had lost his seat three times – at Tonbridge in 1906, Dudley in 1921 and Taunton in 1922 – and failed to get elected twice (East Denbighshire in a 1906 by-election and Dudley at the January 1910 election).

The seat found for Griffith-Boscawen was Mitcham. The constituency, created in 1918, contained the urban district of Mitcham and the neighbouring areas of Carshalton, Wallington and Beddington to the south. It was a county constituency of Surrey, but the area's population growth reflected its development as a London suburb. In the 1910s and 1920s, traditional pursuits such as growing lavender and other medicinal plants were giving way to housing and the nascent chemical industry, and large houses were being sold for residential development. Mitcham's inaugural contest in December 1918 returned Thomas Cato Worsfold as a coalition Unionist in 1918 with a large majority in a straight fight with a Liberal; he held the seat comfortably in 1922. It looked safe enough for the Tories, even with Boscawen as the candidate.

Worsfold was a solicitor and a member of a notable local family. He was not a very active MP, making only three full-scale speeches during his membership of the Commons. He resigned his seat on 12 February 1923, citing ill health and the pressure to attend a parliament with a much smaller majority than that in 1918–22. Bonar Law wrote to Worsfold suggesting that he smooth the way for Griffith-Boscawen to be his successor. It was widely believed at the time that this was a pretext to clear the way for Boscawen, but Worsfold strenuously disputed such assertions, to the lengths of bringing his doctor onto an election platform to rebut the allegation that Worsfold's illness was a diplomatic convenience. Worsfold lived until 1936, remaining active in local and civic life, medical advice notwithstanding.

Boscawen's campaign in Mitcham hit trouble almost immediately. His ministerial brief as Health Secretary included housing. The main problem was rent control. Limitations on working-class rent were legislated as a wartime measure in 1915 and extended into higher-rent properties by the coalition government in 1920. The Conservative government wanted to revert to market rents but feared that doing so without an increased supply of houses would simply cause massive price increases. The issue had been put to a committee of inquiry under Lord Onslow, which with exquisite timing reported just before the by-election campaign started. Onslow recommended phasing out rent control in three stages by June 1925, decontrolling higher-rental properties first. The press and Tory MPs exploded; they feared that in the initial stages, middle-class households would lose their homes, squeezed between escalating rents at the high end and protected tenancies in smaller houses. Housing dominated the Mitcham hustings.

Boscawen's response was less than resolute. He was ideologically in favour of decontrolling rents and promised a housing Act to get back to the pre-war situation of 95 per cent of houses being privately built, but he was under huge electoral pressure in Mitcham. On Friday 16 February, he ruled out decontrolling higher rents as early as June 1923, amid much relief and celebration by the Tories and the press, but he subsequently said that he had been misinterpreted: the higher-rent decontrol would take place in June 1924 and the rest in 1925. The next zigzag was to promise to vote against early decontrol if a single Mitcham elector would lose out by doing so. It was grist to the mill of the internal Tory opposition to Bonar Law; the Rothermere press dubbed the government in general and Boscawen in particular 'wobblers'. Around a third of the electorate in Mitcham were paying enough rent to be affected by the government's irresolution, and the focus remained on housing throughout the election.

The next blow was the emergence of a Labour candidate, James Chuter Ede. Ede was an active local politician, a teacher who had once been a Liberal but had moved over to Labour. He was the only Labour member of Surrey County Council and sat on Epsom Urban District Council, where – a sign of cross-party respect – he chaired the housing committee. Ede was an ideal candidate for Mitcham – respectable, sober, able to win over Liberal votes and non-manual workers and work with the trade unions. Tory press accusations that he was a candidate of 'disruption and disintegration' seemed ludicrous. On his own initiative, Ede started addressing meetings in the constituency, the minuscule local party and national headquarters endorsing him as a fait accompli. Labour in and around London, under the influence of Herbert Morrison, was taken with the concept of 'scientific management' as part of the appeal to the clerical middle class (the 'black-coated workers' in contemporary parlance) and Mitcham was a test bed for this approach to campaigning. The low turnout in the general election was interpreted as evidence that there was a significant latent Labour presence in the electorate that had not voted then but could be mobilised in the by-election.

Labour's campaign in Mitcham did not neglect the traditional business of public meetings but focused on the doorstep. The party's principal innovation was the 'mass canvass'. This was where party volunteers descended on a street. Some would knock on doors to rouse residents while another would set up a chair and deliver a short speech to people who had come to see what the fuss was about. The 1920s mass canvass was a predominantly female activity – the volunteers and the voters during the day were mostly women. The *Daily Telegraph* ruefully admitted after the result:

> The Labour organisation at Mitcham was immensely superior to that of either the Conservatives or the Liberals, though the Labour party had never contested the constituency before. Its volunteer workers were better trained; they were fired to a whiter heat; and their new methods of mass-canvassing can only be countered by imitation.

The Liberal campaign in Mitcham did not catch fire. They selected Ernest Brown, who had contested Salisbury in 1918 and 1922. He was eloquent, had the support of both the Lloyd George and Asquith wings and was solid on the housing issue, but the contest was between the Tories and Labour.

Nominations closed on 23 February. Fifteen minutes from the noon deadline, a surprise candidate entered the fray. The fourth man was an Independent Conservative, John Catterall. His candidacy emerged from the scheming of Tory ex-coalitionists against Bonar Law; he was funded by Oliver Locker-Lampson, a Birmingham Tory MP who had been (1919–21) parliamentary private secretary to the then Conservative leader Austen Chamberlain and supported by the Rothermere press (the *Daily Mail* and the *Daily Mirror*), which were out to cause trouble. Catterall's platform was to delay decontrol of middle-class rents, support France's punitive invasion of the Ruhr and pull out of Iraq and Palestine. Boscawen was incandescent, repeatedly calling the Catterall campaign 'rank treachery'.

The campaign was short and sharp. Between them, the four candidates spoke at around 200 indoor meetings in ten days and many more outdoor stump speeches. Boscawen's meetings were frequently disrupted by heckling; communists were believed to have been mostly responsible and were repudiated by the Labour campaign. But Boscawen was a poor platform speaker and needlessly antagonistic even to well-intentioned questions from the floor at his meetings. Labour's hopes rose during the campaign; the prospect of Conservative votes being split between Boscawen and Catterall meant that what had started as a 'propaganda' effort now had a real chance of victory.

On polling day, Saturday 3 March, the Conservatives were confident that Boscawen would hold on, but Labour's intensive canvassing gave them a more accurate picture. During the day, the parties ferried their supporters to the polling stations in fleets of motor vehicles; unusually, Labour had all the cars their campaign needed in Mitcham. As the parties and candidates waited for the Monday count, news came from the day's other by-election at Willesden East: a Liberal gain in a straight fight with the Conservatives.

Ede took the lead quickly as the votes were counted, as the first boxes came from the Mitcham urban end of the constituency. The votes from Carshalton and Wallington saw Griffith-Boscawen claw back some of the deficit, but it was not enough. Labour had won by a narrow but clear majority of 833 votes — but with only 38 per cent of the vote. The result was announced to an excited crowd of around 2,000 people who had assembled outside Mitcham Vestry Hall. Ede credited mistrust of the government and its housing policy above all but also mentioned his local credentials and the inspiring effect of Labour's role in parliamentary opposition.

The Mitcham result, together with the Liberal gain in Willesden East on the same day and another Labour win at Liverpool Edge Hill on 6 March, was an unforced setback for the new Conservative government. The *Evening Standard* quipped: 'If the government cannot produce houses for the people, neither shall they find seats for homeless Ministers.' The gambit of calling by-elections to allow defeated ministers a passage back to Parliament had backfired badly, and subsequent governments were wary of attempting it; Patrick Gordon Walker's experience at Leyton in 1965 reinforced the lesson.

Boscawen resigned from the Health Ministry; Mitcham was the end for his jinxed electoral career and he never tried to return to Parliament although he lived until 1946. The vacancy at Health was filled by Neville Chamberlain, the start of a rise to power that culminated with a term as Prime Minister in 1937–40. Mitcham forced a generational change on the Tories, the dynamic Chamberlain replacing the old warhorse Boscawen.

In terms of policy, Mitcham was the death blow to radical decontrol of rents and therefore to any Conservative attempt to restore the pre-war status quo. Neville Chamberlain's Rent and Mortgage Interest Restrictions Act of 1923 postponed decontrol of existing tenancies to 1925. Back in the Health Ministry after October 1924, Chamberlain baulked at decontrol even then and rent control was extended several times, the law remaining in place into the 1930s. Chamberlain's Housing Act provided subsidies for private and public housebuilding. The first Labour government's Wheatley Housing Act of 1924 expanded the role of council housing and in the 1930s low interest rates made mortgages and owner occupation ever more affordable. Mitcham was part of the trend, adding council estates like Border Gate in Mitcham itself and swathes of new suburbia in Carshalton. The private rented sector went into continuous decline, squeezed between owner occupation and social rent.

Labour's winner Chuter Ede had only a brief but energetic term as MP for Mitcham. The December 1923 general election was a straight fight between Labour and the Conservatives, and despite a lower turnout, the number of votes for both parties was up on where it was in the by-election. The new Conservative candidate Richard Meller prevailed over Ede by 952 votes (4.6 per cent). Meller and Ede faced each other again in October 1924, and Meller boosted his majority to a relatively safe 6,208 votes (24 per cent). Meller held the seat until his death in June 1940; his successor was defeated by Labour in 1945, but Mitcham returned to the Tories in 1950 and stayed with them until major boundary changes in 1974. The successor seat, Mitcham & Morden, was the scene of an unusual by-election in June 1982 when the Conservative Angela Rumbold gained it despite her party being in government.

Ede left Mitcham after his decisive loss in 1924 and was elected MP for South Shields in May 1929; he represented it until he stood down in 1964, except for the 1931–35 parliament. Coincidentally, the Liberal winner in 1931 was Harcourt 'Crinks' Johnstone, who gained Willesden East from the Tories on the same day that Ede had won Mitcham. Ede had an important ministerial career. In the wartime coalition, he was the Labour deputy to 'Rab' Butler at Education and played a major part in the Education Act of 1944. In the Attlee government, he was Home Secretary from 1945 to 1951. He was appointed Lord Chuter-Ede in 1964 and died in November 1965.

Ernest Brown went on to be Liberal MP for Rugby in 1923–24 and had a longer stint as MP for Leith in 1927–45. In 1931, Brown followed Sir John Simon into the Liberal Nationals and close co-operation with the Conservatives. He served in the National and wartime governments and died in 1962.

Mitcham was interpreted by the Conservatives and the press as being mostly the result of the housing issue driving a wedge between the government and the middle-class electorate and of Conservative in-fighting. The prospect of Labour being the government less than a year after Mitcham still seemed fantastical. Austen Chamberlain thought it showed that electors were increasingly responding on the 'mood of the day' rather than deeper party loyalty. However, the enthusiastic response in working-class areas of Mitcham as soon as an organised Labour campaign appeared suggests that new political loyalties were being forged. As well as commanding a core vote, Mitcham showed that Labour could also, in the right conditions, be a suitable receptacle for middle-class protest. With a century's perspective, Mitcham's position as Labour's first win in a commuter suburb seems significant – a flash in the pan in the class-dominated 1920s but a symbol of the voters Labour aspired to reach for the rest of the twentieth century.

Lewis Baston is a writer on politics, elections and history and the author of Borderlines *(Hodder, 2024), a history and travel book about European borderlands.*

22

WESTMINSTER ABBEY

19 MARCH 1924
CONSERVATIVE HOLD

LORD LEXDEN

Result: Otho Nicholson (Conservative), 8,187, 35.9 per cent; Winston Churchill (Constitutionalist), 8,144, 35.8 per cent; Fenner Brockway (Labour), 6,156, 27.0 per cent; James Scott Duckers (Liberal), 291, 1.3 per cent
Size of majority: 43
Swing: N/A
Name of previous MP and party: John Nicholson (Conservative)
Reason for by-election: Death of incumbent
Result at previous general election: John Nicholson (Conservative) elected unopposed
Date by-election called: 4 March 1924
Date by-election took place: 19 March 1924
Size of total electorate: 36,999
Total number of votes cast: 22,778
Turnout: 61.6 per cent

It was a question that everyone in political life wanted to discuss during the first weeks of March just over a century ago. They spoke of little else as a by-election campaign proceeded in the Westminster Abbey parliamentary constituency. 'Everyone here is agog about the Westminster Election,' one senior Conservative told his wife. Winston Churchill was one of the candidates. In the first editions of the newspapers after votes had been cast on 19 March, he was hailed as the victor.

The constituency, created in 1918, stretched from Pimlico in the west to the Strand in the east, with Oxford Street marking its northern boundary. Tories abounded, filling most of the grand mansions of Belgravia and fine houses elsewhere and rejoicing in the presence of royal palaces and the institutions of government in their midst.

These sedate supporters of the Tory Party were, however, disinclined to dirty their hands with the rough business of electioneering. Billboards, leaflets, rallies were not for them. Such tasks fell to the deferential shopkeepers who served them, to the market traders of Covent Garden, to the petit bourgeois of Soho and to the denizens of theatreland in and around Drury Lane, who always rallied in some number to the Tory cause. There were not many left-wing luvvies in 1924.

While possessing some of the best housing in the country, the constituency also had some of the very worst. Foul slums, known as Devil's Acre, lay within half a mile of the Houses of Parliament. Lord Shaftesbury, the famous nineteenth-century philanthropist, had constantly exhorted MPs to make the short journey to visit the scenes of abject misery. Few bothered.

The grinding poverty which others ignored gave the Labour Party a significant presence in this right-wing stronghold in 1924. The Liberals were of little consequence, trailing hopelessly behind the other two parties in this by-election, one of the most remarkable of the period.

At the beginning of March 1924 when the campaign began, the first Labour government had been in office just over a month, following an indecisive general election. In a restless hung parliament, the balance of power lay with the Liberals, led by Asquith in uneasy association with Lloyd George. They used their votes to put Labour into office, gaining no concessions in return, a rather surprising feature of this deadlocked parliament.

For their part, the Tories under Stanley Baldwin accepted the Labour government with reasonably good grace, having lost their majority at the general election. It was obvious that Labour was in no position to launch a red revolution in Britain, even if they had wanted to. As they settled into their new roles, Ramsay MacDonald's ministers gave no sign that they minded in the slightest that they lacked the power to impose socialism on the country.

That did not stop Winston Churchill sounding the alarm in order to aid his career. He never did anything by halves. The alarm rang loudly. There was a red menace abroad, he warned, even if its full danger had not yet become apparent. The Labour government, he thundered, wanted to 'undermine the commercial and business activities of the country'. He called 'the enthronement in office of a Socialist Government a national misfortune such as has usually befallen great States only on the morrow of defeat in war'. No one should be in any doubt about the threat posed by 'the apparition of this Socialist monstrosity'.

Churchill, then aged forty-nine, was desperate to get out of the political wilderness where he had languished for well over a year. As an ex-Liberal Cabinet minister, he had been thrown out of his safe Dundee seat at the general election of November 1922, going down to another defeat as a Liberal in Leicester West in December 1923. ('From marmalade to ladies' underclothing,' Baldwin joked, referring to products prominently associated with the two constituencies.)

There was no place in the Liberal Party for the virulent anti-socialism which Churchill began to preach at the start of 1924 to revive his fortunes. His policy U-turn meant that he needed a new political home. He made urgent overtures to the Tory Party, which he had abandoned twenty years earlier when he had been one of its rising stars.

Though not all his colleagues agreed (some could not stand the sight of the turncoat), Baldwin was rather pleased to hear of this potential 're-ratting', in Churchill's well-known phrase, especially as the renegade said that he could get some thirty to fifty Liberal MPs to follow his example. Churchill was assured by the Tory leader that a safe seat would be found for him at the next general election. Some arrangement to bring over restive Liberal MPs might be possible in due course. Churchill must be patient.

Patience was not a virtue that this re-ratting politician possessed. Many rank-and-file Tories in the constituencies, delighting in Churchill's fierce anti-socialist rhetoric, saw no reason why he should be kept waiting. This view was prominent among members of the Westminster Abbey Constitutional Association, as the local Tory organisation was known. They invited Churchill to come and address them when in late February the death of their sitting member, Brigadier-General John Nicholson DSO, an undistinguished parliamentarian who had had a majority of over 11,000 at the last contested election in 1922, precipitated what was to become a momentous by-election. With unseemly haste, Churchill announced that he would fight the by-election on 22 February, the day after Nicholson's death.

Churchill made it absolutely plain that he would not call himself a Conservative. Surprisingly, that did not worry Conservative Central Office, which said he should be adopted, completely contrary to normal practice, on his own terms. Despite his earlier reluctance to move hastily, Baldwin did not demur. On 23 February, Churchill wrote to tell his wife that 'at Baldwin's suggestion I had a long talk with him yesterday of the friendliest character'. Conservative Central Office was 'working tooth and nail to secure me the support' of the local association. 'Of course if I stood as a Cons it wd almost certainly be a walk over.' But he wanted the votes of 'moderate Liberals' in the constituency as well, a not unreasonable hope even though he had burned his boats with the Liberal Party leadership but a totally unnecessary aspiration in a constituency of 40,000 electors where the Liberals had never polled more than just over 3,000 votes. Nevertheless, it was as an Independent and anti-socialist that he would stand.

All this careful planning was in vain. The local association would not have him. Its members, who loved a quarrel, had fallen out over the choice of candidates at previous elections. This time they split completely. On 3 March, Otho Nicholson, nephew of the former member with a family fortune based on gin, was adopted as the official Conservative candidate. The runner-up, John (later Sir John) Gatti, a senior local councillor and prominent theatre manager with a wide range of business interests, marched off with his supporters, who included the association chairman, to form a rival band of Tories to campaign for Churchill. Their candidate pledged 'to work effectively with the Conservative Party in resistance to the rapid advance of Socialism'.

Nicholson should withdraw, Churchill told Baldwin on 7 March, or at least be disowned by Central Office. 'I am sure that you do not wish to be compelled by technicalities to fire upon reinforcements I am bringing to your aid. Act now with decision, & we shall be able to work together in the national interest.' He adopted the arrogant tone of a man expecting to be obeyed.

Decisive action was impossible. Leading figures in the party copied the example of the Westminster Tories and took sides for and against

Churchill. 'I am afraid that turbulent, pushing busybody Winston is going to split our party,' William Bridgeman, recently Home Secretary, complained. 'I can't understand how anyone can want him or put any faith in a man who changes sides just when he thinks it is to his own personal advantage to do so.'

Others rushed to welcome him. Lord Wargrave, a former Tory MP, hailed him as 'the most brilliant recruit'. Philip Sassoon, a future junior minister, told him: 'I am so glad you are standing. You are bound to get in.' By 10 March, support for Churchill was being organised in all nine wards of the constituency by Conservative MPs.

Baldwin felt that he could do no more than stop members of his shadow Cabinet making the divisions worse. All invitations to speak either for Nicholson or Churchill must be resisted, he decreed. The official candidate did not even receive a letter of support from his leader. An exasperated ex-Cabinet minister, Leo Amery, furious about Churchill's attempt 'to create disruption in our Party for his own ends', wrote to Nicholson on 14 March. Churchill was incensed when the letter appeared in the press. Amery's 'public action against me' had broken Baldwin's 'self-denying policy'. He retaliated with a much bigger gun. A letter to Churchill from Arthur Balfour, the former Tory leader, went to the newspapers. It said: 'Your absence from the House of Commons at such a time is greatly to be deplored.'

Baldwin despaired. 'We had succeeded up to that moment in keeping our differences out of the papers, and now the enemy have had a glorious time.' He added that 'the issue is very open'. Some were prepared for the very worst. Lord Derby, former War Secretary, feared that Churchill 'may so split our vote that the Socialist will get in'.

That prospect was beyond the wildest dreams of the clever, impressive Labour candidate, Fenner Brockway, writer, pacifist and ardent advocate of the socialism against which Churchill ranted. He explained: 'When I was invited to contest the seat, I asked what was the chance of success. I was told none. My purpose was not to gain the seat, but to take up Mr Churchill's challenge to socialism.' This he did most effectively, aided by a series of articles in the Labour-supporting *Daily Herald* on 'wealthy Westminster's housing scandals', and vigorous canvassing which included the servants working in the royal palaces.

Brockway nearly tripled the Labour vote, taking it to within 2,000 of Churchill's total, a fine achievement which heartened MacDonald's government.

In the end, the issue was simple: could Churchill win enough Tory voters to beat the official Tory candidate into second place? He threw himself into the battle to get them with characteristic zest. By his own later account, people flocked to his standard from all quarters: 'Dukes, jockeys, prize-fighters, courtiers, actors and businessmen, all developed a keen partisanship. The chorus girls of Daly's Theatre sat up all night addressing envelopes and dispatching the election address.'

It recalled a bygone age when elections were fought with no holds barred. *The Times* described it as 'the most remarkable election known in Westminster since the Ballot Act [of 1872] did away with the hustings'. On 20 March, the day after polling, it reported:

> Visitors from the Continent arriving at Victoria may have been misled into thinking that a carnival rather than an election was in progress. Cars, decorated with heather, balloons, streamers and huge rosettes toured the streets; cheering children rode round in lorries and young men motored through the residential districts shouting appeals through megaphones to people in upper flats.

Churchill was pelted with turnips in Covent Garden. At an election meeting off the Strand, he 'buttoned his coat and remained with arms folded for five minutes while the audience booed and cheered'. Rowdiness sometimes led to fighting on the streets. Brendan Bracken, Churchill's hero-worshipping man of mystery from an Irish republican family who was put in charge of the campaign, got caught up in it and was stabbed, an incident recorded by Churchill's faithful detective, Inspector W. H. Thompson.

Were there dirty tricks? Labour thought so. An article in the *Socialist Standard* of April 1924 gave the (slightly far-fetched) details:

> During the closing days of the campaign, the newspapers reported that a motor-car, carrying the Labour Party placard, persistently followed Mr Churchill's car, and whenever he attempted to speak drowned his

voice with motor horns, rattles and shouting. The incident must have swung some hundreds of votes to Mr Churchill, as the 'waverers' in both Liberal and Tory camps would vote for him under these conditions, because he was not getting fair play. The Labour Party stated that the car was not officially connected with them, despite its labels. The suspicion arises that the hooligan car was run by Mr Churchill or his supporters.

As the last votes were being counted, someone told Churchill: 'You're in by a hundred.' This got to the press, which put out reports of victory. They were replaced by news of a narrow defeat when the result was officially declared. Overall, 8,144 had voted for Churchill, 8,187 for Nicholson. He had lost by forty-three votes. A prominent Labour supporter observed that Churchill 'wept unashamedly', which rather shocked him; it was the first time he had ever seen a man cry in public.

How regrettable it was, Lord Crawford, a former Conservative Cabinet minister, reflected, that 'the local association preferred the nonentity' as their candidate and turned down Churchill. 'What will his future be? I have no hesitation in saying that our party ought to find him a good place at any early election.' It did so. Eight months later, he was MP for the safe seat of Epping – and Baldwin's new Chancellor of the Exchequer.

Lord Lexden OBE *is a Conservative peer who writes and lectures on modern British political history. His most recent publication is* Horace Farquhar: A Bad Man Befriended by Kings *(Conservative History Group, 2023). His next work,* From Charles II to Margaret Thatcher: Essays in Conservative History, *will be published in 2026.*

23

SMETHWICK

21 DECEMBER 1926
LABOUR HOLD

JAMES BIRD

Result: Oswald Mosley (Labour), 16,077, 57.1 per cent; M. J. Pike (Conservative), 9,495, 33.7 per cent; Edwin Bayliss (Liberal), 2,600, 9.2 per cent
Size of majority: 6,582
Swing: 9.4 per cent from Conservative to Labour
Name of previous MP and party: John Davison (Labour)
Reason for by-election: Resignation due to ill health
Result at previous general election: John Davison (Labour), 14,491, 52.3 per cent; M. J. Pike (Conservative), 13,238, 47.7 per cent
Date by-election called: 6 December 1926
Date by-election took place: 21 December 1926
Size of total electorate: 35,864
Total number of votes cast: 28,172
Turnout: 78.6 per cent

Smethwick, on the outskirts of Birmingham in the West Midlands, has long been associated with having a turbulent political past. The toxic mix of industrial relations, racial integration and charismatic politicians have played a big role in Smethwick's reputation on the political landscape. But one campaign there in particular remains perhaps Smethwick's most significant political moment; the 1926 by-election that saw the renowned Oswald Mosley capitalise on the instability of the interwar years.

In the mid-1920s, many changes were coming together. Men over the age of twenty-one, and women above thirty, were now able to vote.

The returning soldiers from the First World War were promised a 'land fit for heroes' by the Liberal Prime Minister, David Lloyd George. However, the loss to foreign markets of the staple industries – coal, iron and steel, shipbuilding and cotton – led to a rapid rise in unemployment. The continued policy of deflation and consequent wage reductions led to major industrial unrest and political turmoil. In 1926, the General Strike was called.

It started as an industrial dispute between the miners and the mine owners over reduced pay for more hours of work. The National Union of Mineworkers (NUM) pushed the government to nationalise the mines. However, the Samuel Commission – established by the Conservative Baldwin government to resolve the deadlock – released its report in March 1926, omitting a recommendation for nationalisation. Instead, it proposed wage reductions and the nationalisation of royalties.

Miners then looked for, and received, support from other workers. When the Trades Union Congress (TUC) declared its support for the strike, other industrial workers, including those in road transport, rail, docks, electricity and gas, printers and iron and steel all walked out, and it became the first ever General Strike for Britain.

The strike lasted nine days, though the miners struggled on until November. The action secured no concessions, and the miners eventually returned to work with less money and more hours.

Enter Oswald Mosley and another opportunity to return to Parliament for an already well-established political figure.

Mosley was first elected as a Conservative in 1918 as the youngest sitting MP in the House at just twenty-one. He quickly established himself as a man noted for his speaking skills. As the *Westminster Gazette* said:

> Mosley is the most polished literary speaker in the Commons. Words flow from him in graceful epigrammatic phrases that have a sting in them for the government and the Conservatives. To listen to him is an education in the English language. Also in the art of delicate but deadly repartee.

But his tendency to criticise his own party made him unpopular on the

Tory benches. He opposed the violence of the Black and Tans in Ireland, intervention in Russia and cuts to housing programmes under the Geddes Acts. Disillusioned, he crossed the floor and sat as an Independent in 1920 and was re-elected as an Independent in the 1922 and 1923 elections.

The December 1923 election only exacerbated political instability, producing a hung parliament. Labour cobbled together a minority government under Ramsay MacDonald with the support of a fractious Liberal Party.

Mosley began to view the Labour Party more favourably, and in March 1924, he joined their ranks. MacDonald welcomed him enthusiastically. The Labour Party was in desperate need of a boost to its image, and they believed that having an aristocrat like Mosley on their side would lend them the respectability they sought.

In less than a year, however, that government fell apart. In the subsequent general election, Mosley stood against Neville Chamberlain in Birmingham Ladywood. The contest was razor-thin – he lost by just seventy-seven votes. This narrow defeat was partly due to accusations that the Labour Party had become a 'Red' organisation, under the influence of the Communist Party.

That election, indeed that decade, marked the decline of the Liberal Party, which won only forty seats in 1924 compared to 401 in 1906. Squeezed between Labour and Conservatives, it would see these two parties go on to dominate politics thereafter.

Out of the Commons, Mosley remained a significant force and became a figurehead of the 1926 General Strike. He toured the country. He made generous donations to miners. He led the most significant protest during the strike: a two-mile procession across Birmingham on May Day. The *Birmingham Gazette* said 15,000 to 25,000 people followed Mosley from Victoria Square to Ward End to hear his address on the justice of the miners' cause.

Then, in the region where he had forged a new celebrity for himself, the most fortunate of opportunities came to Oswald Mosley. A by-election was called for 21 December 1926, caused by the resignation of Smethwick's Labour Party MP John Davison. He had represented the constituency since its creation in 1918 but resigned over ill health. Davison would die the following year.

The main parties sought to get their candidates in place quickly. Before the date of the by-election was called, the Conservative association adopted Marshall James Pike on 1 December. At thirty-one years of age, and the son of a miner, he had joined the 2nd Battalion, South Staffordshire Regiment, at the outbreak of the war. He was in the retreat from Mons when he lost an arm in Ypres. He had contested the Smethwick seat at the previous general election in 1923.

On the same evening, the Liberal association adopted Edwin Bayliss as its candidate, the first Liberal to stand in the seat since its creation in 1918.

Mosley's path to selection was more complicated than perhaps it should have been. Having been nominated by the local association to contest the seat for Labour, the fact that his nomination was being made without any reference to the national executive was an infringement of party rules. Labour politicians complained. It was pounced on by the press. They saw it as the Labour Party being split on Mosley's candidacy.

A special deputation was sent from Labour HQ to Smethwick to resolve the matter, with the Smethwick executive agreeing to a readoption meeting in which Oswald Mosley would be the only nominee.

At the council house on Friday 10 December, nominations for the three candidates were received by the Mayor of Smethwick, councillor Frank Jones. By pure chance, the candidates visited the council house at the same time and were introduced to each other by the mayor, whereby they were reported as spending a considerable amount of time chatting together about any other subject in the world other than the by-election.

The strategy for both sides was clear from the outset. Mosley, whom Conservative Prime Minister Stanley Baldwin described as 'a cad and wrong 'un', doubled down on the government policy of deflation, consequent wage reductions and unemployment which had led to strikes and major industrial unrest and placed the blame squarely at Baldwin and the government's door.

The Conservatives sought to emphasise Mosley's aristocratic background, looking to place him at odds with the Smethwick electorate, highlighting his wealth, holidays in Venice and bringing his glamorous wife Lady Cynthia into the fray – claiming she had a taste for fur, dresses and jewels. The *Daily Express* said he was 'playing the part well', suggesting he was pretending at being a socialist by wearing 'an old overcoat and battered hat and calling Lady Cynthia "the missus"'. They also questioned his ties with Russia.

Mosley pounced early in the campaign when Prime Minister Baldwin was alleged to have said 'that all wages would have to come down'. The following day, large posters attributing the statement to the Prime Minister were put out by the socialists across Smethwick. The posters contained the words 'Mr Oswald Mosley says that higher wages lead to prosperity: lower wages lead to ruin'.

This put the Conservatives on the back foot. Baldwin was forced to write a letter to *The Times*, entitled the 'Power of Trade Unions', where he denied the accusation, instead saying that 'I have always believed, that wages should be as high as industry can bear'. Baldwin grimly warned the country that the men who will bring wages down are the men who are trying to ruin industry by waging the socialist class war.

The press kept coming back to Mosley's background. Beaverbrooks's *Daily Express* published a special interview with Mosley's father, in which he underlined everything the Conservatives were seeking to show about Mosley.

'I could never understand the line my son has taken,' he said.

He was born with a gold spoon in his mouth – it cost £100 in doctor's fees to bring him into the world. He lived on the fat of the land and never did a day's labour in his life. If he and his wife want go in for Labour, why don't they do a bit of work themselves, or why doesn't Lady Cynthia sell her pearls for the good of the Smethwick poor?

The crossfire on rhetoric was matched with disorder during the campaign, occasionally turning violent. In his first public meeting, Conservative candidate Pike was shouted down by a considerable number of men at the back of the room, before moving to another meeting held at Brasshouse Lane School where it was reported by *The Times* that a number of socialists were determined to prevent him being heard.

One notorious event saw Mosley and the Conservative candidate exchanging unparliamentary language. Pike was holding a rally when Mosley happened to drive by. Both camps exchanged more unpleasantries, before Mosley sprang out of his car, pushed through the crowd and tried to climb onto the running board of Pike's car. Mosley was hustled off, retreating to his supporters before the meeting broke up in disorder.

The event got so heated, a Conservative reserve speaker, one Mrs Laws, suffered two broken ribs when she got separated from her supporters.

Away from Pike and Mosley, the Liberal candidate Edwin Bayliss found himself squeezed in the middle. He was described by Mosley as like an old play actor interfering in the struggle of two strong armies by standing on his head in no man's land. Bayliss – who was twice injured in the war – took offence, but none of his followers could hold any hope of being anywhere other than at the bottom of the poll.

And then, the former Prime Minister and Labour leader Ramsay MacDonald came to campaign for Mosley on the Saturday before the vote. Addressing a crowd estimated at tens of thousands in Victoria Park, he dismissed Liberalism as a serious factor in modern-day politics. A Liberal rally nearby secured less than a hundred people.

As the campaign was coming to a close, the Prime Minister's own family would provide a headache for the Conservatives. In what was described as a 'piquant' situation by the *Sunday Mercury*, Baldwin's socialist son Oliver spoke in support of Mosley. Miss Betty Baldwin, the daughter of the Prime Minister, was noted as supporting the Conservative candidate. An embarrassment for Baldwin to have the family split, it would underpin Mosley's credentials.

When election day came, Mosley increased the Labour majority from 1,253 in the 1924 general election to 6,582.

The Liberal candidate lost his deposit of £150, having failed to take one-eighth of the total votes cast. A crowd of around 4,000 people waited for several hours for the result, singing 'The Red Flag' and Christmas carols.

Interviewed after the count, Mosley described the result as a decisive struggle between Labour and 'pressocracy' in which Labour had triumphed, demanding the resignation of the government. Pike blamed the loss on having to contend with systematic rowdyism and the notorious wages 'lie' which was 'very skilfully exploited by the Socialists'.

The by-election in the short term enabled Mosley to establish himself as a Labour star. He was re-elected in 1929 and helped to secure a Labour-led government; the first time Labour had the most seats in Parliament. His oratory skills, the glamour of his wife Lady Cynthia and his charm added to his political allure and helped give credibility to this new Labour administration.

Mosley was given the non-Cabinet post of Chancellor of the Duchy of Lancaster. Encouraged to bring bright ideas by Prime Minister Ramsay MacDonald, he presented forward-looking job creation and road-building schemes. But all of his ideas were buried by the rest of the Cabinet.

In the end, Mosley became so frustrated that he resigned his ministerial position and began the process of moving out of the Labour Party and his journey to fascism. Mosley said of his resignation: 'I felt quite simply that if I lent myself any longer to this cynical holoclone, I should be betraying completely the people to whom we had given solemn pledges to deal with the unemployment problem.'

In strife, Mosley saw more opportunity. The impact of the Great Depression, and the lack of progress on unemployment, led to him setting up the New Party, which was crushed in the 1931 election. He then launched the British Union of Fascists (BUF) in 1932, blending his economic programme with antisemitism. He led marches in working-class areas seeking to gain support, notably the East End, tapping into local resentment against Jewish landlords and small business owners.

In the late 1930s, his links to fascism developed further, being on friendly terms with Mussolini while getting married to Diana Mitford (his second wife) at the home of Nazi Propaganda Minister Joseph Goebbels. Hitler was a guest of honour.

Viewed as a suspected enemy sympathiser and potential head of a pro-German puppet regime if the Nazis invaded the UK, Mosley was imprisoned in May 1940. He was released in 1943. Disgraced by his fascist ties, Mosley later moved abroad, although briefly returned to the political fray standing for the Union Movement in the 1959 and 1966 general elections in London seats. He died in France on 3 December 1980.

The Smethwick by-election of 1926 had grit, violence and glamour. It was at the centre point of a shift in British politics, signalling the decline of Liberal influence and the rise of Labour in industrial areas, solidifying the foundation of today's two-party system. Mosley's tactics and rhetoric, his force of personality, played a crucial role in Labour's ascent to the largest party in Westminster for the first time.

With Mosley in the mix, more radical policies began to gain traction within Labour, setting the stage for debates that would shape the party for years to come. For Mosley himself, one of the twentieth century's most enigmatic and controversial figures, the Smethwick campaign provided the comeback and attention he sought. It established him as a prominent player in national politics, while also lending visibility – and a troubling credibility – to the demagoguery that would follow. Despite his ambitions, Mosley's frustration ultimately led him down a more obscure path – an ironic twist for someone once tipped as a potential leader of both Labour and the Conservatives. A compelling 'what might have been'.

James Bird is a corporate affairs professional, former Birmingham City councillor and two-time Conservative parliamentary candidate, offering extensive expertise in strategic communications and political campaigning.

24

WESTMINSTER ST GEORGE'S

19 MARCH 1931
CONSERVATIVE HOLD

SIR ROBERT BUCKLAND

Result: Alfred Duff Cooper (Conservative), 17,242, 59.9 per cent; Ernest Petter (Independent Conservative), 11,532, 40.1 per cent
Size of majority: 5,710
Swing: N/A
Name of previous MP and party: Laming Worthington-Evans (Conservative/Unionist)
Reason for by-election: Death of incumbent
Result at previous general election: Laming Worthington-Evans (Conservative), 22,448, 78.1 per cent; Joseph George Butler (Labour), 6,294, 21.9 per cent
Date by-election called: 6 March 1931
Date by-election took place: 19 March 1931
Size of total electorate: 54,188
Total number of votes cast: 28,774
Turnout: 53.1 per cent

The outcome of the short, sharp 1931 by-election at Westminster St George's was the deciding factor as to whether the Leader of the Opposition and Tory leader since 1923, Stanley Baldwin, would remain in charge. Although the rival candidates were themselves people of note, the contest was really one between Baldwin in one corner and the press barons Lords Beaverbrook and Rothermere in the other.

The constituency itself lay at the heart of London. Originally known as St George Hanover Square from its creation as a seat with the boundaries of that civil parish in 1885, in 1918 it was expanded and renamed Westminster St George's, consisting of the Hanover Square area, Mayfair, several royal parks and Buckingham Palace, Knightsbridge, part of South Kensington and all of Belgravia, Victoria and Pimlico.

Other than a surprise result in a 1921 by-election orchestrated by Rothermere, the seat had been held for decades by Conservatives or Liberal Unionists with enormous vote shares, usually about 75–80 per cent. The complete extension of the vote to women in the 1920s did not see any change in this trend. The denizens of the drawing rooms and salons of Mayfair and Belgravia, not to mention their male and female household servants, could be relied upon to support the Tory cause. This by-election was one of the first to be held after universal suffrage, and it was also one of the first to be a significant media event.

The sitting MP since the 1929 general election, whose death on 14 February 1931 caused the by-election, was Sir Laming Worthington-Evans, known as 'Worthy', who had been in the Commons since 1910. At the 1929 election, he had abandoned his Colchester seat to seek election for St George's. His career matched his nickname. It was impressive but not well remembered. A solicitor by training, he was a junior minister in Lloyd George's wartime coalition government and then entered the Cabinet as Minister of Pensions in 1919. Most notably, he served as Secretary of State for War until the fall of the coalition in 1922 and then, after a brief stint as Postmaster General from 1923 to the fall of Baldwin's first government in January 1924, he returned to the War Office for the duration of the 1924 to 1929 second Baldwin government. In 1929, Sir Laming had won with 78.1 per cent of the vote. Even in a bad year, St George's was the safest Tory seat in the country in that parliament.

The background to the by-election within the Tory Party could hardly have been worse. Bad feeling over the question of Dominion status for India, plus a perception that Baldwin was more interested in other things led Sir Robert Topping, general director of Conservative Central Office, to write a memorandum to the party chairman, Neville Chamberlain, outlining dissatisfaction with Baldwin in all sections of the party. With the economic situation darkening, Baldwin had already indicated to the king's new private secretary, Ralph Wigram, that if the Labour Prime Minister Ramsay MacDonald resigned, all Baldwin could offer was a dissolution of Parliament because he could not have formed a government. Chamberlain, who had an eye on the leadership himself, consulted some senior colleagues about the Topping memorandum. They were virtually unanimous that Baldwin should go.

On 1 March, Baldwin was sent the memorandum and decided that he would resign. One of his old allies and supporters, former Home Secretary and First Lord of the Admiralty Lord Bridgeman, strongly opposed Baldwin's resignation and, arriving at Baldwin's house that evening, told him to stand fast and even contest the by-election himself. This resulted in a U-turn. Baldwin summoned Chamberlain, who came to see him on the morning of 2 March wholly expecting Baldwin to resign but instead was faced with Baldwin's new plan, much to the surprise and consternation of his most likely successor. It was Chamberlain who ended up relinquishing the party chairmanship and it was Baldwin who then managed to enlist a willing volunteer.

Enter Alfred Duff Cooper. Duff, whose father was the noted society doctor Sir Alfred Cooper and whose mother, Lady Agnes Duff, was a descendant of one of William IV's illegitimate children, was educated at Eton and New College, Oxford, before entering the Foreign Service in 1913 and was released for military service in 1917, being awarded the DSO for conspicuous gallantry in the advance to the Albert Canal in August 1918. His marriage to the beautiful, clever and quirky Lady Diana Manners in 1919 was opposed by the Rutland family, on the grounds that Duff had no money and lived the life of a promiscuous gambler that was consciously modelled on that of Charles James Fox. It was only through earnings made by Diana on the London stage that Duff was able to enter the Commons in 1924 when he was elected at Oldham, the old seat of his close friend Winston Churchill.

Duff was made Financial Secretary at the War Office in early 1928, working closely with Worthington-Evans as his Secretary of State, who allowed Duff to shoulder much of the burden. Duff lost Oldham in the 1929 general election defeat for the Tories but healed his wounds by writing an acclaimed biography of Talleyrand. Duff had been selected as candidate for Winchester by 1930 and had been nursing it assiduously, but on 28 February 1931, the original Tory candidate for St George's, John Moore-Brabazon, withdrew because he could no longer support Baldwin.

Brabazon's withdrawal from the by-election contest meant that Baldwin had considered resigning his seat at Bewdley and fighting St George's himself, but Duff Cooper's name was suggested by Geoffrey Dawson, editor of *The Times*, to Baldwin, who liked the idea that Duff, who was a great speaker and campaigner, would fly the flag for his leader. Baldwin and Duff could see that this was now a matter of principle: did the Conservative Party choose its own leaders or were they governed by the barons of the press? Duff decided to seek selection for St George's and promptly told his friend Lord Beaverbrook, who tried to dissuade him as he was sure that Duff would lose.

Max Aitken, Lord Beaverbrook, was a controversial figure to say the least. A Canadian by birth and upbringing, he achieved his great wealth via interests in engineering, banking and some newspapers, but he made his initial fortune through his involvement with a cement production enterprise and a company merger process that seemed highly dubious at the time. Arriving in Britain in the 1900s, his rise through the ranks of public life was dramatic, despite the opposition of King George V, thanks to the favour of Andrew Bonar Law and Lloyd George. He became an MP in 1910, was knighted and then awarded a peerage and Cabinet role during the Great War. By the early 1930s, his *Daily Express* was the largest mass-circulation newspaper in the world, selling 2.25 million copies a day.

For much of his life, Beaverbrook had campaigned for Empire Free Trade and, indeed, a fiscal union between Britain and the Dominions. He had formed an unlikely alliance with the man who should have been his greatest rival: Lord Rothermere.

Harold Harmsworth, Viscount Rothermere, was one of thirteen children, many of whom achieved remarkable feats, most notably his elder brother Lord Northcliffe, who founded the *Daily Mail* and with whom he owned Associated Newspapers. Like his brother, Rothermere was prone to severe mood swings and was innately sceptical and pessimistic about the future of the country. Like Beaverbrook, the king disliked him intensely. Rothermere was virulently anti-Baldwin and the 'one-nation' Conservative tradition.

By 1930, after a ridiculous demand in a letter from Rothermere after the 1929 election that he should have a right of veto over Baldwin's Cabinet appointments to secure the support of the *Daily Mail*, he and Beaverbrook set up the United Empire Party. Unlike Beaverbrook, Rothermere viewed Empire Free Trade as a useful pretext for fermenting discontent and unrest within Tory MPs and among the membership in order to remove the party leader. Baldwin responded strongly by publicly exposing Rothermere's veto demand and won the support of Conservative MPs in two leadership polls that year.

In a run of by-elections, independent Conservative candidates who were backed by Beaverbrook and Rothermere in the name of the 'Empire Free Trade Campaign' had been performing strongly at the ballot box and indeed won a by-election at Fulham in 1930, and this by-election presented the press lords with a golden opportunity to unseat Baldwin, who they hated, as leader of the Conservative Party. With the right wing of the Tory Party in ferment over the question of Dominion status for India, it was proving difficult to attract a Conservative candidate. The Empire Free Trade candidate, Sir Ernest Petter, who enjoyed the full backing of the *Daily Mail* and the *Daily Express*, was proving too much of a threat for potential Tory candidates.

Sir Ernest was a very different character from Duff Cooper. Born in Yeovil in 1873 with an identical twin and thirteen other siblings, Petter went to local schools and then to Mount Radford School in Exeter, later to see a young Tommy Cooper within its walls. Petter left school at seventeen and, apprenticed to his father and working with his twin brother Percy, built the Petter Horseless Carriage in 1895, the first British motor car with a top speed of twelve miles per hour. After a few years' manufacturing small motor carriages, he and his brother moved into industrial and agricultural engine production, bought the company from their father and built James B. Petter & Sons into a major British engine manufacturing company. In 1915, the Petters set up Westland Aircraft Works at Yeovil, building military aircraft. Westland was eventually spun off twenty years later and we remember it as a major helicopter manufacturer whose future became caught up in a famous political crisis in 1986.

Petter was knighted in 1925 as he had been a commissioner of the hugely successful British Empire Exhibition of the previous year. A former president of the British Engineers Association, he was also involved in politics and stood twice as a Conservative for Parliament just after the end of the First World War. By the time of the by-election, Sir Ernest was disenchanted with the leadership of Stanley Baldwin and so was a ready recruit to the Beaverbrook/Rothermere bandwagon.

The constituency was not easy to canvass, as political meetings had to compete with the attractions of the West End and there was no good time to canvass busy domestic servants. Cooper's worry was that the only newspapers that servants would see were the *Express* or *Mail* in the mornings and then the anti-Baldwin *Evening News* or *Standard* in the afternoon. Nonetheless, many great houses started to sport posters either for Duff or Petter, and there were open-air meetings in places like Bond Street and Grosvenor Square. After a disturbing report from a Tory canvasser that a butler in Mayfair had said he was voting for *Sir* Ernest as he was a gentleman rather than *Mr* Cooper, 'who had been a clerk and in a foreign office too', friendly newspapers referred to the Conservative candidate as 'Duff Cooper DSO'.

Thanks to the involvement of Lady Diana Cooper and her sister-in-law 'Kakoo', Duchess of Rutland, the campaign acquired an eighteenth-century air, with echoes of another famous Westminster election campaign when Georgiana, the Duchess of Devonshire, traded kisses for votes in the 1780s. Lord Ashfield had laid on a car for the Coopers, with a fresh white camellia to pin in Diana's cap each day. Diana was booked for a series of meetings, where she read messages from Duff, adding her own idiosyncratic interjections.

Every evening after campaigning, the Coopers and their supporters enjoyed hot soup and other restoratives at Lady Stanley's in Grosvenor Street, Lady Juliet Duff's in Belgrave Square or Londonderry House in the heart of the constituency, which Duff described in his memoirs as a 'fortress of generous hospitality and loyal support'.

In an interesting move, Elizabeth, Duchess of York, who was close to Kakoo Rutland and whose 145 Piccadilly address meant that she was a constituent but prevented by convention from voting, instead sent a busload of servants up from Royal Lodge at Windsor to help with Duff's campaign and demonstrated her strong feelings about the matter by dropping an election leaflet from Sir Ernest that had been inexplicably delivered to the Yorks' house into her wastepaper basket.

It was not a calm campaign. Lord Castlerosse, the dissipated side-kick to Beaverbrook, threatened to evict Lady Castlerosse from their house in Cheyne Row if she displayed a Duff poster in their window. Undeterred, she put one on their motor car. Frankly, that was a better option, bearing in mind the fact that Chelsea was not even in the constituency! Empire Free Trade vans toured the patch, no doubt urging butlers, footmen and parlour maids to vote for *Sir* Ernest.

In one lively meeting at the Grosvenor Gallery, the doughty dowager Duchess of Rutland had to take refuge under a table as chairs were thrown around the hall. Tory supporter Emerald, Lady Cunard, would go early to public meetings and took to sitting ostentatiously in the front row reading the *Daily Telegraph* or *The Star*, which of course were rival newspapers to those of Beaverbrook and Rothermere, and would mutter 'degenerates, they're both degenerates' every time those press barons were mentioned. In return, Rothermere's *London Evening News* carried the banner headline with the improbable assertion: 'Gandhi is Watching St George's'.

It was Baldwin, however, who dominated proceedings. Conservative Central Office swung into action, with 132 messages of support for the leader from local associations across the country. In a direct attempt to appeal to Liberal voters who had no candidate, the Liberal peers Crewe, Grey and Reading issued a statement condemning the irresponsibility of 'amateur politicians' seeking to mislead readers by weapons of distortion and suppression. How familiar this message sounds today! By contrast, Petter failed to woo the Liberal vote by refusing to provide a statement to the local branch of the League of Nations Union because he said he was too busy. This was to prove costly, bearing in mind the importance of the 'peace' vote at that time.

There was also a helpful development in India, with Gandhi calling off the civil disobedience campaign because of a compromise with Viceroy Lord Irwin (Edward Wood, later Earl of Halifax). Baldwin's Commons speech a week before poll on 12 March welcoming progress in India was seen as a strong performance by Tory MPs, helping to calm things considerably within the party.

Then, at Queen's Hall on 17 March, Baldwin gave the finest speech of his political career. As protesters paraded up and down outside, with sandwich boards saying, 'A Vote for Duff Cooper is a Vote for Gandhi', Baldwin excelled. Borrowing a memorable phrase from his first cousin and friend Rudyard Kipling, he described Beaverbrook and Rothermere as seeking 'power without responsibility, the prerogative of the harlot throughout the ages'. Lady Diana Cooper described the 'reporters … jumping out of their skins to a man' when Baldwin uttered those scathing words.

Election day came two days later. Lord Beaverbrook continued to telephone Lady Diana regularly throughout the campaign, although it was only on the day itself that he conceded defeat to her. In her view, Beaverbrook never quite forgave Duff, however.

The emphatic victory meant an early return to the Commons (flanked by Baldwin himself as one of his sponsors) for Cooper, who, at the age of forty-one, was to return to the War Office as Secretary of State and then to the Admiralty as First Lord, before resigning over the Munich Agreement and later joining the Churchill government in various roles, before going to Paris as ambassador in 1944. He was ennobled as Viscount Norwich and died at sea in 1954.

Westminster St George's marked the end of the United Empire Party and was the moment when Baldwin's leadership was secured. In many ways, this by-election was really an internal quarrel between the various parts of the Tory Party, as the Labour government increasingly struggled with the effects of the economic slump and dramatically increased unemployment.

This led to the seismic events of the economic crisis of late summer 1931, the formation of a National government and Baldwin's continued political influence and leadership for much of the 1930s. Just as today we face distortions and misinformation from unaccountable social media owners, the press barons of those years tried to wield similar power. By unifying around their leader and resisting the siren calls of right-wing populists, the Tory Party was able to come back to power swiftly. This is a most valuable lesson for today.

Rt Hon. Sir Robert Buckland KBE KC *was Conservative MP for South Swindon from 2010–24, Solicitor General 2014–19, Minister of State for*

Prisons and Probation 2019, Lord Chancellor and Secretary of State for Justice 2019–21 and Secretary of State for Wales 2022. He is Third Church Estates Commissioner, senior counsel and head of policy at Payne Hicks Beach LLP, a barrister at Foundry Chambers and a member of the DAC Beachcroft Policy Unit. Robert was the Conservative candidate in the 1995 Islwyn by-election.

FULHAM EAST

25 OCTOBER 1933
LABOUR GAIN FROM CONSERVATIVES

T. G. OTTE

Result: John Wilmot (Labour), 17,790, 57.9 per cent; William J. Waldron (Conservative), 12,950, 42.1 per cent
Size of majority: 4,840
Swing: 29.2 per cent from Conservative to Labour
Name of previous MP and party: Kenyon Vaughan-Morgan (Conservative)
Reason for by-election: Death of incumbent
Result at previous general election: Kenyon Vaughan-Morgan (Conservative), 23,498, 68.7 per cent; John Maynard (Labour), 8,917, 26.1 per cent; John Greenwood (Liberals), 1,788, 5.2 per cent
Date by-election called: 9 October 1933
Date by-election took place: 25 October 1933
Size of total electorate: 51,644
Total number of votes cast: 30,740.
Turnout: 59.5 per cent

General elections, Lewis Namier once suggested, are 'locks in the stream of British democracy, controlling the flow of the river and its traffic'. By-elections have a similar function. They are minor sluices that sometimes divert, frequently slow down and occasionally speed up the craft that ply their trade on that stream.

The Fulham East by-election of 1933 affected the flow of politics in a number of ways. In the first place, it was a stupendous victory by the opposition Labour candidate over a Conservative who stood for the

(Tory-dominated) National government that had taken office after the break-up of Ramsay MacDonald's minority administration during the financial emergency two years previously. The successful candidate, John Wilmot, overturned a Unionist majority of 14,521, the largest such feat until Eric Lubbock's success at Orpington in 1962. The swing from the Conservatives to Labour was 29.2 per cent, the biggest until the 1967 Hamilton by-election (there have been larger swings since, of course). At 26.6 per cent, the drop in support for the incumbent was the largest until the 1948 Glasgow Camlachie by-election, and the corresponding increase in Labour's vote share of 31.8 per cent was not bettered until the Liberals' defeat of the Conservatives at Sutton & Cheam in 1972.

It was not the scale of Labour's victory but a broader interpretation that was put on the result which turned Fulham East into a national event — and, it has been suggested, into a 'political myth'. It soon came to be seen as a manifestation of popular pacifism and hence a constraint on the government in its dealings with foreign dictators. 'You will remember the election at Fulham,' said Stanley Baldwin, by now Prime Minister, in the House of Commons on 12 November 1936, 'when the seat which the National Government held was lost by about 7,000 [*sic*] votes on no issue but the pacifist ... That was the feeling in the country in 1933.' It would have been impossible for the government to ignore that sentiment: 'Had the Government, with this great majority, used that majority to do anything that might be described as arming without a mandate ... it would have defeated entirely the end it had in view.' Baldwin's first biographer even claimed that 'the nerve injured in October 1933, the East Fulham nerve, never quite healed'.

Whatever the Fulham effect on the Tory leader's outwardly usually stolid disposition, Baldwin's statement is problematic on a number of counts. For one thing, at 4,840 votes (or 15.8 per cent), the margin of defeat was less startling. More importantly, there was no single issue but a range of factors that affected the result of the Fulham contest. This, then, raises the questions of why he — and others — suggested otherwise and how their version came to be accepted.

But first a word on the constituency itself. Unlike neighbouring Chelsea, it was a predominantly working-class district, although there was also a fairly large residential element in the Barons Court and West

Kensington areas. It contained a considerable number of factories, workshops and wharves along the river, but like many London divisions, this was a 'dormitory' constituency. Prior to the First World War, its large artisan population consisted in many cases of men employed in the building industry, by definition a transient population, constantly on the move in search of work, and so difficult to organise and mobilise. The character of the district had changed somewhat in that there were now many railway workers in it but also, as the borough medical officer observed in 1930, 'a good sprinkling of "black-coated" [i.e. clerical] workers'.

By 1933, the effects of the global depression had reached the constituency. Unemployment was high. In January, the unemployment rate stood at 13.9 per cent, dropping to 9.4 per cent by October, significantly lower than the national average, which reached 25 per cent at the beginning of the year, and a far cry from the desperate situation in some of the industrial heartlands, such as the Rhondda where four in ten people were out of work. Unemployment was marginally lower in Fulham than in other boroughs in the capital (the average for the year was 11.9 per cent). The local building trade, however, was hard hit, hard enough for the mayor of the borough to appeal to residents to spend their savings on home improvements to put local people back to work.

The appeal did little to address the most pressing issue in Fulham: an acute shortage of affordable housing. The cubic space per person failed to reach even the low standards set by London County Council byelaws. Overcrowding – a direct consequence of poverty – had eased by 1933 on account of the new housing scheme at Fulham Court, but there were still just under 3,000 dwellings condemned as not fit for human habitation. Since the Conservative candidate was closely involved with housing, the issue gained particular salience during the by-election.

The constituency was established in 1918 when the old Fulham division was split into two, and it had been held by the Conservatives ever since. Unionism, in fact, had a strong presence in the district for decades. Only once before, in the Liberal landslide of 1906, had the Tories lost Fulham. Between 1885 and 1910, their candidates won on average 53.9 per cent of the vote, a fairly comfortable margin by the standards of Victorian and Edwardian politics and a reflection of the strength of Conservatism among the local shopkeepers and clerks. That strength remained unabated. The party's average share of the vote between 1918 and 1931 was 58.2 per cent, significantly higher than before 1910. But this fact disguises a more complicated situation. It may be argued, in fact, that the party's long local hegemony came to an end at the general election of 1923, when it secured only 43.9 per cent of the vote, still enough to retain the seat with a majority of 2,074 (9.4 per cent) but far less comfortably than the 49.9 and 36.5 per cent margins in the elections of 1918 and 1922. The result in 1929 confirmed that trend, the Conservatives holding on by 1,705 votes (or 4.9 per cent). In many respects, the two subsequent general elections of 1924 and 1931 were exceptions to this trend. In the former, in a backlash against the experiment of a Liberal-tolerated Labour minority administration, the Conservative vote rose to pre-1923 levels (61.6 per cent); and in 1931, under the extraordinary circumstances of that summer, it reached 68.7 per cent, though this was still below the 69.4 per cent the party had won in 1918. The Conservatives' position in the constituency, then, was more precarious than the bald numbers of the 'freak' 1931 election might suggest. Against this weakening of Unionist allegiances stood the steady rise in Labour's vote, from 2,883 (19.5 per cent) in 1918 to 13,425 (39.4 per cent) in 1929. Even in 1924, the party increased its tally; only in 1931 did it lose votes (at 13.3 per cent this was a larger swing against Labour than the national average, as was – and is – so often the case in London).

The Liberals still had a significant presence at Fulham, their vote share rising from 11.1 per cent in 1918 to 21.6 per cent in 1923. The local organisation appears to have been in decline, however, and the party did not contest the 1924 election. It still managed to win 16.3 per cent in 1929 but only 5.2 per cent in 1931. Although a now much diminished force locally, the presence or absence of a Liberal candidate could make a difference.

This was the case in 1933, and it was a contributing factor to the Tory defeat. Prior to deciding whether to field a candidate, local Liberal leaders sent questionnaires to the other two candidates, seeking their views on a range of political questions, including disarmament, free trade and the representation of minorities. The Labour candidate engaged with this process; the Conservative did not. The former's answers were judged to be satisfactory, and the Liberals urged their voters to support Labour. This was perhaps no great surprise since Lloyd George, the leader of the rump-Liberals, had appealed to his supporters in early 1933 to vote Labour whenever there was no free trade candidate. However, even if all 5,551 voters who had voted Liberal in 1929 had gone over to Labour (an absurdly improbable proposition), it would not have given Labour a majority.

The Liberals' questionnaire nevertheless speaks to another crucial aspect of the by-election: the professionalism of Labour's candidate and its local organisation. Wilmot was a Woolwich-born war veteran in his late thirties who had cut his teeth in Lewisham local politics before being adopted as the party's parliamentary candidate for Fulham East (he was later to become a minister in the Attlee government). A perceptive election postmortem in the *Glasgow Herald* (no natural Labour supporter) noted that he was 'a strong candidate who made a good impression at every meeting, and [who] was in truth a formidable opponent'.

The same could not be said of alderman William J. Waldron, the Conservative candidate, who despite his nearly three decades in local politics proved an unimpressive campaigner. There were allegations – unproven and probably untruthful – that he profited from excessive rents. More significantly, he received little active support from Conservative Central Office, where he was suspected of harbouring die-hard views on India and of not being sufficiently sympathetic to the party's official embrace of protectionism. This mattered all the more because the local party organisation had fallen into disrepair, Fulham Tories having relied on the undoubted popularity of the late MP Sir Kenyon Vaughan-Morgan to see them through. By contrast, the local Labour organisation was impressive, as one of its later MPs, the future Foreign Secretary Michael Stewart, recalled in his memoirs. The contest now provided an opportunity for 'a concentrated Labour attack', noted the *Glasgow Herald*'s political correspondent. The party flooded the constituency with canvassers from all over London: 'Meetings were held at almost every street corner ... while placards were displayed

everywhere. The other side could not compete with this powerful electioneering machinery.' Ironically, the newly built Fulham Court Estate,
designed to ease overcrowding in the borough, served as 'a new field for
recruitment of Labour supporters'.

An uninspiring candidate and a ramshackle local party are serious
handicaps, but they are not necessarily decisive. What issues, then,
mattered to the voters at Fulham East? In the absence of polling and
other survey data, answers to this question must remain hypothetical.
We simply cannot know for certain what made individual voters cast
their ballot for a particular candidate. It is, however, possible to draw
conclusions about likely motivating factors on the basis of the issues
prioritised by the candidates. They would, after all, not have done so
had they not thought that these had some traction with voters.

Domestic issues indisputably played a prominent role. Although
London was more shielded from the fall-out of the Depression, and
although conditions in the capital were improving in 1933, there was
an all-pervasive atmosphere of gloom. The Labour campaign naturally focused on social discontent, just as it had done in other by-
elections in 1932 and 1933. The acute shortage of affordable homes was
an acknowledged source of local discontent, and the fact that the Tory
candidate was an alderman and a landlord was an open invitation for
some Labour muckraking. Neville Chamberlain, then Chancellor of
the Exchequer, lost 'not ... a minute's sleep over it', as he confessed to
his sister Ida after the election:

> The press put it all down to Housing and lies about war. Both no
> doubt were factors but I heard yesterday from a friend who had been
> talking to a speaker (street corner) from Fulham what I had suspected
> all along, that the real attack was on the means test.

What about the 'lies about war'? Eleven days before polling day, Adolf
Hitler announced that Germany would withdraw from the Geneva
Disarmament Conference and then leave the League of Nations altogether. According to the *Glasgow Herald*'s analysis, this event produced
a 'psychological effect' that was 'the greatest element in the [Conserv-
ative] defeat'. The reasons for this are not difficult to fathom. The true

nature of the Hitler regime and its ideological aspirations were only imperfectly understood by many in Britain at the time. More important was a conviction which had taken root that the arms races before 1914 had plunged Europe into world war. It was a somewhat crude view, and modern historians have developed a more nuanced understanding of the matter, but in the 1920s and 1930s, it drove demands for some form of arms control, often referred to as 'disarmament'. The 1929–31 Labour government had been instrumental in securing an international conference at Geneva to discuss the question. The National government remained committed to it, Ramsay MacDonald as a matter of internationalist principles – he had little else left now – and Stanley Baldwin, the de facto Prime Minister who often deputised for MacDonald in defence matters, because he despaired at the thought of another major conflict in Europe. In November 1932, he voiced his fears: 'The bomber will always get through.' If war returned to Europe, the young would be blamed for having allowed 'old men' to make a mess of things: 'When the next war comes ... then do not let them lay the blame on the old men. Let them remember that they, they principally and they alone, are responsible for the terrors that have fallen upon the earth.' If he sought to shock domestic opinion into addressing the problem of aerial disarmament, in practice it was little more than an appeal to Britain's youth to rally to the cause of pacifism.

The government's approach to the disarmament conference reflected the confusions of its own policy, the vagaries of international diplomacy and the unresolved question of a viable European security order. With Britain's maritime position secure and no army of any European significance, and given Britain's presumed vulnerability to attack from the air, the government's chief interest was twofold: to secure some form of air defence agreement and to facilitate an understanding between the two major Continental powers, France and Germany. Here lay the real stumbling block. It was a simple problem and an insoluble one. France wanted security; Germany demanded equality. The French ambition had complicated Anglo-French relations since 1919, since it entailed a British security guarantee, which no British government was prepared to give, while the Germans' aspiration was within reach by the time the delegates assembled at Geneva. The British proposed a compromise solution, offering Berlin 'equality of status within a system of security'. It was an imaginative play with words, but it was also impracticable. London wanted an easy success but without having to make any difficult decisions. In September 1933, the French tried to break the deadlock by offering Germany full equality, effectively removing all Versailles restrictions on the country, in return for a British security guarantee against any future German breach of faith. London first stalled and then rejected the proposal, fearful of the destabilising effect of a renewed continental commitment on the nation's finances; and with the government staring through the telescope of imperial preference, events on the Continent seemed far away.

To complicate matters further, the French offer of equality was for a four-year probationary period only, a perfect pretext for Hitler to quit the Geneva talks. French obduracy had played into his hands, but the collapse of the disarmament conference was also a failure of British policy. At that point, Baldwin's 'the bomber will always get through' warning recoiled on his party's hapless candidate at Fulham. It fuelled a 'confused apprehension' in the constituency, especially among female voters, one journalist observer noted. Waldron made a feeble attempt to justify a modicum of rearmament, yet more ammunition for the Labour candidate whose supporters canvassed 'at the doorstep on the text "Mr Wilmot and no war"'. Wilmot was no pacifist, as his successor but one, Michael Stewart, noted, but stood in the mainstream of pro-league Labour opinion, and he exploited the government's foreign embarrassments to maximum electoral effect. He drove home the point in his maiden speech in Parliament on 13 November. The government was driven by 'a sense of impending disaster ... I believe that it is that feeling, that the Government lost control of the situation ... which is responsible for the somewhat remarkable results in recent by-elections.' Public opinion 'among ordinary men and women is in advance of the Government', he concluded: 'Something must be done soon to prevent the whole elaborate machinery of collective peace ... from crumbling away.'

Significantly, this was also a view shared by leading members of the National government. Sir John Simon, the Foreign Secretary, a former Liberal, suggested one week after the election that 'the good people of Fulham naturally use[d] the opportunity to show that they do not mean to send their sons to France and Flanders'. Simon especially, but also Baldwin, supported persisting with efforts at disarmament and advocated appeasing the revisionist powers abroad.

Fulham was the most dramatic and the only actual government defeat in a series of half-a-dozen bad by-election results over the course of five weeks. At a time when the National government faced significant domestic and international challenges, such reverses were not, perhaps, surprising. A poor candidate, a lacklustre campaign and insufficient central support compounded the Tories' problems. But it was the explosive effect of the 'peace question' that turned the expected poor result into a Labour landslide. Whatever the emotional pull of the 'peace' question, it suited the interests of senior ministers to treat Fulham as a 'peace ballot' *avant la lettre*. Simon and MacDonald were ideologically wedded to internationalism. Baldwin lacked the courage to confront public opinion. Therein lay the real significance of the Fulham East by-election.

T. G. Otte is a professor of diplomatic history at the University of East Anglia. He is the author of over twenty books, including the award-winning July Crisis: The World's Descent Into War, Summer 1914 *(Cambridge University Press, 2014),* Statesman of Europe: A Life of Sir Edward Grey *(Allen Lane, 2020) and* Leuthen: Great Battles *(Oxford University Press, 2024).*

26

OXFORD

---

27 OCTOBER 1938
CONSERVATIVE HOLD

SIMON HEFFER

Result: Quintin Hogg (Conservative), 15,797, 56.1 per cent; Alexander (Sandy/Sandie) Lindsay (Independent Progressive), 12,363, 43.9 per cent
Size of majority: 3,434
Swing: 6.7 per cent against Conservative
Name of previous MP and party: Robert Bourne (Conservative)
Reason for by-election: Death of incumbent
Result at previous general election: Robert Bourne (Conservative), 16,306, 62.8 per cent; Patrick Gordon-Walker (Labour), 9,661, 37.2 per cent
Date by-election called: 13 October 1938
Date by-election took place: 27 October 1938
Size of total electorate: 36,907
Total number of votes cast: 28,160
Turnout: 76.3 per cent

The Oxford City by-election of October 1938 is one of the most renowned in British political history; though much of that renown stems from an interpretation of the circumstances of the domestic and international political situation of the time that has, in recent years, started to undergo a process of re-evaluation. The contest came about because the sitting member for the seat, Captain Robert Bourne, who was also a deputy Speaker of the House of Commons, dropped dead aged just fifty, having just come out of church on a Sunday morning in August 1938. Bourne's death came at a time of mounting international tension in which the National government, led since May 1937 by Neville Chamberlain, was playing a role increasingly distasteful to many in the country, especially but not exclusively on the left. A growing number in the Conservative Party – the overwhelming majority grouping in the National government – disliked Chamberlain's policy of seeking to reason with Adolf Hitler, up to a point where the Prime Minister was prepared on behalf of the country to make concessions to the Nazi dictator.

The left were opposed to fascism on principle, hostile not merely to Hitler but also to the regime of Benito Mussolini in Italy – with whom Chamberlain had been seeking to make an alliance against Hitler, unsuccessfully, and at the cost of the support of his Foreign Secretary, Anthony Eden, who had resigned over the issue the previous February. The left's ire was also inflamed by the activities of the fascistic Nationalist side in the Spanish Civil War, then just entering its third and final year, under the leadership of General Francisco Franco. However, for all the left's opposition to fascism and the threat it manifestly presented to Europe's remaining democracies, the Labour Party under its leader, Clement Attlee, religiously still voted against the defence estimates when they came before the House of Commons, on the grounds that they still opposed rearmament. Despite his being accused of weakness towards the dictator, Chamberlain was steadily increasing arms expenditure, particularly on the RAF, and had been lobbying for such a policy since his time as Chancellor of the Exchequer in the mid-1930s.

A general election was scheduled to be held before the end of 1940 and, although the Conservative-dominated National government was in domestic terms pedestrian and somewhat ordinary, the Labour Party was far from being in a winning position. The National government had been formed in August 1931, when the king persuaded Stanley Baldwin, the then Conservative leader, and leading Liberals to accept a coalition led by the former Labour Prime Minister Ramsay MacDonald. MacDonald had lost the support of almost all his own parliamentary party in 1931, when his MPs refused to back his economically essential policy of cutting public spending to avoid national bankruptcy. The country had reacted badly against what voters considered to be Labour's irresponsibility, and the party was crushed in the 1931 general election, finishing with just fifty-two seats. It rebuilt its position at the 1935 election but still had just 154 seats.

Chamberlain met Hitler three times in September 1938, culminating in his agreement (in league with the French Prime Minister, Édouard Daladier) on 30 September to allow Hitler to annex the Sudetenland. The redrawing of boundaries at the Treaty of Versailles in 1919 had left a large German population in the Sudetenland under Czech rule. That annexation was the cause of outrage among many in the political class, but the general public reacted very differently. That autumn, and indeed right up until the winter of 1940, Chamberlain was one of the most popular politicians in the country. Much of what we understand as the history of this period has been seen through the prism of Winston Churchill – and not least the history he wrote of it in his own six-volume account of the Second World War.

Chamberlain acted as he did towards Hitler not because he was stupid or craven but because a declaration of war over the Sudetenland would have been futile. The chiefs of the defence staff had made clear to the Prime Minister before his first trip to Germany that the new RAF that was being built was far from ready; the Royal Navy too had had a expansion programme, but its main focus in 1938–39 was on Japanese activity in the Far East and the Pacific, where British possessions such as Hong Kong, Singapore and the vital entrepôt of Shanghai were deemed under threat; and the army had been moribund since 1918, a problem Chamberlain had only recently begun to address with the appointment of the impressive, and much underrated, Leslie Hore-Belisha as Secretary of State for War. The political situation in October 1938 needs to be seen in that context and not with the benefit of abundant hindsight.

The writ for the by-election was moved after Parliament reassembled in October; and it had the benefit of using a new electoral register that had just come into force. Six other by-elections took place around the same time. The Conservative Party chose its candidate, Quintin Hogg, on 7 September. He was the 31-year-old son of Lord Hailsham, a former Lord Chancellor and influential Conservative grandee. Hogg was a barrister, like his father (whom he venerated and would, eventually, emulate by becoming Lord Chancellor himself), a fellow of All

Souls but hamstrung by a reputation for arrogance and conceitedness. His pedigree, brains and his standing in Oxford all propelled him to the candidacy; once he was chosen, the other parties set about finding their own representatives. In his memoirs half a century later, Hogg would describe what was about to happen as 'the most spectacular and widely-reported by-election of the century'.

This contention was certainly reasonable, because events then took an unexpected turn. On 12 October, the master of Balliol College, Dr Alexander 'Sandy' Lindsay, an Oxford graduate who had before taking up that post in 1924 been professor of moral philosophy at the University of Glasgow, indicated that he was prepared to stand as an Independent Progressive candidate, arguing against what he and his supporters perceived to be Chamberlain's policy of appeasement of Hitler. Lindsay had just finished a term of three years as vice-chancellor of the university and was, therefore, one of the most prominent people in the city. He was an avowed socialist and the first openly to profess such sympathies who had ever become head of an Oxford college. He had been approached by a group of people in Oxford who wanted a high-profile anti-Chamberlain candidate to take on Hogg; among the students in the coalition that assembled to support him were 22-year-old Edward Heath and eighteen-year-old Roy Jenkins, as well as people such as Richard Crossman, Denis Healey and Harold Wilson who would later make great political careers. Lindsay let it be known he was prepared to stand but only if other candidates stood down and gave him a clear run. They did, though Labour's national executive sought unsuccessfully to persuade their candidate, Patrick Gordon-Walker, a tutor at Christ Church who had fought the 1935 election for Labour, not to withdraw. Gordon-Walker was indeed reluctant to do so and required a great deal of persuasion. The orchestrator of this development was an Oxford don, Frank Pakenham, later better known as Lord Longford. Ivor Davies, the 23-year-old Liberal candidate, was willing to do so as soon as he heard of Lindsay's intentions, and he met no opposition from within his party. Lindsay at this stage made what Hogg considered to be a fatal error: he promised he would not stand again at the next general election, which would come within two years. Hogg said this would leave Oxford with a 'dummy Member' were Lindsay to be elected.

Lindsay called his supporters a 'stage army of the good'. The principal argument in his campaign would be that, given the grave uncertainties of the international situation, it was vital to have a foreign policy on which the whole country could unite, which was not the case after Munich. He believed, given the vote against Hogg would not be split, that he had a serious chance of defeating him. As things turned out, he was not wildly mistaken. The local Labour Party in Oxford defied the national executive and on Sunday 16 October made a formal approach to Lindsay to represent their interests, which he agreed to do. He remained a member of the Labour Party throughout the campaign.

On 12 October, fifteen days before the poll, Hogg had been formally adopted as Conservative candidate, and his father came to address his adoption meeting in Oxford. Hailsham pointed out that the House of Commons had overwhelmingly endorsed Chamberlain's policy the previous week, and the French National Assembly had supported its government's decision, and there was nothing to be achieved by disunity. His son echoed the sentiment and added that 'there were some people foolish enough to think that by voting against the National candidate they would be making a gesture of defiance against dictatorship, but they were making a great mistake'. He unwittingly emphasised what would be one of the most unusual features of this in any case unusual contest: that it would, effectively, be all about just one policy, appeasement, and whether it should be continued or abandoned.

Hogg, in another speech the next day, asserted that he was 'the National candidate in the national interest', saying that Chamberlain's efforts for peace had been 'brave' and 'devoted' and that through his leadership he had secured 'peace with honour'. Hogg knew Chamberlain through his father and knew he was not the amoebic figure his opponents were alleging him to be. He would fight a vigorous campaign, convinced of the rightness of his cause and believing sincerely that Chamberlain had bought vital extra time that the nation needed if it were to rearm effectively. In that he was absolutely right. For the rest of his life, Hogg never doubted Chamberlain had made the right decision at Munich: without Hurricanes and Spitfires, which arrived in considerable numbers over the next nine months, the RAF would have been shredded by the Luftwaffe.

The loss of one by-election, however high profile, fought entirely on the question would not have deterred a man of Chamberlain's epic self-belief from continuing his policy. It would certainly not have forced his resignation. However, it would have caused a small political earthquake and might well have undermined Chamberlain's position and forced him out of office sooner than would otherwise be the case. However, Lindsay was playing for high stakes. The two candidates who had stood down said they had done so because they were 'deeply concerned with the gravity of the present situation, and recognis[ed] the urgent need of uniting all the democratic forces of the country'. Lindsay took over a Liberal committee room as his headquarters and a campaign committee comprised of Liberals and Labour activists came together to support him: by the time they did, the campaign would be just ten days long.

He said a lasting peace could not be built because there was no means of uniting behind Chamberlain's policy – not least because, he claimed, no one knew what it was. He pointed to a record of indecision over Spain, China and now the Czechs. He said he craved a positive, and not a negative, foreign policy – not against fascism or Bolshevism but in favour of democracy.

Lindsay did himself no favours, however, by clouding the issue by calling for a revival of the League of Nations, which for some time had been viewed as terminally ineffectual, and then calling for rearmament provided it did not commercially benefit private arms companies and was used to tackle unemployment (which had already fallen in many areas because of the existing rearmament policies and which was not an issue in Oxford because of the success of the local motor industry). Lindsay was on sounder ground in arguing for the prioritisation of the RAF in rearmament, understanding how crucial the achievement of air supremacy would be in any war fought against Germany.

He held his first public meeting on 19 October. It was chaired by Roy Harrod, the economist, who later became the biographer of Keynes and a disruptive unofficial adviser to Harold Macmillan during his premiership; Macmillan too was one of the leading parliamentary opponents of Chamberlain's policy. Lindsay's radical politics and take-no-prisoners manner had made him enemies among the Oxford establishment, some of whom (including H. A. L. Fisher, the Liberal former Education Minister and current warden of New College) came out publicly in favour of Hogg, as did several former heads of house.

The campaign was conducted in the fashion traditional of the times: public meetings, door-to-door canvassing and much tramping about the streets. Because of the unusual nature of the contest, the coverage in the national press was considerable; it was a rare by-election on which the nation's focus was fixed, certainly in the week or ten days before polling day. The short campaign became famous for the slogans used by Lindsay's supporters: the best known was 'A vote for Hogg is a vote for Hitler', but there were also 'Oxford wants Lindsay. Hitler wants Hogg' and somewhat less catchy 'Hitler says: Don't dare vote for Lindsay'. Lindsay himself said he was appealing to 'men and women of all parties who are profoundly disturbed at the outlook before us and the policy which the present government seems to propose to follow'. Hogg described the name-calling as 'unscrupulous' and retorted: 'Vote for Hogg and save your bacon.'

The huge news coverage of the election and the contentiousness of the single-issue fight helped increase turnout considerably, but Hogg's energetic campaign, in the face of a very serious challenge from a man who was more than his intellectual equal, paid off, and he won by the relatively narrow margin of 3,434 votes. Hogg appeared to be assisted by Lindsay's reputation for radicalism – many electors simply saw him as a socialist in sheep's clothing, and in those days, Oxford was not ready for such a thing. The by-election made Lindsay realise how damaging it was for radicalism that two parties should espouse it and split its support. He said in 1939, when invited to address a Liberal summer school, that Labour was 'a party with no leaders worth mentioning', while the Liberals were 'leaders with no party worth mentioning'.

Lindsay never fought another parliamentary election, but in 1945 Attlee gave him a peerage and he went to the House of Lords as Baron Lindsay of Birker. He remained master of Balliol until 1949, when he became founding principal of the University of North Staffordshire, the first new British university of the twentieth century and which later became known as Keele University. He had long been an advocate of a 'people's university' and, when forced on reaching the age of seventy to retire from Balliol, becoming involved at North Staffordshire was a means of putting long-held principles and beliefs about education into practice. In 1952, he died after just three years in the post but having laid the foundations of the institution.

Despite his vociferous support for Chamberlain during the by-election, Hogg voted against him in the Norway debate and thus helped force him from office in May 1940. He enjoyed a long and distinguished career as a Conservative frontbencher, dying in 2001 at the age of ninety-four. He served briefly as Under-Secretary for Air in the 1945 caretaker government but to his annoyance succeeded his father as 2nd Viscount Hailsham in 1950 and moved to the House of Lords. He declined office under Churchill, preferring to focus on his career at the Bar, but in 1956 accepted Eden's offer to become First Lord of the Admiralty. Macmillan made him Minister of Education on becoming Prime Minister in January 1957 but that autumn moved him to become Lord Privy Seal and chairman of the Conservative Party. He presided in that role over the party's handsome victory at the 1959 general election and served as Lord President of the Council and Leader of the House of Lords. He renounced his peerage in 1963 in order to seek the leadership of his party, unsuccessfully. The climax of his career was to serve as Lord Chancellor under Edward Heath from 1970 to 1974 and again under Margaret Thatcher from 1979 to 1987.

In the short term, the Oxford by-election (together with several others held that autumn in which Munich and appeasement were central issues) shored up the Chamberlain administration and its foreign policy; though it also gave a clear signal that there were serious divisions in the country about the policy and warned Chamberlain that he could give Hitler no more leeway. Thus it was, the following March, when the Nazi dictator occupied the rest of the Czech lands, that Chamberlain promised that such a move against Poland would cause Britain to declare war. That he did, with great reluctance, on 3 September 1939; the eleven months' time he had bought had allowed the armed forces to get to a state of readiness to credibly allow them to fight it. The long-term consequence of the by-election was that it became something of a symbol, in 1945, of the unfitness of the Conservative Party to govern and why Labour should be elected instead. This was ironic, given the Labour Party's enthusiasm for disarmament right up to the spring of 1939, when they at last merely abstained upon, rather than voted against, the defence estimates. And the contest also became a symbol of the wrongness of Chamberlain's policy, to the point where it appears, still, to have ruled out a mature analysis of that policy and to have killed the notion that there are two sides to every story.

Simon Heffer is a professor of modern British history at the University of Buckingham and a columnist for the Daily *and* Sunday Telegraph. *His latest history book is* Sing As We Go: Britain between the Wars *(Hutchinson Heinemann, 2023).*

27

BRIDGWATER

---

17 NOVEMBER 1938
INDEPENDENT PROGRESSIVE GAIN FROM CONSERVATIVES

ALUN EVANS

Result: Vernon Bartlett (Independent Progressive), 19,540, 53.2 per cent; Patrick Heathcoat-Amory (Conservative), 17,208, 46.8 per cent
Size of majority: 2,332
Swing: 31.6 per cent from Conservative to Independent Progressive
Name of previous MP and party: Reginald Croom-Johnson (Conservative)
Reason for by-election: Resignation on appointment as High Court judge
Result at previous general election: Reginald Croom-Johnson (Conservative), 17,939, 56.9 per cent; Norman Blake (Liberal), 7,370, 23.4 per cent; Arthur Loveys (Labour), 6,240, 19.8 per cent
Date by-election called: 16 October 1938
Date by-election took place: 17 November 1938
Size of total electorate: 44,651
Total number of votes cast: 36,748
Turnout: 82.3 per cent

The voters of Bridgwater probably knew little about the Sudetenland Germans in the early autumn of 1938. Yet when, in October, German troops marched into and occupied that region of Czechoslovakia, the expansionist policies of Hitler and how Britain should respond to them were to play a central role in the domestic politics of that rural Somerset constituency. Effectively, the appeasement strategy of Prime Minister Neville Chamberlain was over. Although the Munich Agreement of the previous month, signed by Chamberlain and Hitler, had ceded the Sudetenland to German control, the immediate invasion that followed unequivocally signalled the Führer's future intent. Bridgwater, like the Oxford by-election held the previous month, became a vivid symbol of the tensions between those people who supported continued appeasement and those who wanted a far more robust strategy for tackling the fascist threat from mainland Europe.

Through most of the late 1930s, there had been limited co-ordinated opposition to the Prime Minister's strategy. In the second half of the decade, Winston Churchill had, consistently, opposed Chamberlain's policy, but he was seen as a lone, and at times isolated, figure. By the time of Munich, the official opposition Labour Party was also opposed to the agreement. However, unlike in other European countries, notably Spain and France, there was no 'popular front' of socialist, communist and other radical parties uniting against the growing fascist threat. The Labour Party dominated centre-left politics and its leader, Clement Attlee, saw few benefits of joint activity with the small and relatively insignificant British Communist Party, as well as plenty of downsides. Attlee's biographer, John Bew, has commented that while Attlee thought 'a popular front might be useful if democracy was in danger in Britain … it was not'.

In October, the Conservative MP for Bridgwater, Reginald Croom-Johnson, was appointed a High Court judge, requiring him to resign his seat and thereby precipitated a by-election. This meant that, within two months of the Munich Agreement, there were to be two immediate tests of public opinion – in the Oxford and Bridgwater by-elections. The Bridgwater contest was set for 17 November, three weeks after Oxford.

The local Conservative Party picked as their candidate Gerald Heathcoat-Amory. Aged twenty-six, he was a member of the Heathcoat-Amory family who were to hold the neighbouring Devon seat of Tiverton for much of the twentieth century. He was something of the classic establishment candidate – young and politically inexperienced, but it was thought he would be able to win easily the largely rural seat which contained few large urban areas. In the previous general election of 1935, Croom-Johnson had comfortably won the seat with a healthy majority of over 10,000. However, in the 1935 contest, both the Labour and Liberal parties had fielded candidates and, between them, taken over 43 per cent of the vote.

Richard Acland, a left-leaning Liberal MP for Barnstaple in north Devon, immediately spotted an opportunity. He had been elected in 1935 and, from the following year, had been an early proponent of a popular front in Britain. As soon as the by-election was called, Acland urged the progressive forces of the left and centre to unite and field a single candidate at Bridgwater so as to take on the government through an electoral coalition of the Liberals, Labour and other sympathisers. Post Munich, Acland's view was that if a single anti-appeasement candidate could be agreed, then victory at Bridgwater was possible.

Acland approached Vernon Bartlett to persuade him to be the candidate. Bartlett was an inspired choice. First, because he was relatively well known, being a newspaper and radio journalist as well as an author. He had a charismatic style and a flair for public speaking, perfectly suited to the qualities needed to fight what would be a high-profile by-election. But, in addition, he was an expert on foreign affairs, having worked previously for the League of Nations. Being London-based, he faced some criticisms for not being a local man, but these initial strictures soon faded. Bartlett would clearly have more weight and depth than the young and inexperienced Conservative candidate. Acland firmly believed that, if the by-election could be focused relentlessly on opposition to the Munich Agreement, a single popular front candidate could defeat the Conservatives. Bartlett was to be that candidate. He would campaign as an 'Independent Progressive'.

The Liberal Party readily agreed to support Bartlett, but the Labour Party was, initially, somewhat wary of the proposed arrangement, having already selected their candidate, Arthur Loveys, to contest the next general election. Loveys had been the Labour candidate in 1935, but he soon agreed to step down and support Bartlett as the unity candidate. Acland believed that if Bartlett stressed his independence from the two main parties, this would do most to draw in undecided centrist voters. Neither the Liberal leader, Archibald Sinclair, nor Attlee took any part in the campaign or visited the constituency. Attlee, in particular, given his scepticism about the notion and value of a popular front in Britain, remained unconvinced by the overall approach, even at one point suggesting that Labour MPs who publicly supported Bartlett's candidacy might be disciplined by the party.

Acland was determined to fight a lively campaign using the support of local members from both main opposition parties as well as some communists and others. In addition, Bartlett's candidacy benefited enormously from the support, campaigning and canvassing of members of the Left Book Club. The Left Book Club was a publishing phenomenon of the late 1930s. It had been founded in 1936 to campaign specifically for a united centre-left popular front to oppose Hitler and the rise of fascism in Europe. It was particularly focused on the Republican cause in the Spanish Civil War and in its support for the popular front in Spain. The club had been the brainchild of the left-wing publisher Victor Gollancz. Every month, Gollancz and his two editorial colleagues – Harold Laski and John Strachey, both prominent members of the Labour left – chose a monthly book for circulation to members of the club. Gollancz hoped, when he started the club, to sign up a few thousand members. Within a year, it had over 40,000 members and by 1939, at its peak, had 57,000 members, all of whom received at least one book a month. Not only that but the Left Book Club set up local branches which held regular meetings to discuss the issues raised by the books and to campaign for causes such as Spain and the popular front.

Acland had been an early member of the club and was later an author for it. He recognised that, in club members, there was a potential resource to deploy in Bridgwater in support of Bartlett. So, the campaign for the by-election when it commenced was high profile and relied on support from the local political parties as well as non-aligned Left Book Club members. A somewhat maverick local vicar, the Reverend Cresswell Webb, who had been a wartime friend of Bartlett from nearby Exmoor, became Bartlett's campaign agent and managed his campaign. But it was Acland who was the driving force. Tom Wintringham, a communist and Spanish Civil War veteran, came to Bridgwater to support Bartlett and described Acland as 'tall, lanky and earnest – an inspired but intuitive public speaker [who] waved his arms around and shouted exultantly like a revivalist preacher'.

Bartlett led a punishing schedule of public meetings through the constituency. Records of the campaign show that, for example, on one evening Bartlett addressed four meetings in two and a half hours: at

Woolavington, East Huntspill, Highbridge and Burnham-on-Sea. The focus of the campaign was almost exclusively on international politics, opposition to appeasement and how to avert war in Europe. This played to Bartlett's undoubted strengths and expertise. Heathcoat-Amory backed appeasement throughout the campaign, saying at Highbridge that 'I support the Prime Minister and the whole of his policy completely and without reservation'. Like the by-election in Oxford, the Bridgwater contest attracted national attention. Prime Minister Neville Chamberlain wrote in support of the Conservative candidate, saying that 'it is easy for those who have no responsibility on their shoulders to criticise and misrepresent the policy of others upon whose decisions rest the issues of peace or war'. And he added, putting the Munich Agreement centre stage in the Bridgwater contest: 'Would our opponents who criticize us today have plunged the world into war in order to keep the Sudeten Germans under Czechoslovak rule?'

The former Liberal Prime Minister David Lloyd George sent a letter of support to Bartlett, saying that 'unless the people rose above party considerations and placed the safety and honour of the country above every partisan appeal, it was clear that this chronic blundering [by the government] would end in our muddling into irretrievable disaster'.

The Oxford by-election was held three weeks before Bridgwater and the failure of the popular front candidate in that constituency did not appear to damage Bartlett's cause at all. If anything, it inspired his supporters to campaign even more vigorously. Again, the Left Book Club members were prominent.

When the results were declared, Bartlett had won decisively, if not overwhelmingly. He received 19,540 votes (53.2 per cent), compared to Heathcoat-Amory's 17,208 votes (46.8 per cent). A gain from the Conservatives and for the 'Independent Progressive' candidate. At 82.3 per cent, the turnout was exceptionally high – and some 10 per cent higher than at the general election three years earlier. By way of comparison, the turnout at Oxford was eight percentage points lower at 76.3 per cent.

What caused such a remarkable result? Three main factors. First, the rapid agreement and unity among the anti-government parties and associated supporters to unite around a single anti-government candidate. Acland must take much of the credit for delivering this. Second, the inspired choice of Bartlett as the Progressive Independent candidate – given his credibility and expertise on international affairs which left his younger inexperienced opponent deeply exposed as the fascist threat increased. But finally, the campaign itself mattered and contributed to the high turnout which favoured Bartlett. The enthusiasm and sheer hard work displayed by Bartlett's team, including the marshalling of Left Book Club members, undoubtedly influenced the high turnout and, in all probability, the result.

After the event, Victor Gollancz said that the Left Book Club (LBC) and its members had been decisive in Bartlett's victory:

> Looking to the future then it becomes exceedingly important for the LBC members to assess correctly the part played by the Club in this victory; and after a careful investigation, and the receipt of several detailed reports from the spot I feel justified in saying that had there been no LBC there would have been no Bridgwater.

Given Gollancz was the publisher of the Left Book Club and had a financial interest in its future, these comments were hardly surprising. Yet even many political historians of the 1930s, who were far more sceptical of the longer-term influence of the Left Book Club, such as Ben Pimlott in *Labour and the Left in the 1930s*, have acknowledged that Bridgwater was the high-water mark in terms of its reach and influence. The Left Book Club tactics and the use of its members campaigning at local level mirrored, to some extent, the way in which the Liberal Democrat Party similarly managed to exploit by-election opportunities some half a century later.

But did Bridgwater make any significant contribution to British politics more widely? Possibly not in the very short term. Chamberlain's government continued to pursue appeasement for ten more months until the Nazi–Soviet pact and the German invasion of Poland sounded its death knell. What Bridgwater did was show that there was the potential for a united opposition to Chamberlain's policy and, when in 1940 Chamberlain resigned, that body of opinion swung itself firmly behind Churchill, Attlee and the National coalition government and with very little opposition. Bartlett himself remained in national politics until 1950, holding on to the Bridgwater seat in the Labour landslide of 1945. He stood again as an 'Independent Progressive', supported by the Liberals but opposed this time by both Labour and Conservative candidates. In 1950, Bartlett did not stand and the Conservatives regained the seat. They have held it in every general election since.

Alun Evans *is a political historian. Previously, he was, for many years, a UK civil servant, serving in a number of departments, including at No. 10. He is the author of* The Intimacy of Power *(Biteback, 2024), a study of the role and history of the private office in British politics.*

28

KINROSS & WESTERN PERTHSHIRE

21 DECEMBER 1938
UNIONIST HOLD

AMY GRAY

Result: William McNair Snadden (Unionist), 11,808, 52.9 per cent; Katharine Stewart-Murray (Independent), 10,495, 47.1 per cent
Size of majority: 1,313
Swing: 13.2 per cent against Katharine Stewart-Murray
Name of previous MP and party: Katharine Stewart-Murray (Conservative and Unionist)
Reason for by-election: Resignation of incumbent
Result at previous general election: Katharine Stewart-Murray (Unionist), 15,238, 60.2 per cent; Mary Isabella MacDonald (Liberal), 10,069, 39.8 per cent
Date by-election called: 24 November 1938
Date by-election took place: 21 December 1938
Size of total electorate: 33,488
Total number of votes cast: 22,303
Turnout: 66.6 per cent

What happens when an MP falls out, irrevocably, with their local association over a point of principle? Katharine Stewart-Murray, Duchess of Atholl, Scotland's first female MP and the Conservatives' first female minister, was the only opponent of appeasement brave enough to ask her electorate to back her position – and paid the highest political price for it.

A gifted pianist from an ancient Perthshire family of baronets and academics, she had married the Marquis of Tullibardine in 1899 after a long secret engagement. Unable, to her lifelong sadness, to have children, she nursed his soldiers in South Africa in 1901 and in Egypt after Gallipoli in 1915, becoming interested in welfare work and determined not to see another war. She repeatedly worked herself to the point of exhaustion serving on dozens of committees at the same time as writing a detailed military history of Perthshire and supporting her husband's political career. She initially opposed women's suffrage, feeling that women needed more experience of local government before they were given the national vote.

After her father-in-law's death in 1917, her husband became the 8th Duke of Atholl and had to give up his seat in the House of Commons. The new duchess turned the ducal seat at Blair Castle into a hospital and met former suffragettes running a military hospital near the Western Front. After the Armistice, she was elected to the Perthshire Education Authority, where she became convinced that women must be represented where issues concerning them were decided.

By the time the Liberal Prime Minister David Lloyd George suggested that she should stand for Parliament, she was one of the most prominent women in Scotland. After local (male) political leaders asked her to stand, she was elected in 1923 for her home constituency of Kinross & Western Perthshire, winning her husband's old seat back from the Liberals. Less than a year later, her good friend Stanley Baldwin invited her to become the parliamentary secretary to the Board of Education. She was a diligent and well-respected minister, but on her return to the back benches after Labour's victory in 1929, she embraced a number of causes which were regarded by colleagues as increasingly quixotic.

Atholl convened a cross-party committee to campaign against female genital mutilation in British colonies and then published one of the earliest exposés in English of the horrors of Soviet forced labour camps. By 1932, she had aligned herself with Winston Churchill and the Tory diehards against the Government of India Bill, under which India would gradually be granted self-government. Unlike the other diehards, Atholl opposed the measures initially out of concern for the impact of rapidly devolved power on Indian women and children.

Four months after being one of the few MPs to speak in support of Randolph Churchill when he stood against the official Conservative candidate in the Liverpool Wavertree by-election, she resigned the National government whip, with four colleagues, in protest at the India Bill and Baldwin's pursuit of what they thought were profoundly un-Tory policies. She retook the whip a few months later during the Abyssinia crisis to demonstrate her support for the government. However, at the 1935 general election, she persuaded her association executive to agree that she could take a separate line on foreign policy from the government – an agreement she would test to breaking point.

Having taken a contrary position on the defining political issue of the early 1930s, she did the same on the most polarising issue of the mid-1930s: the Spanish Civil War. Her passionate support of the Spanish Republican side, and her willingness to share a platform with communists when fundraising for Spanish relief, led to her being nicknamed 'the Red Duchess'.

When Atholl read the German edition of Hitler's *Mein Kampf*, she realised – ahead of most of her contemporaries – that the most violent passages had been omitted from the much shorter English translation. Visiting countries like Austria and Czechoslovakia persuaded her that Britain was far too complacent about the Nazi threat. She feared that if the fascist General Franco won in Spain with German and Italian support, a wider European war was inevitable.

Her committee brought 4,000 Basque refugee children to Britain, but her lengthy absences from Perthshire to fundraise for the children divided opinion. She even visited Republican Spain with the Labour MP 'Red' Ellen Wilkinson. Local Catholics whipped up opposition to her. While Baldwin had affectionately tolerated her rebellions, the new Prime Minister Neville Chamberlain was unwilling to allow dissent. When Atholl publicly criticised his policies on non-intervention in Spain and in central Europe, he withdrew the whip.

At a special general meeting of the West Perthshire Unionist Association, Colonel Patrick Blair, the Scottish whips' secretary, sat with the local officers as a resolution was carried to support the Prime Minister's position. The national party leadership's view was clear: they wanted her gone. Although she regretted the loss of friends in the association, Atholl still thought that most of her electors supported her. 'I can't say that I think I have much reason to fear a by-election,' she wrote to her husband three days later, 'if I have Labour opinion + can get Highland Glen opinion also – as well as a good proportion of ordinary Unionist votes!' But she was on her way to address another meeting on Spain in Glasgow and was accused of smiling as the communist anthem 'The Internationale' was played. The infuriated association executive ensured a motion not to readopt Atholl was passed.

The duke, a gregarious and serially unfaithful former cavalry officer who was the local Unionist association president, was worried. He understood the local personalities much better than his wife, having commanded many of the men in his military days. He had tried to mollify them but was increasingly struggling to hold the association together. He was not helped when Atholl spent over a month in North America raising money for the Spanish children while Chamberlain made his three trips to see Hitler and triumphantly brought home the Munich Agreement. 'I can't think of anything so disgraceful in our history,' raged Atholl about Britain's betrayal of Czechoslovakia, now convinced that war was certain.

She was in Washington when the four-day Commons debate on Munich began with Duff Cooper's resignation from the Admiralty. In a blistering oration, Churchill thundered against the 'total and unmitigated defeat' he believed Hitler had inflicted on British policy but could do nothing. Fewer than thirty Conservative MPs abstained from the vote. On Atholl's return home, she circulated a pamphlet to every household in the constituency setting out her views. The association executive began actively courting an alternative candidate to fight the expected 1939 general election, and when Atholl found out, she resigned her seat to trigger a by-election.

William McNair Snadden, a local cattle farmer twenty years Atholl's junior, was hastily selected to fight her. The association realised an external candidate would struggle to compete in the fifth largest constituency in the country. Snadden had worked for Atholl at successive elections but was among those who had become disillusioned. 'I have not a little admiration for her capabilities, but I will frankly say that her views frighten me somewhat,' he had written to the duke. The campaign machine which the Atholls had built up over three decades of dominating the county's politics was now deployed against them, with the added weight of everything Conservative Central Office could spare.

Fatefully, Atholl decided to stand as an Independent, hoping that Labour and Liberal supporters would feel more comfortable voting for her. She assumed that her personal vote was strong enough to retain a sufficient number of existing Unionist voters. The Liberal candidate was forced to stand down by her party leadership, splitting local Liberal opinion, and a potential Labour candidate withdrew. It was a straight fight between Atholl and Snadden.

Seventy Conservative and Unionist MPs signed a public letter condemning Atholl's views in a clear signal to other would-be rebels. Vulnerable after his October speech, Churchill was told he would be deselected in Epping if he travelled to Perthshire. Instead, he regularly telephoned Atholl and sent a public letter of support which *The Times* reprinted in full. He began by defending her view of the proper function of MPs, saying that 'the idea that they should be delegates of a party organisation has always been abhorrent to those who understand the spirit of the British Constitution'. He concluded with a rallying call to Perthshire's voters to support their duchess as 'outside our island your defeat at this moment would be relished by the enemies of Britain and of freedom in every part of the world'. But otherwise the higher profile 'Glamour Boy' opponents of appeasement stayed in their smoking rooms and waited to see what would happen.

Atholl's most prominent supporters were instead the same, mostly left-wing names who had backed Sandy Lindsay in Oxford and Vernon Bartlett in Bridgwater, along with dozens of idealistic young volunteers from the Spanish Relief movement. They borrowed a van with loudspeakers which broadcast less than catchy slogans like 'All Conservatives, Liberals, Labour and Non-Party Voters should vote for the Duchess in her magnificent stand for world peace' and 'Remember her long and distinguished services to this district and the people of Perthshire.'

With such a short campaign, the candidates focused on public meetings. The Conservatives organised 101, with Snadden speaking at sixty-one. Their campaign strategy was a simple one. 'Remember: A vote for Snadden is a vote for Chamberlain,' read his leaflets, hoping the Prime Minister's popularity as a peace-bringer would secure victory. Snadden promised pointedly that he would not spend his time overseas. Dozens of MPs were ordered north to campaign for him, and speakers at his meetings included Scotland's second female MP Florence Horsbrugh and Chamberlain's parliamentary private secretary Lord Dunglass (later known as Alec Douglas-Home), who had been with him at Munich. Women made up more than half of the electorate and were targeted by unscrupulous canvassers suggesting that Atholl actively wanted a war which would see their husbands and sons called up.

Journalists flooded the constituency because, as the *Daily Express* put it, '*anything* the Duchess does is news'. The duke, prevented from campaigning by a back injury, held court from his bed in blue pyjamas. He blamed local Catholic priests and landowners for stirring up opposition to his wife and lamented that Perthshire people were not as loyal to his family as they should have been. The scale of his debts had forced him to accept financial support from his heir's in-laws, and the Atholls could no longer entertain in feudal style.

The local Unionist lairds co-ordinated attacks on her. Rent rebates were reportedly given to tenants who promised to support Snadden, Tory leaflets were included in rent bills, the district nurse was among those told she would lose her job if she voted for Atholl and shopkeepers were too scared to display her posters. The Tories made much of the Communist Party's (unwanted) support for Atholl and a telegram supposedly from Stalin reading: 'MOSCOW IS PROUD OF KATHARINE THE EVEN GREATER' (which seems most likely to have been a prank). No wonder the last line of Atholl's election address reminded voters that 'THE BALLOT IS SECRET'. She even felt that she needed to put out an additional leaflet imploring: 'Please don't believe all the things you may hear said about me in this election.'

Mass Observation's researchers attended many of the meetings for both sides and observed that although the speeches were focused on foreign policy, questions were not. Agriculture remained the biggest local issue, and many voters felt it was being ignored. Atholl's posters may have exhorted them to 'Send Hitler your answer/VOTE FOR THE DUCHESS', but international issues seemed a long way from Dunkeld or Pitlochry. The impact of the Milk Marketing Board was of much more immediate interest.

Without the campaign infrastructure to organise and publicise meetings, Atholl could not manage as many and had fewer proxies to speak for her. She did not speak at all in Crieff, one of the largest towns in the constituency, focusing more on the villages, and her audiences were often small. She would spend the morning at home working on correspondence, then hop in the car to be driven to four or five meetings each afternoon and evening, fuelled by homemade game sandwiches. She travelled with a large map of Europe which she would use to illustrate the dangers of Hitler's expansionist policy. Well after midnight, she would head home, her five-foot frame curled up on the car's back seat to sleep.

Appalling Scottish winter weather was one of the major deciding factors. Snadden was followed by a second car in case the first had an accident, while the duke insisted Atholl always packed a snow shovel. The days before polling were marked by blizzards. With eight inches of snow still lying on the ground on polling day, turnout was much lower than in Bridgwater and Oxford. The London newspapers revelled in stories of voters trudging five miles through snow to get to their polling stations or braving boat journeys across the lochs. Snadden's side reportedly deployed 500 cars to Atholl's fifty to ferry their voters to polling stations.

The next day, they gathered in Perth for the result. Wearing a sprig of white heather on her lapel and a red, white and blue rosette, Atholl learned that her pre-planned victory tour would have to be cancelled. Snadden had won by 1,313 votes. After the count, Atholl returned home to play Beethoven sonatas on her neglected piano, always more comfortable expressing her emotions through music than words.

'I was overjoyed at the result of the Perth Election which was far better than I had ventured to hope … I shall have all the merrier a Christmas for it,' wrote a satisfied Chamberlain to his Chief Whip. A Nazi government spokesman smirked that 'we are glad to know that the electorate was not carried away by the demagogic propaganda of this drawing room Bolshevist'.

In the postmortems afterwards, Atholl identified several reasons for her defeat. 'I suffered from an improvised organisation – keen, splendid people, but some new to the work. And I had not everywhere enough cars,' she wrote to a friend. She had expected more help from local Liberals given their national party's position and had not expected the usually supportive local newspapers to be turned against her. 'The main moral of my defeat is the need for paying special attention to the canvassing of women, + meetings for them,' she concluded. She was unable to recognise that her own decision to run as an Independent may have been decisive. She had spent so much time working across parties, particularly with other female MPs, that she had forgotten the power of the party machine and the pull of party loyalty.

The *Dundee Courier* thought that 'if the Duchess of Atholl had won in the contest there is no doubt whatever that the Opposition – in all its varieties – would to-day be calling frantically upon the Government to resign'. Chamberlain did not change his policy. But nine months after the poll, Britain was at war with Germany. The duchess had been right.

Although she was selected as an Independent candidate for the Scottish Universities, she returned to the Tory fold as a member when her friend Churchill became Prime Minister in 1940. After the Second World War, she focused on championing the rights of Poles behind the Iron Curtain, dying at the age of eighty-four in 1960.

Snadden had the unexciting parliamentary career he had promised, speaking almost exclusively on farming in the House of Commons. His loyalty was rewarded with a post as a junior minister in the Scotland Office in 1951, before he retired in 1955 with a baronetcy.

Twenty-five years later, Kinross & Western Perthshire saw another by-election. Lord Dunglass had succeeded his father as the Earl of Home and had been a popular and successful Foreign Secretary. In order to succeed Harold Macmillan (who had supported Atholl's campaign against appeasement) as party leader, he needed a House of Commons seat. Snadden's successor had died, leaving a conveniently Scottish vacancy. Having campaigned against the duchess, Alec Douglas-Home followed her as the MP for Kinross & Western Perthshire in order to become Prime Minister.

Amy Gray's *biography of the Duchess of Atholl,* Red Duchess, *will be published by the History Press in September 2025.*

29

MALDON

---

25 JUNE 1942
INDEPENDENT GAIN FROM CONSERVATIVES

WILL TIMMINS

Result: Tom Driberg (Independent Labour), 12,219, 61.3 per cent; Reuben Hunt (Conservative), 6,226, 31.3 per cent; Richard Borlase Matthews (National Independent and Agricultural), 1,476, 7.4 per cent
Size of majority: 5,993
Swing: 22.1 per cent against Conservatives
Name of previous MP and party: Edward Ruggles-Brise (Conservative)
Reason for by-election: Death of incumbent
Result at previous general election: Edward Ruggles-Brise (Conservative), 17,072, 53.4 per cent; William Toynbee (Labour), 9,264, 28.9 per cent; Hilda Buckmaster (Liberal), 5,680, 17.7 per cent
Date by-election called: 4 June 1942
Date by-election took place: 25 June 1942
Size of total electorate: 44,867
Total number of votes cast: 19,921
Turnout: 44.4 per cent

The Maldon by-election, held on 25 June 1942 at the height of the Second World War, starkly illustrated Britain's evolving political landscape amid escalating public discontent with the war's trajectory. Departing from peacetime conventions, the Conservative, Labour and Liberal parties upheld a pact to avoid electoral opposition to foster national unity. However, of the 141 parliamentary vacancies that arose during the war, sixty-six were uncontested, while seventy-five witnessed

Independents and minor parties seizing the chance to gain ground in the absence of major party opposition.

In early 1942, four Independent candidates unseated coalition incumbents in Grantham, Rugby, Wallasey and Maldon, reflecting widespread discontent. Britain had suffered major setbacks, including the fall of Singapore in February 1942 and defeats in North Africa. The Maldon by-election embodied the growing disillusionment with the government's wartime leadership and intensifying doubts about the prospect of victory.

The by-election was triggered by the death of Sir Edward Ruggles-Brise MP on 12 May 1942. An archetypal Conservative MP, Sir Edward had represented Maldon since 1922, aside from a brief gap between the 1923 and 1924 general elections. As a prominent landowner, he actively farmed his inherited Spains Hall in Finchingfield and, after being educated at Eton and Trinity College, Cambridge, served with distinction in the First World War, earning the Military Cross. In Parliament, he chaired the Conservative backbench agriculture committee and was a redoubtable champion of British farming. Despite a 17.4 per cent swing against him in 1935, he retained a healthy majority of 7,808 votes – a testament to the constituency's long-standing loyalty to the Conservative Party.

The Maldon constituency, rooted in the rural heart of Essex and shaped by the industrial hubs of Braintree, Witham and Burnham, faced unprecedented electoral challenges during the war. By-elections relied on an outdated electoral register from March 1939, which excluded many new voters and failed to account for wartime population shifts. The roll still included absent servicemen, evacuees and redeployed essential workers, while many younger voters went unregistered. Although the pre-war register listed 44,867 eligible voters, local estimates indicated that only 33,000 to 36,000 were able to vote by the time of the by-election – underscoring profound demographic upheaval and difficulties in accurately gauging voter turnout.

Despite the national climate, the local Conservative Party ill-advisedly entered the campaign with misplaced complacency, expecting not merely a win but an unchallenged 'coronation' under the electoral truce. They selected Reuben Hunt – a wealthy ironworks owner and chair of the Saffron Walden Conservative Association – as their candidate. A staunch traditionalist and unapologetic right-winger, Hunt was unwavering in his Conservative convictions, commanding respect among party ranks. Although he resided just beyond the constituency's borders, his selection seemed inevitable; as one local newspaper observed, he had 'practically selected himself'.

Just days after Hunt's selection, two Independent challengers emerged, each distinct in character. The first, Richard Borlase Matthews – a former Liberal candidate and self-proclaimed 'National Independent and Agricultural Candidate' – came from a wealthy Swansea shipping family, owned an all-electric farm and proudly claimed to have advised the Soviet Union on agricultural electrification. Campaigning in a coke-fired, gas-powered car that quickly attracted local interest, Borlase Matthews made unintended local headlines when he drove it into a ditch – a mishap that undermined his claims of engineering expertise.

The second, Tom Driberg, was a flamboyant figure who rejected his middle-class Sussex roots, embracing Anglicanism, socialism and a life of promiscuous homosexuality – a rebellion he termed his 'revolt against Crowborough'. Nearly expelled from Lancing College for a sexual liaison with a fellow pupil, he was saved by a scandal-averse headmaster, finishing the term in isolation. Later, after tutoring, he passed his Oxford scholarship exams on his second attempt.

At Christ Church College, Oxford, Driberg mingled with the satanist Aleister Crowley and joined the Communist Party. Although he left university without a degree, he found his calling when the poet Edith Sitwell secured him a gossip column at the *Daily Express*, where his scandalous 'William Hickey' column made him a favourite of owner Lord Beaverbrook. He was also recruited by MI5 during this time and informed on his communist peers – a betrayal that cost him his party membership.

Throughout his life, he found pleasure in risky, anonymous encounters with young working-class men in public lavatories, yet Driberg skilfully avoided scandal, bragging about bribing and charming police officers to protect his reputation. His closest call came in 1935 when two coal miners he brought home accused him of indecent assault;

Beaverbrook intervened, burying the story and covering legal costs. Driberg's flair for self-preservation was necessary in an era where exposure as a homosexual could ruin lives and careers.

Just before the war, Driberg purchased Bradwell Lodge, an Essex estate that provided a retreat to indulge his aristocratic fantasies and served as a local foothold for his campaign, even though he spent most of his time in London. While not formally aligned with the Communist Party, he remained deeply committed to left-wing causes. In March 1942, he delivered a passionate speech at a rally condemning the ban on the *Daily Worker*, deeming it absurd now that the Soviet Union was an Allied power. Shortly thereafter, *Picture Post* editor Tom Hopkinson encouraged him to run for Parliament.

One evening, weeks after the rally, Driberg heard on the radio that the MP for Maldon had died and saw it as a sign to run. He wasn't alone in this moment; a Canadian soldier, known only as 'S' in Driberg's diary, lay naked by the fire, taunting him, 'You'd never do it – and, if you did, you'd never win.' The thrill of proving S's elegant, athletic figure wrong, coupled with the by-election's unique circumstances – no opposition from major parties, a local seat where he owned property and the chance for status – was irresistible. The next day, he sought permission from Lord Beaverbrook, who dismissed the idea but allowed it, on the condition that Driberg still deliver his columns. Beaverbrook offered him a single piece of advice: 'Buy yourself a hat! British voters won't trust a man who doesn't wear a hat.'

Beaverbrook himself had resigned as Minister of Production in February 1942, frustrated with civil service bureaucracy, ongoing disputes with colleagues and eager to refocus on his newspaper empire. To avoid tensions with the government – and in response to Churchill's concern that Beaverbrook's involvement might signal support for opposition candidates – the *Daily Express* clarified that while Driberg was a valued employee, it did not endorse his candidacy. Overall, the national press showed little interest in the by-election: *The Times*, *Daily Mail* and *Daily Mirror* gave only briefest acknowledgement of Driberg's profession as a journalist, offering virtually non-existent coverage of the campaign.

In the lead-up to polling day, the three candidates articulated their platforms. The obscure Borlase Matthews ran as an Independent and was sharply critical of the government's wartime management and presented himself as a practical choice – a farmer and engineer who could bring hands-on expertise to Parliament. His slogan, 'Action and Agriculture', underscored a commitment to being free from partisan influence. Matthews condemned government inefficiency, appealing to voters who believed that wartime leadership should be driven by technical competence over political loyalty.

Reuben Hunt, the government candidate, centred his campaign around themes of stability and loyalty, urging voters to avoid 'rocking the boat'. His message was bolstered by the support of Churchill, who regarded by-elections as a distraction and public support for the war-time coalition as essential. Hunt's slogan, 'Back Churchill's Choice by Voting for Hunt', aimed to portray him as the safe option in uncertain times.

During the electoral truce, both the local Labour and Liberal parties were expected to rally behind Hunt as the government's candidate. While the Liberals complied, a significant faction within Labour resisted, opting for neutrality over active support. Amid this division, Driberg found a steadfast ally in Father Jack Boggis, subdean of St Mary's Church in Bocking and secretary of both the local Anglo-Russian Friendship Society and the Braintree Labour Party. Defying Labour's official position, Boggis boldly urged the party to reconsider its stance, labelling Hunt the 'worst type of Tory'.

Driberg's visit to Braintree on 11 June 1942 cemented Boggis's loyalty. As the only candidate to attend the opening of an Anglo-Soviet bookshop, Driberg's presence inspired Boggis to resign from Labour and become his organising secretary. Alarmed by this defection, the Maldon Labour Party held an emergency meeting on 14 June 1942, insisting on coalition loyalty and prohibiting support for independents. They enlisted the short-lived former Labour MP Sir Valentine Crittall to reassure members that Labour's role in the coalition was solely in support of the war effort, urging them to back the government.

Boggis was described by Driberg as 'my most active and useful supporter and a personal friend'. With Boggis by his side, Driberg gained credibility and influence, galvanising Labour voters and building crucial momentum against Hunt. Together, they embodied a defiant stand against complacency, igniting a movement to reclaim Labour's core values – and vote – amid a turbulent political landscape.

Philosophically, Driberg positioned himself as a progressive force challenging the political status quo, running an openly left-wing campaign grounded in the 'Nine-Point Plan' created by the 1941 Committee – a group of intellectuals, writers and social reformers, including J. B. Priestley, committed to envisioning a post-war Britain shaped by social justice. The committee advocated for sweeping reforms to bring about free education, full employment and a dignified standard of living for all citizens.

Richard Acland, a Liberal MP disillusioned with the government's wartime policies, began sitting as an Independent before co-founding the socialist Common Wealth Party on 26 July 1942. Recognising a kindred spirit in Driberg, Acland forged a strategic partnership through their shared involvement in the 1941 Committee. Beyond offering moral support, Acland provided Driberg with crucial guidance on electioneering, helping him craft a campaign that resonated deeply with the frustrations of disillusioned voters.

Driberg, branding himself as a 'Candid Friend for Churchill', praised Churchill's wartime leadership but criticised the government's inefficiencies, held back by 'yes-men' and partisan priorities. Acland's public stature as an MP lent Driberg's campaign heightened credibility, and he provided invaluable advice – particularly on handling public meetings – enabling them to present a unified vision of post-war renewal.

The by-election campaign was marked by Driberg's vigorous, dynamic approach, organising an impressive number of public meetings across the constituency in just five weeks. This relentless pace starkly contrasted with Hunt's lacklustre campaign, whose minimal outreach and focus on 'stability' fell flat, especially after recent military setbacks. Hunt's limited public engagements left voters with an impression of complacency, further highlighting Driberg's energetic appeal.

Driberg's campaign garnered significant endorsements from influential figures in the arts like George Bernard Shaw. Shaw urged voters to reject the rigid two-party system in favour of candidates selected for their merit, rather than party loyalty, while Priestley emphasised the urgent need for societal transformation in the wake of the war. These endorsements, widely publicised in local newspapers, dramatically enhanced Driberg's visibility and credibility.

Beyond his extensive public meetings, Driberg strategically utilised local media, contributing a column to the *Burnham Advertiser* titled 'Driberg – the only Candidate who lives in the Division'. This engaging weekly feature, crafted in his signature witty style, effectively promoted his events and highlighted his high-profile supporters, resonating deeply with readers and further solidifying his appeal.

Just a few days before polling, confidence in the war effort was shaken further by the fall of Tobruk, where 30,000 British soldiers were captured. This devastating defeat stunned the public and galvanised Driberg's campaign, inspiring him to release a hard-hitting leaflet titled 'Tragedy at Tobruk', which exposed critical failures in the war effort, from inadequate equipment to questionable leadership. Seizing on public outrage, Driberg rallied support against the government with a powerful call for accountability and reform. In response, the local Communist Party, initially backing Hunt, switched to Driberg after Hunt controversially blamed the North African defeat on Britain's support for Russia. Harold Quinton, secretary of the Braintree Communist Party, urged members to back Driberg, earning a reprimand from the national Communist Party.

On the eve of the poll, Driberg's momentum was undeniable. He managed to attend five meetings in Burnham, Maldon, Witham, Silver End and Braintree, arriving in Braintree at 10 p.m. to find a crowd of 6,000 people still waiting in the market place – a testament to his campaign's energy and resonance with the electorate.

Driberg's victory was emphatic, securing 12,219 votes compared to Hunt's 6,226. This triumph was not just a personal achievement; it signalled widespread discontent with the wartime coalition government and a growing demand for change among voters. Churchill's administration recognised that the outcome directly reflected public frustrations over government inefficiencies and military setbacks, particularly the fall of Tobruk.

National newspapers responded to the result with contrasting views.

The Times downplayed concerns, interpreting the outcome as a call for progress that would strengthen national unity. In stark contrast, the *Daily Mirror* celebrated the Conservative establishment's defeat, hailing Driberg's win as a clear indication of public dissatisfaction with conformity and ineffective leadership.

Driberg's place in history was now firmly established. He joined the Labour Party just before the 1945 general election and quickly became a captivating figure in the House of Commons, serving as an MP until 1974 – first in Maldon and later in Barking. His notorious lifestyle and daring views kept him from ministerial office. Instead, he used his platform to champion left-wing causes, serving for almost twenty-five years on Labour's National Executive Committee while maintaining a vibrant journalism career. Ironically, several months before his passing, he was awarded a peerage – an extraordinary honour for a man whose life defied convention.

The result of the Maldon by-election of 1942 ignited discussions about Britain's political future, indicating the electoral salience of a shift toward progressive, egalitarian policies that would shape the post-war era. Voters signalled their desire for leadership prioritising the welfare of ordinary citizens and returning servicemen. The formation of the Common Wealth Party just weeks after the by-election aimed to harness this momentum, although as a political entity, it struggled to gain any significant traction. Ultimately, Driberg's triumph highlighted a transformative political tide, reflecting the electorate's profound desire for change and a bold new direction for post-war Britain.

Will Timmins *is a leadership and executive search consultant. He has previously served as a parliamentary researcher to several MPs and peers.*

30

WEST DERBYSHIRE

---

17 FEBRUARY 1944
INDEPENDENT LABOUR GAIN FROM CONSERVATIVES

JAMES HEALE

Result: Charles White (Independent Labour), 16,336 votes, 57.7 per cent; William Cavendish (Conservative), 11,775 votes, 41.5 per cent; Robert Goodall (Agriculturalist), 233 votes, 0.8 per cent
Size of majority: 4,561
Swing: N/A
Name of previous MP and party: Henry Hunloke (Conservative)
Reason for by-election: Resignation of incumbent
Result at previous general election: Edward Cavendish (Conservative) elected unopposed
Date by-election called: 26 January 1944
Date by-election took place: 17 February 1944
Size of total electorate: N/A
Total number of votes cast: 28,344
Turnout: 65.4 per cent

The Labour landslide of 1945 came as a shock to Britain's governing class. War-weary aristocrats crammed into London's surviving hotels on election night to hear the results come in. As Winston Churchill despaired at Claridge's, in the rival Savoy one horrified grand dame exclaimed: 'They've elected a Labour government – the country will never stand for that!' Yet portents of the Tory disaster were obvious fifteen months earlier, when an independent leftist routed an aristocratic scion.

After the German reversal at Stalingrad, the course of the conflict had shifted decisively in the Allies' favour. Minds in Britain increasingly turned to post-war planning. The Beveridge Report, released in December 1942, became a bestseller, stimulating public discussion which highlighted party differences over reconstruction. A truce between the Conservatives, Liberals and Labour had prevailed since September 1939, preventing the three main parties from fielding candidates against each other when vacancies arose in the House of Commons. Yet with military victory now likely, successive by-elections showed a shift in public sentiment – disguised by the fig leaf of the wartime pact.

Labour boasted a lead of at least 10 per cent in the opinion polls from 1943 onwards. But with Clement Attlee and his comrades bound by the truce, new avenues had to be found to channel this discontent. Independent candidates won in four successive months in Grantham, Wallasey, Rugby and Maldon. From 1942 onwards, the newly formed Common Wealth Party – led by the ex-Liberal MP Sir Richard Acland – offered a fresh outlet for fatigued voters, hungry for reconstruction. The appeal of its progressive message was evidenced in January 1944, when the party seized the longtime Conservative stronghold of leafy Skipton in Yorkshire. It was the sixth time a National government candidate had lost a by-election, with seven further contests being close-run affairs.

A rupture in one of England's great aristocratic families caused another contest that same month. Since the late sixteenth century, the seat of West Derbyshire had served the interests of the Cavendish family, headed by the Duke of Devonshire. In the 1940s, it was considered one of the last remaining 'pocket boroughs'. Of the nineteen elections held in the constituency since 1883, the nominee of Chatsworth House had been returned unopposed on eight occasions. Edward Cavendish, the 10th Duke of Devonshire, had himself served as the Conservative Member of Parliament here from 1923 to 1938 before his accession to the peerage. The ensuing succession was a family affair: Henry Hunloke, Edward's brother-in-law, duly took over the seat.

The outbreak of war saw Hunloke deployed to the Middle East in the Wiltshire Yeomanry. Such a posting was blamed for his resignation from Parliament: Hunloke, it was claimed, felt unable to represent his constituents' interests while he remained on active service. The real reason, however, was the collapse of his marriage to Edward's sister Lady Anne. The Labour MP James Chuter Ede recorded the perception in political circles that Hunloke had been told that 'if you drop out of the Cavendish family you must surrender the family seat'. At the start of 1944, he did just that. Hunloke quit the Commons before divorcing his wife on the grounds of adultery in March 1945, remarrying just ten weeks later.

Wary of another by-election defeat, party managers moved quickly to replace him. On 24 January 1944 – before Hunloke's decision to resign had even been made public – his local association held an emergency meeting to decide a successor. The occasion was a stage-managed affair. The Duke of Devonshire chaired proceedings, with attendees enquiring as to whether his son and heir, the Marquess of Hartington, might care to stand. Upon Devonshire's confirmation of his son's availability, there then followed a short discussion on the improbability of a Central Office candidate being approved in time. It was thus decided that Hartington ought to be adopted unanimously.

It then transpired that the newly selected candidate had – conveniently – already arranged leave from his posting in the Coldstream Guards and was actually waiting outside the meeting room. He duly entered and addressed his selectors to acclaim. The by-election writ was moved just two days later by the Chief Whip James Stuart – another brother-in-law of the Duke of Devonshire. In the Commons, Sir Richard Acland was outraged. 'You can move the Writ now and have it today, but you are not going to get that seat.' The '48,000 citizens' of West Derbyshire, he argued, were 'being treated as if they were the goods and chattels' of the Cavendish family. Yet as the contest began, most in the constituency expected a Conservative victory, in keeping with the seat's tradition.

As Acland's by-election machine geared itself up, a familiar face emerged to challenge the Chatsworth influence. The West Derbyshire seat had been controlled by the family near-continuously for sixty years. A brief exception occurred between 1918 and 1922, when a Liberal cobbler called Charles White twice triumphed against Cavendish-backed candidates. Two decades on, his son 'young Charlie' White now put himself forward to succeed Hunloke as the MP. Closer in his politics to Labour, rather than the Liberals, the younger White had previously fought and lost the 1938 contest. His experience – and local memories of his father – gave him an edge over any outside candidate. Common Wealth duly backed White under the banner of 'Independent Labour'. A third man, Robert Goodall, stood as an 'Agriculturalist', in an explicit appeal to the farming vote.

The three-week contest was a Hobbesian affair: nasty, brutish and short. Both men addressed approximately a hundred meetings, with each campaign bombarding the seat's villages with leaflets, posters and loudspeaker vans. It was effectively a straight fight between the two frontrunners, with significant emphasis on personalities. One constituent told Mass Observation that 'the issue at stake was not whose policy was best but whether people preferred the Cavendishes or the Whites'.

White's supporters had little compunction in playing the class card against Hartington, who was asked several times whether he could milk a cow. Acland toured the constituency, framing the choice as one between 'an ordinary man' and 'the type of man who had been running the country before the last war and who expected to be called "Sir" or "My Lord"'. In the biggest gaffe of the campaign, Hartington suggested at a public meeting that Britain's coal mines were already nationalised – a remark which added to the impression of being 'out of touch'. 'His speeches were very short,' recorded Mass Observation, 'which suggested that he had been told not to say much in case he put his foot in it.' The 26-year-old army officer's campaign amounted to little more than a vague call for unity and vigorous support for Churchill. White, by contrast, pledged in his election address to fight for full employment, housing, demobilisation and implementing the Beveridge Report. He was aided too by discontent among local farmers, unhappy with low wages, high prices and the Ministry of Agriculture's policy of ploughing up meadowland for arable production.

The Prime Minister took a keen interest in the result, wary of the rising opposition to his coalition. Such was his concern that at the beginning of February 1944, the War Cabinet agreed to revise the terms of the political truce. The Duchess of Devonshire had invited Ernest Brown, the Chancellor of the Duchy of Lancaster, to speak in support of her son. The Cabinet agreed to henceforth allow ministers to give 'more positive measures of support' for by-election candidates, including speaking at meetings. The speech by Brown — a National Liberal — subsequently triggered a backlash from rival Liberal MPs, further straining the bonds of wartime partnership.

For Churchill, the change was not enough. Midway through the campaign, he sent a personal letter of support for Hartington, lauding the link between the candidate's family and the West Derbyshire seat. The gesture was ill-judged, given the strength of local feeling against 'the Devonshire interest'. White seized on the letter. He declared it 'unthinkable' that when 'thousands' were dying for freedom, 'we here in West Derbyshire should allow ourselves to be dictated to and interfered with in a by-election by one man. Mr Churchill is not Herr Hitler and England is not Germany – yet!'

The Cavendish family did their best to overcome the inadequacies of their local Tory association, mothballed since the advent of war. Hartington's American wife, Kathleen Kennedy, gained an early taste of political life on the campaign trail: her three brothers John, Robert and Teddy would all later run for the White House. The Duchess of Devonshire proved 'a force on the platform' for her son but later complained to JFK it 'was the worst and dirtiest fight I ever came across in all the nine or ten elections I have fought'. Meanwhile, the majority of White's canvassing was done by up to eighty staff from Acland's 'Common Wealth Circus', drawn from outside the constituency. They brought with them invaluable expertise, gained from previous wartime by-elections. White's chances were further boosted by a split in the local Liberals, with the local chairman and secretary backing different candidates.

The result proved to be a shock, both locally and nationally. On a turnout of 65.4 per cent, White comfortably triumphed with 57.7 per cent of the vote. Sir Richard Acland exulted that it was 'proof that Britain will not be content to return to the old 1939 world when we have defeated the enemy'. Hartington managed just 41.5 per cent. 'Duchesses' kisses are not what they used to be,' remarked his mother, recalling the famous contest of 1784 in which Georgiana, the Duchess of Devonshire, campaigned. The duke, bewildered by the seat's resounding rejection after his ancestors' work for 300 years, lamented: 'I don't know what the people want.' 'I do,' his heir replied. 'They just don't want the Cavendishes.' The dejected loser addressed a thousand local supporters. 'It has been a hard fight and that is the way it goes. I am going now to fight for you at the front,' adding: 'Better luck next time.' He was killed seven months later, picked off by a German sniper in the drive inland from Normandy. White clung on in 1945 by just 156 votes before sensibly retiring in 1950. West Derbyshire thereafter returned a line of Tories – including Matthew Parris and Patrick McLoughlin – until 2024, when its successor seat Derbyshire Dales voted Labour for the first time.

But the lasting significance of the West Derbyshire by-election was in hastening the end of the National government. News of the outcome 'caused a pall of the blackest gloom to fall on the PM', recalled his secretary in his diaries. So upset was Churchill that his initial thought was to call a general election. Always a man drawn to coalitions, he had previously harboured hopes of continuing his administration into peace time. Yet the West Derbyshire result, in the aftermath of Skipton, confirmed that the wartime truce was fraying under the revival of party political sentiments. It spurred efforts to overhaul the national campaign machines, enabling the main parties to independently fight the next election. In October 1944, both Labour and the Liberals formally declared that they would not fight it on a coalition ticket.

Right up until the end of the war, Churchill urged Attlee to maintain their wartime partnership at every stage. But, in the words of the historian Harry Bennett, 'the cumulative effective of the Independent and Common Wealth by-election victories' had helped convince the Labour 'rank and file that it could fight the first post-war election as an independent party'. West Derbyshire let the party political genie back out of the bottle: once it was released, there was no turning back.

James Heale is the deputy political editor of The Spectator *magazine. He has written for* The Times, *the* Washington Post *and* Tatler *among others. He co-authored the Liz Truss biography* Out of the Blue *(Harper-Collins, 2024) which was named politics book of the year by the* Sunday Times *and* The Guardian.

31

MOTHERWELL & WISHAW

12 APRIL 1945
SNP GAIN FROM LABOUR

RICHARD FINLAY

Result: Robert D. McIntyre (SNP), 11,417, 51.4 per cent; Alexander Anderson (Labour), 10,800, 48.6 per cent
Size of majority: 617
Swing: N/A
Name of previous MP and party: James Walker (Labour)
Reason for by-election: Death of incumbent
Result at previous general election: James Walker (Labour), 14,755, 50.7 per cent; Thomas Ormiston (Unionist), 14,325, 49.3 per cent
Date by-election called: February 1945
Date by-election took place: 12 April 1945
Size of total electorate: 41,133
Total number of votes cast: 22,217
Turnout: 54.0 per cent

The Motherwell & Wishaw by-election in April 1945 entered the annals of history because it returned the first ever Scottish National Party (SNP) Member of Parliament, Dr Robert McIntyre.

It was the twelfth of thirteen by-elections that were held in Scotland during the Second World War out of seventy-two Scottish constituencies. Not only were there more Scottish MPs at this time but there were also two idiosyncrasies in the Scottish electoral system. Three MPs were elected by graduates who had an additional vote for the University constituency and while Dundee was one constituency, it returned two MPs bringing the total number of Scottish MPs at this time to seventy-four. The Scottish seats made up 12 per cent of the total then, compared to just under 8 per cent today. Motherwell & Wishaw was the first of two Scottish seats which changed hands during the war and was followed by the Scottish Universities which was announced the next day and returned an Independent, the scientist John Boyd Orr, who would win the Nobel Prize in 1949 and was widely regarded as having nationalist leanings.

These two by-election results were seen as part of a wider movement of Scottish discontent with the current constitutional arrangement that emerged during the war and would arguably peak with the Scottish Covenant Association which would present some 2 million signatures in favour of establishing Scottish home rule in the late 1940s and early 1950s.

The war delayed the normal electoral cycle which meant that the parliament elected in 1935 lasted until 1945. Its longevity together with the circumstances associated with total war undoubtedly contributed to the unusually large number of by-elections that were held during that period. A total of 141 seats fell vacant, which works out at over two a month for the duration of the war. By-elections during the war were subject to a truce among the major parties which stipulated that should a seat fall vacant, only the incumbent party would contest it, with the rest bowing out. The argument behind this arrangement was that it would preserve national unity, although a large number of Labour rank and file were unhappy because it would also preserve the Conservative 200-seat majority.

Some sixty-six seats were uncontested, but in the other seventy-five, non-established parties and Independent candidates, most notably Sir Richard Acland's Common Wealth Party, were able to mount a challenge against the Conservative Party. By-elections are notoriously tricky to utilise to chart political trends at the best of times but were even more difficult to read because of the wartime truce. Pacifists, carpetbaggers, self-publicists and candidates who expressed a general disgruntlement about the conduct of the war were all part of the mix. Yet for all the difficulties, historians have used the results of the by-elections to chart the leftward drift of public opinion during the war, by noting the growing popularity of candidates who articulated a clear left-wing agenda which pointed the way forward to the Labour landslide in 1945.

During the war, there was a persistent nationalist grumbling, some of it stirred up by the Labour Secretary of State, Thomas Johnston, who used the threat of discontent to strengthen his hand in Cabinet negotiations. Despite the protestations of Scottish newspaper editors, 'England' and 'English' was frequently used in government statements and propaganda to describe the nation and state. There were complaints that the Scottish economy was not receiving its due from government intervention, with too much focus on storage rather than production, and concerns about the commitment to post-war reconstruction that would tackle the long-standing problems associated with poverty and poor housing remained.

The SNP was not part of the political truce and in the Argyll by-election in 1940 managed to secure a respectable 37 per cent of the vote against a Conservative candidate, although there may have been a significant protest against Chamberlain, as election day followed the German invasion of Norway.

The SNP failed to capitalise on this good showing due to organisational weakness and internal division over whether the best strategy was to act as a pressure group that would push the Labour and Liberal parties in support of home rule or one that would contest elections to secure an electoral mandate by winning a majority of Scottish parliamentary seats. The party split at the annual conference in 1942 with John MacCormick and his followers going off to form the Scottish Covenant Association, which would act as a cross-party pressure group, while the rump of the SNP would focus on being more of a conventional political party that would demonstrate the popularity of Scottish self-government by winning elections.

The split also tended to reflect more fundamental ideological differences between those who were more devolutionist and moderate and those more in favour of the creation of a separate Scottish state described as fundamentalists. The division was not as hard and as fast as it might seem, because many members of the SNP were also members of the Scottish Covenant Association and MacCormick stood as an Independent candidate in the Paisley by-election of 1948 on a home rule ticket.

In February 1944, the SNP contested the Kirkcaldy by-election. The candidate, Douglas Young, who had been jailed for his opposition to conscription which he argued was contrary to the Treaty of Union and that only a Scottish Parliament had that right, was a larger-than-life character, who had an eye for publicity. A kilt-wearing classicist with a photographic memory who stood at 6ft 7in. made the issue of female conscripted labour a key part of his election campaign because young unmarried Scottish women were being sent to work in factories in England. This caused considerable discontent among many families and was criticised by church authorities which believed that it put young women at 'moral risk'. One factor in the Kirkcaldy by-election that would help Young was that it was a Labour seat and that meant there was no alternative left-wing candidate. Furthermore, a tendency that emerged during the war was that Conservative voters tended to observe the spirit of the wartime truce more than Labour voters, but this was beginning to wear off, with Conservative voters becoming more openly partisan. Young managed to secure over 40 per cent of the vote and came in as a good second.

The reasonable performance of the SNP seemed to vindicate the policy of contesting elections and paved the way for the adoption of a candidate to contest Motherwell when the seat became vacant following the death of the Labour MP James Walker. The SNP chose Dr Robert McIntyre, a medic who was a conscientious objector and started his life in politics as a member of Labour Party while at Glasgow University. In the general election in 1935, Labour had narrowly won against the Tories, which meant that the SNP had an advantage in that as they were the only party to contest the election, they could capitalise on a significant anti-Labour vote. At the tail end of the war, McIntyre focused his campaign on post-war reconstruction and his expertise as a public health specialist was put to good use. Like Gordon Brown, McIntyre was a 'Son of the Manse' and his Presbyterian influence was important in shaping his public speaking skills that made his delivery and style more of a secular sermon that the locals would be both familiar and comfortable with. Hustings were well attended and raucous affairs and, in the days before television, almost functioned as a form of public entertainment – think of the election meeting in *The 39 Steps*. The *Motherwell and Wishaw Advertiser* reported regularly on the campaign and published election speeches verbatim. Motherwell was in easy reach of Glasgow, which meant that activists from Glasgow could readily travel to the constituency to take part in canvassing and campaigning, and opponents conceded that the SNP had run an efficient operation.

The thrust of McIntyre's message was one of local democracy and the need to have safeguards against the powers of an overpowering centralised state. Scottish self-government with the establishment of a parliament and a vibrant local government would act as an antidote against the encroachments of state bureaucracy and standardisation. An important component in McIntyre's thought was the belief that the impersonal forces of capitalism and state socialism or communism were a threat to individual freedom and that bulwarks of local democracy, be that the Scottish Parliament or local councils, were necessary to safeguard the interests of the local community. In his manifesto he argued:

> Scotland has no need of a highly centralised state interfering in the private lives of the people. We have seen enough of that kind of thing whereby homes are broken up at the behest of officials of one kind and another during the war. A self-governing Scotland would depend on the natural organisation of the family and the local community for its stability. The vigour and integrity of local authority in Parish and Burgh must be restored and control of affairs brought as near to people as possible. Let the community of Scotland be reborn.

This had strong echoes of traditional liberalism and would likely have struck a chord with traditional Conservative voters. In many respects, it was more like some of the politics expressed by parties in the Dominion nations of the British Empire than the staple of class-based politics espoused by the Tories and Labour. It also helped to make it more distinguishable from the SNP's British competitors, and a pitch to the centre ground arguably would not alienate the anti-Labour vote.

McIntyre won with just over half of the vote and a slim majority of 617 on a much-reduced turnout of 54 per cent. About a fifth of voters in the 1935 general election stayed home and this worked to the advantage of the SNP, as there was a strong suspicion that Tories turned out to vote against Labour. Certainly, the reaction among the established parties was that the result was a flash in the pan and pointed out the erratic nature of the Motherwell electorate, which had elected a communist in the past. In any case, a general election was surely in the offing with the war coming to an end. There may have been a degree of Labour complacency – a charge that was levelled at the Scottish Party following the 1945 general election when the Scots failed to make the same progress as was the case south of the border.

McIntyre had a short tenure in the Commons – made shorter by the fact that he was elected at the start of a parliamentary recess and only took his seat at the beginning of June and lost it in the general election in July when it was recaptured by Labour, although he secured over 8,000 votes. He did, however, manage to make his mark. Described by Harold Nicolson as a 'sad nuisance', McIntyre immediately ruffled the feathers of the Westminster establishment by refusing to accept parliamentary sponsors, as was the tradition for all new members, on the grounds that he 'owed no loyalty to the English controlled parties' as that was reserved exclusively for 'Scotland and its people'. He approached the Speaker's Chair on his own without sponsors and was immediately chided that the convention from 1688 was that new members had to be introduced to the Table. As McIntyre pointed out, this was a convention of the English parliament before the Union with Scotland in 1707 and, therefore, was this parliament really just the English parliament continuing, rather than a new British parliament established in 1707? He was denied his seat and only took sponsors under protest, but the event did result in publicity with *Punch* publishing a cartoon of McIntyre entitled 'Intirely [*sic*] On My Own'. It was not flattering. He made important contributions to parliamentary debates on broadcasting and health and annoyed Winston Churchill by asking the Prime Minister 'if he will arrange for a referendum in Scotland on the question of the establishing of a democratic legislature in that country, through which the Scottish people would be able to control effectively the affairs of their own country'. 'No, sir,' was the curt response.

McIntyre's election ensured he was significant in the development of the post-war SNP. He was a pacifist and did not believe violence was a legitimate means to achieve political ends. He was also a constitutional-ist and believed that, whatever the means used to achieve it and its consequences for Scottish independence, the Treaty of Union of 1707 was legal and could only be undone by legal means. By demonstrating that winning elections was possible and by putting forward, as he saw it, the Scottish case in Westminster, a start was made towards the objective of securing a majority of Scottish seats to demonstrate an electoral mandate for independence. His election victory helped undermine the idea of using British political parties to secure self-government and while the SNP would become an independent political party and go it alone, it did not endorse the Sinn Féin policy of parliamentary abstentionism. This was the logical consequence of Scottish nationalists, unlike their Irish counterparts, of recognising the legality of the British state.

Richard Finlay is a professor of Scottish history at the University of Strathclyde. He recently published Scottish Nationalism: History, Ideology and the Question of Independence *(Bloomsbury Academic, 2022) and is finishing a book on Unionism and the Conservative Party in Scotland.*

32

BOURNEMOUTH

15 NOVEMBER 1945
CONSERVATIVE HOLD

DAVID HENCKE

Result: Brendan Bracken (Unionist), 22,980, 46.85 per cent; Edward Shackleton (Labour), 16,526, 33.69 per cent; Basil Wigoder (Liberal), 9,548, 19.46 per cent
Size of majority: 6,454
Swing: 10.29 per cent from Conservative to Labour
Name of previous MP and party: Leonard Lyle (Conservative)
Reason for by-election: Elevation to the House of Lords
Result at previous general election: Leonard Lyle (Conservative), 34,544, 55.45 per cent; Basil Wigoder (Liberal), 14,232, 22.85 per cent; Robert Spence Watson Pollard (Labour), 13,522, 21.71 per cent
Date by-election called: End of October 1945
Date by-election took place: 15 November 1945
Size of total electorate: Approx. 90,000
Total number of votes cast: 49,054
Turnout: 56.5 per cent

This Bournemouth by-election had a unique position in modern British politics which it held for seventy-six years. It was, until 2021, the only by-election where the governing party had increased its share of the vote.

Held on 15 November 1945, it was the seventh by-election since Clement Attlee's new Labour government won a landslide victory the previous July, gaining a majority of 145 with 49.7 per cent share of the popular vote. Only Tony Blair in 1997 and 2001 and Sir Keir Starmer, with a majority of 174 on a 33.7 per cent share of the vote, the lowest share on record, beat that.

In Bournemouth, Labour succeeded in slashing a healthy Tory majority of over 20,000 on general election day to 6,454 – a swing against the Conservatives of over 10 per cent. The party also pushed the Liberal Party from second to third place.

Not until Hartlepool in 2021, when Boris Johnson's government succeeded in overturning a Labour majority of 3,500 to a Tory majority of 6,940, a 16 per cent swing to the government of the day, has Bournemouth's 1945 record been beaten.

The by-election was caused by the incumbent Tory MP, Sir Leonard Lyell, being ennobled in September as Baron Lyle of Westbourne. He was born into a shipping family which later became a big player in the British sugar industry. He was very sporty, having competed three years running in the 1920s in the Wimbledon men's single tennis championships, later becoming president of the Lawn Tennis Association in 1932. During the rest of the Labour government's time in office, he took a prominent role fighting the party's proposals to nationalise the sugar industry. The successful campaign featured the catchy cartoon character 'Mr Cube' to popularise the issue.

His Tory successor was Brendan Bracken, a prominent supporter of Winston Churchill. He had lost his North Paddington seat in the Labour landslide in July and now sought a safe Tory seat to get back into Parliament. He had previously been Minister of Information, fighting Nazi propaganda, and First Lord of the Admiralty in Churchill's wartime Cabinet.

Bracken had led an extraordinary early life. Born in County Tipperary in the south of Ireland, the son of a stonemason, he rebelled against his strict Catholic school education at a Christian Brothers and Jesuit College, absconding from the latter and running up hotel bills in Dublin. In desperation, his mother sent him to stay with a cousin in Australia, where he lived a nomadic existence. He returned to England after five years and turned up at Sedbergh public school in Cumbria at the age of nineteen pretending his was a fifteen-year-old Australian boy who had been orphaned in a bush fire but was related to the headmaster of Winchester College. The headmaster did not quite believe him but was impressed with his tale and admitted him to the school.

In the 1920s, he went into publishing and journalism, starting at the *Empire News* where he was introduced to Winston Churchill. The two became close enough for Prime Minister Stanley Baldwin later to describe him as Churchill's 'faithful chela', *chela* being the Hindi word for disciple. He helped Churchill fight unsuccessful by-elections in the 1920s and stood by him in the wilderness years of the 1930s calling for Britain to rearm to fight the Nazis.

He also played a key role in Churchill becoming Prime Minister and wartime leader by advising him to stay silent when he was expected to nominate Lord Halifax as Chamberlain's successor after a deal with the Labour Party. His silence led to Lord Halifax withdrawing his name.

During the war, Eric Blair, better known as the author George Orwell, worked under him fighting Nazi propaganda and there was speculation whether the Big Brother acronym, BB, in the novel 1984 stood for Brendan Bracken. The book's hero was called Winston.

Edward Shackleton, the Labour candidate, thirty-four, was the younger son of the famous Antarctic explorer Ernest Shackleton. Edward Shackleton was an explorer and mountaineer himself, having led the 1932 Oxford University expedition to Borneo. During this trip, he made the first ascent of Mount Mulu, the second highest peak in Sarawak. In 1934, he was on another Oxford University expedition to a remote northern island, Ellesmere Land, in the Arctic Canadian wilderness which led to the naming of its mountain range, the British Empire Range, and its 9,000-foot mountain, Mount Oxford, after the university.

Leaving university, Shackleton joined the BBC as a talks producer in Northern Ireland, which changed his political views from supporting the Conservatives to Labour.

He had a distinguished war record as a pilot in the RAF. He started in the RAF Volunteer Reserve in 1940, ending the war as an acting wing commander. He was mentioned in dispatches in 1944 and in June 1945 was made an OBE in the king's birthday honours. So he had a good war record to present to Bournemouth electors in November.

Basil Wigoder, the Liberal Party candidate, stood in both the general election and the by-election for Bournemouth and also had a good war record. He was the youngest of the candidates at twenty-four. He had served in the Royal Artillery since 1942, when he was twenty-one, and had been promoted to second lieutenant. He was just starting a legal career by studying law at Oxford University where he was also president of the Oxford Union. A year after the by-election, he was called to the Bar at Gray's Inn, where he mainly practised criminal law.

The campaign was remarkably short by modern standards. Local council elections were held on 1 November, so the campaign did not begin until after that. Labour didn't start organising properly until 3 November – twelve days before polling day – so it was even more remarkable that they were able to slash the Conservative majority and push the Liberals into third place.

A letter dated 3 November from Ernest Robinson, the party's election agent, to all local Labour branches, asked them to provide the names and addresses of all people who paid the political levy. It warned: 'the matter is a very urgent one and I shall be glad if you can let me a list of names and addresses at once' – later amended by hand to say at the 'very earliest moment'.

In the next twelve days, party members had to address letters to 90,000 constituents. A novel feature was a form giving members' names and addresses requesting they would NOT be canvassed during the by-election so the party could concentrate on other voters. The party printed 1,000 of these leaflets.

The Labour campaign emphasised Edward Shackleton's military record and his OBE standing as wing commander. The Tories emphasised Brendan Bracken's closeness to Churchill and included bitter attacks on the new Labour government. The Liberals emphasised truth, justice and freedom.

All the campaigns brought in outside speakers to attract the crowds and sought endorsements from celebrities and well-known figures.

Both Winston Churchill, Leader of the Opposition, and Clement Attlee, gave ringing public endorsements to the Tory and Labour candidates, respectively. Churchill was gushing. In a letter to him published in the *Bournemouth Echo*, he wrote:

My dear Bracken, I do not need to recall to the electors of the Bournemouth Division the excellent services you rendered as Minister for Information in the Coalition Government. Still less need I remind them of your gifts of speech, your wide knowledge of affairs, or your keen political insight. But I would emphasise to them the value of these qualities in the present House of Commons where your vigorous personality and advocacy of Conservative principles will be a great help on the Opposition front Bench.

Clement Attlee was equally publicly supportive of Wing Commander Shackleton, describing him as 'a young man with an excellent war record and wide experience. You are well equipped to play an effective part as a member of the Parliamentary Labour Party. I wish you every success in your campaign and shall be glad to welcome you into our ranks in Parliament.'

The twelve-day campaign was very lively, often with three meetings a day. It included meetings when all candidates appeared, including one organised by the Women for Westminster movement. It also attracted what we would now call 'luvvies' to speak in Bournemouth.

The Liberal Party candidate, Basil Wigoder, managed to get John Creasey, the prolific, popular detective and crime writer, to speak at a meeting on 'truth, justice and freedom'.

Edward Shackleton got the actress Dame Sybil Thorndike to make her first election speech, as she said, 'since I was a young girl'. She denounced poverty in Bournemouth as a disgrace and went on to tell electors that the state should be the mother of the household and make sure there were 'fair do's for everyone'.

Brendan Bracken's campaign under the slogan 'Bracken for Bournemouth' got Tory peers, senior military figures and Dame Regina Evans, chief commandant of the Auxiliary Territorial Service, to speak. She backed him over his attack on bureaucrats requisitioning hotels after the war – an issue popular in a resort like Bournemouth which wanted a revival of the tourist industry.

Group Captain Max Aitken, then MP for Holborn and a hero as a former Battle of Britain pilot, also came to back Brendan Bracken and to condemn nationalisation towards the end of the campaign. Brendan was a friend of his father, Lord Beaverbrook. That afternoon, Lord Lyle, the former Bournemouth MP and now a peer, joined Bracken to denounce the socialists as 'quack doctors' giving people a pink medicine and leaving 'the patient in a torpor – not caring whether he lives or dies … Some lucky patients might be sick before they digest it,' he suggested.

Bracken said if he was elected, Bournemouth would have two voices in Parliament – one in the Commons and the Lords, referring to Lord Lyle's elevation.

He also had the prescience to warn against apathy in a Tory stronghold, concerned that people might not vote – he turned out to be right – as the Tory vote fell heavily on 15 November.

Certainly, Labour thought they had a chance. On the eve of poll, Edward Shackleton is quoted at a meeting saying the seat was winnable and that the Tories were finished. He also attacked the Liberal candidate for 'silly remarks' suggesting Labour wanted the state to control everything.

In fact, Shackleton would appear to have been a moderate Labour candidate for the times – he was careful in his speeches to defend the government on the nationalisation of the mines and the Bank of England – but was reassuring voters, especially hoteliers, that Labour was also in favour of private enterprise. 'We are not nationalising this and that for [the] fun of it,' he said at one meeting.

Labour's victory was not to be – but they did increase their vote, pushing the Liberal Party into third place. The Tory vote did come down by nearly 12,000 – but they still won with a majority just under 6,500.

All three candidates went on to do greater things. Brendan Bracken in the same year became the effective founder of the modern *Financial Times* and its headquarters, Bracken House, is named after him. He also founded *History Today* magazine and became publisher of *The Economist*. He also got a peerage but never took his seat in the House of Lords, saying it was 'like a morgue'. He also turned down a job in Churchill's government in 1951. A heavy smoker, he died from throat cancer in 1958.

Randolph Churchill, Winston's son, described him as 'a fantasist whose dreams came true'.

Edward Shackleton became an MP the following year, winning a by-election at Preston. He was a considerable force in Harold Wilson's government, becoming Lord Privy Seal and Leader of the House of Lords. His last piece of work was a report on the Falkland Islands for Labour.

Basil Wigoder tried unsuccessfully to become Liberal MP but got a peerage in 1974 and then became a force in the Liberal Party as party leader in the Lords. He was also a successful barrister.

David Hencke is a freelance lobby journalist writing for Byline Times *and* The Pensioner *magazine. He was previously Westminster correspondent on* The Guardian. *His own blog Westminster Confidential, davidhencke.com, campaigns on pension inequality, whistleblowing, injustice, corruption and lack of accountability.*

33

CARMARTHEN

28 FEBRUARY 1957
LABOUR GAIN FROM LIBERAL

ROGER AWAN-SCULLY

Result: Megan Lloyd George (Labour), 23,679, 47.3 per cent; John Morgan Davies (Liberal), 20,610, 41.2 per cent; Jennie Eirian Davies (Plaid Cymru), 5,741, 11.5 per cent
Size of majority: 3,069
Swing: 6.4 per cent from Liberal to Labour
Name of previous MP and party: Rhys Hopkin Morris (Liberal)
Reason for by-election: Death of incumbent
Result at previous general election: Rhys Hopkin Morris (Liberal), 24,420, 49.5 per cent; Jack Evans (Labour), 21,077, 42.7 per cent; Jennie Eirian Davies (Plaid Cymru), 3,825, 7.8 per cent
Date by-election called: 7 February 1957
Date by-election took place: 28 February 1957
Size of total electorate: 57,243
Total number of votes cast: 50,030
Turnout: 87.4 per cent

In late November 1956, a Britain still digesting the tumult of the recent Suez Crisis paid rather little attention to the death of the MP for Carmarthen, Sir Rhys Hopkin Morris. Suez would have multiple and often complicated impacts – on the political career of Prime Minister Anthony Eden and several of his senior colleagues, on the UK's relationships with its American and French allies and on the country's standing in the world and the future of its empire. Perhaps inevitably, the crisis would come to influence the outcome of the by-election that followed Hopkin Morris's demise. But the by-election would also showcase at least two longer-term domestic political themes: the ailing fortunes of the once-mighty Liberal Party and the interrelated theme of the Lloyd George family's complicated role in Welsh and British politics.

Sir Rhys Hopkin Morris had been deeply involved in the maelstrom of Liberal politics for several decades. Unusually for Welsh Liberals, he had sided with Asquith over Lloyd George in the divisions that affected the party after 1916. In the following few years, Hopkin Morris would be a parliamentary candidate as an Asquithian Liberal, an Independent Liberal and an official Liberal. Successfully elected for the Cardiganshire constituency in 1923, he held his seat through several subsequent elections until quitting Parliament voluntarily in 1932. Astonishingly, Hopkin Morris returned to the Commons in the 1945 general election when, with nearly all of Britain swinging strongly to Labour and the Liberals in further decline, he actually captured the Carmarthen seat for his party from a sitting Labour MP. He then retained the seat through the three subsequent general elections, even as the fortunes of the Liberal Party declined yet further: from only twelve parliamentary seats in 1945 to nine in 1950, and then a mere six MPs in both 1951 and 1955. When Hopkin Morris's fellow Welsh MP Clement Davies resigned as Liberal leader a year after the disappointing 1955 election, Hopkin Morris was thus one of perilously few MPs that could, in theory, have succeeded Davies. But the Carmarthen MP was by then sixty-eight, and as a Commons deputy Speaker since 1951, he had already largely eschewed partisanship. Moreover, Hopkin Morris died just one month later.

The ensuing by-election, in a Liberal-held seat with a narrow majority, posed an immediate problem for new party leader Jo Grimond. In later years, he and subsequent Liberal/Liberal Democrat leaders would often seize upon by-elections as an opportunity for the third party to capitalise on discontent with incumbent governments. For now, Carmarthen offered a much less enticing prospect. Barely into the role of party leader, Grimond was forced into defending one of the few remaining pieces of Liberal territory. This task was rendered even more difficult by a very obvious Liberal split on the dominant issue of the day. Grimond had publicly and repeatedly opposed Operation

Musketeer, Prime Minister Eden's military expedition to take control of the Suez Canal. But the new Liberal candidate in Carmarthen, John Morgan Davies, had supported Eden over Suez, as previously had Hopkin Morris. The Liberals thus got the worst of all worlds – being publicly divided on the main political issue of the day, while their national opposition to Musketeer almost certainly alienated many of the Conservatives who they were dependent on for support in the seat.

The Conservatives had not contested the Carmarthen constituency since 1935. The seat was one of a number of seats where electoral pacts were repeatedly agreed between the Conservatives and Liberals to avoid splitting the non-Labour vote. Conservative support was thus crucial to the Liberals in Carmarthen. Such pacts made a great deal of sense for the Liberals, who by the 1950s struggled to field candidates in many constituencies anyway: in return for standing aside in seats where they stood no chance, they got a clear run against Labour and the possibility of significant Tory support in some places where they might still win. The local pact in Carmarthen held good for the by-election. But it was to prove a final hurrah – there would be no further such Con–Lib by-election electoral pacts, and by the 1959 general election, there would also be a Conservative candidate in Carmarthen.

The timing of Hopkin Morris's death, and the calling of the by-election for the end of February, meant that the campaign ran through the entirety of the Welsh winter of 1956–57 and either side of Christmas and New Year celebrations. Such campaigning would be challenging in any seat. In a large, rural constituency, it was even more so. And yet the by-election, when it came, generated what to modern eyes is an astonishing turnout of nearly 90 per cent of the registered electorate! In part, this was indicative of a broader tradition of political engagement and high turnouts in the constituency – at the previous general election, turnout had been above 85 per cent. But in 1957, there was an additional factor with considerable pulling power – the Labour Party candidate.

David Lloyd George had been inextricably associated with the Liberal Party's success across Britain, and its total dominance of Welsh politics, in the early years of the twentieth century. But the 'Welsh wizard' was also deeply implicated in the subsequent splintering and vertiginous decline of his party. By the post-war period, with the great man now dead and the Liberals apparently politically doomed, his family began to abandon ship. Son Gwilym Lloyd George had (in effect) left the Liberals for the Conservatives in the late-1940s, becoming a Tory Home Secretary in the mid-1950s. But the most politically talented of David Lloyd George's children moved in the opposite direction to her brother. After losing her Anglesey seat to Labour in the 1951 general election, Lady Megan Lloyd George had defected to that party four years later. Now, the Carmarthen by-election offered her an ideal opportunity to come back into Parliament.

Labour needed only a small swing from the previous general election to win Carmarthen. They faced Liberal opponents who were divided on the main political issue of the day and who would be without any personal vote that Hopkin Morris had managed to accrue over his time as an MP. In addition to these significant advantages, Labour had one further card to play in fielding Lady Megan as their candidate. In a rural, largely Welsh-speaking constituency, Labour was able to field a fluent Welsh speaker who was deeply familiar with rural Wales. But she was more than that: Lady Megan was also a highly skilled politician with considerable 'star quality' who could tap into the residual pull that the Lloyd George name still had in much of rural Wales.

The by-election was very much a two-horse race. But there was one other candidate on the ballot paper. Jennie Eirian Davies had first stood for Plaid Cymru in the Carmarthen constituency at the previous 1955 general election, gaining a respectable 7.8 per cent of the vote but still losing her deposit. Like their sister party the SNP in Scotland, Plaid Cymru were still very much a minor force in electoral politics at the time. Their limited support, such as it was, was mostly confined to rural and more Welsh-speaking communities, and it was in these places where Plaid focused their very limited resources. The by-election offered a chance for the party to raise their profile and support with a campaign in precisely this type of constituency, and so it was unsurprising that Eirian Davies was once again nominated to stand for Plaid.

Labour sought to make Suez the main issue in the campaign, with Lady Megan happy to exploit Liberal divisions on the issue and maximise the difficulties that this might give to her main opponent in winning votes from Conservative sympathisers. The Labour candidate also repeatedly emphasised her own roots in Liberal radicalism, a strand of thought that she suggested her former party had now abandoned. The Liberals sought to avoid the Suez issue and focus much more on local matters with their locally based candidate. Plaid Cymru did not pretend that they were likely to win the by-election but did talk up their chances of doubling or even trebling their support from the previous general election – hopes that were not quite to be realised.

Voting took place on the last day of February 1957, the same day as another by-election in Wednesbury in the English Midlands. On a significant but hardly huge swing of just over 6 per cent, the seat changed hands from Liberal to Labour. The majority of just over 3,000 that Sir Rhys Hopkin Morris had enjoyed at the 1955 general election was converted into a very similar sized victory margin for Lady Megan Lloyd George. She would go on to hold the seat, with even larger majorities, in the three subsequent general elections.

Returned to Parliament, Lady Megan mainly focused either on agriculture – of obvious relevance to her rural constituency – or Welsh affairs. She continued her long-standing support for Welsh recognition within the UK. Having been a leading voice within the Parliament for Wales campaign earlier in the 1950s, she also supported the creation of a Secretary of State for Wales: this latter ambition was realised when Jim Griffiths became the first ever Welsh Secretary in 1964. However, neither Hugh Gaitskell nor Harold Wilson ever promoted her to their shadow ministerial team, and she remained a backbench MP when Labour regained power in 1964.

In difficult circumstances, the Liberals' vote in Carmarthen actually held up rather well. But it was not enough to prevent them losing a seat that they had held for over a decade and declining to a mere five MPs in the House of Commons. And through all the subsequent ups and downs in the fortunes of the party and its successors, Liberals have never again come close to winning a parliamentary seat in this part of Wales. Their opposition to the Suez debacle made considerable political sense for the Liberals nationally. But it was ill luck for the party that a by-election that followed so swiftly after the crisis was in a constituency where their stance on the crisis was electorally harmful: splitting the national party from their local candidate and alienating the Liberals from necessary Conservative support.

The great irony of the 1957 Carmarthen by-election was that the person condemning the Liberals to their lowest-ever number of MPs should be someone from the Lloyd George family. But like her brother, Lady Megan had been forced to the conclusion, after years of Liberal decline and failure, that her political ambitions and objectives could best be secured from within another party. Her victory in Carmarthen would not, in fact, turn out to be a further step towards total Liberal extinction, but such hardly seemed implausible at the time. Meanwhile, her own political career had been given a new lease of life. The same could not be said of her two opponents in the contest: neither John Morgan Davies nor Jennie Eirian Davies ever stood for Parliament again.

For the third party standing in the by-election, there was little to celebrate beyond a modest improvement in their vote share. They were still unable to save their electoral deposit. But this modest improvement from a low base was actually the harbinger of, for Plaid, the much more momentous Carmarthen by-election that would follow Lady Megan's own death some nine years later.

Roger Awan-Scully is a professor and dean of arts and social sciences at Hong Kong Metropolitan University.

34

TORRINGTON

27 MARCH 1958
LIBERAL GAIN FROM NATIONAL LIBERAL AND CONSERVATIVE

MICHAEL McMANUS

Result: Mark Bonham Carter (Liberal), 13,408, 37.99 per cent; Anthony Royle (Conservative), 13,189, 37.37 per cent; Leonard Lamb (Labour), 8,697, 24.64 per cent
Size of majority: 219
Swing: 32.84 per cent from National Liberal and Conservative to Liberal
Name of previous MP and party: George Lambert (National Liberal and Conservative)
Reason for by-election: Elevation to the House of Lords following death of father
Result at previous general election: George Lambert (National Liberal), 20,124, 65.05 per cent; Leonard Lamb (Labour), 10,812, 34.95 per cent
Date by-election called: 6 March 1958
Date by-election took place: 27 March 1958
Size of total electorate: 43,790
Total number of votes cast: 35,294
Turnout: 80.60 per cent

At the 1951 general election, the Liberal Party had hit its lowest point, winning just 2.5 per cent of the vote and six seats. Three of those seats were in rural Wales and, in its two English seats, in Bolton and Huddersfield, the party was dependent upon an electoral pact with the Conservatives. The sole other MP was rising star Jo Grimond, in his northern outpost of Orkney & Shetland. By 1955, the party looked like the largest minor party, not the smallest major party. Party leader Clement Davies was so unwell he was barely able to campaign, and it was Jo Grimond, nominally party Chief Whip but increasingly its leader-in-waiting, who fronted the show. In November 1956, Grimond finally took up the reins in a necessary but painful coup. Davies, already in his seventies and in failing health, was reluctant to stand aside, but events at Suez and in Hungary necessitated a livelier and more effective leader.

The Liberal revival had arguably already begun, with an almost unnoticed fillip in the local elections of spring 1956. What would become a familiar post-war pattern was asserting itself, as Liberal fortunes revived during a long period of Conservative government. It wasn't all plain sailing for Grimond, though: in the month he became leader, his parliamentary colleague Rhys Hopkin Morris, the MP for Carmarthen, died suddenly and unexpectedly. Labour's by-election candidate was Megan Lloyd George, formerly deputy leader of the Liberals, who beat a pro-Suez Liberal by 3,000 votes. The Liberal parliamentary party was now perilously reduced to only five MPs.

The Carmarthen result was largely the consequence of strictly local factors, not least the deep local affection for Hopkin Morris and the sheer force of personality of Megan Lloyd George. Although it was a brutal blow, therefore, it was by no means mortal and there were other reasons for optimism. After Suez, a small but significant group of voters and, especially, political activists had detached themselves from the Tories. They were now in search of a new home; and Grimond was a charismatic and persuasive figure.

The following year, 1957, was decisive, as Grimond and his coterie took charge of the party machine and began to build a stronger, more independent profile for the party, taking full advantage of the emergence of television as an influential mass medium. At a by-election in Gloucester in September 1957, Liberal Patrick Lort-Phillips won 20 per cent of the vote in a seat the party had not contested at all in 1955. Then, on 16 December 1957, the Conservative MP for Rochdale died. This was another seat the Liberals had failed to contest in 1955, but they selected well-known broadcaster Ludovic Kennedy as their candidate and threw themselves into the contest with passion.

Labour gained the seat on 13 February 1958 but with a reduced share of the vote. Building on nothing, Kennedy was the story of the night, coming a strong second with over 17,000 votes – 35.5 per cent of the total. For the Tories, it was a humiliation, but for the Liberals, proof that a much-needed parliamentary victory might now be within sight. Television companies had previously kept a safe distance from political controversy, but the lure of Ludovic Kennedy and Mrs Kennedy, aka Moira Shearer of *Red Shoes* fame, proved too much for them: they played an unprecedented, significant role by providing lively coverage of the Rochdale campaign. The Liberal Party was back in business and increasingly media savvy too.

Four days after Rochdale, George Lambert, the first Viscount Lambert, died at the age of ninety-one. His son, also George, succeeded to the title and had to resign as MP for Torrington, which he had won by 9,312 votes in 1955, gaining 65 per cent of the votes cast in a straight fight with Labour. The West Country had strong Liberal traditions and Lambert was one of a number of Tories who stood there under the increasingly anachronistic 'National Liberal–Conservative' label. The by-election was not totally unexpected, given the advanced age and frail health of the first viscount; and although the Liberals had not contested the seat in 1955, they did now have a prospective candidate in place, a 59-year-old local farmer by the name of Ambrose Fulford, who had been nursing the seat for two years. Fulford had, however, warned Grimond and Jeremy Thorpe the previous year that he did not feel he would necessarily be up to the demands of a by-election campaign.

At this time, Jo Grimond was undertaking a Herculean task. Having gained Orkney & Shetland in 1950 against all expectations, he had consolidated his position there considerably but remained desperately fearful that his constituents – a tight-knit and geographically remote bunch of hardy souls – might feel neglected as his national profile grew and revolt against him. So, he continued to commute back to his 'patch' most weekends, while also flying the flag at Westminster and campaigning around the country as best he could.

He needed rapidly to build a team around him of credible, loyal and effective lieutenants. His shortlist for any parliamentary opportunities was headed by Mark Bonham Carter, brother of his wife Laura.

Although, as the grandson of Herbert Asquith, Bonham Carter had dynastic Liberal credentials of the first order, the Tories had long tried to seduce him with promises of a safe seat and rapid preferment, and, in the immediate run-up to the Suez Crisis, he was reported to have been going through the necessary procedures for signing up. Eden's handling of Suez and Grimond's accession had then cemented him back into the Liberal cause. Mark Bonham Carter was not, by all accounts, the easiest of men – he was a somewhat aloof Wykehamist who could appear arrogant, spiky and impatient – but he was highly intelligent, politically astute and, above all, fiercely loyal to Jo and Laura Grimond.

After Rochdale, Torrington looked eminently winnable and Grimond immediately wanted Bonham Carter, who conveniently had fought part of the constituency in 1945 on old boundaries, to be the candidate. It was reported on 24 February that Ambrose Fulford had, indeed, contacted the executive committee of the Torrington Liberals and offered to stand down, in favour a younger man, 'say about 40', though he would still stand if they wanted him to: 'So far as I am concerned, the future of the party is more important than the individual.' There was immediate press speculation about John Foot, Frank Byers – and Mark Bonham Carter. It was not, however, front-page news across the board. Not yet.

The following day, it was reported that Mark Bonham Carter ('36 and a friend of Princess Margaret') was indeed to be invited to meet the executive committee, with a view to becoming their candidate. Herbert Harris, director general of the party organisation, explained that this was 'just a formality'. He was duly selected in his absence. Bonham Carter's mother, Lady Violet, wrote in her diary that 'I can see that Mark's mouth waters for the fray'. With his wife, Mark Bonham Carter then diplomatically spent a weekend at Southcott Barton in the constituency, staying with Ambrose Fulford in an apparent show of unity.

He was still to meet the constituency executive and, in a phrase unlikely to make a comeback, especially in Liberal Democrat circles, denied being 'the n***** in the woodpile', claiming there was no question of his splitting the Liberal vote. When he did present himself to the association the following Friday, he exuded confidence, speaking about the H-bomb, economic policy and foreign affairs and noting how quickly the Conservatives had moved the writ for the by-election: 'They are prepared to face the farmers before the annual price review, but are not prepared to face the country after the Budget.' He was enthusiastically applauded and cheered by a large crowd. A Liberal tide was turning.

Even though the ousted Fulford assured his successor of his full and active support, there was no shortage of local Liberals bemoaning the loss of a local man as their candidate. The party's candidate for Falmouth & Camborne, Alan Gibson, publicly criticised the party, saying Fulford had been 'stabbed in the back by party headquarters' and he hoped Bonham Carter would lose his deposit. Under the new dispensation, Gibson was rapidly summoned before his own executive committee to give an account of himself and only partially retracted his sentiments: 'I believed the matter was badly mishandled, but, because Liberalism so obviously responded to the country's needs, I was prepared to give my support to Mr Bonham Carter.' Thereafter, things would improve rapidly, beginning with a carefully choreographed mass defection of Young Conservatives in Exeter, who came en masse to campaign at the by-election.

There was a significant degree of national interest in the contest, with some early articles focusing on the candidates' wives. Mrs Mark Bonham Carter was the former Lady St Just and a daughter of the US publishing magnate Condé Nast (one piece affirmed she 'has not only good looks and a friendly manner, but is useful secretarially'); whereas Mrs Anthony Royle, wife of the National Liberal–Conservative candidate, was better known as the celebrated model Shirley Worthington. In contrast, Mrs Leonard Lamb, wife of the Labour candidate, an engine driver, said she was 'no glamour girl'. Mrs Lamb was a formidable local presence in her own right, however, and no stranger to making 'stump' speeches. Lamb was the one truly local candidate in the contest – a county councillor, a Justice of the Peace and chairman of the Newton Abbot Urban Council. He had also fought the seat before, so, at the outset of the campaign, there was a genuine belief he might even win, in a three-cornered contest.

It was largely an orthodox campaign. There were a number of opinion polls and they consistently showed the Liberal candidate slightly ahead, which suited the Liberals perfectly. Perhaps this was even the wellspring of the party's infamous 'neck-and-neck' literature? Bonham Carter's one slip of the campaign came when a piece of his election literature appeared to suggest he wanted to 'Ban the Bomb'. In meetings, he stuck rigidly to the party line, against an independent deterrent but not a unilateralist.

The government did, in the event, announce both a 1 per cent cut in the base rate and also, less helpfully to Anthony Royle, some cuts to farming subsidies, a severe, possibly mortal, blow to his campaign: 600 or so square miles of the constituency were dominated by dairy tenant farmers and both milk and egg subsidies were cut. The liveliest moment of all came when the redoubtable Bessie Braddock encountered Anthony Royle in front of the town hall at Crediton. Forewarned of her presence, Royle offered her a chocolate Easter egg, inscribed with the message 'To Bessie, with love from Tony' and tied with a blue ribbon. She brushed it aside and it smashed on the pavement, to the delight of the local canine population. Royle withdrew for a time, then returned, to be verbally abused by hecklers who ended up with a police warning.

Mark Bonham Carter undertook a testing timetable, involving a daily press conference at 9.30 a.m., followed by a full day's campaigning and a series of meetings every evening. His mother Lady Violet and Jeremy Thorpe threw their full weights behind the campaign, she memorably likening the Conservative candidate to the 'hind legs of a Tory pantomime horse'. Grimond spent one full day in the constituency, addressing three meetings and being pleasantly surprised by the welcome he received. At the last meeting, in Bideford, he had an audience of around 1,200 people, the biggest of the campaign. Ludovic and Moira Kennedy also attended.

An eve-of-poll editorial in the *Daily Telegraph* hyperbolically warned of 'Fratricide at Torrington' between Bonham Carter and Royle:

If the Socialist candidate were to slip into the seat under their clashing swords, the electors of the Right who had voted Liberal would look very foolish. The question would have to be asked in all marginal constituencies: what is to be done about Liberals who insist on using the Right-wing vote to help the Left into Parliament? That is the real danger at Torrington tomorrow: that a vote for Liberalism turns out in the end to be a vote for Socialism.

What a powerful reminder that still all-too familiar argument provides, of the cyclical nature of politics. There is indeed little (or nothing) new under the political sun.

On the eve of poll, Mark Bonham Carter said he believed he was poised to win 16,000 votes, which would deliver victory. In the event, 13,408 votes sufficed and he did win the seat, after a recount, by a slender but historic margin of 219 votes, on a remarkable turnout of just over 80 per cent of the electorate (10 per cent higher than at the 1955 general election): the first Liberal gain at a by-election since March 1929. Lady Violet was ecstatic, likening the revived Liberals of Torrington to a liberating army and sending out a message to like-minded folk elsewhere – 'Hold on, hold on, we are coming!'

Grimond penned an article in the *News Chronicle*, on 29 March 1958, conceding that it could be argued that a Liberal vote was a protest vote but then 'all votes are' in some sense and, at least, a Liberal vote 'isn't a protest vote against one particular thing ... It is a protest against the whole of politics since the war ... It is a protest against broken promises and bumbledom [a direct antecedent of "the blob"].' But most important of all was: 'Our opponents used to say that a Liberal vote was a wasted vote. Torrington has killed that dead.' Subsequent analysis showed the Liberals had taken two Conservative votes for every one socialist vote: 39 per cent of Bonham Carter's supporters had voted Tory in 1955 and 54 per cent of his voters were women.

When Mark Bonham Carter took his seat in the House of Commons, the faint cheers of his new colleagues were drowned out by laughter and jeers from the other parties. He soon established an unchallengeable position as Jo Grimond's closest confidant and, for a time, his most important parliamentary lieutenant. With a reliable parliamentary seat, he would in all probability have given Jeremy Thorpe a run as Grimond's successor, but, in 1959, he lost at Torrington by 2,265 votes.

Four by-elections in a row – at Gloucester, Ipswich, Rochdale and now Torrington – had served Liberal purposes very well and, for the remainder of the 1955 parliament, the party would devote a considerable amount of effort and of its limited resources to contesting residential and agricultural seats at by-elections. Harold Macmillan was beginning to make his mark as Prime Minister, however; and as 1958 progressed, the initiative was slipping away from the opposition parties. In the House of Commons, Aneurin Bevan tried to patronise Macmillan by dubbing him 'Mr MacWonder'. 'What a bloody silly thing to say,' Jo Grimond whispered to Mark Bonham Carter. Grimond was among the first to realise that, for all his old-world mannerisms, this new Conservative Prime Minister was going to prove far more formidable than most people had foreseen.

Michael McManus is an author and playwright. His biography of former Liberal leader Jo Grimond, Towards the Sound of Gunfire, *was published in 2001 and, in spring 2024, his play* Party Games *had a national tour, produced by the Yvonne Arnaud Theatre.*

35

ORPINGTON

14 MARCH 1962
LIBERAL GAIN FROM CONSERVATIVES

LORD NORTON

Result: Eric Lubbock (Liberal), 22,846, 52.9 per cent; Peter Goldman (Conservative), 14,991, 34.7 per cent; Alan Jinkinson (Labour), 5,350, 12.4 per cent
Size of majority: 7,855
Swing: 26.8 per cent from Conservative to Liberal
Name of previous MP and party: Douglas Sumner (Conservative)
Reason for by-election: Promotion to a county court judge
Result at previous general election: Donald Sumner (Conservative), 24,303, 56.6 per cent; Norman John Hart (Labour), 9,543, 22.2 per cent; Jack Omar Galloway (Liberal), 9,092, 21.2 per cent
Date by-election called: 20 February 1962
Date by-election took place: 14 March 1962
Size of total electorate: 53,779
Total number of votes cast: 43,187
Turnout: 80.3 per cent

In the 1959 general election, the sitting Conservative MP for the Kent seat of Orpington, Donald Sumner (he had beaten Margaret Thatcher to be the candidate in 1955), was re-elected with a majority of 14,760. The Labour candidate narrowly squeezed out the Liberal candidate to come in second, by 9,543 votes to 9,092.

In October 1961, Sumner, a barrister, was appointed a county court judge, thus causing a by-election. The writ was not moved until the following year. For the election, the Conservatives selected, from a very lengthy application list, a high-flying and academically gifted member of the Conservative Research Department, Peter Goldman, who was expected to make it to high ministerial office once in Parliament. The Liberal Party selected a local councillor, Eric Lubbock, after the candidate from the general election, Jack Galloway, decided reluctantly to withdraw. (He was under threat of scandal, having apparently entered a bigamous marriage.) Labour selected a young trade unionist, Alan Jinkinson.

Goldman, described by *The Times* as '37, suave, decisive, newly married', was a good speaker – he reportedly 'spoke brilliantly' at his adoption meeting – and fought what Alistair Horne described as an 'energetic and capable campaign'. However, he was fighting in what was not the most auspicious of circumstances. The principal problems were not of his making. Locally, the Liberals had done well in elections to Orpington District Council, pushing Labour into third place, and were viewed now as the main challenger to the Tories in the seat. Lubbock, although he had not lived in Orpington for long, was able to claim to be a local through his family – he was now living in the family home in the constituency, his children going to local schools – as well as by having been elected as a local councillor. He was aided by an energetic campaign team, which helped offset the fact that he was not an especially good speaker; he focused instead on knocking on doors. Nationally, the Macmillan government had hit a bad patch and was losing support. This affected the campaigning in by-elections. (A by-election was taking place in Blackpool North the day before the Orpington election.) Rising prices were adding to the government's unpopularity, as was a pay pause, introduced by Chancellor Selwyn Lloyd to counter inflation and which was affecting Orpington's white-collar workers. Lloyd had introduced an emergency Budget in 1961. These conditions contributed to a perception of an administration that was starting to flounder. At the start of the year, polling from National Opinion Polls (NOP) published in the *Daily Mail* indicated that Goldman enjoyed a narrow 1.1 per cent lead over Lubbock. Jinkinson was trailing a poor third.

Although an excellent speaker, Goldman attracted criticism. He suffered from the fact that he was seen, even by some local Conservatives, as a candidate who had been parachuted into the seat. (Sumner, in contrast, had been selected in 1955 as the local candidate; he was the association chairman at the time.) Although Goldman's wife was from Kent, and he promised that if elected he would make a home in the constituency, he was portrayed by his Liberal opponents as someone who could not be expected to understand local problems. Although good at addressing meetings, he was not as adept at knocking on doors as Lubbock – he toured in a campaign caravan, essentially holding court for anyone who wished to meet him – and appeared a somewhat cerebral figure. A survey undertaken for the Liberals found that some electors felt he had become the candidate 'simply so that he could get into Parliament'. He may also have suffered from some antisemitism – he was a Jew who had converted to the Anglican faith – though there is little evidence to indicate that this was a significant factor.

Blackpool North polled on 13 March and, although the Conservatives held the seat, it was with a massively reduced majority. The 1959 majority of 15,587 was reduced to one of 973, with the Liberals coming in second place. The result in Orpington was even more stunning. Lubbock got 22,846 votes to Goldman's 14,991, a Liberal majority of 7,855. Jinkinson came third, with 5,350 votes, losing his deposit. The result, according to *The Times* the following day, 'was the most severe blow the Conservatives have suffered since they returned to power in 1951'.

The by-election set two firsts. It was the first where the count was broadcast on television. Television coverage of elections was coming of age in the 1950s and the declaration of the result in Orpington was shown on screen, with Lubbock smiling as the returning officer read out the totals, Goldman's figures being announced first and Lubbock's last. It was also viewed as the first in which tactical voting was seen as decisive in determining the outcome. The Liberals had established themselves as the principal challengers in the seat and former Labour voters switched to vote Liberal in order to turn the Conservatives out. A Liberal post-election survey found that 62 per cent of working-class voters had voted Liberal, as against 44 per cent of middle-class voters, suggesting a much greater shift of Labour supporters to Lubbock than of traditional Conservative voters. On the morning of the poll, the

Daily Mail had published an NOP poll showing that the Liberals were narrowly ahead of the Conservatives, thus establishing that the candidate best placed to turn the Conservatives out was the Liberal.

It was a blow to Prime Minister Harold Macmillan. As Alistair Horne observed, the fact that the Labour vote had virtually disappeared was a blow rather than a consolation: 'The emergence for the first time of tactical voting, with Labour voters deserting their own candidate to support the better-placed Liberal candidate, meant that scores of traditionally safe Conservative seats might now be at risk.' Macmillan also saw it as bolstering right-wingers in his party, who attributed the defeat to the government pursuing overly liberal policies. Other ministers, such as Iain Macleod, who was essentially Goldman's mentor, saw it more straightforwardly as a consequence of the government's pay policy.

The result also exercised psephologists who identified a potential partisan dealignment, with post-industrial society producing electors who were more self-made white-collar workers – the product of grammar schools – as distinct from the established professional middle-class and the manual working class. The phenomenon of 'Orpington man' was created. It exercised Macmillan, who in Cabinet was to argue that public spending should be increased to win over both Orpington man and the traditional working class.

The fear of what Orpington man presaged for the fate of the Conservative Party had an immediate effect in terms of panicking the previously unflappable Macmillan. He confided to his diary: 'We have been swept off our feet by the Liberal revival.' The Liberals did well in a subsequent by-election in Derby North, coming second in a seat they had not contested in 1959. On the day of another by-election, in Leicester North East, Macmillan decided he needed to reconfigure his government, engaging in the 'Night of the Long Knives', unceremoniously dismissing seven members of his Cabinet. In sacking Selwyn Lloyd as Chancellor, he told him that the situation was desperate and something had to be done quickly. In the by-election, the Liberals again came second in a seat they had not contested at the general election. The combination of Macmillan's drastic reaction and the party's poor polling performance reinforced speculation as to Macmillan's future. Scandals added further impetus to the move to replace him.

The principal effect of the Orpington by-election was not, as the Liberals hoped, and as Macmillan feared, the rise of Orpington man and a resurgence of the Liberal Party. If anything, Orpington man was stillborn. Although there was something of a bounce for the Liberals in terms of local election results and party membership, support in subsequent by-elections gradually tailed off and only nine Liberals were elected in the 1964 general election. If anything, the Liberals suffered from believing that Orpington man did exist, focusing on trying to mobilise support from what was a small part of the electorate.

Archival research by York Membery found that at a private meeting of senior party figures, Goldman attributed the loss of the seat to a number of factors which were specific to the time and the seat rather than a wider change in the nature of the electorate. He attributed his loss to general discontent with the government, demographic changes in Orpington, pressures on financially stretched middle-class voters and the meanness of the Conservative-controlled Orpington Council. Two of these were, then, specific to Orpington and may have served to exacerbate the scale of the defeat. The other two derived from the performance of government in handling the affairs, not least the economic affairs, of the nation. This was borne out by a post-election survey, commissioned by Macleod as Conservative Party chairman, which found that it was the pay pause and general dissatisfaction with the government that were to blame. The local factors may have played to the Liberals' capacity to win the seat, but the others were just as, if not more, exploitable by the Labour Party.

Insofar as there was a notable political impact, it was in effecting, or at least helping trigger, the demise of the Macmillan era. Macmillan's panicked reaction to the by-election and his handling the following year of the Profumo affair led to pressure for him to go. His image as the unflappable Prime Minister was gone and the perception of a man out of touch was exploited by the newly elected leader of the Labour Party, Harold Wilson. The chairman of the Conservative 1922 Committee, John Morrison, along with two other members of the 1922 Committee, decided it was time for a change of leadership and began the task of identifying who should replace Macmillan.

At a more personal level, the result had consequences for the two leading candidates and did no harm to the career of the third. Eric Lubbock held the seat at the subsequent general election and was again returned in 1966, losing the seat to the Conservatives in 1970. He was reported as saying, 'In 1962 the wise, far-seeing people of Orpington elected me as their Member; in 1970 the fools threw me out.' As an MP, he was active, serving for most of the time as his party's Chief Whip and contesting unsuccessfully the leadership in 1967. In 1971, he succeeded his cousin as Baron Avebury and served as an active peer until his death in 2016. He had been elected as a Liberal Democrat hereditary peer in 1999 and by the time of his death was the longest-serving Liberal Democrat peer. He achieved a reputation as a notable human rights activist.

Whereas the by-election propelled Lubbock into the public realm as an active parliamentarian, it served to consign Goldman largely to political obscurity. On 4 May 1962, *The Times* reported that he had been 'courteously informed' by the chairman of the local Conservative association that the executive council had begun 'to look for a new – and local – candidate'. Goldman said that he hoped to fight another seat at the general election and that he had not been deterred by what had happened: 'It would have happened to anybody in the present climate of politics.' He continued as director of the Conservative Political Centre, before in 1964 being appointed as director of the Consumers' Association. 'This does not mean I am leaving politics for good', he said, 'or that I won't stand as a candidate again.' He was never selected as a candidate again. He proved a long-standing director of the Consumers' Association, occasionally appearing in press reports on consumer affairs, but the glittering political career predicted in 1962 eluded him.

As for the Labour candidate, Alan Jinkinson, he went on to fight another seat – Hendon North – in the 1964 general election, significantly reducing the Conservative majority, but made his mark instead in the trade union movement, serving as general secretary of his union, the National and Local Government Officers' Association (NALGO), before becoming the first general secretary of the public services union, UNISON.

The Orpington by-election entered history as a dramatic political event, even though its most significant impact was not the effect initially claimed (or feared by Macmillan) – a Liberal revival – but its contribution to the ending of one political career (Macmillan's) and the stifling of another (Goldman's). The decision of Donald Sumner to accept a place on the bench seemed unremarkable at the time, but it was to trigger an event that was to become a memorable part of British political history.

Philip Norton (Lord Norton of Louth) is a professor of government, and director of the Centre for Legislative Studies, at the University of Hull. His latest book is The 1922 Committee: Power Behind the Scenes *(Manchester University Press, 2023).*

36

STRATFORD

15 AUGUST 1963
CONSERVATIVE HOLD

SCARLETT MAGUIRE AND
PATRICK J. MAGUIRE

Result: Angus Maude (Conservative), 15,846, 43.61 per cent; Andrew Faulds (Labour), 12,376, 34.06 per cent; Derick Mirfin (Liberal), 7,622, 20.98 per cent; M. S. Blair (Independent), 281, 0.77 per cent; David Sutch (Teenage), 209, 0.58 per cent
Size of majority: 3,470
Swing: 13.74 per cent from Conservative to Labour
Name of previous MP and party: John Profumo (Conservative)
Reason for by-election: Resignation following the Profumo affair
Result at previous general election: John Profumo (Conservative), 26,146, 68.51 per cent; Joseph Stretton (Labour), 12,017, 31.49 per cent
Date by-election called: 6 June 1963
Date by-election took place: 15 August 1963
Size of total electorate: 49,660
Total number of votes cast: 36,334
Turnout: 73.2 per cent

On 16 August 1963, an increasingly dispirited and ill Harold Macmillan confided to his diary:

> [Angus] Maude won by 3,500. This is bad. The Labour poll is constant at 12,000 but the Liberals have polled 7,000 (they did not contest this seat at the General Election). I think the Liberals must have taken our votes. I fear this will be thought bad for us, both by our friends and our enemies.

Macmillan was struggling to come to terms with the result of the Stratford by-election the day before, which had been more damaging to his government than anticipated. Stratford was supposed to be one of the Conservative Party's safest seats. The Conservatives had won at the 1959 general election with 68.5 per cent of the vote, and the party Central Office had projected a more comfortable by-election Conservative majority of around 5,000, not the 25 per cent collapse in the Conservative vote that transpired. Macmillan's despair was compounded by the belief of his officials that the Liberal revival so evident at the Orpington by-election of the previous year had peaked in 1962 and was now receding. This was despite the by-election in Colne Valley on 21 March that saw the Conservatives relegated to third place by the Liberals, who enjoyed a 13.7 swing and finished with 39.5 per cent of the vote.

Macmillan might have taken some solace from the extremely unusual background to the forced poll. While we have become more than accustomed to by-elections resulting from the scandalous behaviour of MPs, Stratford was unusual at the time for not being occasioned by an incumbent's death or elevation to higher office. Instead, this by-election was triggered by the forced resignation of a government minister, John Profumo. And it was a resignation that had been especially mired in scandal, attracting ongoing, lengthy and sensationalist media coverage.

A Harrow- and Oxford-educated D-Day veteran who had risen to the rank of brigadier and was then serving as Macmillan's Secretary of State for War, Profumo was meant to be a rising star in the party. His resignation was brought about not just because he was having an affair with a nineteen-year-old but because that nineteen-year-old, Christine Keeler, was also having an affair with Yevgeny Ivanov, a senior naval attaché at the Soviet embassy and an operative of the GRU (the Soviet military intelligence agency). The Profumo affair was not just sexually scandalous; it had the potential to threaten national security.

In some ways, this chimed with the succession of espionage scandals which had plagued Macmillan's governments: the Portland spy ring, the trial of George Blake, the official White Paper on the defections of Burgess and Maclean and, in January 1963, the escape of MI6 double agent Kim Philby from Beirut to Russia. This last incident was particularly embarrassing to Macmillan as, while Foreign Secretary in 1955, he had proclaimed Philby's innocence to the House, saying there was 'no reason to conclude that Mr Philby has betrayed the interests of his country, or to identify him with the so-called "third man"'.

The election in Stratford got off to a bad start. Even the calling of the by-election attracted some controversy, with both the Liberal and Labour parties objecting to the moving of the writ in the Commons on 23 July following the announcement of Profumo's resignation on 5 June. Profumo stood down, admitting that he had lied to Parliament when he had originally declared there was 'no impropriety' in his relationship with Keeler, whom he said he had only met on a few occasions. This was political suicide at the time. The veteran Labour MP Manny Shinwell objected on a number of grounds to the apparent 'unseemly haste' in calling the by-election so soon (by comparison, the Colne election had been five full months after the death of the incumbent). Most importantly, Shinwell criticised the timing, 'because there may be something in the Denning Report [commissioned to examine the scandal] which may have some impact on the electors'.

Unsurprisingly, the Profumo affair had attracted a great deal of media interest, particularly in what Macmillan referred to as 'the gutter press'. It involved a Conservative minister and his leading actress wife (Valerie Hobson), a teenager and a Russian spy, and its tentacles reached out from London high society – the Astors had hosted the dinner party that led to Profumo's first encounter with Keeler – to the seedy underbelly of Notting Hill. That being said, it was the nineteen-year-old Keeler who bore most of the opprobrium. She was depicted as a common prostitute with pretensions who had entrapped Profumo to provide a 'kiss and tell' story to sell to newspapers (she obtained a £200 advance from the *Sunday Pictorial* with a further £800 to be paid on publication, which Profumo squashed with a libel writ). Equally vilified was the osteopath and artist Stephen Ward who had introduced Keeler to both Profumo and Ivanov. On being found guilty of living off immoral earnings, a devastated Ward committed suicide with an overdose of barbiturates, finally dying on 3 August, just twelve days before polling day in Stratford.

It was against this fevered backdrop that the Stratford by-election was fought, and, thanks to the Profumo affair, it would be the most high-profile by-elections in years. And unlike at the 1959 general election, this would not be a straight Conservative–Labour contest but a five-way fight. Indeed, the by-election is notable not only because of the circumstances surrounding its origins but because of its candidates. Angus Maude was an identikit senior Conservative politician of the time. Educated at Rugby and Oxford and held as a prisoner of war in Italy during the Second World War, he became a journalist at *The Times* before going into politics. He was first elected to Parliament as MP for Ealing South in 1950 and served as the director of the Conservative Political Centre from 1951 to 1955. Macmillan described him in 1957 as 'an able but disappointed politician, somewhat soured as he has seen others pass him in the race'. Maude did in fact resign in 1958 to become editor of the *Sydney Morning Herald*, citing the lack of influence of backbenchers. He first sought to return to national politics in the South Dorset by-election of 1962, losing by just 704 votes. The defeat was largely due to the intervention of an anti-Common Market candidate who won 5,057 votes and split Conservative support. After his narrow win in Stratford, Maude would go on to become a minister under Ted Heath and a prominent supporter of Margaret Thatcher before being elevated to the House of Lords in 1983.

His Labour opponent, Andrew Faulds, cut a somewhat different figure. A respected Royal Shakespeare Company actor, he campaigned on the front foot and happily accused Maude of 'carpet bagging' in pursuit of a television career. Even though he only increased Labour's vote share by 2.57 per cent, he came close enough to victory that after the result, he claimed 'there are defeats that have the taste of victory'. Out of luck in Stratford, he later became MP for Smethwick in Labour's 1966 landslide and remained as a Labour MP (later for Warley East) until 1997.

The Liberal candidate, Derick Mirfin, had already lost two election contests in 1955 and 1959, before appearing again at Stratford. A one-time chair of the Union of Liberal Students and president of the Cambridge University Union, he was an archetypal 'new Liberal': young, self-confident and assertive. It was his 7,622 votes that so concerned Macmillan on 16 August. After his defeat, Mirfin abandoned national politics to concentrate on local affairs and would reach his personal pinnacle by becoming the first Liberal Democrat Mayor of Basingstoke in 1998.

Completing the field were two independent candidates. The first was an anti-Common Market local farmer, M. S. Blair (the National Farmers' Union was considerably animated by the perceived threat of the Common Market). Blair considerably underperformed the candidate in Dorset, largely thanks to de Gaulle's veto, which prevented the UK joining the European Economic Community, and finished with just 281 votes. The second independent was the eccentric musician David Sutch, who self-styled as 'Screaming Lord Sutch'. Although he would go on to be a serial contestant in by-elections, Stratford was Sutch's debut on the political scene. This time around, he finished with just 209 votes. He campaigned in a top hat and tails for votes at eighteen, the abolition of dog licences and commercial radio, under the banner of the National Teenage Party – underlining the fact that Profumo had had an affair with a teenager while the minimum voting age was still twenty-one. Sutch would go on to stand in thirty-nine by-elections and form the Monster Raving Loony Party.

Looking back, perhaps one of the more peculiar aspects of the by-election was the initial omertà of the leading candidates about what was now widely termed the Profumo affair. Indeed, Faulds did not reference it at all throughout his campaign. *The Times* reported one week before polling day that 'all candidates have agreed that there should be no reference to the events which gave rise to the by-election'. It was Maude who, potentially inadvertently, broke the silence. The press reported that he had proclaimed that people should regret 'the tragic events which gave rise to the by-election' at a local campaign meeting. Mirfin then seized the opportunity to denounce the portrayal of Profumo as a victim and sought to add the affair to the serial failures of the Macmillan government.

Maude prolonged the controversy by responding to Mirfin that 'if the ruining of a Minister is not a tragedy, I do not know what is'. Not surprisingly, neither the deceased Ward nor the soon-to-be imprisoned

Keeler received any such public condolences. As a *Spectator* columnist wrote after the result had been declared, 'whilst Profumo was not a significant factor in undermining the Conservative vote, the general line that "you can't trust these Conservatives" had gained a good deal of force from the traumatic effects of the incident. Some Tory abstentions and Liberal conversions may well have stemmed from this malaise.'

Despite the considerable media attention, there were other issues that mattered to Stratford voters during the campaign. Three local ones featured especially prominently: the closure of the direct rail link to London following the Beeching cuts, a planned housing expansion on the site of an old POW camp at Ettington, as well as the loss of the village station. Nationally, as had been the case at every by-election since 1961, Macmillan and Chancellor Selwyn Lloyd's staggeringly un-popular anti-inflationary 'pay pause' also loomed large.

The Stratford by-election was the beginning of the end for Macmil-lan's government. Indeed, Macmillan rapidly accepted the inevitable and became determined to resign. Initially, he intended to do so in a carefully staged manner, after the Conservative Party conference in October, but his hand was forced by hospitalisation during the con-ference. To much surprise at the time, it was Sir Alec Douglas-Home who succeeded him and went on to lead the Conservatives to a narrow defeat at the 1964 general election.

As more recent Conservative Prime Ministers could no doubt attest, Macmillan had clearly been worn down by the succession of by-election defeats which had marked his last two years as Prime Minister. In his bleakest moments, he envisaged a 1945-style Labour landslide:

> We have been swept off our feet by a Liberal revival, [it] seems to in-dicate a real movement representing or expressing real grievances or emotions … It is the revolt of the middle classes … We have killed the class war and the fear of Socialism. So … we have made it possible for people to gratify their exasperation at minor difficulties by voting against the government … We have made England safe for Liberalism.

In the end, while Macmillan was right to have some concerns, he was perhaps being overly pessimistic. As was frequently the case, the

Stratford by-election was a poor indicator of voting performance at a general election. The Liberal tide was receding, as indeed it had looked like before the by-election. They did go on to achieve 11.2 per cent of the vote in 1964 (although largely because they contested a further 149 seats) and returned nine MPs to Parliament. In an odd postscript, the author of the by-election underwent a relatively rapid rehabilitation. Profumo was awarded a CBE in 1975 for charitable work and was even seated next to the Queen at Margaret Thatcher's seventieth birthday party in 1995.

While the Conservatives held on to Stratford in what was in many ways an unremarkable result, the extraordinary circumstances under which the poll was triggered make it one of the most striking by-elections of the decade.

Scarlett Maguire is a pollster and founder of the strategic research company Merlin Strategy. Scarlett is a regular guest on BBC News, BBC Radio 4, Sky News, Bloomberg, Politico and Fox, providing analysis on political and electoral developments in the US and the UK.

Patrick J. Maguire was a social and political historian who was the head of humanities at Brighton University and a specialist in social class and Labour politics. He co-founded the Centre for Memory, Narrative and Histories in 2008 and was active in the History Workshop movement and the Workers' Educational Association. He co-wrote this chapter with his daughter Scarlett before passing away on 28 April 2025.

37

BRISTOL SOUTH EAST

20 AUGUST 1963
LABOUR GAIN FROM CONSERVATIVES

LEE EVANS

Result: Tony Benn (Labour), 20,313, 79.7 per cent; Edward Martell (National Fellowship Conservative), 4,834, 19.0 per cent; Marguerite Lloyd (Independent), 287, 1.1 per cent; Geoffrey Pearl (Anti-Socialist, Liberal Conservative), 44, 0.2 per cent (withdrew)
Size of majority: 15,479
Swing: N/A
Name of previous MP and party: Malcolm St Clair (Conservative)
Reason for by-election: Resignation of incumbent
Result at previous by-election: Tony Benn (Labour), 23,275, 69.5 per cent (disqualified); Malcolm St Clair (Conservative), 10,231, 30.5 per cent (elected)
Date by-election called: 2 August 1963
Date by-election took place: 20 August 1963
Size of total electorate: 60,382
Total number of votes cast: 25,492
Turnout: 42.2 per cent

As votes were cast in the 1963 Bristol South East by-election, nobody doubted the result. The Labour candidate, Anthony Wedgwood Benn, in later years better known as Tony Benn, faced no opposition from the Conservatives or the Liberals and he was elected with almost 80 per cent of the vote. It was the most predictable of outcomes. Yet the road to Benn's victory – featuring a death, two by-elections, a court case and an Act of Parliament – was one of the most dramatic and unpredictable of the twentieth century.

Benn was first elected as Member of Parliament for Bristol South East in 1950, replacing the former Labour Chancellor Stafford Cripps. From the moment he took his seat in the Commons, Benn knew his time there could be limited – if not by the voters of his constituency, then by his father's mortality. Benn's father, William Wedgwood Benn, had been a Liberal-turned-Labour MP before being elevated to the House of Lords during the Second World War. The title Viscount Stansgate would be his for life, but as a hereditary peerage, it would then be passed on to his eldest male descendant. At the time of the senior Benn's ennoblement, this was the destiny of his eldest son, Michael; when Michael died in 1944, the heir became his younger brother, Tony.

While there were many privileges to being a hereditary peer at the time, for a select few – members of the House of Commons – it was a demerit. MPs who became peers were immediately booted off the green benches and forced to sit, should they wish to remain in Parliament, on red ones. Benn, a fierce opponent of the hereditary system, was keen to avoid this fate and tried to introduce a personal Bill in 1955 to renounce his peerage. It was rejected. His father sought to achieve the same on his son's behalf via a public Bill, only for peers to vote it down. Try as he might to avoid his fate, when the first Viscount Stansgate died on 17 November 1960, Tony Benn acceded to the title.

Benn resolved not to accept his peerage. Initially, he tried to carry on as normal and turned up to the House of Commons, but the Speaker had made an order to keep him out of the Chamber. Next, he attempted to return his father's letters patent, the document establishing the peerage, only to have them sent back to him. They were, whether he wanted them or not, his – and so was the peerage. The press dubbed Benn 'the reluctant peer'. He protested and asked instead to be labelled 'the persistent commoner', but few indulged him in this act of self-branding.

With no MP representing Bristol South East, the first of two by-elections was called for 4 May 1961. Benn stood and hoped to strike a blow for democracy against what he considered the absurdity of the hereditary principle. This was how Benn framed his battle, as he did so many in his life: him, on the side of the people, against the establishment. But the reality was rather more mixed. While the Prime Minister, Harold Macmillan, said that Benn could not become an MP, irrespective of the result ('That is the law and this by-election cannot change it'), a figure no less established than Winston Churchill pledged his support to Benn and even donated £10 to his election fund. Buckingham Palace was also rumoured to be on Benn's side, with the Queen said to believe that 'however dear the Monarchy is to the British people, I can't think that the conscription of unwilling peers is a necessary prop to the popularity of the Crown'.

The 1961 by-election was a straight fight between Benn and the Conservative Malcolm St Clair. There was much uncertainty about the outcome: would Bristol's voters support a peer's right to choose which House of Parliament he sat in, even if it risked leaving them unrepresented? The question took on a new dynamic when Benn's rival was asked, 'Are you, by any chance, connected with the peerage yourself?' St Clair confessed that his cousin was a hereditary peer. The predictable question followed — 'Who is your cousin's heir?' — and St Clair uttered the words which made the whole contest a farce: 'I am.' Voters in Bristol were being asked to choose between a peer who could not represent them and a peer-in-waiting who was just a heartbeat away from being unable to represent them. Benn joked that he would campaign for St Clair's right to represent the seat in Parliament, if only he could win it. When voters went to the polls, they made it clear he could not: Benn was re-elected with a majority of 13,044.

With the authority of the voters of Bristol, Benn sought to take his seat in the Commons once again. 'Here', he said, 'was the response from the people I represented.' But the voters of Bristol, vote as they might, could not change the law. As Benn approached the Commons Chamber, the doorkeeper told him, firmly and unmistakably, 'You cannot enter, sir.' Benn's frustration turned to fury when he tried to light his pipe outside the distinguished Strangers' Gallery only to be told, 'You can't smoke here.' Benn protested, 'What do you mean? I always do' but was admonished: 'You're not a Member.' Benn later admitted in an interview: 'I absolutely lost my temper ... I really attacked him.' But the doorkeeper was right. Benn was still not an MP.

The question of who would represent Bristol South East was decided by an election court. Benn chose to represent himself and made his case over twenty-two hours, totalling 135,000 words. His argument may have been persuasive, but it was inconsistent with the law and Benn knew it. St Clair, with a negative majority way into five figures, was declared Bristol South East's representative. Benn offered his sympathy to St Clair: 'I think he must be the unhappiest man in England.' St Clair was indeed unhappy. When he first took his seat, a large number of Labour MPs walked out in protest. He then waited sixteen months before making his maiden speech and, when he finally did so, began in an apologetic tone: 'I understand that it is customary for an honourable member to crave the indulgence of the House when making a maiden speech. I must crave the indulgence of the House even more … since I arrived here in rather peculiar circumstances.'

As Benn marked the first anniversary of his father's death, he was still out of Parliament, the people of Bristol South East were represented by someone they did not vote for and their new MP was embarrassed about having to represent them. To break the impasse, St Clair offered to resign. Keen to avoid a repeat of the current farce, he cautioned Benn: 'Before I do resign I must have your assurance that you would not assent to nomination at any by-election or election in this constituency.' Benn refused, in no small part because he didn't actually want St Clair to resign. If another by-election was called before he was able to disclaim his peerage legally, then voters would be asked the same question again: do you want Benn, who cannot represent you, or do you want someone else? There may only be so many times that his constituency party and the voters would stick with him through meaningless by-elections before selecting or electing someone else. Having failed by every other means, Benn knew that his only way back into the Commons was through a change in the law and he wanted St Clair to hold his place until it happened. 'That', he said, 'will keep [the issue] alive.'

A joint committee of the Commons and Lords was established to determine what reform the Chambers and the parties within them could agree upon. For the most part, it was an uncontroversial process; it was widely accepted that the current position was unsustainable. The committee proposed that peers, such as Benn, should be able to disclaim their title. Their work gave Benn great confidence and by July 1962, speaking in an interview, he felt able to express his belief that a Bill giving effect to the committee's proposals would be passed before the next general election.

Until then, Benn needed to maintain the support of the Labour Party – locally and nationally. Local support proved steadfast, but the national leadership of the Labour Party was far more equivocal. While he agreed with him in principle, Labour leader Hugh Gaitskell often appeared uninterested in Benn's plight, once telling him: 'You can't expect the Party to make a fuss over you.' After the 1961 by-election, Gaitskell recommended that in the event of a repeat contest, Benn's wife, Caroline, should stand in his place – something Benn was keen to avoid. In January 1963, Gaitskell died and the leadership of the Labour Party was fought out between two men: George Brown and Harold Wilson. The former, Gaitskell's deputy, was hostile to Benn's case. Back in 1961, he had told Benn that 'I'm dead against you myself. I would strongly object to your fighting the seat again.' He subsequently slammed Benn as 'with the middle class' and told him: 'You would never have got anywhere without the advantage of being your father's son and it will do you well to suffer from the disadvantages.' Wilson, on the other hand, was an ally. He pledged to support Benn and, much to Benn's relief, was victorious in the contest to replace Gaitskell. Wilson put the party foursquare behind the reluctant peer, supported the measures to change the law and encouraged Benn's readoption as candidate. 'His interest', recalled Benn, 'has made a sensational difference.'

By summer 1963, everything was fitting into place. Benn had been readopted as candidate and the Peerage Bill, which would allow Benn to disclaim his title, was on its way to becoming an Act. But fate put one final hurdle in Benn's way and it seemed serious. In mid-July, Benn felt unwell after giving a speech in Bristol. He was admitted to hospital and his wife rushed to his bedside as tests were undertaken to find what was wrong. Eccentrically, Benn asked the doctor to take a hypodermic full of blood and put it in a test tube for him as a reminder of the 'noble blood' which he hoped he would soon be able to forfeit. As the doctor mixed it with anticoagulant, to ensure the gruesome memento wouldn't clot, Benn's blood turned blue – 'most appropriately', he observed. Happily, his health scare proved just that – a scare – and Benn was soon discharged with a prescription to rest. But there would be little time for that.

The Peerage Act became law on 31 July 1963 and Benn became the first peer to renounce his title. Having signed the instrument of disclaimer, he declared, 'I am the first man in history who, by Act of Parliament, is prevented from receiving a hereditary peerage. I am statutorily immunised.' St Clair was true to his word and resigned as MP. His political fate was not a happy one: while he remained ambitious to serve in Parliament and sought selection elsewhere, he never managed to return to the Commons. Of the hereditary peerage that had been so widely mocked in 1961, his cousin, the 17th Lord Sinclair, outlived him by two months.

The by-election was called as soon as practicable for 20 August. The Liberals and Conservatives accepted Benn's claim to the seat and did not stand. The decision was not uncontroversial; Sir Kenneth Brown, chairman of Bristol Conservatives, felt compelled to issue a statement urging all Conservative supporters to 'follow the lead the officers have given them – that is that we are not going to fight'. The local Labour Party responded by agreeing to only a limited campaign, with 'an Election address to be distributed by hand, and a simple window bill and to campaign for only a few days at the end'. They need not stretch themselves much further. There was, in effect, only one issue in the campaign: Benn's right to represent his constituents, and that argument had been ceded to him. To make his case to the voters, Benn left a pre-planned family holiday in France and deployed a novel approach to campaigning. Starting at 6 a.m., he would go and greet people in the bus queues, board the bus and meet everyone he could before getting off at the next stop. 'People are delighted as they have nothing to do or read on a bus and are anyway quite captured.'

Benn's only real opponent was the dogged libertarian Edward Martell, 'a brilliant publicist' in Benn's own account, who stood as a National Fellowship Conservative. Martell kept Benn working, but the outcome was never really in doubt. Benn won with 20,313 votes, more than 15,000 ahead of Martell. Despite the margin of victory, Benn somehow managed to appear ungracious in victory, turning his fire on

Martell – the first non-major party candidate to save his deposit in seventeen years – in his victory speech. 'I could not, in all honesty, say that Mr Martell had put up a fair fight,' complained Benn, before being victoriously towed in his car from the count to party HQ, a Bristol Labour tradition. With the declaration over, Benn was, undeniably, back in the Commons. He took his seat after the summer recess and wrote in his famous diary, 'Today was the day I have been dreaming about for many a year.'

Safely back in the Commons, Benn became one of the most prominent Labour politicians of the second half of the twentieth century. In Wilson's government, he served as Postmaster General and Minister of Technology. Later, in the 1980s, he became a thorn in the side of successive Labour leaders with his campaigns for Labour Party democracy and the party's deputy leadership. Benn lost Bristol East, the successor to the seat he had fought so hard to represent, in Margaret Thatcher's 1983 landslide victory. A year later, he returned to Parliament as MP for Chesterfield – the fourth by-election he fought in his career – before leaving the Commons in 2001, more than five decades after he was first elected. By this stage, although his political power was declining, he was on his way to becoming a national treasure. When he died in 2014, another self-styled Tony, this time Blair, said, 'Benn was one of those rare things: a genuine radical for all his life. He was a fearless campaigner and a legendary figure for the Labour movement.' Blair was right and few episodes demonstrated Benn's radicalism and fearlessness as well as his battle to remain MP for Bristol South East.

Lee Evans is the John Ramsden Fellow at the Mile End Institute at Queen Mary, University of London.

38

KINROSS & WESTERN PERTHSHIRE

7 NOVEMBER 1963
SCOTTISH UNIONIST HOLD

ANDREW HOLT

Result: Alec Douglas-Home (Scottish Unionist), 14,147, 57.4 per cent; Alistair Duncan Millar (Liberal), 4,819, 19.5 per cent; Andrew Forrester (Labour), 3,752, 15.2 per cent; Arthur Donaldson (SNP), 1,801, 7.3 per cent; Ian Smith (Independent Unionist), 78, 0.3 per cent; William Rushton (Independent), 45, 0.2 per cent; Richard Wort (Independent Conservative), 23, 0.1 per cent
Size of majority: 9,328
Swing: N/A
Name of previous MP and party: Gilmour Leburn (Scottish Unionist)
Reason for by-election: Death of incumbent
Result at previous general election: Gilmour Leburn (Scottish Unionist), 16,256, 68.2 per cent; Gregor Mackenzie (Labour), 4,008, 16.8 per cent; Arthur Donaldson (SNP), 3,568, 15.0 per cent
Date by-election called: 15 August 1963
Date by-election took place: 7 November 1963
Size of total electorate: 32,428
Total number of votes cast: 24,665
Turnout: 76.1 per cent

In August 1963, a junior Scottish Office minister in Harold Macmillan's Conservative government died from heart failure while on holiday. 'A warm, outgoing, friendly personality, with an unpretentious manner,' Gilmour Leburn had turned fifty just weeks earlier. Leburn had represented Kinross & Western Perthshire, a safe Unionist seat in central Scotland, since 1955. (Scottish Unionists took the Conservative whip at Westminster.) In the 1959 general election, he retained the seat with a majority of over 12,000. The Unionists could expect to hold Kinross & Western Perthshire. As their candidate, they selected George Younger, still in his early thirties and eldest son of the 3rd Viscount Younger of Leckie. Polling day was set for 7 November.

The by-election campaign was to take place against a backdrop of growing pressure on the Macmillan government. The Conservatives had been in office since 1951. Macmillan himself had been Prime Minister since January 1957, succeeding Anthony Eden in the aftermath of the Suez Crisis. In October 1959, he led the party to its third successive general election victory while increasing the government's overall majority. By autumn 1963, however, Macmillan was considering his position. Speculation over his future had grown since his major reshuffle in July 1962. Dubbed the 'Night of the Long Knives', Macmillan jettisoned a third of his Cabinet, including his Chancellor of the Exchequer, Selwyn Lloyd. More acute pressure came over the summer of 1963. Already damaged by the Vassall affair, the government was left reeling by the resignation of Secretary of State for War John Profumo amid public revelations about his involvement with Christine Keeler. Scandals aside, there were mutterings that the world had moved on. Macmillan's Edwardian persona seemed increasingly out of step with the mood of the early '60s. With another general election due in 1964 – by which time Macmillan would be seventy – the Prime Minister was actively considering retirement.

A chain of events that began in Downing Street in early October imbued the Kinross & Western Perthshire poll with unexpected significance. Macmillan had finally resolved to continue as premier and informed Buckingham Palace accordingly on the morning of 8 October. He had spent the previous night in severe pain, however, and later that day was admitted to hospital. The Prime Minister underwent an emergency prostate operation on 10 October and decided to tender his resignation. In the meantime, Conservative Party members were gathering in Blackpool for their annual conference. Much has been written about the manoeuvring that followed. In the end, it was the

Foreign Secretary, the 14th Earl of Home, who ultimately emerged as Macmillan's successor, ahead of Rab Butler and Lord Hailsham (Quintin Hogg). The choice of a peer, and the way in which it transpired, was not without controversy. Nevertheless, having managed to form a Cabinet – albeit without Iain Macleod or Enoch Powell – Home kissed hands on Saturday 19 October.

It had become generally accepted that a Prime Minister could not sit in the House of Lords. No peer had been appointed to the role since the 3rd Marquess of Salisbury, who left office in 1902. Even Home's appointment to the Foreign Office in 1960 had proved controversial. While Home was able to fend off Labour leader Harold Wilson's attack on his status by noting that the Leader of the Opposition was himself 'the fourteenth Mr Wilson', there was never any question that Home would have to seek election to the House of Commons. Benefiting from the campaign of Tony Benn (2nd Viscount Stansgate) to be able to renounce his hereditary peerage, Home disclaimed his titles on 23 October. The opening of Parliament was postponed from 29 October so that Sir Alec Douglas-Home, as he became known, could find a seat. For nearly three weeks, the Prime Minister of the United Kingdom served without holding a place in either House of Parliament and without holding the leadership of a political party.

The large rural seat of Kinross & Western Perthshire was the obvious place for Douglas-Home to stand. George Younger offered to step aside and was promised the next available safe Scottish seat. (Younger would eventually enter Parliament as MP for Ayr in October 1964 and rose to serve as Secretary of State for Defence under Margaret Thatcher, 1986–89.) John Robertson would serve as Douglas-Home's agent. Robertson had already been active in canvassing the constituency with Younger, who also continued to support Douglas-Home's campaign. With the stakes so high, there was a nervousness in the Unionist camp. They were keen that Douglas-Home should win with an overall majority and were targeting a turnout of over 70 per cent. There could be no room for complacency.

Douglas-Home's selection by the Unionists prompted a wider spread of candidates than had contested the seat in 1959. The Liberals – who were absent from the 1959 contest – chose local farmer Alistair Duncan

Millar, son of barrister and former Liberal MP John Duncan Millar. SNP leader Arthur Donaldson, a journalist from Forfar, stood again after finishing in third place last time around. Labour's candidate was Andrew Forrester, a young teacher married only days earlier who was forced to campaign with his right forearm in plaster. There were also three independent candidates, all motivated by unhappiness with the way in which Douglas-Home had assumed office. The most colourful of these was *Private Eye* co-founder Willie Rushton, whose impressions of Macmillan were a highlight of the BBC's satirical show *That Was the Week That Was*. Ian Smith was a garage owner and ex-RAF officer who claimed to be representing 'disgruntled rank and file Tories'. The seventh and final candidate to join the race was Richard Wort, a maths teacher at an independent school in London. Claiming to represent the Independent Light Blue Conservative Party — which he renamed the Light and Dark Blue Conservative Party — Wort stood on a platform of opposition to the disclaiming of peerages to achieve government office, arguing that Douglas-Home should have governed from the Lords. Wort collected the ten signatures necessary for his nomination with less than thirty minutes to spare. His newly appointed agent then surprised his Labour counterparts by asking them the polling date.

The campaign commanded international media attention. Press and television reporters struggled to navigate central Scotland's minor roads as they tried to locate town halls in small villages. Hotel rooms were in short supply. Douglas-Home based himself in the Comrie home of his friend Major Andrew Drummond-Moray. It was a small house and every available chair was needed for the press conferences held there. While local issues could not be ignored, the by-election provided an opportunity for the new Prime Minister to introduce himself to the country. The level of media reporting necessitated numerous different speeches and Douglas-Home delivered nearly fifty. He was supported by a young Nigel Lawson and John MacGregor from the Conservative Research Department, who ensured he was well prepared for each location. Conservative canvassing was sparse, but supporters who spoke for Douglas-Home included Lady Tweedsmuir, John Maclay — ousted as Scottish Secretary by Macmillan in July 1962 — and William Whitelaw. Television played a very limited role because Duncan Millar refused to appear.

The campaign was a short one. Douglas-Home arrived on the evening of 25 October and set out his stall in a speech at Perth cattle market the following day. He promised no lurch to the right and outlined a seven-point programme covering expansion, modernisation, spreading prosperity, education, housing, welfare and health. He would frequently address three meetings per evening, speaking to audiences as small as fifty. Venues included school rooms and timber halls, including some decked-out for Halloween. By 3 November, Douglas-Home had covered nearly 1,000 miles. He embarked on a final tour of polling stations on 7 November. Throughout, he had to balance campaigning with his responsibilities as Prime Minister, returning to London for Cabinet meetings.

Other candidates struggled to compete for attention in a race dominated by the presence of the Prime Minister. They would sometimes appear at the same event, such as a gathering of farmworkers and shepherds at the small hamlet of Amulree on 28 October. The Liberal candidate Alistair Duncan Millar compensated for his aversion to television by addressing up to five meetings per night. Labour drew canvassers from teachers and farmers, while the SNP claimed to have over 400 canvassers. The usual SNP slogan of 'Home Rule for Scotland' proved unhelpful when deployed against the former earl, however, while high winds hindered Donaldson's progress in the literal sense as they rattled the loudspeakers attached to his car. Such setbacks did not diminish his optimism. Donaldson produced a series of articles ranking candidates' likelihood of success. By polling day, he had concluded that 'the fight is now between ourselves and Lord Home'. (Donaldson was ultimately to lose his deposit.) Smith, meanwhile, had to quickly correct posters that suggested his speaking engagement would be displacing a village bingo night. There were also some less savoury allegations and incidents. On 30 October, Millar claimed that 'social forces' were being exerted to persuade farm and estate workers to vote for Douglas-Home, while Forrester received a death threat. With none of Douglas-Home's challengers making significant headway, Wort said on 3 November that he had written to the other candidates proposing that they all withdraw in favour of the Prime Minister's closest challenger.

Douglas-Home won the by-election with over 57 per cent of the vote and a majority of over 9,000. While this was lower that Leburn's figure from 1959, Douglas-Home faced a wider range of candidates, including a Liberal. In the event, the Liberals actually received a lower share of the vote than in 1950 — the last time they had contested the seat. Labour's organisation had improved since considerably but to little effect. Their vote share also fell. Like the SNP's Arthur Donaldson, the independents all lost their deposits. Douglas-Home soon returned to Downing Street. When asked whether he planned to buy a house in his new constituency, he replied, 'I have too many houses to live in already.' With his place in Parliament secured, Douglas-Home was elected as leader of the Conservative Party on 11 November. Parliament sat again the following day and Douglas-Home returned to the green benches for first time since 1951.

The Conservatives had less to cheer from another poll held on the same day as Kinross & Western Perthshire. In Luton, Labour overturned a National Liberal (effectively Conservative) majority of over 5,000. Douglas-Home had suggested that 'Luton was the last page of the old chapter and Kinross & Western Perthshire is the first page of the new'. Five further by-elections that took place in 1963 did not support this prediction, as the Conservative vote fell and Labour strengthened its position. Douglas-Home had little time to make an impact and the upcoming general election could never be far from his mind. The uncertainty provided by the impending poll hindered the government in taking the initiative internationally, but it did act decisively when necessary. The government's most notable measure was the abolition of resale price maintenance (RPM). Douglas-Home served as Prime Minister until his narrow defeat to Harold Wilson's Labour Party in October 1964. He retained his seat and increased his personal majority to nearly 12,000 but resigned as party leader in the summer of 1965. When Ted Heath brought the Conservatives back to power in 1970, Douglas-Home once again became Foreign Secretary. He continued to serve as MP for Kinross & Western Perthshire until 1974, stepping down between the February and October general elections that year. He subsequently returned to the House of Lords with a life peerage as Baron Home of the Hirsel.

The 1963 Kinross & Western Perthshire by-election provided an unusual spectacle. It saw a sitting Prime Minister travel a constituency in a way that would have been impossible in the midst of a general election. The campaign had elements of anachronism, with a visible clash between the old and the new. Media attention was intense and journalists from across the world descended on small Scottish villages. Douglas-Home made use of professional speechwriters and wider political support from Conservative Central Office in a way that was to become commonplace. On the other hand, Douglas-Home's campaign was based on making multiple speeches in small local venues. He met prospective constituents face to face, shaking hands and signing autographs. Television's relevance was diminished by the reluctance of one candidate to appear. While the result was expected, it was a unique scenario that is unlikely to be repeated.

Andrew Holt is the author of The Foreign Policy of the Douglas-Home Government: Britain, the United States and the End of Empire (*Palgrave Macmillan 2014). He holds a PhD in history and is a fellow of the Royal Historical Society.*

39

LEYTON

21 JANUARY 1965
CONSERVATIVE GAIN FROM LABOUR

RICHARD JOHNSON

Result: Ronald Buxton (Conservative), 16,544, 42.9 per cent; Patrick Gordon Walker (Labour), 16,339, 42.4 per cent; Alistair Mackay (Liberal), 5,382, 14.0 per cent; Jeremiah Lynch (UK & Commonwealth), 157, 0.4 per cent; George Delf (Disarmament), 156, 0.4 per cent
Size of majority: 205
Swing: 8.7 per cent from Labour to Conservative
Name of previous MP and party: Reginald Sorensen (Labour)
Reason for by-election: Elevation to the House of Lords
Result at previous general election: Reginald Sorensen (Labour), 23,640, 50.4 per cent; Ronald Buxton (Conservative), 15,714, 33.5 per cent; Alastair Mackay (Liberal), 7,598, 16.2 per cent
Date by-election called: 15 December 1964
Date by-election took place: 21 January 1965
Size of total electorate: 66,860
Total number of votes cast: 38,578
Turnout: 57.7 per cent

In October 1964, Harold Wilson became the first Labour Prime Minister in thirteen years. The new government's popular mandate was weaker than expected. Labour had actually won fewer votes than at the previous election, but a six-point drop in the Conservative vote share and lower turnout had given Labour a parliamentary majority.

Immediately, the new administration announced that the Conservatives had left the country's finances in a more ruinous condition than expected. The outgoing Chancellor Reginald Maudling said to his successor Jim Callaghan on the way out the door, 'Sorry, old cock, to leave it in this shape.' An £800 million deficit faced the government, and tough decisions needed to be made.

One of these decisions was to delay an increase in old-age pensions. Soon, backbench Labour MPs were facing the wrath of angry pensioners in their constituencies. To make matters worse, the government had proceeded with an increase in MPs' pay, leading to accusations that MPs were stuffing their own pockets while picking those of the elderly. One embarrassed Labour MP, Leo Abse, announced that he would donate his extra income to an old-age charity in Pontypool until pensioners were given their pension top-ups.

In addition to negative stories about pensioners, another dark cloud hung over the new Labour government: backlash to increased levels of immigration. Under the Conservatives, immigration to Britain had increased substantially, especially (ironically) when the government announced it would introduce restrictions on Commonwealth arrivals. Although the increase had happened under the Conservatives, Labour was seen to be more pro-immigration, having vigorously opposed the Conservatives' Commonwealth Immigrants Act of 1962.

It was against this backdrop that Patrick Gordon Walker, the shadow Foreign Secretary, shockingly lost his seat at the 1964 general election. His constituency, Smethwick, had seen several thousand immigrants move to the area in the previous decade. The immigrants were mostly from the Punjab, where Gordon Walker had coincidentally spent some of his childhood, when his father was a colonial judge in Lahore. Considered 'Labour's foremost Commonwealth expert', Gordon Walker was one of its greatest champions and welcomed the new arrivals to the town (where he did not live). As the local MP in 1961, he opened Guru Nanak Gurdwara Smethwick, the largest Sikh gurdwara in Europe. The building was subsequently graffitied with 'N*****s Out', 'Gordon Walker Traitor' and 'Long Live England', foreshadowing the contentious election three years later.

Even though there had been a national swing of 3.5 per cent from the Conservatives to Labour across the country, in Smethwick the

Conservatives received a 7.2 per cent swing in their favour. It was an extraordinary result, which could be blamed on a disreputable local Conservative campaign. The informal, shameful slogan of that campaign was, 'If you want a n***** neighbour, vote Labour'. The Conservative candidate Peter Griffiths, a local councillor and schoolteacher, had spent the preceding years using a local newspaper column to indulge in the worst insinuations about the behaviour of Smethwick's new residents, including claims that Asian men were grooming white girls. Rumours also circulated that Gordon Walker had a Black wife. His wife, Audrey, had been born in Jamaica, but she was white, the daughter of a coconut plantation owner.

When Harold Wilson heard the news of his shadow Foreign Secretary's defeat on election night, he was said to have turned white, and his political secretary Marcia Williams burst into tears. Wilson decried the 'utterly squalid' campaign and accused the Smethwick Conservatives of 'degrading politics to about the lowest level I have known in my lifetime'. When the new parliament assembled in the House of Commons for the first time, Wilson singled out the new Conservative MP for Smethwick, hoping he would be treated like a 'parliamentary leper'. With these explosive remarks, as one journalist put it, 'Wilson blew up the Commons'.

In an extraordinary move, Harold Wilson ignored the verdict of the voters of Smethwick and appointed their ex-MP to his Cabinet as Foreign Secretary, anyway. In fact, Wilson appointed two Cabinet ministers who were members neither of the House of Commons nor of the House of Lords, the other being Transport and General Workers' Union (TGWU) general secretary Frank Cousins as Minister of Technology. While technically possible under Britain's flexible constitution, the convention that members of the executive must simultaneously serve in the legislature meant that seats in the House of Commons needed to be found as soon as possible.

In order to manufacture this, Wilson created vacancies by elevating two Labour MPs to the House of Lords. Of course, all of the MPs had just been re-elected, and voters might not appreciate being sent back to the polls so soon and unnecessarily. But in spite of having a majority of just four, Wilson disregarded these concerns. For Cousins, the constituency of Nuneaton was chosen. The incumbent MP, Frank Bowles, had a reputation for making infrequent visits to the town and would not be missed. Bowles was promptly elevated to the House of Lords and made captain of the Queen's Bodyguard of the Yeomen of the Guard.

For Gordon Walker, it was initially thought he might stand in the north, but he requested a London constituency, which would make it easier for him to campaign while simultaneously serving as Foreign Secretary. A seat was located in the north-east London suburb of Leyton. The incumbent MP, Reginald Sorensen, was seventy-four and had first been elected an MP in 1929. Sorensen, a former factory worker, was one of the most left-wing Labour MPs and initially rebuffed the idea of becoming a peer. However, the Prime Minister placed him under 'tremendous pressure' to consider the wider interests of his party and country and on 15 December 1964, he agreed to become Lord Sorensen of Leyton.

Some in the Leyton Labour Party were not impressed with the left-wing idealist Sorensen being replaced by Gordon Walker, who was on the right of the party. Gordon Walker had been an acolyte and personal friend of Wilson's predecessor (and rival) Hugh Gaitskell. Gaitskell's untimely death in 1963 caused him to display rare emotion on the radio the following day, telling listeners, 'I have lost my best friend.'

Yet it was precisely because Gordon Walker was on the right that he was seen by Harold Wilson as such a valuable member of his Cabinet. Unlike Keir Starmer, who as Labour leader sought to purge the party of his ideological adversaries, Harold Wilson very much believed that the Labour Party needed to be a 'broad church' and endorsed Labour MP Ian Mikardo's comment that Labour needed a left and a right wing to fly. Although emerging from the left of the party, Wilson appointed right-wing figures to some of his most important ministries after the 1964 election, including his two chief finance ministers, Jim Callaghan and George Brown. Mikardo described Gordon Walker as 'as far to the right as you can get in the Labour Party without toppling over the edge'.

Patrick Gordon Walker was a child of the British Empire, with both his father and grandfather having been officials in the Indian civil service, and a man who by conviction believed in a multiracial Commonwealth of equals to replace it. Before entering Parliament, he had been a fellow at Christ Church, Oxford, where his colleagues included Albert Einstein, Gilbert Ryle, Frederick Lindemann and Sir Keith Feiling. He was elected to Parliament in 1945 in a by-election caused when the MP for Smethwick was killed in a car crash one day after becoming an MP. Gordon Walker rose to the Cabinet within just five years. Labour Prime Minister Clement Attlee believed Gordon Walker had 'exceptional ability' and was a great improvement on his predecessor as Commonwealth Secretary Philip Noel-Baker, whom Attlee described as 'talkative but not illuminating'.

Gordon Walker's faults, which became apparent in the 1965 Leyton by-election, included a rather stiff, demure personality. He was not a natural campaigner. An American journalist observed: 'As a campaigner, he has the political sex appeal of a turtle.' Earlier in his career, Nye Bevan rather uncharitably described Gordon Walker as a 'dreary' man 'rooted in nothings'. Tony Benn described him as 'the laziest man I have ever known'. David Pearce, editor of Gordon Walker's diaries, is perhaps more accurate when he says that the image of a posh Oxford don was 'good copy' for the press. In the finest tradition of British parliamentary democracy, here was 'a disdainful patrician Foreign Secretary having to beg for the votes of the plebs'.

If the Labour leadership had expected the Leyton by-election to be a mere formality, they were sorely mistaken. Once again, the issues of race and immigration reared their ugly heads. Gordon Walker's first campaign event was invaded by the far right. He was met with jeers of 'Keep Britain white', 'Send the blacks back' and 'Go back to Jamaica'. Flour bombs were thrown at the stage. In the ensuing fracas, the Defence Secretary Denis Healey punched the neo-Nazi leader Colin Jordan, an incident broadcast to millions of homes on television. Healey later proudly recalled: 'I knocked him off the platform and he fell on a journalist in the front row of the hall and broke his spectacles.'

The historian Marc Collinson has recently argued that race and migration were not significant issues in the by-election and that the pension freeze issue was dominant, but this is not convincing. Collinson's sources, public leaflets and private letters by campaigners in the Sorensen collection, cannot be taken purely at face value. Local campaigners, even Labour ones, would have had an incentive to downplay the racism of their own community. As Elizabeth Buettner has argued in her article, 'This is Staffordshire, not Alabama', Britons did not like to think of their country as having the same kind of racial strife that was so widely documented in America that decade. Contemporary media reports paint a very different picture, with issues of race and immigration said to have 'dogged' the Foreign Secretary's Leyton campaign. In a private letter to Gordon Walker a few weeks after the by-election, Harold Wilson wrote: 'There can be no doubt that on this subject [immigration/race] politics is plummeting to an all-time low.'

Race was salient from the moment the campaign began. Cabinet colleague Richard Crossman observed that Gordon Walker had 'taken the taint of Smethwick with him into this gloomy North London suburb'. Minutes before nominations closed, a man in blackface arrived at Leyton Town Hall with a sign saying he was 'Walker Gordon [*sic*]: The Race Mixing Candidate. Make Britain Black!' When told he would need to pay a £150 deposit if he wished to be a candidate, he told the council officials to take it out of national assistance and stormed off.

Racist stunts continued throughout the campaign. A protester paraded in front of the Leyton Labour headquarters in a monkey suit, carrying a sign reading: 'We immigrants are voting for Gordon Walker.' On a different occasion, Labour Party volunteers arrived to find their building had been covered in swastikas. I side with David Pearce, who believed that the Leyton by-election 'was dominated by race'.

Nonetheless, Collinson's contention about the pension freeze should not be dismissed entirely. The Conservative candidate Ronald Buxton was not the source of the racist antics. A patrician Tory, he presented a different image from the populist Peter Griffiths in Smethwick. Buxton's leaflets show that the public-facing message of the Tory campaign was focused on the pension freeze and the MPs' pay increase.

On the ninety-ninth day of the Labour government, Buxton was declared the new Conservative MP for Leyton by 205 votes. Patrick Gordon Walker had been rejected by yet another constituency in just three months. He resigned immediately as Foreign Secretary. It was a huge embarrassment for the new Labour government. Three days later, however, Winston Churchill died and headlines quickly shifted, much to Wilson's relief.

The Leader of the Opposition Alec Douglas-Home, however, would not allow Labour to forget the result. He told the Commons, 'The best epitaph on the 100 days of Socialist Government so far is the arrival in the House today, by popular vote, of my honourable friend, the Member for Leyton.' The Leyton result spooked Wilson and restrained some of the bravado he had shown in appointing the non-MPs Cousins and Gordon Walker to his Cabinet in the first place. As David Butler and Anthony King record one MP saying, 'The Prime Minister was becoming just a technician. Leyton forced him to remember what it was to be a political leader.'

After the defeat, Patrick Gordon Walker's political career would never be the same again. A month later, Llywelyn Williams, the MP for Abertillery, died. It was one of the safest Labour seats in the country, won by the party with 88 per cent of the vote in 1964. The local General and Municipal Workers' union branch invited Gordon Walker to be the Labour candidate, but he declined. He could not bear to face another by-election campaign so soon after the humiliation of Leyton. If Williams's death had come just a few weeks earlier, Gordon Walker's political career might have been saved.

Instead, Wilson sent Gordon Walker on tours of south-east Asia and America, promoting the Labour government's foreign policy. In 1966, he stood again in Leyton and was elected. Ronald Buxton never returned to Parliament. Wilson initially wanted to appoint Gordon Walker as Commonwealth Secretary, but the new Foreign Secretary George Brown objected on the grounds that Gordon Walker's focus on the Commonwealth would make negotiations over entry into the European Economic Community too difficult. Wilson instead made Gordon Walker 'Minister without Portfolio', a serious relegation from his previous status.

Wilson came to regard Gordon Walker as cursed. Cecil King said that after Leyton, Wilson looked upon him as 'someone with a hoodoo; nothing ever goes right for him'. He eventually appointed Gordon Walker as Education Secretary, but the tenure was short-lived.

After just seven months, Wilson sacked him from the Cabinet, using what Marcia Williams called his 'feather duster', rather than 'pickaxe', approach. In compensation for relegation to the back benches, Gordon Walker was made a Companion of Honour. The Prime Minister told him that he would be given a peerage – but only after the dissolution of Parliament. Wilson could not afford another by-election in Leyton.

Dr Richard Johnson is a senior lecturer in politics at Queen Mary, University of London. He is the author of two books on Labour Party history: Camaraderie: One Hundred Years of the Cambridge Labour Party, 1912-2012 *(with Ashley Walsh) and* Keeping the Red Flag Flying: The Labour Party in Opposition since 1922 *(with Mark Garnett and Gavin Hyman).*

40

ROXBURGH, SELKIRK & PEEBLES

24 MARCH 1965
LIBERAL GAIN FROM CONSERVATIVES

SIR PETER RIDDELL

Result: David Steel (Liberal), 21,549, 49.2 per cent; Robert McEwen (Unionist), 16,942, 38.6 per cent; Ronald King Murray (Labour), 4,936, 11.2 per cent; Anthony Kerr (Independent Scottish Nationalist), 411, 0.9 per cent
Size of majority: 4,607
Swing: 7.3 per cent from Unionists to Liberals
Name of previous MP and party: Charles Donaldson (Scottish Unionist/Conservative)
Reason for by-election: Death of incumbent
Result of previous general election: Charles Donaldson (Unionist), 18,924, 42.8 per cent; David Steel (Liberal), 17,185, 38.9 per cent; Ronald King Murray (Labour), 7,007, 15.8 per cent; Anthony Kerr (SNP), 1,093, 2.5 per cent
Date by-election called: 2 March 1965
Date by-election took place: 24 March 1965
Size of total electorate: 53,788
Total number of votes cast: 43,838
Turnout: 81.5 per cent

The Roxburgh, Selkirk & Peebles by-election was one of the most consequential in post-war history, not for the change in votes or its immediate impact on party fortunes but because David Steel, the victor, became a highly influential figure in British politics over the following four decades.

The contest attracted national attention at the time – and the attendance of many leading national politicians as well as eager young Liberal canvassers from across England – because it was seen as a potential upset. The by-election was the second part of a contest which started at the previous autumn's general election when Steel had achieved a near 9 per cent swing to the Liberals from the Unionists, as the Conservatives were still generally known in Scotland, cutting the majority of the elderly incumbent Commander Charles Donaldson to just 1,739.

The large Borders constituency which changed its boundaries over the decades had mainly been represented by Unionists or their allies since the First World War, though it had been closely fought with the Liberals who had briefly held the seat between the 1950 and 1951 general elections. While having a rural image, most of the population lived in the traditional textile towns of Galashiels, Jedburgh and Kelso which had a radical tradition. The unnamed Scottish correspondent of *The Times* expressed a popular, if distinctly patronising and even then dated, view in one of his by-election reports: 'As the snow fades on the hills, the lambs are limbering up and in the towns the well-dressed mill girls of the prosperous tweed and knitwear industries are acquainting themselves with spring fashions.'

The constituency was generally prosperous with low unemployment and the main concern was depopulation as younger people moved out of the area, with 9,000 overall leaving the constituency and adjoining Berwickshire since 1951. So, the dominant issue was how to combat this trend, and the parties produced rival, though rather similar, plans for what many decades later would be called 'levelling-up'. Unlike the central belt between Edinburgh and Glasgow, there was no desire for a new town but rather for government support for new employment and improving transport links, as well as a new regional hospital.

Steel had originally been picked for Edinburgh Pentlands but switched to Roxburgh in January 1964 since it was regarded as a winnable seat. Still in his mid-twenties, he had already been involved in a number of by-elections as assistant general secretary of the Scottish Liberal Party and was a protégé of national party leader Jo Grimond.

During the October 1964 general election, he not only did well in Roxburgh but also featured in a national election broadcast. Immediately afterwards, he began working for BBC Scotland's current affairs department. However, less than two months after polling day, Commander Donaldson died during minor surgery in London. Steel was immediately put on gardening leave by the BBC until the end of the following March, which meant that the licence fee payer was in practice funding him to be a candidate preparing for the inevitable by-election – which was not formally called until the beginning of March.

The Unionists picked Robert McEwen, a member of a well-known Borders family from Marchmont House and later holder of the family baronetcy, though his brothers Alex and Rory were better known at the time for their popular folk singing. McEwen offered a traditional image compared with the self-consciously fresh and modernising approach of Steel. Labour retained its candidate from 1964 for the by-election in Ronald King Murray, a successful Edinburgh advocate. Anthony Kerr, who lost his deposit in fighting the seat for the Scottish National Party, stood again but as an Independent Scottish Nationalist having been disowned by his former party.

When the campaign formally started in March 1965, Liberal hopes were high. Steel had achieved the third highest Liberal vote among the fifty-four seats where the party had come second in 1964 and the party had gained three seats in the Scottish Highlands. For the Unionists, it was a matter of showing resilience after the party had gone into opposition after thirteen years in power, not least since Sir Alec Douglas-Home, the former Prime Minister, was very much a Borders man. For Labour, there was no expectation of victory but, rather, of weakening the Conservatives.

As *The Times* reported on 3 May, the importance of the by-election was shown – 'ascertained', in the more formal language of the time – by the parties' lists of speakers which 'contain the names of more well-known politicians than are usually involved for such a contest in Scotland'. National Conservative leaders included Quintin Hogg (later Lord Hailsham), Reginald Maudling, Iain Macleod, Sir Keith Joseph and Edward Heath, as well as more colourful backbenchers like Sir Gerald Nabarro. Labour's list included deputy leader George Brown,

Michael Stewart, Richard Crossman, as well as Scottish Secretary Willie Ross. There was a constant ferrying of London luminaries from Turnhouse, now Edinburgh, airport, prompting one Labour courier to be reported as saying, 'If only all this energy could be diverted into the export drive.'

The Liberals had fewer stars but their big names – party leader Grimond, Jeremy Thorpe, Emily Hooson, Lord Byers – all came. Nonetheless, Steel was not overshadowed by the party leaders and he took centre stage at the campaign meetings, always making the final speech and answering the questions.

Both main campaigns had several full-time organisers – eight for the Unionists and six for the Liberals, who had several hundred, some claimed up to a thousand, helpers come in on the final weekend, notably student activists in buses from across England. To many, Steel was, like Grimond, a symbol of a new, more modern liberalism.

It was in one sense a traditional campaign with several meetings attended by 400 to 500 people and often a number of meetings each night in the various towns in the constituency. When McEwen had to take to his bed for a couple of days suffering from a kidney stone, his wife stepped in and read his speech at two meetings one evening.

Yet the Liberals introduced what were seen as novel campaigning themes, at least for the Borders, linked in with the youth of their candidate. Posters, tin badges, car stickers and a glossy election address all focused on the candidate, and there was what later became a familiar campaigning tool, especially for the Liberals, a propaganda free-sheet called *The Border News*, which looked like a newspaper.

It was a turbulent time internationally with the re-elected Lyndon Johnson grappling with the worsening Vietnam War and the internal turmoil over civil rights as Martin Luther King led the bloody Selma march in Alabama in the middle of the campaign. Herbert Morrison and King Farouk died in March. But the outside world hardly intruded, apart from some rumblings over levels of agricultural support and inflation.

There were familiar campaign excitements: a poster of the Liberal candidates had been whirling round on machinery in a mill and a shotgun was said to have been discharged over the heads of Liberals posting bills in the country. There was even a rumour – as there invariably is with Liberal and now Liberal Democrat campaigns – about a last-minute poll favouring Steel. It was never published, partly to avoid problems of electoral law and expense limits. The later explanation was that the poll was nothing to do with the Scottish Liberals but had been commissioned by the London party for research. As often is the case, what mattered was the rumour not the existence or veracity of the poll.

The message was, however, that the Liberals were doing well and this was reflected in the bookies' odds. On the eve of the poll, Ladbrokes had Steel at six to four and McEwen on two to one on. There was a sense that it was the Liberals' opportunity. *The Times* correspondent noted in mid-campaign that the main change since the general election was that in October 1964,

> it was more difficult for the Liberals to get their message across because of all the weight of national publicity devoted to whether Home or Wilson was going to be Prime Minister and the Tory vote was held up in a way it would not be in a by-election. Now we have inevitably a number of people who dutifully voted Tory last time who will not do so this time.

In an eve-of-poll report, the same correspondent wrote that McEwen 'may not have cut enough of a personal dash with the electorate in these rolling hills and prosperous little towns as some of the actively involved Tories wish'.

By contrast, Steel was undoubtedly cutting a dash and creating a mood of youthful excitement – prompting party leader Grimond to claim at a final packed rally: 'There can be little doubt that the Boy David is not only going to knock over one Goliath but two.'

In the event, Steel did even better than expected in the by-election, which was held on a Wednesday, not the now invariable Thursday. His majority was double the size that had been expected, and the later editions of *The Times* on Thursday 25 March reported 'Liberals Sweep in at Roxburgh'. The *Scottish Daily Express* had a headline proclaiming: 'It's the Boy David'.

Of the other candidates, Ronald King Murray resurfaced five years later to win Edinburgh Leith for Labour, serving from 1970 until 1979, becoming Lord Advocate and later a senior Scottish judge.

Steel's victory was seen as a personal triumph and it was not the start of a broader Liberal revival. On the same day, the party had lost its deposit in the Saffron Walden by-election, called to fill the vacancy caused by the departure from the Commons of R. A. Butler. The main press coverage focused on the Conservatives and the position of Home. Some isolated rumbling about his position quietened down with the approach of the local elections. But Home stepped down in July. For Harold Wilson, the result made no difference to his precarious majority in the Commons, though it confirmed that the Conservatives were in no position to mount a real challenge. A general election was delayed for another eleven months.

The real importance of the by-election was in making Steel an MP, where he remained for thirty-two years, despite a narrow scrape in 1970. Unlike other Liberal MPs who often survived for just a few general elections if that, Steel's longevity from his base in the Borders ensured that he could make a national impact: in piloting through a major relaxation of the abortion laws in 1966–67; then a decade later in negotiating the Lib–Lab pact with James Callaghan; and then in organising the electoral pact with the new SDP from 1981 onwards, which led to a partial merger and the emergence of the Liberal Democrats after the 1987 election. Without the Roxburgh by-election, some of these events might still have happened but not in the same way or at the same time.

David Torrance, Steel's biographer, described election night in Jedburgh when the new MP was carried shoulder-high down the street and Steel himself recalled that night as being 'the most thrilling and memorable of his career – it was the beginning of a wonderful adventure that is the political life'.

Sir Peter Riddell *was a political journalist (*Financial Times *and* The Times*), a former director of the Institute for Government and Public Appointments Commissioner. He is currently an honorary professor at the Constitution Unit at UCL and commentator on standards in public life. He has written nine books on British politics.*

41

KINGSTON UPON HULL NORTH

27 JANUARY 1966
LABOUR HOLD

NICK THOMAS-SYMONDS

Result: Kevin McNamara (Labour), 24,479, 52.2 per cent; Toby Jessel (Conservative), 19,128, 40.8 per cent; Laurie Millward (Liberal), 2,945, 6.3 per cent; Richard Gott (Radical Alliance), 253, 0.5 per cent; Russell Eckley (Independent), 35, 0.1 per cent; Kelvin Woodburne (Independent), 33, 0.1 per cent
Size of Majority: 5,351
Swing: 4.4 per cent from Conservative to Labour
Name of previous MP and party: Henry Solomons (Labour)
Reason for by-election: Death of incumbent
Result at previous general election: Henry Solomons (Labour), 20,664, 43.3 per cent; Michael Coulson (Conservative), 19,483, 40.8 per cent; Laurie Millward (Liberal), 7,750, 15.9 per cent
Date by-election called: 3 January 1966
Date by-election took place: 27 January 1966
Size of total electorate: 61,433
Total number of votes cast: 46,873
Turnout: 76.3 per cent

When Henry Solomons, the Labour MP for Kingston upon Hull North, died in Westminster Hospital on Sunday 7 November 1965, the then Labour government's working parliamentary majority was cut to the smallest number possible: one. A former councillor and trade unionist with the Union of Shop, Distributive and Allied

Workers, Solomons had gained the seat from the Conservatives at the general election of 15 October 1964 by the narrow margin of 1,181 votes. Then aged sixty-one, he might have expected a longer parliamentary career, but his health was poor; in June 1965, he had collapsed during an all-night Commons sitting and he passed away on his sixty-third birthday. Just days after his death, on 11 November 1965, Labour held the seat of Erith & Crayford in a by-election, increasing the government majority to two, but the situation remained precarious.

The political outlook for the government was, however, promising. On Friday 19 November, an opinion poll in the *Daily Mail* showed a Labour lead of 18.5 per cent, with 73 per cent of people declaring they were satisfied with Harold Wilson as Prime Minister. Labour then moved to select its candidate for the by-election swiftly. A shortlist of six was produced by Monday 22 November and included the nominee of the Union of Shop, Distributive and Allied Workers: Thomas Torney, one of their organisers, but he was based at Derby. Guy Barnett, who had served as MP for Dorset South from a by-election victory in 1962 until losing the seat in the 1964 general election, also made the list. However, it was a local candidate who triumphed when the local constituency party executive met on the Wednesday: a 31-year-old lecturer in law at the Hull College of Commerce who had lived in the city since 1952. *The Times*, announcing his selection on 25 November, referred to him as 'Mr Joseph McNamara', but he was to be known by his second name. Kevin McNamara became a well-known Labour figure, serving as an MP until he stood down in 2005, and was shadow Secretary of State for Northern Ireland from 1987 to 1994.

The Conservatives selected Toby Jessel, a company director, also thirty-one. A councillor in the London Borough of Southwark who had stood at Peckham in 1964 and was, later, to be MP for Twickenham, Jessel focused on the cost of living. At his adoption meeting, he produced a basket of groceries, emphasising by how much their price had increased under Labour. The Liberals reselected the local candidate who had stood for them in 1964: 36-year-old Laurie Millward, a Hull City councillor.

Aside from the three main contenders, there were two Independents on the ballot paper who made little impression: Russell Eckley had put himself forward for Parliament before, including at the Pontefract by-election in 1962 when he said he was standing for 'the legions of God'; Kelvin Woodburne, meanwhile, argued for 'world government'. Another Independent candidate, Lieutenant-Commander W. G. Boaks, a former naval officer, asked for nomination papers but did not in the event become a candidate. This was part of a pattern; he had done the same thing with both the Erith & Crayford and Cities of London & Westminster by-elections, though he had gained eighty-nine votes as an Independent at the West Walthamstow by-election back in 1956.

In the event, it was another non-mainstream candidate who caught the eye and presented a worry to Labour regarding taking enough left-of-centre votes away from the party to hand the seat to the Conservatives. Richard Gott, a 27-year-old journalist who had written *Guardian* leaders, stood as a 'Radical Alliance' candidate focusing on the Labour government's support for the American bombing of North Vietnam. Labour had hoped he might stand aside given that the government majority was tiny, but Gott was determined to press on, calling the Labour government's position 'an unforgivable crime'.

He was a colourful character. On 16 January, Gott attended the first meeting of McNamara's campaign. In the presence of Home Office Minister Alice Bacon and Minister of Overseas Development Anthony Greenwood, Gott challenged McNamara on his view of the American bombing. The chair ruled that Gott, not being a voter, did not have the right to ask a question and he was escorted out. In *The Times* on 9 January, it had already been concluded that

a red-bearded radical and a pretty, blonde babysitter are, politically speaking, the most significant people in Britain today. It is not stretching a point to say that until the date of the crucial by-election in Hull North, they will control the fate of the Government more surely than the Conservative and Liberal parties put together.

The beard – and a fur hat – were certainly Gott's. The babysitter, Christine Tennison, was caring for the newly born baby of the Liberals' Laurie Millward, who, at this point, was only thirteen weeks old.

The date of the by-election was set for Thursday 27 January. There was an argument for waiting a few more weeks, as an updated electoral register would be in place in mid-February: the Conservatives were expected to do well with postal voters on the existing register and many newly registered electors might be thought to favour Labour, but the party's buoyant opinion poll position pushed towards going earlier.

Wilson was in a strong position, despite major issues presenting themselves to him. On Armistice Day, 11 November 1965, Rhodesian Prime Minister Ian Smith had announced his Unilateral Declaration of Independence in a ploy to maintain the minority rule of the white settlers over the African population. That evening, Wilson broadcast to the nation, declaring the Smith regime illegal and announcing sanctions. It was a statesmanlike response, enhancing his reputation. Back at home, earlier that autumn, on 16 September, the Labour government published its National Plan for a 25 per cent increase in national output over five years with expanded productive capacity and improved efficiency. The Cabinet had made its National Board for Prices and Incomes a statutory body, meaning wage and price disputes could be referred to it for settlement with enforcement powers. While Wilson was finding challenges in controlling prices and incomes, the very idea of the government doing this caused splits in the Conservative opposition which were exploited by the Prime Minister during the by-election campaign.

Over the weekend of 15 and 16 January, Wilson attacked the Conservatives: 'On the national plan, their spokesmen condemned it on television, they supported it in Parliament, and finally abstained from committing themselves … On prices and incomes, half of them condemn the idea of a policy at all.' Angus Maude MP, the Conservatives' spokesman on the colonies, had written in *The Spectator* that the party had completely lost 'effective political leadership'. Paul Williams, chair of the right-wing Monday Club and a former MP, supported Maude, saying that 'the Opposition has become a meaningless irrelevance … consumed with a host of committees studying largely irrelevant details of policy'. Heath struck back at Williams: 'I am not going to be deflected by any criticism from the chairman of the Monday Club. It is of no account.' On 18 January, Heath called Maude for a meeting at his flat in London, and his colonies spokesman resigned: 'I have now come to the conclusion that my views, which I believe in the interests of the party ought to be put before the country, can be more satisfactorily expressed from the backbenches.' The Conservative leader turned his fire on Labour's attempts to keep prices down: 'The Government are trudging through the sands of failure towards the quagmire of a compulsory early warning system.' Heath warned where the approach would end up: 'If this fails the Government's path leads on to the introduction of compulsion on wage levels, leading in turn to Government control on overtime and promotion. This is a downward road, ending in severe restrictions on individual freedom and on the proper role of trade unions.' He followed this up with a message to Jessel on 20 January, urging the voters of Hull North to pass judgement on the Labour government's 'bungling and mismanagement' focusing on rising prices for household necessities and 'higher taxes on petrol, cars, beer, spirits, and tobacco, with the surcharge on imports, with increased postal charges, radio and television licences'. These, with the greater cost of fuel and fares in the nationalised industries, were 'hitting every family harder and harder'.

Wilson did have a slight wobble, holding a meeting in his Commons office with party officials the next day to discuss the progress of the campaign. That same day, a Gallup poll in the *Daily Telegraph* showed a fall in the Labour lead from the end of 1965 from 8 per cent to 4.5 per cent. Wilson had already sent in the big guns: since Bacon and Greenwood's appearance alongside McNamara, Roy Jenkins MP, the Home Secretary, had visited to speak in favour of the by-election candidate on 17 January, as had Sir Dingle Foot, the Solicitor General. The momentum of visiting senior speakers was maintained: the following day, it was Barbara Castle MP, Minister of Transport; on 19 January, it was Tony Benn MP, Postmaster General; on 20 January, it had been Tony Crosland MP, Secretary of State for Education and Science. As Wilson pondered the final week of the campaign, visits were already scheduled from George Brown MP, deputy leader and Secretary of State for Economic Affairs, on 23 January; from James Callaghan, Chancellor of the Exchequer, on 24 January; from Kenneth Robinson MP, Minister for Health, and Bessie Braddock, MP for Liverpool Exchange and a combative campaigner, on the final day before polling, 26

January. It was an impressive list. The Conservatives sent former Prime Minister Alec Douglas-Home MP while the Liberal leader Jo Grimond MP was joined on his party's speaker list by colleagues David Steel MP and Lord Wade.

Wilson was taking no chances. He sent a message to McNamara that was to become famous: Hull was to become a link between the north and the Midlands and western Europe, with the building of the Humber Bridge. This would bring significant benefits to local people, including to the voters about to go to the polls:

> Linked by a bridge, Humberside – north as well as south of the river – could become one of the most promising areas for really large-scale new town development. Within a matter of months the preliminary surveys of this area will be completed so that a decision can be taken on detailed planning.

The Prime Minister defended the government's record on inflation: 'The Government has kept many prices steady for eight months, and has helped to make manufacturers and shopkeepers more cost-conscious.' With one eye on the threat posed by Gott, Wilson also referred to foreign affairs in the same message: 'On Vietnam, no nation, no Government has done more to get parties to the conference table, and we shall continue our efforts.' He added, on Rhodesia: 'We are determined to bring to an end the illegal regime so that the country can move forward to a fresh start within the Commonwealth. I know that the people of Britain are behind us.'

The shadow Chancellor, Iain Macleod MP, was savage in his criticism, calling the promise to build the Humber Bridge a 'pre-election bribe'. He added: 'First, one of the junior Transport Ministers said that one was not needed. Then came the by-election. The same junior Minister promptly became much more enthusiastic about a new bridge.' Macleod went on: 'The by-election continued to turn against Labour and something more was needed. So Mrs Castle says in Hull that one day there will be a new bridge. After the publication of today's Gallup Poll, I expect Mr Wilson to arrive himself early next week and promise you a tunnel.' He added: 'Hull folk are pretty hard-headed. They look a gift bridge carefully in the mouth – and they know why it has been thrust at them.' Macleod tried to turn the debate back to the cost of living and rising prices, the fault for which lay with the Labour government:

> Mr McNamara, the principal Labour candidate, has made a charge so serious that he must either substantiate his allegations or withdraw them. He has said that political motives were behind recent rises in the price of bread. Let Mr McNamara now name the firms he considers guilty. It is of course the Socialist Government which is the guilty party.

In the final days of the campaign, attention turned to an increase in the local rates by the Hull Corporation's Finance Committee. A meeting of its members on 25 January, forty-eight hours before polling day, in the words of *The Times*, 'can not have improved Labour's chances'. While the chair, Sir Leo Schultz, said an estimated rise of 4s 6d to 18s 6d in the pound would be more than halved, it was still an increase and yet another squeeze on the cost of living. Indeed, *The Times*' prediction was that 'everything now points to a Conservative victory', especially with other candidates likely to split the Labour vote.

The reality was to prove very different. Labour more than quadrupled its majority, to 5,351, taking 24,479 votes to 19,128 for the Conservatives. *The Times*' coverage changed dramatically; on 29 January the newspaper hailed the Prime Minister: 'The young master has done it again. Mr Harold Wilson has won Hull North handsomely. The victory is his.' It was a blow for Heath, but there was no challenge to his leadership. Angus Maude, in Edinburgh the day after the by-election, said Heath would be a 'long lived and effective leader of the Conservative Party'. Heath himself tried to lift his party: 'We are not dispirited by this defeat. Indeed, from it we will create the means to victory. I call on each member of our party to use every effort to make our new policies known to the country and to expose the growing weaknesses of the Government.' The Liberals were a distant third, on 2,945 votes; the Chief Whip, Eric Lubbock MP, put on a brave face and told the annual dinner of the Orpington Liberals that 'Labour's overwhelming victory was not due to any merit of their own, but to the complete and utter failure of the Tories as a credible alternative Government'. The argument was that in seats where the Liberals were the leading challengers to the Conservatives, they would benefit. Gott, meanwhile, trailed in with 253 votes; Eckley took only thirty-five and Woodburne thirty-three.

With the parliamentary arithmetic as it was, a general election was in any event coming soon, but Wilson was emboldened: there could hardly be a better time after a swing to the government in a by-election. On 28 February, the Prime Minister called a general election for 31 March and won a landslide majority of ninety-seven seats. The 1.4-mile Humber Bridge opened to cars on 24 June 1981, before its formal opening the following month, by Her Late Majesty Queen Elizabeth II, on 17 July. Today's ministers, whose behaviour to take decisions to their party's political advantage is tightly regulated under the Ministerial Code, must look back at this by-election campaign with a wry smile.

*Rt Hon. **Nick Thomas-Symonds** MP is the Paymaster General, a fellow of the Royal Historical Society and an acclaimed political biographer. His most recent book is* Harold Wilson: The Winner *(Weidenfeld & Nicolson, 2022).*

42

CARMARTHEN

14 JULY 1966
PLAID CYMRU GAIN FROM LABOUR

SAM BLAXLAND

Result: Gwynfor Evans (Plaid Cymru), 16,179, 39.0 per cent; Gwilym Prys Davies (Labour), 13,743, 33.1 per cent; D. Hywel Davies (Liberal), 8,650, 20.8 per cent; Simon Day (Conservative), 2,934, 7.1 per cent
Size of majority: 2,436
Swing: 18.0 per cent from Labour to Plaid Cymru
Name of previous MP and party: Megan Lloyd George (Labour)
Reason for by-election: Death of incumbent
Result at previous general election: Megan Lloyd George (Labour), 21,221, 46.2 per cent; D. Hywel Davies (Liberal), 11,988, 26.1 per cent; Gwynfor Evans (Plaid Cymru), 7,416, 16.1 per cent; Simon Day (Conservative), 5,338, 11.6 per cent
Date by-election called: 23 June 1966
Date by-election took place: 14 July 1966
Size of total electorate: 55,407
Total number of votes cast: 41,506
Turnout: 74.9 per cent

Megan Lloyd George, the incumbent Labour member for the Carmarthen constituency at the 1966 general election, must have known she was dying by the time that campaign took place. She was confined to her home with the final stages of cancer, went to no hustings and made no speeches. But she was part of the great Welsh dynasty – daughter of the former Prime Minister David Lloyd George and a sparkling character in her own right – and comfortably won the seat anyway with the largest majority she had ever had. Her victory was part of an excellent general election result for Labour in Wales. Six weeks later, she died. One of the great 'what ifs' of Welsh politics is what would have happened had Lady Megan not contested the seat. In that scenario, there would have been no Carmarthen by-election in 1966, and far fewer people would ever have heard of Gwynfor Evans, who shocked observers and pundits by winning that contest and becoming Plaid Cymru's first MP. Although Plaid (as it is often shortened to) have never come close to overtaking Labour as the dominant political force in Wales, and although this is the only Westminster by-election the party has ever won, Carmarthen 1966 was its springboard into the mainstream. Arguably, by promoting nationalism and specific Welsh causes, it helped change the course of Welsh politics for the rest of the twentieth century more than any other single event.

Megan Lloyd George had herself become the MP for Carmarthen at a by-election in 1957 (see Chapter 33). The seat, in south-west Wales, was largely rural, with some industrial coal mining areas in the east. It contained a large number of Welsh speakers and had for some time been a Liberal–Labour marginal, with the last Liberal MP, Rhys Hopkin Morris, being a typical old-fashioned Nonconformist. The local Conservatives even supported him into the mid-1950s, in the hope of stopping Labour from winning the constituency. Megan Lloyd George's Liberal roots (she had previously been a Liberal MP for the north Wales seat of Anglesey) would undoubtedly have worked in her favour. She died on 14 May 1966, and the writ for the by-election was received on 23 June. It was called for 14 July – Bastille Day.

The contest was a lively one, with relatively traditional campaigning methods used, including speeches, town hall meetings, the distribution of flyers and election addresses, the tacking up of posters and the erecting of large hoardings featuring pictures of 'Gwynfor' – he was often simply referred to by his first name. In fact, knowing that Megan Lloyd George was going to die, Plaid had begun to prepare, quietly but effectively, for the by-election in the weeks before it was called and had been able to pre-prepare some of this material. The specific timing of the by-election helped the party, too, because it coincided with a college break, and a range of Plaid Cymru-supporting students were able to travel to

Carmarthenshire to take part in the campaign. The performance of the government, whose popularity had already dipped dramatically since the general election, was the subject of much criticism by Plaid. In his campaigning literature, Evans spoke directly to the agricultural workers of the constituency and robustly criticised the Selective Employment Tax on farmers imposed by the Chancellor of the Exchequer James Callaghan. 'When you ask for help today,' he wrote, 'you are given promises for tomorrow.' Pressure on the pound, rising interest rates and suspicion that the government was likely to close more coal pits and rural schools also featured as part of Plaid's messaging.

More generally, Evans stressed how this part of rural south-west Wales was often forgotten by central government, with industrial expansion of other parts of the country leading to the increasing marginalisation of Carmarthenshire. In the typical section of the election address given over to the candidate's wife, Rhiannon Evans spoke directly to 'the mothers of Carmarthenshire', urging them to vote Plaid Cymru out of hope for more employment opportunities for their children in the local area, which, she said, was 'where they belong'. But Plaid's campaigning was subtle and clever. Different parts of the constituency received alternative leaflets, with literature in more rural areas using language about the nation, whereas material dispersed in the more industrial eastern part of the seat concentrated on themes like 'work in Wales'.

Being able to cite a connection to the constituency has always been an especially important part of political campaigns in Welsh seats, across all parties. Evans played heavily on the fact that he was deeply rooted in the constituency and those campaigning for him reminded voters of this as often as they could. He had been the first ever Plaid Cymru county councillor in Wales, elected in Carmarthenshire in 1949. Labour's candidate, Gwilym Prys Davies, was, unlike Evans, not from the area and was deemed shy and even a little condescending. He was very nationalistic by the standards of Labour politicians and had been a leading proponent of setting up a national assembly for Wales. In particular, he was a great champion of the Welsh language. On both of these fronts, however, few could match Gwynfor Evans, Plaid Cymru's long-term leader. Prys Davies was additionally tarred by his association with a troubled Labour government. Many in the local Labour Party, who had been enthralled by Megan Lloyd George, were lukewarm about campaigning for someone they thought too nationalistic.

The Conservatives were rarely in contention for these kinds of rural, Welsh-speaking seats, but even by their standards, they chose an unsuitable candidate. It was always good practice in such Welsh-speaking heartlands to pick someone who was proficient in the language, because some campaigning and public meetings would be conducted in Welsh. While the Tories always failed to field a clean sweep of Welsh speakers in these kind of constituencies at general elections, to reselect their monolingual English speaker, Simon Day, for a prominent by-election exposed one of the party's failings in Wales. Conservative Central Office lamented that they had been forced to do so because of the proximity of the by-election to the general election, with no time to find someone better. Day's unsuitability was reflected by a measly 2,934 votes – a figure that was especially poor given that the Conservatives were the main opposition party to the Labour government in Westminster. Day even lost his deposit.

Despite the circumstances looking favourable for Plaid Cymru, few if any expected the party to actually win. Some local bookmakers were reportedly offering odds of 2,000 to one on Evans taking the seat. Everyone in Plaid Cymru involved in the campaign thought that coming second would be an excellent outcome, including Gwynfor Evans himself. His victory, therefore, represented, in the words of Evans's biographer, 'one of the greatest [by-election] shocks ever'. Plaid witnessed nearly a 23 per cent swing to the party when compared to the general election held only three months beforehand, with Evans winning a majority of 2,436. That represented an unprecedented swing against an incumbent government up to that point. Given that a cash-strapped Plaid Cymru had lost twenty-one of its twenty-three deposits at the 1964 general election, and then polled fewer votes in 1966, the result in Carmarthen really was extraordinary. Evans's leap from a poor third place to a relatively healthy victory reflected a well-fought campaign and a typical kind of by-election kick-back against the government. One observer of the campaign noted after the result that Evans's victory represented both a 'craving for Welshness' but also a rebuke of Labour under Harold Wilson, with voters thinking that the Prime Minister's 99-seat majority was 'as much as he deserves at present'.

The announcement of the result, from the balcony of Carmarthen's Guildhall, was captured on film. Most of it was drowned out by roars from an enormous crowd gathered below, who began chanting 'Gwynfor! Gwynfor! Gwynfor!' Speaking calmly and with his characteristic dignity in both Welsh and English, Evans told his supporters (in English and in his relatively Anglicised accent) that the result meant 'Wales is at last on the march'. After descending into the crowd, he was carried aloft to the party's small headquarters in the town of Carmarthen.

In many ways, it is the consequences and the aftermath of this by-election that are the most significant. As Evans's obituary in *The Times* noted, his victory in Carmarthen in 1966 was enough to convince some that they had found 'a new political messiah'. On the day he first travelled by train to Parliament, he was reportedly greeted by crowds bearing gifts at various Welsh stations. When he arrived in London, an enormous crowd of supporters gathered in Westminster, with one member of staff in the palace noting that the last time he had seen a reaction like that had been when the Beatles visited. Newspapers across the political spectrum found things to like in Evans – from his left-leaning views on a variety of issues to his patriotism and respect for tradition.

Moreover, the election was a game changer for Plaid Cymru. It altered how the party saw itself and how others perceived it. Having a prominent MP leading the party attracted a range of new members and different kinds of supporters, including more young people. Its profile expanded and the party began to establish itself as the dominant force in the handful of Welsh seats in the rural north-west that would end up being its heartland in later decades. Two by-elections in the Welsh seats of Rhondda West and Caerphilly, both of which were normally rock-sold Labour, nearly saw those constituencies fall to Plaid Cymru in 1967 and 1968 – results that seriously unnerved Labour, which had long thought of itself as the de facto party of Wales. But a Plaid Cymru surge, akin to what eventually happened with the SNP in Scotland, was not to be. Plaid has never been the strong force that some predicted or hoped it would be in the late 1960s. Since that period, the Conservatives have normally performed better at elections across Wales. Evans himself lost Carmarthen in 1970, failed to regain it (by three votes!) in February 1974, won it back in the October election of that year, only to lose it again in 1979. He stood a final time in 1983 and came in third place.

Gwynfor Evans's presence in Parliament, however, especially in the late 1960s, where he was dubbed 'the member for Wales', and his relentless promotion of all things Welsh, including the language and the 'need' for a parliament, undeniably changed the narrative about Welsh identity. There is a tendency among historians writing about Wales in the twentieth century to see everything that happened in the post-Second World War period as part of a story that led to the reawakening or 'rebirth' of 'the nation'. The culmination of this is presented as the establishment of the National Assembly for Wales – what is now called the Senedd. In reality, history is more complicated than that, but Evans did play a real role in making the political weather in Wales. The Welsh Office under Margaret Thatcher in the 1980s responded, in part, to nationalist pressure and promoted things like bilingualism to such an extent that it reinforced Welsh distinctiveness. Evans's threat to kill himself by fasting to death if the Tories did not introduce a Welsh-language television channel played a major role in ensuring that channel – called S4C – began broadcasting in 1982.

In short, by helping to shore up a sense of Welsh identity, Evans was part of creating the conditions in which devolution was eventually palatable to enough voters to make it a reality, even if they turned down the idea in a referendum in 1979. They voted for it – just, by the tiniest margin – in 1997. When Gwynfor (he continued to be known by his first name) died in 2005 at the grand age of ninety-two, Wales lost a politician who had been truly influential. He would almost certainly not have had the chance to make that impact had it not been for Carmarthen, 1966: one of the most consequential by-elections in modern Welsh history.

Sam Blaxland is a lecturer at UCL who specialises in the history of post-war Britain, particularly Conservatism, higher education and students. His most recent book is The Conservative Party in Wales, 1945–1997 *(University of Wales Press, 2024).*

43

HAMILTON

---

2 NOVEMBER 1967
SNP GAIN FROM LABOUR

MICHAEL RUSSELL

Result: Winifred Ewing (SNP), 18,397, 46.0 per cent; Alexander Wilson (Labour), 16,598, 41.5 per cent; Iain J. A. Dyer (Conservative), 4,986, 12.5 per cent
Size of majority: 1,779
Swing: 37.9 per cent from Labour to SNP
Name of previous MP and party: Tom Fraser (Labour)
Reason for by-election: Promotion to chair of North of Scotland Hydro-Electric Board
Result at previous general election: Tom Fraser (Labour), 27,865, 71.2 per cent; Iain J. A. Dyer (Conservative), 11,289, 28.8 per cent
Date by-election called: 12 October 1967
Date by-election took place: 2 November 1967
Size of total electorate: 53,394
Total number of votes cast: 39,981
Turnout: 74.9 per cent

Professor James Mitchell gave his excellent study of the 1967 Hamilton by-election the subtitle 'the by-election that transformed Scotland'. Certainly, modern distinctive multi-party Scottish politics, in which the constitution looms large, can be said to have properly begun at Hamilton as a result of a spectacular result for the Scottish National Party which had previously won only a single Westminster wartime by-election in a seat which it lost three months later.

However, since Hamilton, the SNP has had continuous representation at Westminster, with the (so far) high point reached in the 2015 general election, at which the party won fifty-eight of the fifty-nine Scottish seats. While the result of the 2024 general election restored a measure of dominance in Scotland to the Labour Party, at the time of writing, the SNP remains the devolved government of the country with the largest representation in the Scottish Parliament, a Parliament whose very existence is in part due to the shock to the UK political system that the voters of Hamilton delivered on 2 November 1967 when there was (for that time) a record-breaking 37.9 per cent swing from Labour to the SNP.

The Labour Party had represented Hamilton since the seat was created in 1918. Every commentator expected the result to be, as the leading Labour-supporting Scottish newspaper the *Daily Record* put it at the start of the campaign, a 'foregone conclusion'. Indeed, so great was the complacency that the Saturday before polling, the Labour candidate took the day off, saying that his decision came from '90 per cent confidence and 10 per cent need'.

However, the next day, Scotland's *Sunday Mail* newspaper, stablemate of the *Daily Record*, reported on a survey in one Hamilton council estate which found that out of thirty electors, eighteen intended to vote SNP, with only five declaring for Labour, one for the Tories and six who either didn't know or wouldn't vote.

Then two days later – on the Tuesday of election week – the *Daily Record* headlined another rudimentary local poll with the headline 'Labour is far from home in Hamilton'.

They were right.

The by-election was caused by the appointment of the sitting Labour MP, Tom Fraser, as chairman of the state-owned North of Scotland Hydro-Electric Board. His salary for the post, which included membership of the board of another Scottish electricity generator and of the new Highlands & Islands Development Board, was more than double that of a backbench MP.

In seeking the post, Fraser was following in the footsteps of the great Labour MP Tom Johnston, who had been wartime Secretary of State for Scotland but who left politics in 1945 to chair the Hydro Board, as it was known.

Fraser had been an effective minister, first as a junior in the Scottish Office in the Attlee administration and then as Transport Minister in Harold Wilson's Cabinet, introducing the 70-mph speed limit on motorways, although he also presided over the decimation of Scotland's – and Britain's – railway network.

Wilson fired him in a December 1965 reshuffle, but he stood again in the March 1966 general election, recording his eighth consecutive victory since he won Hamilton in a 1943 by-election. However, there were persistent rumours in his constituency that he was seeking an alternative occupation and these persuaded a small group of local Scottish National Party members to start preparations so that they would not be wrong-footed if a by-election was suddenly called.

The SNP had been seen as, in the words of one commentator, a largely irrelevant party of 'monomaniacs and poets' for much of its 33-year existence. However, a period of professionalisation within the party was now underway, with a steady increase in the number of members, branches and elections fought, although in the 1966 UK general election, it had still only managed to put up twenty-three candidates, leaving forty-eight seats vacant. The total vote share for the party in that election was 0.5 per cent.

Now SNP activists in Hamilton were keen to show that they could compete and they considered a number of possible candidates before settling on a 37-year-old Glasgow solicitor, Winifred Ewing, who had not stood anywhere before but was gaining a reputation in the party as both a talented and a glamorous politician. She was formally selected on 20 July 1966, six days after the Welsh nationalist Gwynfor Evans won a by-election in Carmarthen, giving Plaid Cymru its first ever representation at Westminster.

That victory over Labour added to the woes of the incumbent Labour government. Since the highly successful general election on 31 March 1966, which gave the party an overall majority of ninety-seven (and forty-six of the seventy-one Scottish seats), there had been ministerial resignations, a compulsory wage freeze, national strikes by seamen and dock workers and by-election defeats, including at Glasgow Pollok which was snatched by the Conservatives but with the SNP unexpectedly securing over 28 per cent of the vote. These difficulties would culminate in the devaluation of the pound some two weeks after the Hamilton by-election.

Internationally, the Vietnam War and the pressure from the US for British backing was also causing tensions within the Labour Party.

All these factors meant that holding an immediate by-election in Hamilton would have been risky. Conventional wisdom and past results suggested that the Conservatives were the party most likely to take Hamilton, but the SNP had been slowly growing in confidence and experience, and recent by-election showings had not only indicated the party's potential but also a substantial increase in membership and on-the-ground organisation.

Given the prevailing political circumstances, Tom Fraser's appointment was not confirmed until July 1967, which meant that Winnie Ewing was able to campaign for a full year without any other candidates in the field. She used that time to enthusiastically work the constituency and to identify herself with it and its landmarks.

One of those was the huge globe that sat outside the birthplace of missionary David Livingstone in Blantyre, and an abiding image of her campaign – reproduced many times, including on the cover of her biography published in 2004 – is the picture of her perched on it, with the caption being words she spoke in her victory speech in Hamilton Town Hall: 'Stop the World, Scotland wants to get on.'

Winnie Ewing was just what the Hamilton constituency needed. Energetic and personally attractive with a fondness for 'campaigning by shopping' in the high streets and villages of the constituency, she was well supported by her accountant husband Stewart, who devised a whole series of innovations including colourful and noisy car cavalcades. In addition, she was an experienced public speaker and debater, having learned useful lessons in the testing arena of the Glasgow criminal courts.

She was also what the media was looking for at a time when politics seemed stale. The possibility – no matter how remote – of a political upset caused by such a personality with a fresh message meant that much of the press and broadcast media enthused about her to the detriment of the other two more staid candidates.

Her bright and refreshing approach also extended to her policy prospectus, which was liberal and internationalist, and gave the lie to the narrow and insular outlook which long-term enemies of the SNP such as Labour Scottish Secretary Willie Ross imagined was the nationalist norm.

Although the SNP leader was still the 66-year-old Arthur Donaldson, who had been interned at the start of the Second World War, a new generation of capable, credible, left-leaning and modernising key figures was emerging, including the future leader Billy Wolfe who had performed well in elections in his local West Lothian constituency.

Winnie Ewing's candidacy was complemented by the genius of her agent, a teacher called John McAteer, who brought to the role an unrivalled eye for detail and a phenomenal capacity for hard work. He, in his turn, was backed up by a small but highly effective national structure in the SNP, spearheaded by a former Ayrshire farmer Ian Mac-Donald as the national organiser and Angus MacGillivray, a former West Lothian painter and decorator, who was the fundraiser.

They motivated the party and encouraged members across Scotland to volunteer to help from an early date. They were also willing to spend money on the constituency to help canvassing and provide materials. By the end of the campaign, the SNP nationally had spent almost a quarter of its annual budget on Hamilton.

The decision by the Liberal Party not to field a candidate in the by-election gave a considerable boost to the SNP campaign, and this was increased when Ludovic Kennedy, one of the Liberal's key media voices, left his party and spoke in Winnie Ewing's favour. She also received a range of other celebrity endorsements, including from the *James Bond* star Sean Connery (a lifelong supporter of the SNP) and locally popular personalities.

The Conservatives ran their candidate from the 1966 general election, another Glasgow lawyer called Iain Dyer. Their negative campaign was strongly focused on the SNP after their early canvass returns indicated that the Conservatives not only were out of serious contention but might not even take second place.

Labour's candidate, Alex Wilson, was in the mould of his predecessor, a former miner supported by the trade unions. There was some bad feeling in the local constituency Labour Party (CLP) about Tom

Fraser's decision to leave politics for a well-paid job, as well as about his supposed lack of gratitude to his local supporters. Wilson was also something of a drab figure when contrasted with Winnie Ewing, and the Labour campaign was mistaken in its view that a former mining constituency would not take well to a woman and particularly a young professional woman who aspired to be their MP. In fact, she proved very popular, especially with female voters.

Local Labour resentments and a limited level of support from outside the constituency for the Labour candidate – only sixteen Labour MPs visited during the campaign – presented a further obstacle to success, particularly when it became clear that SNP members across Scotland were highly motivated with support for their presence in the constituency coming from the SNP at national level.

The SNP campaign organisers tried to make the work enjoyable and the reception on the doorsteps helped encourage participation. There was a competition among branches to see which could contribute the most man and woman power. As the campaign progressed, word got out that something significant might be happening on the ground which also drove increased volunteering.

The SNP had a huge presence on the ground in the last few days, and on election day itself, it was able to staff all the twenty-nine polling stations continuously, including the very smallest at Rosebank in the Clyde Valley. When the polls closed, activists gathered outside Hamilton Town Hall waiting for the result and rumours began to fly that an upset was likely.

The counting was efficient and quick and the result was declared just after midnight. A huge crowd, almost entirely SNP activists who had been in the constituency working all day, reacted with enormous excitement and Winnie Ewing was carried shoulder-high to the town's Zambezi Hotel, where copies of the hastily produced special second edition of the weekly local paper the *Hamilton Advertiser*, blazing the result on its front page, were eagerly passed from hand to hand.

Winnie Ewing had overturned a Labour majority over the Tories of 16,500 and with a swing of nearly 40 per cent had come from nowhere to take one of Labour's safest seats. The shockwaves were enormous and lasting – for a start, Labour and the Conservatives were both forced to address what appeared to be deep dissatisfaction with their approach to Scotland. They did so by slowly extending administrative devolution and promising further change.

However, as the threat receded and subsequent Scottish by-elections failed to produce further SNP victories, with Labour holding the Glasgow Gorbals seat in October 1969 with over 50 per cent of the vote and South Ayrshire in March 1970 (where the SNP came third), so the promises began to evaporate.

It would take the SNP successes of the two 1974 general elections, including not just eleven seats won but second place in almost every other constituency, to make alarm bells ring again at Westminster and renew the process started by Hamilton which eventually resulted in the establishment of a devolved Scottish Parliament in 1999, which in turn led to the election of the SNP to government in 2007 and the independence referendum in 2014.

The failure of the SNP to make any significant breakthrough in the June 1970 UK general election was also a factor in temporarily reducing the panic and muting the promises. In that election, Winnie Ewing lost the Hamilton seat, although she secured a creditable 35 per cent of the vote, while the 1967 by-election loser Alex Wilson was finally returned as the Hamilton MP, which he represented until his death in March 1978. He was succeeded at another Hamilton by-election – the third in forty-five years – by George Robertson, later UK Defence Secretary and then secretary general of NATO.

However, the very last result declared in 1970 – on the day after polling – saved the SNP's face when Donald Stewart, the former Provost of Stornoway, won the Western Isles, removing from Parliament one of its longest-serving Labour members, Malcolm K. Macmillan, who had been elected in 1935 at the age of twenty-two.

Winnie Ewing had a difficult time in her three years as the MP for Hamilton. The hostility to her among Labour MPs was palpable and the scrutiny intense. Every absence was noted and had it not been for the support of fellow rookie MP Gwynfor Evans, she would have suffered even more greatly. At one stage, she had to formally complain to Labour's Chief Whip about being stalked by a Scottish Labour member who was forced to apologise to her.

More positively, she was in great demand in Scotland and campaigned tirelessly for the SNP the length and breadth of the country. She was the SNP's first popularly recognised figure and received a great deal of media exposure.

All that made it even harder for her when she returned to her previous occupation as a solicitor in 1970, so it was no great surprise that she was much sought after by SNP constituency parties looking for a high-profile candidate for a future election.

She became an MP again in February 1974, for the Moray constituency in the north-east of Scotland, unexpectedly defeating the sitting Secretary of State for Scotland Gordon Campbell who, in a demonstration of pique, refused even to shake her hand at the count.

Losing that seat in 1979 (the SNP in the 1970s, in the words of Alex Salmond, having 'gone up like the rocket and down like the stick'), she defied all predictions once more by being elected to the European Parliament only weeks later in the first direct elections to that body. Liberal MP Russell Johnson, who like Winnie Ewing had been a nominated Member of the European Parliament (MEP) since 1975, was the overwhelming favourite to take the newly created seat, but her very visible campaigning across a huge area (the constituency covered almost a quarter of the Scottish land mass and contained most of the offshore inhabited islands) secured her a narrow victory.

Winnie Ewing remained an MEP for twenty years, recording larger and larger majorities and earning the sobriquet of 'Madame Écosse', until she retired in 1999 in order to stand for the newly created Scottish Parliament where she served a single term as a regional MSP for the Highlands and Islands.

As the oldest member elected to that parliament, she chaired the first formal session on 12 May 1999, memorably declaring: 'I want to start with the words that I have always wanted either to say or to hear someone else say – the Scottish Parliament, which adjourned on March 25, 1707, is hereby reconvened.'

She is still the only person ever to have served as an elected Member of the Scottish Parliament, the Westminster Parliament and the European Parliament.

Winnie Ewing was the president of the SNP from 1987–2005 but retired from active politics after leaving elected office, though she made a campaign intervention during the 2014 independence referendum.

Winnie Ewing died in Glasgow on 21 June 2023, aged ninety-three. Two of her three children became Members of the Scottish Parliament and Scottish government ministers, and one of them, Annabelle, also served as an MP at Westminster from 2001 to 2005.

Michael Russell is a former MSP and Scottish government minister and was president of the SNP from 2020–23. Currently chair of the Scottish Land Commission, he has worked as a columnist and television producer, is the author of seven books and edited Winnie Ewing's biography Stop the World *(Birlinn Ltd, 2004).*

44

ROCHDALE

26 OCTOBER 1972
LIBERAL GAIN FROM LABOUR

ALISTAIR BURT

Result: Cyril Smith (Liberal), 19,296, 42.29 per cent; Lawrence Cunliffe (Labour), 14,203, 31.12 per cent; David Trippier (Conservative), 8,060, 17.66 per cent; Jim Merrick (Independent), 4,074, 8.93 per cent
Size of majority: 5,093
Swing: 11.89 per cent from Labour to Liberal
Name of previous MP and party: John 'Jack' McCann (Labour)
Reason for by-election: Death of incumbent
Result at previous general election: Jack McCann (Labour), 19,247, 41.57 per cent; Cyril Smith (Liberal), 14,076, 30.40 per cent; M. Andrew (Conservative), 12,978, 28.03 per cent
Date by-election called: 3 October 1972
Date by-election took place: 26 October 1972
Size of total electorate: 66,344
Total number of votes cast: 45,633
Turnout: 68.78 per cent

'There can be few people in Rochdale who have not heard of Cyril Smith, but you can bet your bottom dollar, or 50 pence piece, that they all will have in the next three weeks.'

Thus, the press introduced a wider world to alderman Cyril Smith of Rochdale. If you wish for a textbook example of personality and its impact in English politics, of the dominance of an individual in a

348

by-election, then look no further than Rochdale '72. It was all about Cyril, and it was always going to be.

Rochdale is a proud mill town to the north of Manchester, at the foot of the Pennines. Its politics are famously bound in nineteenth-century history by association with Richard Cobden and John Bright, with community and the Co-Op movement and with Methodism. Largely, but not exclusively, represented regularly throughout the twentieth century by Labour and Liberal members, the 1972 by-election arose from the death of Labour MP John 'Jack' McCann, who had won five elections since 1958. On a poor night for Labour nationally, as Ted Heath's Tories surprised pundits with a win at the general election, Jack McCann held Rochdale for Labour in 1970 with 41.6 per cent of the vote and a majority of 5,171.

Within five days of his death on 16 July, his Liberal opponent of 1970, Cyril Smith, made clear to his party and the press that he wished to stand again. We were off.

Parties moved quickly to select their candidates. McCann's death came just before the summer recess, with an expectation of the writ being moved very smartly on return of the House. It was on 3 October, with the election date set for Thursday 26 October. The Conservatives went local – and young. But 26-year-old David Trippier, a Rochdale stockbroker, had already made his mark and was a local councillor there. He had become well known for spearheading a campaign to save a much-loved public garden area and was a fluent and highly regarded public speaker and communicator for the party in the north as a prominent Young Conservative.

The Labour Party went for the 44-year-old Lawrence Cunliffe, from a shortlist of Union candidates with sponsorship behind them. A family man and an experienced councillor, the mining engineer from the Bolton district of Farnworth was chosen in preference to two Rochdale councillors, one of them being Roger Stott, who would later find a seat in Wigan. At the time, it must have seemed a sound choice; Farnworth was surely local enough to hold Labour members loyalty, knowing that every vote counted. It was an early error in the campaign.

But both Trippier and Cunliffe, who would become good MPs in their own right, were supporting cast.

Cyril Smith *was* Mr Rochdale, and his controversial star was about to move into the ascendant. While the first thing you would notice about Cyril (as universally known) was the 22 stone 6ft 2in. frame, the second thing you would learn would be his local history and what people thought of him. There was a charming 'our Cyril' element; still living in a two-up, two-down Rochdale home with his mum, a town hall cleaner he had made his mayoress, his devotion to the town was obvious. But there were other stories and comments. He had begun a political career as a Liberal, moved to Labour, then Independent and back to the Liberals. This had not gone down well with all. By 1972, Cyril had already been on Rochdale Council for twenty years and was embedded in its committees, on various other bodies as well as running a successful manufacturing company. Opinions on him were not hard to find for the national press giving the by-election a rundown: 'As many chins as he has had parties', 'Everyone has a story about Cyril, trouble is no one can prove any of them', 'He may be the Party's best candidate, but ideologically he is a disaster'.

David Trippier remembers the man and campaign well:

> From the start, it was all about Cyril. There were posters of him everywhere, focusing on 'Cyril Smith – The Man'. Labour councillors were caustic about him; Conservatives remembered that he had approached them before defecting to the Liberals, but we wouldn't have him, because of what he had said about the Tories before.

Labour's rush to move the writ was probably based on a desire to move quickly before the Liberal organisation got going. Campaign manager Paul Carmody was an experienced regional organiser for Labour and understood it was Labour's to lose. The national background seemed propitious enough. Ted Heath's government, the narrow winner of the 1970 election, was struggling with rising inflation, mixed messages on the economy led by Chancellor Anthony Barber's ill-fated dash for growth, industrial unrest and above all had seen unemployment top 1 million at the end of 1971 for the first time since the 1930s, accompanied by bitter demonstrations. No opposition could have asked for more.

But although early expectations suggested quiet confidence for Labour, there was unease right from the start about 'Smithery'. Labour was not universally seen as the answer to the government, and reporters sensed the unease of voters for both main parties. And there was always the perennial possibility of a 'Liberal revival'.

Shortly before nominations closed, a fourth candidate joined the fight. Jim Merrick, a former Tory from Bradford, expelled from the party because of his views, was to stand as an Independent representing the British Campaign to Stop Immigration. Rochdale, in common with other northern mill towns, had encouraged labour, principally from Pakistan, to fill the night shifts in the cotton factories. By 1972, there were some 7,000 such residents, representing 4.6 per cent of the population. On the surface of the town, there appeared few issues associated with this. There were community relations groups, and the Pakistani community had integrated into local politics, mostly through their identification as 'workers' with the Labour Party. There was no shortage of housing, and unemployment stood at 4.9 per cent. But it was not hard for practised exploiters to seize upon opportunities, and a visiting journalist had noted that 'there was enough resentment about their presence to give him [Merrick] between 100 and 1,000 votes'.

The campaign began in earnest with traditional launches among crowds of supporters, and the initial pitches of the candidates set the tone for the issues of the following three weeks. Cyril Smith at a 'packed Town Hall' said the country was in a 'pathetic state', lacking in honest and firm leadership. He spared few horses. 'A state where violence, terrorism and anarchy raise their heads, where respect for law and order diminish, and trade union thuggery shows its hand.' His platform highlighted law and order (he was already well known as a supporter of corporal punishment, having stated that local ringleaders of a school riot deserved a 'damn good hiding'), industrial relations, education and fair rents in housing. But he also made much of Rochdale and its future, believing 'we can be pioneers in the future as much as the past'.

David Trippier also made a confident start in front of 300 people at the town hall, who had escaped the rival attractions of a football match and the Christadelphians in another room. He made 'an impressively positive speech' but also focused on law and order, speaking for those who were afraid to go out at night.

Lawrence Cunliffe's first public meeting led on the topics of his campaign: unemployment, the link between high inflation and high unemployment and an early mention of 'cuts in school milk', the issue which was first to put Mrs Margaret Thatcher 'milk snatcher' in the headlines for many who had previously never heard of her. Interestingly, another national political story was emerging of which we were to hear much more. The tussle between union power and government was beginning to be noticed. The *Rochdale Observer*, the local paper of record, noted early in the campaign that, in recent industrial disputes, 'we have seen miners win concessions, which may well have been right, by brute force methods, which are undoubtedly wrong'. By February 1974, the issue 'Who runs Britain?' was to be the key question of the general election that month.

The Rochdale campaign played out through well-attended public meetings, with all the trappings – big political guns from Westminster, hecklers and a steady increase in temperature and anxiety as the shape of the campaign began to emerge. To David Trippier, it became clear at an early stage that the real politics of the by-election were not whether and to what extent the governing Conservatives received a bloody nose from the Lancashire electorate – they were never in the fight – it was all about the Liberals overhauling Labour from the 1970 election:

> I thought within the first week that Cyril would win. He was very tough on Labour and Cunliffe in particular, treated him unfairly, I thought. He was critical both in front of him and behind his back. Smith was a superb performer at meetings. He shone. He had done his homework, had his notes and spoke well. And his poster campaign was first rate, and highly personal, local and with very simple messages.

It was that local element which was key. Challenged by the press that he was focusing too much on Rochdale, Smith would reply it was what mattered to his electors – not the worst charge he could face. He promised to set up a people's panel of locally qualified experts, from the health service to industry, to guide him on his votes in Parliament.

Smith's agent, Jim Spiller, also banked on the likelihood that Liberals who had not supported him in the 1970 general election, due to the party infighting and sheer disturbance that Smith caused, would return to the fold. This turned out to be correct, and local canvassers were joined by many from all over the country as word got out that a win was on.

MPs and household names came along, the Liberals led by party leader Jeremy Thorpe. Emlyn Hooson, Russell Johnston, John Pardoe and David Steel among them. David Trippier counted on Cabinet minister Jim Prior, Mark Carlisle, Christopher Chataway, Patrick Jenkin and the young Winston Churchill. Labour was smaller in number but made up for it in star power with Merlyn Rees, Barbara Castle, Michael Foot and Jim Callaghan.

As the election moved towards the last week, the newspaper talk was of panic in the Labour ranks, as the numbers of MPs canvassing was interpreted not as the usual 'get out the vote effort' but as a worried reaction to the growing sense that Smith was taking votes from disaffected Tories, who knew their candidate would not win and wanted to stop Labour, and taking them also from the residual Labour vote.

There was another group of voters moving from Labour to Liberals. The Pakistani community was shifting. Firstly, there was strong engagement from Cyril Smith personally. He went to the mills at the end of night-time shifts. Unlike Labour, he made contacting him a personal matter, not one delegated to a council colleague. In addition, Harold Wilson's support of India had not gone unnoticed in a fragile time in the relationship between the two states in the subcontinent. And a rising issue of concern among the Bangladeshi Rochdale community for the safety of current Bangladeshi prisoners of war was picked up by Jeremy Thorpe, who promised he would send Smith as his envoy to the region if he was a Westminster MP. (It did not happen.)

As the campaign closed, a degree of bitterness broke out. Cunliffe made an allegation that 'buffoonery' was triumphing, along with 'cranks, turncoats and self publicists', and had to avoid the calls to 'name the buffoon', which he did not. The pundits spoke of a photo finish. The Liberals had gone a bit shy of predicting victory. Except Cyril, who believed he was 'well in'.

The count confirmed that Smith was right. The 1970 poll result was reversed, and the Liberals had a new MP by a majority of over 5,000, an astonishing turnaround from 1970. Smith was triumphant and went round the market the next day accompanied by his mother. Praise was generous in recognising that whatever success the Liberal Party had, it was Cyril Smith who had won, by winning over the floating votes of former Conservatives and Labour supporters. Each of the main candidates made respectful speeches, acknowledging Smith's outsized role in his victory, which continued what had been for the main part, the awkwardness between the Liberals and Labour aside, a personally courteous contest between all except Merrick, who was disliked by the rest. Those who looked beyond Smith wrote again of Liberal revival and noted that a by-election in Sutton & Cheam was anticipated soon. Would the revival carry? (Spoiler, yes it did, for that by-election.)

Labour had lost a by-election, only the fifth time since 1929 an opposition had done so, but would bind up its wounds in time for 1974's two elections, before heading into the perils of the winter of discontent and opening the doors for Mrs Thatcher.

But, away from Liberal triumph, there was a 'disquieting' vote. The anti-immigration candidate had not polled 100 or 1,000 but north of 4,000. This was seen as a significant and unexpected shock and much commented upon. Cunliffe said he was astounded. There were reports during the day of harassment of Pakistani voters by Merrick's people, challenging their identity and right to vote. Labour councillor Abdul Choudhry said that he was disappointed to realise that '10 per cent of the town don't want us here'. In a changing England, this was not to be the last time that race and immigration was to be a local factor in a national Rochdale electoral contest.

Smith was to hold the seat for twenty years and gain honours and renown, but his reputation was deeply diminished after his death in 2010, when allegations of child abuse were made against him, and it was revealed that the CPS believed on evidence presented to them that he should have been charged with serious offences and indeed that a cover-up at a high level had taken place.

Both of his major party opponents in 1972 had long and distinguished parliamentary careers as well-liked Lancashire representatives.

David Trippier was well regarded in the contest, described by one paper as 'a live wire, facts at his fingertips and of firm convictions'. He became MP for Rossendale & Darwen and served in the governments of Margaret Thatcher and John Major and was latterly High Sheriff of Lancashire.

Lawrence Cunliffe, who accepted the description of himself as 'left of centre with his feet on the floor', became MP for Leigh and served for twenty-two years.

Rt Hon. Alistair Burt *is the pro-chancellor of Lancaster University, UK commissioner to the ICMP in The Hague and a devotee of non-league football. He was an MP for thirty-two years between 1983 and 2019, holding several ministerial and opposition roles, on domestic and foreign affairs. This chapter was written with many thanks to the Local Studies Centre, Rochdale Public Library, and staff.*

45

SUTTON & CHEAM

7 DECEMBER 1972
LIBERAL GAIN FROM CONSERVATIVES

CONNOR HAND

Result: Graham Tope (Liberal), 18,328, 53.6 per cent; Neil Macfarlane (Conservative), 10,911, 31.9 per cent; David Miller (Labour), 2,937, 8.6 per cent; Chris Frere-Smith (Anti-Common Market), 1,332, 3.9 per cent; Edgar Scruby (National Independence), 660, 1.9 per cent
Size of majority: 7,417
Swing: 32.6 per cent from Conservative to Liberal
Name of previous MP and party: Richard Sharples (Conservative)
Reason for by-election: Resignation on being appointed Governor of Bermuda
Result at previous general election: Richard Sharples (Conservative), 23,957, 58.1 per cent; John Dowsett (Labour), 11,261, 27.3 per cent; Nicholas McGeorge (Liberal), 6,023, 14.6 per cent
Date by-election called: 15 November 1972
Date by-election took place: 7 December 1972
Size of total electorate: 60,735
Total number of votes cast: 34,194
Turnout: 56.3 per cent

In early 1973, the Liberal Party's executive committee convened to discuss their momentous by-election victory in Sutton & Cheam, staged just before Christmas the previous year. Tucked away in the corner, the leader Jeremy Thorpe and his eventual successor, David Steel, had disengaged from the presentation on the party's strategy and were quietly discussing other matters. Party president Trevor Jones, the architect of their stunning success, objected to this lack of attention to his seminar, regarding them like recalcitrant teenagers in a classroom. He drew a whistle from his jacket pocket and blew it hard.

'Attention is the most important word in the English language,' Jones said curtly, his glare fixed on Steel and Thorpe. 'Now I have yours, this is what you need to hear.'

As well as showcasing his abrasive nature, this episode captures Jones's approach to political messaging. To him, generating attention was everything. A businessman and master publicist, Jones was an enthusiastic exponent of 'community politics', a belief that the Liberals could build electoral success by focusing relentlessly on local issues rather than the national messaging. Community politics had yielded impressive results in Liverpool, where Jones was a councillor, and with the Liberals returning just six seats in the 1970 general election, he was determined to prove his methods could rejuvenate the party.

Sutton & Cheam, a constituency with a Conservative majority of over 12,500, where the Liberals had narrowly clung on to their deposit in 1970, provided an opportunity to prove his point. Jones's techniques delivered such a totemic triumph that the *Daily Telegraph* called the party's candidate, Graham Tope, 'the outstanding by-election winner of the last 40 years'. Yet the significance of this by-election was not just confined to the substantial swing achieved by Tope; it catalysed the Liberals' revival in the early-to-mid 1970s, showing the effectiveness of community politics in areas where the party had little previous support or organisation. Indeed, the principles adopted in Sutton & Cheam would guide them, and their successors the Liberal Democrats, for decades.

Since 1954, Sutton & Cheam had been represented by Sir Richard Sharples, an Old Etonian and Home Office minister under Ted Heath. After eighteen years presiding over the constituency, Sharples accepted an offer to become Governor of Bermuda, seduced by the promise of sunnier climes and a salary of £160,000 in today's money. Even Sharples, who'd already earned a reputation as an absentee MP, realised that addressing constituency matters from the Caribbean was unfeasible and thus signalled his intention to resign in June 1972. Incidentally, Sharples was assassinated after just six months in post by Erskine

Burrows, a Black Power advocate who became the final person to be executed under British rule in 1977.

On the face of it, conditions could hardly have been more propitious for a challenger party. At the turn of the year, unemployment figures had reached 1 million, with inflation and industrial action compounding the problem. Heath's principal promise in 1970 had been to curb the pressure families faced at the till. Inflation, though, remained above 7 per cent. Meanwhile, a seven-week miners' strike forced the government to declare a state of emergency and a three-day working week in February 1972, culminating in significant pay concessions to the National Union of Mineworkers (NUM). Heath also struggled to contain his fissiparous party on whether to join the European Economic Community (EEC). Fortunately for the Prime Minister, Harold Wilson's Labour Party, similarly divided over the EEC, were unable to capitalise on the government's capitulation to the NUM, given 70 per cent of the public perceived Labour as being too close to the unions.

With the Liberal Party polling at just 8 per cent nationally, there was little to suggest they could translate discontent into votes. Jones understood these dismal ratings posed a strategic problem. Simply put, irrespective of the major parties' difficulties, the Liberals would likely generate little traction by concentrating on their national positions. Fortunately for Jones, the party's prospective candidate was Graham Tope, a 28-year-old member of the Young Liberals, who accepted that, to stand any chance in the by-election, they must ruthlessly target local grievances. With few in the party or media believing Sutton & Cheam was in play for the Liberals, Jones closed his pitch to lead Tope's campaign with a simple proposition: 'Give it a try, you've got nothing to lose.' Tope took the gamble and fully embraced the essence of Jones's motto, often using it in campaign material and conversations with voters.

Tope set off on his honeymoon in July 1972, leaving Jones to survey the relatively affluent suburban seat, noting observations into a pocket-sized metal Dictaphone. Accompanying Jones was Des Wilson, a future party general election campaign director and president. Wilson was struck by Jones's ability to recognise and capitalise on marketing opportunities. He was particularly impressed by the Welshman's opportunism when he noticed a woman trip on an uneven pavement. Bolting out of his car to tend to the woman's injuries, Jones grabbed his camera and snapped the jagged pavement remarking that it would 'look good on a leaflet'.

Though the lamentable state of the constituency's pavements was consistently highlighted by Tope's campaign, Jones's first *Focus* leaflet targeted road safety. Pioneered by Cyril Carr, Jones's mentor at Liverpool City Council, *Focus* was adroitly engineered to trumpet local grievances, featuring a 'grumble sheet' which encouraged residents to detail their issues. On his weekly visits to the Sutton & Cheam constituency, Jones transported thousands of leaflets from his Liverpool printers in his flamboyant white Triumph Stag, clocking 10,000 miles over the course of the campaign. Years spent perfecting attention-grabbing leaflets exuded from the inaugural *Focus*. Entitled 'Death Stalks the Crossroads', these leaflets featured a shot of North Cheam crossroads flanked by a cartoon of a menacing-looking car, with grills that matched the teeth of the skull beneath it. At the wheel was a figure donning a cowboy hat, creating a sense of lawlessness hammered home by a local resident's testimony which read: 'It's so dangerous to cross… The only safe way to the other side would be to be born there!'

The material in *Focus* instantly resonated. Tope recounted how he 'came back from my honeymoon having never heard of *Focus*' yet was inundated with letters and phone calls responding to it. Such was the impact that, fearing reputational damage, the Licensed Taxi Drivers' Association demanded the Liberals clarify that the presence of a black cab in the photo was purely coincidental. Tope conceded that 'not a great deal of policy' appeared in *Focus* but argued its intention was to 'connect with people', brushing aside criticism from other candidates and even his own party.

That connection, along with practical action, delivered results, the 'Fair Fares' campaign being a case in point. Inspired by grumble sheet feedback, already proving to be a wellspring of ideas, election agent Gerry Watkin realised anger over concessionary bus fares had significant campaigning potential. Unlike twenty-four other London boroughs, Sutton only offered discounted rates to pensioners on concessionary benefits. Tope organised a petition contesting this, arguing they should be universally available. Perhaps unsurprisingly, in an area with the highest proportion of pensioners of any London borough, he amassed 5,000 signatures within weeks. The compromise he extracted by mid-September doubled the council's spending on concessions. This proved Tope could tackle dissatisfaction by taking on the council, building his credibility as a vehicle for expressing frustration with the two major parties while also presenting himself as an effective potential MP.

Adding to these headwinds were problems experienced by the Conservatives and Labour at local level. Insurance manager David Miller was selected for Labour but ran an ineffective campaign after being refused time off work. Only able to canvass half of the constituency, one uncomplimentary report at the time suggested that poor Miller resembled 'a man out for a spin in a Mini in the middle of a Grand Prix'. The Conservatives, meanwhile, were divided on multiple fronts. Their councillors sparred over plans to reduce the number of grammar schools as well as the choice of candidate. Experienced local councillor Tag Taylor, who many considered the obvious choice, was overlooked in favour of Neil Macfarlane, a 36-year-old oil executive parachuted in from Maidenhead. Importing an unknown candidate undoubtedly played into the Liberals' hands, fuelling the suspicion that the Conservatives were taking traditional voters' support for granted. It further cemented the growing contrast between Tope's championing of local issues and Sharples's indifference towards constituency matters.

By mid-October, 200,000 *Focus* newsletters had been delivered across the constituency, highlighting issues ranging from an unpopular proposed flyover at Angel Hill to the challenges posed across the constituency's roads. Tope, for example, was pictured taking a pickaxe to a drain which had been clumsily tarmacked over by workmen. What's more, Tope's cause was boosted by Cyril Smith's victory for the Liberals at the Rochdale by-election on 26 October, which was presented as evidence of their rise nationally – a crucial currency for disruptor parties, as the Liberals discovered during their seminal victory at Orpington in 1962.

It is clear, though, that Thorpe was still sceptical of their chances, an attitude reflected by the paltry support offered to Tope's campaign by the national party. He still relied on a handful of mainly local volunteers to distribute leaflets. The starkest betrayal of this lack of confidence, however, was from Steel. In November, he argued it was unconscionable for Harold Wilson's whips to delay a by-election in Lincoln, where Dick Taverne had resigned as the Labour MP to fight for Democratic Labour. As this would be leaving the constituency 'unrepresented … [for] six months', Steel signalled he would happily move the writ on Taverne's behalf. Chris Frere-Smith, one of Sutton & Cheam's two anti-Common Market candidates, quickly pointed out that Sharples's seat would soon effectively reach a similar milestone and yet no such offer was forthcoming. The reasoning was clear: Taverne would likely inflict an embarrassing defeat for the Labour Party, but with the *Sutton Advertiser* forecasting a comfortable Conservative majority of 8,000, there was no urgent political incentive for the Liberals to seek a by-election date for Sutton & Cheam.

This perception was soon punctured. Two weeks after the *Advertiser*'s prediction, a poll commissioned by Liberal peer Lord Beaumont put the party at 28 per cent in the Sutton & Cheam constituency, nearly double what they achieved in 1970. This suggested that the Conservatives' choice, Neil Macfarlane, could be beaten, convincing Thorpe to reallocate activists away from Uxbridge where another by-election was taking place on the same day as the Sutton & Cheam by-election.

Though initially earmarked for internal use only, the poll rather cunningly found its way into the local and national papers, raising the plausibility of a Liberal upset. This change in the political atmosphere was palpable and even filtered across the Atlantic. At a Downing Street dinner, Pierre Trudeau, the Liberal Prime Minister of Canada, mischievously and audibly asked Thorpe, also in attendance, 'How is it going in Sutton, Jeremy?', playing on the anxieties of Heath and the Conservatives.

A week from polling day, finally set for 7 December, Macfarlane sensed that the Liberals posed a real threat. With Labour destined to finish a distant third, he attempted to juxtapose his hawkish positions on law and order, including stiffer sentences for murderers, against Tope's history of activism.

At a hustings event, Macfarlane claimed constituents did not wish to 'indulge the rabble-rousing techniques of the Young Liberals'. He was referring to Tope's arrest in Czechoslovakia in 1969, where he was accused of protesting against the Russian occupation, and then Tope's involvement in 'Stop the Seventy Tour', a campaign in which activists dug up cricket pitches in a bid to prevent the Apartheid-era all-white South African side touring England in 1970. Many viewed such activity with suspicion, and reports suggest Macfarlane's attack registered with parts of the electorate. On the eve of the poll, for instance, Tope was forced to defend his actions to residents of Bramble Acres old people's home in Sutton, insisting that many 'church councils, other MPs and the majority of the country' opposed the South African team's arrival.

As Macfarlane's attacks intensified, Tope benefited from the strategic direction of John Spiller, the mastermind of Cyril Smith's recent victory in Rochdale, who marshalled an army of canvassers which had swelled from around twenty to over 800 people. This army included Liberals from Manchester, the Midlands, Devon and the Netherlands. Even former leader Jo Grimond was tempted south to this London constituency. For Liberals, this rare public appearance was, as the *Daily Mail* put it, 'the nearest thing to the Second Coming and Father Christmas rolled into one'. The Conservatives also deployed big hitters. Visits from Peter Walker, president of the Board of Trade, and Home Secretary Robert Carr illustrated their confidence that the seat would be retained. Indeed, on polling day, the bookies still offered Macfarlane at 1/4 to win with the Liberals at 5/2. Yet Tope felt sufficiently emboldened by his chances that he called the offices of the *Evening Standard* to inform them that it would 'be another Orpington tonight'.

His confidence was well founded. Astonishingly, the Liberals surged from third place in 1970 to over 53 per cent of the vote, delivering a majority of 7,417. At the campaign's outset, Thorpe dismissed Jones's claim that he could produce a margin of victory greater than the majorities of all six Liberal MPs combined. He achieved this with 1,000 votes spare; not that being proved wrong bothered a jubilant Thorpe. Before a rapturous crowd at the Liberal Party's annual ball at the Savoy Hotel, he hailed Tope's victory as 'Orpington-plus' and though his words might have seemed hyperbolic, they were backed up by data. In overturning the Conservatives' majority, Tope surpassed the 26 per cent swing in Orpington and left *The Times'* political editor, David Wood, reaching for the 1933 Fulham East by-election as a point of comparison for the 'scale [and] possibly significance' of the achievement.

In many ways, though, to appreciate the full magnitude of this victory, it is necessary to factor in 7 December's other contest – Uxbridge. Here the Liberal candidate, Ian Stuart, fared poorly, forfeiting his deposit, a result which emphasised the importance of the tactics employed in Sutton. Though Sutton was undoubtedly a blow for the Prime Minister, winning in Uxbridge abated the Conservatives' blushes. Labour's failure to capture Uxbridge, despite all the pressures facing the government, exacerbated the party's pitiful performance in Sutton & Cheam. Humiliatingly, Miller lost his deposit, while the two anti-EEC candidates attracted fewer than 2,000 votes between them, roughly half what they were expecting.

Over the next two years, the impact of this by-election reverberated around the country to the particular detriment of Heath's Conservative Party. In 1973, the momentum sparked by Sutton & Cheam helped the Liberals deliver three more victories: Berwick-upon-Tweed, Ripon and the Isle of Ely, deposing the Conservatives on each occasion. More importantly, it provided them with the impetus to take advantage of a volatile electorate in the first general election of 1974, where Thorpe's party attracted 6 million votes and won fourteen seats, more than double their haul at the last election. Though this election was hardly a smashing of the major parties' duopoly in terms of seats, it was the first time their combined share dropped below 80 per cent since 1929, producing the first hung parliament in forty-five years. The result presented Thorpe with the choice of whether to join the Conservatives in a coalition government. He declined, passing up the opportunity to become Home Secretary. Yet the transformation in the party's fortunes compared to the electoral nadir of 1970 could not be clearer.

Tope ultimately only served as an MP for fifteen months, eventually being defeated by Macfarlane in both elections of 1974, becoming a Liberal Democrat peer in 1994. While his time as an MP was fleeting, his win has left an indelible imprint on the party's campaigning strategy. In fact, along with continued use of *Focus* leaflets to this day, the emphasis on community politics provided the blueprint for the party, as it restored national credibility under Paddy Ashdown in the 1990s and later propelled Sir Ed Davey's revitalisation of the Liberal Democrats which was largely achieved through key by-election victories fought against the Conservatives on local issues.

Before Sutton & Cheam, David Steel told Trevor Jones that people in the party were 'not quite ready for [his] methods'. With characteristic confidence, Jones replied, 'No, but they are ready for my results.' Fifty years later, the Liberal Democrats' continued focus on championing local issues stands as a vindication of his words.

Connor Hand is a journalist and senior newsgathering producer at LBC Radio.

46

LINCOLN

---

1 MARCH 1973
DEMOCRATIC LABOUR GAIN FROM LABOUR

JULIA LANGDON

Result: Dick Taverne (Democratic Labour), 21,967, 58.2 per cent; John Dilks (Labour), 8,776, 23.3 per cent; Jonathan Guinness (Conservative), 6,616, 17.5 per cent; Reg Simmerson (Democratic Conservative Against Common Market), 198, 0.5 per cent; Malcolm Waller (Majority Rule), 100, 0.3 per cent; Jean Justice (Independent for Hanratty Inquiry), 81, 0.2 per cent
Size of majority: 13,191
Swing: 43.0 per cent from Labour to Democratic Labour
Name of previous MP and party: Dick Taverne (Labour)
Reason for by-election: Resignation of incumbent
Result at previous general election: Dick Taverne (Labour), 20,090, 51.0 per cent; Richard Alexander (Conservative), 15,340, 39.0 per cent; Gilbert Blades (Independent), 3,937, 10.0 per cent
Date by-election called: 9 February 1973
Date by-election took place: 1 March 1973
Size of total electorate: 51,199
Total number of votes cast: 37,738
Turnout: 72.6 per cent

In many ways, the remarkable Lincoln by-election of 1973, staged as it was just two months to the day after the accession of the United Kingdom into membership of what everybody then called the Common Market, would prove to be emblematic of the myriad problems the relationship with Europe would throw up for the country's political

parties for the next half century and beyond. The stance so purposeful-
ly struck by Dick Taverne, a committed European and the triumphant
victor, who had stood down as the Labour MP to contest his own seat
as an Independent, was also indicative of the growing authority of the
Labour left wing and would point towards the corrosive party divisions
within the next decade which would lead to the formation of the Social
Democratic Party.

The outcome of the historic election – giving victory for the first
time in a post-war English by-election to an Independent candidate
– can be seen now, with the passage of time, as an outlier. It did seem
possible in its immediate aftermath, however, that it might herald a
fundamental realignment of the British political system, as was then
being widely advocated by sections of the British media.

The by-election threw the national spotlight on the specific role of
any MP in a representative democracy and the (unresolved) question
of the extent to which an elected member of the House of Commons
is the creature of the local party. 'Who do you want as your MP?' Dick
Taverne demanded in his final leaflet before polling on 1 March. 'A
man or a mouse?'

At the end of a thrilling campaign, which fully engaged the citizenry
of Lincoln, turning the small cathedral city into the focus of nationwide political attention and importing a host of celebrities to pound
its ancient pavements, the voters responded with a turn-out of 72.6
per cent – equivalent to that of a general election – and gave Taverne a
thumping 58.2 per cent majority and more votes even than he had won
as the official Labour candidate in the preceding 1970 general election.
Dick Taverne was hailed by the political record-keepers as having secured the greatest personal election success in British political history.

He achieved it with the help of a lacklustre official Labour candidate, a sparkling eccentric for a Conservative opponent and busloads of
helpers who rolled in on the A15 from all over the country. Old school
friends and college chums from Charterhouse and Balliol, Oxford,
turned up in town in his support and some of his colleagues from the
Bar also found the time to come and help him. At least one Conservative MP, Patrick Mayhew, a future Attorney General, made the journey.
The cross section of those who chose to campaign on his behalf were

similar sorts to those who would later sign up for the SDP. He found particularly strong backing from *The Times* newspaper whose editor, William Rees-Mogg (yes! Charterhouse and Balliol), was at the time in favour both of UK membership of Europe and the idea of a radical new centre party in British politics. Many of Taverne's local friends and supporters would join the Lincoln Democratic Labour Association which would, if only briefly, run the City of Lincoln Council. Further assistance to his eventual success was provided by the Liberals deciding not to run a candidate.

There were two significant factors in the background to the by-election: the ambivalence of the Labour Party's view of the Common Market and Dick Taverne's own relationship with his local party at what was becoming an increasingly divisive time in party politics. The coincidence of Britain signing up as a member of Europe while the Labour Party's internal controversy on the issue was far from settled brought about the head-on political car crash in Lincoln between the MP and his local party which made the by-election inevitable.

Dick Taverne was born in 1928 of Dutch parents in the Dutch East Indies and was subsequently raised in Holland until the Nazi invasion brought the family to England. It is of little surprise, therefore, that he would become an enthusiastic European. He went to Oxford in 1947, regarding himself initially as a 'mild Marxist' but swiftly discounting communism in favour of the Labour Club. His contemporaries in the club, of which he became chairman, included Bill Rodgers and Shirley Catlin (later Williams), two of the 'Gang of Four' founding members of the SDP; one of his best friends was the television journalist Robin Day. In 1954, he qualified as a barrister (taking Silk in 1965) and in 1959, in Harold Macmillan's 'You've never had it so good' election, he stood unsuccessfully as the Labour candidate in Putney and managed to reduce the Conservative majority. Meanwhile, he had become close-ly involved with a group of other supporters of the party leader, Hugh Gaitskell, in the formation of the Campaign for Democratic Socialism, the body which sought to fight the (Aneurin) Bevanite-left, primarily against nuclear disarmament.

In 1962, when a by-election was called in Lincoln, the Gaitskellites were anxious to replace the Labour MP, Sir Geoffrey de Freitas, one of their number who had been appointed High Commissioner to Ghana, with another moderate, as the by-election was viewed as a crucial test of public opinion. An unashamedly rigged shortlist of three candidates, all Gaitskellites, was presented to the local party, including Taverne who had impressed Gaitskell himself when he spoke at the last party conference in Blackpool and who personally suggested him. The by-election would be nothing like as crucial as 1973 – Taverne increased the previous Labour majority – but the way in which the shortlist of candidates had been compiled caused a walk-out in protest at the selection by a local party official, Leo Beckett. Before the by-election had taken place, a week after the selection conference, left-wingers in the party took control of the main levers of its local power, the party executive and the management committee. Thereafter, the party was dominated by the left, which was committed, among other things, to unequivocal opposition to Europe. Leo Beckett became the party chairman in 1972 and his name would resonate in the city for many years to come.

Political discussion of Britain's role in Europe was largely theoretical in the 1960s. The UK first applied to join in 1961 but was knocked back twice by Charles de Gaulle's opposition – for his own nationalist reasons relating to the French–German axis. When he stood down in 1969, the path was cleared for what proved a successful application. I was on the *London Evening News* at the time, where the back bench featured a brilliant headline writer, Phil Wrack. His contribution on this occasion: 'It's Oui, Oui, Oui All The Way Home'. Edward Heath, who had headed the negotiations for Britain's membership in the early 1960s, his enthusiasm fuelled in part by his active fighting experience in the Second World War, then took over as Conservative Prime Minister in 1970, determined now that his place in history would be as the man who led Britain into Europe. He could scarcely have anticipated that the European issue would in fact help bring about the fall from office of each of his successors as party leader for generations to come.

Harold Wilson's position, having succeeded Gaitskell as Labour leader, was every bit as problematic by the time of the by-election. Although his government had embarked on negotiations to join and secured the approval of the Commons to do so by 488 votes to sixty-two, after Heath took office the tide turned. By then, Labour had come to regard Europe as a capitalist club, with the exception of the former Gaitskellites, most significantly led by Roy Jenkins, who contrastingly viewed membership of the European Community as a political totem. Wilson would later square this circle in his next government with the 1975 referendum on continued membership, but for the vote of principle, on accession, Labour imposed a three-line whip to oppose joining. On 28 October 1971, the House of Commons voted by a majority of 112 in favour of the Heath government's motion, a figure which included the rebellious votes of sixty-nine Labour MPs who defied the whip, including Dick Taverne.

His first few years as the Lincoln MP had been marked by what he termed in his memoirs 'a slightly fragile sense of political unity'. This was assisted initially by Labour's victories in the 1964 and 1966 elections, but the contractual compromises which make up so much of government policy is always going to attract criticism from the party ranks and so it proved then. Nuclear disarmament was one touchstone for the left; another was incomes policy, which was regarded as an attack on the working class. Taverne had joined the government as a junior minister at the Home Office in 1966 and then moved to the Treasury, first as a Minister of State and then as Financial Secretary. When his party ordered him to resign from government in protest at its anti-socialist policies – increased prescription charges was a particular resentment – he refused. When Labour lost the 1970 election and the Common Market became an issue, open warfare was declared. Taverne made it clear to his party in Lincoln that he planned to support the Heath government's vote in principle, and they told him that he would be deselected as Labour MP if he did so. He went ahead and so did they. They voted seventy-five to fifty to deselect him.

There ensued the usual messing around in which the Labour Party specialises, featuring allegations of improper practices, a committee of inquiry, a report whose findings were then sensationally overturned – but the upshot was always going to be a resignation and a by-election. Taverne's parliamentary colleagues tried to persuade him to lie low and roll with the party's strictures until the tide turned, as it surely would – and did. Taverne refused to compromise. It meant that he would not get the support in the by-election of his natural political friends, from

Roy Jenkins down. He was ticked off by Wilson – who never liked him and once described him as 'silken' and 'treacherous' at a Parliamentary Labour Party meeting. Taverne had had enough. In the autumn of 1972, he applied for the Manor of Northstead, an office of profit under the Crown and thus a device for resigning from the House of Commons, and the battle was joined. There was a universal view that he was on a hiding to nothing. The *Sunday Times* said his action was 'suicidal'.

But Taverne had set up the Lincoln Democratic Labour Association and a third of the members of Lincoln Labour Party had joined. He had been denounced by Tony Benn, then the Labour Party chairman, in his closing speech at Labour's annual conference as someone who was neither democratic nor Labour but a creature of the media who was destined for defeat. The Labour Party decided to delay the by-election for as long as was decently possible to enhance the chances of exactly that. The writ was only moved by the Labour Chief Whip, Bob Mellish, after his then Liberal equivalent, David Steel, proposed that he would do so – the party having been under great pressure from the radical likes of the young Peter Hain (then a member of the Liberals) who believed that they should have fought the seat.

And something else was blowing on the chilly Lincolnshire wind through that winter. An opinion poll conducted by London Weekend Television at the end of the Labour conference (after Taverne's resignation) suggested that 49 per cent of his Lincoln electorate would support their existing MP, 16 per cent would support the Tories and a mere 14 per cent would back any official Labour candidate. Taverne understandably thought it was too good to be true, but a Granada TV *World in Action* programme, produced by a young John Birt, had dramatised the raw politics of what was playing out in the city and this, along with Benn's ill-judged Blackpool speech, had made these little local difficulties into a topic of national interest. When Taverne called a meeting in Lincoln to explain his mission, he was astonished when 700 people turned up at the town hall, a location which could only accommodate 450. The overflow listened to the meeting on loudspeakers outside and heard Taverne supported by the brilliant author, journalist and broadcaster Bernard Levin, then at the height of his fame, and the controversial Mervyn Stockwood, Bishop of Southwark, a famed supporter of CND and right-on left-wing causes – such as would not normally include the likes of Taverne. He made a visionary speech about Europe, which much later he revealed was entirely written by Oswald Mosley, the former Labour MP who became a fascist. The bishop told Taverne that Mosley had thought he would need some help – 'but thought that if he supported you it might not do much good. So he said I should go and he would write my speech.'

Mosley was by then in his late seventies and had a further vicarious influence on the by-election. He had married Diana (née Mitford) in Nazi Germany in 1936 at the home of Joseph Goebbels, with Adolf Hitler as guest of honour. He was thus stepfather to Jonathan Guinness (now the 3rd Lord Moyne), then chairman of the right-wing Monday Club and chosen by the Conservatives as their candidate for Lincoln. This was, of course, a gift for the press who baited Guinness at every press conference with considerable success. He was funny and assertive and handled journalists with aristocratic insouciance, but he was in-experienced. Having said at a press conference that the death penalty should be reinstated, he was questioned about arrangements to prevent convicted murderers from committing suicide and was then somehow trapped into proposing that they should be provided with razor blades to enable them to do so and thus save the state the cost of their prison upkeep. He was nicknamed 'Old Razor Blades' by the media thereafter, assisted with helpful planted questions from party supporters when al-lowed out in public and treated as a joke. Election day brought him a good luck telegram signed 'Gillette'.

It probably deprived him of second place because he was only 2,000 votes short of John Dilks, the Labour candidate, whose campaign was badly wanting. The party had sent a reputed 100 MPs to knock doors in an attempt to help Dilks, a chunky good-looking character who ticked all the party boxes: he was leader of Derby Council and his exciting day job was in management at the Co-Op. But he was beyond help. Throughout the campaign, he refused ever to utter Dick Taverne's name, an extraordinarily pointless exercise, which he justified when challenged by saying, somewhat peevishly: 'I'm not interested in what he is doing.' But everybody else was. The Labour Party even sent a team from *Labour Weekly*, the party newspaper, to produce a Lincoln by-election edition for distribution to every home in the constituency. I was part of the team. I wrote the no-holds-barred interview with the candidate. It was an unedifying exercise and the atmosphere at Labour Party headquarters, devoid as it was of its core membership, was grim, rising only to the occasional gloomy.

And here's the thing: one of the greatest curiosities of the by-election was that Dilks was the only serious candidate even to raise the subject of Europe. The public didn't want to know about it. Reg Simmerson, a long-time anti-Europe candidate at by-elections, was happy to bore for Britain on the subject and was rewarded with 198 votes for his effort. The candidate at 'Taverne House', the drill hall which served as Democratic Labour's headquarters, was more interested in airing the man-or-mouse question, and the Tory Party was trying to keep Guinness quiet in the apparent belief that a victory for Taverne would be the most damaging outcome for Labour on the national political stage. There were diversionary side interests provided by the candidacy of Jean Justice, the 'A6 Murder candidate', a man campaigning for a posthumous pardon for James Hanratty, who had been hanged for murder (which DNA evidence would later prove he had committed) and whose case for such a pardon had reputedly been blocked by Taverne as a Home Office minister. Malcolm Waller, founder of the Majority Rule Party, wanted to discount the views of MPs if they were not shared by the majority. That got him 100 votes, nineteen more than for Justice. But Europe? Not an issue.

The *Daily Telegraph* ran an opinion poll a week before election day giving the rebel Taverne a 2 per cent lead over his official Labour challenger. How wrong could they be? The early hours of 2 March revealed a stunning 35 per cent lead. It would send a searing shock through the political wiring of the national parties and seemed a possible harbinger of real change. Yet Taverne played it wrong: he dissipated his victory and although his Lincoln local loyalists staggered on – running the council until 1979 – it was not until 1981 that the SDP would be formed in its short-lived attempt to reform the structure of British politics.

Where are they now? Dick Taverne over-reached his ambition by setting up a Campaign for Social Democracy (to echo the CDS) and putting up four additional candidates in February 1974. It was a disastrous mistake. When Roy Jenkins and the Gang of Four did split from Labour, Taverne joined their party, came second in the 1982 Peckham by-election as the SDP candidate and third in Dulwich in 1983. He joined the Liberal Democrats when the parties merged and was appointed to the House of Lords in 1996. Margaret Jackson, the Labour Party research officer, who would eventually depose Taverne in the October 1974 general election, winning by 984 votes, became the second Mrs Beckett in 1979. She stood in Lincoln in February 1974 and reduced Taverne's majority to 1,293 as an interim. Interestingly, the Labour Party had decided the way to beat Taverne was by choosing a female candidate. I know this because they asked me.

Beckett lost Lincoln in 1979 and won Derby South in 1983, where she remained an MP until 2024. More than half a century later, some of the main players live on in old age; the aspirations of a generation which sought to rewrite the social democratic centre of British politics are well and truly dead.

Julia Langdon is a journalist, author and broadcaster who has been covering politics since even before Lincoln in 1973. Tales from the Ancient Onion Wood: A celebration of friendship and wild garlic will be published later in 2025.

47

GLASGOW GOVAN

8 NOVEMBER 1973
SNP GAIN FROM LABOUR

GERRY HASSAN

Result: Margo MacDonald (SNP), 6,360, 41.9 per cent; Harry Selby (Labour), 5,789, 38.2 per cent; John Mair (Conservative), 1,780, 11.7; Peter McMillan (Liberal), 1,239, 8.2 per cent
Size of majority: 571
Swing: 26.7 per cent from Labour to SNP
Name of previous MP and Party: John Rankin (Labour)
Reason for by-election: Death of incumbent
Result at previous general election: John Rankin (Labour), 13,443, 60.1 per cent; Gerald F. Belton (Conservative), 6,301, 28.2 per cent; Michael Grieve (SNP), 2,294, 10.3 per cent; Thomas Biggam (Communist), 326, 1.5 per cent
Date by-election called: 9 October 1973
Date by-election took place: 8 November 1973
Size of total electorate: 35,114
Total number of votes cast: 15,168
Turnout: 43.2 per cent

Govan is situated on the Southside of Glasgow. Historically, it was an early Christian settlement and later became renowned for its industry, shipbuilding and radicalism – from rent strikes in the First World War to the Upper Clyde Shipbuilders' (UCS) work-in of the 1970s. Immortalised as the home of Rab C. Nesbitt and Mary Doll in the TV sitcom, and long affected by poverty, the area has been patronised by many – a phenomenon caricatured in Stanley Baxter's *Parliamo Glasgow*.

Govan has for decades held a place in political mythology as an urban Brigadoon – a parliamentary seat which appears and disappears every decade or so as a critical battleground in the struggle between the Labour Party and the SNP for dominance in Scotland.

In late 1973, a by-election was called after the death of the Labour MP for Govan John Rankin, who had held the seat in 1970 with a 7,142 majority (31.9 per cent) over the Conservatives, with Labour winning 60.1 per cent of the vote.

However, the timing of the contest was fortuitous for the SNP who were on the rise again and had in March of the same year nearly snatched the Labour stronghold of Dundee East with Gordon Wilson slashing the party's majority to 1,141 (and who would go on to take the seat in February 1974).

The SNP's high-profile campaign 'It's Scotland's Oil' was having an impact and making waves. The totemic Upper Clyde Shipbuilders (UCS) work-in of 1971–72 had concluded victoriously and put the cause of the workers and industry on the Clyde centre-stage. Alongside this, the Kilbrandon Commission on the Constitution that emerged from Labour's panic post-Hamilton and Harold Wilson's need to be seen to be acting on devolution would publish its recommendations on Scottish home rule during the campaign. This was all set against the backdrop of the growing unpopularity of Ted Heath's Conservative government.

Despite this, many senior figures in the Labour Party in Scotland were deeply complacent about the SNP challenge. Labour believed that the SNP were 'a one-woman sensation' after Winnie Ewing was unable to retain her Hamilton seat in 1970, after winning it in 1967, or indeed unable to make a national breakthrough that year beyond winning Western Isles – their first ever gain at a UK general election. To Labour loyalists, the SNP were 'Tartan Tories' who stood for 'Still No Policies', as their opponents described the catch-all protest nature of their appeal.

Jimmy Allison, Scottish Labour organiser, worked on the 1973 Govan campaign (as well as 1988) and witnessed first-hand the denial about the SNP threat. He spoke to Peter Allison (no relation), Scottish Secretary, and Harry Selby, the Labour candidate, in the midst of the campaign: 'Peter Allison regarded the SNP as unimportant and during a meeting in his office, attended by myself and Harry Selby, I lashed into both of them highlighting the political climate which was favourable to the SNP and pointing out their Scotland's Oil campaign.'

Despite Hamilton and the recent Dundee East contest, complacency was widespread within Labour. One Labour Party official early in the campaign noted with supreme confidence: 'We are clearly out in front, with the Tory a poor second.' For them, the Nationalists did not even warrant a mention.

Added to these difficulties and arrogance was the Labour candidate Harry Selby. Jim Sillars, then a young Labour MP, campaigned in the contest and recalled Selby: 'Harry was a revolutionary socialist firmly entrenched in the 1930s, utterly convinced that his Marxist analysis was an open sesame to understanding the world's problems.'

Selby was a Trotskyite, had been a Revolutionary Socialist League member and, following a split in 1948, was the leading figure in a small group called the Left Faction. This group had significant influence in the Govan local party, leading to Selby becoming the candidate in 1973. Selby, his friends and family ran Govan Labour Party as a small, closed shop which Jimmy Allison described in the following terms: 'Harry was a devout socialist who did not allow people into the party unless they were familiar with Marx and Engels. No wonder it was such a small CLP.'

Alongside this was the quality of the SNP candidate Margo MacDonald, who was everything Selby was not. Margo was a rising star with charisma, thirty years of age (Selby was sixty-one), and had already been noticed in the 1970 election in Paisley for her media and publicity suaveness. There was potential peril in the SNP choosing MacDonald, for as one contemporary observer put it: 'Govan had a male dominated culture so choosing a young woman as a candidate was a bit of a risk and could have backfired.' Allison took a different view: 'My fear of losing the seat increased when the SNP chose Margo MacDonald.'

Margo MacDonald was born in 1943 in Hamilton, went to Hamilton Academy where according to journalist Alison Downie she was remembered as 'a big girl with a big personality', going on to become a physical education teacher at East Kilbride High School. She became involved in the SNP in the wave of Winnie Ewing's Hamilton victory, standing in Paisley in the 1970 election winning 7.3 per cent of the vote.

Speaking about Govan, MacDonald told Downie about her political awakening:

> There was a time when I thought it was possible to retain a sense of nationhood in Scotland while not being involved politically. It took me some time to realise this wasn't possible, and although I joined the SNP five years ago, I still feel it's more of a cause than just a party – that's why it has this appeal to young people, who are not on the whole politically conscious.

Sillars painted a bleak picture of the Labour campaign in his 1986 autobiography *Scotland: The Case for Optimism*. Even though he was writing from the retrospective lens of a SNP convert, much of the picture rings true and is corroborated by others. He was visibly shocked by the state of Govan and the attitude of the local Labour Party. Upon seeing a burned-out car abandoned in a street which a resident had complained to him about, he told Selby it needed to be cleared, to which the candidate replied: 'I know about that car, we use it to stand on when drumming up support for rent demonstrations.'

Another example on polling day involved Willie Ross, previously Secretary of State for Scotland and then the most senior Scottish Labour politician. Sillars wrote: 'About 8.00 p.m. we packed it in when Willie Ross toured past us in a car shouting through the loudspeaker system: "Noo's the day and noo's the hour for Govan to kick out Tory power."' He then reflected on the incongruity of the situation: 'Labour controlled the area and the city of Glasgow. It was Labour power and what was done or not done with it that lay at the heart of the by-election.' This was a reaction many Labour outsiders to the city were to have when they encountered a desolate, bleak world and a local Labour insouciance that it was any of their responsibility.

Margo MacDonald won the seat by 571 votes, with 41.9 per cent of the vote to Selby's 38.2 per cent – representing a swing of 26.7 per cent from Labour to SNP in what was then described as 'scenes of near-hysteria'. Instantly, she became a national figure, known simply as

'Margo', causing an impact nearly as great as when Winnie Ewing won Hamilton six years previously and, critically, showing that the SNP could no longer be dismissed as irrelevant.

The *Glasgow Herald* announced on its front page: 'SNP shock for Labour in Govan', with Scottish political correspondent William Clark describing it as 'a debacle' for Labour and showing that 'no Labour seat is safe from Nationalist assault'. An editorial said that Labour's defeat in Govan, along with its failure the same day to make any progress in the Tory seat of Edinburgh North (held by Alex Fletcher with a tiny 0.6 per cent swing from Tory to Labour), were 'the worst ever' by-election results for Labour in Scotland.

Margo reflected on her experience of campaigning and the moribund nature of such local Labour parties, telling me in 2010: 'They appeared to people on the inside as normal, even vibrant, as they never noticed the long-term decay. In reality in places like Govan they had become the equivalent of rotten burghs with little connection to working people and their concerns.' She concluded that 'what made it worse is that they did not even notice or seem to care how cut-off and self-serving they had become, and hence part of the problem'.

Tony Benn observed in his diaries:

> The Govan by-election has already gone bad on us in a big way. These by-elections do provide some sort of a test of how we are going to do and there is a great deal of anxiety about them. Particularly as the Scot Nats have made such a tremendous impact. I think it is the effect of the oil giving them more impact.

Margo saw her triumph in the context of the crises of the period, reflecting to me: 'The Govan victory was cataclysmic in Scottish and British politics. It was a bolt-like shock to the British establishment and our very own well-entrenched establishment here in Scotland.' She concluded: 'One thing we know about establishments is they do not like being threatened. Winning in Govan produced a reaction which we in the SNP looking back were not fully prepared for.'

MacDonald's hold on Govan was short-lived. Ted Heath called an election in early 1974 and Selby regained the seat in February 1974 with a 543 majority over MacDonald, aided by altered boundaries and the addition of more Labour areas. He increased his majority to 1,952 in October 1974 and represented Govan until the end of the 1979 parliament when he retired.

Margo MacDonald had made an impact and shown the electoral vulnerability of Labour at the centre of its Scottish heartland. The SNP built on the momentum of Govan and in the February 1974 election, despite Margo losing in Govan, increased their Westminster representation from one in 1970 to seven, taking four seats from the Tories and two from Labour, winning 21.9 per cent of the Scottish vote. In the second general election in October, SNP representation rose to eleven, taking a further four seats from the Tories and achieving 30.4 per cent of the Scottish vote, 5.9 per cent behind Labour, well ahead of the Conservatives who were reduced to third place in votes (but not seats). What was more, in thirty-five of Labour's forty-one Scottish seats, the SNP were in second place as the clear challenger.

The 1970s were to be shaped by the challenge of the SNP and the politics of devolution, but it was not to prove plain sailing for the Nationalists. A Labour government with a wafer-thin then non-existent majority meant that the votes of the SNP group mattered, and internal party divisions could be painfully exposed on such votes as aircraft and shipbuilding nationalisation, leaving aside devolution and the 1979 referendum.

Another dimension of MacDonald's win, aided by Ewing's earlier victory in Hamilton, was the effect this had on the macho monocultural male entitlement culture that was Scottish politics and in particular Scottish Labour. The Scottish political scene in the 1960s and early 1970s was dominated by dull, mediocre, elderly men who seemed to have held safe Labour and Tory seats for decades and had little connection to modern Scotland. There were in 1970 a mere two female MPs sitting for Scottish seats out of seventy-one constituencies (and in 1979 it fell to one: Judith Hart, MP for Lanark).

Margo's victory electrified politics and it is no accident that MacDonald was quickly dubbed 'the Blonde Bombshell': a sobriquet underlining the grip of everyday sexism in Scottish politics. She was also the target of much unreconstructed criticism for daring to be a young woman (and mother of two children) who had been elected to Parliament.

Condescending remarks were made about Margo's husband Peter running a pub: the Hoolet's Nest in Blantyre, Lanarkshire, with their home above. Just after her election, with acres of newspaper coverage profiling her and her life, Margo felt the need to state: 'They're going about asking people if they want a part-time barmaid representing them. They're trying to suggest that I pull pints instead of working as an MP.' When she made her maiden speech in the Commons in December 1973, Tam Galbraith, Tory MP for Glasgow Hillhead, commented in the House that while her speech 'did not please my ears, everything that my eye saw was a delight'.

Scottish politics was to take too long to overthrow such reactionary attitudes from dinosaurs and never fully arrived in the modern world until the establishment of the Scottish Parliament in 1999. It was not perfect and there were still prejudicial and outmoded attitudes, but with forty-eight out of 129 MSPs women and election by proportional representation, it did feel more like the diverse, pluralist Scotland had arrived.

Margo was elected to the 1999 Scottish Parliament as a list MSP for the Lothian Region and quickly made an impact as an effective parliamentarian and debater, but at the same time she fell foul of the command-and-control mindset of the SNP leadership who effectively deselected her for the 2003 Scottish elections.

This was but a brief inconvenience in the second coming of Margo, and in the 2003 elections, she was easily elected as an Independent in the Lothian region, being re-elected in 2007 and 2011. This could be seen as a golden age for Margo where she worked across party barriers, established effective relationships with former sworn Labour enemies, while allowing her independence of mind to sit with her passionate support for the cause of independence.

In her latter days, Margo was diagnosed with Parkinson's, advocated for assisted dying and worked as an active politician until close to her death in April 2014 at the age of seventy – five months before the historic independence referendum. By this time, a politician who had broken through so many barriers had become 'a national treasure'

– according to former SNP activist and academic Isobel Lindsay – an affectionate accolade which was fitting and long-overdue.

Lindsay assessed the contribution of Margo to public life, writing in 2016: 'Margo was one of the public faces most associated with the SNP over the last forty years, even though she was only an MP and MSP for the party for little over four years.' Yet her legacy is bigger and more complex: 'Her passion, zeal and independent mind made her a natural campaigner, but less a successful party politician.' Margo was always motivated by 'more of a cause than just a party' as she herself said, and she should be remembered as someone who was more than a party politician but a campaigner and principled supporter of causes close to her heart.

Govan had made an impact with Margo's victory. The modern SNP began with Hamilton. Govan Act One proved the SNP was not a flash in the pan but a permanent feature in Scottish politics. Govan Act Two would serve to remind Labour it should never forget this fact.

Dr Gerry Hassan is a writer and academic, author and editor of more than two dozen books on Scottish and UK politics, whose latest book is Britain Needs Change: The Politics of Hope and Labour's Challenge *(Biteback, 2024). He is co-founder of Kirkcudbright Fringe Festival in Dumfries and Galloway. Many thanks to Denise Davie of the Special Collections of the Mitchell Library, Glasgow, for checking and verifying various historic electoral figures.*

48

WOOLWICH WEST

26 JUNE 1975
CONSERVATIVE GAIN FROM LABOUR

AMBER WHAPSHOTT

Result: Peter Bottomley (Conservative), 17,280, 48.78 per cent; Joseph Stanyer (Labour), 14,898, 42.06 per cent; Sheilagh Hobday (Liberal), 1,884, 5.32 per cent; Ruth Robinson (National Front), 856, 2.42 per cent; Ronald Mallone (Fellowship), 218, 0.62 per cent; Frank Hansford-Miller (English National), 140, 0.39 per cent; Reginald Simmerson (Conservative, Anti-Common Market), 104, 0.29 per cent; Peter Bishop (Independent), 41, 0.12 per cent
Size of majority: 2,382
Swing: 7.61 per cent from Labour to Conservative
Name of previous MP and party: William Hamling (Labour)
Reason for by-election: Death of incumbent
Result at previous general election: William Hamling (Labour), 19,614, 47.09 per cent; Peter Bottomley (Conservative), 16,073, 38.59 per cent; J. P. Johnson (Liberal), 5,962, 14.31 per cent
Date by-election called: N/A
Date by-election took place: 26 June 1975
Size of total electorate: 56,359
Total number of votes cast: 35,421
Turnout: 62.85 per cent

The victory of the Conservative candidate Peter Bottomley in the 1975 by-election of Woolwich West was significant for the fortunes of the Conservative Party, spearheaded by the recently elected leader Margaret Thatcher. The result reduced Labour's already slim majority in the House of Commons from three seats to one seat, including that of the Labour Party's John Stonehouse, who was absent in Australia.

The by-election was the first to take place since the general election of 1974. The campaign presented a considerable test for the Wilson government and its weak majority. In October 1974, Prime Minister Harold Wilson had won a majority of three seats, the narrowest in modern British history. This election took place just eight months after the general election of February 1974, which had led to a hung parliament. After the Conservative Party failed to secure a coalition with other parties such as the Liberals and the Ulster Unionists, Wilson went on to form a majority government after a second general election that October.

Arguably even more so, the election represented an early challenge for Margaret Thatcher, who had been elected Conservative Party leader just four months prior, succeeding former Prime Minister Edward Heath.

For both Harold Wilson and Margaret Thatcher, the by-election represented a crucial turning point for their respective leaderships. Wilson aimed to utilise the by-election to demonstrate the continuing support for the Labour Party, while Thatcher was afforded an opportunity to solidify her leadership against the backdrop of early concerns about her ability to effectively lead the party. Some of the electorate opined that the Conservative leader stumbled through initial interviews, lacking natural appeal and a certain warmth, and struggled to command authority over the parliamentary party in Westminster.

Further significance of the Woolwich West by-election lies in Thatcher's decision to canvass personally in support of Bottomley, thereby abandoning the assumption that party leaders did not campaign in by-elections.

Labour had held the Woolwich West seat in the 1974 general election with a majority of 3,541, and this was the first by-election that the Conservatives had fought under Thatcher's leadership. Thatcher displayed conviction in the party's ability to overturn this majority when she broke precedent and campaigned personally in the constituency. This breaking of convention resulted in a significant and timely victory for the party and for Thatcher's leadership.

The political and economic landscape surrounding the by-election was marked by high inflation, worsened by a rise in oil prices and high wage growth. The rate of inflation reached approximately 25 per cent during this time. Combined with social unrest and an ongoing trend of industrial action and strong trade union power, Wilson's already insubstantial majority was precarious at best. These factors depreciated the already tenuous political authority of the Labour government.

It was against this backdrop that the by-election of Woolwich West, a lower middle-class suburb on the outskirts of south-east London, commenced. The by-election was triggered by the death of the constituency's standing Labour MP, William Hamling, on 20 March 1975. Hamling, a Royal Marines officer, had held the seat since winning it from the Conservatives at the 1964 general election.

Hamling had held the seat in the October 1974 general election, receiving 47.1 per cent of the vote compared to Conservative candidate Peter Bottomley's 38.6 per cent. At this election, the Liberal candidate J. P. Johnson received 14.3 per cent of the vote, although the Liberal vote share would be squeezed at the by-election in the following year.

There were eight candidates for the seat in 1975. The Labour and Conservative candidates won over 90 per cent of the vote share combined, with the Liberal candidate achieving 5.32 per cent. The other parties, which included National Front and English National candidates, won a modest 1,359 votes combined, of the 35,421 votes cast.

Peter Bottomley, the Conservative candidate, had campaigned for the seat in both of the February and October general elections of 1974. He had joined the Conservative Party in 1972, at the age of twenty-eight. Bottomley had come to know the area well and had fostered strong local connections, including with the previous MP, William Hamling. A friendship was formed to the extent that Bottomley was a regular visitor to Hamling's bedside at Westminster Hospital following a heart attack.

Joseph Stanyer, the Labour candidate, was a local councillor and housing chairman. Stanyer supported the European Common Market and was not particularly on the left of the party. Both the Conservative and Labour candidates were well known locally.

Richard West of the *New Statesman* followed Peter Bottomley around the borough as he attempted to gain support for his campaign. West noted that inflation and the resulting pay demands, particularly the rail strikes that had been threatened, were a local concern as many in the area commuted by train. Several rail strikes had taken place in 1974 and 1975. During a time of significantly inflated costs, it is unsurprising that the electorate could be concerned about their ability to attend work in the event of rail strikes.

The European Common Market was another key issue for the electorate. Early June 1975 had seen a non-binding referendum take place to ask the electorate whether the country should remain in the European Economic Community, which it had joined in January 1973 under Heath's Conservative government. People in Woolwich West praised the part that Heath played in the debate, particularly citing his televised speech on the matter to the Oxford Union.

During the campaign, distinctions between perceived extremists and Marxists compared to the 'moderates' in the Labour movement recurred as a topic of discussion. Bottomley himself and the electors were nervous about the threat that 'extremists' on the left could pose, and the people of Woolwich seemed to be strongly on the side of the moderates.

According to West, Bottomley 'did not explain what his party would do to check inflation that it had not tried and failed to do when in office'. He declined to say whether he favoured Sir Keith Joseph's economic remedies, which advocated for free-market conservatism and the economic theory of monetarism. Bottomley's victory despite the absence of clear policy on the issue of soaring inflation is perhaps indicative of the strength of the electorate's concerns over the Labour Party.

Bottomley recalls Thatcher's office telephoning a week before the election to discuss the possible result. He recollects that 'unlike national predictions, the local bookmakers had odds of 4–1 on, even though Labour had over 4,000 members'.

Bottomley remembers:

They called again the next day. The odds had not changed. We expected to win. The nervousness may have reflected the uncertainty then dogging Mrs Thatcher's leadership of the party. We fought the election hard all day every day until we got to Saturday lunchtime … We were determined to win. Leaders of parties normally stayed away from by-elections. If the election was not won it could be blamed on the leader. Credit for success went to the candidate. Margaret was keen to come. She was new; she was different. What do you do with the leader? We invited her to officially open the new Association office. On the last Saturday we waved to shoppers in Eltham sitting on the folded roof of a Triumph convertible. It was a success. By coming, Margaret's presence made a significant contribution to our campaign. She boosted morale and levels of activity.

This recollection aptly summarises the gamble that Thatcher was taking in the early stages of her leadership, when she faced pervasive doubts of her capability inside and outside of the party. Bottomley himself has since ventured that if he had not been victorious, there would have been a 'heavy movement' to topple Thatcher.

As it happened, Peter Bottomley was victorious for the Conservative Party with 48.78 per cent of the vote share. Bottomley won by 2,382 votes, signifying a considerable shift to the Conservatives of 7.61 per cent. If such a shift took place in a general election, this would mark the advent of Britain's first female Prime Minister, Margaret Thatcher.

Labour's candidate, Joseph Stanyer, received 42.06 per cent of the vote.

The morning after the by-election, the *Daily Telegraph* described the result as a personal victory for Thatcher and signifying a vote of no confidence in the Labour government. Harry Boyne, the paper's correspondent, described the swing to the Conservatives as a warning that 'inflation is the dominant issue in politics today'. Boyne predicted that if inflation continued at the present rate, Labour would concede subsequent by-elections and possibly the next general election. The results in several subsequent by-elections and the general election of 1979 would serve to confirm Boyne's predictions.

The *New York Times* reported how the by-election 'eliminates Labour's effective majority in the Commons'.

The result had a series of consequences for both the Labour and

Conservative parties. Undoubtedly, the result did not instil confidence in Wilson's government at a time in which this was much needed. The significance did not lay in the ability of the by-election to affect policy, which was unlikely, but rather the revealing of concerns over divisions and conflicts within the Labour Party and comparative support for the Conservative Party.

The narrowness of the Labour government's majority in 1974 eventually resulted in a gradual loss of this majority by 1977 through a series of by-election losses, including in Woolwich West. This trend led to the eventual defeat of the Labour government following a motion of no confidence in March 1979. Margaret Thatcher succeeded James Callaghan as Prime Minister in May 1979.

For Thatcher, the by-election served to silence early doubts surrounding her leadership, at a time in which cementing her strength as leader was vastly important.

The Woolwich West by-election proved to be the first in a succession of by-election wins for the Conservative Party under Thatcher's leadership, including in Walsall North and Workington in November 1976, Birmingham Stechford in March 1977 and Ilford North in March 1978.

Following his successful campaign, Peter Bottomley held the Woolwich West seat until its abolition for the 1983 general election. Bottomley then secured Eltham, the successor seat, and from 1997 to 2024 represented Worthing West in West Sussex. On the back benches, Bottomley became president of the Conservative Trade Unionists in 1978. Bottomley went on to become a member of Margaret Thatcher's government, where he was appointed as the Parliamentary Under-Secretary of State at the Department for Employment in 1984. In 1986, he became Minister of Roads and Traffic in the Department for Transport.

Bottomley became the longest-serving MP following the 2019 general election, where he retained his seat. Thereafter, he became Father of the House until the following general election.

Amber Whapshott is a policy adviser and graduate of history from the University of Oxford.

49

WALSALL NORTH

4 NOVEMBER 1976
CONSERVATIVE GAIN FROM LABOUR

JOHN BARNES

Result: Robin Hodgson (Conservative), 16,212, 43.4 per cent; David Winnick (Labour), 11,833, 31.6 per cent; Sidney Wright (Independent), 4,374, 11.7 per cent; Joseph Parker (National Front), 2,724, 7.3 per cent; Fran Oborski (Liberal), 1.212, 3.2 per cent; James McCallum (Socialist Workers), 574, 1.5 per cent; Marian Powell (National), 258, 0.7 per cent; Jonathan Tyler (Ecology), 181, 0.5 per cent; Bob Boaks (Air, Road, Public Safety, White Resident), 30, 0.1 per cent
Size of majority: 4,379
Swing: 22.6 per cent from Labour to Conservative
Name of previous MP and party: John Stonehouse (Labour/English National)
Reason for by-election: Resignation following conviction for fraud
Result at previous general election: John Stonehouse (Labour), 28,340, 59.5 per cent; Robin Hodgson (Conservative), 12,455, 26.1 per cent; W. Gill (Liberal), 6,337, 13.4 per cent; J. Richards (Communist), 465, 1.0 per cent
Date by-election called: 15 October 1976
Date by-election took place: 4 November 1976
Size of total electorate: 72,593
Total number of votes cast: 37,398
Turnout: 51.5 per cent

The Walsall North by-election was one of three held on 4 November 1976 in what were regarded as bedrock Labour seats. Two fell to the Conservatives, the more remarkable loss being Walsall North where the swing to the Conservatives was 22.6 per cent and the Labour vote down by 27.9 per cent. It remains the largest by-election swing ever from Labour to the Conservative Party. The Conservative candidate, Robin Hodgson, turned a Labour majority of 15,855 (33.4 per cent) into a Conservative majority of 4,379 (11.8 per cent). Notably, a well-regarded local Independent, councillor Sid Wright, finished in third place, capturing 11.7 per cent of the vote.

Until January 1975, Wright had been a Labour councillor and chairman of the borough's finance committee, but he had broken with his own party over its 'lunatic spending' and had subsequently been deprived of his membership of all committees. He had signalled publicly that he intended to run in the by-election when it was called but had expected that to be in weeks rather than months. By the time the by-election took place, Labour had lost ground in successive borough elections and Wright had been restored to the finance chair by a disparate coalition of Conservative, Independent and Ratepayer councillors. Almost certainly he was correct when he insisted that not all his votes in the by-election had come from Labour, but his decision to run against his former party had undoubtedly been a factor in its defeat.

At least part of Wright's disillusion can be traced to the way in which the long-serving Labour MP for Walsall North, William Wells, had forfeited the seat to John Stonehouse, the Labour MP for Wednesbury. After the 1970 general election, the constituency boundaries on which the next general election would be fought had been redrawn. Wednesbury had disappeared as a constituency and its six Willenhall wards were transferred to Walsall North to replace wards transferred to the new constituency of Aldridge-Brownhills. As Robin Hodgson recalled, Stonehouse could be ruthless when his career was at stake. He was reputed to have played some part in the ousting of the previous MP from Wednesbury in 1957 and had gone on to win the subsequent by-election. When he competed with Wells for the Walsall North's constituency Labour Party's nomination, he triumphed by sixty-four votes to twenty-one. After the executive had voted, Wells complained that there were many faces at the meeting whom he did not recognise and reports from trustworthy sources confirm that a number of trade union delegates had been created in the Wednesbury constituency and bussed in on the night to take part in the selection. While no breach of party rules had been committed, Sid Wright, who had served as Wells's election agent, was angered by what had happened, and a new election agent had to be found to work with Stonehouse.

The seat remained a Labour stronghold. In the February 1974 general election, fighting the new Conservative candidate, Robin Hodgson, Stonehouse had a comfortable victory by 32,458 votes (63.6 per cent) to 17,754 (34.8 per cent), with a Communist a very distant third. With a Liberal candidate intervening in October 1974, Stonehouse's victory was even more comfortable. He took 59.5 per cent of the total vote to Hodgson's 26.1 per cent and the Liberal's 13.4 per cent. Although he had served in the previous Labour government, he was not included in Wilson's new administration.

Little more than a month later, on 20 November 1974, he disappeared, apparently drowned while swimming off a beach in Miami. When no body surfaced, rumours that he might have staged his own disappearance began to circulate, although they soon had to compete with stories of his possible murder by the Mafia. Allegations, which later turned out to be false, were made about financial irregularities in regard to money raised for the new government of Bangladesh, and it was reported that he might have gone into hiding because he was about to be exposed as a Czech spy. The Prime Minister told Parliament on 17 December that the spying allegation had been investigated in 1970 and that no evidence had been found to substantiate it. A week later, on Christmas Eve, Stonehouse was identified in Melbourne as an illegal immigrant and arrested. He had assumed the identity of a deceased constituent and intended to make a new life in Australia with his secretary and mistress, Sheila Buckley.

The long-drawn-out saga which followed frustrated his constituents and damaged the reputation of politics more generally. With scant regard for the presumption of innocence, the press highlighted Stonehouse's financial malpractices, the way in which he had defrauded family and friends, the life policies he had taken out shortly before his 'death' and the transfer of sufficient sums to his new persona to enable a comfortable start to his new life. If that was not sufficiently destructive of his reputation, fresh evidence emerged to indicate that, while a minister, he had been in the pay of the Czech secret service. For sound constitutional and legal reasons, the government was reluctant to expel him from Parliament or seek to hasten his prosecution. Stonehouse was able, therefore, to return to the Commons and voice increasingly severe criticism of both the Labour government and the way in which British politics operated. Eventually, he crossed the floor of the House to join a fringe party campaigning for an English Parliament. It was July 1976 before he was finally brought to trial. Choosing to defend himself, he was found guilty on all but one of eighteen counts with which he was charged and sent to jail for seven years. He vacated his seat on 25 August, but even then, the by-election could not be called until Parliament reassembled.

While this drama was playing out, much had happened to suggest that the government was no longer in control of the country's economic destiny. Inflation had climbed as high as 25 per cent in 1975 and the danger of a wage/price spiral had been such that the TUC volunteered a period of pay restraint. Unemployment mounted, but the continued adverse balance of payments meant that any reflation would have to be export led. In the spring, there was what looked like a deliberate attempt by the authorities to lower the value of the pound. A new agreement was reached with the TUC in April, but the value of the pound continued to slide. Wilson's successor as Prime Minister, James Callaghan, was frustrated by what he saw as a problem inherent in Britain remaining banker to the sterling area. Despite two Budgets, two rounds of spending and a $5 billion loan with a six-month term, all of this since the beginning of 1976, sterling continued its downward slide. Inevitably, there was discontent in the Parliamentary Labour Party and division in the Cabinet. The extent of the rift between the government and its supporters was exposed when the national executive agreed on 7 September to vote for the nationalisation of the main clearing banks and insurance funds. Despite the Prime Minister's response – he termed the proposal an 'electoral albatross' and would oppose its inclusion in an election manifesto – conference adopted the proposal by a six to one majority; and it also rejected the government's White Paper on public expenditure, promising support to any local council that refused to implement the proposed cuts. In his speech to conference, the

Prime Minister had made clear his view that Keynesian economics was dead, an admission that can only have delighted his new opponent, Margaret Thatcher. On 29 September, with the pound under further pressure, the Chancellor announced that the government would seek a $3.9 billion loan from the International Monetary Fund (IMF), to which conference responded with a resolution combining support for the government's defence of sterling with a determination to resist any loan conditions that required further cuts in public spending. Continued pressure on sterling led to the Minimum Lending Rate being raised to the unprecedented level of 15 per cent, but the Conservatives remained the only party looking to bring the government down. To add to its woes, the month-on-month figures suggested that inflation was rising again by as much as 1.8 per cent a month.

This was hardly the most propitious background against which to launch three critical by-elections. With the government's overall majority at stake, however, it was clear that as soon as the House reassembled on 11 October, the by-election writs would be moved and that the poll would take place on 4 November. Nominations closed on 25 October, at which point it was clear that the English National Party had withdrawn their candidate.

Nine would fight the seat, among them the irrepressible Bill Boaks seemingly determined to forfeit yet another by-election deposit. An eccentric retired naval officer, he campaigned with an armoured bicycle concealed in an iron bedstead and was a convinced opponent of both the motor car and the establishment. Even his further tag of 'White Resident' was misleading as he disliked the National Front intensely and saw it as a means to undermine them.

The Ecology Party was fighting its first by-election, although under the name of People and the Movement for Survival, it had taken part in the 1974 general elections. Its candidate, Jonathan Tyler, lectured on transport at the University of Birmingham and was president of the party's executive committee. The National Party had broken away from the National Front after a long-drawn-out factional struggle, but only a quarter of the National Front's branches followed their lead. Maureen Powell, fighting the seat on its behalf, had permission from the party's chairman to do so, but a major row over the candidature developed within the party's executive. Eventually, she was instructed to withdraw in favour of the National Front but refused to do so.

Under the leadership of John Tyndall, the National Front had reverted to racist ideas and was seemingly in decline as a result. Nevertheless, it thought it could exploit the growing racial tensions in Britain to its political advantage, although its failure to secure the election of a single councillor in the 1976 local elections was telling. Its by-election campaign began with a demonstration on 25 October to which the Socialist Workers Party (SWP) responded with a counter demonstration. Both marches passed off peacefully, but a breakaway group from the SWP then sought to disrupt the National Front's rally, and the police were forced to make twenty-two arrests. The local branch of the National Council for Civil Liberties subsequently argued that both marches should have been banned. But while they fought one another, it became clear that the race issue was playing surprisingly little part in the campaign. Both Hodgson and Winnick seemed determined to play it down, and Wright, while arguing for a halt to immigration, went out of his way to emphasise that he had no issue with – indeed got on well with – those already settled here. Joseph Parker's campaign never caught fire nor did it ever seem likely that he would get near the 12.5 per cent vote required to reclaim his deposit. Nor was the Socialist Workers Party likely to make much headway, not only because its candidate was on bail for civil disorder offences but more because the Labour candidate, David Winnick, stood well to the left in his own party.

What was more amazing, and harder to explain, was the collapse in the Liberal vote. The Liberal Party had not had the best of years. Constant references in the press to Norman Scott's claim of a homosexual relationship with its leader, Jeremy Thorpe, had led to his resignation and a bruising leadership contest had followed. The new leader, David Steel, had called for a 'Government of National Unity', a call repeated at the by-election by the Liberal candidate, Fran Oborski, on 21 October. This echoed Edward Heath's message at the October 1974 election and raised the pertinent question of why the Liberal Party had turned down Heath's offer of coalition in February 1974. Her survey in the constituency listed unemployment, prices and the economy as the top issues with housing also mentioned, but the only Liberal answer vouchsafed seemed to be a 'Government of National Recovery'.

There is little indication of where former Liberals gave their vote, but some may have been attracted by Wright's candidature. He was fifty-four, had served with the Eighth Army during the war and was well known as a congenitally cheerful stallholder in Walsall Market. As a long-standing Labour member of the council, where in addition to the finance committee he had been chair of the planning committee, he had recently served as mayor. Although the press dubbed him 'king of Bloxwich', he was well liked throughout the borough. Many shared his view that the creation of a West Midlands Council was wholly unnecessary and backed his call for its abolition. His decision to break with his party commanded respect and his argument that the country's first priority was to get inflation under control was widely accepted. Public expenditure must be cut and bureaucracies pruned nationally and locally. 'People are utterly fed up with professional politicians always promising jam tomorrow,' he concluded. 'They're glad to see a local face.'

The importance the government attached to the by-election was signalled by the number of frontbench speakers deployed in the campaign. Barbara Castle, dropped from the Cabinet by Jim Callaghan, spoke on 19 October and was followed by five Cabinet members, Tony Benn, Peter Shore, Walsall-born and educated David Ennals, Michael Foot and Shirley Williams. Their presence was somewhat at odds with Winnick's seeming determination to focus on local issues, although he had earlier identified jobs and prices as the major issues in the campaign. He was also embarrassed by continual questioning as to how he, a former member of the Tribune Group, critical of the government's economic policies, would be able to support it in Parliament. He had a ready answer. Whatever the government's faults, a Tory government would be worse, bringing higher unemployment and threatening the NHS.

However, it was fast becoming impossible to dispute the truth of the Conservative claim that the government was no longer in full control of the economy. The pound had fallen to a new low of $1.55 on 25 October and the IMF team were coming to London on 1 November to discuss the terms for its loan. GDP had fallen in the second quarter, the money supply was increasing at an annual rate of 17.5 per cent, well above target, and inflation was expected to be running at 13–14 per cent by the end of the year. The Manpower Services Commission forecast on 1 November that at best unemployment would not fall before 1978/79 and that it could get worse. There were also reports as the IMF team flew in that public expenditure cuts of $1 billion would be required to secure the required loan. Callaghan had gone public with his doubts about the sterling area on 25 October, controversially hinting that British troops might have to be withdrawn from Germany if the problem were not resolved. On 2 November, Healey warned Labour MPs that a mini Budget would be required before Christmas to cut the Public Sector Borrowing Requirement (PSBR), hinting that this might be achieved through a mix of tax rises and public spending cuts. The *Birmingham Daily Post* had already warned that increases in VAT and duties on cigarettes, alcohol and petrol were likely to form part of the package. There were reports that he had also confirmed that moves were afoot to end sterling's role as a reserve currency, although that would require a loan of at least $7 billion, almost twice the $3.9 billion currently under discussion. Britain's reserves had fallen again by £287 million in October with the only good news being a rise in the value of the pound to $1.59.

From the outset, Hodgson had made the collapse of Labour's economic policy his target, noting that almost 5,000 were already out of work in the Walsall area and that employment prospects were bleak. He too had powerful support with the party chairman, Lord Thorneycroft, William Whitelaw and Geoffrey Howe addressing public meetings. Mrs Thatcher chose instead to speak with shoppers in both Willenhall and Bloxwich on 27 October, defying SWP hecklers as she did so. It was a major coup when Edward Heath also agreed to speak for Hodgson. He delivered a scathing attack on the government's economic failure to an audience of almost 500, a good deal more than the fifty who listened to Shirley Williams the same night.

The Conservatives went into polling day quietly confident. They were heartened by what seemed a sign of desperation on the part of their opponents, the decision by the Tribune Group to bus in their

MPs to support Winnick. The Conservatives promptly dubbed it the 'blunderbus' and were probably right to think it would remind the electorate that Winnick favoured left-wing policies, including import controls as well as the nationalisation of the banks and leading in-surance companies. Their canvassing returns suggested a 19 per cent swing from Labour to their own party and they were agreeably sur-prised when the Birmingham *Evening Mail* carried a Marplan poll on 1 November forecasting a 19.3 per cent swing. That was a good deal more than might have been inferred from the national polls, favourable though they were. Gallup's October poll, carried out on 14–18 October, showed the Conservatives on 48 per cent with an 11.5 per cent lead. By mid-November, support was to rise to 55 per cent and the lead to 25 per cent.

Defeat did not come as a complete surprise to Winnick, therefore, but the scale of it was a shock. He blamed his defeat on low turnout, the Stonehouse legacy and the government's policies. His victorious opponent discounted the Stonehouse factor and named rising prices and unemployment as the consequences of two and a half years of Labour government. 'You must understand that 80 per cent of the con-stituency is made up of skilled or semi-skilled people, and two thirds of them live in council houses,' he told *The Times*.

> During the past few years their standard of living has fallen, partly due to inflation and partly due to them finding themselves in a higher tax bracket because of the system of progressive taxation. When Mr Healey said he was going to hammer the rich, they did not realise they were among the people he was talking about. Against this they see the abuse of the social security system.

Allowing for the evident political bias, this probably comes close to explaining why so many working men had chosen to switch their vote: their wives were probably more influenced by the price rises they faced on a weekly basis.

While the result here and at Workington deprived the Labour gov-ernment of its overall majority and thrust them back on the support of the nationalist parties, it had less impact in the short term than Mrs

Thatcher might have hoped. In the New Year, fearing electoral annihilation, David Steel offered a grateful James Callaghan a pact which allowed his government time to recover. However, many of the factors that temporarily delivered Walsall North to the Conservatives were to be evident in Mrs Thatcher's general election victory in 1979. But Walsall North remained a bridge too far for them, Winnick regaining the seat, and that remained the case until 2017.

John Barnes taught history at Gonville and Caius College, Cambridge, before becoming a lecturer in government at the LSE. He was the unsuccessful Conservative candidate at Walsall North in the 1964, 1966 and 1970 general elections.

50

WORKINGTON

MICHAEL MULLANEY

Result: Richard Page (Conservative), 19,396, 48.2 per cent; Dale Campbell-Savours (Labour), 18,331, 45.6 per cent; Bernard Wates (Liberal), 2,480, 6.2 per cent
Size of majority: 1,065
Swing: 13.2 per cent from Labour to Conservative
Name of previous MP and party: Fred Peart (Labour)
Reason for by-election: Elevation to the House of Lords
Result at previous general election: Fred Peart (Labour), 22,539, 56.0 per cent; Richard Page (Conservative), 12,988, 32.3 per cent; J. Burns (Liberal), 4,728, 11.8 per cent
Date by-election called: 23 September 1976
Date by-election took place: 4 November 1976
Size of total electorate: Approx. 54,100
Total number of votes cast: 40,207
Turnout: 74.2 per cent

It has become a fashion at recent general elections to have a key voter in a named place that is seen to typify the key voter/seats at the election. So the 1992 election had 'Basildon man' in Essex, after the Essex seat which narrowly voted Conservative in the Tory landslides of 1983 and 1987, and where its remaining Tory in 1992 signified the surprise Tory win nationally. In 1997, 'Worcester woman' was seen to typify the voters being targeted by Tony Blair's New Labour and Labour's easy capture of the seat from the Tories in 1997 encapsulated the Blair landslide.

In the 2019 general election, the key voter was 'Workington man'. He was supposed to typify the type of voter who lived in previously safe Labour seats in the north and Midlands but who, due to a combination of Boris, Brexit and Corbyn, was open to voting Tory. In the end, Workington did go Conservative in 2019, as did the country. However, while Workington had a reputation as a safe Labour seat, it was in fact the scene of another close Labour/Tory battle in the past. Back in 1976, a close-fought by-election took place in Workington.

Workington in 1976 was in theory an ultra-safe Labour seat. It was, after all, one of the 1931 Labour seats: the just fifty-two seats that elected a Labour MP in the 1931 general election, the worst election for the Labour Party since it had begun competing on a national stage. It was also one of just sixteen seats that had voted Labour at every general election since 1918. However, while history may have made it seem an ultra-safe Labour seat, the data suggested otherwise. By October 1974, Workington was only the 149th safest Labour seat and the swing to the Conservatives required to lose it was 11.9 per cent, something that would seem certainly achievable against a struggling government in a by-election. If history pointed to an easy win for Labour in Workington, the data would suggest otherwise.

One crumb of comfort for Labour in defending the seat, though, was the low level of Liberal votes in the constituency. The Liberals received 11.8 per cent, and in those days a lost deposit, in the seat in October 1974. With much of the switch to the Tories nationally coming from the collapsing Liberal vote at the time, the fact the Liberals started from a low base was at least one positive for Labour in their efforts to defend the seat.

The MP for Workington at the time was Fred Peart, who had been the MP there since 1945. He'd held a number of Cabinet roles including Leader of the House of Commons and since 1974 had been the Agriculture Secretary.

Peart was most notable for being both a Labour Party moderate and Eurosceptic. Even though the rows in the Parliamentary Labour Party over membership of the European Common Market in the 1970s could be seen as a left-right issue, things were rather more complicated. While the leading Anti-Common Market figures were from the left (Tony Benn, Michael Foot, Barbara Castle) and the leading Pro-Common Market figures were from the right (Roy Jenkins, Shirley Williams, Roy Hattersley), there was a key group of MPs in the centre and right of the party who were also Eurosceptic. Peart was among them and in fact organised a group of centre and right-wing Labour MPs in what was known as the 'Peart Group', including Peter Shore, Douglas Jay and John Gilbert, to press the case against the Common Market in the early 1970s. When Roy Jenkins sought to become deputy leader of the Labour Party against left-winger Michael Foot in 1971, what should have been a fairly easy win was reduced by Peart standing for deputy as a Eurosceptic moderate. Jenkins only just received a majority of Labour MPs votes, winning 133 (53.6 per cent) to sixty-seven for Foot (27.0 per cent) and forty-eight for Peart (19.4 per cent). The existence of MPs like Peart meant that in the 1970s, Labour, despite being dominated by the centre and right of the party (at least in Parliament), would tend towards being a Eurosceptic party opposing entry in 1971 and being divided in the Common Market referendum of 1975.

In October 1974, Labour had been elected with a narrow majority of three seats. By 1976, the Labour government had lost its majority following the loss of Woolwich West to the Conservatives in a June 1975 by-election, and then former Labour MP John Stonehouse joined the English National Party on 4 April 1976.

James Callaghan had succeeded Harold Wilson as Prime Minister on 5 April 1976, the day after Stonehouse's defection. While the government's position in the Commons was perilous, the situation in the Lords – then dominated by overwhelmingly Conservative hereditary peers – was even worse. In the 1975–76 parliamentary session, the government had endured a remarkable 126 defeats. This was to be the most for any government until it was overtaken by the 128 defeats inflicted on the Conservative government by the Lords in 2021–22. The Labour group in the Lords was fairly small and Callaghan felt it could do with having some added ballast. He therefore persuaded a reluctant Peart to resign his Workington seat and go to the House of Lords to lead the Labour group. Peart resigned his seat to take up the role of Leader of the House of Lords and Lord Privy Seal on 23 September.

The by-election was set for 4 November 1976. Remarkably for a government without a majority, there were to be three by-elections in Labour seats on the same day, none caused by the death of the sitting MP. Walsall North would take place due to the conviction of John Stonehouse for insurance fraud. Newcastle Central was to take place due to Ted Short becoming chairman of Cable and Wireless. While Workington may have been perceived as a safe seat, it was in fact by far the most marginal of the three being fought that day – the Labour majorities in Walsall North (33.4 per cent) and Newcastle Central (55.3 per cent) being substantially above the 23.7 per cent Labour majority in Workington.

While more recent by-elections often attract long lists of candidates standing for a variety of radical parties or single-issue campaigns, or just candidates seeking attention, the Workington by-election would see only three candidates vying to succeed Peart.

For Labour, defending the seat was 33-year-old Dale Campbell-Savours. Campbell-Savours was the managing director of a clock and metal component manufacturing company. He had briefly served as a Ramsbottom Urban District Councillor between 1972 and 1974 before it was abolished under local government reforms of the time. He had fought the Darwen parliamentary seat in both the 1974 elections, finishing 5,651 votes behind the Conservatives in the October election.

For the Conservatives, looking to gain the seat was 35-year-old Richard Page. Page worked for Page Holdings, a property and automotive company, and had been a district councillor in Banstead in Surrey 1968–71 and had contested Workington in both the 1974 elections. He finished a clear second on both occasions, 9,551 votes behind Peart in the October election.

Finally, the Liberal candidate was Bernard Wates. The oldest candidate at fifty-six, Wates lived in Selside in Cumbria and was a part-time teacher, having been deputy director of Education for Westmorland from 1962 to 1974. Wates had contested Westmorland at the October 1974 election. The seat was one of the better Liberal prospects. The candidate in February 1974 had come a clear second to the Tories, 6,534 votes behind. It was also one of just ten seats where the Liberals had finished second at each of the four general elections between 1959 and 1970. However, despite getting a large number of votes at both the February 1974 (6 million and 19.3 per cent) and October 1974 elections

(5.3 million and 18.3 per cent), the Liberal Party at that time was unable to convert a large number of votes into seats, electing just fourteen MPs in February and thirteen in October. Wates was to come a clear second in Westmorland in October 1974 but to finish 7,715 votes short of winning.

The campaign was a fairly short one, with just six weeks separating Peart's elevation to the Lords on 23 September and polling day in Workington on 4 November. Given the Liberals' poor, deposit-losing showing in Workington in October 1974 and the party's poor performance in the polls exacerbated by the events around former leader Jeremy Thorpe who resigned in May of 1976, it would clearly be a two-horse race between Labour and the Tories.

The national opinion polls had begun to turn against Labour by this time and the Conservatives were beginning to build up solid leads. Of the polls published during the by-election campaign, the NOP for the *Daily Mail* at the end of September showed a 6 per cent Tory lead over Labour nationally. This widened to a 15 per cent Tory lead in the NOP poll in early October and then to 18.5 per cent in the NOP poll published mid-October. Gallup for the *Daily Telegraph* in mid-October showed a more modest but still sizeable Tory lead of 11.5 per cent. The NOP poll published in early November had an 11 per cent Tory lead.

Margaret Thatcher, then Leader of the Opposition for eighteen months, sensed the opportunity of a gain from the government. With the government's majority eroded, a win for the Tories in Workington and Walsall North on the same day would further destabilise the Labour government and would help solidify her own position as Tory leader against internal party critics. Thatcher visited the constituency during the campaign in support of Page, touring the main population settlements of Maryport, Cockermouth as well as Workington. During the campaign, she visited the Workington Conservative Club. Conservative Workington town councillor Margaret Jones claims that when Thatcher arrived at the club, a man barred her path to the bar because it was 'for men only'. A sexist slight one can't imagine anyone daring to try on Margaret Thatcher in later years when she was in her pomp as Prime Minister!

The election took place on 4 November. The turnout in Workington would be remarkably high for a by-election at 74.2 per cent. A drop of just 1.5 per cent compared to the October 1974 general election, while on the same day there were much bigger falls in turnout in Walsall North (-15.1 per cent) and Newcastle Central (-17.4 per cent). The high turnout seems to have helped stem the loss of votes for Labour as the drop in Labour's vote share in Workington (-10.4 per cent) was a lot less than the drop in Walsall North (-27.9 per cent) and Newcastle Central (-24.2 per cent). It wasn't quite enough for Labour to hold Workington, though, as Page took the seat for the Conservatives with a narrow 1,065 vote majority on a 13.2 per cent swing.

Speaking at the Finchley Conservatives' autumn fair on the Saturday after the by-election, Margaret Thatcher hailed the win in Workington as well as Walsall North as a sign that the Conservatives were heading to victory: 'The by-election results had a clear message. The people have had enough ... The people's verdict on the Labour government in Walsall and Workington was clear. Get out!'

The defeated Labour candidate Campbell-Savours had his own explanation for the loss of the seat. In the summer of 1976, a phenomenon had begun to excite the press: the existence of 'scroungers'. Press coverage of people who were allegedly deliberately unemployed and living a life of apparent luxury became widespread. As such, when he lost Workington, Campbell-Savours said it was due to 'the reaction of ordinary working-class people to so called social security scroungers'.

The loss of Workington as well as Walsall North put the Labour government into even more of a minority in the House of Commons. A few months later, a motion of no confidence from the Conservatives forced Callaghan to form the Lib–Lab pact with Liberal leader David Steel in order to keep the government in office.

What of the post-by-election careers of the three candidates?

Of the six Conservative gains from Labour in the 1974–79 parliament, four were to revert to Labour at the 1979 general election. Workington was among them, with Page losing the seat by 5,756 votes. His absence from Parliament was to be brief, though. The Tory MP for South West Hertfordshire, Geoffrey Dodsworth, resigned from Parliament in October 1979 and Page was selected to replace him, being elected to Parliament on 13 December 1979. He was to serve as a Parliamentary Under-Secretary for Trade and Industry towards the end of the John Major government and retired from Parliament in 2005.

Dale Campbell-Savours was given a second chance by the Workington Labour Party, fighting the seat in the 1979 general election, gaining it back from the Conservatives. He was to serve as an opposition spokesman from 1991–94 for international development and then agriculture, before resigning due to ill health. He held Workington until 2001 and now sits in the House of Lords.

Bernard Wates, the Liberal candidate, was never to stand for Parliament again and was to pass away prematurely in 1982 aged sixty-one.

In conclusion, the Workington by-election did not need to take place. Peart was reluctant to go to the Lords. The government had no majority and was defending two other seats on 4 November. Though Workington had been one of just fifty-two seats to stay Labour in its crushing defeat of 1931 and had been one of an even smaller group of seats that had been Labour consistently since 1918, it was by the mid-1970s a solid Labour seat but not a super-safe one.

A swing of less than 12 per cent was needed for Labour to lose Workington in the by-election – a size of swing that could easily be suffered by a government in difficulty. The government had been enduring a series of defeats in the Lords so there was a case for putting someone of Peart's heft in the Lords. However, was this worth losing a Labour seat in the Commons to the Tories when the government had no majority?

On 28 March 1979, the Labour government was to narrowly lose a vote of no confidence by 311 to 310, prompting a general election and Labour's removal from office. The unnecessary Workington by-election of 1976, which saw a Labour seat go Conservative, can then be added to the list of decisive factors in that one vote defeat. A defeat that saw a general election and the return of a Conservative government in May 1979 with Labour having to wait eighteen years in opposition until a radically transformed 'New' Labour under Tony Blair took Labour back to government in 1997.

Michael Mullaney is a borough and county councillor in Hinckley and leader of the Liberal Democrat Group on Leicestershire County Council. He was the Liberal Democrat parliamentary candidate in Hinckley & Bosworth at the 2024 election.

51

ASHFIELD

---

28 APRIL 1977
CONSERVATIVE GAIN FROM LABOUR

ROBERT WALLER

Result: Tim Smith (Conservative), 19,616, 43.1 per cent; Michael Cowan (Labour), 19,352, 42.5 per cent; Hampton Flint (Liberal), 4,380, 9.6 per cent; George Herrod (National Front), 1,734, 3.8 per cent; June Hall (Socialist Workers), 453, 1.0 per cent

Size of majority: 264

Swing: 20.8 per cent from Labour to Conservative

Name of previous MP and party: David Marquand (Labour)

Reason for by-election: Promotion to European Commission in Brussels

Result at previous general election: David Marquand (Labour), 35,367, 63.4 per cent; Richard Kemm (Conservative), 12,452, 22.3 per cent; Hampton Flint (Liberal), 7,959, 14.3 per cent

Date by-election called: 7 April 1977

Date by-election took place: 28 April 1977

Size of total electorate: 76,273

Total number of votes cast: 45,535

Turnout: 59.7 per cent

Balliol College, Oxford, the night of 29–30 April 1977: a group of undergraduates, keen amateur psephologists, gathered to await the results of two parliamentary by-elections taking place simultaneously. When the results came through, they were so astounding, taken together, that they decided to phone the *Daily Telegraph* for confirmation that they were correct (no internet and smartphones in those days).

The reason for the dumbfounded confusion of the bright young things at that elite institution was that the Labour government had retained Great Grimsby, although suffering a negative swing of 7 per cent, but they had lost Ashfield, a 'mining seat' in Nottinghamshire that was much safer on paper, on a catastrophic swing of nigh on 21 per cent. At the October 1974 general election, Ashfield's Labour majority had been 21,486, Great Grimsby's only 6,982. I was one of those shocked students, engaged especially as I was about to commence doctoral research into the history of the Nottinghamshire coalfield. The phenomenal result certainly still needs explaining – especially in light of the subsequent intriguing electoral history of Ashfield, which still continues to surprise with highly dramatic results in the mid-2020s.

The first thing that needs to be understood is the circumstances in which the Ashfield by-election was called, especially in contrast to Great Grimsby's. The latter's MP, Anthony Crosland, a distinguished theorist of social democracy (*The Future of Socialism*, 1956), was serving in James Callaghan's Cabinet as Foreign Secretary when he died suddenly on 19 February 1977 in Oxford, following a cerebral haemorrhage, at the age of fifty-eight. This tragic cause contrasted with the situation at Ashfield.

David Marquand, the member since 1966, was not a miner. He was an intellectual and an academic, educated at Magdalen and St Antony's Colleges, Oxford, and the University of California at Berkeley, then a lecturer in social studies at Sussex from 1964 to his election in 1966. His political mentor was the doyen of right-wing Labour, Roy Jenkins, who had finished third in the first ballot for party leader (tantamount to becoming Prime Minister) on Harold Wilson's unexpected retirement in March 1976. It is said that Jenkins wanted to be Foreign Secretary in the victor James Callaghan's government – but the post was given to Crosland instead. Jenkins almost immediately left British politics (for the time being), accepting the presidency of the European Commission from 6 January 1977. (Labour lost the by-election for his Commons seat, Birmingham Stechford, on 31 March 1977, just four weeks before that at Ashfield.) The 42-year-old Marquand resigned his seat at Ashfield to become Jenkins's chief adviser in Brussels. Unlike Grimsby, it was seen locally as an unnecessary by-election – which often results in a worse result for the defending party.

The constituency of Ashfield is located in western Nottinghamshire, close to the Derbyshire border, halfway up the county: north of Nottingham and just south of Mansfield, the second largest community. The Ashfield electorate was mainly to be found in three medium-sized towns: Hucknall, Kirkby-in-Ashfield and Sutton-in-Ashfield. The last named was the largest, with 30,250 electors at the time of the by-election, compared with 20,200 for Hucknall and 17,200 for Kirkby. The total electorate was just over 76,250, the remainder being made up of a few wards then in the rural district of Basford: Annesley, Felley and Selston parishes. Rural or not, these fitted the overall character of the Ashfield seat: this was based on industry and, in particular, on coal. Selston had a colliery until 1968, Annesley/Newstead till 2000. These may be added to the mines associated with the three main towns, such as Kirkby (closed 1969), Teversal (1980), New Hucknall (1981), Linby (1988), Sutton at Stanton Hill (1989), Silverhill (1992) and Bentinck (1998).

For the context of the by-election campaign, the history of Nottinghamshire's coal miners needs to be outlined. The 1977 by-election took place less than seven years before the great strike of 1984–85, when Arthur Scargill faced off against Margaret Thatcher, after calling a national strike without a national ballot and crucially without united support. Nottinghamshire, in particular, felt itself to be less threatened with mine closures and was known for the number of its working miners. They clashed vigorously and, in a couple of instances, fatally with flying pickets and their supporters. A split formed the breakaway Union of Democratic Mineworkers (UDM), still regarded as scabs by many in striking areas. Neil Greatrex, who became president of the UDM, was from Kirkby-in-Ashfield and worked at Bentinck Colliery in this constituency. Its other early leader, Roy Lynk, was from Sutton-in-Ashfield.

But the UDM split was not an entirely new development. Back in 1926, an organisation called the Nottinghamshire Miners' Industrial Union (NMIU), had been formed to co-ordinate a return to work after the General Strike. It broke with the official Nottinghamshire Miners' Association and embarked on an eleven-year split until 1937. The NMIU was more widely known as the Spencer Union after its founder and leader, George Spencer, who – as in the 1980s – represent-ed a tradition of autonomy from national unions and their decisions. Since 1918, Spencer had been the Labour MP for Broxtowe – which is not to be confused with the current seat of the same name, which is in a different part of the county. That Broxtowe was the direct predecessor of the Ashfield constituency.

As for the national political background to the by-election cam-paign, by April 1977, hammer blows to the incumbent Labour govern-ment were not unexpected. The key issues in their unpopularity were economic. The 'social contract', by which unions were supposed to restrain pay demands in recognition of increases in government social spending, had been completely ineffective. By the summer of 1975, in-flation was over 25 per cent, more than double that at the end of 1973 and the highest in the developed world, so once the EEC referendum was out of the way, in July 1975 the government returned to a statutory pay policy: increases of £6 per week but no increases for those on more than £8,500 a year.

In the early part of his government from April 1976, James Cal-laghan faced an economic crisis of extreme severity that had necessi-tated recourse to the International Monetary Fund (IMF) for a loan of $3 billion in exchange for the guarantee of £2 billion government spending cuts. At the time and for some years afterwards, it was the largest package the IMF had ever agreed with any member country. But this required tough measures on fiscal policy (government spend-ing cuts) as IMF conditionality. Callaghan had to fight Tony Benn in the Cabinet to ensure that we accepted the conditions rather than going protectionist with import controls. It was a traumatic episode that shook the unity of the government, with an overvalued pound and wage costs driven up by powerful unions and ineffective industrial management and political leadership that could not solve the country's problems without external aid.

So by 1977, most people had suffered a three-year squeeze in their standard of living with the prospect of more to come as pay policy continued, inflation was still in double figures, the policy to control inflation on which the government had won the 1974 elections (ap-peasing the unions) was seen to have failed, unemployment was high by the standards of the day and rising, sterling had collapsed and the government had had to accept IMF help on IMF conditions to underpin it. It was no great surprise that by-elections didn't go well.

Nominations in Ashfield closed on Tuesday 19 April with five candidates: as well as Labour, Conservative and Liberal, there was George Herrod of the National Front, described as a former miner and ex-Guardsman, and June Hall of the Socialist Workers Party, a Trotskyist group that usually did not contest bourgeois-democratic elections. The Conservative was Tim Smith, a 29-year-old chartered accountant and company secretary who had been educated at Harrow and Oxford. He did not seem a natural fit for a strongly working-class constituency in the East Midlands with notably lower-than-average educational qualifications. However, Labour's standard-bearer was Dr Michael Cowan, an intellectual and writer on local government, selected against the wishes of the local miners (according to Peter Rose who wrote the 1974–79 chapter in *By-Elections in British Politics*, edited by Chris Cook and John Ramsden). He was a Nottinghamshire county councillor – not for a division within the Ashfield constituency but rather for Wollaton in the west end of the city of Nottingham (a ward lost to the Conservatives on the first Thursday of May 1977, a week after the Ashfield by-election, although Cowan was not a candidate).

Neighbouring MPs helped Tim Smith's Conservative campaign, such as Jim Lester, MP for Beeston, as reported by his local paper, the *Beeston & Sandiacre News*, on 21 April, while Lynda Chalker spoke at Hucknall, reported on 19 April as saying that the supreme priority in the campaign was the control of inflation and that 'Ashfield has the chance to stop the draining of all our energies in Labour's whirlpool of socialism'. The primary Tory line in the campaign was that public spending should have been cut back in 1975 and there would not now be a million unemployed. Their second priority was a co-ordinated system of benefits and taxation to encourage people wishing to work longer hours. Number three was cutting bureaucracy. Tim Smith argued that for local purposes there needed to be a productivity deal in a pit-by-pit incentive scheme.

The Liberal candidate Hampton Flint prioritised the liberty of the individual but also that society should despise 'those layabouts and parasites who sponge on others' – 'as far as I am concerned they can starve'.

In his campaign, Labour's Michael Cowan also condemned those content to claim benefits but said there were also 'scroungers' in other groups such as accountants and small shopkeepers who 'fiddle their income tax returns and expenses sheets – they were diddling Britain out of far more than fraudulent benefit claimants [were]'. More should be done for pensioners.

The SWP candidate attacked both Labour and the Conservatives by condemning 'the Tory policies of the Labour government, which would put tens of thousands of school leavers in the dole queue in the summer to come'. The National Front candidate claimed food prices were rising directly because of Common Market membership and 'both Tories and Labour were in thrall to Brussels'.

When the results were declared, Labour's share dropped from 63.4 per cent to 42.5 per cent, a numerical fall enhanced by the lower turn-out, of just over 16,000. The Conservatives almost doubled, from 22.4 per cent to 43.1 per cent and actually increased in number by over 7,000. The Liberals went down by 4.7 per cent and lost their deposit (it was then set at 12.5 per cent, one-eighth of the vote). The National Front took 1,734 votes, nearly 4 per cent, and was well ahead of the Socialist Workers in last place with just 453 (1 per cent). Altogether, there were 11,000 fewer casting ballots than in the general election.

There was some suggestion that Labour lost in Ashfield because the miners stayed at home, but in fact at 59.7 per cent, the turnout was almost 13 per cent higher than that at Grimsby (46.9 per cent) and, with a fall of 15 per cent, had not dropped as much as Grimsby's did (22.5 per cent). A turnout of 60 per cent is well above average, both for the 1974–79 parliament and by 21st-century standards. There was clearly a genuine swing of opinion, not just differential abstention.

How was the astonishing Ashfield result explained locally? The verdict of the *Nottingham Evening Post* on Friday 29 April was that Cowan and his organisation had been unable to get out the full strength of the traditional Labour vote to the polling booths and also that Ashfield electors had given an early warning to Prime Minister Callaghan that the miners were thoroughly disenchanted with his pay policy; the local electors had given the thumbs down to the Liberals as well for their 'alliance with the Labour party'.

It was said that only 15 per cent were canvassed by Labour and that only two dozen workers from outside the constituency were brought in on polling day, while 100 were in Nottingham on the same night help-ing to return a district councillor. There were, inevitably, suggestions that Labour had focused on Grimsby and ignored Ashfield, perceived as the safer of the two; but Austin Mitchell, the victor in the former, insisted this was not the case.

In the national press, there were other interpretations of the cam-paign and result. On 9 May, the *Daily Mirror*'s Joe Haines described the Ashfield result as being 'almost Jim Callaghan's Hiroshima ... because Ashfield is mining country and Labour has its roots in coal'. Haines ascribed this to a lack of loyalty because the union's man Frank Haynes had not been selected. One miner said he felt ashamed for voting Conservative and there was rumoured to be a blacklist of miners who had shown Tory window bills or publicly admitted voting Conservative. But one who did talk to Joe Haines said he had to work seven days a week to put meat on the table and was bothered about the tax deducted from his wages – a payslip showed a third removed from the gross sum. Another complained about 'prices up all the time', yet another that people on benefits were getting more than they were.

Haines summed up the reasons for the defeat as the failings of the Labour Party organisations in Nottinghamshire and London and the malice of the union. The failure to select a candidate more acceptable to the miners could be considered a local gaffe; the success at Grimsby on the same day would seem to prove that there were no specific na-tional Labour gaffes during the period of the campaign.

Clearly, in an overall assessment of the campaign and outcome of the Ashfield by-election, the national background has to be taken into account, especially the economic problems and the general 'midterm blues' of the Labour government, just over halfway into its term. But the very different result on the same day in Grimsby means that local factors were also very significant: the causes being a voluntary departure to a less than overwhelmingly popular institution abroad and the selec-tion of a candidate not approved by the miners, who were themselves in a discontented mood, in a part of Britain with a complex industrial and political tradition.

What was the future for those who contested the Ashfield by-election? In 1981, Michael Cowan became a Nottinghamshire county councillor, for Bilborough in Nottingham, retiring from that role in 1989. He never entered Parliament. Tim Smith was only MP for Ashfield for a week over two years. In the general election of 3 May 1979, although Mrs Thatcher became Prime Minister with an overall majority of forty-four seats, Frank Haynes regained the seat for Labour with a majority of nearly 8,000, though this still represented an adverse swing since October 1974 of 14.4 per cent. Although a Londoner, Haynes was sponsored by the NUM. However, that was not the end of Smith's parliamentary career. In 1982, in a by-election in Beaconsfield in south Buckinghamshire, he easily retained the seat vacated by the death of Sir Ronald Bell. The Labour candidate, lagging in third place, was a 29-year-old barrister in his first contest – by the name of Anthony Charles Lynton Blair. Smith held the seat until the 1997 general election, when he stood down after being implicated in the Mohamed Al Fayed 'cash-for-questions' affair: the same issue that affected Neil Hamilton, who contested his Tatton seat and was defeated by the anti-sleaze Independent, Martin Bell.

As for David Marquand, his stay in Brussels was relatively short, ending in 1978. He returned to Britain and to academia as professor of politics at Salford and Sheffield universities and principal of Mansfield College, Oxford. Among his best-known books was a long and authoritative biography of Ramsay MacDonald, the first Labour Prime Minister, who was expelled from the party after he formed a coalition government in 1931 and fought an election against the rump of Labour. Marquand became a member of the SDP after the split in the early 1980s.

The short-term significance of the Ashfield by-election was that it was one of six losses for the Callaghan government within just two and a half years. It never recovered the lost ground. Having decided against an autumn 1978 general election, Callaghan endured the 'winter of discontent' and then was defeated in a no-confidence motion in the Commons, which forced the May 1979 general election. Labour lost three more in a row and the party was out of office for eighteen years.

Long term, Ashfield went on to have a fascinating and unpredictable electoral history. Its loyalty to Labour remained very questionable. In the twenty-first century, there emerged what could be called the 'Z' factor, first at local level: in 2007 Jason Zadrozny was first elected as a Lib Dem councillor for Sutton-in-Ashfield North and became, aged twenty-six, the youngest council leader in the country. In 2010, he stood for Parliament for Ashfield losing by only 192 votes to Labour's Gloria De Piero. By 2015, Zadrozny was an Independent, now representing Larwood ward (named after the famous cricket fast bowler of the 1930s, who was from Ashfield), and in May 2019 his group took thirty out of thirty-five council seats.

Then, in the December 2019 general election, it was a classic 'red wall' seat, falling to the Tories for the first time since 1977. The new MP was Lee Anderson, a former miner who went on to become an active and controversial deputy chairman of his party from February 2023, then in March 2024 defected to become the first ever MP for the Reform Party.

Ashfield was the one and only red wall seat that Labour did not regain in July 2024. Lee Anderson successfully defended with a majority of 5,508. Zadrozny took 16 per cent, leaving Labour and the Conservatives between them with only 37 per cent. Whether Ashfield is untypical or a harbinger for Reform and realignment is too early to tell as of the time of writing. But one thing that is clear is that it is still a highly individual, highly volatile constituency, that no one can take for granted – just as it was back in that late spring of 1977.

Dr Robert Waller *is a historian and psephologist. His doctoral thesis at Oxford University was on the Nottinghamshire coalfield, published as* The Dukeries Transformed *(Oxford University Press, 1983). His* Almanac of British Politics *is now updated online at https://vote-2012.proboards.com/ board/186/vote-almanac-british-politics-boundaries.*

52

GREAT GRIMSBY

28 APRIL 1977
LABOUR HOLD

JOHN BOWERS

Result: Austin Mitchell (Labour), 21,890, 46.88 per cent; Robert Blair (Conservative), 21,370, 45.76 per cent; Andrew De Freitas (Liberal), 3,128, 6.70 per cent; Michael Stanton (Socialist Workers), 215, 0.46 per cent; Peter Bishop (Sunshine), 64, 0.14 per cent; Max Nottingham (Malcolm Muggeridge Fan Club), 30, 0.06 per cent
Size of majority: 520
Swing: 7.03 per cent from Labour to Conservative
Name of previous MP and party: Tony Crosland (Labour)
Reason for by-election: Death of incumbent
Result at previous general election: Tony Crosland (Labour), 21,657, 47.10 per cent; K. C. Brown (Conservative), 14,675, 31.91 per cent; D. M. Rigby (Liberal), 9,487, 20.63 per cent; J. McElrea (Independent Labour), 166, 0.36 per cent
Date by-election called: 7 April 1977
Date by-election took place: 28 April 1977
Size of total electorate: Approx. 65,000
Total number of votes cast: 46,697
Turnout: N/A

James Callaghan's government was deeply unpopular when Tony Crosland, the Foreign Secretary, died unexpectedly of a cerebral haemorrhage at the Radcliffe Infirmary in Oxford on 19 February 1977 aged just fifty-eight. I had met him only five days earlier at a student event in Oxford. He had held the Great Grimsby seat since 1959, when he won it with a majority of 100.

Most pundits expected that Labour would lose Grimsby because the party had just surrendered Stechford in Birmingham with a swing against them of 17 per cent as they sought to replace Roy Jenkins, who had been a close friend of Crosland at Oxford and became the EU president. The party 'mislaid' a 14,000 majority in that West Midlands stronghold. A key difference from Grimsby was that there was little Liberal Party presence in the Midlands seat, whereas the Liberals had a strong presence in the Humberside town.

The Tories needed only half of that Stechford swing to take Grimsby, even though Crosland had built up a 6,982 majority. This caused the journalist Matthew Coady to remark that for Callaghan, a win in Grimsby would be 'as welcome as a dove for Noah'. The desperation in the Labour camp was demonstrated by the fact that this was said even though Grimsby had been held by Labour for a continuous period of thirty-two years. It was indeed crucial because Callaghan had a minority of two in the Commons and was being buoyed up by the Lib–Lab pact.

Could anyone rescue the seat for Labour? That was the desperate cry across the compact fishing town. There was only one man who might do so, thought senior figures in the local Labour Party. He was the local(ish), gregarious 42-year-old, well-connected Yorkshire TV personality who was wildly popular locally (despite being a Yorkshireman). These were the days when the local TV news programme (especially in the north) had a major following. He had previously presented the BBC's *24 Hours* late-night programme, a forerunner to *Newsnight*. He was also celebrated for having interviewed Brian Clough, Harold Wilson (when he resigned) and Marcia Williams.

This man was Austin Mitchell, who at first sight was as far different to Crosland as it was possible to be. Crosland was patrician and distant; Austin, the son of a dyer, was down to earth and sometimes in your face. He grew up in Baildon (part of Bradford Urban District Council) and went to Bingley Grammar School, whereas Crosland spent his early years in Highgate, a posh private school, the son of a senior civil servant. Crosland had a penchant for whisky; Austin never touched the stuff. Crosland had been a Euro enthusiast, although he became increasingly sceptical of it as Foreign Secretary; Austin was a life-long Brexiteer (indeed before the word gained currency, as were many Grimsby folk). The intellectual and austere Crosland had not been the most assiduous of constituency MPs – Mitchell said he came up to the town once a month, watched a football game (once taking along a bemused Henry Kissinger who, having been born in Germany, was a serious football fan) and then headed straight back to London to watch *Match of the Day*.

Austin was given to stunts; he even changed his name for a while much later to Austin Haddock to fight for the Grimsby fishing industry; Crosland was seriousness personified. Austin was described in *The Times* as a 'likeable, affable, singularly unstuffy man'.

Yet they *did* have much in common: both were centrists in terms of the Labour Party; both had a deep love of everything Grimsby (and both spent long periods on Grimsby trawlers). Crosland's ashes were scattered at sea near Grimsby. Both were active Fabians and both had journalist wives. Crosland had been a politics fellow at Trinity College, Oxford, while Austin operated as the same, virtually around the corner, at Jesus and Nuffield Colleges. At Nuffield, Austin was originally David Butler's co-author on *The British General Election of 1970*, until TV beckoned. Mitchell's PhD was a thesis on Regency politics.

The Mitchells were staying in Nantucket at Jared Coffin House, a smart hotel in Massachusetts, when they heard the news that Tony Crosland had died. Austin was sad but thought little more about it until Jack Franklin, the redoubtable Fabian chair of the local party (and a friend of my family), contacted him a few days later. Mitchell had already put his name forward for two Yorkshire seats (Sowerby and Leeds West) for Labour, but long-time trade unionists had won both selections, as usually happened in those days in northern seats. Austin often said that he (Franklin) did not know who he (Austin) was when he rang up, but I somehow doubt this as everyone in Grimsby knew the popular local TV star (who appeared nightly on the *Calendar* news show) and most wanted to share the sprinkling of stardust he brought. Joe Ashton, a leading right-wing MP, also put Austin's name forward for the seat.

In response to Franklin's approaches, Mitchell expressed keen interest. It was, however, not a good start when he found a 'death to yorkies' sign in huge letters besides the road as he entered the town (this is a traditional welcoming Humberside greeting with which he became familiar; no harm was intended and no offence taken). Grimsby had always been in Lincolnshire before the Humberside county confection was introduced in 1972. The Humber Bridge had been promised by the Wilson government to win votes in the crucial Hull North by-election in 1966.

Echoing this resentment of outsiders, Andrew De Freitas, the Liberal candidate, claimed during the by-election campaign that the River Humber had proved to be too great a barrier for Mitchell to cross, while Mitchell himself said he 'was the only immigration issue in the town' (there being few immigrants from abroad).

There was a shortlist of six for the Labour selection, including a key lieutenant of Tony Crosland (Dick Leonard, a pro-EU political adviser who had held the Romford seat 1970–74 and was assistant editor of *The Economist*), but those at the top of the local party knew it had to be Mitchell and he duly won selection on the first ballot. The press scoffed that he was picked so as to appeal to housewives, and someone while he was canvassing her spoke of his 'dreamy blue eyes'. He was selected just three days before the election writ was issued.

The Conservative candidate was the amiable and softly spoken Robbie Blair, who had lived in the town for thirty years (although born in Aberdeen) and ran the big Birds Eye frozen food factory, one of the biggest food processors in the world. His son Alistair was a fish merchant, having been at St John's College, Oxford, at the same time as another A. Blair (later known as Tony). Robbie thought the UK was stumbling rapidly towards communism. At fifty-one, he was ten years older than Austin. He replaced a barrister from London who had won the Tory nomination but had not gone down well locally.

Andrew De Freitas (who died in 2024), the Liberal candidate, was born in Guyana and had been a councillor for some six years. He worked in accounts on the docks (or 'down dock', as Grimbarians say). The complement was completed by a docker standing for the Socialist Workers Party and no-hopers from the Muggeridge Fan Club and Sunshine Party.

The Labour by-election campaign leading up to the election on 28 April was turbo-charged by the national party HQ. In his entertaining memoir *Confessions of a Political Maverick*, Mitchell said, 'I glided into Parliament. In by-elections candidates are power assisted rather than left to struggle on their own.' Min Birdsall from Labour's head office was sent to take charge of his PR. Austin and his journalist wife Linda McDougall took a flat over a Cleethorpes fish and chip shop for the duration of the campaign. It was important to locals that Austin agreed to live in Grimsby if elected, although this came as a surprise to his wife.

Linda was born in New Zealand and met Mitchell when he was working there originally as a politics professor at the University of Canterbury and then a TV presenter. She was a BBC and Granada TV director and recently the author of an excellent book on Marcia Williams, with whom Austin had conducted a famous interview. Grimsby is a town where rumours spread easily even before the advent of the internet (often turbo-charged by my late mother). A particularly bizarre story circulated that Linda was a sister of Arthur Scargill (the hard-left general secretary of the National Union of Mineworkers), even though she in fact spoke with a New Zealand accent!

Fishing was inevitably the key election issue. At that time, 18 per cent of locals had jobs linked to fishing, often in ancillary industries. The Grimsby folks felt that the industry had been strangled by the ban on fishing off the Icelandic coast arising from the so-called 'Cod Wars'. One local wag said that Grimsby fishermen would eventually only be able to fish in a Grimsby park pond. The local demand was for a coastal fishing zone of fifty miles which was properly policed and enforced. The EU had a 200-mile limit and this is partly what fuelled resentment of the European Project in the area.

During the campaign, what was known locally as 'Show Day', the then important Easter holiday fish catch, was poor and this heightened the concern of those in the vital industry. It also did not help that Boston Deep Sea Fleet (a major trawler owner) laid up four trawlers during the contest.

The Liberals campaigned for the abolition of Humberside County Council, which felt to many like a shotgun marriage between the north and south banks of the Humber, which were traditionally fierce rivals. Prices featured as another key problem so that Robbie Blair produced a shopping basket entitled 'the housewife's nightmare' to dramatise the issue. He claimed that the basket now cost £2.42 but had been yours for only 99p when Labour came to power. Labour lost ground because of the highest April unemployment figures ever announced during the campaign. Overall, 7.5 per cent of the town were unemployed and there were and still are pockets of real deprivation in the borough. The construction of better roads to Grimsby was also an election theme (and is still a bugbear of locals). Goodies were, however, showered on the town during the campaign, as it gained the development area status it had long craved from the Labour government.

Mitchell proved to be an inspired campaigner, always stopping to chat to people, so that he was way behind his team of canvassers as they progressed more rapidly down a street. Everyone felt they knew him as 'our friend from the telly' and everyone wanted to be photographed with him. Some thought he was in fact *Warren* Mitchell from the telly, the 'star' of the apparently racist comedy programme *Till Death Us Do Part*. Of course, the three main candidates were all at Blundell Park for the game against Lincoln City, local derby rivals.

These were the days of the big political meeting, complete with hecklers. The town was visited by more big names than ever before (or since). David Owen (who had replaced Crosland as Foreign Secretary at the age of thirty-eight) and Michael Foot (the popular Secretary of State for Employment and darling of the left) spoke at large public meetings. It was somewhat jarring that Owen gave a packed audience an elegant defence of the EU after Mitchell's speech vehemently denouncing it. David Steel, the Liberal leader, and Cyril Smith were the star Liberal turns.

The local paper reported that 1,400 turned up to see Edward Heath, with some 500 turned away. Margaret Thatcher came straight from a visit to China and got more than she bargained for on the Fish Docks as she was kissed in full public view by a burly and gruff fish merchant (who told the press that until then he had been a Labour supporter). William Whitelaw also spoke.

Roy Hattersley, Geoffrey Howe and Shirley Williams completed the big-name Bill. Enoch Powell had been slated to speak on the EU at a rally in Grimsby, but this was postponed because of the by-election. Susan Crosland also visited to canvass.

There were three debates between the candidates. The best one-liner inevitably came from Austin, who said of Thatcher: 'She is egalitarian in her willingness to talk down to everyone.'

Famous journalists trod the town's streets, including Marge Proops, the *Daily Mirror* columnist who wrote a piece very sympathetic to Austin in what was then the second largest selling newspaper. Proops even referred to Austin's 'beautiful teeth'.

There was, however, the usual sneering by outsiders at the oddity of the town. Michael Parkin said that the term Grimbarian used to describe those from the town like myself 'sounds like a cross between Grim and barbarian'. One article was headlined: 'Fish town where the chips are down'; another proclaimed 'they have gone fishing for votes'.

Throughout the hard-fought contest, the expectation was that Labour would lose as they did lose the Ashfield by-election held the same day, a seat vacated by David Marquand so that he could take on a role in Europe as adviser to Jenkins (he was later principal of Mansfield College, Oxford). The difference was perhaps because Mitchell was a big local personality and perhaps because Ashfield was an unnecessary by-election. James Fenton, the political correspondent of the *New Statesman* and later a professor of poetry, said that the smell of defeat hovered over Labour during the campaign. The bookies were indeed laying odds of four to eleven on Blair to win. Mitchell said he did not believe betting odds as they were determined by the amount of money placed and the Tories had all the money! It was even reported that the best champagne had been ordered at the local Tory Party HQ for their assumed victory party. The ITN poll on election night predicted a Tory win. Austin wrote later that he went to the count at the beautiful Victorian Grimsby Town Hall with his loser's speech ready.

While there was a swing of 20.9 per cent to the Conservatives in Ashfield, which was just enough for them to win the seat, the Labour to Conservative swing in Grimsby was only 7 per cent and Mitchell managed to poll more votes than Crosland had at the previous general election. In fact, Mitchell won by 520 votes, which was a majority far down from Crosland's 7,000 margin of victory. Austin Mitchell gained 21,890, Robbie Blair 21,370 and Andrew De Freitas 3,128, with the other three trailing far behind. At the next election, in 1979, Mitchell increased his majority to 6,241 votes. At 69.8 per cent, turnout was higher than at the previous general election.

Blair did not stand again, while De Freitas continued as a councillor for many years and was leader of the council for a while.

Austin proved to be a popular constituency MP but never gained ministerial office, partly saddled with the fact he worked for the Murdoch empire through Sky TV on a series called *Hard Talk*. This led to his dismissal from a trade spokesman role under Kinnock. He was perhaps too much known as the clown.

He stood down at the 2015 general election, at the age of eighty. At this time, there had only been three Grimsby MPs since the end of the Second World War.

His obituary said: 'Maverick is a word which is often used in a pejorative manner, especially when it's used to describe a politician. It was a word which was often used to describe Austin Mitchell, but in his case I think it was used in an affectionate manner.'

He had several parliamentary victories. He was ultimately successful in his campaign for televising Parliament and he brought down the legal costs of house purchase. He believed that his greatest achievement was getting compensation for Grimsby fishermen who became redundant when the industry collapsed. It was a long fight.

John Bowers KC hails from Grimsby and still owns a house there. He is the principal of Brasenose College, Oxford, and a barrister at Littleton Chambers. His latest book is Downward Spiral: Collapsing public standards and how to restore them *(Manchester University Press, 2024) and he has written fourteen books on employment law, including* A Practical Approach to Employment Law, *now in its eighth edition.*

53

GLASGOW GARSCADDEN

13 APRIL 1978
LABOUR HOLD

MARK PEEL

Result: Donald Dewar (Labour), 16,507, 45.4 per cent; Keith Bovey (SNP), 11,955, 32.9 per cent; Iain Lawson (Conservative), 6,746, 18.5 per cent; Shiona Farrell (SLP), 583, 1.6 per cent; Sammy Barr (Communist), 407, 1.1 per cent; Peter Porteous (Socialist Workers), 166, 0.5 per cent
Size of majority: 4,552
Swing: 3.6 per cent from Labour to SNP
Name of previous MP and party: William Small (Labour)
Reason for by-election: Death of incumbent
Result at previous general election: William Small (Labour), 19,737, 50.9 per cent; Keith Bovey (SNP), 12,100, 31.2 per cent; John Corbett (Conservative), 5,004, 12.9 per cent; Michael Kibby (Liberal), 1,915, 5.0 per cent
Date by-election called: 20 March 1978
Date by-election took place: 13 April 1978
Size of total electorate: Approx. 54,700
Total number of votes cast: 36,364
Turnout: 69.1 per cent

The Glasgow Garscadden by-election held on 13 April 1978 was the first by-election in Scotland for nearly five years and had long-term ramifications, given the changing political dynamics north of the border.

Ever since 1707, England and Scotland had been bound together by the Act of Union, but that union had begun to fray by the 1960s as industrial decline in Scotland bred a growing disillusionment with the political status quo.

This growing disillusionment was reflected in the rise of the Scottish National Party (SNP), which had rocked the Scottish Labour establishment with a dramatic by-election win at Hamilton in November 1967. Their cause was further boosted by the discovery of oil in the North Sea in 1970, and by cleverly deploying the slogan 'It's Scotland's oil', they gained an unprecedented breakthrough in the two general elections of 1974. In the second of those elections in October which saw the Wilson government re-elected with a minuscule majority, they won eleven seats on 30 per cent of the vote in Scotland — only 6.4 per cent behind Labour — posing a real threat to them in their urban heartlands.

Elected in February 1974 as a minority government on a pledge to restore industrial harmony following an era of bitter strikes during the Heath government, Labour's generous pay settlements with the trade unions helped unleash rampant inflation and a balance of payments deficit. Faced with the collapse of sterling in September 1976, Chancellor of the Exchequer Denis Healey felt obliged to ask the International Monetary Fund for a $3.9 billion loan. The loan was granted that December but only if the government (now under Jim Callaghan who'd replaced Wilson earlier that year) made deep-seated cuts in public expenditure at a time when high inflation and unemployment were seriously eroding its popularity. A plethora of by-elections in late 1976 and 1977 saw Labour lose safe seats such as Walsall North and Ashfield to the Conservatives on 20 per cent swings, depriving it of its Commons majority. Their exposed parliamentary position, despite its pact with the Liberal Party, was reflected in the Scotland Bill establishing an assembly in Edinburgh, given the various pitfalls it faced from rebellious Labour backbenchers, who thought it would lead to separation.

It was against this background that the Labour MP for Glasgow Garscadden, William Small, died on 18 January, aged sixty-eight. An active member of the Amalgamated Engineering Union, Small had been elected MP for Glasgow Scotstoun in 1959, a seat he held until it was abolished in the February 1974 general election, when he moved to the new Glasgow Garscadden constituency, winning it comfortably.

In the fight to succeed him, the Garscadden Labour Party, strongly influenced by Jimmy Allison, Labour's chief Scottish organiser, an honest but wily political operator, narrowly chose Donald Dewar as their new candidate over Ian Leitch, a Dumbarton councillor.

An alumnus of the elite Glasgow Academy and Glasgow University, where he forged his reputation as an accomplished debater, Dewar won the marginal seat of Aberdeen South in 1966, becoming an able, conscientious MP with strong pro-devolution sympathies. Defeated in 1970, he sought a safe seat elsewhere, but his moderate, pro-European sentiments were out of kilter with local Labour parties, and he was rejected on countless occasions. Becoming a children's reporter in Lanarkshire before entering a private law practice, he began to despair of ever returning to Parliament until the Garscadden vacancy gave him a lifeline.

In a by-election featuring six candidates – the Liberal Party chose not to field anyone – Dewar's main challenger was the SNP's Keith Bovey, a fifty-year-old Glasgow lawyer and leading pacifist stemming from his military service in Japan at the end of the Second World War. Having fought Glasgow Hillhead for the SNP at the February 1974 election and Garscadden that October, he looked to maintain his party's recent momentum with a historic win before the impending general election.

The Conservative candidate was Iain Lawson, a 25-year-old local shop manager. His immediate priority was to regain those Conservative voters who'd switched to the SNP, primarily for tactical reasons, by stressing traditional Tory values such as law and order.

Of the three fringe candidates, perhaps the most interesting was Shiona Farrell, a law graduate from Strathclyde University now working as an immigration counsellor and the wife of the executive chairman of the breakaway Scottish Labour Party, established in January 1976 to secure a Scottish assembly with strong executive powers. After a difficult year when the party had been infiltrated by the far left, the by-election would help determine whether it had a viable future.

The two other candidates were Sammy Barr, a former leader of the Upper Clyde Shipbuilders' sit-in and convener of shop stewards at Govan, for the Communist Party, and Peter Porteous, a shop steward at Yarrow's, for the Socialist Workers Party, both of whom sought publicity for their radical policies to combat poverty.

The Garscadden constituency in north-west Glasgow, an electorate of 54,500 in which 91 per cent lived in council housing, many on the sprawling Drumchapel estate, appeared rock-solid Labour territory, but following recent job losses there, the party was taking nothing for granted. The writ for the by-election was moved on 20 March for Thursday 13 April, two days after Healey's likely tax-cutting Budget, and Allison, a shrewd political strategist, knowing that Labour's supremacy in Scotland was on the line, mounted a high-profile campaign. Prime Minister Callaghan addressed the Scottish Council of the Labour Party at Dunoon on 18 March and gave Dewar his enthusiastic endorsement; later Cabinet ministers Michael Foot, Tony Benn, Shirley Williams, David Owen and Roy Hattersley visited the constituency, as party activists poured in from all over Scotland to see off the SNP.

Although Labour had clawed back some ground in the national polls with an improving economy – the Conservatives won the Ilford North by-election on 2 March with a mere 6.9 per cent swing – a Marplan poll for *The Sun* put them two points behind the SNP in Garscadden. Bovey predicted an SNP win by 5,000, but for all his experience, he seemed the wrong man to fight a constituency which bordered the Govan, Scotstoun and Yoker shipyards. His conviction that armaments should be phased out of Yarrow's, specialists in defence contracts, and replaced by the building of merchant ships alienated many of its 5,600 workers. His comments were seized upon by George Younger, an opposition Scottish affairs spokesman, who dubbed him a 'clueless idiot', and Teddy Taylor, the shadow Scottish Secretary, put down a parliamentary motion challenging SNP MPs to defend Bovey's position. None of them did so.

Days later, Bovey's gaffe was compounded by the SNP Provost of Cumbernauld, Gordon Murray, who praised Scottish conscientious objectors in 1939 for refusing to fight 'England's war'. Replying to this charge, Dewar said it was a rewriting of history of which the National Front would be proud and a calculated insult to thousands of Scots who were prepared to die in the fight against the Nazis.

Knowing Labour's vulnerability on unemployment, which had risen in Scotland under their watch from 91,000 to 191,000, the SNP, downplaying their commitment to independence, resolved to attack them over their handling of the economy, but Dewar raised the stakes with a scathing denunciation of the SNP at the Scottish Council of the Labour Party. Determined to make independence the core of his campaign, he attacked them for offering a vision of an intolerant and mean society. 'There is an anti-Englishness about their Garscadden campaign which must be outfaced and outfought. "It's up with the drawbridge, and I'm alright, Jack." We have had a bonanza in the North Sea and it's "Gimme, Gimme, Gimme".' The great tragedy was that the SNP was lulling voters on false pretences by claiming that independence was not a major issue in the campaign.

Dewar continued his assault on nationalism when Bovey accepted his challenge for a public debate before a capacity audience at Knightswood Church Hall, chaired by the renowned broadcaster Magnus Magnusson on 29 March. He claimed that independence would ruin Scotland's export trade and increase unemployment. It was ludicrous to assume that English firms and an English government would continue to give orders to Scottish firms if the Scottish Parliament was keeping the proceeds from North Sea oil to itself.

His attack won appreciation from most of the audience, but he in turn was forced onto the defensive when the debate focused on the economy, not least the closure of several local businesses. His claim that government contracts would create more jobs was shouted down by the sceptics.

Dewar was also on shaky ground when he disputed news of 200 redundancies and 700 layoffs at Govan Shipbuilders, owing to a delay in the building of thirteen Polish ships. He said he'd contacted Gregor Mackenzie, a Scottish Office minister, and was told of a plan to avert layoffs by switching some of the men to maintenance work and diverting others to the Scott Lithgow yard at Greenock. His claim was news to both management and unions who denied any knowledge of such a plan. 'We most certainly will not conduct negotiations through the mouths of the prospective parliamentary candidates,' declared Jimmy Airlie, the Govan shop stewards convener.

Another leading issue was the vexed question of abortion in a constituency where 35 per cent of the electorate were Roman Catholic. In *Flourish*, the journal of the Archdiocese of Glasgow, Archbishop

Thomas Winning wrote that abortion was one of the most important issues in the by-election and urged Catholics to reflect carefully on how they voted, but his spokesman later denied that he was backing the SNP candidate because of his anti-abortion stance. (Iain Lawson, the son of a Church of Scotland minister, was also anti-abortion, as was Shiona Farrell, a committed Catholic, but, deploring the antics of the militant anti-abortionists, she believed it should be an issue of individual conscience.)

Dewar, in contrast, because he had supported the 1967 Abortion Act, was pilloried by the pro-life lobby. Aside from plastering the constituency with crude posters of aborted foetuses, protesters turned up at his meetings and once caused a disruption by walking in file to the front to drop flowers at his feet for the dead babies. At crowded meetings organised by the Society for the Protection of Unborn Children on 3 and 4 April, he conceded that the 1967 Act needed reviewing. He didn't believe in abortion on demand but accepted the case for it if the mother and baby were in danger. On such occasions, it was up to the individual conscience, but the law should not preclude the possibility of abortion.

Despite the *Scottish Catholic Observer* denouncing him for his stance, abortion didn't swing that many votes, partly because Bovey's opposition to it was tempered by his atheism. A poll taken after the by-election found that 61 per cent of Roman Catholics had voted Labour.

The last week of the campaign was enlivened by a visit from the Leader of the Opposition Margaret Thatcher, who ignored loud heckling from the Socialist Workers Party in a Drumchapel shopping centre, and ministers Michael Foot, Tony Benn and Shirley Williams. They descended on the Yoker shipyard at lunchtime on the final day, along with the radical journalist Paul Foot, who was supporting the Socialist Workers Party, and Margo MacDonald, winner of the 1973 Govan by-election and the SNP's deputy leader. (It was there that Dewar complained to MacDonald about her party's leaflet depicting him as a public-school carpetbagger.)

Amid all the tumult, the tide was beginning to turn in Labour's direction. A redoubtable campaigner, Dewar bonded with voters on the doorstep, especially with one, also called Donald Dewar, who hailed from the same street as his grandfather in Lochgilphead. Always interested in their concerns, he listened intently and often went back to provide further assistance. According to John Rowan, then a young trainee agent from Glasgow Southside, he treated everyone the same. When Rowan, out canvassing with a local councillor, froze in front of a television camera, Dewar just laughed and said it could have happened to anyone.

As the campaign entered its final stages, the tide began to turn in Labour's direction. A small drop in unemployment in Scotland, a public endorsement from the Scottish TUC and Healey's Budget of limited tax cuts suggested Dewar's stance on the economy and devolution were cutting through. (This was later confirmed by an exit poll which found that a favourable reaction to the Budget influenced 28 per cent of Labour voters.) A local opinion poll put Labour seven points ahead of the SNP, a System Three poll in the *Glasgow Herald* had them five points ahead in Scotland and even the SNP camp admitted the result was too close to call, a far cry from their confident prediction weeks earlier.

Dewar, for his part, thought he'd edge it, provided his supporters turned out. His fears about electoral apathy were heightened by the miserable weather on polling day. 'It's going,' he predicted as he and Alf Young, Labour's research officer in Scotland, left an old people's home in mid-afternoon. Not for the first time, his pessimism proved unfounded. On an impressive 69.1 per cent turnout, Labour romped home with a 4,552 majority over the SNP, the swing of 3.6 per cent against them the lowest to date in the Parliament. At the count at Knightswood School, a clearly delighted Dewar said:

> Obviously I am thrilled to have won this magnificent and decisive
> victory for the Labour Party. Those people who said that Labour was
> dead or dying in west/central Scotland haven't been near Garscadden
> in the last four or five weeks. We have taken the attack to the enemy,
> and we have beaten them out of sight.

As he emerged from the school to greet his supporters, he was subjected to taunts from disillusioned SNP activists and narrowly missed being hit by a full beer can.

In a by-election which had generated huge media coverage, almost all of it pro-unionist and pro-Labour in the case of the *Daily Record* and *Daily Mirror*, he thrived in that atmosphere, proving a formidable campaigner, the best Scottish Labour by-election candidate that Allison witnessed during his time as a full-time official. Calling Dewar's victory the most serious setback the SNP had faced for eleven years, the *Glasgow Herald* wrote: 'Labour was helped by the fact that it fielded an exceptionally able candidate while the performance of the SNP candidate was not as dynamic or incisive as his supporters had hoped.'

'Dewar destroyed the SNP candidate Keith Bovey, in debates on TV, at the shipyards, in the Press and on the doorsteps with a ruthlessness never seen before or since in Scottish politics,' recalled George Galloway, later a left-wing Glasgow MP and no fan of Dewar's.

'His knock-out blow that Glasgow winter's night flattened the SNP for a generation.'

Although the SNP had improved their vote, the result was a crushing disappointment, especially after all their inflated expectations about winning the seat. Compared to Dewar, Bovey proved a lacklustre campaigner who never made a convincing case for independence, and according to Professor James Mitchell in his book *Strategies for Self-Government*, 'by SNP standards, the campaign was a disaster. The Parliamentary Group distanced themselves from Bovey's views on defence – and the election agent publicly admitted that canvass returns showing the SNP doing spectacularly well were bogus.'

Bovey contested Monklands West in the 1987 and 1992 general elections, but with his party still in the doldrums, he didn't come close to winning.

For Lawson, an able and energetic campaigner, the result was a trifle disappointing, but he succeeded in winning back the lost votes of October 1974 with 18.5 per cent of the vote. After nearly winning Dumbarton for the Conservatives in 1983, he defected to the SNP three years later over the Conservative government's failure to protect the Scottish steel industry, helping Jim Sillars to a memorable by-election victory at Govan in 1988.

While all three fringe parties secured a mere 3 per cent of the vote between them, most galling was the result of the SLP, which attracted only 583 votes. Despite having an impressive candidate in Shiona Farrell, the party was totally overshadowed by the larger parties, and after failing to win any seats at the 1979 election, it disbanded in 1981. Farrell never contested another election and in time became a convert to New Labour. Peter Porteous, who gained 166 votes, didn't stand again either, in contrast to Sammy Barr, who fought the 1979 and 1983 general elections in Garscadden but with less success than his 407 votes in the by-election.

By-elections are rarely consequential, but Garscadden certainly was, because it revived the political career of Donald Dewar and gave him the opportunity to become one of Scotland's greatest statesmen. A committed advocate of Scottish devolution at a time when many of his colleagues remained lukewarm, he led the opposition to Conservative rule in Scotland during the Thatcher and Major eras, and when Labour returned to government in 1997, he delivered on his vision of a parliament in Edinburgh. Once it was established in 1999, he became Scotland's inaugural First Minister, and although his premature death in October 2000 limited his impact in office, his legacy to the country has earned him a special place in its history.

Mark Peel taught history and politics at Fettes College before turning to writing. The author of seventeen books, many on cricket, he has also written biographies of Donald Soper, Shirley Williams, the 14th Duke of Hamilton and Donald Dewar.

54

LIVERPOOL EDGE HILL

29 MARCH 1979
LIBERAL GAIN FROM LABOUR

LORD RENNARD

Result: David Alton (Liberal), 12,945, 64.1 per cent; Bob Wareing (Labour), 4,812, 23.8 per cent; Nicholas Ward (Conservative), 1,906, 9.4 per cent; Joan Jonker (Law & Order), 337, 1.7 per cent; Ann Walker (Socialist Unity), 127, 0.6 per cent; Michael Taylor (Gay Liberal), 40, 0.2 per cent; Bill Boaks (Democratic Monarchist), 32, 0.2 per cent
Size of majority: 8,133
Swing: 30.6 per cent from Labour to Liberal
Name of previous MP and party: Arthur Irvine (Labour)
Reason for by-election: Death of incumbent
Result at previous general election: Arthur Irvine (Labour), 13,023, 51.9 per cent; David Alton (Liberal), 6,852, 27.3 per cent; Stephen Perry (Conservative), 5,208, 20.8 per cent
Date by-election called: 1 March 1979
Date by-election took place: 29 March 1979
Size of total electorate: 35,368
Total number of votes cast: 20,199
Turnout: 57.1 per cent

The brilliant play *This House* by James Graham powerfully describes the tensions in the House of Commons Whips' Offices as Labour struggled to remain in power in the second half of the 1974–79 parliament. Labour's majority in the general election of 10 October 1974 had been just three and it had become a deficit by 1977 as a result of by-election losses. James Callaghan's government had to be propped up by David Steel's thirteen Liberal MPs from March 1977 until September 1978 to avoid a general election. When their collaboration ended, Callaghan failed to call the expected general election.

There is a minor role in the play for Sir Arthur Irvine, the MP for Liverpool Edge Hill, whose severe ill health became a significant source of stress to the Labour whips during this time as they feared that he might not be well enough to vote or even survive the parliament (he didn't). They needed every vote that they could get to avoid Commons defeats, including on matters of confidence. Irvine, a former Liberal candidate who became Solicitor General under Harold Wilson, had been the MP for the seat since 1947. He died aged sixty-nine on 15 December 1978, leaving the fate of the Labour government hanging in the balance, even with Unionist support based on a promise of more constituencies for Northern Ireland.

The Edge Hill constituency, on the outskirts of the city centre and stretching out four square miles, was one of only a handful of seats in which the Liberals had come second in October 1974. The young and very energetic candidate, David Alton, a peripatetic teacher and local Liberal councillor, had obtained 26.7 per cent of the vote. In February 1974, he had been the first Liberal to fight the constituency since 1950 and it had been a Conservative–Labour marginal in the late 1950s.

Alton had formed the Edge Hill Liberal Association in 1972 with just four members including himself. The other three who met in his bedsit for the meeting were his then girlfriend, who brought along her sister and a teaching friend from her school, Ann McTegart, who was made chair and later the accommodation officer for the by-election. Alton always worked closely on election campaigns with the legendary Sir Trevor 'Jones the Vote' and by 1973 they had overseen the Liberals winning all twelve city council seats in the Edge Hill constituency. At the same time, the Liberal Party won forty-eight of the ninety-nine city council seats, making Liverpool the first city in modern times to be run by the party.

Liberal campaigning in Edge Hill was always frantic, seven days a week throughout the year. But preparations for a parliamentary by-election saw them stepped up in 1977. This was as a result of Irvine being deselected by the Edge Hill Labour Party, to be replaced by the more left-wing Bob Wareing, and Irvine saying that he would resign as an MP in response. Liverpool Liberals took him at his word, but he never did resign.

This was the era in which the Trotskyite Militant Tendency was successfully infiltrating the Liverpool Labour Party, although Wareing was not a member of the group. Irvine had attracted considerable flak from all quarters for spending only a few hours a month in the constituency. This was when he came up from London to hold a surgery and stayed overnight in the nearby Adelphi Hotel, which was much grander in those days than it is today and where Harold Wilson stayed when MP and visiting his Huyton constituency.

The time was difficult for the Liberals, who suffered a massive backlash in response to the 'Lib–Lab pact'. In the Liverpool local elections in May 1977, Conservative candidates won twenty of Liverpool's thirty-three wards in the county council elections, including some most unlikely ones. But the Alton-led Liberals in Edge Hill retained three of the four wards in the constituency, only very narrowly losing the fourth.

The flow of monthly *Focus* leaflets, as first pioneered in Liverpool for the party's first breakthrough in the city with Cyril Carr in Church ward in 1962, continued across each of the Edge Hill wards. These local community-based leaflets had spread across the city under the influence of Jones and others. Alton was a Young Liberal in Brentwood when he decided to do his teacher training in Liverpool as a result of reading the accounts in the weekly *Liberal News* of what Jones and Carr were doing in the city. Alton and Jones began a close working partnership, with Alton successfully fighting the Low Hill ward in 1972 and becoming a councillor at the age of twenty-one.

After some disappointment with the general election results in 1974, the campaigning continued. A great flow of *Focus* leaflets in Edge Hill during the 1970s was supplemented by regular door knocking based on residents' surveys, street letters discussing action about the many issues raised and well-attended advice centres held by the Liberal councillors across all parts of the constituency.

The summer of 1977 saw celebrations of Queen Elizabeth's Silver Jubilee. The local Liberals worked with residents to get permits to close many of the roads for street parties. Jones's ship chandlers' business provided large quantities of bunting. Appeals were made in the *Focus* leaflets for Edge Hill constituency residents who were aged eighty and over and who were alive at the time of Queen Victoria's Diamond Jubilee. Over 100 of them came forward and the party provided commemorative plates marking the Jubilee and certificates to be presented by Alton at the parties. One leaflet headed 'Queen's Visit to Edge Hill' made much of the fact that the royal car had to travel three miles through the constituency on the way to the town hall and some people allegedly credited Alton with arranging her visit. Meanwhile, vigorous campaigns were being run against unpopular school closures in the constituency and in support of retaining, or reopening, local police stations.

The Rowntree Trust generously sponsored work to support the very large volume of casework being dealt with, as well as providing funds to employ a young Liverpudlian, Robert Littler, to work from Alton's Edge Hill home. This modest house was effectively a full-time HQ and the widely advertised personal phone number never stopped ringing with people wanting help.

At the same time, the relevance of the Liberal Party locally increased and it had real influence improving people's lives through running the city council after regaining control of the town hall in 1978. Alton was Jones's deputy leader on the city council and chair of the housing committee. This helped to obtain favourable coverage in the *Liverpool Echo* every night and allowed him to drive forward a key aim of helping many residents redevelop their old terraced homes. Grants were made available in many areas to pay most of the costs of replacing outside plumbing with modern indoor bathrooms and other improvements.

With Arthur Irvine still failing to make good his threat to resign his seat, a general election was widely expected in the autumn of 1978. The Liberal Party had few realistic hopes for that election, but Edge Hill was one of them. Liberal candidates across the four Edge Hill wards had obtained an aggregate 56 per cent vote share in May 1978, compared to 25 per cent for Labour and 18 per cent for the Conservatives, with Alton polling 67 per cent of the vote in his own Low Hill/Smithdown ward. The leaflets and special deliveries like Christmas cards to every household continued almost weekly and all but one of the thirteen Liberal MPs (the exception being Jeremy Thorpe who was a friend of Irvine's) began making regular visits to Edge Hill.

A first leaflet for the general election was printed and bundled in readiness for distribution in the evening immediately after Callaghan was expected to use a TV broadcast to open the general election campaign. Over a dozen of us gathered in the front room of Alton's house to watch the broadcast in readiness to begin the distribution of the leaflets across the constituency. We were dumbfounded when we heard the Prime Minister announce that there would be no general election that autumn.

Speculation continued as to whether the ailing Irvine would yet resign or survive until there would be a general election. In December 1978, Irvine finally passed away. But it was not clear if there would be a by-election with a general election certain to be not many months away. Sleight of hand was involved in ensuring that it occurred. The Liberal Chief Whip at the time was the wily Alan Beith. Private discussions took place about whether Labour were going to move the writ and enable a by-election to take place. The argument was made by Beith and the Liberal leader David Steel that while the Liberals could not possibly win, they would come a good second and create a damaging result for the Conservatives as the general election approached. The writ was moved on 1 March for polling to take place on 29 March 1979. Of course, the Liberals knew that we could win in spite of the party's parlous state in the national opinion polls, around 6 per cent at the beginning of the year.

But before that there was a threat to Alton's candidature which could have derailed the by-election campaign. In late 1977, Alton had acted as the election agent for two council by-elections in the next-door Kirkdale constituency. Both were won by the Liberal candidates, but Labour challenged the election expense returns which Alton submitted and questioned his account of the costs of the multiplicity of leaflets delivered. As a result of this, he was charged with election offences which would have disqualified him from standing as a candidate. Fortunately, the sympathetic local press led with the headline 'Liberal hits out at dirty tricks' as a smear campaign against him was alleged. Three days of committal hearings, with his defence led by the brilliant

Liverpool solicitor Rex Makin, saw Labour's case torn to shreds and the charges thrown out by the stipendiary magistrate. It was a great start to his by-election campaign.

A 'Good Evening' leaflet was distributed to every household at the outset of the campaign. The first public meeting was held on Alton's twenty-eighth birthday and saw veteran Labour councillor Hughie Carr walk to the podium to announce his defection to the Liberals. The deputy Labour leader on the city council was also there trying to heckle noisily, but he was put down effectively by the crowd and by Cyril Smith, then the Liberal MP for Rochdale.

The by-election leaflets were classic Trevor Jones style. One led on the problems of burst water pipes with the headline: 'Try bathing five children without water'. An eve-of-poll leaflet was based on news about the dispute over bin collection. An 'Alton Shock' was promised in one leaflet if he was elected to Parliament. He was pictured campaigning four years previously with local mothers demanding a nursery school and which had been opened two years ago, with '54 toddlers' now attending.

Media profiles during the campaign included Anne Robinson in the *Liverpool Echo* saying that, 'if he [Alton] appeared on Mastermind and had Edge Hill as his subject, then he would walk away with all the prizes'. More than a thousand Liberal volunteers were regularly coming to canvass and deliver leaflets in the final weeks of the campaign. The Conservatives had once had a sizeable base in the constituency, but people now knew who the choice was between. Ken Dodd, leading his 'Diddy Men' on a march in support of the Conservative candidate Nick Ward, failed to lift his campaign.

The Labour campaign, and candidate Bob Wareing, also failed to impress. There were more allegations of dirty tricks when nominations closed, and someone appeared on the ballot paper as a 'Gay Liberal'. This was while Jeremy Thorpe was still a Liberal MP but faced the charge of conspiring to murder his lover Norman Scott. Alton was also as yet unmarried. The brilliant local investigative reporter Ian Craig tracked the 'Gay Liberal candidate' down. He had signed a blank nomination paper when approached in a local pub and thought that he was standing for the National Front. Craig identified the source of the operation with the Gay Liberal's deposit being paid by the chairman of one of the Labour ward associations within the constituency.

Nothing could sidetrack the Liberal bandwagon. Eleven very well attended public meetings were held for people to hear Alton speaking with a clutch of senior Liberals, including Lord Michael Winstanley, briefly MP for Hazel Grove in 1974 and who was famous for his Granada TV programme *This Is Your Right*. The eve-of-poll rally was a tricky event. John Pardoe, David Penhaligon and Cyril Smith were all due to speak at it. But then there was to be a vote of no confidence in the government that night. The Liberal MPs needed to vote against the Labour government as the party sought to recover from the damage of having been seen to prop up Callaghan's government earlier in the parliament. The Commons vote was on a knife edge. A call from the government Whips' Office came to the by-election HQ. They hoped that Clement Freud might 'accidentally' miss the last train from Lime Street to get him to the Commons to vote that night. In return, they pledged support for his Private Members' Bill to provide for Freedom of Information. The issue had then to wait another twenty years as Freud made the vote.

Everyone in the Liberal campaign felt confident of victory in the next day's by-election if no general election was called. But if the government lost the vote and a general election was called, then polling would go ahead in the by-election the next day, with the outcome seeming less certain. The government fell by one vote and the first day of the 1979 general election campaign was fought on the streets of Edge Hill.

Volunteers delivering the famous Liberal 'Good Morning' leaflet before polls opened at 7 a.m. were treated to breakfast cooked by Clement Freud in a local Italian cafe near the HQ. Twenty-seven committee room organisers for the twenty-seven polling stations managed hundreds of volunteers calling on supporters seven or eight times until they voted.

The count in St George's Hall was a joyous affair for the hundreds of Liberal supporters who gathered in the foyer confident of victory and singing 'Lloyd George Knew My Father' and other Liberal anthems as the result was declared with Alton gaining 64.1 per cent of the vote, an

8,133 majority and being elected as the youngest MP in the Commons aged twenty-eight. The Conservative lost his deposit.

The next day, the *Daily Mail* (northern edition) ran with the headline: 'Liberals by a landslide'. Liberal poll ratings nationally increased from less than 6 per cent to over 10 per cent, enough of a lift combined with David Steel's impressive TV performances to save the Liberal Party in the 1979 general election after the turbulence of the Lib–Lab pact and the scandal surrounding Jeremy Thorpe. The Liberals won eleven seats, compared to thirteen in 1979, and two years later Steel was able to form the Liberal–SDP Alliance with Roy Jenkins and others.

Bob Wareing became the MP for Liverpool West Derby in 1983. He earned the nicknames 'Serbian Bob' and the 'member for Belgrade' because of his pro-Serb positions. After serving as the MP for Edge Hill for just three days prior to the general election, Alton was re-elected comfortably in the 1979 general election. But to his great consternation, the Boundary Commission announced that it was abolishing the small Edge Hill constituency in 1982. The new much larger Mossley Hill constituency was theoretically a Conservative seat with a majority over 9,000, with the Liberals in third place, 4,000 votes behind second-placed Labour. He appointed me to be his election agent and he won re-election to Parliament in 1983 with the biggest swing against the Conservatives anywhere in England. He stood down from the Commons and left the Lib Dems in 1997 to become an Independent crossbench peer.

Lord Rennard was a volunteer in the Edge Hill by-election campaign 1976–79 and David Alton's election agent for Mossley Hill in 1983. He worked professionally for the Liberals/Liberal Democrats for twenty-seven years, becoming the national director of campaigns and elections with Paddy Ashdown in 1989 and chief executive with Charles Kennedy in 2003. In this time, he oversaw thirteen Lib Dem parliamentary by-election victories, including Eastbourne, Newbury and Christchurch. He became a Lib Dem peer in 1999. His memoir Winning Here *was published by Biteback in 2018.*

FERMANAGH & SOUTH TYRONE

9 APRIL 1981
ANTI-H-BLOCK GAIN

TOBY HARNDEN

Result: Bobby Sands (Anti-H-Block/Armagh Political Prisoner), 30,493, 51.2 per cent; Harry West (UUP), 29,046, 48.8 per cent
Size of majority: 1,447
Swing: N/A
Name of previous MP and party: Frank Maguire (Independent Republican)
Reason for by-election: Death of incumbent
Result at previous general election: Frank Maguire (Independent Republican), 22,398, 36.0 per cent; Raymond Ferguson (UUP), 17,411, 28.0 per cent; Austin Currie (Independent SDLP), 10,785, 17.3 per cent; Ernest Baird (UUUP), 10,607, 17.0 per cent; Peter Acheson (Alliance), 1,070, 1.7 per cent
Date by-election called: 20 March 1981
Date by-election took place: 9 April 1981
Size of total electorate: 72,283
Total number of votes cast: 62,818
Turnout: 86.9 per cent

The two tumultuous by-elections of 1981 in Fermanagh & South Tyrone marked a turning point in the Irish Troubles and cemented Prime Minister Margaret Thatcher's reputation as the 'Iron Lady' who would brook no compromise. They took place in geographically the largest constituency in the United Kingdom. The first contest elected the MP whose death after twenty-five days ended the shortest tenure in Parliament since 1945, while the second saw the highest turnout in any election during the same period. Both winners, aged twenty-seven and twenty-eight, were the youngest MPs in Parliament. Although Winston Churchill had famously spoken in 1922 of 'the dreary steeples of Fermanagh and Tyrone', in fact the Northern Ireland constituency was mostly sprawling farmland, with a long border with the Irish Republic, across which was smuggled everything from pigs and poteen to guns and explosives.

Few had foreseen political drama in Fermanagh & South Tyrone, even though the April by-election was called against the backdrop of an IRA hunger strike in which ten inmates, some of them convicted murderers, had vowed to starve themselves to death if they were not granted the rights of prisoners of war. In 1976, seven years after the modern Troubles had begun, the 'special category status' enjoyed by IRA prisoners had been withdrawn.

The leader of the hunger strike was Bobby Sands, who was serving fourteen years for possession of a pistol after he'd been captured in Belfast in 1977 outside a Protestant furniture store he had just blown up. Known to his IRA comrades as 'Geronimo', Sands, whose family had been expelled from their home in North Belfast by loyalist mobs, had spent eight consecutive Christmases in prison by 1980. He was a zealous believer in Irish unity by whatever means necessary but also had a romantic and intellectual streak. He wrote poetry and songs and his reading included the revolutionary theories of Frantz Fanon and Che Guevara as well as the works of Irish martyrs James Connolly and Patrick Pearse, executed by the British in 1916.

During his time in Cage 11 in 1973, his commander was Gerry Adams, interned as an IRA suspect. Adams, more than four years older than Sands, would become a key figure in the by-election drama, which cemented his status as a future leader of Sinn Féin, the IRA's political wing.

Sands had stepped down as the IRA commanding officer inside the Maze Prison – referred to as long Kesh or the H-Blocks by Irish republicans – when his fast began on 1 March 1981, a week short of his twenty-seventh birthday. A previous hunger strike had ended in ignominy for the IRA at the end of 1980 after fifty-three days. Before that, there had been blanket protests, in which IRA men refused to wear prison clothes, and dirty protests, in which they smeared their cells with faeces. This protest would not be called off prematurely. 'We accept the tragic consequences that most certainly await us and the overshadowing fact that death may not secure a principled settlement,' Sands, using his codename Marcella, had written. The Irish writer Fintan O'Toole detected a fanaticism: 'Blowing up furniture for Ireland did not exactly equate to the deeds of James Connolly and Patrick Pearse. Perhaps this was part of Sands's implacability – he had something to prove and only one way to prove it.'

Tragically, Sands and the other nine hunger strikers who were to die in 1981 had pitted themselves against someone who was equally intransigent. 'There is no such thing as political murder, political bombing or political violence,' Margaret Thatcher said in a speech in Belfast on 5 March. 'There is only criminal murder, criminal bombing and criminal violence. We will not compromise on this. There will be no political status.' Outside the prison, the Troubles claimed sixty-nine victims across Northern Ireland during the eight months of the hunger strikes.

The fateful April by-election was triggered by the unexpected death that night of Frank Maguire, fifty-one, who collapsed at his home above the pub – Frank's Bar – he owned in Lisnaskea, Fermanagh. Maguire was a former IRA man who was strongly sympathetic to the hunger strikers. Although not an abstentionist (as Sinn Féin MPs have remained for the past thirty-nine years since Adams was first elected as an MP in 1983), Maguire was known as the 'invisible man' at Westminster. Since being elected in October 1974, Maguire had never given a Commons speech or asked a parliamentary question. Despite his absenteeism, he had managed to bring down a government in March 1979, by abstaining from supporting Labour when Prime Minister James Callaghan faced a no-confidence motion. Paddy O'Hare, a Fermanagh journalist and politician, summed up the nationalist attitude to Parliament in London: 'Westminster? We hold the damn place in contempt. We use it only as a means of informing the world of the evils of partition.'

Bernadette Devlin McAliskey, a republican activist who had been elected as MP for Mid Ulster at age twenty-one in 1969 before losing her seat in 1974, had floated the idea of an H-Blocks candidacy even before Maguire's sudden death. Her pitch to Maguire was to be that Sinn Féin would 'borrow' the seat to boost the case of the hunger strikers. By an inadvertent quirk of the Criminal Law Act of 1967, which abolished the distinction between felonies and misdemeanours, a person convicted of a serious crime was eligible to be an MP.

With Frank Maguire's death, it was initially assumed that his brother Noel Maguire would stand and inherit the seat with relative ease. McAliskey, who had been shot nine times by loyalists in January 1981, then indicated she might enter the fray. Fermanagh & South Tyrone was firmly divided along sectarian lines and splintering the votes of Catholics – who outnumbered Protestants by about 5,000 in the constituency – would almost guarantee a Unionist victory. Austin Currie, of the moderate nationalist Social Democratic and Labour Party (SDLP), wanted to compete but agreed to stay out in favour of Noel Maguire. Behind the scenes, Sinn Féin had adopted a proposal by activist Jim Gibney that Sands be the candidate.

Twelve minutes before the deadline for nominations, Noel Maguire withdrew, stating: 'I have been told the only way of saving Bobby Sands's life is by letting him go forward in the elections. I cannot have the life of another man on my hands.' McAliskey declared she would not stand and signed the nomination papers of Sands. It was a masterly orchestration by Adams, who had become the key figure behind Sands's candidacy. Although Sands stood under the label 'Anti-H-Block/Armagh Political Prisoner', it was clear that Sinn Féin was pulling the strings.

The IRA man's opponent was to be the reluctant and lacklustre Harry West, sixty-three, an old-style Unionist and farmer who had been a Cabinet minister in the waning years of the old Stormont parliament and briefly an MP in 1974. He had retired from active politics in 1979 after a stinging defeat in the European elections. A better choice would have been Roy Kells, an Ulster Defence Regiment part-timer who had survived two IRA assassination attempts and been suggested by Reverend Ian Paisley as a Unionist unity candidate.

The April by-election campaign, which only lasted twenty days, was marked by very little activity out on the stump. Sands, plainly, could not campaign and Humphrey Atkins, the Northern Ireland Secretary, banned him even from being interviewed in prison. BBC impartiality rules meant that they therefore couldn't speak directly to West. The result, *The Guardian* noted, was that 'people peripheral to the contest are having all the say and the two candidates none'. West described his own campaigning as 'low key', and it was mostly conducted via loud-speaker from his Peugeot saloon. Even then, West preferred to remain silent, deferring to his colleague John Taylor, later Ulster Unionist MP for Strangford from 1983 to 2001 and now Baron Kilclooney. 'I'm hoping he'll be doing much of the shouting through the microphone,' said West. 'He likes that sort of thing.'

Both candidates made token efforts to reach across the sectarian divide. A hastily printed manifesto by Sands delivered to every home read in part: 'I was born in a predominantly Protestant area of Belfast. I was keen on sports and won a lot of medals and ran for Protestant clubs.' West ran an ad in Catholic newspapers urging: 'If you believe in peace, democracy, law and order, you have responsibility to vote Harry West.' In reality, the key to victory for each candidate was to maxim-ise turnout on their side of the religious fence. In Britain, there was a struggle to fathom that Sands could win. The *Daily Telegraph* initially dismissed him as 'a token candidate', while *The Observer* opined that for a Catholic 'to vote for an IRA man is tantamount to saying that they do not mind their Protestant neighbours being murdered'. But Sands began as the favourite – the challenge for his team was to ensure high Catholic turnout.

There was, of course, violence. Two days before the by-election, the IRA shot dead Joanne Mathers, twenty-nine, a Protestant census worker in Belfast, disgusting moderate Catholics. On polling day itself, a 300-pound IRA bomb was defused in the Protestant townland Tat-tymore, near Roslea, in an apparent attempt to stop Unionists voting. Sinn Féin adroitly framed Sands's campaign as about saving the hunger striker rather than endorsing the IRA campaign. Echoing – perhaps not coincidentally – the words of Noel Maguire, the Sands campaign slogan was 'his life is in your hands'. A bitter Austin Currie described it as a 'shrewd and unprincipled campaign to persuade voters that voting for Sands did not entail supporting violence'.

Bobby Sands listened to the election result on his radio in the Maze. On the forty-first day of his fast, weakening and having lost two stone in weight, he had eked out a victory by just 1,447 votes or 2.4 per cent. His election manager Owen Carron delivered the victory speech in Enniskillen, declaring that the people had 'voted against Unionism, voted against the H-Block, and it's time Britain did what she should always do – get out of Ireland'. West described the result as a 'sorry sight', while Harold McCusker, an MP from Paisley's Democratic Unionist Party, said it was the equivalent of 30,000 Catholics standing at the grave of Joanna Mathers and giving three cheers for her murderer.

The by-election was a severe setback for Thatcher, exacerbated by the death of Bobby Sands on 5 May, who succumbed after starving himself for sixty-six days, leading to widespread nationalist rioting. While public opinion in Britain backed her stance against the IRA, the plight of the hunger strikers became an international cause célèbre. Streets in Tehran and Paris were named after Sands, and NORAID, which raised funds for the IRA in the United States, raked in £125,000 in donations. A Dane and a Norwegian from the European Court of Human Rights had rushed to be at the bedside of Sands. Britain's enemies took advantage. Iran's ambassador met Sands's campaign team and Muammar Gaddafi's Libya stepped up arms shipments to the IRA.

On 7 May, Sands was buried in West Belfast with full IRA honours after a funeral procession that drew an estimated 100,000 people. Carron told mourners that Sands was the victim of a 'cruel murder' by the British state, adding: 'Today we repledge ourselves to drive England from our soil.' Two miles away, Paisley spoke at a rival memorial service for IRA victims, booming: 'The world focuses its attention on an IRA gunman in prison who committed suicide. Those we remember had no choice.' The day before, a Royal Ulster Constabulary (RUC) officer had been shot dead by an IRA sniper.

Toby Harnden was the Ireland correspondent for the Daily Telegraph from 1996 until 1999. He is the author of Bandit Country: The IRA and South Armagh (Hodder, 1999) – widely considered to be one of the best books about the Irish Troubles. An Orwell Prize winner, his fourth book is due to be published by Simon & Schuster in 2026.

FERMANAGH & SOUTH TYRONE

20 AUGUST 1981
ANTI-H-BLOCK HOLD

TOBY HARNDEN

Result: Owen Carron (Anti-H-Block Proxy Political Prisoner), 31,278, 49.1 per cent; Ken Maginnis (UUP), 29,048, 45.6 per cent; Seamus Close (Alliance), 1,930, 3.0 per cent; Tom Moore (Workers' Party Republican Clubs), 1,132, 1.8 per cent; Martin Green (General Amnesty), 249, 0.4 per cent; Simon Hall-Raleigh (The Peace Lover), 90, 0.1 per cent
Size of majority: 2,230
Swing: N/A
Name of previous MP and party: Bobby Sands (Anti-H-Block/ Armagh Political Prisoner)
Reason for by-election: Death of incumbent
Result at previous general election: Frank Maguire (Independent Republican), 22,398, 36.0 per cent; Raymond Ferguson (UUP), 17,411, 28.0 per cent; Austin Currie (Independent SDLP), 10,785, 17.3 per cent; Ernest Baird (UUUP), 10,607, 17.0 per cent; Peter Acheson (Alliance), 1,070, 1.7 per cent
Date by-election called: 28 July 1981
Date by-election took place: 20 August 1981
Size of total electorate: 72,834
Total number of votes cast: 64,531
Turnout: 88.6 per cent

The Conservative government and most of the House of Commons opposed holding another by-election while the hunger strike continued – once it was over, other Irish nationalist parties could contest the seat. Sinn Féin enlisted the help of Dafydd Jones, a Welsh nationalist MP, to move the writ for the by-election which party leader Gerry Adams fervently desired. The canny manoeuvre worked and on 28 July a 23-day campaign was announced. By this time, eight hunger strikers had died, among them Kieran Doherty, who had been elected to the Irish parliament on 11 June. Not only had the nationalist votes for Bobby Sands failed to save his life, they had given renewed impetus to the IRA hunger strike – five of those who were to die had stopped eating after the election of Sands.

There were signs, however, of fractures within the republican ranks. Raymond McCreesh, the third hunger striker to die, had indicated he might want to give up his fast. According to a British government document, McCreesh's brother, a priest, pushed back, telling him: 'Your brother and I were proud to carry the coffins of Bobby Sands and Frank Hughes [the second to die]. They are in heaven waiting for you.' Other families tried to pressurise the IRA to end the strike because Thatcher seemed immovable. On 31 July, Paddy Quinn's fast had been ended at the request of his mother. To this day, some republicans charge that Adams prolonged the strike, leading to more deaths, because of the political benefit he was reaping.

For the 20 August by-election, Carron was chosen as the republican 'Anti-H-Block Proxy Political Prisoner' candidate. By this time, the government had changed the law so that convicted criminals could not become MPs. The softly spoken, bearded Carron, an unemployed history teacher, had no terrorist convictions and was not known to be in the IRA, which meant he could campaign and appear on television. He would be charged with possession of a rifle in 1986, flee to the Irish Republic and be held in prison there for two years while successfully fighting extradition; he always denied IRA membership.

The Unionists jettisoned the hapless West and selected Ken Maginnis, a moustachioed major in the Ulster Defence Regiment (UDR) who resigned his commission after eleven years in uniform to fight the by-election. Maginnis, forty-three, attempted to campaign on economic issues – unemployment was 23 per cent in much of the constituency – but knew his main hope of winning was boosting Protestant turnout and hoping for nationalist disillusionment with the IRA. He was unrelenting in his criticism of republican violence, which resonated in rural areas where many Protestant farmers, often part-time UDR men, had been picked off and murdered. He rejected any criticism of the RUC or the UDR, which republicans painted as brutal, sectarian forces. 'The only dirty and nasty thing that I've experienced about being a member of the UDR is that you're likely to get killed or maimed by people who don't give a damn about the community,' he said.

Carron, a Fermanagh native, proved an effective campaigner, travelling in a large pink bus filled with young supporters wearing yellow T-shirts with 'Vote Carron, the prisoners' candidate' in green letters. Sands, he said, was an Irish hero 'who hurled his frail body against the juggernaut of British imperialism'. He was accompanied by a brother of Sands and two sisters of another dead hunger striker, Thomas McElwee. It was notable that he received an enthusiastic reception in moderate nationalist areas where the SDLP would normally prevail: the hunger strikes had radicalised Northern Irish Catholics.

The death of Michael Devine, the tenth and final hunger striker to perish, was announced on the day of the by-election, probably giving Carron a boost. Maginnis received two more votes than West, but Carron improved on Sands's tally by 785. Unionists, with some credibility, claimed massive election fraud by republicans. At Coalisland, five Catholics were detained on the instructions of the presiding officer, while the RUC said on election day that twenty-seven people had been arrested for personation and scores more had been turned away. Maginnis said the election had been a 'travesty of the democratic system' due to 'mass intimidation' by republicans. Carron immediately confirmed that he would not take his seat at Westminster, foreshadowing the Sinn Féin policy of abstentionism.

The hunger strikes ended in October with the kind of ambiguous deal that could have been achieved much earlier had the IRA leadership and Thatcher so desired. The IRA secured a more favourable prison regimen and over the course of the 1980s, paramilitary prisoners in the Maze achieved POW status in all but name. In September 1983, thirty-eight IRA prisoners managed to escape. In March 1997, another mass breakout was thwarted when a seventy-metre tunnel was discovered. I was among the reporters who visited the prison shortly afterwards and met a highly disciplined set of IRA prisoners, with a military command structure, operating essentially as they desired. Padraig Wilson, the senior IRA prisoner, appeared to be a more powerful figure than the governor.

Despite her public stance, Thatcher privately admired the courage of the IRA hunger strikers. She wrote at the time: 'You have to hand it to some of these IRA boys … What a waste! What a terrible waste of human life!' Charles Moore, Thatcher's official biographer, concluded that she had, in fact, negotiated with terrorists to end the hunger strike. 'She never quite admitted this, even privately, but it was so.' The Prime Minister, however, had become a figure of unparalleled loathing by Irish republicans. Danny Morrison, a senior republican who had been spokesman for Sands during the April by-election, described her as 'the biggest bastard we have ever known'. In October 1984, the IRA almost killed her in the bomb that decimated Brighton's Grand Hotel.

Probably the most significant ramification of the 1981 by-elections was that they gave Adams and Sinn Féin the springboard to become a force in electoral politics. In October 1981, Morrison called for republicans to seize power with 'a ballot box in one hand and an Armalite in the other'. Adams concluded that the hunger strikes made it 'easier to argue for an electoral strategy within republican ranks'. Brian Keenan, a senior IRA commander, backed Adams, concluding: 'We must never forsake action but the final war to win will be the savage war of peace.' Thus, Sinn Féin and the IRA embarked on a course that would ultimately lead to the 1998 Good Friday Agreement, after which all paramilitary prisoners were freed from the Maze. It was, however, a long and bloody road to an imperfect peace. 'Ten men achieved a terrible finality, but outside the prison, nothing was concluded,' O'Toole observed.

The eventual outcome, moreover, was far from the one Bobby Sands advocated. Indeed, one of the fiercest critics of the Adams strategy has been Bernadette Sands McKevitt, younger sister of Bobby Sands and wife of the late Mickey McKevitt, who led the breakaway Real IRA. 'Bobby did not die for cross-border bodies with executive powers,' she said in 1998. 'He did not die for nationalists to be equal British citizens within the Northern Ireland state.'

Owen Carron lost his seat to Ken Maginnis in the June 1983 general election, when the nationalist vote was split, but Adams won in West Belfast, becoming Sinn Féin's first MP. Maginnis became a staunch advocate of reaching an accommodation with republicans. He held Fermanagh & South Tyrone until 2001, when he was created a life peer. After his 1983 defeat, Carron faded into relative obscurity, though he remains a committed republican. Today, Sinn Féin is the largest party in Northern Ireland. It holds seven of the province's eighteen Westminster seats, including Fermanagh & South Tyrone, and the post of First Minister in the devolved government.

Toby Harnden *was the Ireland correspondent for the* Daily Telegraph *from 1996 until 1999. He is the author of* Bandit Country: The IRA and South Armagh *(Hodder, 1999) – widely considered to be one of the best books about the Irish Troubles. An Orwell Prize winner, his fourth book is due to be published by Simon & Schuster in 2026.*

56

WARRINGTON

16 JULY 1981
LABOUR HOLD

PAUL LINFORD

Result: Doug Hoyle (Labour), 14,280, 48.4 per cent; Roy Jenkins (SDP), 12,521, 42.4 per cent; Stanley Sorrell (Conservative), 2,102, 7.1 per cent; Neil Chantrell (Ecology), 219, 0.8 per cent; Daniel Hussey (United Democratic Labour), 149, 0.5 per cent; Iain Leslie (Citizen's Band Radio), 111, 0.4 per cent; John Fleming (Independent Labour), 53, 0.2 per cent; Donald Kean (Social Democratic), 38, 0.1 per cent; Bill Boaks (Democratic Monarchist), 14, 0.1 per cent; Harry Wise (English Democratic), 11, 0.0 per cent; Tom Keen (More Prosperous Britain), 10, 0.0 per cent

Size of majority: 1,759

Swing: 23.0 per cent from Labour to Liberal/SDP

Name of previous MP and party: Thomas Williams (Labour)

Reason for by-election: Resignation on being appointed a High Court judge

Result at previous general election: Thomas Williams (Labour), 19,306, 61.6 per cent; G. Povey (Conservative), 9,032, 28.8 per cent; Iain Brodie Brown (Liberal), 2,883, 9.2 per cent; C. Campbell (SDP), 144, 0.5 per cent

Date by-election called: 1 June 1981

Date by-election took place: 16 July 1981

Size of total electorate: 44,059

Total number of votes cast: 29,508

Turnout: 67.0 per cent

Margaret Thatcher's decisive victory in the 1979 general election sent the politics of the British centre-left into a state of flux from which it would not emerge for the best part of a decade. Without the discipline of power to hold it together, the splits that had been bubbling below the surface in James Callaghan's Labour Cabinet before the election burst into the open as Tony Benn launched his crusade for party 'democracy' – left-wing code at the time for bringing the mainly right-wing parliamentary party under the control of activists and the unions.

Callaghan, who was significantly more popular with the public than his party, had stayed on as Labour leader following the election defeat, ostensibly in order to 'take the shine off the ball' for Denis Healey, his erstwhile Chancellor and natural successor, but any hope of a smooth handover soon imploded amid the party infighting, with Benn constructing a seductive 'betrayal' narrative in which the parliamentary party's perceived failure to adhere to Labour's socialist ideals was entirely to blame for its defeat.

The Bennites' radical prescriptions, notably mandatory selection contests for MPs, unilateral nuclear disarmament and withdrawal from the European Economic Community (EEC) – a left-wing cause back then – inevitably gave rise to chatter about a 'centre party', perhaps made up of Labour's more moderate elements alongside those of the Liberal Party, which had soldiered on as a third force in British politics since last tasting power in the 1920s, enduring several false dawns along the way.

Such talk drew much of its inspiration from the Lib–Lab pact formed in 1977 which had enabled Callaghan to continue governing after he lost his parliamentary majority. By the chaotic standards of the mid-1970s, it was generally regarded as having been a successful and relatively stable period of government, and it was only when the Liberal leader David Steel ended the arrangement in the summer of 1978 that Callaghan's administration had started to fall apart.

It was against this somewhat febrile backdrop that Roy Jenkins prepared to step back into British politics, having spent four years in Brussels as head of the European Commission. The former Home Secretary and Chancellor had once been strongly tipped to succeed Harold

Wilson as Labour leader, but his star faded after he defied the Labour whip in 1972 to support Britain's entry to the EEC, and he came a poor third to Callaghan in the leadership election four years later.

But Jenkins retained a significant following among that section of educated, middle-class, moderate-minded voters – today you'd call them Centrist Dads – who didn't warm to Mrs Thatcher but didn't want too much red-blooded socialism either, and the BBC, which in those days was of a similar sort of ideological bent, had given him a platform by inviting him to deliver its prestigious Richard Dimbleby Lecture in November 1979.

Entitled 'Home Thoughts from Abroad', it turned into a searing critique of how the two-party system had taken post-war Britain for a 'queasy ride on the ideological big dipper', citing the thirty-year journey from nationalisation to denationalisation to renationalisation to privatisation as an example of 'superficial and quickly reversed political change without much purpose or underlying effect'.

With the hindsight of more recent political history, the lecture now reads as a classic statement of the 'Third Way' centrism later adopted by Tony Blair and New Labour, for example: 'We need the innovating stimulus of the free market economy without either the unacceptable brutality of its untrammelled distribution of rewards or its indifference to unemployment.' Or:

> You want the class system to fade without being replaced either by an aggressive and intolerant proletarianism or by the dominance of the brash and selfish values of a 'get rich quick' society … These are some of the objectives which I believe could be assisted by a strengthening of the radical centre.

It was that phrase 'strengthening of the radical centre' which really set the hares running – as explicit a call for a new party as Jenkins could have made without actually saying so. He also drew a clear link between his proposed antidote to Britain's see-saw politics – proportional representation – and the possibility of new parties emerging, arguing:

> The great disadvantage of our present electoral system is that it freezes

the pattern of politics. Everyone assumes that if a party splits it will be electorally slaughtered. I am not so sure. I believe that the electorate can tell a hawk from a handsaw, and that if it saw a new grouping, with cohesive and relevant policies, it might be more attracted by this new reality than by old labels which had become increasingly irrelevant.

Fast forward twenty months to July 1981, and the political situation had been transformed. Callaghan had resigned and been replaced not by Healey but by the old romantic hero of the Labour left, Michael Foot. The party had committed itself to a new system of electing its leaders which gave the unions the biggest say. Benn had launched a challenge to Healey for the deputy leadership which threatened a fresh lurch to the left. And three moderate ex-Labour ministers, Shirley Williams, David Owen and Bill Rodgers, had joined together with Jenkins in setting up, in March 1981, the Social Democratic Party.

The newly formed SDP quickly agreed an electoral pact with the Liberals and took a commanding lead in the opinion polls. But the overarching question remained: how would the new party – and specifically Jenkins, who, given his long experience of government, naturally aspired to lead it – fare when people got the chance to cast their votes in an actual election? The answer would come at Warrington.

The SDP–Liberal Alliance's subsequent by-election victories at Crosby, Glasgow Hillhead and Bermondsey would come to represent the zenith of its fortunes, and naturally all of them are covered in this volume. Yet those famous triumphs were arguably only made possible by what happened at Warrington, a narrow defeat described by Jenkins at the time as 'by far the greatest victory' of his career.

Unusually, the by-election was triggered by the appointment of the incumbent MP Sir Thomas Williams as a High Court judge. This in itself amounted to something of a political curiosity, in that Williams was the last Member to vacate a seat for an actual paid role, as opposed to the fictitious appointments to the Chiltern Hundreds and the Manor of Northstead which are still used as pretexts for MPs to resign from the Commons.

Williams had held the seat for twenty years, since a previous by-election in 1961, and Labour had held it since the end of the Second

World War, so it scarcely looked winnable for a party whose image inevitably looked rather middle class. But as Anthony Sampson noted at the time: 'Like other northern towns, Warrington was not the rugged proletarian stronghold of southern clichés: it was lively and socially mobile, with an attractive new town whose electors seemed quite intrigued by this odd caravan arriving from London.'

Labour's candidate might well have been Margaret Beckett, who had lost her Lincoln seat at the 1979 election and later went on to become a leading figure in the Blair government, but she lost out in the selection contest to Doug Hoyle. He had also lost his seat in 1979, at Nelson & Colne, and was both a member of Labour's national executive and president of the powerful white-collar ASTMS union run by that other famous Jenkins of '70s and '80s politics, Clive – 'the maverick left-wing leader of a union whose members mainly voted Tory', as Healey once waspishly described him.

Unsurprisingly, Clive Jenkins was to the fore in a combative Labour campaign which portrayed the SDP as class traitors, openly mocked 'Woy' Jenkins's rhotacism with talk of 'Wawwington' and gleefully threw some of the 'Gang of Four's' earlier comments about a breakaway party back in their faces, notably Shirley Williams who had previously said that a centre party 'would have no roots, no principles, no philosophy and no values'.

Jenkins, though, was undeterred. Seeking to shake off his image as a burgundy-swilling Brussels grandee, he toured the constituency tirelessly, eschewing the gloves-off style of his opponents and seeking to make a positive case for the new politics. In this respect, Labour's resort to class warfare in its campaign strategy played into his hands somewhat, given his analysis of Britain's addiction to class-based politics as central to the country's ills.

By the end of the campaign, there were as many SDP posters in the windows of the terraced houses around the old centre of town as Labour ones, and when the votes were counted, Jenkins had come within 1,759 votes of an astonishing triumph, the Tory vote collapsing in the SDP's favour alongside a 23 per cent swing away from Labour to the newly formed party.

There was not a trace of magnanimity from Hoyle in his victory speech. He continued to denounce the SDP as a 'media party' and predicted its defeat would lead to its swift demise. By contrast, Jenkins's own words – 'this is the first election I have lost in many years, but it is by far the greatest victory in which I have ever participated' – made Hoyle's look somewhat petty and vindictive.

Jenkins was proved right. The SDP's strong performance at Warrington not only re-established him as a key player in British politics but showed the Alliance was a credible contender for power, providing the springboard for the by-election wins that followed. But those, of course, are other stories.

Ultimately, the centre-left realignment triggered by the Thatcher hegemony played out as the Alliance evolved into the Liberal Democrats, and Labour slowly returned to the middle ground, first under Neil Kinnock, who denounced the 'grotesque chaos' of the hard left, then under John Smith, who introduced 'one member, one vote' for parliamentary selections, and finally under Tony Blair, who fully embraced the Thatcherite settlement, synthesising her economic liberalism with more centre-left social policies.

The ascent of Blair provided Jenkins with a last opportunity, nearly twenty years on from his Dimbleby lecture, to put proportional representation back on the political agenda. Blair had a grand ambition to heal the Labour–Liberal split which, in his eyes, had 'handed the twentieth century to the Conservatives', and asked Jenkins, who had been something of a mentor to the young Labour leader, to chair an independent commission to look into possible changes to the voting system.

His report, published in December 1998, proposed a system under which some MPs would be elected by the alternative vote, with additional members elected from top-up lists to give a proportional result. But PR was anathema to tribal Labour politicians such as John Prescott and Jack Straw, and the Jenkins Report was duly kicked into that corner of St James's Park where they can't quite get the mower.

Jenkins died in 2003, aged eighty-two. His long-term legacy will probably rest less on his failed attempts to 'break the mould' than on his record as the reforming 1960s Home Secretary who abolished the crime of buggery and supported Steel's Private Members' Bill legalising abortion. He remains the bête noire of social conservatives such as Peter Hitchens who blame him for the decline of 'traditional values' in Britain, but one suspects such an epitaph would not have displeased him.

So much for the gallant loser of that July 1981 contest – what of the victor? Doug Hoyle was to remain an MP throughout Labour's long years of opposition, only standing down at the 1997 election which saw the party finally return to power under Blair after its eighteen years in the wilderness

Although initially seen as a man of the left, he became a strong supporter of Kinnock in his attempts to modernise the party in the 1980s and was elected chair of the Parliamentary Labour Party in 1992 when Smith took over.

Hoyle bequeathed a different sort of legacy to British politics – his son Lindsay, who went on to become MP for Chorley and then Speaker of the House of Commons, in which role he proved a rather gentler character than the pugnacious father who had denounced the SDP.

Hoyle lived to the ripe old age of ninety-eight, serving in the Lords until retiring from the Chamber in 2023, and died in April 2024, only a matter of months before this account of his most famous hour came to be written.

Paul Linford *is a former political editor of Newcastle-based daily newspaper* The Journal *and worked as a parliamentary lobby correspondent from 1995 to 2004. In addition to his freelance political writing, he is the editor-proprietor of the journalism trade website HoldtheFrontPage.*

57

CROSBY

26 NOVEMBER 1981
SDP GAIN FROM CONSERVATIVES

MATTHEW COLE

Result: Shirley Williams (SDP), 28,118, 49.07 per cent; John Butcher (Conservative), 22,829, 39.84 per cent; John Backhouse (Labour), 5,450, 9.51 per cent; Richard Small (Ecology), 489, 0.83 per cent; Tarquin Biscuitbarrel (Raving Loony), 223, 0.39 per cent; Tom Keen (Independent), 99, 0.17 per cent; Bill Boaks (Democratic Monarchist), 36, 0.06 per cent; John Kennedy (Independent), 31, 0.05 per cent; Donald Potter (Independent), 31, 0.05 per cent
Size of majority: 5,289
Swing: 25.47 per cent from Conservative to SDP/Liberal Alliance
Name of previous MP and party: Graham Page (Conservative)
Reason for by-election: Death of incumbent
Result at previous general election: Graham Page (Conservative), 34,768, 56.95 per cent; Tony Mulhearn (Labour), 15,496, 25.38 per cent; Anthony Hill (Liberal), 9,302, 15.24 per cent; Peter Hussey (Ecology), 1,489, 2.44 per cent
Date by-election called: 4 November 1981
Date by-election took place: 26 November 1981
Size of total electorate: 82,680
Total number of votes cast: 57,297
Turnout: 69.3 per cent

The by-election at Crosby produced a very significant swing, but that was not its most distinctive characteristic: it brought into the Commons the first elected MP of a new party, the Social Democratic

Party (SDP), founded only eight months earlier. Other parties have broken their duck at by-elections – the Scottish and Welsh nationalists and UKIP, for instance – but Crosby did greater damage at the time to both main parties than these. Its longer-term significance is more complex and had a stronger message for the losing parties than for the winner.

The context of the Crosby by-election starts on 26 March 1981 with the foundation of the SDP by four members of the Labour government which had lost office two years earlier. Roy Jenkins, David Owen, Shirley Williams and Bill Rodgers left Labour following its shift to the left and internal reforms strengthening the hand of trade union leadership: the SDP started amid a blaze of publicity, attracting thirty MPs – all but one from Labour – and 80,000 members from all parties and none.

The SDP established an alliance with the Liberals, which identified a 'Programme for Government' based on shared policies and anticipating the sharing of parliamentary candidatures. The first of these gave rise to periodic tensions; the second was a more immediate and sometimes intense issue, most urgently as a string of by-election contests arose while no agreed procedure had been established for determining which party would fight each seat. At the first, in Warrington, Jenkins was given a free run and came close to snatching a solid Labour seat; the next, at Croydon, was more contentious, and Liberal candidate Bill Pitt won after resisting national pressure to withdraw in favour of Shirley Williams, who had declined the contest at Warrington.

The Crosby vacancy arose with the death of Sir Graham Page, its Conservative MP for nearly thirty years, on 1 October, though the Conservatives waited over a month before moving the writ to open the by-election campaign formally. Stung by criticism over Warrington and her exclusion from Croydon, Williams was determined to fight Crosby, and during the first stage of the SDP's conference at Perth, she gained the support of Liberal Leader David Steel. By chance, however, Crosby Liberals had on the eve of Sir Graham's death confirmed Anthony Hill, a local councillor who had maintained a respectable vote in 1979, as their candidate. Neither Hill nor his supporters were consulted before Williams, in a meandering speech brought to focus by a hastily scribbled prompt from Rodgers placed in her eyeline, publicly declared she would stand at Crosby to the acclaim of the SDP's conference, by now meeting at Bradford.

Some Liberals bristled at this presumption, and Williams owed her success at the by-election very heavily to Hill's gracious withdrawal from the nomination and her own performance at a tense meeting with his association two weeks later. This was accounted for partly by Hill's self-sacrifice and Williams's charm; partly by Steel's pressure on resentful Liberals to secure the return of Williams to Parliament and give 'payback' for Croydon; but also because Crosby was a tough prospect. Williams wrote in *The Times* that week that it was a high mountain, but the highest of mountains had to be scaled.

On paper, Crosby was indeed one of the least attractive contests for an SDP candidate. It was the eighth-safest Conservative seat, as well as the second largest of any by population, and marked by strong class divisions. In 1979, the Liberals had come third with 15 per cent of the vote. The constituency lay between Liverpool and the affluent resort of Southport and had three main population centres – Crosby itself, Formby and Maghull. The first of these was a Merseyside commuter suburb, the latter bordered working-class Bootle, and in between lay Lancashire farmland, while the coastal areas were dominated by older retirees. Overall, the constituency had a significantly higher proportion of owner-occupiers, middle-class voters and golf courses than most seats. Williams characterised it dramatically in her memoir:

> One end of the constituency, nearest to Liverpool's declining dockland, Seaforth and Waterloo, had wretched housing and high levels of unemployment. Nearby Thornton had one of the biggest council estates in the northwest, where problem families were dumped together. In Crosby itself, respectable middle-class families lived behind looped lace curtains in Victorian houses – it was as if they were pulling their skirts above their ankles to escape the degradation of a Liverpool that was running down and beset by riots and crime.

Though unpromising for the Alliance in its class and electoral background, Crosby's Merseyside location allowed the SDP to point to evidence of decay in the social and political fabric which they could attribute to the 'old' parties. Deprivation and division had given rise in July to sustained rioting in Toxteth less than ten miles away, sharpening criticism of the Thatcher government's approaches to the economy, housing, education and policing; meanwhile, Labour's Liverpool City Council group was coming under the control of the Trotskyist Militant Tendency – one of the longest-standing activists in which, Tony Mulhearn, was president of Liverpool District Labour Party and had fought Crosby in 1979. Williams's letter to electors stressed that the by-election gave them 'the opportunity to begin the fightback for Britain', issuing appeals to both sides to 'use your vote to warn this Conservative Government that a policy built on mass unemployment will not do' and that Labour 'does not offer a sane or safe alternative. It is being taken over by extreme leftwingers.'

It is difficult to overstate the impact of Shirley Williams's campaigning charisma. Firstly, her stamina seemed unlimited throughout fourteen-hour days of press conferences, canvassing and public meetings: she was dubbed the 'tiny tornado'; one supporter even compared her to Joan of Arc. And then there was her character. Though from a privileged background, she could draw voters of all classes into conversation; despite a reputation for indecision, she was resolute and candid in asserting her opinions when arrived at; and, if not noted for humour, she listened to others patiently and responded thoughtfully. Her supporters saw in her an uncommon combination of reason, goodwill and sincerity, with a welcome deficiency of hubris. Even the *Daily Telegraph*'s Charles Moore acknowledged her reputation as 'that rare thing, the human being in politics'. *The Times* agreed in an eve-of-poll endorsement:

> It is hard to think of any politician today who can inspire the warmth and trust that she does. Her party will be the stronger and political life in the country will be healthier if she is once again in the House of Commons – good enough reasons for the voters of Crosby to send her there tomorrow.

The reaction to Williams in Crosby testified to this, and she led local polls for over a month before polling day: one journalist set her pace on a street canvass at a hundred yards an hour because of voters' eagerness to speak to her. Her first public meeting set the tone for the campaign, attracting an audience of over 1,000, while 1,500 supporters journeyed to Crosby from across the country to help her campaign. The awkwardness of Williams's public bid for the nomination was forgotten as figures from the Liberal half of the Alliance lent their vital weight to her task: Liberal leader David Steel and his predecessor Jo Grimond were joined by David Alton, MP for neighbouring Edge Hill, and leader of Liverpool City Council Trevor Jones, nicknamed 'Jones the Vote' and displaced Liberal candidate Anthony Hill. Accompanied by these and the leading Social Democrats, and her lack of ostentation notwithstanding, Williams was happy to motor around the constituency on the back of a lorry with the theme tune from *Chariots of Fire* playing over the tannoy in a carnival atmosphere with more than a touch of knowing irony. To symbolise his party's claim to classless appeal, Bill Rodgers brought Williams's workers claret and chips, a combination which became the title of a book about the SDP the following year. The *Liverpool Echo* was prepared to say: 'She's tough and swift in answer, slams anyone who starts to be critical, and all in all behaves like the seasoned campaigner she is.' Importantly for the candidate of a party with no elected MPs, 'Shirley Williams gives the impression of one sure she is going to win.'

The candidates of the two main parties – teacher John Backhouse for Labour and accountant John Butcher for the Conservatives – had local credentials but could not match the campaigning style and celebrity of Williams. Neither stood again as a parliamentary candidate. The Conservatives in Crosby were not used to close contests and their organisation and messaging were exposed as ineffective. Butcher – not to be confused with his namesake who was already a Conservative MP in the Midlands – was taunted at daily press conferences by a pack of national journalists such as *Newsnight*'s Vincent Hanna who, according to ITN's David Walter, 'made mincemeat of the unfortunate Mr Butcher'. The daily press conferences were suspended, and a rearguard knocking-copy campaign against Williams under the slogan 'Once a Socialist, Always a Socialist' failed to land a punch. Butcher was forced to withdraw a claim that Williams had encouraged violent picketing in the 1977 Grunwick dispute, and his father, Commander Butcher, was embittered enough to bring a *Daily Telegraph* reporter before the Press Council for criticising Butcher junior after applying for the Conservative nomination himself. A clutch of independents – including a Cambridge University student standing for the Monster Raving Loony Party after changing his name by deed poll to Tarquin Fin-tim-lin-bin-whin-bim-lim-bus-stop-F'tang-F'tang-Olé-Biscuitbarrel in homage to the Monty Python election night sketch – failed to make the airtime or column inches normally enjoyed by such candidates at by-elections with high media profile.

The campaign was not without its challenges for Williams: as well as starting from a limited electoral base, she was at every public meeting asked about SDP policy across the full range of issues, on many of which it remained embryonic. Williams's confident command of public affairs meant she could use this latitude to conjure policy spontaneously better than most candidates could have hoped to, challenging one critical reporter to 'ask me any question you like, and I'll tell you what the SDP policy is'. On two questions in particular, however, she faced more critical scrutiny and demonstrated her instinctive robustness: private education and fertility rights.

Five years earlier, Williams had as Education Secretary deprived direct grant grammar schools (which ran on a mixture of state funding and fees) of their government support and questioned whether fee-paying schools generally deserved charitable status. Three former direct grant schools, all of which had become wholly private, were in the constituency and the Conservatives encouraged criticism of Williams's alleged hostility to them from the Independent Schools Information Service. Williams made no concession to them, except to reassure anxious parents that the SDP's commitment to the European Convention on Human Rights meant that they would never be able, even if they wished it, to abolish private education. But she argued that charitable status had to be earned by public service, of which she saw little in such schools. She described an enthusiastic defence of educational standards in private schools from Old Etonian Jo Grimond at one of her meetings as 'a sock in the jaw'. Williams spoke at one local private school,

Merchant Taylors', where governors had voted by a majority of only one to send her an invitation, but the question of private education was not raised. She ended the visit observing that the students showed themselves to be bright – 'as they are at the Sacred Heart Comprehensive down the road', she added.

Williams's views on abortion were the source of more toxic criticism. A practising Catholic, she could hope for a sympathetic hearing from the quarter of Crosby's voters who shared her faith. It was certainly noted that she attended services more frequently than the church strictly required during the campaign and in more than one place. The other side of the coin, however, was the expectation her faith raised that she would make a strict declaration against abortion. Anti-abortion campaign group the Society for the Protection of Unborn Children (SPUC) challenged Williams to commit herself to follow their guidance on any future proposed legislation. Williams reminded them that she had voted against David Steel's Act decriminalising some abortion but refused to give an open-ended commitment to any group on measures not yet proposed. The SPUC prepared leaflets calling for her defeat to be distributed at Catholic churches across Crosby, and it took a call from Williams to the Archbishop of Liverpool, Derek Worlock, to block their activities. Asked at a press conference about her relationship with the church, she invited her questioner to call archdiocesan press officer Father Thompson.

It was such pressures rather than the Conservatives' own campaign that offered the greatest threat to the SDP bandwagon, though Williams suspected that some apparently non-partisan stunts were being managed at a distance by the Tories – even including the 'mooning' of a dinner she had with Roy Jenkins through a restaurant window by a local rugby club!

On a turnout only 6 per cent below that of the previous general election, Williams won a majority of over 5,000 votes, while the Tories lost nearly 12,000 and Labour lost its deposit.

Unsurprisingly, the SDP allowed themselves to see Crosby as symptomatic of a wider malaise in British politics from which they expected sensational benefits: Roy Jenkins noted the warmth of the audience at an edition of BBC's *Question Time* on the evening of the result, feeling himself 'rowing with the current'. But they were not alone in this. *The Times* called it 'the biggest upheaval in any by-election in recent history' and *The Observer* declared 'enter the era of the three-party system'. Crosby was global news: the *New York Times* reported that 'Mrs Williams's success established the new force in British politics as an equal contender for political power'; Williams featured on the front of *Time* magazine and, with Steel and Jenkins, was presented on the cover of *The Economist* as 'Her Majesty's New Opposition'. While the 'Shirley' factor secured the scale of the victory, the swings achieved at Warrington and Croydon would have been enough for a win. Even the usually cautious *New Statesman* pollster Peter Kellner acknowledged that, together with other by-election results, the Alliance's impact was 'unprecedented': 'Liberal gains at Orpington in 1962 and Sutton and Cheam a decade later registered swings on the same scale as we are now seeing: but they were isolated events. Those *were* the days of the localised, tactical protest vote: today something different is happening.'

In December, a Gallup poll found that over 50 per cent of respondents said they supported the Alliance.

The successful candidate can be forgiven a little exuberance. Her acceptance speech quoted Dryden – ''tis well an old age is out, and time to begin anew' – and, describing the SDP as not a party but a crusade, predicted that the Alliance would form the next government: 'The mould of British politics has been totally shattered.' SDP campaigners drank champagne until the morning singing 'We Shall Overcome'.

Both of the main parties consoled themselves publicly that the result was a reflection of conventional mid-term protest voting, with the added value of Williams and the novelty of a new party, conditions which would not be repeated. Internally, however, both Labour and the Conservatives knew there was a problem but were divided about how to react.

Labour leader Michael Foot blamed the party's humiliation on statements from the far left which 'were anti-parliamentary and gave ruinous advantage and opportunities to our Social Democrat enemies', and in the month after Crosby, a National Executive Committee inquiry into the Militant Tendency was begun. On Labour's left, Tony Benn – who, visiting Crosby, predicted a Labour win – despaired in his diary after the result that Foot was 'trying to clean up the party so that the SDP will rejoin'. Deputy leader Denis Healey later acknowledged with uncharacteristic self-doubt that 'for a moment it looked as if Roy Jenkins was right, and that the new centre grouping had broken the mould of British politics'; and even the left's house journal *Tribune* feared on the day of the result that 'Labour is two years from disaster', asking 'will the growing challenge from the SDP push Labour back into a 1931-type position?'

The chief victims on this occasion, however, were the Conservatives. The *Sunday Telegraph*, recognising the Tories' hold as 'vulnerable', had already begged its Crosby readers embarrassingly to 'remain loyal to Mrs Thatcher, who is only carrying out the very policies the voters supported only two years ago'. Thatcher regretted in her memoirs that the by-election had allowed Williams 'to get back into the Commons' and noted that she herself was then rated as the most unpopular Prime Minister in polling history. Admiring biographer Charles Moore describes Thatcher then 'in a state of tension which made her very difficult to work with'. Five days after the Crosby result, she burst in uninvited – and, according to one present, 'quite full of whisky' – to a late-night pre-Budget meeting between Chancellor Geoffrey Howe and his officials. Dismissing Howe's speech, she told him: 'If this is the best you can do, then I'd better send you to the hospital and deliver the statement myself.' Ted Heath, the predecessor whom Thatcher had displaced, mischievously stoked the fire beneath her by offering to form a coalition with the SDP.

The atmosphere of triumph was short-lived. Williams soon recognised with typical candour in a leaked off-the-record interview with American journalists that her support at Crosby was 'broad and frothy, without much organisational support or intellectual underpinning' and that most SDP members were 'political novices, easily put off by the nitty-gritty and infighting of the process'. Certainly, as she wrote in her memoir, the by-election represented the SDP's 'high tide': in fact, the waters receded further and faster than the most realistic analysis might have anticipated.

Big wins by new parties at by-elections can be, as UKIP and Respect later discovered, false dawns. Following unfavourable boundary revisions which she speculated might have resulted from a joint submission to the commissioners by Labour and the Conservatives, Williams lost Crosby in 1983, earning her the unique discomfort of being the only person to lose two different seats for two different parties at two consecutive general elections. All but five of the twenty-seven SDP MPs seeking re-election then were defeated too. Following internal tensions, the impact of the Falklands War and because of the cruel effect of the electoral system, the SDP–Liberal Alliance gained a quarter of the vote but only twenty-three seats.

However, though the mould of British politics had not been broken, and the SDP itself did not survive beyond the following general election, cracks in the foundations of the party system were widening in a way of which Crosby gave spectacular notice, demonstrating not the strength of the SDP crusade but the fragility of the main parties' defences. Its incursion foreshadowed the fall of Labour's base vote then, in 1987 and in 2010 to under a third of the poll, and the Conservatives' to under a third in 1997 and 2001 and under a quarter in 2024. The destination of the vote, and the parliamentary representation, for parties other than the Conservatives and Labour has fluctuated dramatically, but its scale has grown, since the 1950s, when it consisted of six MPs and less than one vote in twenty. At the first general election after Crosby, it rose to 30 per cent of the vote; and in 2024, it edged over a hundred seats and towards half of the vote. Crosby was an important milestone on that journey which still has lessons for strategists on all sides.

Matthew Cole is an associate of the Regional Heritage Centre at Lancaster University and has written extensively about the SDP–Liberal Alliance and the north-west. He worked for the BBC as a political analyst at the last nine general elections.

58

GLASGOW HILLHEAD

25 MARCH 1982
SDP GAIN FROM CONSERVATIVES

ANDREW MARR

Result: Roy Jenkins (SDP), 10,106, 33.4 per cent; Gerry Malone (Conservative), 8,068, 26.6 per cent; David Wiseman (Labour), 7,846, 25.9 per cent; George Leslie (SNP), 3,416, 11.3 per cent; Jack Glass (Protestant Crusade against the Papal Visit), 388, 1.3 per cent; Roy Harold Jenkins (Social Democrat), 282, 0.9 per cent; Nicolette Carlaw (Ecology), 178, 0.6 per cent; Bill Boaks (Public Safety Democratic Monarchist White Resident), 5, 0.0 per cent
Size of majority: 2,038
Swing: 23.9 per cent from Conservative to SDP
Name of previous MP and party: Tam Galbraith (Conservative)
Reason for by-election: Death of incumbent
Result at previous general election: Tam Galbraith (Conservative), 12,368, 41.0 per cent; Richard Mowbray (Labour), 10,366, 34.4 per cent; Marshall Harris (Liberal), 4,349, 14.4 per cent; G. Borthwick (SNP), 3,050, 10.1 per cent
Date by-election called: 3 March 1982
Date by-election took place: 25 March 1982
Size of total electorate: Approx. 37,500
Total number of votes cast: 30,289
Turnout: 76.4 per cent

Few by-elections promise to change the course of British political history; the spectacular and often hilarious one that took place in Glasgow Hillhead, in the artistic, prosperous and academic West End heart of the city, did promise that; although history, sad to relate, never kept its side of the bargain.

Hillhead was really the final chance for Roy Jenkins, former Home Secretary, former Labour Chancellor of the Exchequer and creator of the breakaway two-year-old Social Democratic Party, to re-enter Parliament as its leader and, he hoped, 'break the mould of British politics' and perhaps become Prime Minister. A former president of the European Commission, Jenkins had narrowly failed at the Warrington by-election of the previous July. He was no longer the obvious leader of the so-called 'Gang of Four' and he felt that three by-election attempts would be one too many, making him thoroughly ridiculous. It would be Glasgow Hillhead, in short, or bust.

As a 23-year-old jobbing reporter for *The Scotsman*, I was enthralled by the coming contest. These were wild times politically. Margaret Thatcher was in the middle of her early period of struggle as Prime Minister and hugely unpopular, although the start of the transformational Falklands War, which began in early April of the year, was just weeks away. Labour, still under the leadership of Michael Foot, was in the throes of the bitter fight between trade union-backed traditionalists and the Bennite hard left – a brutal war which had driven out the SDP. Everything in politics seemed shaken and unpredictable. In the early spring of 1982, it seemed that 'Thatcherism' would be unable to cope with the huge rising unemployment numbers and the effects of deindustrialisation and would be itself consigned to the scrapheap at the next election. Yet Tony Benn's socialist crusade was hardly popular among the British middle classes, and Foot, the unworldly bibliophile, was widely derided. The times seemed perfect for a centrist reshaping.

On top of all of this, the Glasgow Hillhead by-election promised a rich human story. Roy Jenkins had been, in some sense, the architect of the swinging '60s. He was now a rotund, bibulous grandee in late middle age, whose speech impediment, prosperous years in Brussels and thirst for good claret disguised a searching intelligence and fierce ambition but also made him an easy target for *Private Eye* and the newspaper cartoonists.

Hillhead was, as it happened, of the most cultured and highly educated constituencies in all of Britain, crisscrossed by grand orange-pink sandstone boulevards, beautiful parks and fine public buildings. But it was still Glasgow; and Roy Jenkins did not seem a Glasgow kind of boy. He compared his bemusement on arriving and seeing its skyline 'as mysterious to me as the minarets of Constantinople' had been to Russian troops in their war with Turkey — a typically orotund 'Royism'. The campaign would bring more.

This by-election had been brought about by the death of 'Tam', or Sir Thomas Galloway Dunlop, Galbraith at the early age of sixty-two. Tam Galbraith had been a pillar of the Scottish Unionist Party, as the Conservatives were generally known then, since winning the seat in 1948 and surviving a brush with scandal during the so-called 'Vassall' Soviet espionage affair.

He was hardly an obscure figure, but so little focused had Jenkins been on Scottish politics, that when he was phoned at home to say that 'Galbraith had died', he assumed it was his friend, the famous economist J. K. Galbraith.

Then there was the Scotland issue. Jenkins did not know Glasgow well and indeed had described it as 'slightly sinister' before the SDP were able to persuade the Scottish Liberals to stand aside for the contest after a secret summit in London.

Once Roy brought down all his London and SDP friends, it felt to Scottish reporters as if we were receiving a culturally alien, if perhaps benign, influx. Who were all these people in fancy clothes, with screechily incomprehensible English voices, driving posh cars and Land Rovers past the university and Kelvingrove Park? Even among the Glasgow middle classes, there was a lot of twitching of curtains and bemused shaking of heads.

Jenkins would inevitably be seen as a carpetbagger. And in Gerald Malone, the Tories had a local candidate, Glasgow-born, Glasgow-educated. Malone would later become Tory MP for Aberdeen South, and then for Winchester, ending up as Health Minister under John Major. In Glasgow, however, sectarian bigotry was still rampant. Each year there would be large, drum-and-fife headed Orange marches, with platoons of stern-looking men stomping along in their bowler hats and mackintoshes. The Tories' local name, 'Unionists', emphatically did not refer to the Union of 1707, and Pastor Jack Glass, a militant Protestant campaigner, did the Roman Catholic Malone no favours.

This would not be an easy fight on any side. One of the anti-SDP candidates changed his name to Roy Jenkins and stood under a banner designed to confuse voters; and Labour was well dug in in parts of the constituency, fighting a campaign very much based on Jenkins as a pampered, posh, ignorant outsider.

What, perhaps, everybody had underestimated was quite how hard the 63-year-old would work, making endless trips to the constituency, striding along long and windy streets with a trail of hacks behind him, almost sprinting up twisting flights of stone stairs in old tenement buildings, listening and learning, beaming and nodding, every step of the way. In a film by the documentary maker Michael Cockerell later on, Jenkins said that he personally counted every hand he shook and that he had shaken more than 5,000. That equates to about half of his eventual majority.

The opinion polling was all over the place for the first three weeks of the campaign, and it was hard for reporters like me to distinguish between real enthusiasm for Jenkins and hype whipped up by the arrival of exotic London stars such as Shirley Williams, who had recently won the Crosby by-election, and David Owen, the former Foreign Secretary and later Jenkins's deadly rival.

The daily press conferences once the campaign got going properly crackled with energy and occasionally were genuinely funny. I remember Jenkins informing us, with a very straight face, that he knew Glaswegians were warming to him because of the number of people who waved back at him when he stood at various windswept crossroads in the constituency. Hardly scientific, we suggested: 'Not at all. Studying significant waving from nodal points has been a pwinciple of entire my political life.'

He enjoyed the comedy. A little later, he confessed to me that his wife had slightly deflated him. In those days, the SDP–Liberal Alliance often used an orange lozenge-shaped logo. Jenkins said he had been 'much gwatified' by the number of them on the back of cars running up and down the Byres Road in the centre of the constituency: 'Wather twagically, Jennifer gently pointed out to me that if one looked more closely, they all read "Child on Board".'

Never mind: the physicians, academics, accountants and the rest of the professional class of West End Glasgow, a place then remote from the allure of Scottish nationalism, or indeed Thatcherism, found they were warming to the optimistic rhetoric and sheer, gleeful energy of the veteran politician.

In the last days of what had been a chilly and occasionally wet March, the sun came out and the dogs in the street had a pretty clear sense of what was about to happen. Coming in at just over 2,000 votes, his final majority over Gerry Malone was hardly enormous – certainly by the standards of by-elections in recent years – but it put him in a pivotal position to take the leadership of the SDP in a year when many expected the party to overwhelm Labour and beat the Conservatives at the next election. It must have seemed as if the prime ministership was almost in his grasp at last. His biographer John Campbell wrote that, 'on a personal level Jenkins's victory at Hillhead was perhaps the highpoint of his political life'.

He liked to draw the parallel of Asquith, one of his great political heroes, winning a by-election at Paisley in 1921. He was about as natural an adoptive Glaswegian as if Angela Rayner had found herself adopted for Henley or Jacob Rees-Mogg as the MP for Bermondsey. But, unexpectedly, Glasgow became a great enthusiasm. He bought a flat there, revisiting the city constantly, and gloried in its extraordinary Victorian architecture and its energy, coming to prefer it greatly to Edinburgh, which he compared to 'a splendid salmon laid out on a slab'. Handsome but dead.

Sadly for him, his by-election triumph was about as good as it got. On the back of her triumph over General Galtieri in the South Pacific, Margaret Thatcher was transmuted into the Iron Lady and won a smashing general election victory in 1983, just a little over a year after the by-election. Although the SDP–Liberal Alliance came close to Labour in its share of the popular vote, it won just twenty-three seats compared to the 209 Labour MPs – not the first or last victim of Britain's brutal first past the post electoral system.

Jenkins was left as the admiral of a coracle. He was already loathing his return to the House of Commons, where he was obliged to sit near aggressive and hostile Labour MPs such as Dennis Skinner and far from the reassuring brass and wood authority of the dispatch box. More significantly, the atmosphere in British politics was by now very different – much more aggressive as the whirlwind of Thatcherism blew ever more strongly. The Thatcherite MP and diarist Alan Clark recorded an early attempt by Jenkins to take her on: 'He was so portentous and long-winded that he started to lose the sympathy of the House about half way through and the barracking resumed. The Lady replied quite brightly and freshly, as if she did not particularly know who he was, or care.'

After the election, when he retained Glasgow Hillhead, and after being privately humiliated by the liberal leader David Steel, who had suggested that he take second place to him in the campaign, Jenkins realised his grand dream of reshaping British politics was over. Under pressure from David Owen, he gave up the leadership and watched, increasingly unhappily, as Owen took the SDP further to the right.

Jenkins became an increasingly admired author – he had always been a brilliant writer – and an elder statesman out of step with the state. His unashamed enthusiasm for high culture and the finer things of life, and his plummy voice, which he had originally created out of a working-class Welsh one, turned him into something of a figure of fun.

But had he triumphed – which means, I suppose, had the Argentinians never invaded the Falkland Islands, and had Labour never found within itself, in Neil Kinnock, the means of its survival and revival – then British history in modern times would have been very different. Jenkins was a passionate European who would certainly have driven us towards the single currency; he wanted to use the great bonanza of North Sea oil and gas revenues to rebuild public services and he was a genuine, Keynesian opponent of Thatcherite economics.

That more 'civilised' Britain never happened, and it is frankly impossible to imagine Jenkins as a British politician today. But the whirlwind of the Glasgow Hillhead by-election, with its laughter, its shocking undercurrent of sectarianism and its sheer unexpectedness, was one of the great nearly turning points of modern times. As a young reporter at the back of the hall, with a certain ingrained prejudice against the SDP, I quite quickly realised I was in the presence of a kind of greatness.

Andrew Marr *has been a political journalist for forty-five years and covered the Glasgow Hillhead by-election for* The Scotsman. *He is a former editor of* The Independent *and political editor of the BBC. He presented the Sunday morning* Andrew Marr Show *from 2005–19. He is currently presenter of* Tonight with Andrew Marr *on LBC and political editor of the* New Statesman.

59

BERMONDSEY

24 FEBRUARY 1983
LIBERAL GAIN FROM LABOUR

SIR JOHN CURTICE

Result: Simon Hughes (Liberal), 17,017, 57.7 per cent; Peter Tatchell (Labour), 7,698, 26.1 per cent; John O'Grady (Real Bermondsey Labour), 2,243, 7.6 per cent; Robert Hughes (Conservative), 1,631, 5.5 per cent; James Sneath (National Front), 426, 1.4 per cent; David Sutch (Monster Raving Loony), 97, 0.3 per cent; Jane Birdwood (Independent Patriot), 69, 0.2 per cent; Michael Keulemans (New Britain), 62, 0.2 per cent; Barry Giddings (Independent Labour), 50, 0.2 per cent; Robert Gordon (Communist), 50, 0.2 per cent; George Hannah (Ecology), 48, 0.2 per cent; Fran Eden (Revolutionary Communist), 38, 0.1 per cent; Ann King (National Labour), 25, 0.1 per cent; Alan Baker (United Democratic), 15, 0.1 per cent; David Wedgwood (ACMFT), 15, 0.1 per cent; Esmond Bevan (Systems Designer), 8, 0.0 per cent
Size of majority: 9,319
Swing: 44.2 per cent from Labour to Liberal
Name of previous MP and party: Bob Mellish (Labour)
Reason for by-election: Resignation of incumbent
Result at previous general election: Bob Mellish (Labour), 19,338, 63.6 per cent; Alexander Duma (Conservative), 7,582, 24.9 per cent; Thomas Taylor (Liberal), 2,072, 6.8 per cent; James Sneath (National Front), 1,175, 3.9 per cent; Anthony Moore (Workers Revolutionary), 239, 0.8 per cent
Date by-election called: 31 January 1983
Date by-election took place: 24 February 1983
Size of total electorate: 51,096

Total number of votes cast: 29,489
Turnout: 57.7 per cent

The Bermondsey by-election, held on 24 February 1983, occasioned one of the most controversial campaigns in British by-election history and concluded with the biggest swing in party support ever recorded. Yet while the contest had a long-term impact on the electoral landscape of the constituency itself, it proved to have little political impact beyond its borders. However, the character of the campaign did rebound on the victor many years later.

The by-election was caused by the decision of the incumbent MP, Bob Mellish, to stand down after being appointed by the Conservative government as deputy chair of the London Docklands Development Corporation (LDDC). Mellish, a former trade union official whose father had been a dock worker, was Labour's Chief Whip from 1969 to 1976 and had been the Labour MP for the area – predominantly working class and dominated by social housing – since winning a by-election in 1946. He had always been elected with massive, albeit recently slightly declining, majorities ever since.

However, Labour was a restive and much divided party in the early 1980s, as it reacted to the shock of defeat in 1979 after a troubled spell in government. Many in the party wanted to push it to the left, and their standard-bearer, Tony Benn, had only been narrowly defeated for the party's deputy leadership in 1981. Michael Foot, the party's leader since 1980, had made his name as the most eloquent and widely admired rhetorician on the left of the party but now found himself struggling to maintain party unity. The most serious blow to his leadership was the defection in 1981 of four former senior Labour Cabinet members from the right of the party. They founded their own party, the Social Democratic Party (SDP), which had since formed an electoral alliance with the Liberal Party.

In one of many such instances of local disunity, a hitherto largely moribund local Labour Party in Bermondsey was taken over in 1980 by a group of left-wing party officers who were concerned in particular about the quality of social housing and the possible impact of the re-development of the Thames riverside being undertaken by the LDDC on the availability of housing for local people. Mellish, who was very much on the right of the party, had decided to stand down at the next election and had, against the wishes of his party, already taken on the role of unpaid deputy chair of the LDDC. At the beginning of November 1981, the local Labour Party selected as his replacement Peter Tatchell who, originally from Australia, was now secretary of the local party and an active community and human rights campaigner. Though on the left of the party, he was not associated with the Trotskyite Militant Tendency, which was to be proscribed the following year by Labour for engaging in entryist tactics. Unhappy at Tatchell's nomination, Mellish resigned from the Labour Party in July 1982 and threatened to trigger a by-election, a decision made more likely by the fact that doing so would enable him to be paid for his work as deputy chair of the LDDC.

But left-wing activism was not all that was stirring in the constituency. The local Liberal Party, inspired by the 'community politics' local activism that had been taken up during the 1970s by many Liberals, had also begun to be an active presence in 1980, again focusing on the issue of housing. They were rewarded with 16 per cent of the vote and second place (ahead of the Conservatives) in the 1981 Greater London Council (GLC) election, more than twice the party's tally locally in the 1979 general election and a much more impressive advance than the party achieved generally across the capital. Their candidate had been Simon Hughes, a barrister and active Christian.

Meanwhile, the formation of the SDP and its Alliance with the Liberals had had a dramatic impact on the electoral landscape. For a while between the autumn of 1981 and the outbreak of the Falklands War in April 1982, the new Alliance enjoyed an unprecedented lead in the national opinion polls, with one Gallup poll even crediting the party with 50 per cent. Spectacular by-election gains were recorded in Croydon, Crosby and Glasgow Hillhead. However, the successful conclusion of the Falklands campaign was followed by a revival in the Conservatives' fortunes, and while the Alliance was still running above 20 per cent in the opinion polls, subsequent by-election performances had been less impressive. Indeed, just a few months before the Bermondsey contest, the challenge from the Alliance (represented in this instance by an SDP candidate) had been fended off with relative ease by Labour in a by-election in next door Peckham.

However, Tatchell's selection as Labour's nominee had proven particularly controversial. Earlier in 1981, he had written in the journal *London Labour Briefing*, which circulated among the left, that 'we must look to new, more militant forms of extra-parliamentary opposition which involve mass popular participation and challenge the government's right to rule'. In the wake of Tatchell's success at securing his party's Bermondsey nomination, James Wellbeloved, a defector from Labour to the SDP, challenged the Labour front bench about these remarks in a Commons debate. He then raised the issue again in an oral question to the Prime Minister the following month. After the Prime Minister responded that she assumed anyone wanting to become an MP would uphold parliamentary democracy, Foot intervened to say that 'since the matter has been raised, may I say that the individual concerned is not an endorsed member of the Labour Party, and, so far as I am concerned, never will be endorsed'. (What Foot meant, of course, was that Tatchell was not an endorsed candidate for the Labour Party.)

Subsequently, Labour's National Executive Committee (NEC) was persuaded by Foot to reject Tatchell's nomination as Labour's candidate, albeit only by one vote. The constituency nomination process was to be rerun – but with Tatchell allowed to run again. With the by-election now looming, in January 1983 the local party stuck by their original selection, a decision that the NEC, including Foot, now accepted. But the row ensured that Tatchell had become a highly controversial candidate, not only within Bermondsey but also in the pages of the tabloid press, who had been denounced by his own leader.

To his reputation as a left-winger was added the fact that Tatchell was gay. Although private sexual activity between men over twenty-one had been decriminalised in 1967, it was still far from being socially accepted. The British Social Attitudes survey of 1983 reported that half the population (50 per cent) felt that sexual activity between two adults of the same sex was 'always wrong', while just one in six (17 per cent) believed it was not wrong at all. Not a single MP was openly gay – in the 1974–79 parliament, the first openly lesbian MP, Maureen Colquhoun, had come close to being deselected and eventually lost her Northampton North seat on an above average swing. This was not a propitious portent for Tatchell, now thrust into the position of being the first gay rights advocate to be standing as a mainstream party candidate.

Meanwhile, having initially lost out on his party's nomination, in September 1982 Simon Hughes became the Liberal candidate after the party's selection process was rerun in the wake of the formation of the Liberal–SDP Alliance. Then, in November, Mellish finally became Steward of the Chiltern Hundreds in order take up his paid position at the LDDC, thereby triggering the by-election.

Rather than keeping silent, let alone back Labour's nominee, Mellish supported the candidature of John O'Grady, former Labour leader of Southwark Council, who stood as the 'Real Bermondsey Labour' candidate. Labour's divisions in the constituency – and thus also nationally – were now clearly to become one of the key issues in the election campaign. Indeed, O'Grady proved to be one of no fewer than sixteen candidates, a new record high for any by-election.

That campaign was distinguished by two features. The first was widespread vilification and intimidation of Tatchell, through hate mail and phone calls, graffiti and physical attack, including at and on his home (most notably, a live bullet was posted through his letter box), together with a series of adverse tabloid news stories. The attacks were motivated in part by the status he had acquired as a symbol of an allegedly more left-wing Labour Party but more especially by his sexual orientation. In the press, for example, it was falsely suggested he had abandoned the Bermondsey campaign to attend the Gay Olympics in San Francisco. In another article, he was described as a 'rather exotic Australian canary who sings some odd songs'.

The innuendo was not confined to the press. Some of Tatchell's opponents, including Liberal activists, appeared willing to make his sexuality an issue too. For example, O'Grady was filmed touring the constituency on the back of a horse and cart, singing a song which referred to Tatchell 'wearing his trousers back to front'. Meanwhile, while out canvassing, some gay male Liberal campaigners allegedly sported a badge saying, 'I have been kissed by Peter Tatchell', a move that perhaps was intended as a joke but which, if so, appeared at least to be in poor taste. Similarly, in an attempt to persuade voters that their candidate had the best chance of defeating Tatchell, a Liberal leaflet was headlined: 'Simon Hughes: The Straight Choice', a headline that, in the circumstances, could be thought deliberately to convey a double meaning.

However, most controversial of all was a leaflet that was circulated anonymously. It juxtaposed two pictures, one of 'Her Majesty' Queen Elizabeth II in a regal pose, the other of '"Red Pete" Tatchell'. Above the two pictures ran the headline: 'Which Queen Will You Vote For?', and a text that, inter alia, referred to Tatchell's republican views and his decision to leave Australia in 1971 in order to avoid the draft for the Vietnam War. In short, the leaflet combined an oblique reference to Tatchell's sexual orientation with an attack on his political views. It has been suggested – but never confirmed – that the leaflet, which also gave details of Tatchell's home address and phone number, was the work of some associated with the Liberal campaign.

No fewer than four polls of vote intention were conducted during the campaign. The first, conducted by the NOP in early January, shortly before the by-election was called, put Labour well ahead, though its 47 per cent support represented a marked drop on the 64 per cent that Mellish had won in 1979, let alone the 70 per cent or more that he usually won in the constituency. As many as 37 per cent of those who had voted Labour in 1979 said they disapproved of the party's decision to nominate Tatchell. However, at this stage, it appeared that the opposition vote was divided, with both Hughes and O'Grady on around 20 per cent, leaving Labour still well ahead.

A second NOP poll released just over a week before polling day indicated, however, that Labour's lead had narrowed significantly during the campaign, while Hughes was now clearly ahead of both O'Grady and the Conservative candidate, Robert Hughes. Then an ORC poll five days later put the Liberal candidate neck and neck with Tatchell and it was evident that Hughes did have a serious chance of winning. Thereafter, a final poll released in *The Sun* on the eve of the poll indicated that Hughes had indeed now pulled ahead.

In short, this looked like a by-election in which the polls had an unusually important influence. Poll figures that showed Hughes had the best chance of defeating Tatchell seemingly helped persuade voters to back the Liberal candidate. Indeed, concern that this had been the case led Douglas Hoyle, who had only narrowly fended off a by-election challenge from the SDP two years earlier in Warrington, to introduce shortly after the by-election a Ten-Minute Rule Bill that would have banned the conduct and publication of polls of vote intentions during an election campaign. The pollsters themselves were inclined to downplay any suggestion that they had any undue influence and suggested they were simply registering changes of mind for which they were not necessarily responsible.

As the statistics at the start of the chapter show, Hughes not only won but did so in a record-breaking fashion. At 44.2 points, the 'swing' from Labour to Liberal Democrat, that is, the changes in the Labour and Liberal Democrat shares of the vote divided by two, was and still is the biggest swing ever to have been recorded in a UK by-election. It is also one of only three by-elections where the winning candidate increased their party's share of the vote by more than fifty points as compared with the previous general election. The publicity surrounding the contest also helped bring voters to the polls, with turnout only down marginally on the general election, much as had been the case in the other by-elections in the 1979–83 parliament where the Liberal–SDP Alliance had been serious contenders. Meanwhile, the challenge posed by the Real Bermondsey Labour candidate faded badly, though he did both manage to save his deposit and condemn the Conservatives into a rare fourth place, a far from discreditable performance for an independent candidate.

With the prospect of a general election in the offing, the Alliance hoped this remarkable by-election success would help revive the party's fortunes in the polls. Indeed, for a while it did. In the month following the by-election, the party stood at just under 30 per cent and was challenging Labour for second place. Meanwhile, doubts that many had about Michael Foot's ability to lead Labour into a successful general election campaign were only reinforced by the outcome, and the Labour leader, who had been deeply embarrassed by his inability to control developments in the constituency, found it necessary to issue a statement after the result was declared indicating his determination to fight the next election.

Indeed, after Bermondsey, it looked as though the Labour leader's fate would be determined by what happened in a by-election due to be held a month later in Darlington, a marginal Labour seat for which the Alliance now had high hopes. Yet in the event, the Alliance challenge there fizzled out and Labour retained the seat against the still second-placed Conservative candidate. The pressure on Foot eased, while support for the Alliance in the polls slipped back to where it had been before the Bermondsey contest. Spectacular though Hughes's success had been, ultimately it made little difference to the national political picture.

Yet it did have a long-term impact on the electoral politics of Bermondsey. Despite the constituency's strongly working-class character, Hughes not only retained the seat in the general election the following June but managed to turn it into a personal fiefdom, the only one of the four successful Alliance by-election candidates in the 1979–83 parliament to do so. He only eventually lost the seat (to Labour) in 2015 when support for the Liberal Democrats fell heavily across the country in the wake of its coalition with the Conservatives in the 2010–15 parliament.

Although not originally part of the Liberal Democrat ministerial team in the coalition (instead he became his party's deputy leader), Hughes did secure a role in government when he was appointed a Justice Minister in 2013. An attempt to regain his seat in 2017 ended in failure, and the constituency is now a safe Labour seat once more, albeit still with a substantial Liberal Democrat presence. Tatchell, meanwhile, forged a highly successful career as a human rights activist, both in the UK and abroad, including not least in campaigning for the civil partnership legislation that in 2005 afforded legal recognition of same-sex relationships. Public attitudes towards same-sex relationships (less than one in ten now think they are 'always wrong') are now very different from those that bedevilled Tatchell's candidacy in 1983.

There is, however, a poignant coda to this story. In January 2006, Hughes decided to stand for the leadership of the Liberal Democrats following the resignation of Charles Kennedy. Later that month, *The Sun* published evidence that Hughes, whose sexuality had long been the subject of speculation by others and evasion on his own part, had used a gay chat service. Hughes found himself forced to admit for the first time that he was bisexual, having had relationships in the past with both men and women.

Tatchell has stated he had been aware of Hughes's sexuality at the time of the Bermondsey by-election (he has also said he was propositioned by Mellish). Nevertheless, he had since accepted Hughes's apologies for the treatment that he, Tatchell, had suffered in that contest. Strikingly, in the wake of Hughes's admission that he was bisexual, Tatchell indicated that if he were a Liberal Democrat member, he would vote in the party's leadership contest for Hughes (who, in the event, came third). The two men have on several occasions shared public platforms on human rights issues and recollections of the Bermondsey by-election. Only one of them could be the winner of the Bermondsey by-election, but it was a battle that, perhaps, proved to be the making of both of them.

*Sir **John Curtice** is a professor of politics at the University of Strathclyde and senior fellow at the National Centre for Social Research and the 'UK in a Changing Europe' think tank. He has been a regular member of the BBC's election night team since 1979.*

60

DARLINGTON

24 MARCH 1983
LABOUR HOLD

FRANCIS BECKETT

Result: Ossie (Oswald) O'Brien (Labour), 20,544, 39.5 per cent; Michael Fallon (Conservative), 18,132, 34.9 per cent; Anthony Cook (SDP), 12,735, 24.5 per cent; David Sutch (Monster Raving Loony), 374, 0.7 per cent; Arthur Clark (Independent), 164, 0.3 per cent; Thomas Keen (Tactical Voting Annihilates Bennite Tatchellites), 27, 0.1 per cent; Jitendra Bardwaj (Yoga and Meditation), 15, 0.0 per cent; Peter Smith (Republican), 10, 0.0 per cent
Size of majority: 2,412
Swing: 1.3 per cent from Conservative to Labour
Name of previous MP and party: Edward Fletcher (Labour)
Reason for by-election: Death of incumbent
Result at previous general election: Edward Fletcher (Labour), 22,565, 45.5 per cent; Timothy Kirkhope (Conservative), 21,513, 43.4 per cent; K. Walker (Liberal), 5,054, 10.2 per cent; H. Outhwaite (National Front), 444, 0.9 per cent
Date by-election called: 25 February 1983
Date by-election took place: 24 March 1983
Size of total electorate: Approx. 65,000
Total number of votes cast: 52,001
Turnout: 66.6 per cent

After losing a previously safe seat, political parties tend to avoid presenting themselves to the electorate again any time soon. So after Labour's disaster in Bermondsey, everyone assumed that Chief

Whip Michael Cocks would delay moving the writ for the pending by-election in Darlington, hoping for better times. He could decide the timing because Labour had held the seat.

So when Cocks went straight to the House of Commons and ensured that Darlington would vote on 24 March 1983, exactly a month to the day after Bermondsey had inflicted a crushing defeat on his party, he caught everyone by surprise.

Cocks thought Bermondsey was so bad that his party had to show at once that it was a one-off. Darlington was as good a prospect as he could hope for: a northern seat, far from the metropolitan maelstrom, with the most reassuring of candidates already in place – a thoughtful, articulate, likeable 55-year-old local lecturer, a Catholic, a family man (code for 'not gay') with middle-of-the-road views, called Oswald (Ossie) O'Brien.

But it was a gamble. Darlington's long-standing Labour MP Ted Fletcher, who had died the previous month aged seventy-one, had a frail 1,052 vote majority over the Conservatives at the 1979 general election. The Liberals had come a decent third, and their vote was substantially bigger than Fletcher's majority.

Since then, four former Cabinet members had formed a breakaway from the Labour Party called the Social Democratic Party (SDP), and they had an alliance with the Liberals. The Liberals had fought and won Bermondsey, so it was the SDP's turn to fight Darlington. Their candidate was a popular and charismatic Tyne Tees television presenter called Tony Cook, with an easy, folksy manner and the local following that only a regional TV personality could muster.

The smart money was on Cook, but the Conservatives were also in it to win, fielding a clever and fluent 31-year-old Conservative Party researcher, Michael Fallon.

Michael Cocks's decision caught the Conservatives and SDP by surprise, as it was intended to, but it also caught out Labour's own director of communications, Nick Grant, who was instantly on the phone to me, to ask if I happened to be free to spend the next month in Darlington, as Labour's press officer. I was a freelance journalist but had handled by-elections for Labour before.

So, if I had nothing particular to do that afternoon, would I kindly get on a train to Darlington at once, if not sooner, as there was a press conference to launch the campaign the following morning and no one there had ever dealt with national media?

I stayed that night with the agent, Terry Johnston, and borrowed a clean shirt from him to chair the press conference.

I found a fluent, clever and humorous candidate and an efficient agent, Terry Johnston. Labour leader Michael Foot sent us a safe pair of hands to manage the campaign, the experienced and reassuringly right-wing Copeland MP Jack Cunningham.

Labour had to win. Foot's leadership would surely go down if we lost, and it might take the party with it. And if Labour lost to the Liberal–SDP Alliance, there was a real possibility that they would replace Labour as the alternative governing party in Britain.

Labour's route to victory lay in destroying the Alliance momentum – even if that helped the Conservatives. So there was the occasional discreet conversation between Jack and his Tory counterpart, and me and mine, about isolating the Alliance and undermining its candidate.

Labour strategists were, therefore, surprisingly cheerful when they found that the Conservative campaign, though low-key, was effective and well organised, and Michael Fallon was an able and well-briefed candidate.

The Alliance strategy was rather similar. As SDP founder Bill Rodgers has written: 'Our best hope was always to push one of the old parties into third place and then collapse their vote.'

An opinion poll taken two days after the Bermondsey result showed the Alliance in the lead, and a fortnight later on 9 March, *The Times* reported: 'SDP man slightly ahead.' Yet I do not remember a moment, in all our many daily conversations, when either I, or Ossie, or Jack or Terry thought it at all likely. All four of us believed we were going to win.

The BBC's Vincent Hanna, at that time the face of by-elections, rode into the town like a conquering hero. His enemies said that Hanna was full of his own cleverness, which was true, but he did have a lot of cleverness to be full of. In Darlington, he was to play an even bigger role than usual.

He once told me that politicians were invented for his amusement, and he enjoyed making candidates look foolish. On his own admission, he failed with the Conservative: Michael Fallon was a pro. Why, said Vincent, did Fallon not sit on the terraces at lowly Darlington Football Club?

'I do.'

'When was the last time?'

'In November.'

'What was the game?'

'Darlington v. Bury.'

'What was the score?

'It was 2–1. Darlington scored first.'

But he found it disconcertingly easy to make Tony Cook look foolish. Cook was not the first broadcaster to suppose that his presentational skills would see him through in politics. He was not on top of policy and floundered badly in his early press conferences on such matters as railways and health, at one point telling Hanna to 'sod off'.

Cook thought Hanna was his nemesis and that Hanna was working for Labour. I met Cook in the street outside my hotel once, and he almost begged me to call Hanna off. I knew Hanna well – we were both on the executive of the National Union of Journalists. But I had not set Hanna on him and could not call him off even if I wanted to.

Cook's problem was not Hanna. His shaky grasp of policy was reported in detail by top-class local newspaper journalists and by Peter Dodson of Radio Cleveland. I watched him, with Fallon and O'Brien, face an audience of local sixth formers. Fallon and O'Brien gave detailed policy answers to their questions. Cook talked down to them, and you could feel the resentment in the room.

Labour's vulnerability was the left, identified in people's minds with the party's unsuccessful candidate in Bermondsey, Peter Tatchell, and with the Trotskyite Militant Tendency. The SDP tried hard to capitalise on this, rushing to the newspapers whenever they spotted a known Militant giving out Labour leaflets.

The *Daily Express* tried to help, sending Peter Hitchens to Darlington to search for Militant. Each morning, Peter would try to hijack Labour's morning press conference. If he could get Ossie or our visiting frontbencher to say something – anything – about Militant or engage in yet another exchange on defence policy (where Labour was vulnerable), that could be presented as the main story of the day. I chaired the press conferences, and I saw it as my job to stop him. The resulting exchanges were described by Vincent Hanna in an article in *The Journalist*:

> Francis would splutter at him for several minutes and Hitchens would wonder why he never won. I explained that Francis is the best splutter-er in the business; he has medals for it. When President of the NUJ he would outsplutter NEC troublemakers like me for hours at a time. 'Is there no way to silence him?' asked Hitchens.

One day, Hitchens wrote triumphantly that he had found a notice on the Labour headquarters noticeboard advertising a Militant meeting. That afternoon Terry Johnston told me, 'I've taken down that Militant notice.' I said, 'Please put it back up, in exactly the same place as before.' The next morning, Peter arrived at the press conference and went straight to the noticeboard. His face fell when he saw the notice was still there. Its precipitate absence was to have been his story.

'Still there,' I said, a little smugly. Peter, who is a courteous man, smiled and congratulated me.

Darlington was almost certain to be the last by-election before the next general election. It was thought to be the Alliance's one chance to break the mould, and Labour's one chance to stop them. It really mattered.

So everyone pulled the stops out. Labour flooded the place with canvassers, in a way that neither the Conservatives nor the SDP could match. The trade unions rallied round – the unions still thought of the Labour Party as part of their movement, in a way that they ceased to do during the Blair years. Bill Rodgers writes that Labour 'fought a skilful campaign with massive resources ... At times, it seemed as if every full-time trade union official was in Darlington, complete with a Granada 2.3.'

The big guns from all three parties were wheeled in, put in front of press conferences, then sent out onto the streets, and in the evenings they addressed big meetings in the town. Many of them visited the

Shildon railway engineering works, where 2,000 jobs were threatened under a British Rail closure plan. Labour and the SDP promised to save it, and the government produced a plan that was supposed to save some of it (but didn't).

Former Prime Minister Jim Callaghan came and told everyone who would listen that he was there 'because Ossie O'Brien is my sort of Labour candidate'.

Drawing the biggest crowds in March 1983 was a very new member of Labour's shadow Cabinet, just then the most exciting politician in Britain – Labour's education spokesman, Neil Kinnock.

A short, sturdy, noisy young man with ginger hair and a loud hounds-tooth suit stepped smartly off the London train, borrowed £5 from me and took everyone he found in the nearby party headquarters to the pub. In Darlington in 1983, you could buy a substantial round of drinks with £5.

In the pub, he did not stop talking for a moment. A stream of ideas tumbled out of him, each one perfectly wrapped in an evocative phrase.

Eventually, we dragged him across to the biggest hall in town, which seated hundreds and was packed out. He spoke for a full hour, making his audience laugh and cry in turn. 'Now, the Cabinet wets – by the way, do you know why they call them that? It's because that's what they do when she shouts at them.'

Then I took him to a private room and whispered that I had overheard a plot to get rid of Michael Foot. He buoyed me with his optimism, and for a good five minutes we both believed that soon Michael Foot would be Prime Minister.

In the end, Labour had everything it hoped for from Darlington. The Tories came second and the Alliance a poor third.

Everyone had been pretty sure for a few days, and I had been under siege from Vincent and ITN's David Walter, each wanting to get the winning candidate on air first. I opted for Vincent, and told David so, which led to an unseemly scrimmage as Ossie came off the platform. ITN technicians blocked my way with cables and started to push me out of the way, while David took Ossie's arm.

But we had told Ossie to follow Nita Clarke, whom Labour HQ had sent to Darlington for the last couple of days to help me. She led

Ossie to Vincent. I was able to join them a few minutes later and shepherd Ossie round at least a dozen television and radio interviews, in the order in which I had scheduled them.

The myth has grown up that Vincent Hanna delivered it for Labour. But Cook's deficiencies as a candidate would have been apparent without Vincent, and the SDP attempt to make Labour look extreme was always going to founder on the rock in the middle of the road called Ossie O'Brien.

Would things have been different with a better Alliance candidate? Probably not. Bermondsey had been fought on what we now call culture wars. Darlington was supremely uninterested in culture wars and only needed reassuring that Labour was too.

At the time, I felt elated and grateful that I had been given a major part to play in saving from oblivion the party I had first joined as a student at the end of the 1960s. But three months later, Labour was crushingly defeated in the general election, and I wonder if Darlington really made much difference.

It saved Michael Foot's leadership. I overheard the plotting from visiting frontbenchers and knew that a defeat at Darlington would mean a challenge to Foot. There is no knowing where that might have led – perhaps to Denis Healey becoming leader and a rather less crushing defeat in the general election.

It almost certainly caused Margaret Thatcher to call the 1983 general election, because it showed her that Labour was on the road to recovery. She did not have to go to the country until May 1984, but she was returned with a massive majority in June 1983.

Was Darlington the reason the Alliance never replaced Labour as the party of opposition? I think not. Bermondsey really was a one-off, a shout of rage, like Orpington in 1962.

Ossie O'Brien was an MP for just seven weeks, losing Darlington to the Conservatives in Labour's general election rout in June. He went on to work for Alcohol Concern and contributed to the literature on the problem of drugs in society. He died in 1997, a month short of his sixty-ninth birthday.

Michael Fallon had a distinguished career. He defeated O'Brien at the general election and held the seat until 1992 when he lost it to

Labour's Alan Milburn. He returned to the House of Commons as MP for Sevenoaks in 1997, held a succession of government posts, got into the Cabinet and stood down at the 2019 general election.

And Tony Cook? During the by-election, he told Vincent Hanna that if he lost, he would try to negotiate his job at Tyne Tees back. If he tried, he seems to have failed, and he is thought to have immersed himself in local voluntary projects. You cannot find him by putting 'Tony Cook' into Google. But if you put in 'Tony Cook Darlington', you get Vincent Hanna's Wikipedia page.

Francis Beckett is a journalist, author and playwright. His books include biographies of four Prime Ministers – Attlee, Macmillan, Blair and Brown – and a biography of 1956. His most recent play is MEGA – Make England Great Again, *about a future election won by the Britons First Party.*

61

CHESTERFIELD

1 MARCH 1984
LABOUR HOLD

GREG ROSEN

Result: Tony Benn (Labour), 24,633, 46.5 per cent; Max Payne (Liberal), 18,369, 34.7 per cent; Nick Bourne (Conservative), 8,028, 15.2 per cent; Bill Maynard (Independent Labour), 1,355, 2.6 per cent; David Sutch (Monster Raving Loony), 178, 0.3 per cent; David Bentley (Four-Wheel Drive Hatchback Road Safety), 116, 0.2 per cent; John Davey (Independent), 83, 0.3 per cent; Thomas Layton (Independent Ecology), 46, 0.1 per cent; Helen Anscomb (Independent – Freight on Rails Not Roads), 34, 0.1 per cent; Jitendra Bardwaj (Yoga and Meditation), 33, 0.1 per cent; Donald Butler (Independent – Buy Your Chesterfield in Thame), 24, 0.1 per cent; Paul Nicholls-Jones (The Welshman), 22, 0.0 per cent; Sid Shaw (Elvisly Yours Elvis Presley), 20, 0.0 per cent; Christopher Hill (I Am Not a Number), 17, 0.0 per cent; Giancarlo Piccaro (Acne), 15, 0.0 per cent; David Cahill (Re-classify The Sun Newspaper a Comic), 12, 0.0 per cent; John Connell (Peace), 7, 0.0 per cent
Size of majority: 6,264
Swing: 7.9 per cent from Labour to Liberal/Alliance
Name of previous MP and party: Eric Varley (Labour)
Reason for by-election: Resignation on being appointed CEO of Coalite
Result at previous general election: Eric Varley (Labour), 23,881, 48.1 per cent; Nick Bourne (Conservative), 23,881, 32.4 per cent; Max Payne, 9,705, 19.5 per cent
Date by-election called: 6 February 1984
Date by-election took place: 1 March 1984
Size of total electorate: 68,942

Total number of votes cast: 52,992
Turnout: 76.9 per cent

The 1984 Chesterfield by-election was won by Tony Benn with a majority of 6,264 votes over the runner-up, Liberal candidate Max Payne. Yet it symbolised Benn's greatest defeat.

Less than a year earlier, Benn had considered himself Britain's next Prime Minister but one. If Labour lost the 1983 general election, the ageing Michael Foot would retire, and Benn was best placed to succeed. Labour now conducted its leadership elections under a new electoral college that had actually been crafted by Benn's supporters specifically to benefit their candidate. So long as he hung on to Labour's leadership long enough, his supporters believed that the alienation of voters from Mrs Thatcher's divisive government would make a Benn premiership inevitable. In the unlikely event that Labour actually won the election, if Foot didn't retire swiftly, he could be ejected. The 1980 defenestration of Labour's victorious GLC leader Andrew McIntosh and replacement by Ken Livingstone was regarded by commentators as precedent for such a move. What could possibly go wrong?

Voters gave Benn his answer. At the June 1983 general election, the electorate rejected Labour, and in Benn's constituency of Bristol East, voters dumped him for his Tory opponent Jonathan Sayeed. Benn, out of Parliament, was ineligible for any leadership election. Michael Foot resigned swiftly, giving his charismatic young Bevanite protégé Neil Kinnock a run at the leadership without Benn in the contest. Benn could but watch as the Kinnock bandwagon hoovered up votes across Labour's centre and left. With most trade unions endorsing a 'dream ticket' of Kinnock and his Gaitskellite rival Roy Hattersley in either combination of leader and deputy, the vainglorious leadership candidature of Benn's ally Eric Heffer served only to highlight the political weakness of Labour's hard left without a parliamentary champion of Benn's charisma and celebrity.

Labour's 1983 leadership election saw Kinnock triumph with more than 71 per cent of the electoral college vote. Hattersley secured 19 per cent, but Heffer managed 6 per cent. Benn was the future once. To be so again, he needed to crowbar himself back into Parliament. He had done it before, when his father's death in 1960 had forced Anthony Wedgwood Benn, as he then styled himself, to accept the Viscountcy of Stansgate and the seat in the House of Lords that came with it, threatening to derail his prospering political career. Only by changing Britain's constitution to allow hereditary peerages to be disclaimed could Benn return to the Commons. To secure such constitutional change was unprecedented. Undaunted, Benn doggedly pursued constitutional change, and the Conservative government helped out – passing a law in 1963 that enabled Benn to return to the House of Commons. The helping hand of Labour's new Prime Minister Harold Wilson gave Benn ministerial office and responsibility for putting the white heat into the technological revolution. Soon 'Wedge Benn of Min-Tech' was renowned for his championing of Concorde, hovercraft and atomic power – a household name tipped for future leadership.

Ironically in view of the public persona he later crafted as a rebel, Benn built his political career as a consummate insider, a minister throughout the Wilson and Callaghan governments, burnishing his leadership credentials all the way. To fall at the last hurdle, to be prevented from standing for the leadership under the electoral college he and his supporters had specifically engineered to favour his chances – it could not be allowed to stand. He had to get back into Parliament. And while the voters of Bristol might have thwarted him, the rivalries of Westminster insider politics gave Benn a ladder back to Parliament.

Benn secured the advance tip-off available only to a Westminster insider from the Chief Whip Michael Cocks (who was seeking revenge, having fallen out with new leader Neil Kinnock), that Chesterfield MP Eric Varley intended to resign his seat to accept a job in business. Benn phoned a friend: miners' union leader Arthur Scargill. Benn's diary entry of 11 November 1983 recounts that Scargill 'had a word with Peter Heathfield, who is a member of the GMC [General Management Committee] of the Chesterfield Party' and then telephoned Benn back to tell him, 'You must move quickly. We will get statements put out in the constituency to the effect that they will like you, and you must be ready to say that you would be pleased to respond.' Benn was nervous, recounting to his diary on 13 November:

Current opinion in Chesterfield is that the GMC will be 60–40 against my candidature, and the word is spreading that if I was the candidate Labour would lose the seat. On the other hand work is going on. The AUEW [engineering union – now part of Unite] is being approached, and Chesterfield is a good left-wing district council.

Even in 1983, there was a perceived advantage for a local candidate over those seeking to parachute in from afar, so on 18 November Benn

decided to do a bit of research on Chesterfield. I thought to myself: I wonder if I have got any local connections with Chesterfield. So I went to the family tree that Debrett's had produced and discovered that my grandfather, my great-grandparents and my great-great-grandparents were all born within a 45-mile radius of Chesterfield.

His diary is silent on whether rival candidates also enjoyed the assistance of Debrett's handy guides to local antecedents.

Nevertheless, despite the assistance of Debrett's, Benn was clearly worried that not all Labour's leading players shared Scargill's enthusiasm for him. Benn wrote a letter to Neil Kinnock protesting at press reports that Kinnock was 'working to prevent my selection for Chesterfield' which he took to Labour's national executive meeting, intending to deliver it by hand. Kinnock's failure to appreciate the virtue of Benn's candidature may have been shared by inanimate objects, as on the way to the NEC meeting, Benn recounted to his diary, 'I got stuck in the lift … which was slightly frightening', but like a good cub-scout, Benn 'managed to force the door with a penknife'. Sabotage continued throughout the day: 'At home, in the office Julie was struggling with the word processor … both my telephones were out of action and I discovered I hadn't paid the bill.' It was all a great burden for the people's champion. And it got worse. On 11 December, Benn 'caught the train to Chesterfield to meet party members. The train didn't actually stop in Chesterfield station but went straight through, then halted…' Not to be thwarted, the ever-resourceful Benn 'opened the carriage door and jumped onto the line and walked back half a mile. I couldn't afford to be late.'

Having triumphed against the forces of British Telecom and British

Rail, barely a couple of days later Benn records in his diary the attempts of the media to sabotage his candidature, principally the BBC and *The Guardian*:

> *Newsnight* had a programme on the Chesterfield by-election including a poll ... It is clear that they are trying to prevent Chesterfield from selecting me. The purpose of the poll, financed partly by *The Guardian* and *Newsnight*, was to suggest that, although it was a safe Labour seat, if I was the candidate it would become a three-way marginal.

On 6 January, Benn was shocked to receive a telephone tip-off 'after midnight' that Chesterfield Executive Committee had not shortlisted him. 'So I rang [nearby MP] Dennis Skinner, who said he would talk to people in Chesterfield,' Benn recorded. Within forty-eight hours, Benn had been added to the shortlist. 'Observers in the selection conference [15 January] noted that when a delegate had a sudden epileptic fit during his speech the candidate instantly checked his stop-watch to keep a check on stoppage time while the man received help,' the *Politicos' Dictionary of Labour Biography* reveals. Benn won; his defeated rivals included Chesterfield Council leader Bill Flanagan, later national chairman of the Coalfield Communities Campaign. Decades later, Flanagan's *Guardian* obituary declared Flanagan 'probably contributed more to the regeneration of Britain's coalfield communities than any other single person'.

Now that he was candidate, Benn told Kinnock he wanted the by-election as soon as possible, and they agreed on 1 March. Chesterfield was the first by-election since Kinnock had become Labour's leader that October. At Penrith, in July 1983, the only other by-election since the general election, the Liberals had almost seized victory from the incumbent Conservatives, while Labour lost its deposit. At Chesterfield, the Liberal–SDP Alliance were out to steal the seat, hoping the high-profile candidature of such a totemic left-winger as Benn would generate countervailing enthusiasm for their candidate. Phil Woolas, later Labour MP and minister and then the Labour candidate for NUS president, spoke alongside Benn at Chesterfield campaign rallies. Woolas recalls: 'Had we lost the by-election, the Alliance would have been in a very strong position, either leading to defections to SDP or swifter modernisation.'

But Chesterfield was less demographically propitious for the Alliance than Penrith or other seats where the Alliance had surged. Chesterfield was a compact market town of traditional brick-built terraces and semis, making cars unnecessary for campaigning. Labour's campaign HQ was at the offices of the Derbyshire National Union of Mineworkers, in the centre of town next to the football stadium. Most homes were rented from the council and Coal Board. 'Not wealthy but well kept,' recalls John Mann, later a Labour MP and peer, who as the then chair of the National Organisation of Labour Students (NOLS) organised many of the campaign activists. In addition to mining, other dominant local employers tended to be large shift-based workplaces, especially engineering, with strong trade union organisation.

Andy McSmith, subsequently a leading lobby journalist and author, was then a Labour HQ press officer and seconded to Benn's press team. He remembers Labour's regional organiser Peter Coleman as 'very effective' and the campaign's media chief Monica Foot (ex-wife of journalist Paul, the nephew of Michael) as a seasoned professional. 'Kinnock feared Benn's return but feared loss of a by-election this early in his leadership even more,' McSmith recalls. 'So he wanted Benn to win.' Far from Labour's leadership being out to sabotage Benn, they were concerned he would sabotage himself.

Nevertheless, Benn didn't trust Labour's official apparatus and fell out with Monica Foot early on. Benn had a parallel operation with support from Ken Livingstone's team, including GLC chief press secretary Nita Clarke, who was seconded to the campaign.

A massive campaign advantage for Labour was the sheer scale of Labour activists visiting the constituency: 'We were able to spend an hour on the doorstep,' recalled John Mann, who describes the campaign as a traditional 'Mikardo system election done well'. Labour campaigners could engage voters in miners' welfare and pubs and clubs, many of whom worked routine-based shifts. 'I was going into people's houses to persuade them, sitting down and having cups of tea, that's how we got turnout so high,' recalls Mann. Moreover, the scale of mainstream Labour activists prevented Militant from hijacking Labour's campaign.

The Liberals weren't able to match the numbers of Labour activists and their leaflet-based campaign proved less effective. Unable to compete with Labour's 'ground game', the media began to sense Liberal momentum slipping, and wider media coverage became framed through that lens. Liberal leader David Steel garnered unflattering media coverage trying on a punk wig he had been handed at a haircut awards ceremony in London.

While Labour's campaign was focused and effective, the candidate was less so. Mann recalls Benn 'spending afternoons doing radio interviews with foreign media' and 'pushing international politics and CND, neither of which were vote winners'. But Benn was an A-list celebrity. He was a 'name' that voters had heard of above and beyond politics, 'not a left-wing celebrity but a celebrity', recalls Mann. 'Somebody beats nobody,' McSmith recalls: 'Benn was a celebrity and the Liberal candidate was not. Benn had "star quality".'

In previous by-elections, it had been usual for the candidates to hold daily press conferences. 'I refused to hold press conferences,' Benn's diary records, 'obliging the "media circus" to follow us round the constituency as we canvassed and addressed public meetings.' In one meeting, Benn publicly claimed BBC *Newsnight*'s Vincent Hanna (who was married to the daughter of SDLP founder Gerry Fitt) was 'the SDP candidate for Chesterfield and wanted a Liberal victory'. Hanna was furious. Benn claimed he was trying to pre-empt hostile media by attacking a prominent journalist.

It was the era of rallies, not yet of debates. The highlight saw Labour's former deputy leader Denis Healey join Benn on the platform. Double the hall capacity turned up, leaving many stuck outside. At the rally, Labour's general secretary Jim Mortimer gave himself the central chair on the platform, between Healey and Benn. As a media pro and former BBC journalist himself, Benn wanted TV pictures of himself and Healey next to each other. When Mortimer stood up to introduce the speakers, Benn nipped into the middle chair. A witness recalls that Mortimer didn't notice and sat down on Benn's lap. Healey, in his speech, said, 'Tony and I are like Torvill and Dean of politics', at which point a huge banner collapsed behind them. But Labour's campaign soldiered on to victory.

While Max Payne was Benn's most challenging opponent, he was not the most famous: TV actor and celebrity Bill Maynard stood against Benn as Independent Labour but would garner only 2.6 per cent of the vote. Phil Woolas recalls bigger TV celebrities canvassing for Benn: Cherie Blair's father Tony Booth and *Corrie*'s Pat Phoenix.

Other candidates secured still fewer votes than Maynard, including Monster Raving Loony chief David Sutch and a local furniture shop owner campaigning for 'a Chesterfield for Chesterfield'.

They all failed. But so, strategically, did Benn. Benn's diary records Chesterfield as 'a triumph for the left and showed that socialist policies are not a deterrent'. But his hope that his Chesterfield victory would restore his trajectory to greater power proved misplaced. Benn returned to Parliament a backbench passenger in a Labour Party where Neil Kinnock and his team were firmly in the driving seat.

During the Chesterfield campaign, Benn was challenged on his leadership ambitions by the media. Woolas recalls that Benn promised that he wouldn't run against Kinnock if elected, though he refused to rule out running against deputy leader Roy Hattersley. In 1988, Benn nevertheless ran for Labour's leadership against Kinnock and was over-whelmingly defeated. Far from being the candidate of working people, Benn found trade unions underwhelmed by his disloyalty: they backed Kinnock by 99.2 per cent to 0.8 per cent.

Of all the Chesterfield candidates, only one subsequently achieved power: Tory Nick Bourne, who in the by-election came third. In the Blair era, he became leader of the Conservative Group in the Welsh Assembly and subsequently a lord and Tory minister at Westminster 2015–19. Benn became president of the Stop the War Coalition. Speaking to *Socialist Review* in 2007, Benn said: 'I would be ashamed if I thought I'd ever said anything I didn't believe to get on, but making mistakes is part of life, isn't it?'

Greg Rosen *is a senior counsel at SEC Newgate UK and a Labour histori-an. His books include* Serving the People, Old Labour to New *(Politico, 2005) and Politico's* Dictionary of Labour Biography. *A former vice-chair of the Fabians and visiting fellow at Goldsmiths, University of London, he is chair of the Labour History Group.*

62

GREENWICH

NIGEL FLETCHER

Result: Rosie Barnes (SDP), 18,287, 53.0 per cent; Deirdre Wood (Labour), 11,676, 33.8 per cent; John Antcliffe (Conservative), 3,852, 11.2 per cent; Graham Bell (Green), 264, 0.8 per cent; Malcolm Hardee (Rainbow Dream Ticket), 124, 0.3 per cent; Ian Dell (BNP), 116, 0.3 per cent; Joe Pearce (National Front), 103, 0.3 per cent; Kate Marshall (Revolutionary Communist), 91, 0.3 per cent
Size of majority: 6,611
Swing: 16.1 per cent Labour to SDP
Name of previous MP and party: Guy Barnett (Labour)
Reason for by-election: Death of incumbent
Result at previous general election: Guy Barnett (Labour), 13,361, 38.2 per cent; Arthur Rolfe (Conservative), 12,150, 34.8 per cent; Timothy Ford (SDP), 8,783, 25.1 per cent; Ian Dell (BNP), 259, 0.7 per cent; Ronald Mallone (Fellowship), 242, 0.7 per cent; F. Hooks (Communist), 149, 0.4 per cent
Date by-election called: 3 February 1987
Date by-election took place: 26 February 1987
Size of total electorate: 50,637
Total number of votes cast: 34,513
Turnout: 68.2 per cent

I might be biased, but I can't help thinking that Greenwich, the town and borough, has a unique place in the political history of the United Kingdom. From the late fifteenth century, when the Tudor palace was built by the river, it has frequently been the site of high politics and low plotting. During the turbulent reigns of Henry VIII, Mary Tudor and Elizabeth I, it was at the absolute centre of the country's governance. Later, in the nineteenth century, its riverside taverns became noted political salons, with Tory and Liberal leaders venturing down the river from Westminster to enjoy regular whitebait suppers with their senior colleagues and formulate their plans for the parliamentary session.

From 1868, Greenwich was represented in Parliament by the Prime Minister himself, William Gladstone, though in common with most MPs of the time, he never lived there. In more recent times, the town has seen one of its actual residents achieve the highest office, albeit briefly. After a year as Foreign Secretary, Liz Truss became Prime Minister in 2022 and moved with her family from their home in Greenwich to 10 Downing Street. Her ill-fated economic plans had been formulated during walks in Greenwich Park with the man she would appoint as her Chancellor, Kwasi Kwarteng, who also lived nearby. When her tenure ended after just forty-nine days, it was to Greenwich that she returned.

As a parliamentary constituency, it has also had more than its fair share of by-elections. In the three decades between 1846 and 1873, it saw no fewer than seven of them, through a mixture of the deaths, resignations and appointments to office of incumbent MPs. It was then nearly a century before the next one occurred in 1971, when Labour's Richard Marsh resigned to become chairman of British Rail. His replacement, Guy Barnett, successfully held the seat and served as Greenwich's MP for the next fifteen years, until his untimely death on Christmas Eve 1986 necessitated another by-election.

That campaign, in February 1987, would attract significant attention from the national media and become one of the best-remembered such contests in the post-war period. It would deliver a shock to the political system, with the Social Democratic Party (SDP) overtaking both the Conservatives and Labour to win the seat. Their stunning victory would stoke predictions of a surge in support for the SDP–Liberal Alliance and raise expectations of a breakthrough for the party at the looming general election.

Having been a Labour-held seat for decades, much media speculation immediately turned on who would be that party's choice to defend the seat. With Neil Kinnock having made his battle with the hard left a defining theme of his leadership, it was seen as an important test of his modernising agenda. Guy Barnett had been a moderate, but the local party in Greenwich now tended leftwards. A number of likely left-wing contenders were mentioned, including former Lambeth Council leader Ted Knight, trade union official (and future Corbynite NEC member) Peter Willsman, and former GLC member Valerie Wise. Some reports also suggested that local Greenwich councillor Eddie McPartland, a 'staunch Marxist' and supporter of the Militant Tendency, could also stand.

However, most early media reports identified the most likely left-wing candidate as Deirdre Wood, a member of the Inner London Education Authority who had previously stood unsuccessfully against Guy Barnett at his mandatory reselection meeting. She was on the hard left and had been a member of the GLC, where she had supported Ken Livingstone in numerous controversial causes, including welcoming members of Sinn Féin for tea at County Hall during the IRA's bombing campaign. Such credentials led one local observer in December 1986 to predict that if she was selected, it would be 'worth several hundred votes to the SDP'. It turned out to be rather more than that.

The Labour selection was delayed until after Guy Barnett's funeral, and during the next few weeks, other names entered the fray, including the MEP Richard Balfe and the chair of the London Labour Party, Glenys Thornton, a moderate who was close to Kinnock and viewed as the leadership's favoured candidate. But in the end, it was Deirdre Wood who comfortably won the selection at the start of February, to the obvious delight of the other parties, whose representatives openly speculated that her views and record would alienate voters and damage Labour's chances.

One of those making this prediction was the local SDP candidate, Rosie Barnes, who was quoted saying Wood's selection 'can only do us an enormous amount of good'. Barnes herself was a forty-year-old professional market researcher who had lived in Greenwich for sixteen years and whose husband Graham was an SDP councillor in the borough. She had only been selected for the seat a couple of months before, after the previous candidate Timothy Ford stood down, complaining that he was receiving no support from the party nationally and was effectively a paper candidate. The SDP had instead been concentrating its efforts on the neighbouring constituency of Woolwich, where it had a sitting MP, John Cartwright. In Greenwich, the SDP had come a respectable third in 1983, with Ford polling 8,783 votes (25 per cent of the vote).

But it was the local Conservatives who, on paper, were the main challengers to Labour, having come within 1,211 votes (and 3.4 points) of winning the seat. They also had a new candidate, with the previous contender, Arthur Rolfe, having chosen not to seek reselection the previous summer. To replace him, members had selected 25-year-old John Antcliffe, a Greenwich councillor for the Blackheath ward, who had grown up in nearby Eltham and been active in the local Young Conservatives before going to Cambridge University. After graduation, he had gone to work in the City and by the time of the election was a financial adviser at the merchant bank Rothschild's. He was also gay, though in the homophobic climate of the 1980s, this was not something he felt able to disclose publicly. He was nevertheless pointedly referred to as 'a bachelor' or 'unmarried' in many media reports, while others focused on his youth and status as a 'City whizzkid'.

As regards the smaller parties, Graham Bell, an electrician from Lee Green, was selected by the Green Party and Kate Marshall by the Revolutionary Communist Party. On the far right, voters would have a choice between the British National Party's Ian Dell and the National Front, who selected one of their Barking activists (as it were), Joe Pearce. The traditional by-election role of joke candidate was provided, rather literally, by Malcolm Hardee, an anarchic local comedian who ran a comedy club next to the Blackwall Tunnel in East Greenwich. He became the candidate for the 'Rainbow Dream Ticket, Beer, Fags and Skittles Party' and would later publish an autobiography claiming that in 1986 he and others were questioned after he stole Freddie Mercury's fortieth birthday cake. By an odd coincidence, he would not be the only candidate for whom a fortieth birthday cake would cause trouble.

As the party holding the seat, the timing of the by-election was in the hands of the Labour Party, and their by-election team had

convened at the start of January to discuss possible dates. They decided to go for 5 March, or 26 February if the Liberals/Alliance chose
that date for the pending Truro by-election (which they did). The fact
the Labour candidate was not due to be chosen for several weeks did
not hold things up, and the party got on with securing a campaign
HQ (the old Co-Op at 17 Old Dover Road), commissioning a private
poll of the constituency from MORI and drafting a special edition of
'Greenwich Labour News' to go out to households the following week.
Relations with the local constituency Labour Party were described as
'excellent', and the by-election was given top priority by the leadership,
who recognised that a good result would be an important boost to the
party's prospects ahead of the general election.

From the outset, it was Labour's to lose. The private poll they commissioned showed 52 per cent of respondents planning to vote Labour,
with the Conservatives on 28 per cent and the SDP–Liberal Alliance
trailing on 18 per cent. A Harris poll for *The Observer* published on 11
January had an even more emphatic result – Labour on 60 per cent,
with the Conservatives on 25 per cent and the SDP–Liberal Alliance
on 15 per cent. This would have translated into a huge 10,000 majority
and suggested that Labour was set to romp home in the contest.

How on earth, then, did they manage to lose? Much of the blame
must fall on their selection of Deirdre Wood, who proved to be as
much of a gift to her opponents as they had predicted. This combined
with other factors to generate what one historian has called a 'perfect
storm' for the SDP to prevail. It was not all of their own making, but
it provided them with an opportunity which they were able to exploit
to the fullest.

Certainly, the SDP ran a slick and effective campaign, with the
party's national organiser Alec McGivan using it as a testbed for new
campaigning techniques he had imported from America. The local
campaign benefited from an influx of volunteers, with up to 150 activists a day flooding into the seat, and these were sent out onto the
doorsteps from early in the campaign, enabling 70 per cent of the constituency to be canvassed. The data harvested allowed highly person-
alised computer-generated letters to be targeted at individual voters,
matching key campaign messages to those likely to be most receptive

to them. Such ruthless targeting is now well understood by the best political strategists (and has indeed been used to good effect by local Conservatives in recent successful Greenwich Council by-election campaigns), but at the time the novelty of this 'high-tech' operation led to much media comment during and after the campaign.

The SDP also had the significant benefit of a candidate who was local, down to earth and personable. In the glare of an intensive media spotlight, Barnes became familiar to the local electorate in a way that few candidates can hope to match, and the more voters saw of her, the more they seemed to like her. This was reflected in the media coverage, which contrasted her easy manner and moderate appeal with her Labour opponent's hard-left reputation and awkwardness in front of the cameras.

For the Conservatives, the campaign was an opportunity to paint Labour as an unreconstructed, extreme party. John Antcliffe responded to the selection of Deirdre Wood by saying she was 'a classic representative of the loony left within the Labour party' whose views were 'totally alien to those of traditional Labour voters'. This message was heavily reinforced by a barrage of negative media coverage highlighting the left-wing positions taken by Wood and her husband, a trade union official, with the *Daily Mail* dubbing them 'Mr and Mrs Hard Left'.

As campaigning formally got underway, a constituency poll for the BBC's *Newsnight* showed Labour still comfortably in the lead, on 48 per cent, with the Conservatives and SDP vying for second place on 26 per cent and 24 per cent, respectively. The parties each deployed heavy hitters to the streets of Greenwich from the start: SDP leader Dr David Owen arrived to support Rosie Barnes, Conservative Party chairman Norman Tebbit joined John Antcliffe and Labour's deputy leader Roy Hattersley put on a show of support for Deirdre Wood, smoothing over media questions about her views on NATO and being photographed helping her cut a birthday cake to celebrate her fortieth birthday. This innocuous-looking stunt backfired later in the campaign when, in a peculiar development, Wood was accused in the press of 'fibbing' about her age, and Labour was forced to admit that their candidate was in fact forty-four years old.

After a week of campaigning and sustained media coverage, the contest reached a crucial turning point as a series of new polls showed Labour's lead slipping further. Neil Kinnock was reported to have 'hit the panic button' at the news and ordered every available Labour MP to hit the doorsteps in Greenwich. In a delicious coincidence, these headlines appeared on the very day Deirdre Wood was being joined on the campaign trail by *Dad's Army* actor Clive Dunn, famous as Corporal Jones for his 'don't panic' catchphrase.

More significantly, the polls showed the SDP moving decisively ahead of the Conservatives and establishing themselves as the main challengers to Labour. Despite regular campaign visits by government ministers in support of John Antcliffe, local Conservatives privately complained that Conservative Central Office was holding back on resources: 'They've left the A team at Smith Square and sent us the Z team,' one was quoted as saying. The energetic Antcliffe was left making the best of it, sprinting around the constituency fuelled by Mars bars provided by his campaign minder, the Lewisham MP and Olympic rowing silver medallist Colin Moynihan. But he was clearly losing the race. Even a surprise endorsement from the former Labour MP for the constituency, Dick Marsh, did little to revive the flagging Conservative campaign.

As the campaign entered its closing stages, the possibility of the SDP causing a serious upset began to gain credence. An NOP poll for the *Evening Standard* put them on 35 per cent, just five points behind Labour on 40 per cent. The Conservatives were well behind on 23 per cent. A bandwagon began to roll. Newspaper profiles of a smiling Rosie Barnes suggested she could be on the brink of overtaking Labour and winning the seat. The media, sensing a dramatic finish to the race, talked up the prospect and by doing so gave a clear signal to Conservative voters and Labour moderates that a tactical vote for the SDP was the best way to defeat the Labour left-winger.

As Rosie Barnes basked in the warm glow of sympathetic media profiles, Deirdre Wood continued to be relentlessly attacked by the Conservative-supporting press. This reached a dramatic climax on the final weekend of the campaign when Labour called a press conference to denounce the actions of the *News of the World*, which they accused of running a smear campaign against their candidate. They revealed that the newspaper had been planning to run an intrusive story about Wood's father, who had died of alcohol poisoning in a Salvation Army hostel. After threats of legal action from Labour, the paper dropped the story. But giving her response at the press conference, Wood was reduced to tears as she set out details of her late father's violent abuse of her and her mother.

The incident provoked a wave of sympathy, including from political opponents. Even the Prime Minister was dragged into the row. Margaret Thatcher was challenged to condemn the behaviour of the journalists and did so, publishing a letter in which she said she knew 'from bitter experience' how upsetting such abuse can be and that she utterly deplored personal attacks on those in public life and on their families. Labour strategists, meanwhile, started to suggest that the backlash could help swing votes back towards Labour in the closing days of the campaign.

It was now a two-party fight to the finish. Labour was worried, with an internal political intelligence briefing noting that 'virtually no section of the electorate is immune to SDP incursion'. This seemed to be borne out by the feeling on the streets, where former SDP leader Roy Jenkins arrived to support Rosie Barnes and declared: 'I scent victory.'

He was right. After a frantic effort by all parties to turn out their vote on polling day, the result was an overwhelming victory for Rosie Barnes and the SDP, who won 53 per cent of the vote, with Labour's beleaguered Deirdre Wood nearly twenty points behind on 33.8 per cent. The scale of the triumph could be explained by looking at the Conservative vote share, which suffered a dramatic collapse. John Antcliffe won just 11.2 per cent – down nearly twenty-four points from the result at the previous general election. The 2 a.m. front page of *The Times* neatly summarised what had happened: 'Tactical vote gives Alliance huge victory.'

The immediate consequence of the result was to provide a significant boost for the Alliance while raising worrying questions for Neil Kinnock as he prepared to contest his first general election. We tend to forget now, but that election was, in the words of New Labour's strategic guru Philip Gould, 'the fight for the survival of Labour as the major opposition party in British Politics'. With the Alliance having run Labour close in vote share in 1983, it was not fanciful to imagine that in 1987 an SDP–Liberal surge could see them overtake Labour and fulfil their dream of reshaping British politics. Greenwich seemed to herald just such a result.

For the Conservatives, it was a mixed outcome. On the one hand, it demonstrated that Labour was still suffering badly from the impression that it harboured a 'loony left' agenda behind Kinnock's more moderate public platform and Peter Mandelson's 'red rose' rebranding. But on the other hand, they had failed to reap the reward, with the SDP instead becoming the recipients of disaffected and tactical anti-Labour votes. This looked set to cause them trouble in other seats where the SDP could position themselves as the moderate alternative to Labour.

In the event, the Alliance bandwagon not only stalled but went into reverse. They made a net loss of one seat at the general election in June and saw their national vote share fall. Margaret Thatcher won another landslide victory, while Labour made modest gains and secured its place as the main party of opposition. In Greenwich, the general election saw a rematch between the top three candidates, all of whom were selected again by their parties. John Antcliffe doubled the Conservative vote share, finishing with 23 per cent, while Deirdre Wood only managed to increase Labour's by a single point, allowing Rosie Barnes to hold the seat with a reduced majority and 40 per cent of the vote.

Despite this second win, the SDP's days were numbered. A year later, Barnes and her neighbouring MP John Cartwright opposed the party's merger with the Liberals and instead joined David Owen's 'continuing' SDP. Then, after that party was dissolved in 1990, she contested the 1992 general election as an 'Independent Social Democrat' but narrowly lost to Labour's Nick Raynsford, who had by then replaced Deirdre Wood as the party's candidate. Wood continued to serve on the Inner London Education Authority until that body was abolished in 1990.

Meanwhile, the Conservatives' young 'City whizzkid' John Antcliffe lived up to that label with a successful career in business. He became a highly regarded figure in the world of financial public affairs, but in 2010, he died suddenly of a brain haemorrhage at the age of just forty-eight. Margaret Thatcher attended his memorial service, and there is now a memorial fellowship in his name at Churchill College, Cambridge.

Looking back from a distance of nearly four decades, the Greenwich by-election still stands out as a memorable campaign. We can see now that it marked the last hurrah of the SDP and was the first and only time that the party won a seat from Labour. But for a few months in 1987, it looked as though Greenwich had once again played host to a political event that would have national repercussions.

Dr Nigel Fletcher is a political historian and the co-founder of the Centre for Opposition Studies. He served as a councillor in the Royal Borough of Greenwich for thirteen years, ending up as Leader of the Opposition there until losing his seat in 2022. He is now a visiting fellow at King's College London and in 2025 was appointed the Ken Young Memorial Research Fellow at the Mile End Institute, Queen Mary University of London.

GLASGOW GOVAN

10 NOVEMBER 1988
SNP GAIN FROM LABOUR

GERRY HASSAN

Result: Jim Sillars (SNP), 14,677, 48.8 per cent; Bob Gillespie (Labour), 11,123, 36.9 per cent; Graeme Hamilton (Conservative), 2,207, 7.3 per cent; Bernard Ponsonby (SLD), 1,246, 4.1 per cent; George Campbell (Green), 345, 1.1 per cent; Douglas Chalmers (Communist), 281, 0.9 per cent; Lord Sutch (Monster Raving Loony), 174, 0.6 per cent; Fraser Clark (Independent), 51, 0.2 per cent
Size of majority: 3,554
Swing: 32.2 per cent from Labour to SNP
Name of previous MP and party: Bruce Millan (Labour)
Reason for by-election: Promotion to European commissioner
Result at previous general election: Bruce Millan (Labour), 24,071, 64.8 per cent; Alasdair Ferguson (SNP), 4,562, 12.3 per cent; Janet Girsman (Conservative), 4,411, 11.9 per cent; Felix McCabe (SDP), 3,851, 10.4 per cent; Douglas Chalmers (Communist), 237, 0.6 per cent
Date by-election called: 9 October 1988
Date by-election took place: 10 November 1988
Size of total electorate: 49,994
Total number of votes cast: 30,104
Turnout: 60.2 per cent

Govan Act Two took place fifteen years and two days after the first act. The context was even more dramatic: an unpopular Tory government just elected the year before with a huge UK parliamentary majority, the rising salience of the Scottish question fuelled by the Tory

Party having their Scottish representation more than halved and the burning question of the poll tax being imposed on Scotland without popular consent and legitimacy – and a year earlier than for England and Wales.

It had all seemed simpler for Labour a year previously in Scotland. In the 1987 election when Thatcher won an overall majority of 102, Scotland had turned decisively against the Tories – reducing their number of seats from twenty-one to ten. Labour was returned with fifty out of seventy-two Scottish seats, a gain of nine, and were quickly dubbed 'the fighting fifty'. Yet the question of the Tory lack of a mandate (which became known as 'the Doomsday Scenario') was to come back to bite Labour, a pro-unionist party which could not ultimately 'out nat' the Scottish Nationalists, with Alex Salmond calling the Labour contingent 'the feeble fifty'.

This Labour conundrum provided the backdrop to Govan. Neil Kinnock's keynote address to the Scottish Labour conference in March 1988 made not one mention of a Scottish Parliament. When questioned afterwards about this in a TV interview, he commented that he had also 'not mentioned the weather in the Himalayas either'.

Such tensions were particularly acutely felt on the poll tax, the legitimacy of which was being openly questioned in Scotland. Its implementation a year ahead of England and Wales was radicalising opinion, with deliberate non-payment considered by a large swathe of society and adopted by the SNP.

This debate was reflected inside the Labour Party and highlighted in a special conference held in Govan Town Hall in September 1988: a sign itself of the weakness of the leadership on the issue in the party. The party's divisions were publicly displayed. Constituency parties were behind non-payment, with the leadership only able to hold the line because the bulk of the union block votes rowed in behind Donald Dewar and the Scottish executive.

Pre-Govan, Labour also began to move hesitantly towards a more radical home rule stance. Dewar stated in a speech at Stirling University in October 1988 that 'Scots will have to live a little dangerously for a while'. This meant support for the proposals in *A Claim of Right for Scotland* published in the summer for a cross-party Constitutional

Convention to agree a plan for a Scottish Parliament. Dewar, a seasoned Labour right-winger, made this move by overcoming resistance from traditional allies such as the MP Sam Galbraith and Scottish general secretary Murray Elder.

This is the backdrop to Govan Act Two, which arose because Bruce Millan (who won the seat in 1987 with a 19,509 majority) became a European commissioner, leaving Labour facing a challenging by-election caused by its own actions.

The SNP selected Jim Sillars, a former Scottish Labour MP, as the party's candidate and ran a campaign filled with energy, buzz and excitement. Supported by activists and celebrities such as Craig and Charlie Reid of the Proclaimers, there was a sense of momentum and belief that the SNP could win. A Labour press officer drafted in from London recalled the Proclaimers 'driving round Govan on the back of a flatbed truck urging everyone to kick Labour where it hurt'. Sillars was standing as 'SNP Anti-Poll Tax Candidate'; adding to the frenetic energy and intrigue, between Govan 1973 and this campaign, he had married Margo MacDonald who won the seat for the SNP fifteen years previously.

Sillars told me, looking back on the campaign:

> The decision taken by the NEC well before we knew there was going to be a by-election in Govan, to become part of the anti-poll tax campaign, proved to be of critical importance. That the SNP was involved in encouraging mass non-payment, and was known to be there on principle, meant that we could place our anti-Thatcher, anti-poll tax position, front and centre of the campaign and be believed.

The Labour campaign was beset by problems from the start. The local party was small, numbering 170, many retired and politically inactive. Their candidate Bob Gillespie was a seasoned trade union negotiator, originally from Glasgow, who worked for the print union SOGAT in London and took on the likes of Robert Maxwell, the owner of the Labour-supporting *Daily Mirror* and *Daily Record*.

This was to have fateful consequences for press coverage of the campaign in the usually loyal *Record*. Gillespie later reflected on his stand against the press baron: 'Maxwell always put gagging orders on people. He would never have been able to do that if you only spoke as an MP in the Palace of Westminster. So he went after me.' The result was that Labour faced a universally hostile press environment where it could not even bank on its usual allies at the *Record*.

Neither the Scottish nor UK party had wanted Gillespie. The latter did not trust the Scottish party and took control of the then daily press conferences in an attempt to control their candidate. As a memento from his navy days, he had 'Hong Kong' tattooed on his knuckles: something which he was made to feel over-conscious of in press conferences and even asked whether he and 'his background' were 'a liability', replying that he found that 'an incredible question', as well as insulting and patronising.

Gillespie was inspired in his youth by the politics of Communist Willie Gallacher, later recounting his influence: 'He said: "Whenever I am confronted by a question of policy, I always ask myself the question, how will this affect the working class?"' Such sentiment might have gone down well in Govan, but Gillespie was not allowed to express such views by his handlers.

Reflecting on this, Sillars comments:

> Woven into that scenario was the Labour party contribution. In placing itself against non-payment of the poll tax, it was not placing itself on the side of the people. It didn't like the poll tax, but would not do the one thing that would defeat it. I am sure Bob Gillespie took the same view as me, but was not allowed any leeway, and had to stick to the party line.

A pivotal moment in the contest were two TV debates. The second, on STV, was held in the last week as opinion polls showed the gap between Labour and SNP closing significantly. The STV format allowed candidates to cross-examine each other, and Sillars questioned Gillespie on European funding on the technical subject of 'additionality'. Jimmy Allison, Scottish Labour organiser, later wrote: 'It was obvious that he did not know what the word meant and could not handle the situation.' He concluded: 'It was an unmitigated disaster, and you could see that Sillars smelled victory.'

In the by-election on 10 November, Sillars won by 48.8 per cent to Labour's 36.9 per cent, a majority of 3,554 on a swing of 32.2 per cent. The BBC/NOP exit poll showed the most important issues in the contest as: 32 per cent representing Scotland's interests, 21 per cent poll tax, 19 per cent unemployment, 16 per cent NHS, 12 per cent benefit changes and 10 per cent candidates; 32 per cent supported non-payment of the poll tax; meanwhile 58 per cent supported home rule compared to 16 per cent independence. Finally, the performance of Scottish Labour MPs was seen as good by 37 per cent and bad by 55 per cent.

Tony Benn recounted in his diary the following day on Govan: 'There had been no socialist politics in our campaign – just the idea that if you keep your head you'll win. A 19,000 majority, the seventeenth safest seat in Britain, was transformed into a 3,000 SNP majority.' Benn went on to make a prescient point: 'It revealed that if you don't offer people analysis they go for separatism, and it was also a reflection of our failure to discuss constitutional questions, which are at the core of the devolution argument.'

Doug Chalmers, the Communist candidate, finished sixth with 281 votes (0.9 per cent) and reflects now that Sillars won because 'the SNP were talking with the grain of the times. There was dissatisfaction with the neglect and de-industrialisation of Scotland and with Labour's complacency and presumption that they owned the voters of Govan.'

Unlike most by-elections, the story of Govan does not end with the result but the aftershocks it induced. In the immediate aftermath, Sillars acted magnanimously and called for greater co-operation between the opposition parties against the Tories. Labour went and licked its wounds; the pro-home rule Scottish Labour Action (SLA), writing in its newsletter, summed it up: 'Gubbed in Govan: Lessons for Labour' and declared that 'people felt Labour doesn't fight hard enough for Scotland' and that 'the election of another Labour MP would do little for Scotland's interests'.

Yet from this electoral earthquake, things did not pan out completely as expected. Scottish Labour within days of Govan formalised its support of *A Claim of Right* and a cross-party convention, moves which had already been afoot but which now had greater urgency.

Meanwhile, the SNP after their initial conciliatory tone got carried away with their soaring poll ratings as they hit 32 per cent and were within 4 per cent of Labour. They then decided to boycott what they suddenly called 'Labour's rigged Convention', seeing the entire exercise as a 'devolution trojan horse' into which Labour were trying to entrap them and prevent independence from being raised.

This hubris cost the SNP at the time, allowed Labour to regroup, join the convention and come up with a workable plan for a parliament in association with the Lib Dems, Greens and others. This along with a more professional Labour electoral approach saw Labour's Mike Watson see off Alex Neil of the SNP in the nearby Glasgow Central by-election of June 1989 with a 6,462 majority on a 15.1 per cent Labour to SNP swing; on the same day, the Euro elections across Scotland saw Labour win seven seats to the SNP's one and 41.9 per cent to 25.6 per cent.

Jim Sillars was a high-profile campaigning MP for Govan, but Labour targeted the seat at the April 1992 general election and put significant resources behind their candidate, the combative Ian Davidson, who was returned with a 4,125 majority.

Did Govan second time around change anything, or was it just another example of by-election protest blues? Bernard Ponsonby, candidate for the 'Social and Liberal Democrats' (renamed Liberal Democrats), went on to become STV's political editor and had the ignominy of finishing fourth in the contest with 1,246 votes (4.1 per cent).

Years later, he still remembers his brush with the democratic process fondly but downplays its significance, stating: 'Govan '88 produced a kind of political fever as the activist classes debated what it all meant.' He concludes: 'Now I was there every single step of the way and I regarded this as a classic protest.'

The publication *Radical Scotland* in an editorial at the time took a contrary line, arguing that politics would never quite be the same: 'This was no "blip", no "flash flood". The instant judgement of the London press – that this was just a protest vote which will conveniently disappear again – shows only their total lack of understanding.'

Jim Sillars now takes a long view of the importance of Govan, stating:

I believe the Govan result was a seminal moment in Scottish politics.

It wiped out the stain of the 1979 vote of confidence disaster that befell the SNP and restored it to being a party that people respected and were prepared to listen to. The 'Tartan Tory' gibe that had served Labour well and had handicapped the SNP was no longer accepted by the people.

The effect on the Labour Party was profound. It realised that it faced a real threat that enabled the devolutionist wing to remove control of the constitutional issue from its unionist wing. The Govan result can be viewed as having contributed to Labour's recommitment to, and then, creation of a Scottish Parliament.

Doug Chalmers states:

It created a symbol that the cosy two party system that had long existed in Scotland was broken, and that it was possible for alternative voices to break through. This gave heart to those such as SNP voters and dissatisfied Labour voters that their votes weren't necessarily wasted and that the status quo could be challenged – as it was, in the coming years.

The myths of Govan continued long after the by-election battle buses packed up and after Labour revenge on Sillars. In 1997, Mohammad Sarwar stood for Labour after a bitter internal selection battle against Mike Watson and defeated SNP rising star Nicola Sturgeon. This contest produced significant media interest and increased Labour nerves after their publicised party troubles, but Labour held the seat with a reduced 2,914 majority. This was in New Labour's landslide year, and Scottish Labour HQ had the foresight to treat the seat as a marginal, allocated resources to it and assured the local party that 'the SNP had never in its history won a Glasgow seat at a Westminster election' (this not happening at a Westminster contest until the 2015 SNP landslide).

Two years later in the first Scottish Parliament elections, Sturgeon lost to Labour's Gordon Jackson by 1,756 votes. On polling day, I took a group of international visitors to meet all the main candidates, who were generous with their time. It was clear from his demeanour that Labour's Jackson thought he was going to lose, and when asked by one of the visitors 'Why has Labour legislated for a devolved Parliament?' he answered with a weary resignation: 'You know I have often asked myself that very same question.'

Jackson proved to be a part-time MSP who refused to give up his lucrative highly paid work as an advocate, went on holiday in the middle of the 2003 campaign and still narrowly won, and eventually, on the third occasion, lost to Sturgeon in 2007 by 744 votes. Govan was subsequently abolished for the 2005 Westminster and 2011 Scottish Parliament, but it lives on in political memory and folklore and may someday return to haunt others.

One aspect of the 1988 Govan contest seldom reflected upon was its all-male nature with eight male candidates. No one in mainstream media mentioned it at the time, in the TV debates or in contemporary analysis of the result.

Retrospectively, neither Sillars nor the late Bob Gillespie ever touched upon it – proof of the continued hold of a certain male view of politics, particularly on the left. 'The overall impression was of a pretty homogeneous group of men, at ease in their unexamined masculinist privilege,' reflects Lesley Orr, academic and feminist, 'operating with taken-for-granted assumptions about politics, labour, work and power, in a fast-changing industrial economy.' The silences were telling in Govan in 1988 and still exist in too many places today.

Govan represents many things: frustration and anger among voters and even the love story between Margo MacDonald and Jim Sillars. It was a kick against the political establishment which produced results – a Labour Party which worked cross-party for a Parliament, and an SNP which eventually recognised it needed to think long term and which ultimately contributed to the establishment of the Scottish Parliament in 1999.

Dr Gerry Hassan is a writer and academic and author/editor of more than two dozen books on Scottish and UK politics; his latest being Britain Needs Change: The Politics of Hope and Labour's Challenge *(Biteback, 2024). He is co-founder of Kirkcudbright Fringe Festival in Dumfries and Galloway.*

64

EASTBOURNE

---

18 OCTOBER 1990
LIBERAL DEMOCRAT GAIN FROM CONSERVATIVES

TIM BALE

Result: David Bellotti (Liberal Democrats), 23,415, 50.8 per cent; Richard Hickmet (Conservative), 18,865, 41.0 per cent; Charlotte Atkins (Labour), 2,308, 5.0 per cent; David Aherne (Green), 553, 1.2 per cent; Theresia Williamson (Liberal), 526, 1.1 per cent; Lady Whiplash (Corrective), 216, 0.5 per cent; John McAuley (National Front), 154, 0.3 per cent; Eric Page (Ironside), 35, 0.1 per cent
Size of majority: 4,550
Swing: 20.0 per cent from Conservative to Liberal Democrats
Name of previous MP and party: Ian Gow (Conservative)
Reason for by-election: Murder of incumbent by the Provisional IRA
Result at previous general election: Ian Gow (Conservative), 33,587, 59.9 per cent; Peter Driver (Liberal), 16,664, 29.7 per cent; Ash Patel (Labour), 4,928, 8.8 per cent; Ruth Addison (Green), 867, 1.6 per cent.
Date by-election called: 20 September 1990
Date by-election took place: 18 October 1990
Size of total electorate: 75,904
Total number of votes cast: 46,115
Turnout: 60.8 per cent

The contest in Eastbourne was brought about by the murder, via a car bomb, of Ian Gow, MP for the constituency since 1974, by the Provisional IRA on the morning of 30 July 1990. He was the third Conservative MP to be killed in the Thatcher era by Irish Republican terrorists, the first being Airey Neave in 1979 and the second Anthony Berry (in the Brighton bombing) in 1984. Five years previously, in November 1985, Thatcher had controversially signed the Anglo-Irish Agreement, prompting Gow, who had been her uber-loyal parliamentary private secretary, to resign from his junior ministerial role at the Treasury. Gow had, nonetheless, remained one of her doughtiest defenders, even as she and her government grew increasingly unpopular, particularly in the wake of the introduction of the poll tax in the spring of that year.

An opinion survey released by ICM on the day before Gow died had the Conservatives on 36 per cent of the vote and Labour, then led by Neil Kinnock, on 52 per cent. The evident public antipathy toward the Community Charge (as the poll tax was officially known) might have given a younger Margaret Thatcher pause for thought. Likewise, perhaps, the fact that sixty Tory MPs had failed to support her when, in the autumn of 1989 following the Tories' poor performance in that summer's elections to the European Parliament, one of their colleagues had dared (albeit more symbolically rather than seriously) to challenge her for the leadership. But after a decade in No. 10, she was becoming less and less inclined to listen and more and more inclined to think that only she knew best.

Gow's death, however, was, for her, first and foremost, a personal rather than a political tragedy. Certainly, neither she nor many of her critics thought that the inevitable by-election would result in anything other than a Conservative victory. There was no sympathy for the IRA in the constituency, and Gow was a popular MP who had held it with a majority of nearly 17,000 at the 1987 general election. Labour, which had failed to reach even a 10 per cent vote share in the seat in that contest, stood absolutely no chance. Meanwhile, the Liberal Democrats – the party created in March 1988 from the merger of the historic Liberal Party and the Social Democratic Party that had broken away from Labour in 1981 – were only on 7 per cent nationally in ICM's survey. Nor had they performed very impressively at the ballot box: the European Parliament elections had seen them win just a 6 per cent vote share – a result that had seen them beaten into third place by the Greens. And although the Conservatives had lost well over 200 seats at local elections in the spring of 1990, the Lib Dems had gone backwards too, shedding nearly eighty councillors nationwide.

It may have been this – along with the fact that in only one of the eleven by-elections so far fought under his leadership had his party achieved anything more than a third-place finish – that led Paddy Ashdown, the Lib Dem leader, to decide in the first instance that his party should not contest Eastbourne. But he was persuaded at the last minute to rethink his position by the Lib Dems' head of campaigns, Chris Rennard, who fired off a forthright fax outlining several reasons why not standing would be a mistake. First, Rennard argued, there was a precedent – and an encouraging one: not only had the Liberal Party fought the Enfield Southgate by-election triggered by the death of Anthony Berry in the IRA's bombing of the Grand Hotel in Brighton in 1984; it had significantly increased its vote (albeit not sufficiently to prevent a young Michael Portillo entering the Commons for the first time). Second, at the local elections in Eastbourne the previous May, the Lib Dems had actually outpolled the Tories, suggesting that the seat might be winnable; if it did fall to the Lib Dems, it could be the start of something big – after all, Rennard reminded Ashdown, support for the Liberal Party in the early 1970s had shot up after a series of by-election successes. Finally, the decision about whether to fight Eastbourne wasn't just a matter for the leader but for the federal executive and, most of all, the local party. Ashdown was annoyed, even angry, but could see the sense in all this and relented. Eastbourne Lib Dems, it transpired, were well up for the fight, and Rennard put together a crack team (which included future Lib Dem MPs Paul Burstow and Norman Baker, as well as local agent Paul Jacobs) to assist them in every way possible.

The Conservatives, meanwhile, were confident that they would retain the seat even if it were contested. In a move that surprised those who assumed they would 'go long' and hold the election after a memorial service planned for Gow on 22 October, they announced it would be held the previous week. This would give their opponents as little time to organise as possible and might see the party benefit from any bump in popularity resulting from its annual conference, due to be held in Bournemouth the week prior to polling day on the 18th.

They also selected their candidate in fairly short order, lighting, from a longlist of 230 aspirants, on Richard Hickmet, a London barrister, who had been elected to the Commons for the highly marginal constituency of Glanford & Scunthorpe in 1983, only to lose the seat at the next election in 1987.

Whatever Hickmet's personal qualities, however, his selection may not have been the wisest decision. He was clearly not local (as the Lib Dems, who quickly selected East Sussex councillor David Bellotti, predictably never tired of pointing out). And his family was originally from the Turkish community in Cyprus – problematic when a number of Eastbourne's hospitality businesses were run by Greeks and Greek Cypriots who made no secret of their opposition to being represented by someone prepared to recognise the self-styled Turkish Republic of Northern Cyprus. Moreover, the fact that Hickmet was a 'retread' – a defeated MP seeking to make it back into Parliament – allowed the Lib Dems to suggest (albeit not in terms) that the Tories were offering the town's voters sloppy seconds.

None of this would have been sufficient, in all likelihood, to deliver victory to the Lib Dems, whose early private polling (understandably never released) had them on just 11 per cent. However, there were other, even more important, factors at play.

The poll tax was, inevitably, a problem for the Conservatives. But it was not the only one: inflation was running at just under 11 per cent and interest rates stood at an equally eye-watering 14 per cent; pensioners (who made up nearly a third of the town's voters) were feeling squeezed and so were local businesses, symbolised by a number of boarded-up hotels along the town's otherwise impressive seafront. Against this difficult background, the government's announcement the week before polling day that it was taking the UK into Europe's Exchange Rate Mechanism (ERM) and was therefore cutting interest rates by 1 per cent failed to provide its campaign with much of a boost. Nor, it seemed, could the government do much to assuage voters' anxieties about the state of the NHS – not least because one of the Tories' first campaign guides included in its list of local hospitals one that had been recently demolished, allowing the Lib Dems (who also had some success with a petition protesting car park charges at one of the hospitals still standing) to press home their attack on Hickmet as an out-of-touch carpetbagger.

But it was another Tory leaflet that probably proved the real turning point. Under the headline 'Friend and Colleague of Ian Gow', it suggested that 'any result, other than a massive vote for Richard Hickmet, will be a moral victory for terrorism'. This prompted a flurry of furious letters to the weekly local paper, Saturday's *Eastbourne Herald*, the front page of which went on to scream 'Campaign is "emotional blackmail"'. Rather than rowing back, however, Hickmet doubled down, suggesting, first, that a victory for any of his opponents 'would mean that you could kill a MP because you do not believe his views and change the colour of the seat. That cannot be right for democracy' and, second, on the eve of polling day: 'If the political representation of this seat were to change ... the IRA will have achieved something.' Bellotti took care not to criticise his opponent's approach directly, but the widespread distaste it prompted probably meant he didn't have to.

The Lib Dems were also lucky in their other opponents. Unlike Margaret Thatcher, Neil Kinnock may have taken time out to visit the town, but Labour's prospects weren't helped by its national executive preventing the local party's chosen candidate standing over his refusal to pay the poll tax, replacing him in short order with a London-based trade union press officer, Charlotte Atkins. Although she later made it into Parliament (and into the junior ranks of government) as MP for Staffordshire Moorlands between 1997 and 2010, she only saved her deposit in Eastbourne by just three votes – not surprisingly, perhaps, given an NOP exit poll for BBC *Newsnight* found that 55 per cent of those who had voted Labour at the general election had switched to the Lib Dems in the by-election.

Those Labour–Lib Dem switchers, however, were not as important to the Lib Dems' victory as the sense of momentum they managed to generate. This was achieved in part by traditional means – namely, bringing in activists from all over the country to join what was already a healthy local party in contacting voters (this time by telephone as well as on the doorstep) and carpet-bombing the constituency with Day-Glo posters and garden signs. But it also owed much to Rennard, a couple of days out from polling day, releasing the returns of a canvass from that weekend, supposedly covering over half of the electorate and carried out by over 800 activists. In contrast to a telephone poll carried out by the local television station a week before that had the Tories comfortably ahead, Rennard's returns had Bellotti on 33.6 per cent, only just behind Hickmet on 37 per cent, with Atkins trailing badly on 7.9 per cent and some 16 per cent of voters still undecided. This set the scene nicely for Paddy Ashdown to visit the town for a high-profile rally in the run-up to polling day – an event that apparently trumped the Conservatives' own get-together, guest-starring Cecil Parkinson (now back in the Cabinet after his resignation amid a scandal in the early 1980s), which was held across town the same day. By then, Rennard was all but convinced that Bellotti would emerge the winner, but he kept his counsel in order (successfully, it turned out) to increase the shock value of the Lib Dems' victory on the night itself.

In the days that followed, Richard Hickmet's friends in the Conservative Party pushed back against what they saw as an underhanded attempt by Central Office, by unnamed ministers and even by disappointed local party members to blame him for the defeat: Michael Brown, MP for Brigg & Cleethorpes, for instance, insisted to journalists that Hickmet 'was nothing other than the reader of the scripts for a campaign which was totally run by Central Office'. The party's agent in Eastbourne, however, insisted that the decision to put out the infamous leaflet was taken locally, although it was later reported that it had been drafted by Tony Garrett and Mark Fulbrook, director and deputy director of the campaigns unit at Central Office and been approved (possibly reluctantly, possibly not) by Kenneth Baker, the party chairman. Whatever the truth of the matter, however, the by-election effectively ended the losing candidate's political career: Hickmet never re-entered the Commons and instead returned to his legal practice.

That said, the by-election did not mark the beginning of a glittering future for the Liberal Democrat victor. David Bellotti served (faithfully but with no particular distinction) at Westminster for less than two years – until he was defeated at the 1992 election by the Tory candidate, Nigel Waterson, who added nearly 13,000 votes to Hickmet's total, beating the incumbent by just under 5,500 votes on a share of 52 per cent. Bellotti then tried and failed to win a seat in the European

Parliament in 1994, after which he returned to local government in East Sussex before leaving the area under something of a cloud as the CEO of Brighton & Hove Albion who presided over the sale of its historic stadium without the club having another permanent home to go to. By the time of his death in 2015, however, he had resumed his Lib Dem political career – this time in local government in the West Country.

The political impact of the by-election, however, was genuinely massive. For the newly merged Liberal Democrats, electing the first fully fledged Lib Dem MP to Parliament allowed them to push back against the worryingly widespread accusation that they were less than the sum of their parts – accusations that the party was further able to scotch by winning by-election victories in Ribble Valley and Kincardine & Deeside in the spring and autumn of 1991. Although both constituencies were, like Eastbourne, won back by the Tories in 1992 general election, Paddy Ashdown's party won a far-from-disastrous 18 per cent of the vote and twenty Commons seats.

It was for the Conservatives, however, that the by-election proved truly momentous – in spite of the fact that the NOP exit poll suggested that, had Eastbourne been contested at a general election rather than a by-election, the Conservatives would have won by much the same majority as in 1987. The loss of the government's twenty-sixth safest seat (particularly in a contest precipitated by an event which many had assumed would garner sympathy for the party of the MP who had been brutally murdered by a terrorist organisation) may only have reduced its majority to ninety-six; but it confirmed the feeling among Tory MPs that they stood a good chance of losing their own seats unless they moved against their increasingly unpopular leader and Prime Minister.

Two weeks after the by-election, the long-suffering Geoffrey Howe resigned as Deputy Prime Minister, making a devastating speech in the House of Commons calculated to precipitate a challenge to Margaret Thatcher by her long-term rival Michael Heseltine. Some three weeks later, she herself was gone, to be replaced as Prime Minister by her Chancellor, John Major, by the end of the following week. From what had looked like a hopeless position in the opinion polls before he took over, his administration turned things around in order to win a stunning general election victory in April 1992, albeit one that quickly turned to ashes when the UK's withdrawal from the ERM on 'Black Wednesday' that September – along with the evident inability of some particularly Eurosceptic, right-wing Conservative MPs to get over their heroine's defenestration two years earlier – trashed the Tories' reputation for governing competence.

Tim Bale *is a professor of politics at Queen Mary University of London. He is the author of* The Conservative Party After Brexit, *the updated, paperback edition of which was published in early 2025, and the co-author of the forthcoming* The British General Election of 2024.

65

NEWBURY

6 MAY 1993
LIBERAL DEMOCRAT GAIN FROM CONSERVATIVES

ELINOR GOODMAN

Result: David Rendel (Liberal Democrats), 37,590, 65.1 per cent; Julian Davidson (Conservative), 15,535, 26.9 per cent; Steve Billcliffe (Labour), 1,151, 2.0 per cent; Alan Sked (Anto-Federalist League), 601, 1.0 per cent; Andrew Bannon (Conservative Candidate), 561, 1.0 per cent; Stephen Martin (Commoners'), 435, 0.8 per cent; Screaming Lord Sutch (Monster Raving Loony), 432, 0.7 per cent; Jim Wallis (Green), 341, 0.6 per cent; John Browne (Conservative Rebel), 267, 0.5 per cent; Lindi St Clair (Corrective), 170, 0.3 per cent; Bill Board (Maastricht Referendum for Britain), 84, 0.1 per cent; Jonathan Day (People & Pensioners), 49, 0.1 per cent; Colin Palmer (21st Century Independent Foresters), 40, 0.1 per cent; Mladen Grbin (Defence of Children's Humanity Bosnia), 33, 0.1 per cent; Alan Page (SDP), 33, 0.1 per cent; Anne Murphy (Communist), 32, 0.1 per cent; Michael Stone (Give the Royal Billions to Schools), 21, 0.1 per cent
Size of majority: 22,055
Swing: 28.4 per cent from Conservative to Liberal Democrats
Name of previous MP and party: Judith Chaplin (Conservative)
Reason for by-election: Death of incumbent
Result at previous general election: Judith Chaplin (Conservative), 37,135, 55.9 per cent; David Rendel (Liberal Democrats), 24,778, 37.3 per cent; Richard J. E. Hall (Labour), 3,962, 6.0 per cent; Jim Wallis (Green), 539, 0.8 per cent
Date by-election called: 14 April 1993

Date by-election took place: 6 May 1993
Size of total electorate: Approx. 79,900
Total number of votes cast: 56,250
Turnout: 70.4 per cent

I have two abiding memories of the Newbury by-election in May 1993: neat housing estates peppered with tired-looking For Sale signs; and the Chancellor, Norman Lamont saying, in the words of the French singer, Édith Piaf, that he had no regrets about Britain being forced out of the Exchange Rate Mechanism. One other thing I didn't notice at the time, but was arguably more consequential, was Nigel Farage's first bit part in politics.

The Newbury by-election was the first after the general election of 1992 which the Conservatives had unexpectedly won, despite being in the middle of the second worst recession since the war. Since then, politically, things had got worse for the Tories. The humiliating failure to keep sterling within the agreed bands for the Exchange Rate Mechanism had destroyed the central plank of the government's economic policy and with it what was left of its reputation for economic competence. It also inflamed the splits within the Conservative Party over Europe, which drowned out any glimmers of good news on the economy.

On top of that, Norman Lamont had unveiled a highly unpopular Budget earlier in 1993 aimed at getting spending under control. In a foretaste of the anger about the withdrawal of the winter fuel allowance by Labour shortly after the 2024 election, there was an outcry about the imposition of the VAT on domestic fuel bills, particularly as it had been ruled out by the Conservatives before the election.

Some things had improved. Interest rates had come down, as they were no longer needed to maintain parity with the Deutschmark. So too had inflation and the government was increasingly confident that after all the false dawns, the economy was finally beginning to recover. But unlike previous recessions, this one had hit the south of England – and Newbury is slap bang in the middle of southern England, halfway down the M4 corridor. And here they were still reeling from it.

What had once been a quiet market town, surrounded by villages and racing gallops, was boosted by the opening of the M4 in 1972. Situated on an intersection between the new motorway and main roads between the south coast and the Midlands, it became a distribution hub and a magnet for company headquarters. The expansion was symbolised by the opening of a huge Vodafone site in the mid-1980s. Other factories sprung up around it, the majority employing fewer than twenty-five people.

New housing estates were built to accommodate the growing workforce. In the ten years to 1992, the population had increased by more than 13 per cent. Many of the families who bought those houses took out large mortgages, confident that they would continue to prosper in an area which seemed to be an advertisement for the Thatcher dream.

The recession in Newbury when it came was nothing like as bad as it had been in many northern towns, as it benefited from not being dependent on just one large industry. But there had been a fivefold increase in unemployment between January 1990 and January 1993, when it reached 4,000 – that in a constituency where the problem before had been finding workers. Possibly most damaging politically was the effect on house prices, as houseowners struggled to cover the size of their mortgage when they came to sell. While nationally, repossessions had fallen by 18 per cent, in Newbury they were up 3 per cent. The phrase 'negative equity' had become part of the political lexicon. In its by-election guide, the Liberal Democrats described the town as 'the negative equity capital of England', an assertion they later had to admit they had picked up in the press, and subsequently had to withdraw, but it stuck anyway.

For Prime Minister John Major, the by-election was not just a political headache but a personal blow. It was triggered by the death of Judith Chaplin, who before entering Parliament had been one of his closest aides. When he thought of resigning after Black Wednesday, she was one of those who told him not to.

Chaplin had had a majority in 1992 of 12,357 over the Liberal Democrats, making it in general election terms a comfortably safe Conservative seat. Surrounded by affluent villages, it had tended to elect patrician, rather wet Conservatives. Judith Chaplin herself had links to the former Tory Prime Minister Sir Robert Walpole. She hadn't expected to lose in the 1992 election, but her majority, like the national result, was as much due to fear of letting in a Labour government under Neil Kinnock as an endorsement of John Major's Conservative Party. Still less was it an endorsement of the Conservatives' handling of the recession. By-elections, as they had been in the previous parliament, though, were an opportunity to take revenge on the government.

For the Liberal Democrats, Newbury was an ideal place to get people voting tactically, as the Labour vote had been squeezed to 6 per cent at the general election, and there was never any realistic chance of them winning. There was even a debate within the local Labour Party as to whether they should field a candidate. But the then Labour leader, John Smith, was against anything which could be portrayed as co-operation with the Liberal Democrats, so despite his doubts about the slick techniques used by Peter Mandelson when he was Neil Kinnock's communications director, Smith sent him down to Newbury to manage the campaign there.

The Labour candidate was a local man, Steve Billcliffe, a former director of Friends of the Earth, who Mandelson dubbed 'Sergeant Bilko'. But not even his supposedly Machiavellian powers could do much to help the candidate. He managed all the usual by-election events, like the daily press conferences and a walkabout for John Smith, who said that the voters had seemed very friendly, without knowing the ones he met had been hand-picked. But Mandelson took a more light-hearted approach to the campaign than he would have, had he thought it was a winnable seat. On one occasion, driving around, he met the Natural Law Party candidate, whose main boast was that he could ascend into the air unaided. Mandelson wound down his window and shouted, 'Levitate the car, levitate the car.'

The Liberal Democrats, on the other hand, took the campaign extremely seriously. The previous parliament had been very difficult for them, particularly at the start, destroying their dreams of replacing Labour as the national opposition to the Conservatives. The Alliance with David Owen's SDP had fallen apart, amid much mockery from Labour, and they began to look increasingly irrelevant. Mrs Thatcher described them as a 'dead parrot'. In the early part of the parliament, they weren't even winning by-elections. But as the recession got worse, and outrage about the poll tax increased, they began to be beneficiaries of the protest vote in Conservative-held seats. At the general election, though, they failed to get any more than the ten seats they held before.

By-elections, though, remained their life blood, and Chris Rennard, the Liberal Democrat campaign manager, saw Newbury as a chance to establish the Liberal Democrats as the opposition to the Tories in the south of England. Before the campaign even started officially, he quite literally got out the Liberal playbook and showed activists the tactics they had used in previous by-election victories. Voters would be bombarded with leaflets combining opposition to national policies with local grievances which it was hoped would help council candidates fighting elections on the same day. Different leaflets would be sent to different sectors of the electorate. Such tactics had often been attacked as 'dirty tricks' by their opponents, who claimed the Liberal Democrats contradicted themselves, depending on who they were targeting. But a BBC investigation in Newbury was unable to prove this.

The Liberal Democrats began with the advantage that they controlled the council and generally got good press in the local paper. Their candidate, David Rendel, was himself a local councillor who had fought the seat twice before, including at the previous election. He had family connections with the Liberal Party going back to Gladstone, and while he wasn't actually Newbury born and bred, he lived in the constituency and was married to a local doctor. An Old Etonian and rowing blue, he had an impeccably polite manner on the doorstep. Mandelson tried to ridicule him, by referring him to as 'Dave' following his agent's attempts to present him as a common man in one of the more run-down parts of the constituency. But regardless of where he went to school, he came across as a solid citizen with a proven commitment to the town.

The Conservatives played into Liberal hands by selecting a candidate from outside the constituency. Julian Davidson, a Dorset councillor, had fought the Liberal Democrat leader, Paddy Ashdown, in Yeovil, and presumably local Tories thought that would have taught him how to deal with the Orange Peril. At his selection meeting, he vigorously attacked 'the Liberals' and beat John Maples, a former minister, to the nomination. But he made the mistake early on of admitting he had only visited Newbury 'on a few odd occasions'.

The Liberal Democrat campaign, though, wasn't without its tensions. Chris Rennard, the party's agent, carried out research in the constituency early on, which showed that while his party scored highly on the economy and defending public services, local voters were very nervous about any association with the Labour Party. The Liberal leader had to be reluctantly persuaded not to use one of his speeches in Newbury to promote the idea of co-operation between the two parties, much to the relief of David Rendel, who was more of a Liberal at heart.

The Conservatives tried to fight their campaign on the economy, pointing to the signs of improvement like the unemployment figures, though they were yet to have much impact in Newbury. What is more, fighting on the economy meant bringing the Chancellor, Norman Lamont, to the town. And he had been very unpopular even before Black Wednesday. A poll carried out in Newbury by Rennard showed he had a -64 per cent popularity rating.

He had displayed an astonishing lack of empathy with voters. Famously, he said in the middle of the recession, unemployment and high interests were a 'price worth paying to get inflation down' and stretched the credibility of hard-pressed voters by saying he could see the 'green shoots' of recovery long before they could. Shortly after Black Wednesday, on a trip to Washington, he was asked how he felt about being forced out of the European Exchange Rate Mechanism (ERM). He replied by saying his wife had heard him 'singing in the bath for the first time in a long time'. Which was hardly the party line of a government that spent millions of pounds trying to stay inside the mechanism.

All these quotes were manna from heaven for his political opponents – and the pack of journalists who descended on Newbury hoping to witness him putting his foot in it again. Asked which of these quotes he regretted most, he replied injudiciously: '*Je ne regrette rien.*' The media later blamed the Tories' poor performance on these words, which was probably fanciful, but John Major makes it clear in his autobiography that it was another factor in convincing him that the Chancellor had become a liability.

A bigger problem for Julian Davidson was how far to distance himself from Lamont's unpopular Budget. The nearest he got to criticism was to say if he was elected, he would fight to stop the VAT rise being extended. But he was pretty lukewarm in his endorsement of the government's claims that the economy was recovering, admitting the roots were 'fragile'. In an angry exchange of letters, Norman Lamont hit back at Paddy Ashdown for talking down the economy, but the Liberal Democrats welcomed almost anything that put their leader in the headlines, as one of their central objectives in the campaign was to raise his profile as the voice of public anger about broken promises.

As usual, the Lib Dem by-election printing machine rolled into action. Thirty different leaflets, many tailored to particular groups, piled up on doormats, distributed by more than 1,000 activists who flooded the constituency. Signatures were collected for two petitions, one on VAT and the other demanding a new hospital. On the eve of the poll, they sent out a leaflet to former Labour voters, illustrated by a cartoon of a tubby Lamont in his bath with the rather baffling message: 'You can help Norman Lamont sing in his bath by voting Labour.'

There were plenty of other options for protest voters. In total, there were nineteen candidates, more than in any previous by-election. There were the usual publicity seekers like Lord David Sutch for the Monster Raving Loony Party as well as potentially more serious parties like the Greens and the Anti-Federalists, one of three anti-Maastricht parties. It was led by Dr Alan Sked, an academic, and based on the Anti-Corn Law League of the early nineteenth century. He invited Enoch Powell to Newbury, which provided a drive-on role for a then little-known Nigel Farage who acted as his chauffeur. It was Powell's last public speaking engagement and he packed out the hall. For Nigel Farage, it was, he said, the 'thing that got him involved in politics'.

During the campaign, it had become clear that the Liberal Democrats could win, but the scale of their victory shocked the Conservatives. Rendel won by 22,055 votes, a swing of 28 per cent from the Conservatives — among the record-breaking swings for Conservative seats falling to the Liberals/Liberal Democrats in by-elections — which was demoralising for the Conservatives who had held the seat since 1924. Labour lost its deposit with just 2 per cent of the vote. The Conservatives tried to dismiss it as the usual 'mid-term' protest vote, but as the Liberal Democrats pointed out, one year after the election hardly counted as 'mid-term'. Their tactic of persuading former Labour voters to vote tactically for them had worked, but it was former Tories who were responsible for the size of the victory.

The Liberal Democrats had repeatedly said during the campaign that the by-election was a chance to send a message to Major – to sack Lamont. And it seemed to have worked. Later in May, the Prime Minister decided to get rid of Lamont as Chancellor because he had become a liability. He offered him the job of Environment Secretary, but Lamont refused, retiring to smoulder on the back benches among other Eurosceptics. But they failed in their campaign to get the VAT increase, introduced by Lamont, reversed immediately. However, the by-election had shown how unpopular the tax was, and the government was defeated the following year by a Conservative rebellion when it tried to introduce the second stage of the increase Lamont had proposed. The vote had become entangled in the continuing war within the Tory Party over Europe but also reflected worries among backbenchers about the unpopularity of the tax as shown by recent by-elections.

For Labour, the result was a reminder of how far they were from being a national party and prompted further discussions about what kind of relationship they should have with the Liberal Democrats. Peter Mandelson tried to make the best of it by claiming that Labour had shaken the electoral tree but that the apple had fallen off into the hands of the Liberal Democrats.

Elinor Goodman *is a UK journalist, best known as political editor of* Channel 4 News *from 1988 to 2005.*

66

CHRISTCHURCH

29 JULY 1993
LIBERAL DEMOCRAT GAIN FROM
CONSERVATIVES

MICHAEL CRICK

Result: Diana Maddock (Liberal Democrats), 33,164, 62.2 per cent; Robert Hayward (Conservative), 16,737, 31.4 per cent; Nigel Lickley (Labour), 1,453, 2.7 per cent; Alan Sked (Anti-Maastricht/Anti-Federalist League), 878, 1.6 per cent; Lord David Sutch (Monster Raving Loony), 404, 0.8 per cent; Andrew Bannon (The Conservative Candidate), 357, 0.7 per cent; Peter Newman (Sack Graham Taylor), 80, 0.2 per cent; Tara Bardot-Jackson (Buy the Daily Sport), 67, 0.1 per cent; Peter Hollyman (Save the National Health Service), 60, 0.1 per cent; John Crockard (Highlander IV Wednesday Promotion Night), 48, 0.1 per cent; Mark Griffiths (Natural Law), 45, 0.1 per cent; Mark Belcher (Ian For King), 23, 0.0 per cent; Karl Fitzhugh (Alfred the Chicken), 18, 0.0 per cent; John Walley (Rainbow Alliance Coalition), 16, 0.0 per cent
Size of majority: 16,427
Swing: 35.4 per cent from Conservative to Liberal Democrats
Name of previous MP and party: Robert Adley (Conservative)
Reason for by-election: Death of incumbent
Result at previous general election: Robert Adley (Conservative), 36,627, 63.5 per cent; Dennis Bussey (Liberal Democrats), 13,612, 23.6 per cent; Alan Lloyd (Labour), 6,997, 12.1 per cent; James Barratt (Natural Law), 243, 0.4 per cent; Adrian Wareham (Chauvinist Raving Alliance), 175, 0.3 per cent
Date by-election called: 7 July 1993

Date by-election took place: 29 July 1993
Size of total electorate: Approx. 71,900
Total number of votes cast: 53,350
Turnout: 74.2 per cent

Towards the end of the contest in Newbury, the Liberal Democrat election chief Chris Rennard got a tip that another south of England contest might be in the offing. Robert Adley, the Conservative MP for Christchurch in Dorset, was gravely ill, Rennard was told. So, after their astounding result in Newbury, Rennard ordered that the party's by-election resources – printers, office furniture, fax machines, telephones, stationery and so on – be sent to Christchurch rather than returned to London.

Rennard privately set a new goal – not just of matching the Lib Dems' huge 28.4 per cent swing in Newbury but of rewriting the by-election record books.

Robert Adley died on 13 May 1993. He had been MP for Christchurch since February 1974, having sat for the marginal Bristol North East from 1970 to 1974. A railway enthusiast, Adley had written several books about steam locomotives during his time as an MP and spent the final year of his life as chair of the Commons Transport Committee, in which role he'd denounced John Major's plans to privatise the railways as a 'poll tax on wheels'.

An affluent constituency, Christchurch curved northwards from the Saxon port of that name on the Dorset coast, through the outer reaches of Bournemouth into the New Forest (not yet a national park). Not since 1906 had the area returned anyone but a Conservative MP, and Adley boasted a majority of 23,015 in 1992 – almost 40 per cent.

Norman Lamont, the Chancellor who had announced in his March 1993 Budget that VAT would be imposed on domestic energy bills, had been replaced by Kenneth Clarke in a post-Newbury reshuffle by John Major. But Major's problems grew, and his reputation diminished further, when Lamont damned the government in his memorable Commons resignation speech as being 'in office but not in power'. The extra fuel tax was bound to prove even more unpopular in this new contest than in Newbury, since Christchurch's seaside communities and rural villages had one of the highest proportions of retired people of any seat in the UK, and older people tend to rely on central heating more than others.

The Liberal Democrats picked as their candidate a 48-year-old councillor from Southampton, Diana Maddock — a friendly but unremarkable councillor and former teacher with a steely coiffure. She'd come a poor third in Southampton Test in 1992 and was her party's regional organiser in Hampshire. Chris Rennard thought Maddock's local credentials were 'quite limited', but that didn't matter since the Conservatives picked someone even less local. The previous year Robert Hayward, forty-four, had lost his seat in the Bristol suburb of Kingswood, where he'd been MP since 1983. Hayward had never held office but had been PPS to three different ministers and was an expert on election statistics. In the 1990 Conservative leadership contest, he had kept the tallies for the John Major team of which MP was voting which way.

Yet astonishingly, Hayward — then known as 'Rob' — never wanted to be the candidate, perhaps because he feared the likely outcome. He says he only applied for the Christchurch selection as practice for trying for other safe Conservative seats later on and was confident there were several local contenders who were much more likely to appeal to Christchurch's Tory members. But these local favourites dropped out one after another — one failed to make the longlist, another withdrew abruptly and unexpectedly, while a third was asked at a meeting by a grande dame of the local association if he could say who she was. He couldn't.

To his growing horror, Hayward realised he might actually win the nomination. In a fraught meeting at Central Office in Westminster, he begged to withdraw. 'But how would it look if it was known John Major's numbers' man had given up on the seat?' a senior official warned, and he advised Hayward to 'throw' the contest — perform poorly before the members. Hayward thought that would be dishonest.

'All the way down to the selection, I was praying my car would break down,' Hayward recalls. It didn't, of course, and he was drawn to speak last. 'I spent my time pacing up and down the field outside thinking: "I don't want to do this."'

Hayward 'was by far the best performer on the night', wrote the party's campaign press officer Jo-Anne Nadler in a subsequent memoir. 'I was greatly relieved when he was announced the winner.'

But Tory bigwigs delayed over setting a date for the by-election, hoping first to get the Maastricht Treaty through the Commons. But the delay only gave time for the Lib Dems to gain momentum and spend huge sums on hundreds of thousands of leaflets before the official campaign spending limits started. Every Maddock leaflet stressed that Hayward wasn't local and had deserted his previous seat. Hayward pointed out that Robert Adley had made the same journey – from Bristol to Christchurch, which may have impressed Tory members but not local voters.

This wasn't a typical Lib Dem campaign of fighting from behind. Instead, a month before polling, a local newspaper poll gave them a 4 per cent lead. 'I never really doubted the result,' campaign chief Chris Rennard said later. The Lib Dems' goal was to aim for a record-breaking majority so as to press the case for change in government policy, including reversal of the VAT on domestic fuel (rather tricky when Lib Dem leader Paddy Ashdown privately supported the policy on environmental grounds).

And the Lib Dems were helped by rumours that Tory ministers were now considering other stringent financial measures, such as charges for food and overnight stays in hospital, charging old-age pensioners for prescriptions and cuts to pensions – all policies unlikely to appeal to the elderly folk of Christchurch. But it was hard for ministers to refute such suggestions when John Major had already broken his 1992 election pledge not to raise income tax. 'I knew it was going to be difficult,' Robert Hayward said years later, 'and it was hell.'

Liberal Democrat activists came to Christchurch in their hundreds – having seen shots on TV of yachts in the harbour and people enjoying themselves al fresco at nice restaurants, many came down hoping for a short holiday. The contest was much less attractive for Tory volunteers. The local party in South Buckinghamshire usually took a coach to by-election campaigns, but this time couldn't get enough members to sign up. Sensing blood, claiming Christchurch was a good way to explore John Major's troubles on the ground, or just a chance to get away from Westminster, journalists descended in large numbers too, along with broadcasters from America and Japan.

Rob Hayward was upset when his Central Office handlers refused to let him attend an early hustings event with other candidates, since his absence made him look frightened and weak. Then he was haunted by an incident from the year before when, as an MP, the whips had persuaded him to 'talk out' – or filibuster – a Private Members' Bill to extend rights for disabled people, a move Hayward had deeply regretted and for which he apologised to the Commons. In Christchurch one morning, a couple of dozen disabled people, many in wheelchairs, ambushed a public meeting Hayward was addressing and heckled him with their protests. At the end, party officials hustled Hayward out through a side entrance, much to his dismay. 'I'd have been quite happy to go and speak to them,' he says, 'for hours if necessary.'

Chris Rennard reveals – astonishingly and unbeknownst to anyone at the time – that the disabled protest was actually organised by the disgraced former Liberal leader Jeremy Thorpe, who had been diagnosed with Parkinson's disease and was trying to work his way back into party favour after his 1979 acquittal on charges of attempted murder.

Rob Hayward also faced an internal party problem – growing rumours that he was gay and that a newspaper was about to run a story about his love life, at a time when no Conservative MP had ever come out. Jo-Anne Nadler first heard the rumour from her boyfriend and in the Tory campaign HQ. She later wrote: 'It soon became obvious from the misplaced double entendres among more senior staff that I was not the only person who had heard of the possible exotic entanglements of our candidate.' Before long, Nadler relates, the Tory campaign office was:

> a hotbed of gossip … The routine jobs of leaflet production, telephone canvassing, envelope stuffing, and poster preparation etc. went on amid a slightly hysterical atmosphere of guffawing and innuendo. Poor Rob, if he ever felt any resentment or diminished enthusiasm, he certainly did not show it. His Tiggerish energy was boundless … his humour always positive. If anything, I rather felt he was getting a bit of a kick out of the whole thing, rather enjoying the 'Carry On' frisson of suggestiveness that now seemed to permeate the whole event.

Nothing became fully public at the time.

During the penultimate week, the Christchurch contest was overshadowed by far weightier events in London. Seven days before polling, the Commons finally voted on the Maastricht Treaty and the British opt-outs which John Major had secured in Holland in late 1991. A revolt by twenty-six Conservative rebels caused the government to lose by eight votes a crucial vote to 'note' Britain's 'opt-out' from the Social Chapter of the treaty. That night, Major called a confidence vote for the next day, Friday, while Conservative HQ pencilled in 2 September for a general election if that Commons vote was lost. In the end, Major won by thirty-eight votes.

Behind the scenes, Lib Dem leader Paddy Ashdown had been meeting John Major to discuss how his MPs might help the government through the Maastricht votes – from the principled position of his party being pro-Europe – though several Lib Dem colleagues would have been unhappy had they known about their leader's clandestine dealings. Ashdown even wrote in his diary that his support for the government might cause his party to lose the by-election.

Having won his confidence vote, John Major did a series of TV interviews. After being questioned by Michael Brunson of ITN – and while both men assumed they were no longer being recorded – Brunson asked Major why he couldn't 'simply sack' three members of his Cabinet who had threatened to resign over the European treaty. That would only make things worse, Major explained. 'You and I can both think of ex-ministers who are going around causing all sorts of trouble. Do we want three more of the bastards out there?'

The exchanges were leaked and dominated the Sunday papers. Major never explained who the bastards were, but the consensus was he had meant Michael Portillo, Peter Lilley and John Redwood.

In Christchurch, the 'bastards' question dominated the Conservatives' Monday press conference. Reporters behaved like gleeful teenage schoolkids suddenly allowed to use a word that was rather more taboo in 1993 than nowadays. One reporter asked: 'Is it true that your motto, as you get stuck into the last week of campaigning, will be "Don't let the bastards get you down?"' That was met with wide laughs, including from Hayward. As far as he was concerned, he replied, the debates over Maastricht were now over. And Hayward boasted of support in his campaign from a 'full range of people' across the party. 'Does that mean you've had some bastards here supporting you?' asked this writer. Hayward laughed even more loudly.

But Maastricht troubles, the confidence vote, then Major's 'bastards' outburst all suggested a badly divided government which had lost its grip, quite beside its economic and financial woes. In the final days, the Tory campaign became a damage limitation exercise. A Lib Dem victory wouldn't change government policy, the Tories briefed reporters, and they were bound to win back Christchurch at a general election – as happened with most Lib Dem by-election victories, they said. A walkabout in Christchurch town centre was reduced from fifty minutes to just twenty as Hayward carefully tried to speak to as few people as possible lest a hostile response be captured on camera.

Yet many of the press sympathised with Hayward; they felt he'd been a good sport in taking on inevitable defeat, and after closing his final press conference, some journalists present gave him a spontaneous round of applause.

Labour's candidate also faced humiliation. Nigel Lickley, thirty-two, was a criminal barrister from Basingstoke who 'looked like a merchant banker', a BBC reporter observed. His main goal was not to do worse than Labour's 2 per cent in Newbury, though his task wasn't helped when transport spokesman John Prescott said on radio that it was 'unrealistic' to assume Labour could win. When Prescott visited Christchurch, a reporter reminded him what he'd said. 'I've completely changed my mind,' Prescott replied. 'I've now met Nigel and we're gonna win by a mile.'

Despite Labour's hopeless prospects, Lickley had support from almost the whole shadow Cabinet – Gordon Brown, Margaret Beckett, Tony Blair, David Blunkett and Jack Straw (both twice), Robin Cook, Donald Dewar, Mo Mowlam, Jack Cunningham and the Oscar-winning actress Glenda Jackson. Labour leader John Smith spent all day campaigning with Lickley, and they drove round together in the same car. 'You do realise,' Lickley's minder, newly elected MP John Denham, told him, 'that you've spent more time with Smith than any of us MPs ever dream of. We're lucky to get five minutes!'

Alan Sked, an LSE historian, stood for the Anti-Federalist League, as he had in Newbury. 'He was really impressive,' Lickley recalls, 'because he really knew his stuff.'

The high-profile nature of the contest attracted fourteen candidates in all, resulting in an eighteen-inch-long ballot paper. One contender wanted Graham Taylor sacked as England manager; others stood to advertise a local nightclub and a video game; and a scantily clad actress/model, Tara Bardot Jackson, came to Christchurch to promote the *Daily Sport* tabloid. A man called Andrew Bannon must have confused some voters by calling himself 'The Conservative Candidate', as opposed to Rob Hayward who was 'The Official Conservative'.

On the Thursday of voting, I toured polling stations from early morning until almost close of poll, conducting my own straw poll after people had cast their ballots. The verdict was stark – the citizens of Christchurch had voted Liberal Democrat by a ratio of two to one. And that was indeed the result as Diana Maddock won a whopping majority of 16,427, trouncing the Conservatives by 62.2 per cent to 31.4 per cent. The swing was a huge 35.4 per cent and the records had to be rewritten. In her acceptance speech, Maddock told John Major: 'Change your policies or change your job.'

Despite Labour bringing all their big-hitters down to Christchurch, Nigel Lickley lost his deposit, having got 2.7 per cent – not quite as bad as Newbury but a much bigger fall in support. Most Labour supporters had switched to the Lib Dems, of course.

As many people had forecast, Diana Maddock kept Christchurch only until the 1997 election when she was beaten by Conservative Christopher Chope (who remains the MP to this day), albeit by only 2,165 votes. She was immediately elevated to the Lords, served as president of the Liberal Democrats in 1998–99 and, in 2001, married former deputy leader Sir Alan Beith. Diana Maddock died in 2020.

Nigel Lickley fought and lost Basingstoke in 1997, then gave up politics to concentrate on the law and is now a senior criminal judge at the Old Bailey.

A week after Christchurch, Alan Sked and his colleagues met and agreed that the name Anti-Federalist League meant little to voters. A few weeks later, they changed it to the UK Independence Party – another mouthful which people would soon shorten to UKIP.

An internal Conservative HQ briefing note said the result was 'especially disappointing as Rob Hayward was such a good candidate'. But Hayward never tried to stand for Parliament again. Not long afterwards, he came out publicly as gay, joined the board of the LGBT group Stonewall and, in 1995, helped found the world's first gay rugby club, Kings Cross Steelers. For three decades, he has advised Conservative HQ on constituency boundary changes, and he became a regular election analyst, respected for his public impartiality despite becoming a Conservative peer. In the Lords, he has worked closely on election law with Chris Rennard, the architect of his 1993 defeat.

Christchurch remained the worst post-war by-election loss for any sitting government, until the Conservatives lost Clacton to UKIP in 2014, but that was exceptional because the UKIP candidate, Douglas Carswell, had defected from the Tories. In the 2024 Wellingborough by-election, the Conservatives suffered an even bigger fall in percentage vote than in Christchurch (37.6 per cent against 32.2 per cent). But looking back after more than three decades, Lord Hayward seems rather proud that one of his records does still stand — Christchurch remains the worst swing from a governing party to another major party in living memory.

Michael Crick *spent thirty-five years as a TV correspondent, with* Channel 4 News, Panorama *and* Newsnight. *His books include biographies of Jeffrey Archer, David Butler and Nigel Farage. His X account* @tomorrowsmps *follows parliamentary selections.*

67

EASTLEIGH

9 JUNE 1994
LIBERAL DEMOCRAT GAIN FROM CONSERVATIVES

MARK GARNETT

Result: David Chidgey (Liberal Democrats), 24,473, 44.3 per cent; Marilyn Birks (Labour), 15,234, 27.6 per cent; Stephen Reid (Conservative), 13,675, 24.7 per cent; Nigel Farage (UKIP), 972, 1.7 per cent; Screaming Lord Sutch (Monster Raving Loony), 783, 1.4 per cent; P. Warburton (Natural Law), 145, 0.3 per cent
Size of majority: 9,239
Swing: 21.5 per cent from Conservative to Liberal Democrats
Name of previous MP and party: Stephen Milligan (Conservative)
Reason for by-election: Death of incumbent
Result at previous general election: Stephen Milligan (Conservative), 38,998, 51.3 per cent; David Chidgey (Liberal Democrats), 21,296, 28.0 per cent; Johanna E. Sugrue (Labour), 15,768, 20.7 per cent
Date by-election called: 17 May 1994
Date by-election took place: 9 June 1994
Size of total electorate: 94,116
Total number of votes cast: 55,282
Turnout: 58.7 per cent

Stephen Milligan came relatively late to parliamentary politics but was widely touted to make up for lost time after his election in 1992 as Conservative MP for the Hampshire constituency of Eastleigh. As a journalist for *The Economist*, the BBC and the *Sunday Times*, he had demonstrated communication skills which John Major's government sorely lacked. Some former newsroom colleagues thought him unduly obsequious in the Commons; but friends, notably a fellow newcomer, Gyles Brandreth, recognised abilities which justified his ambitions. As an unabashed 'Europhile', Milligan's rarity value among the 1992 Tory intake was even more welcome to a government facing the challenge of ratifying the Maastricht Treaty. Milligan was promoted almost immediately, becoming parliamentary private secretary (PPS) to the staunchly Eurosceptic Minister of State for Defence Procurement, Jonathan Aitken.

At forty-three, Milligan was older than most aspiring 'high-flyers' first elected in 1992. He did, though, enjoy the security of a seemingly safe seat for life. Eastleigh, located in Hampshire's Hamble Valley between Southampton and Winchester, had been a marginal when first contested in 1955 as a straight fight between the Conservatives and Labour. The intrusion of a Liberal candidate in Labour's election-winning years of 1964 and 1966 probably helped the Tories to cling on to the seat; after 1970, their margin of victory increased in three-cornered contests.

An insignificant political force in the area before 1964 – they rarely contested seats in either Southampton or Winchester – the Liberals quickly established a strong presence in the new Eastleigh seat. In 1992, for the third election in a row, the party (now the Liberal Democrats) finished comfortably clear of Labour in second place. Its local appeal was registered even more strongly in local elections. In 1988, the newly merged party, under the short-lived 'Social & Liberal Democrat' label, took control of Eastleigh Council – the only English highlight of a dismal night for 'the Salads'. However, in the previous year's general election, Eastleigh's moderate Conservative MP, Sir David Price, had secured more than half the votes and a majority above 13,000. Adopted as the Conservative candidate on Price's retirement, Milligan could feel confident of maintaining this remarkable disparity between voting patterns at local and national level. He matched Price's share of the vote and increased the Conservative lead to almost 18,000.

Having covered serious political stories for most of his professional life, Milligan himself hit the headlines on 7 February 1994 when news broke of his sudden death. Panic-stricken Tory whips initially hinted at homicide, while the Prime Minister initially gave the impression that Milligan must have taken his own life. In fact, he had died accidentally, during solitary sexual activity. The intrusive modern media would always have treated a fatality of this kind as a pretext for prurient speculation. However, in February 1994, coverage was sure to be bound up with the 'Back to Basics' slogan which Major had deployed at the October 1993 Conservative conference. He had hoped to relaunch his beleaguered premiership by appealing to basic British decency as the lodestone for future policymaking. The speech was 'spun' by Major's overzealous entourage as the prelude to a moral crusade, embracing aspects of private conduct. This interpretation was widely accepted: it was what many Conservative conference-goers had wanted to hear, if not what Major had been trying to say.

Stories discreditable to Major had been frequent media features even before (but especially after) 'Black Wednesday' (September 1992). In that month, the Prime Minister's friend David Mellor had been forced out of the Cabinet, following imaginative press coverage of an extra-marital affair. Just a few weeks before Milligan's death, another over-publicised domestic tragedy had prompted the resignation of a junior minister, the Earl of Caithness. Whether or not such developments were relevant to either the real or imagined themes of 'Back to Basics', for the Conservative Party, the 'optics' of Milligan's death could not have been more unhelpful. On hearing the news, the Prime Minister's own *bête rouge*, Edwina Currie, noted in her diary that the media were already 'talking endlessly about sleaze'.

Edwina Currie assumed that Milligan's successor would be chosen on the scheduled date for local elections – 5 May 1994. Although that timetable would deny Eastleigh's voters parliamentary representation for nearly three months, it would follow the previous year's Newbury precedent, with the additional justification that three other (Labour-held) seats were waiting to be filled after deaths in the first weeks of 1994.

Serious campaigning in Eastleigh, in fact, began before Milligan's funeral. The by-election was discussed by senior Liberal Democrats at a meeting of 8 February. On the sensible supposition of a May poll, the party's leader Paddy Ashdown anticipated simultaneous blows against both of its rivals — seizing council seats from Labour while wresting Eastleigh from the Tories. However, for the Liberal Democrats, Eastleigh represented jeopardy as well as opportunity. Labour was sure to fight harder than it had done at either Newbury or Christchurch in the previous year; its lead in national opinion polls had surged, thanks not least to the renewed slew of sleaze stories. More insistently than ever, both of the main parties were likely to argue that voting for the Liberal Democrats would be a pointless protest — an argument inadvertently assisted by a young Lib Dem councillor, Keith House, who seemed flummoxed when *Newsnight*'s Michael Crick asked him on camera to explain what a Lib Dem win in Eastleigh would achieve.

With no realistic chance of holding the seat but hoping to stave off a setback even more severe than its 1993 reverses, the Conservatives suffered a new setback shortly after Milligan's death. In the words of the Hampshire-born journalist John Arlott: 'The very name "Eastleigh" means railways'; the constituency included several stations as well as facilities for locomotive building and repair. The prospect of significant job cuts, resulting from the government's unpopular rail privatisation, extracted only mealy-mouthed answers from ministers (including Major himself).

Nevertheless, the government continued to hope that its candidate could sneak into a face-saving second place, given adequate support and the likelihood of unseemly squabbling between the opposition parties. In 1992, Labour's candidate had trailed by more than 23,000 votes, making the idea of an Eastleigh result which replicated the national opinion polls profoundly fanciful. However, with the Conservatives mortally wounded, Labour strategists had turned their attention to more realistic obstacles to victory in the next general election. As Ashdown had anticipated, Labour had a vested interest in campaigning to stall the Liberal Democrat run of by-election victories, even if this allowed the Conservatives to retain Eastleigh.

The voters of Eastleigh did go the polls on 5 May 1994, and a parliamentary by-election was held on that day. However, the Eastleigh voters were only taking part in the local elections, while the 5 May parliamentary contest was held at Rotherham, to fill the vacancy created by the death of its Labour MP on 25 January. There was no by-election at Eastleigh because the government had decided to delay 'moving the writ' – the process which, by informal convention, prevented by-elections from being held until the incumbent party had given its permission. After its 1993 defeats, Major's government had decided to exploit this provision to drag in its heels. As a result, the writs for Eastleigh and the other pending by-elections were not moved until 17 May, with voting to take place on 9 June.

The postponement of the Eastleigh by-election is easily explained. While not discounting the importance of May's local elections, the Conservatives were far more exercised by the nationwide elections to the European Parliament (EP), scheduled for 9 June. The UK vote could be treated by voters, and presented by commentators, as a sur-rogate referendum on the government's European policy. Fêted in late 1991 even by Eurosceptics as a latter-day Sir Francis Drake for his tough negotiations at Maastricht, by 1994 Major was regarded by the 'Thatcherised' grass roots of his party as a deadlier national foe than the Spanish Armada. If the 1994 local elections went badly, they could be rationalised as a typical and unrepresentative symptom of 'mid-term blues'; a similar (or even greater) reversal in the EP elections would be a different matter. If the Conservatives went into that campaign fresh from a humiliating by-election defeat as well as poor local election results, the depressive effect on grass roots activists would have been greater. It would be particularly dangerous if the by-election gave a further fillip to the Liberal Democrats, whose clear stance on 'Europe' contrasted sharply with Major's uncomfortable fence-straddling. Jittery Conservative MEPs duly found a receptive audience when they lob-bied government managers to delay Eastleigh for as long as decency permitted.

In blissful ignorance of these high-level machinations, the main local parties selected their Eastleigh champions in good time for a May election. In mid-March, the Conservatives chose Stephen Reid, an IT specialist and then leader of Basingstoke Council (a position he was to lose in the May local elections). The Labour candidate was Marilyn Birks, a senior drama lecturer at Winchester's King Alfred's College. On the first of three visits to the constituency, the shadow Home Secretary, Tony Blair, presided over Birks's introductory press conference. Predictably, Blair targeted the Liberal Democrats rather than the incumbent Conservatives, claiming that a vote for Ashdown's party would be wasted since 'they stand for nothing'.

Also before the end of March, the Lib Dems nominated David Chidgey, who had stood for the party in 1992 and performed respectably. He was on a shortlist of three, with the temporarily tongue-tied councillor Keith House and the London-based Jenny Tonge (later MP for Richmond Park, 1997–2005). An engineer and railway specialist with deep local roots, Chidgey's lack of media pizzazz was probably an additional attraction to obtuse local Liberal Democrats, who decided that they preferred his proven track record.

Gamblers on a Liberal Democrat victory at Eastleigh could feel satisfied with their investments after May's local election results. Eastleigh Borough Council returned to Liberal Democrat control, under Keith House's leadership; Labour and the Conservatives contested a distant second place. In the same day's Rotherham by-election, the Lib Dem vote share increased by 17.4 points, chiefly at the expense of the future Conservative minister Nick Gibb, who barely bested the Monster Raving Loony candidate. Kicking Eastleigh into the long grass, it transpired, was unlikely to help the Conservatives to retrieve the electoral ball from Ashdown's rampant team.

By 1994, Euro election day in the UK was well established as a celebration of democratic indifference. However, there was open speculation at Westminster that a disastrous national outcome for the Conservatives could provoke dramatic domestic ramifications, even bringing an end to Major's precarious European balancing act. Indeed, the Prime Minister had exchanged calculations with his party chairman, Sir Norman Fowler, agreeing that his position would be in peril if the Tory tally of MEPs was reduced from thirty-two to less than ten.

One party had lost its leader even before the votes were cast on 9 June; but the felled figure was Labour's John Smith rather than Major. The sudden death of Smith – not long after a campaigning appearance at Eastleigh – caused a temporary cessation of electoral hostilities, nationally and locally. Tony Blair quickly became the overwhelming favourite to replace Smith, not least because his fellow 'moderniser', the shadow Chancellor Gordon Brown, was persuaded not to stand against him.

For Blair's supporters, the unexpected development increased the salience of Eastleigh but also its potential hazards. Blair's 'USP' for the success-starved Labour Party was his probable but unproven appeal to voters in places which his rivals could not reach. Relatively prosperous southern constituencies like Eastleigh seemed unwinnable even by an electoral miracle-worker; but Blair's interventions in the constituency had included ritualistic predictions of Labour victory as well as disparaging comments about the Liberal Democrats. Notionally, at the time of the by-election, Labour was led by a 'caretaker', Margaret Beckett. However, as 'leader-in-waiting', Blair had attracted very extensive and flattering media coverage. If, as he had claimed, Labour had been well placed to win Eastleigh under John Smith, the idea of a more voter-friendly prospective leader should have turned the probability into a certainty. Yet before Smith's death, Labour activists already knew, on the basis of canvassing as well the local election results, that second place at Eastleigh was the best they could hope for, with or without the 'Blair factor'. The Lib Dem bandwagon was rolling too vigorously and its wheels were most unlikely to fall off.

In this context, it is significant that Blair, who was allergic to association with defeat, did not return to Eastleigh on the eve of the poll. This honour was consigned to the dutiful Gordon Brown – not noted for his electoral pulling-power in southern England. The biggest Tory gun was in the repair shop: Michael Heseltine, whose own health issues had been brought into focus by Smith's fatal heart attack, was suspected (as usual) of lurking in the hope of benefiting from Major's misfortunes. The Foreign Secretary, Douglas Hurd, was fielded as a worthy but less than rabble-rousing alternative for Eastleigh Tories.

The full list of Eastleigh candidates – just six – was sharply reduced compared to Newbury and Christchurch. Among the deposit-forfeiting also-rans was Nigel Farage, standing on behalf of the newly dubbed 'United Kingdom Independence Party' (UKIP) while also contesting a free and fair election for the 'undemocratic' EU Parliament. Although Farage won fewer than 1,000 Eastleigh votes, he did surpass Lord David Sutch for fourth place at this early stage of a career which encompassed feats beyond the wildest fantasy of any Monster Raving Loony.

Few observers were surprised that David Chidgey won Eastleigh for the Liberal Democrats. Yet his majority – 9,239 ahead of Labour and 10,798 above the unseated Conservatives – was greater than expected even by Lib Dem number-crunchers. The turnout, way down on Newbury and Christchurch at less than 59 per cent, presumably reflected a local feeling that the result had been a foregone conclusion for too long. At less than 17 per cent, the 'swing' from Conservative to the Liberal Democrats was unremarkable by recent standards – indeed, on the same night more substantial shifts, from Conservative to Labour, were registered at Dagenham (vacated as recently as 17 May by Labour's Bryan Gould) and Barking, where the nascent 'strength and stability' of the Conservative Theresa May attracted fewer than 2,000 votes.

However, Eastleigh was the only by-election that mattered on 9 June and dominated media attention while the votes for the EP were counted over the weekend. For Major's biographer, Anthony Seldon, 'Eastleigh was a moment of truth'. As well as showing that one of the opposition parties could win seats from the Conservatives, even if Labour and the Liberal Democrats engaged in a slanging-match, the outcome confirmed that no south of England Conservative MP could feel safe from Ashdown's insurgents. Notwithstanding the local factors at play at Eastleigh, Major's 'Back to Basics' relaunch had only made a Conservative shipwreck more likely.

However, Ashdown himself was less than ecstatic, reflecting in his diary that Labour's Eastleigh performance 'had taken the gilt from the gingerbread'. His forebodings were confirmed by the delayed EP election results. Thanks to the 'first past the post' system – being used for the final time – the Liberal Democrats won 16.1 per cent of the UK vote, but just two of the eighty-seven seats. Unlike at Eastleigh, the Lib Dems had suffered from the system because Labour supporters in the south of England stuck to their party allegiance rather than voting tactically. Although the Conservatives lost thirteen seats (on less than 27 per cent of the votes), their final tally of eighteen was comfortably clear of the Major–Fowler doomsday scenario.

Leaderless Labour had saved John Major – or, rather, by repelling the Liberal Democrats' southern surge in the Euro elections, it gave the Prime Minister another year, before he resorted to the desperate device of a vote of confidence in himself. Although he defeated his unelectable

1995 leadership challenger, John Redwood, the latter's slogan – 'No change, no chance' – encapsulated the message of the various elections of 9 June 1994. Barring some deeply improbable development – something even more unlikely than a bloodless substitution of Heseltine for Major – Labour was sure to be the largest party after the next general election, under Tony Blair or any other conceivable leader.

The remaining question in June 1994 was whether Labour needed the insurance of some kind of pre-election deal with the Liberal Democrats. For those who looked beyond tactical considerations and envisaged a lasting 'progressive alliance' between Labour and the Lib Dems, the Eastleigh result could not have been more opportune. It helped to convince Ashdown to abandon his increasingly untenable posture of 'equidistance' between the two main parties. The Lib Dem leader was impatient for serious talks with Labour to begin, as soon as Blair took over (21 July 1994). However, the EP elections had strongly suggested that Labour could win nationally, and win big, without the kind of deal which might alienate the party's more tribal members. Ashdown's published diaries show how Blair exploited the combined lessons of 9 June 1994, holding out the hope of meaningful co-operation and even the prospect of radical electoral change, to keep the Lib Dems onside until 1997 without ever committing to a formal pact.

As for Eastleigh, its history since the 1994 by-election has been unusually interesting. David Chidgey retained the seat against the 1997 Labour landslide and increased his majority in 2001 as the gilt began to drop off Blair's gingerbread. He was elevated to the House of Lords before the 2005 general election. His successor, Chris Huhne, enjoyed a pastiche of 'power', becoming a coalition Cabinet minister in 2010. However, he was forced to resign from the Cameron government in February 2012, and from Parliament a year later, eventually serving a prison term for infringements of John Major's 'basics'. The subsequent by-election (28 February 2013) was another blast from the past, with thirteen contestants. As in 1994, there was a 'Beer, Baccy and Crumpet' candidate, although on this occasion this was someone other than Nigel Farage.

Yet there had been dramatic happenings among the electors of Eastleigh since Farage's first stumblings on the electoral stage. Between

1994 and 2013, UKIP was no more than a speck on the Eastleigh horizon. But among the crowded cast of characters in the 2013 by-election, the UKIP candidate (Diane James, later Farage's short-lived successor as party leader) finished in second place, less than 2,000 votes behind the Liberal Democrat winner. In the general elections of 2015, 2017 and 2019, pre-1994 service was resumed, with the Conservatives securing commanding majorities. However, the intervention of a Faragist 'Reform UK' candidate in 2024 was sufficient to turn Eastleigh back to what it had been in 1997 – a Lib Dem seat, vulnerable to assault from all flanks.

Mark Garnett has taught British politics at several universities. He is the author of numerous books and articles, including most recently Keeping the Red Flag Flying: The Labour Party in Opposition since 1922 *(with Gavin Hyman and Richard Johnson, Polity Press, 2024).*

68

DUDLEY WEST

15 DECEMBER 1994
LABOUR GAIN FROM CONSERVATIVES

LUCIA HENWOOD

Result: Ian Pearson (Labour), 28,400, 68.8 per cent; Graham Postles (Conservative), 7,706, 18.7 per cent; Mike Hadley (Liberal Democrats), 3,154, 7.6 per cent; Malcolm Floyd (UKIP), 590, 1.4 per cent; Andy Carmichael (National Front), 561, 1.4 per cent; Mike Hyde (Liberal), 548, 1.3 per cent; Mike Nattrass (New Britain), 146, 0.4 per cent; Marjorie Nicholson (FOREST – Freedom of Choice for Smokers), 77, 0.2 per cent; John Oldbury (Natural Law), 70, 0.2 per cent; Colin Palmer (21st Century Conservatives), 55, 0.1 per cent
Size of majority: 20,694
Swing: 29.1 per cent from Conservative to Labour
Name of previous MP and party: John Blackburn (Conservative)
Reason for by-election: Death of incumbent
Result at previous general election: John Blackburn (Conservative), 34,729, 48.8 per cent; K. J. Lomax (Labour), 28,940, 40.7 per cent; Gerald P. T. Lewis (Liberal Democrats), 7,446, 10.5 per cent
Date by-election called: 23 November 1994
Date by-election took place: 15 December 1994
Size of total electorate: 87,972
Total number of votes cast: 41,307
Turnout: 47.0 per cent

When the results of the Dudley West by-election were declared in the early hours of 16 December, the size of Labour's victory broke the BBC's parliamentary projection model. The 29.1 per cent swing was the largest from Conservative to Labour since 1945. Translated nationally, it would have caused the Conservatives to lose every seat. The model was not set up to display this, so the BBC had to add a single seat to allow the projections to be shown. A Conservative majority of 8.1 per cent in Dudley West in 1992 had been transformed into a Labour majority of 50.1 per cent. At a time when the Conservative government appeared tired, divided and crisis-prone, Dudley West seemed like a powerful sign that Labour was poised to take over.

The by-election was triggered by the death of John Blackburn on 12 October 1994. Blackburn, who had represented Dudley West since 1979, was known as a 'policeman's friend' in the Commons and a 'first-class constituency MP' locally. As Dudley West was a Conservative seat, it was up to the government to choose the by-election's date. The *Birmingham Post* reported that the government might delay 'the likely humiliation' until the new year. However, on 23 November, the date was announced as 15 December, ten days before Christmas.

Dudley West was the first contest of the parliamentary term in a Labour–Conservative seat. The Conservatives had lost three by-elections with double-digit swings, but all three had been to the Liberal Democrats. It was also Tony Blair's first electoral test since becoming Labour leader in July. At that point, New Labour was very new: the term had only been unveiled a few weeks earlier during Blair's first conference speech as leader. With Blair's battle over Clause IV and Labour Party reform just beginning, he needed to prove that New Labour's approach could expand the party's appeal to new groups of voters. As a test of this, Dudley West could hardly have been better. According to Fiona Gordon, the Labour campaign's deputy manager, Dudley West's electorate was a 'microcosm of the coalition of voters' Labour needed to win over to regain power, ranging from 'typical Black Country' areas like Brierley Hill to 'middle-class, prosperous' Kingswinford and Sedgley.

Dudley West's political history was moderately conservative, but this was certainly not core Tory territory. The constituency had only gone Conservative in 1979. Both Labour and Conservative MPs had represented Dudley and Brierley Hill, its two predecessor seats, since 1945. The trend continued beyond 1994. After winning the by-election,

Labour's Ian Pearson held the successor seat of Dudley South for all of the Blair and Brown years, deciding not to seek re-election in 2010, when it returned to the Conservatives. In 2024, Dudley went Labour again.

In 1992, the Conservative majority in Dudley West was solid but not resounding. John Blackburn was re-elected with a nearly halved majority of 5,789, following a 4 per cent swing to Labour, a close reflection of the national result. To win a majority at the next general election, Labour needed to gain fifty-five seats from the Conservatives. Dudley West was the fifty-fourth most vulnerable Conservative seat.

Results in Dudley West tended to match the national picture closely – and the national picture in autumn 1994 was dismal for the Conservative Party. Since their unexpected victory in 1992, the Conservatives' 21-seat majority had begun to ebb away. The loss of Dudley West brought it down to thirteen. In September 1992, Black Wednesday had seen the UK crash out of the European Exchange Rate Mechanism. Public perception of the Conservatives was tarnished by sleaze scandals and blue-on-blue fighting over the Maastricht Treaty. At the time of the by-election, John Major was governing with a minority of four, having suspended eight Maastricht rebels from the Conservative whip. From the start, Dudley West appeared to be a contest which Labour was certain to win.

Given Labour's prospects, the party's candidate selection was fiercely contested. Out of around 200 applicants, four candidates were chosen by the NEC to be put before local party members. By 1997, three of the four shortlisted candidates were in Parliament. The future Home Secretary Jacqui Smith, elected in Redditch in 1997, came second. Ian Pearson described the selection battle as a 'brutal' process, a harder fight than the by-election itself.

Pearson was in many ways the ideal New Labour candidate, combining local roots, strong Labour commitments and 'pro-business' credentials. Fergus Sheppard, the *Birmingham Evening Mail*'s political editor, recalled him as 'illustrative of the new kind of candidate Labour were fielding'. An Oxford PPE graduate, he trained as an accountant before gaining a PhD in industrial studies at Warwick. With the exception of his time at Oxford, Pearson had lived in Dudley West and the two neighbouring constituencies all his life. In 1994, he was joint-CEO of the West Midlands Enterprise Board, a consultancy and investment company. The role was highly enough paid that becoming an MP meant taking a 40 per cent pay cut. Pearson had been a Labour member since the age of fifteen. Although not active at the time of his selection, he had worked part-time in the party's local government research service in the 1980s and served for two years on Dudley Council. Described by Blair during the campaign as 'ministerial material', he went on to serve as a minister from 2001 to 2010, including as Economic Secretary to the Treasury from 2008.

The revelation that Pearson had been a member of Militant Tendency in the 1980s provided some ammunition for other parties. Still, there were no colourful details to cause lasting damage. Pearson's membership of Militant Tendency had been short-lived, abandoned by the time he left school. By 1994, he had 'credentials for fighting Militant more than being a member', viewing it as 'cancerous' for the Labour Party. Despite attempts by rival campaigns to paint him as a more extreme figure, the image he presented to voters was reassuringly moderate.

The other main candidates were similarly dependable choices. Graham Postles, the Conservative candidate, worked for an insurance firm in Brierley Hill and described himself as 'the locals' choice'. He later served two years as chairman of the Conservative Policy Forum and was active in the party until his death in 2020. The Liberal Democrat, Mike Hadley, was a former pharmacist, brought up in the area, who was married to a doctor and ran a medical software business he had founded.

Dudley West voters also had seven minor-party candidates to choose from, including four who made opposition to the Maastricht Treaty a focus of their campaign. Malcolm Floyd of the newly founded UK Independence Party did best, coming fourth with 590 votes. His leaflets included a brief letter from Enoch Powell, urging voters to 'speak for Britain' and 'help to turn out a government which persists in Europe'. Other candidates campaigned on more unusual platforms. Marjorie Nicholson stood for FOREST, Freedom of Choice for Smokers, urging voters to 'light up Dudley West!', while the Natural Law Party's John

Oldbury promised to deliver 'problem-free government' using 'Yogic Flying'. Standing for the National Front, Andy Carmichael came fifth with 561 votes. In 1997, he was revealed in the *Sunday Times* to have been an undercover agent, employed by MI5 to infiltrate the party, later helping to engineer a split within the organisation.

The BBC summarised the campaign as 'fairly low-key', suggesting the voters of Dudley West were more interested in the approach of Christmas than the election, showing little interest in the Cabinet and shadow Cabinet members who visited almost daily. Alongside political visits, the 'star turn' was actor Richard Attenborough at the peak of *Jurassic Park* fame, who visited to support Labour in his green Rolls-Royce. Lord Snape, then MP for West Bromwich East and one of Pearson's minders, said most efforts focused on the 'bread-and-butter doorstep campaign'. The core campaign messaging followed well-trodden paths. The Conservatives attacked Ian Pearson's 'left-wing record', calling him a candidate who kept the 'Left in Labour'. The Labour campaign focused on 'Tory tax lies'. As Pearson told *The Guardian*, the campaign's central issues were 'tax, tax, tax' and 'VAT, VAT'. In one leaflet, the underlined phrase 'you pay more tax' appeared three times. Another leaflet asked voters what they would do 'with £500 extra to spend this Christmas', before saying they'd 'already spent it – on taxes', encouraging voters to give themselves 'an early Christmas present' by voting Labour.

Lord Snape remembers the Labour campaign as 'faultless from start to finish', while the other campaigns were also organised, professional operations. The Labour campaign was the most active but also, with most to lose, especially cautious. Pearson described campaign manager Fraser Kemp, a future MP, as a 'typical election agent', who viewed the candidate as a 'legal necessity' rather than someone who should be kept informed about every detail. He contrasted the contest with his experience standing in Bexhill & Battle in 'third place Sussex' in 1983, where, with far less at stake, he had more freedom in his campaigning. In Dudley West, the general attitude of those around him was 'keep quiet, we're winning'.

There was plenty to encourage Labour through the campaign. The previous year, Kenneth Clarke had questioned the relevance of election promises 'made on a wet night in Dudley'. It was repeatedly quoted by local newspapers and Labour campaigners. The loss of two previously safe Conservative wards on Dudley Council during the campaign did nothing to improve Conservative morale. Nationally, the picture was even less encouraging. While the campaign period was not all smooth sailing for Labour, with rows about Blair's choice of school for his son making the news, the problems the Conservatives faced were on a different scale. On 6 December, the week before the by-election, the government was defeated on plans to increase VAT on domestic fuel, the first government defeat on a Budget measure since 1978. The *Telegraph* described it as a 'humiliating defeat', the 'biggest blow to Mr Major's authority' in his time as Prime Minister. Fiona Gordon recalled Donald Dewar, shadow Social Security Secretary, receiving a 'rockstar welcome' in Dudley the next day because there was a sense that Labour had defeated the government on an issue 'which really mattered to people'.

By the end of the campaign, Coral had stopped taking bets on a Labour victory. A poll by the *Birmingham Evening Mail* predicted a swing of 30 per cent from the Conservatives to Labour. The *Wolverhampton Express and Star* ran the headline: 'Labour alarmed by its huge poll lead'. With all signs pointing towards a resounding victory, Labour's main fears were around getting out the vote and managing expectations.

In the end, Labour had no cause for concern. Ian Pearson was elected with a majority of over 20,000 and a 29.1 per cent swing to Labour. At the count, Pearson said Dudley West had 'spoken for the nation', bringing 'closer the end of this discredited, shambolic, tired, sleazy government'. In his diaries, Alastair Campbell described Pearson as delivering 'our message word-perfect'. A few days earlier, Campbell had emphasised the importance of Pearson mentioning New Labour in his victory speech. He delivered, calling the result 'a positive vote for New Labour under the leadership of Tony Blair'.

Former Conservative chair Norman Fowler wrote in his diaries that there was 'next to nothing' for his party's 'comfort'. The only consolation for Conservatives was low turnout of only 47 per cent, down 35 per cent from 1992. Despite Labour's share of the vote rising by 28 per cent, their number of votes had actually decreased by 540. The Conservatives argued that voters had simply stayed home, not shifted to Labour. On the BBC results programme, Stephen Dorrell, Secretary of State for National Heritage, blamed party disunity for the result, arguing that the Conservatives could recover if they presented a more united front, especially on Europe. This seemed an unlikely prospect. On the same programme, Bill Cash, a prominent Conservative Eurosceptic, said voters were deserting the party because of the economic fallout of the failed attempt to increase integration with Europe. David Dimbleby warned that results like Dudley West risked bringing the Conservatives into a 'vortex of decline', as individual MPs felt their own electoral prospects were best served by breaking with party orthodoxy.

The lessons Labour drew were understandably more positive. The by-election had also provided experience campaigning in the kind of 'weathervane' seat that would decide the next election. The party made use of the tactics and expertise they developed during the campaign. After the by-election, campaign manager Fraser Kemp moved to Labour headquarters. Rejecting the idea that 'general disillusionment' with the government alone had driven the result, Labour argued that the electorate were also interested in what New Labour had to say. Lord Rooker, then MP for Birmingham Perry Barr and one of Pearson's minders, described Dudley West as the campaign where Labour discovered the 'switchers', Conservative voters bypassing the Liberal Democrats and going straight to Labour. During the campaign, Labour held the first of several 'switchers' events, a meeting between Tony Blair and voters changing parties, a tactic which they later used more extensively. Having identified the 'switchers', Labour improved their data collection in future campaigns, allowing them to deliver more targeted messages to voters.

For a governing party, in power for fifteen years, to lose a by-election like Dudley West was hardly surprising. The Conservatives had an unbroken run of ten by-election losses since 1989. Some of these seats had returned to the party in 1992. However, to lose it by such a large margin, without anyone expressing much shock, was disastrous. Pointing to low turnout was useful in suggesting voters had not actually defected to Labour, but it underlined how far Conservative support had fallen. By share of the vote retained, it was the Conservatives' worst result in history, against any party. Only 22 per cent of 1992 Conservative voters in Dudley West supported them. As pollster Peter Kellner told the BBC, the Conservatives were 'staring into an abyss', with every indicator, from polls to local elections, showing they were 'the most unpopular government this century'.

The normality of the campaign reinforced this. The by-election was brought about by the death of a popular local MP, not by any scandal. There were no significant local grievances to motivate voters. The constituency's dynamics meant that tactical voting could play no role in the result. Candidates from all major parties were credible and qualified, supported by competent campaigns. The story of the Dudley West by-election was simply that of voters in a bellwether seat turning away from the Conservative Party in large numbers. As the *Birmingham Post* wrote, the result left 'no hiding place' for the Conservative Party.

The worst Conservative fears about Dudley West's impact did not materialise. Major managed to stay on as Prime Minister. The idea, raised by Robin Oakley on the BBC, that, given the size of the Conservative majority and the age of some Conservative MPs, 'actuarial probability' alone suggested the Conservative majority might not last a full term, proved overly pessimistic. The government limped on until 1997. However, Dudley West set the tone of the following months and years. Fergus Sheppard described it as a 'wind direction is changing kind of by-election', showing that New Labour was 'the rising force in the land'. For David Benjamin, who reported on the by-election for the *Birmingham Post and Mail*, what happened in Dudley West made the results of 1997 a 'foregone conclusion'.

Lucia Henwood is an economic analyst. She has previously worked as a researcher on books by Peter Cardwell, Michael Crick, Isabel Hardman and Jane Martinson and on The Times Guide to the House of Commons 2024 *(Times Books, 2024).*

69

WINCHESTER

20 NOVEMBER 1997
LIBERAL DEMOCRAT GAIN FROM CONSERVATIVES

JACK BROWN

Result: Mark Oaten (Liberal Democrats), 37,006, 68.0 per cent; Gerry Malone (Conservative), 15,450, 28.4 per cent; Patrick Davies (Labour), 944, 1.7 per cent; Robin Page (UKIP), 521, 1.0 per cent; Lord David Sutch (Monster Raving Loony), 316, 0.6 per cent; Richard Huggett (Literal Democrat Mark Here to Win), 59, 0.1 per cent; Rosemary Barry (Natural Law), 48, 0.1 per cent; Roger Everest (Independent Conservative), 40, 0.1 per cent

Size of majority: 21,556

Swing: 19.8 per cent from Conservative to Liberal Democrats

Name of previous MP and party: Gerry Malone (Conservative)

Reason for by-election: Rerun following legal challenges after 1997 general election result

Result at previous general election: Mark Oaten (Liberal Democrats), 26,100, 42.1 per cent; Gerry Malone (Conservative), 26,098, 42.1 per cent; Patrick Davies (Labour), 6,528, 10.5 per cent; Peter Strand (Referendum), 1,598, 2.6 per cent; Richard Huggett (Liberal Democrat Top Choice for Parliament), 640, 1.0 per cent; Derek Rumsey (UKIP), 476, 0.8 per cent; John Browne (Independent), 307, 0.5 per cent; Peter Stockton (Monster Raving Loony), 307, 0.5 per cent

Date by-election called: 28 October 1997

Date by-election took place: 20 November 1997

Size of total electorate: 79,116

Total number of votes cast: 54,384

Turnout: 68.7 per cent

The Winchester by-election of 20 November 1997 was fascinating for at least three different reasons. The controversial circumstances in which it was held would alone warrant its inclusion in this book. Effectively a rerun of the general election contest of 1 May, it took place following a legal challenge that saw the original result rendered void. After a long night of vote-counting chaos, the election had seen the joint closest result in British electoral history announced, with the winner declared by a margin of just two votes. The second-placed candidate subsequently challenged the result, arguing successfully that a small but crucial number of votes ruled technically ineligible should have been counted. The resulting by-election was, therefore, an acrimonious and awkward affair.

The by-election's result was also interesting in itself. Its much clearer result was symbolic of significant national changes. The Liberal Democrats took the seat from the Conservatives comfortably, dealing another hammer blow to the recently defeated party of national government. The losing Conservative candidate had been a government minister at the time of the general election. Winchester had been represented by a Conservative since 1950 and had only elected an MP from a different party on one other occasion across the entire twentieth century. Winchester, therefore, underlined how far the Tories had fallen in 1997.

Finally, the Winchester by-election stands out for the particular role played by the outsiders and oddballs that have long been a hardy perennial of British elections. It represented the last poll contested by the Monster Raving Looney Party's Screaming Lord Sutch, perhaps the most iconic such figure. However, the role of independent electoral troublemaker Richard Huggett was to prove more significant. Huggett ran on a deliberately confusing ticket, seeking to disrupt and interfere in the result, ultimately leading to a national change in the law following the election. This only added to the sense of chaos in what was a fascinating mess of a by-election.

The 1997 general election was itself a remarkable contest, resulting in a historically unusual and sizeable victory for Tony Blair's 'New' Labour. The party's majority of 179 was the largest achieved by any government in the post-war era. Blair's 1997 win followed a surprise victory for John Major's Conservative Party in 1992, won with the largest number of votes ever attracted by a single political party. This turnaround represented a rare true 'landslide'.

New Labour's campaign was extremely professional, with the young, charismatic and then-popular Tony Blair at its heart. A few months after the election, one internal Labour Party poll found a remarkable 93 per cent of the British public thought Blair was doing a good job. But the Conservatives were also tired, having been in power since 1979. The Exchange Rate Mechanism crisis of 1992, which saw the government's economic policy collapse at great expense at the hands of the international money markets on 'Black Wednesday', killed the party's reputation for economic competence. Public services were crumbling and infighting over Europe was rampant. A series of scandals then further damaged the flagging Conservatives. This anti-Tory feeling helped both Labour and the Liberal Democrats. The latter won forty-six seats, at the time the highest number won by any third party in the post-war years. They also recorded over half as many votes as the Conservative Party nationally.

In Winchester, the key contest was between the Liberal Democrats and the Conservative Party and saw the former emerge apparently triumphant. Liberal Democrat candidate Mark Oaten was eventually told he had won the seat by just two votes, despite a messy process that had seen two full recounts, briefly interrupted by a planned wedding reception. Had just one vote gone the other way, the result would have been an exact tie. This would reportedly have seen lots drawn to decide the winner.

It had been a wild ride. The initial count did not conclude until 6 a.m. and put Oaten ahead by 290 votes. After the first recount, Oaten was thought to have lost by twenty-two. His declared victory arrived at 6 p.m. the following day, after yet another recount. It was a major shock for the exhausted participants. The Conservative candidate Gerald Malone had been a deputy chairman of the Conservative Party and Minister of State in the Department of Health. He had entered the election with a majority of over 8,000. Oaten, who would go on to chair the Liberal Democrats from 2001 to 2003 and serve as their home affairs spokesperson from 2003 to 2006, was not yet a nationally recognised figure. Despite this, Malone's presumably exhausted election agent did not initially push for a third recount. Instead, Malone would launch a legal challenge in the weeks that followed.

Malone's case was based on the grounds that fifty-five ballots had been rejected for lacking a perforated strip or stamp that indicated their authenticity. He also argued that two additional rejected ballots should also have been counted. In both cases, Malone's complaint was against the returning officer and those running the election on the ground, rather than his opponent. The lack of stamp appeared a simple administrative error but a significant one. Of the fifty-five rejected ballots, twenty-two were marked for Malone and eighteen for Oaten. Had they been counted, Malone would have been the candidate who won by two votes.

Election annulments are extremely rare in the UK, but Malone's relatively straightforward case nevertheless won the day. Lord Justice Sir Henry Brooke agreed that the election should be declared void after short consideration at the High Court. The Speaker of the House was then required to 'move the writ' and order a by-election, which she did on 28 October. The by-election was fixed for 20 November. Given the nature of the complaint, *The Independent* predicted the rerun election would be 'bitter and closely fought'. In the event, there was plenty of bitterness, even if most of it occurred away from the main participants, but there was little that was close about the result.

Despite his unusual win in the High Court, the Conservative candidate was not initially happy with the judge's decision to hand the result back to the electorate rather than directly to himself, with his opponent remaining Winchester's MP in the interim. In Malone's view, he had won the election and should remain the MP. Malone told *The Guardian* he was still speaking to former constituents who wanted him to continue casework on their behalf: 'But I can't. I won but I am not in Parliament. He lost and he is there.'

The Liberal Democrats did not oppose the High Court's decision to annul the general election result. Oaten expressed his fear of becoming 'a *Trivial Pursuit* question in years to come' by losing his seat in record time in an interview with *The Guardian* but conceded he had already 'become a quiz show question' by being declared winner by such a tight margin in the now-voided original contest. He claimed his team had 'what we wanted' from the court's decision, with the election result handed back to Winchester's electorate for another try rather than overturned.

Oaten's seemingly relaxed approach to the rerun may also have been influenced by his belief that it was his, rather than his Conservative opponent's vote, that had been suppressed in the general election. Some newspapers mused that the rerun favoured the Conservatives, as the 2,000 or so votes won by minor parties tending towards the Eurosceptic right in May were now surely up for grabs in November. However, Labour had won 6,528 votes in May, and some reporting suggested that the party was considering standing its candidate down in November to ensure a Tory defeat. The picture was further complicated by the source of most of the bitterness around the election's rerun: the candidacy of former teacher Richard John Huggett.

Richard Huggett ran as an independent candidate in Winchester during the general election under the banner 'Liberal Democrat Top Choice for Parliament'. He won 640 votes, just 1 per cent of the total but still 320 times the winning margin. Oaten would have been within his rights to assume that at least some of these votes were rightly his, intended for the Liberal Democrats and misattributed by confused voters. Ideally, Huggett would not run again; if he did, Oaten could only hope that increased public attention could help to win some of those votes back.

Huggett was a fascinating and difficult participant in British elections. He pulled a similar stunt in the 1994 European elections in Devon & East Plymouth, where he collected an impressive if not necessarily deliberate 10,203 votes running as the 'Literal Democrat' candidate. The Liberal Democrats lost that seat to the Conservatives by just 700 votes, meaning that it was highly likely that Huggett had deprived the Liberal candidate of victory through the simple confusion of party names and candidates.

Huggett claimed to be an equal opportunities pain in the backside, whose main issue was that he didn't 'believe in political parties' and saw elections as 'a way of challenging their monopoly on political life'. Huggett had also previously stood independently as the 'Conservative Party Candidate for Brighton', winning 2,000 votes there. In Winchester in

1997, Huggett first attempted to claim that he had changed his name to 'Gerry Maclone', hoping to insert himself onto the ballot paper just above the Conservative candidate and hijack his vote. However, Winchester's acting returning officer and chief executive of the council, David Cowan, managed to block this move legally.

His claim that he was not simply a Conservative Party provocateur, therefore, has some merit. However, his denials that his candidature had sought to confuse the electorate, made following the 1994 contest, are a little harder to believe. Huggett told *The Observer* that 'to suggest that 10–11,000 people in Devon are so stupid they can't see the difference [between "Literal" and "Liberal" Democrat] is horrible. You shouldn't patronise people like that. Ninety-eight or 99 per cent voted for me because they wanted new ideas.' This claim was hard to substantiate.

Huggett also clearly had a particular issue with the Liberal Democrats, a political party which his father had been local president of. Huggett claimed the 'most odious and hateful' politicians he had ever encountered were Liberal Democrats, who 'think they have an unassailable right to the moral high ground'. He targeted them with particular enthusiasm. This came to a head in Winchester on 1 May 1997. Huggett claimed in an interview that Oaten had threatened to kill him on the night of the count, which he had found 'quite rude' and reported to the police. Oaten did not deny this but said it had been intended as a joke: 'It had been a long night and I was at the end of my tether.'

Huggett ran again in November's Winchester by-election as a 'Literal Democrat Mark Here to Win'. In the build-up to the contest, Oaten was in no mood for jokes: 'Am I bitter? Yes I am. Look what he's put me through. I don't think he'll get 640 votes this time. But what if he gets 10 and it's as close again?' Oaten combated Huggett's campaign by running under the banner 'Liberal Democrat – Leader Paddy Ashdown'. Whether due to clearer labelling on the part of the Liberal Democrat candidate, increased publicity around the by-election or Winchester's voters simply becoming tired of the 'joke', Huggett won just fifty-nine votes in November's by-election.

Huggett's candidacy was not the only source of bitterness. Acting returning officer David Cowan had a difficult time during and after the general election. After the election he oversaw was successfully challenged by the incumbent, Cowan wrote in the *Local Government Chronicle* that he felt the mechanics of elections should be re-examined. His frustration can only have increased when a chance encounter between himself and the Liberal Democrat candidate during an Italian holiday was reported in the local paper, with conspiratorial (if entirely unevidenced) implications. The legal challenge meant that the general election was subject to extra scrutiny, and two cases of 'personation' were found, whereby voters were found to have voted in someone else's name. A national Liberal Democrat party political broadcast on the eve of the by-election, booked prior to confirmation of its date in anticipation, brought about a complaint of breaching election law, as it had not been included in the party's official election expenses. The complaint was quickly dropped but added to the sense of controversy and chaos.

The unusual and controversial circumstances of the by-election, as well as Huggett's persistent involvement, drew plenty of attention outside of Winchester. While the main three parties retained the same candidates, minor parties chopped and changed their candidates. The Referendum Party, founded by Sir James Goldsmith, had stood in the original 1997 election and garnered 1,598 votes. Goldsmith died in July, and the party rebranded itself a 'political movement', no longer standing candidates. This was expected to aid the Conservatives, although the growing UK Independence Party did stand in both general election and by-election, putting on forty-five extra votes in the rerun competition. This increased vote may have been due to their candidate, former journalist and presenter of television's *One Man and His Dog* Robin Page, being slightly better known than previous candidate Derek Rumsey.

The 1997 Winchester by-election was also notable as the final election contested by David Sutch, founder and leader of the Monster Raving Loony Party, before his suicide in 1999. 'Screaming Lord Sutch' was a serial election contestant, standing in thirty-nine such contests. He won 316 votes in Winchester. The previous candidate, Peter Stockton, had claimed his lost deposit back from the now-voided general election. In keeping with the party's long-standing tradition, Sutch then lost his own deposit in the by-election that followed.

Away from the madness, a relatively traditional campaign was conducted. With another by-election set to take place in Beckenham the same day, but otherwise little else on, Conservative Party leader William Hague and most of the shadow Cabinet visited Winchester, as did Liberal Democrat leader Paddy Ashdown. Winchester Liberal Democrats held media events in a local optometrist's, highlighting their party's national pledge to make eye tests and teeth checks free and drawing attention to the Conservative candidate's record as a Health Minister.

Their campaign portrayed Malone as an entitled poor loser, with his slogan 'Winchester Wants Gerry Back' (reported elsewhere as 'Winchester Needs Gerry Back'), seen as debatable after an election result that had been far from decisive. As Lord Rennard's memoir *Winning Here* recalls, the Liberal Democrats' description of Malone as 'like the batsman given out by the umpire, but refusing to walk' seemed to stick. Malone's attempts to rapidly reshape his public image by joining a local protest against student fees and promoting green issues do not seem to have changed the electorate's mind, given his five years as Winchester's MP.

Contemporary reporting noted that Malone's campaign claimed Oaten had underperformed during his short tenure as Winchester's MP, an attack repeated by the Labour candidate and local councillor Patrick Davies. Oaten spoke just twice in the Commons in his six-month tenure, including his maiden speech, and reportedly asked no questions, leaving himself vulnerable to this line of attack.

So there was certainly some bitterness to be had, if not quite fear and loathing. *The Observer*'s Andrew Rawnsley reported on the 'paranoia' which was 'haunting' both camps, whose 'mutual nightmare' was that the closeness of the initial result meant that any single voter who promised their vote to a candidate this time round could potentially change the result if they failed to follow through.

Ultimately, Liberal Democrat Oaten won a decisive and clear victory, garnering 37,006 votes and a majority of 21,556 over second-placed Conservative candidate Malone. Labour's position was also relevant. The Conservatives had hoped that Labour supporters who had voted tactically for the Liberal Democrats in the general election would return home, damaging the Liberal vote. The Liberal Democrats hoped

Labour would not run a candidate at all. Both were disappointed, but the Liberal Democrats won the day.

Labour's Patrick Davies contested both of Winchester's elections in 1997. Like independent Richard Huggett, his November result was a fraction of that achieved in May. Labour's Winchester by-election result was historically terrible, with the party finishing third but registering just 944 votes, or 1.7 per cent of the total, and losing the party's deposit. The party was focused on the Beckenham by-election the same day, which they believed they had a better chance at but which the Conservatives won. Labour scarcely campaigned in Winchester. They even privately offered information to help the Liberals. Their same candidate had won 6,528 votes, or 10.5 per cent of the total, in the now-voided general election. Despite Conservative hopes, tactical voting against them appeared to have played a larger, rather than a smaller, role in the by-election.

The by-election had some significant long-term effects. Huggett's involvement in Winchester was at least partly responsible for a change in the law. The Registration of Political Parties Act of 1998 required political parties to be registered, making Huggett's weird wheeze illegal in future elections. Equally, running as an 'Independent Conservative', as seen in Winchester in both 1992 and in the 1997 by-election, was effectively banned.

Mark Oaten MP would go on to run for the leadership of the Liberal Democrats in 2006, following a stint as the party's home affairs spokesperson that saw him develop an approach he branded 'tough liberalism'. However, he dropped out of the leadership race after his campaign failed to garner support. His position was then derailed after the *News of the World* revealed that he had been paying a male sex worker while married. He stepped down as an MP in 2010. He came out as gay in a 2019 interview, saying he was in a happy relationship. He has published two books, including a memoir entitled *Screwing Up: How One MP Survived Politics, Scandal and Turning Forty*.

Dr Jack Brown *is a lecturer in government studies at the Strand Group, King's College London. He teaches and studies London-wide and national government. He is author of* No. 10: The Geography of Power at Downing Street *and* The London Problem *(Haus Publishing, 2019).*

70

SOUTH ANTRIM

21 SEPTEMBER 2000
DUP GAIN FROM UUP

RICHARD BULLICK

Result: William McCrea (DUP), 11,601, 37.95 per cent; David Burnside (UUP), 10,779, 35.26 per cent; Donovan McClelland (Social Democratic and Labour), 3,496, 11.44 per cent; Martin Meehan (Sinn Féin), 2,611, 8.54 per cent; David Ford (Alliance Party of Northern Ireland), 2,031, 6.64 per cent; David Collins (Natural Law), 49, 0.16 per cent
Size of majority: 822
Swing: N/A
Name of previous MP and party: Clifford Forsythe (UUP)
Reason for by-election: Death of incumbent
Result at previous general election: Clifford Forsythe (UUP), 23,108, 57.49 per cent; Donovan McClelland (Social Democratic and Labour), 6,497, 16.16 per cent; David Ford (Alliance Party of Northern Ireland), 4,668, 11.61 per cent; Hugh Smyth (Progressive Unionist), 3,490, 8.67 per cent; Henry Cushinan (Sinn Féin), 2,229, 5.55 per cent; Barbara Briggs (Natural Law), 203, 0.51 per cent
Date by-election called: 15 August 2000
Date by-election took place: 21 September 2000
Size of total electorate: 71,047
Total number of votes cast: 30,567
Turnout: 43.02 per cent

Historically, by-elections in Northern Ireland have been few and far between. Yet those rare occurrences have often had a significance far beyond the election of a single Member of Parliament. The elections of Bernadette Devlin in 1969, Bobby Sands in 1981 and Robert Mc-Cartney in 1995 all played an outsized role in reshaping the politics of Northern Ireland.

The stunning by-election victory for the Democratic Unionist Party (DUP) in South Antrim in September 2000 was as consequential as any of its predecessors. It marked a pivotal moment in Northern Ireland's political history, showcasing the rapidly evolving landscape of Northern Ireland politics following the Belfast (Good Friday) Agreement of 1998 and reframing unionist politics for the next two decades.

In the years leading up to the Belfast (Good Friday) Agreement, unionism was largely united. By contrast, in the years following the agreement, unionism splintered into pro and anti-agreement camps.

For some unionists, the compromises involved in supporting the agreement were a price worth paying for the hope of peace and political stability. Others could not reconcile themselves to the prospect of Sinn Féin in government prior to the decommissioning of IRA weapons, the early release of paramilitary prisoners or fundamental reform of the Royal Ulster Constabulary.

These divisions within unionism crystallised around a titanic political battle for its heart, soul and future between Ian Paisley's DUP and David Trimble's Ulster Unionist Party (UUP). After the 1997 Westminster election, the UUP had ten Members of Parliament and the DUP only two. By 2017, the DUP had achieved virtually complete ascendancy within unionism, holding not only ten of eleven unionist seats in the Commons but the balance of power at Westminster.

While the rise of the DUP neither started nor finished in South Antrim, few could deny that it was a seminal event in its rise to become the largest unionist party and the long and painful fall of the UUP.

The Ulster Unionist Party emerged as a leading force in opposition to Irish Home Rule in the years after 1905. Dominated by an alliance of traditional Ulster landed gentry with key industrial families and closely linked to the Orange Order, the party played a significant role in the creation of Northern Ireland in 1921. It subsequently led the government at Stormont until the collapse of devolution in 1972. For almost 100 years, it was Northern Ireland's largest party, often with little unionist opposition.

In the tumultuous years from the late 1960s as the Northern Ireland

'Troubles' began, a plethora of small unionist protest parties were established but almost all rapidly disappeared. Only the DUP, founded in 1971 by Free Presbyterian minister, the Reverend Dr Ian Paisley, provided an enduring challenge. Before the 1998 agreement, the party never seriously threatened to eclipse its larger rival, remaining primarily a party of working-class loyalists and rural evangelicals.

On Good Friday, 10 April 1998, the shape of unionist politics was fundamentally altered when agreement was reached on a future political settlement for Northern Ireland. The Belfast (Good Friday) Agreement would establish a local assembly led by a power-sharing executive made up of both nationalist and unionist parties. It was supported by the UUP leadership under David Trimble, parties representing loyalist paramilitaries and the two main nationalist parties, the SDLP and Sinn Féin, but was vehemently opposed by the DUP.

Though the agreement was endorsed at a referendum in May 1998 by 71.1 per cent of voters in Northern Ireland, unionists were bitterly divided. By the time of the subsequent Assembly election held on 25 June 1998, it was clear that a new and deep fracture had emerged within unionism. These divisions existed not only between the UUP and the DUP but also rapidly emerged *within* the Ulster Unionist Party, with many rank-and-file members opposing the leadership's position.

The months after the 1998 deal were not easy times for David Trimble's UUP. The failure of the IRA to decommission its weapons delayed the establishment of devolution and deepened divisions in the party.

The UUP finally agreed to set up a power-sharing executive in December 1999 without decommissioning having been delivered. However, the government was forced to suspend the political institution in February 2000. Three months later, the executive was restored but deep disharmony within the UUP remained.

On 27 April 2000, in the midst of Trimble's difficulties, Clifford Forsythe, the Ulster Unionist Party MP for South Antrim, died suddenly. At any other time and in any other circumstances, the by-election that followed would have seen the almost inevitable election of the UUP's candidate of choice. Not so this time.

The parliamentary constituency of South Antrim lies to the north of Belfast and encompasses the outer suburbs of Belfast, Glengormley,

Templepatrick and Newtownabbey, the county town of Antrim and the smaller towns of Ballyclare, Randalstown and Crumlin. It is a constituency with an overwhelming unionist majority: around two-thirds of the population being Protestant and less than a third Catholic.

To say that South Antrim was an Ulster Unionist Party heartland would be an understatement. In the 1979 general election, James Molyneaux, later leader of the UUP, had the largest majority of any MP in the United Kingdom. Indeed, the DUP had not even contested the Westminster seat for seventeen years prior to the 2000 campaign. Clifford Forsythe, the UUP MP since 1983, won over 70 per cent of the votes at the 1992 general election.

By contrast to previously sedate South Antrim elections, the contest that followed Forsythe's death was widely billed as a titanic struggle between the unionist 'Yes' and 'No' to the agreement camps, though as with most Northern Ireland politics, the reality was more complex.

The campaign for South Antrim was 'ground zero' in the battle for the future direction of unionism. Contemporaries recognised that it would be a crucial indicator of the strength of the unionist parties post-Good Friday Agreement. The DUP had not yet developed serious alternative proposals for government – rather, the campaign was a referendum of the UUP's handling of the peace process.

The DUP selected its former Mid Ulster MP, Dr Rev. William McCrea, a hard-working constituency representative on the traditional wing of the party.

There was speculation that the UUP would field Jim Wilson, a pro-agreement Member of the Northern Ireland Assembly, which would have provided a straightforward choice for unionist voters: a firm Trimble supporter versus an anti-agreement stalwart. In the event, they chose David Burnside, who had established a reputation in public relations with British Airways, having spearheaded the airline's infamous battle with Virgin Atlantic.

At one level, Burnside appeared an ideal candidate for the UUP: a highly qualified well-regarded unionist with a pre-existing network at Westminster. Yet some felt he failed to connect with grassroots unionists in South Antrim. Further, his position on the agreement was ambiguous. At a hustings event in early September, boycotted by William McCrea, who refused to share a platform with the Sinn Féin candidate, Burnside advised the electorate he had voted 'Yes' on the agreement in 1998 on the basis of pledges from the British government, particularly around decommissioning, but that if he had known they would not be honoured, he would have voted 'No'. Burnside's position of soft opposition could neither secure the support of middle-ground opinion nor compete with William McCrea's anti-agreement credentials.

The campaign burst onto the media scene in August when a number of letters attacking David Burnside appearing in local newspapers were discovered not to be authentic. The politically damaging material was signed in the names of real people, using their legitimate addresses, but on investigation, all the letters were false. It was insinuated that DUP activists may have been responsible.

Burnside fought the campaign on the pledge to unite unionism, but such a message stood in contrast with the divisions that were all too apparent within the UUP.

William McCrea had a simple dispatch of opposition. He was clear about the message that was delivered by voters. In an interview before polling day, he said:

> On the doorsteps I'm finding that people are sick about what is happening to the RUC and disgusted by the early release of terrorist prisoners. They feel betrayed by the appeasement process and by Sinn Féin's participation in government even though not one bullet has been handed in by the IRA.

Whether a more unambiguously pro-agreement Ulster Unionist candidate could have won in September 2000 is a matter of debate. But Burnside was neither fully 'Yes' nor 'No'. He tried to straddle both camps and failed. Burnside talked about uniting both wings of the UUP, but an agreed policy is required to achieve unity and none was forthcoming. Instead, he was confusingly supported by diverse figures from within the party, with totally different views on the way forward.

The day of the election itself was marked by heavy rain reflecting the mood of unionism in the wake of the Belfast (Good Friday) Agreement and ultimately affecting the overall turnout.

At the early stages of the count, few were predicting a William McCrea victory, but around 1 a.m. the mood changed and it was becoming clear that McCrea was in front.

Newtownabbey Times correspondent David Gordon noted: 'South Antrim counts were never like this … The drama in the early hours … was in stark contrast to previous parliamentary contests.'

When the votes were counted, the DUP's William McCrea defeated David Burnside of the UUP by 822 votes with a 43 per cent turnout out of an electorate of just over 70,000. The UUP vote had fallen by 22 per cent from its 1997 general election showing and, from a position of not having contested South Antrim at the previous Westminster election, the DUP won 38 per cent of the vote.

The victory was also notable for the DUP's strong constituency-level organisation. The division and poor organisation of the UUP during the South Antrim contest contrasted with the military precision of the DUP campaign led by the then director of elections and deputy leader Peter Robinson.

After the election, Burnside reflected: 'The Ulster Unionist Party was weak on door-to-door canvassing and compared to the DUP election machine we were weak on numbers … Less than half the Assembly party and only half of our Members of Parliament came in to give support.'

In the immediate aftermath of the count, the message from the two unionist candidates was surprisingly similar: the government had to listen to this result and so did the UUP leadership. Burnside confessed that the UUP faced much soul-searching. However, he was keen to stress that this was a short-term protest vote, which would be countered by the re-establishment of strong and straightforward unionist credentials by the party.

McCrea proclaimed that South Antrim had 'lit a fire' on behalf of traditional unionism that could not be put out. Ian Paisley likened the victory to his own performance in Bannside in 1969, when he narrowly lost out to UUP leader and Prime Minister of Northern Ireland Captain Terence O'Neill and fatally undermined O'Neill's premiership with his strong performance.

The significance of the result was widely recognised at the time. The next day, the BBC News headlines proclaimed that the election was a

'Blow to NI Peace Deal'. The Secretary of State for Northern Ireland, Peter Mandelson, conceded that the peace process was in trouble.

The day after the result was declared, the unionist-leaning *Belfast News Letter* reported that 'London, Dublin and Washington were dismayed by the stunning DUP victory and its implication for the future of the peace process'.

The defeat in South Antrim also sent shock waves through the UUP.

In subsequent weeks, the press concluded that the message to UUP leader David Trimble was loud and clear: unionism would tolerate no further concessions – on either policing or decommissioning. The by-election also prompted significant speculation on the future of Trimble's leadership.

The *Newtownabbey Times* declared that the by-election was 'the electoral nightmare that could finish off Trimble'. Little over a month later, Jeffrey Donaldson would narrowly fail to win the battle for the party leadership.

The DUP's victory in South Antrim marked a significant shift in Northern Ireland politics. In the short term, it represented a defeat for the UUP and pro-agreement unionism. In the longer term, it foreshadowed a wider shift in voter sentiment and the decline of a party which had dominated Northern Ireland politics for almost 100 years.

The feeling that the Union was no longer in safe hands was not one that would be easily overcome. One anonymous newspaper correspondent accurately predicted electoral oblivion for the UUP and concluded there was 'not a single UUP MP, councillor or Assembly man who can be utterly sure of being re-elected'. The Young Unionist leadership proclaimed the defeat was 'potentially a precursor to complete electoral annihilation' for the UUP.

Indeed, Arlene Foster, then UUP honorary secretary, described South Antrim as 'probably the worst electoral result in the UUP's history'.

The DUP's success reinforced the perception that unionists were increasingly rallying around a more assertive and uncompromising stance, which would shape future negotiations and government in Northern Ireland.

Burnside would go on to win South Antrim at the subsequent general election only to lose it to McCrea again in 2005, but the by-election signalled a fundamental and wider shift in Northern Ireland politics.

The victory in South Antrim was a critical junction for unionism, marking not only the beginning of the DUP's rise to dominance but the beginning of its journey into the mainstream of unionist politics, becoming a party of government rather than opposition, and the inevitable compromise with Sinn Féin.

It was still three years before the DUP would eclipse the UUP in a province-wide election and almost seven before the DUP would restore devolution with Sinn Féin, having negotiated changes to the Belfast (Good Friday) Agreement at St Andrews. By that time, it was not the UUP and SDLP that would lead the executive but the DUP and Sinn Féin. As so often is the case in Irish history, the rise of a more uncompromising political stance is followed by a process of renegotiation, redefinition and agreement.

South Antrim was a remarkable beginning: the loss by the UUP of what had been one of the safest seats in the United Kingdom heralded a fundamental reshaping of the landscape of unionism. After South Antrim, the invincibility of the UUP had gone and internal party discipline deteriorated, with a number of leading members including Peter Weir and future leaders, Arlene Foster and Sir Jeffrey Donaldson, defecting to the DUP in the following years.

The South Antrim by-election was a pivotal event in Northern Ireland politics encapsulating the struggles and transformations within the unionist community in the post-conflict era. In the early autumn of 2000, circumstances contrived to ensure that the South Antrim contest was the most consequential by-election within unionism in a century, with long-lasting implications for party dynamics and political discourse in Northern Ireland. It shaped the trajectory of unionist politics for the first two decades of the twenty-first century.

The once dominant UUP is yet to come close to regaining its position as the leading voice of unionism.

In all likelihood, it never will.

Richard Bullick worked as a special adviser in the Northern Ireland Executive for much of the period since 2000, including for the First Minister from 2008 to 2017 and 2021 to 2022. He was part of the DUP campaign team for the South Antrim by-election.

71

BRENT EAST

18 SEPTEMBER 2003
LIBERAL DEMOCRAT GAIN FROM LABOUR

JOE PIKE

Result: Sarah Teather (Liberal Democrats), 8,158, 39.1 per cent; Robert Evans (Labour), 7,040, 33.8 per cent; Uma Fernandes (Conservative), 3,368, 16.2 per cent; Noel Lynch (Green), 638, 3.1 per cent; Brian Butterworth (Socialist Alliance), 361, 1.7 per cent; Khidori Fawzi Ibrahim (Public Services Not War), 219, 1.1; Winston McKenzie (Independent), 197, 0.9 per cent; Kelly McBride (Independent), 189, 0.9 per cent; Harold Immanuel (Independent Labour), 188, 0.9 per cent; Brian Hall (UKIP), 140, 0.7 per cent; Iris Cremer (Socialist Labour), 111, 0.5 per cent; Neil Walsh (Independent), 101, 0.5 per cent; Alan Hope (Monster Raving Loony), 59, 0.3 per cent; Aaron Barschak (No description), 37, 0.2 per cent; Jiten Bardwaj (No description), 35, 0.2 per cent; Rainbow George Weiss (www.xat.org), 11, 0.1 per cent
Size of majority: 1,118
Swing: 29.0 per cent from Labour to Liberal Democrats
Name of previous MP and party: Paul Daisley (Labour)
Reason for by-election: Death of incumbent
Result at previous general election: Paul Daisley (Labour), 18,325, 63.2 per cent; David Gauke (Conservative), 5,278, 18.2 per cent; Norsheen Bhatti (Liberal Democrats), 3,065, 10.6 per cent; Simone Aspis (Green), 1,361, 4.7; Sarah Macken (ProLife Alliance), 392, 1.4 per cent; Iris Cremer (Socialist Labour), 383, 1.3 per cent; Ashwin Tanna (UKIP), 188, 0.6 per cent
Date by-election called: N/A
Date by-election took place: 18 September 2003

Size of total electorate: 57,558
Total number of votes cast: 20,852
Turnout: 36.2 per cent

On 17 July 2003, Dr David Kelly bumped into Ruth Absalom, an elderly neighbour, on her afternoon walk. She was with her dog Buster. 'Oh hello, David, how are things?' she said.

'Not too bad,' Kelly replied.

The next person to see Kelly was dog-owner Louise Holmes the following morning. At 8 a.m., her dog picked up a scent in the woods at nearby Harrowdown Hill and led her to Kelly's body, slumped by a tree.

His death would go on to cause political resignations, wild conspiracy theories and a hotly debated public inquiry. A biological warfare expert and former UN weapons inspector, Dr Kelly had been named as the source of quotes used by the BBC's Andrew Gilligan in reports that claimed the UK government had 'sexed up' its dossier about Iraq and weapons of mass destruction (WMDs).

The political summer of 2003 was hot with debate over Prime Minister Tony Blair's decision to join the US invasion of Iraq.

The House of Commons had voted for military action. But more than 100 Labour rebels joined Charles Kennedy's Liberal Democrats in opposition. Around 1 million people marched the streets of London with an anti-war protest, the biggest political demonstration the UK had ever seen.

Blair, the cartoonists had decided, was US President Bush's poodle.

The domestic challenges facing Blair, from private sector investment in the NHS to university tuition fees, are remarkably similar to today. But it was Dr Kelly's death and the war which were to prove decisive.

The Brent East by-election was the government's first electoral test after troops went into Iraq.

The fact of a by-election there was hardly a surprise for Labour whips and party organisers. The MP Paul Daisley had been seriously ill even before entering Parliament. An operation to remove a tumour in his colon followed by weeks spent in a coma meant he couldn't even campaign for himself when he won in 2001.

As leader of Brent Council, Daisley claimed to have transformed the borough from being rife with factionalism and corruption into a 'model Labour authority'. That record helped Daisley become MP for Brent East, the seat vacated by the new independent Mayor of London Ken Livingstone.

But illness meant Daisley hardly spoke in the Commons. In late 2002, he announced he had terminal cancer. Just six months later on 19 June 2003, Speaker Michael Martin told MPs that he had died.

One of Labour's first decisions about the contest was perhaps its most ill-advised – going long. The government Chief Whip did not move the writ immediately, meaning instead of a swift contest before the summer, the campaign would last almost three months.

Some had been concerned that a swift race would be disrespectful to Daisley's family. Others worried a low-profile campaign just before the summer risked an embarrassingly low turnout as with Hilary Benn's victory in the 1999 Leeds Central by-election when only 19.9 per cent of those eligible voted.

The advice from the former Brent East MP (and independent mayor) Ken Livingstone was to wait until after the summer holidays, set up a proper Labour campaign operation and ensure that turnout was high. The party listened to Livingstone.

Brent East was supposedly safe. Daisley had won in 2001 with a majority of 13,047 and 63 per cent of the vote.

They quickly selected an experienced candidate with local links: Robert Evans, a sitting Labour Member of the European Parliament for nine years, most of that representing north-west London including Brent.

To his supporters, Evans was capable and a Blairite. To his detractors, he was a Blairite.

The Conservatives picked a local community nurse and councillor. Mauritian-born Uma Fernandes had to dissuade her 23-year-old lawyer daughter Suella also from applying for the nomination. 'You should let Mummy have a chance,' she told the future Attorney General and Home Secretary.

The Liberal Democrats had already chosen 29-year-old Sarah Teather, a charity worker and Islington councillor. They believed Brent was a long-term target. Party strategists predicted that after a couple of election cycles and some boundary changes, a new winnable constituency would appear in north London including some of Brent East. So why not start working towards that now?

Teather had joined the party in her first week at Cambridge University and after helping Susan Kramer's 2000 campaign to be Mayor of London, she had been encouraged to apply for the candidates' list. Because it was to eventually be a Lib Dem target seat, Teather was questioned by local members and faced a grilling by a 'star chamber' of party veterans.

But as a health and social care policy analyst at Macmillan Cancer Relief, she couldn't afford to take a sabbatical for the campaign. 'I couldn't take three months unpaid leave,' Teather told me. 'That was just unthinkable.'

So aside from a few days off work at the start and end of the campaign, Teather campaigned in her evenings and weekends.

The Greens chose London Assembly member, auctioneer and charity shop owner Noel Lynch. Perhaps partly due to the debate around Iraq, there were a slew of other left-wing candidates from Socialist Alliance to Independent Labour to Socialist Labour. 'All very People's Front of Judea,' joked one involved.

Sixteen was a lot of candidates, even for a by-election. Perhaps the most startling person on the ballot paper was Aaron Barschak, the self-styled 'comedy-terrorist' who earlier in the year had gatecrashed Prince William's twenty-first birthday at Windsor Castle dressed as Osama bin Laden.

Barschak's candidacy – as with his scaling the castle walls – seemed to be a publicity stunt to boost attendance at his Edinburgh Fringe show. But the critical reception he received in the Scottish capital was almost as galling as the paltry thirty-seven votes he would win in Brent East. A one-star review in *The Guardian* said Barschak 'has outstayed his 15 minutes of fame, and even the merkin he wore on that fateful day cannot cover his lack of material or talent as a stand-up'.

The tense British summer was compounded by the arrival of a European heatwave, the hottest the Continent had weathered since 1540. Beyoncé's debut solo album *Dangerously in Love* had been released to rave reviews. The Black Eyed Peas, Dido and Gareth Gates were battling it out in the charts. So in north-west London there was, at least initially, very little media interest in a by-election in a safe Labour seat.

Uma Fernandes did not fancy her chances. 'Let's not kid ourselves,' was the Conservative candidate's assessment to one journalist. The Liberal Democrats seized on the gaffe and it soon became the focus of leaflets intended to 'squeeze' Tory votes. 'Even the Conservative candidate doesn't think they can win here, so why not vote Lib Dem and give Labour a lesson?'

Public anger about Iraq was palpable and here Labour candidate Robert Evans bore the brunt. He remembered one awkward moment while leafleting outside a school. 'One little child was given a Labour balloon,' he told me. 'And her mum snatched it away from her and said, "When the Prime Minister takes his troops out of Iraq, you can have a balloon." So the child went off crying.'

Evans separately met an older voter who was seething about 'what you lot have done to poor Henry Kelly'. Henry Kelly was an Irish television and radio presenter. She meant David Kelly. 'I had to say, "We've not done anything to Henry Kelly," but she wasn't taking any of it.'

Ken Livingstone was not even in the party, but the mayor put on a red rosette to return to the campaign trail in his former seat. There were few hustings, but Labour strategists argued there was little to be gained and they'd likely be infiltrated by anti-war demonstrators.

From the beginning, Sarah Teather felt privately optimistic. 'I had a really strong instinct from the start that there was a chance that we'd win it,' she told me. Teather would present herself on stickers and leaflets as 'The REAL Alternative'.

With low expectations, the small and young Lib Dem team seemed to be enjoying themselves the most. 'We ate curry and ice cream in alternating measures,' Teather recalled. 'It was a fun atmosphere. There was nothing to lose because we were in third place and we had very few local party members and no infrastructure and everything to gain.'

The party tried to learn lessons from US Democratic presidential wannabe Howard Dean, who had recently used the increasingly influential internet to raise tens of millions of dollars. Instead of fundraising focused on a few wealthy donors, the Dean team solicited smaller donations online.

Liberal Democrats innovation supremo Mark Pack later wrote that 25 per cent of Brent East by-election campaign funds had been raised online via email-based appeals. Facebook and Twitter/X were yet to be invented. The real advantage, the campaign found, was the popularisation of email, which helped the party corral members to join the effort in north-west London.

Rather suddenly, in the final week of campaigning, word spread that a major upset was possible. So a media circus soon landed.

On election night, the count at Brent Town Hall was packed, tense and at points ill-tempered. Some remember a fight breaking out. It is unclear who was involved. Aaron Barschak turned up wearing a red military jacket and was pictured holding a pint and kissing a female police officer on the cheek.

Labour candidate Robert Evans was waiting in a local hotel as most of his campaign team sampled ballots at the count to try to predict the result. 'I think it was Barry Gardiner, then MP for Brent North, who took me aside and said, "You've got to brace yourself, because they think we could be losing it by 500,"' Evans remembered.

'That was the first time it really dawned on me, although I always knew it was a possibility, that I'd got to brace myself for the fact that I might lose.'

Sarah Teather was told to come to the town hall but wait outside in the car. 'It's looking close,' her campaign manager said. 'And just brace yourself. It's mad in there. There's just an unbelievable number of press.'

Teather found herself unable to write a speech until she was sure of the result. 'I was scribbling notes on the back of a bit of paper in the car,' she said. 'In the end, I had to go and hide in the toilets in order to try and draft it.'

Jon Craig, Sky News' new signing, who would go on to broadcast from more than forty by-election counts, announced Labour's loss even before the returning officer had stood up. Evans tipped him off that Labour had lost by 1,000 votes and Craig passed on the revelation on live TV.

When the result was announced, Sarah Teather had a message for the Prime Minister: 'Tony Blair, I hope that you are listening tonight.

The people of Brent have spoken for the people of Britain. They want you to listen. They want you to deliver.

'But there is no comfort in this result tonight for the Conservative party,' she added. 'They are irrelevant to constituencies like this. The tide may be turning against Tony Blair and New Labour, but the tide remains far out for the Conservatives in this country.'

'Lib Dems Stun Blair by Taking Brent East,' wrote *The Independent*. 'By-election upset which will send shockwaves through Tony Blair's government,' declared *The Guardian*.

Overturning a 13,000 Labour majority was a shock. It was the first time Labour had lost a seat in a by-election for fifteen years. The 29-point swing, the biggest in almost a decade, was a huge achievement for the Lib Dems.

Timing, turnout and tensions over Iraq had all contributed to the dramatic result. A September by-election had allowed the Liberal Democrats months to pool resources from across the capital and build their campaign operation. For Labour, the timing was doubly awkward, providing as it did a painful prelude to their annual party conference a fortnight later in Bournemouth.

While a turnout of 36.2 per cent was far from a surprise, Robert Evans was convinced that controversy over Iraq meant that not just Labour voters but even some in the CLP stayed at home. 'I'm sure all party members in Brent East didn't vote Labour that day,' he said. 'And many of them will have just decided to register their protest by not voting.'

Low turnouts are expected in uncompetitive by-elections, but this was a closely fought contest and two-thirds of voters stayed at home.

The Guardian's Martin Kettle also warned of the danger to Labour of minor (often left-leaning) parties. 'More than one in 10 votes went to the 13 "fringe" candidates,' he wrote. 'Between them they polled 2,286 votes. Put another way, they polled more than twice Teather's 1,118 majority over Labour's Robert Evans.'

Andrew Rawnsley argued in his *Observer* column that after 'months of relentless battering', the Brent East result was a 'bloody nose' for Labour. 'Indisputably a blow, this defeat rips another tear in the suit of invincibility that once armoured Tony Blair.'

The result was also an embarrassment, albeit smaller, for Tory leader and self-styled 'quiet man' Iain Duncan Smith, whose party was shunted into third place.

He didn't take the result quietly, accusing the Lib Dems of using 'deceit and double standards' to achieve victory. 'To win the seat the Liberal Democrats used the usual tricks, faithful to the words of their secret campaign handbook: Be wicked, act shamelessly, stir endlessly,' he said.

Within weeks, Duncan Smith had told his party conference, in a message of defiance: 'The quiet man is here to stay and he's turning up the volume.' Within weeks of that, he had lost a vote of confidence among MPs and resigned.

If the Brent by-election had happened just a year later, a different political force would have been added to the mix. In 2004, George Galloway founded his Respect Party, largely out of the Stop the War movement.

Sarah Teather immediately became a hero for the reinvigorated Lib Dems. She had unseated David Lammy – another London by-election victor – as Baby of the House. Young, passionate and articulate, her first day at Westminster was celebrated and the party wheeled her out for another victory lap at party conference.

She went on to increase her majority in 2005, beating future Labour MP Yasmin Qureshi and future Conservative Chancellor Kwasi Kwarteng.

Teather was soon promoted to the Lib Dem front bench and, alongside Ed Davey, she put pressure on Charles Kennedy to stand down as leader. In the coalition government, she was Children's Minister for two years.

Disillusioned with Nick Clegg's leadership on the party's approach to social justice and immigration, she stood down in 2015 and was until recently director of the Jesuit Refugee Service.

Robert Evans stood down from the European Parliament in 2009 to pursue a career as a consultant and part-time lecturer. He is one of two Labour councillors on the 81-seat Surrey County Council. And while Evans does not regret standing in the Brent East by-election, he says losing 'wounds you for life'.

For the prolific pen of government communications director and diarist Alastair Campbell, the result received a brief mention.

'Woke up to news we had lost Brent East by-election to the Libs, then back to preparing,' Campbell wrote.

He was preparing to give evidence to the Hutton Inquiry into the circumstances surrounding David Kelly's death.

Brent East was a spectacular victory for the Liberal Democrats, the first electoral outlet for public fury over Iraq. It set the scene for gains in 2005, the coalition government in 2010 and then the scrapheap in 2015.

Joe Pike *is the politics and investigations correspondent for the BBC. He was previously at* Newsnight, Sky News and ITV. *He is the author of* Project Fear *(Biteback, 2015), the acclaimed behind-the-scenes account of the 2014 Scottish referendum campaign.*

72

CREWE & NANTWICH

22 MAY 2008
CONSERVATIVE GAIN FROM LABOUR

LORD PARKINSON

Result: Edward Timpson (Conservative), 20,539, 49.5 per cent; Tamsin Dunwoody (Labour), 12,679, 30.6 per cent; Elizabeth Shenton (Liberal Democrats), 6,040, 14.6 per cent; Mike Nattrass (UKIP), 922, 2.2 per cent; Robert Smith (Green), 359, 0.9 per cent; David Roberts (English Democrat), 275, 0.7 per cent; The Flying Brick (Monster Raving Loony), 236, 0.6 per cent; Mark Walklate (Independent), 217, 0.5 per cent; Paul Thorogood (Independent), 118, 0.3 per cent; Gemma Garrett (Independent), 113, 0.3 per cent

Size of majority: 7,860

Swing: 17.6 per cent from Labour to Conservative

Name of previous MP and party: Gwyneth Dunwoody (Labour)

Reason for by-election: Death of incumbent

Result at previous general election: Gwyneth Dunwoody (Labour), 21,240, 48.8 per cent; Eveleigh Moore-Dutton (Conservative), 14,162, 32.6 per cent; Paul Roberts (Liberal Democrats), 8,083, 18.6 per cent

Date by-election called: 30 April 2008

Date by-election took place: 22 May 2008

Size of total electorate: 71,963

Total number of votes cast: 41,498

Turnout: 57.7 per cent

'They moved the writ before they'd even buried her.'

The Crewe & Nantwich by-election caught us by surprise in Conservative Central Office. I was working on the party's target seats campaign at the time. One of our team had the macabre job of being on 'by-election watch' — monitoring the health and indiscretions of Members of Parliament to be on the lookout for potential polls.

Though Gwyneth Dunwoody, the veteran Labour MP, was seventy-seven and had been MP for Crewe, then Crewe & Nantwich, since February 1974 (having previously sat for Exeter, 1966–70), her seat was not on our radar. A scratch from a cat led to blood poisoning, emergency heart surgery and her unexpected death on 17 April 2008, which shocked her many friends and admirers across the political spectrum.

A small team of us from Central Office visited the constituency on 30 April to prepare for the coming campaign. Flags flew at half-mast for the popular former MP. As we drove round with the local Tory chairman and election agent, we were stunned to hear the news that the writ for the by-election had been moved in Parliament. The campaign had begun — more than a week before Dunwoody's funeral on 8 May. Stephen Gilbert, the party's head of campaigning, cancelled our plans to return on the train that evening; we booked ourselves into whichever hotels had vacancies, borrowed some laptops and set to work. It was not until the following weekend that we were allowed to return to London to pick up fresh underwear and clothes for the month ahead.

In one — vital — respect, we were not playing catch-up. We already had an excellent Conservative candidate in place: Edward Timpson, a local barrister, had been selected the previous summer and had established himself as an energetic campaigner, collecting a 3,000-strong petition against local Post Office closures and delivering it personally to Downing Street; just a fortnight earlier, he had run the London Marathon to raise money for the cancer unit at Leighton Hospital, where his three children had been born. For some reason, the Liberal Democrats ditched their existing candidate, Marc Godwin, within hours of the vacancy arising. He resigned from the party in anger, accusing it of 'a shabby backroom deal'. In his place, they selected Elizabeth Shenton, a councillor from Newcastle-under-Lyme — only half an hour's drive away but enough for us to label her an 'outsider' from the West Midlands. (She returned her party's favour by defecting to Labour over the coalition government's 'damaging policies' in 2013.)

Labour, meanwhile, looked even further afield, selecting a candidate from 175 miles away: Gwyneth Dunwoody's daughter, Tamsin. She lived in Pembrokeshire, where she had been a Member of the Welsh Assembly until being defeated by the Tory Paul Davies in 2007. In many senses, she was a shrewd pick: it was clear how proud most people were to have been represented by her fiercely independent and hard-working mother. Our focus groups had shown how voters – particularly women – thought she would follow very suitably in her footsteps. At that time, we used Experian's 'Mosaic' framework to segment the electorate by demographic types. Our analysis told us that around a third of the electorate in Crewe & Nantwich could be classed as solid Labour, while less than 10 per cent were solid Conservatives. The rest fell into our top target types and 'toss-up' categories: the campaign to win them over was on.

By-elections impose additional strain on candidates. Though he was intelligent, energetic and knew the local area well, I remember the expression on Edward Timpson's face when he came into Central Office for a briefing earlier in April. After a long day being passed from department to department, overwhelmed with information, legal guidance and press briefings, he was greeted by Lord Ashcroft, the deputy chairman of the party in charge of target seats. 'Well, there you go,' Michael said with a characteristic glint in his eye. 'You've been told what to do. Don't fuck it up.'

To help him avoid this, Angela Browning, the experienced MP for Tiverton & Honiton, was appointed as 'candidate's friend' – basically a chaperone, confidante and counsellor. She knew the seat well, having stood against Gwyneth Dunwoody in 1987, and enjoyed being back on familiar turf. She raised the spirits of the whole campaign team – not least when she accidentally posted her mobile phone through someone's letterbox while out canvassing and regaled us with the tale of its retrieval. Also posted to the campaign full-time was Eric Pickles, a member of the shadow Cabinet, dispatched by David Cameron to ensure the campaign was treated as a priority by the party at every level. This he did with great gusto and trademark charm. He was stationed in our makeshift campaign HQ, a series of Portakabins on Gresty Road, just yards from the railway station which brought hundreds of volunteers – and the home of Crewe Alexandra football club.

Labour's campaign was run by Steve McCabe, MP for the Hall Green division of Birmingham. Their decision to try to paint Edward Timpson as 'the Tory Toff from Tarporley' became a dominant feature of the campaign and backfired spectacularly. Labour leaflets branded Timpson 'Out of touch Teddy' and pointed out that his family's business had a turnover of £100 million – something I recalled wryly in the summer of 2024, when his brother James, its chief executive, was raised to the peerage and appointed as a Labour minister in the House of Lords. Two Labour staffers were dressed in morning suits and top hats and sent to gate-crash Tory campaign events – but succeeded mainly in turning off voters and Labour activists alike. (I befriended one of them, John Greenshields, a couple of years later, when we worked on the cross-party NOtoAV campaign.) Under slogans such as 'One of Us vs One of Them' and 'Do you want a Tory conman or a Dunwoody?', Labour flyers carried doctored photographs of Timpson with a top hat on. When Labour circulated a photograph of Tory campaigners delivering leaflets in a Bentley, they were sharply reminded that the high-quality cars were made in Crewe, proudly employing 4,000 local people. We did not need to point out that Tamsin Dunwoody was the granddaughter of a baroness or that she appeared in *Burke's Landed Gentry*; the negative Labour campaign turned off its own supporters. One Labour activist told the press: 'I'm two steps away from sending money to the Tory campaign.' The party's deputy leader, Harriet Harman, pulled out of a planned trip after distancing herself from the campaign's tactics.

The Lib Dem campaign was little better. Conservative campaigners bore the scars of previous by-elections. At Cheadle three years earlier, Conservative activists had turned up to their campaign office on polling day to find the locks filled with glue. It was never established who had done it, but suspicions lingered. After all, the infamous guidance from the Association of Liberal Democrat Councillors advised their campaigners to 'be wicked, act shamelessly, stir endlessly … Positive campaigning will NOT be enough to win control.'

While Labour dressed in top hats and tails, Conservative campaigners dressed up as giant 10 pence pieces. This was to highlight Gordon Brown's decision to scrap the 10p starting rate of income tax, hitting 5.3

million of the lowest-paid families in the country – including 10,000 families in Crewe & Nantwich. The change had been made in his last Budget as Chancellor but came into effect at the start of the new tax year, making Crewe & Nantwich the first parliamentary election since people began to feel its pinch. The Labour campaign inflamed opinion by claiming it was 'not an issue' locally. It formed a constant backdrop to the campaign: on the morning the writ was moved, the famously intransigent Brown admitted on the *Today* programme having made 'mistakes' in its implementation. As the row escalated, his successor as Chancellor, Alistair Darling, made a statement to Parliament on 13 May outlining a new approach. It was tantamount to an emergency Budget nine days before the by-election – but his changes served only to delay the pain for most. Embowered by such unpopularity, the Prime Minister did not come to Crewe & Nantwich; David Cameron, by contrast, visited four times.

While the 10p tax rate dominated, other issues featured heavily in the campaign, such as Labour's further taxes on petrol and alcohol, and their effect on the rising cost of living. The future of Crewe railway station and Royal Mail sorting office were big issues in the town, while the Green Belt, cuts to NHS first responders and the loss of forty-eight dairy farms since 2001 were prominent in Nantwich and the rural parts of the constituency.

A buoyant Tory Party heeded Eric Pickles's call and came to Crewe in their hundreds. Our brilliant colleague Marion Little helped to plant more than 1,000 posters in people's front gardens (shrewdly, she prioritised the routes she knew the shadow Chancellor George Osborne would take when driving from Tatton so he could admire their handiwork). The Tory campaign team benefited from the skills of George Eustice, David Mackintosh and Nick Timothy, who would all go on to serve as MPs themselves, as well as future Downing Street denizens such as Alan Sendorek, Alex Dawson and Richard Jackson.

Our campaign newspaper, *Change*, bore the influence of Andy Coulson, the former *News of the World* editor who had become the Tories' director of communications the year before. Determined to outdo the Lib Dems, we produced an eight-page newspaper complete with sports page (reporting Crewe Alexandra's narrow escape from relegation from

League One), a word search containing twenty of Gordon Brown's stealthy tax rises and editorials offering the electorate advice on how to vote. For the final weekend, we produced a 'Sunday' newspaper, emblazoned with the date and delivered across the whole constituency in a single day.

On polling day – Thursday 22 May – neither Gordon Brown nor David Cameron stayed up to wait for the result; Cameron set his alarm for 2 a.m. and crept through his home in west London to turn on the television. What he saw made him too excited to go back to sleep, so he woke his wife Samantha to tell her. Edward Timpson had turned a Labour majority of 7,078 into a Conservative one of 7,860. It was a 17.6 per cent swing from Labour to Tory – the biggest since the Ashfield by-election in 1977. It was the first time in my lifetime the Conservatives had gained a seat at a by-election (the last had been in Mitcham & Morden, at the height of the Falklands War, in 1982).

Turnout was unusually high: almost the same as at the previous general election. As the psephological gurus Colin Rallings and Michael Thrasher put it: 'An old-fashioned two-party dogfight saw many former Labour voters switch directly to the Tories. There can be no other interpretation of the result.' Returning to Crewe to greet his newest parliamentary colleague, David Cameron hailed the 'remarkable' victory as marking the 'end of New Labour'. The outspoken Labour MP for Ealing North, Stephen Pound, said ruefully: 'People say it's a kick in the teeth. I feel I've been kicked in another part of my anatomy.' His colleague Graham Stringer was blunter still, telling the *Sunday Times*: 'I want a senior member of the cabinet to start a leadership challenge.'

Edward Timpson went on to serve as Minister for Children and Families and as Solicitor General. (Receiving the customary appointment as Queen's Counsel in July 2022, he was the last QC to be appointed during the reign of Elizabeth II.) He held Crewe & Nantwich at the 2010 and 2015 general elections. After being defeated by just forty-eight votes (after three recounts) in 2017, he re-entered the Commons in 2019 in the neighbouring Eddisbury constituency. Whether or not that made him a 'toff', he was finally the 'Tory from Tarporley'.

Tamsin Dunwoody applied unsuccessfully to be the Labour candidate for Islwyn at the 2010 general election. Contesting her mother's seat just days after her unexpected death must have been an extraordinary ordeal for her and her family. Speaking at her funeral on 8 May, she said: 'It's hard to describe what it's like losing such a wonderful person but at the same time I want to fight for her beliefs. She was such an incredible person and I was incredibly proud of her.' For all the electoral upset of the 2008 by-election, it is clear that her mother's former constituents shared that pride at having had her as their Member of Parliament.

Lord Parkinson *worked on the Crewe & Nantwich, Henley and Norwich North by-elections during his time on the Conservative Party's target seats campaign, 2007–10. He is the chairman of the Conservative History Group and served as Minister for Arts, Heritage & Libraries in the last Conservative government.*

73

HALTEMPRICE & HOWDEN

10 JULY 2008
CONSERVATIVE HOLD

ROBERT EVANS

Result: David Davis (Conservative), 17,113, 71.6 per cent; Shan Oakes (Green), 1,758, 7.4 per cent; Joanne Robinson (English Democrats), 1,714, 7.2 per cent; Tess Culnane (National Front), 544, 2.3 per cent; Gemma Garrett (Miss Great Britain), 521, 2.2 per cent; Jill Saward (Independent), 492, 2.1 per cent; Mad Cow-Girl (Monster Raving Loony), 412, 1.7 per cent; Walter Sweeney (Independent), 238, 1.0 per cent; John Nicholson (Independent), 162, 0.7 per cent; David Craig (Independent), 135, 0.6 per cent; David Pinder (New), 135, 0.6 per cent; David Icke (No description), 110, 0.5 per cent; Hamish Howitt (Freedom 4 Choice), 91, 0.4 per cent; Chris Talbot (Socialist Equality), 84, 0.4 per cent; Grace Astley (Independent), 77, 0.3 per cent; George Hargreaves (Christian), 76, 0.3 per cent; David Bishop (Church of the Militant Elvis), 44, 0.2 per cent; John Upex (Independent), 38, 0.2 per cent; Greg Wood (Independent), 32, 0.1 per cent; Eamonn Fitzpatrick (Independent), 31, 0.1 per cent; Ronnie Carroll (Make Politicians History), 29, 0.1 per cent; Thomas Darwood (Independent), 25, 0.1 per cent; Christopher Foren (Independent), 23, 0.1 per cent; Herbert Crossman (Independent), 11, 0.0 per cent; Tony Farnon (Independent), 8, 0.0 per cent; Norman Scarth (Independent), 8, 0.0 per cent
Size of majority: 15,355
Swing: N/A
Name of previous MP and party: David Davis (Conservative)
Reason for by-election: Resignation of incumbent
Result at previous general election: David Davis (Conservative),

22,792, 47.5 per cent; Jon Neal (Liberal Democrats), 17,676, 36.8 per cent; Edward Hart (Labour), 6,104, 12.7 per cent; John Mainprize (BNP), 798, 1.7 per cent; Philip Lane (UKIP), 659, 1.4 per cent
Date by-election called: 18 June 2008
Date by-election took place: 10 July 2008
Size of total electorate: 69,307
Total number of votes cast: 23,911
Turnout: 34.5 per cent

The 2008 Haltemprice & Howden by-election followed the resignation of the sitting MP David Davis, citing his opposition to the Counter Terrorism Bill for his decision. This was unusual for a number of reasons, although not because Davis was the first member to resign on a point of principle and to offer himself for re-election in the same constituency.

With mixed results, others had done it before. In 1912, George Lansbury, later the Labour leader, quit in Bow & Bromley to register his support for the suffragettes but lost the by-election. In 1938, Scotland's first female MP, Kitty Stewart-Murray (later the Duchess of Atholl), a unionist MP for Kinross & Western Perthshire, resigned to protest against Neville Chamberlain's policy of appeasement. Standing as an Independent, she also lost the by-election and never stood for Parliament again.

In 1986, fifteen Ulster Unionist MPs resigned their seats en masse, to fight by-elections in protest at the Anglo-Irish Agreement. All but one of them were immediately re-elected.

What was unusual about Davis's resignation was that he was shadow Home Secretary at the time; one of the most senior and influential politicians on the opposition front benches. His decision was seen as a personal one, without the support of his leader David Cameron, whom he told only hours before making his move. In 2005, Davis had been the original favourite to win the Conservative Party leadership in the aftermath of the party's third general election defeat, but Cameron had beaten him in the battle to succeed Michael Howard.

For months leading up to his surprise resignation, Davis had led opposition to the Labour government's plans to raise the time a terrorism suspect could be detained without trial. Since 2000, this had increased from the basic forty-eight hours, first to fourteen days in 2003 and then twenty-eight days under the Blair government's Terrorism Act of 2006. By 2008, the new Prime Minister Gordon Brown and his Home Secretary, Jacqui Smith, were arguing that there would be times when the police might need longer to hold a suspect before they could bring charges, because of the 'scale and complexity' of investigations into possible threats.

Brown had staked his authority on winning the 11 June vote, personally calling dozens of Labour MPs to persuade them to back increasing the time limit. His victory, by just nine votes, gave Britain some of the toughest anti-terror laws in the western world. Davis had reportedly warned Cameron that he would resign if Conservative MPs did not oppose this measure, arguing it showed 'the insidious and relentless erosion of civil liberties in Britain'. What the Tory leader did not know, was that his shadow Home Secretary had already decide to fight a single-issue by-election in his Yorkshire seat.

He promptly resigned on the day after the vote. The Speaker of the House of Commons, Michael Martin, refused Davis permission to address the Chamber, so he was forced to make his explanation and press statement outside Parliament. As MPs are not technically allowed to resign, Davis used the mechanism of applying for the position of Steward and Bailiff of the Chiltern Hundreds, nominally an 'office of profit' under the Crown which disqualified him as an MP.

Some observers felt his decision a massive own goal and one which not only let the Prime Minister off the hook but created a crisis for the whole opposition and especially for Cameron as leader. Jacqui Smith said the Conservatives were in 'total disarray' while one of her predecessors as Home Secretary, David Blunkett, described Davis's move as 'childish and immature' – views shared by some in his own party. Cameron publicly acclaimed Davis's move as 'a very brave and courageous decision' and then responded quickly by appointing the libertarian Dominic Grieve as the new shadow Home Secretary. Other Tories wondered if Davis had 'flipped', with one MP saying, 'Here we are on the ropes and he goes and does this. Gordon [Brown] must be in seventh heaven.' Tory grandee and Churchill's grandson Nicholas

Soames MP felt the decision to be 'a disaster for David personally. Words cannot express how foolish he has been,' adding that he felt Davis had let the Conservative Party down.

The director of Liberty (formerly the National Council for Civil Liberties), Shami Chakrabarti, had suggested to Davis that he could have much more influence by attacking the government from the opposition front bench and that a resignation would distract from this. Meanwhile, the former Conservative MP turned journalist Matthew Parris wrote that, had he been asked, he would have 'tried hard to dissuade' Davis from resigning but observed that 'this Tory maverick may touch a surprisingly popular nerve ... A martyr, a man of the people from the council estates who broke the big boys' rules in the Westminster game.'

The left-leaning press was also cautiously sympathetic, with *The Observer* saying his stance 'was a decent aspiration, that a by-election campaign will change minds more effectively than parliamentary debate'. Jan Morris in *The Guardian* went further, arguing that Davis was fighting 'a battle for liberty of the mind, of the identity, of the spirit', hailing him as 'a prophet as well as a politician'.

The constituency of Haltemprice & Howden is a mixture of urban and rural. Haltemprice is a middle-class suburb of Hull adjoining several urban villages and dozens of rural ones following the A63 corridor. Howden is a small market town. The constituency has returned Conservative MPs since 1837, although Davis's majority fell to under 2,000 in 2001.

The Liberal Democrats quickly announced that, in solidarity with Davis and in opposition to the government, they would not be standing a candidate in the by-election. The Labour Party followed suit, claiming that it was a political stunt and believing there was little in it for them. For a while, it looked as if the only serious opposition to Davis might come from the one-time editor of *The Sun* Kelvin MacKenzie. Rupert Murdoch, the head of News International, was very keen on the idea of MacKenzie's candidature, and *The Sun*'s editor Rebekah Wade believed that 'democracy would not be best served by a walkover' for Davis. MacKenzie himself was understood to be 'very hostile' to Davis's opposition to the government's plans to increase the period of detention to forty-two days.

Initially, MacKenzie had claimed he was '90 per cent certain' he would stand, but when the writ for the by-election was moved on 10 July, he wrote in his column that he wouldn't be putting his name forward, for financial reasons. '*The Sun* couldn't put up the cash – so I was going to have to rustle up £100,000 to conduct my campaign.' An early opinion poll had put MacKenzie on just 14 per cent of the vote, had he stood, but clearly his heart wasn't really in it anyway, as he concluded: 'The truth is that I would have been a crap MP.' Murdoch had cooled on the idea so MacKenzie urged *Sun* readers to vote for Eamonn Fitzpatrick, a market stall trader from Northampton who was solidly behind the government's 42-day plan and who had promised to pack up his stall for a month to campaign in the seat. Fitzpatrick eventually polled just thirty-one votes.

Davis might have been disappointed by the absence of candidates from the other major parties and fears were raised that the by-election might become farcical; fears that were, perhaps, confirmed when the East Riding of Yorkshire Council returning officer announced that a record twenty-six candidates had been validly nominated. The electoral commission unusually allowed them to list the candidates in two columns, thereby making the ballot paper A4 in size.

Without a Labour or Liberal Democrat candidate, the contest was always going to be unusual. Andrew Norfolk wrote in *The Times* that while 'extension to what is already the longest pre-charge detention in the free world' was deadly serious, the by-election was 'pantomime politics'. Into this pantomime, in support of Davis, came several serious-minded campaigners including Labour MP Bob Marshall-Andrews, Shami Chakrabarti and London bombing survivor Rachel North. Added to these Davis attracted high-profile supporters including actors Colin Firth and Honor Blackman, singer turned poverty campaigner Bob Geldof and Colonel Tim Collins, of Iraq War fame. Davis believed Shan Oakes, the Green Party candidate, to be his most serious opponent, but although describing herself as the 'real civil liberties candidate', Oakes appeared unlikely to bring about the 'scare' for the Conservatives she predicted. However, along with Joanne Robinson for the English Democrats, she was one of only three candidates, including Davis himself, to save her deposit. A record twenty-three candidates sacrificed their £500 for polling less than the necessary 5 per cent minimum.

Robinson's campaign was wider in its context, calling for a referendum on the EU treaty, an English parliament and an end to 'uncontrolled immigration'; views shared in part by the Christian Party's George Hargreaves who maintained the direction the European Union was going would 'imprison the whole nation for 42 years or more'.

Independent candidate Jill Saward from London, the victim of the notorious and violent Ealing vicarage rape, had made her name as a principled 'campaigner on behalf of the victims of sexual violence'. Andrew Sparrow in *The Guardian* identified her as a serious candidate and 'Davis's most prominent opponent', as she was supported by unnamed 'party politicians'. However worthy Saward's message, her campaign never caught the public's imagination and she polled just 492 votes, finishing sixth.

Two weeks before the by-election, *The Guardian*'s Nick Watt ran several pages on Davis under the headline 'Maverick or freedom fighter?', highlighting his background as a former SAS officer turned 'Tory bruiser' who would take no lectures 'about being soft on terror'. Davis was then joined on the campaign trail by David Cameron, who told the BBC's James Lansdale he was 'delighted to be here … and keen to see David Davis re-elected with a big majority'. Some local residents thought differently, calling the by-election 'a waste of money', 'a waste of time' or serving 'no purpose'. Lansdale also interviewed the Green's Shan Oakes, who repeated her view of the need to oppose the erosion of civil liberties but didn't feel Davis was the right person to do it. Lansdale's 'vox pop' also followed Jill Saward – 'CCTV is important as it helps put criminals behind bars' – and filmed a former Miss Great Britain, the Mad Cow-Girl from the Monster Raving Loony Party, Independent maverick former sports presenter David Icke and David Bishop, standing for the Church of the Militant Elvis Party. The veteran *Newsnight* political correspondent Michael Crick claimed a by-election record when he followed and interviewed a record thirteen candidates in one day, some of whom seemed to have little idea what was going on.

When the result of the by-election was declared, on the floor of a local leisure centre (the stage being too small for twenty-six candidates), Davis had been returned to Westminster with a near record by-election 72 per cent share of the vote. Without candidates from either the governing Labour Party or the Liberal Democrats, a low turnout of voters was feared, but at 34 per cent, it was respectable. Some records were broken at Haltemprice & Howden, from the number of candidates (especially independents) to the record twenty-three lost deposits. The Greens achieved their best result and the Tories their largest ever increase in their share of the vote, up by 24 per cent.

Behind Davis's 17,113 votes, only the Greens and the English Democrats polled in four figures. The rest of the candidates registered derisory shares, with two independents Tony Farnon and Norman Scarth getting a mere eight votes each, fewer than the ten legitimate signatures they had gathered on their nomination papers.

Was it all really worth it? Davis thought so, arguing he had 'fired a shot across the bows of Gordon Brown's arrogant, arbitrary and authoritarian government', adding that he would continue to fight the 42-day detention, ID cards and oppose the 'ever-intrusive state'. He told the BBC Radio 4's *Today* programme that 'the Westminster village' hadn't really understood his principled stand. In answer to a parliamentary question from the Labour MP Peter Kilfoyle, the Justice Minister indicated that the whole contest would have cost the taxpayer in excess of £200,000, with the candidates' own costs on top of that.

Reflecting on his stance, a decade later, Davis drew attention to a 'wave of intrusive new tech creeping up on the population just as social media did before', pointing out that when, in the by-election, he had campaigned on civil liberties, many had felt him 'old fashioned, even eccentric'. Now, he noted, 'people are awake to it. Three quarters of citizens now worry about the impact of these privacy invasions, nine of out of ten want to control what personal data is collected about them, and want tougher punishments for companies that violate their privacy.'

Had he not called the by-election, Davis might well have been made Home Secretary when Cameron formed his coalition government in 2010. The post went to Theresa May (later to become Prime Minister) and David Davis returned to the back benches where he stayed for the whole of the 2015 parliament. He was appointed Secretary of State for Exiting the EU under May's premiership but resigned this position in 2018 and later played a key role in the downfall of Boris Johnson as Prime Minister. Davis became a regular champion for libertarian causes, including suspected and alleged miscarriages of justice – the case of nurse Lucy Letby, being the latest.

As for the plans to detain terror suspects for forty-two days, they were defeated in the House of Lords and abandoned.

Robert Evans was a London MEP from 1994 to 2009. His main achievement was legislation outlawing discrimination against disabled passengers when travelling by air. In 2003, he was the Labour candidate in the Brent East by-election. Evans is a member of Surrey County Council and a visiting professor at Royal Holloway College. In 2022, he gained an MSc in South Asian politics at SOAS.

74

GLASGOW EAST

24 JULY 2008
SNP GAIN FROM LABOUR

LESLEY ORR

Result: John Mason (SNP), 11,277, 43.1 per cent; Margaret Curran (Labour), 10,912, 41.7 per cent; Davena Rankin (Conservative), 1,639, 6.3 per cent; Ian Robertson (Liberal Democrats), 915, 3.5 per cent; Frances Curran (Scottish Socialist), 555, 2.1 per cent; Tricia McLeish (Solidarity), 512, 2.0 per cent; Dr Eileen Duke (Scottish Green), 232, 0.9 per cent; Chris Creighton (Independent), 67, 0.3 per cent; Hamish Howitt (Freedom-4-Choice), 65, 0.2 per cent

Size of majority: 365

Swing: 22.5 per cent from Labour to SNP

Name of previous MP and party: David Marshall (Labour)

Reason for by-election: Resignation due to ill health

Result at previous general election: David Marshall (Labour), 18,775, 60.7 per cent; Lachlan McNeill (SNP), 5,268, 17.0 per cent; David Jackson (Liberal Democrats), 3,665, 11.8 per cent; Carl Thomson (Conservative), 2,135, 6.9 per cent; George Savage (Scottish Socialist), 1,096, 3.5 per cent

Date by-election called: 30 June 2008

Date by-election took place: 24 July 2008

Size of total electorate: 62,052

Total number of votes cast: 26,219

Turnout: 42.3 per cent

On 30 June 2008, David Marshall MP resigned on grounds of ill health, widely assumed to be precipitated by imminent scrutiny of parliamentary expenses used to employ his wife and daughter and claim rent for an office in his own home.

He had represented the people of Glasgow's East End since 1979, as member for Glasgow Shettleston prior to 2005 boundary changes which created the new seat of Glasgow East, mostly out of the former Baillieston and Shettleston constituencies. It encompassed the inner-city tenements of Parkhead, Tollcross and Gallowgate, pockets of Victorian villas and the enormous peripheral council housing schemes including Baillieston and Easterhouse. Marshall was a Labour man to his fingertips – a machine politician in the party's seemingly impregnable heartland. The voters of Glasgow Shettleston sent Red Clydeside ILP leader and housing campaigner John Wheatley to Westminster in 1922, and a Labour stronghold it had remained.

In 2008, this was Labour's third safest seat in Scotland. The area had once been a major industrial workshop for the British Empire. The vast Parkhead Forge – a legendary site of worker militancy during the First World War – employed up to 30,000. But it closed in 1975, followed by Templeton's carpet factory and umpteen small businesses. By the mid-1980s, the East End was in the throes of severe deindustrialisation and long-term economic decline.

The root causes of that decline, and the manifold social, health and environmental effects on alienated communities, were traditional bread-and-butter issues for the 'people's party'; they were nowhere near the top of the UK political establishment's agenda in 2008. Glasgow East had been ignored for many years, wrote Deborah Orr in *The Independent*. 'Now, with a by-election coming up, it has suddenly become a fascinating part of the world' not for its own sake 'but because it will be playing a walk-on part in the great game that is Westminster politics'.

The 'great game' was preoccupied with the fate of a deeply unpopular New Labour government and particularly the flailing leadership of Prime Minister Gordon Brown, who had finally succeeded Tony Blair in June 2007. After equivocating over whether to call a general election, his ratings had plummeted. Amid a recession precipitated by the global financial crash, people were burdened with rising prices, higher bills and insecurity. A Labour government which had abandoned its traditional principles, adopted a post-Thatcherite economic model and was more interested in swing voters seemed blind to the situation of their core working-class supporters. It had lost three by-elections in the space of two months, including a calamitous defeat in Crewe & Nantwich. Rumbles of discontent in the Parliamentary Labour Party were reaching high velocity.

A by-election in Labour's Scottish fiefdom was Brown's worst nightmare. The Scottish Labour Party's hegemony had already been thoroughly rattled in 2007 by the unthinkable – the Scottish National Party (SNP) had taken power in the devolved Scottish Parliament. The SNP had won over urban Scotland by appropriating Labour's left-of-centre mantle, offering hope and promising change. Led by First Minister Alex Salmond, the minority SNP government was enjoying an unusually long honeymoon. The political atmosphere in Scotland had changed. The new regime had no need or desire to defer to the big boys in London but were ambitious to prove their boldness and competence. This by-election was its first significant electoral test, and Salmond approached it with relish. He was clearly an asset to the SNP campaign; Brown was universally regarded as a liability. 'To lose such a seat for the first time since 1922 would not just be a spectacular Labour disaster but an unmissable sign of wider Labour disintegration in Scotland,' wrote Martin Kettle in *The Guardian*. A deep sense of crisis prevailed in the Scottish Labour Party (SLP) – leaderless since Wendy Alexander's resignation under an expenses cloud, in the same week as Marshall.

A general impression of the SLP's exhausted ineptitude was borne out by a farcical start to their campaign. When 24 July was announced as the polling date, the media and SNP were quick to criticise the government for trying to catch the SNP on the hop by making it a short contest with polling day during the Glasgow Fair holiday fortnight. Many voters would be away and there were difficulties for postal voters. If this was Labour's strategy, it came back to bite. Their preferred candidate, George Ryan, failed to show up for the selection meeting. In an SLP hardly overflowing with talent, three prominent figures (Glasgow City Council leader Stephen Purcell, former General Secretary Lesley Quinn and MSP for Glasgow Shettleston Frank McAveety) were pressured and declined. The fifth-choice candidate was finally confirmed on 8 July. Margaret Curran was MSP for Glasgow Baillieston, covering much of Glasgow East. A long-time Labour activist who had been a community education worker and lecturer, Curran was from the East End, but in the first of many gaffes, she was forced to clarify that her claim to be a lifelong resident was a 'slip of the tongue', when it emerged she had been living in a leafy Southside suburb for twenty years.

By the time Curran launched her campaign, declaring 'the Labour fightback starts right here, right now', the SNP had, according to Salmond, 'got off to a flying start' with their candidate John Mason, who was also keen to put his local credentials front and centre. A chartered accountant, he lived in a 'modest Barlanark flat', was a councillor for Shettleston and leader of the SNP's council opposition group. A committed evangelical Baptist lay preacher who had spent three years in Nepal as a missionary, Mason was known for his diligence. A vox popped woman said he had done so much for the community that she didn't want to lose him as her councillor. With Salmond at his shoulder – or, it was hinted, minding him – Mason declared that he would campaign primarily on prices, fuel poverty and the hardships suffered especially by the elderly folk of the constituency. Promising to be 'on your side', his message was that the people of Glasgow East resented being taken for granted by Labour and that there was little to choose between them and the Tories.

Both main candidates in this two-horse race wanted to focus on local concerns, both acknowledged the bleak statistics highlighting the privations of an area blighted by long-term urban decay and both wanted also to stress that there were signs of vitality and community spirit in a constituency where they had decent reputations as hard-working local politicians. They talked up the potential impact of the 2014 Commonwealth Games for east Glasgow regeneration.

But it was Conservative Party leader David Cameron who set the tone for a by-election which generated huge UK media interest. He launched his party's campaign in Gallowgate with a landmark speech in a constituency they would never win. Candidate Davena Rankin – a local woman of colour and trade union activist – was not in the usual Tory mould (she would later join the Labour Party). Iain Duncan

Smith MP accompanied them. He had established his 'compassionate Conservatism' Centre for Social Justice (CSJ) think tank after his 2002 Easterhouse visit sparked a 'Damascene conversion' to seek 'new solutions to poverty'. The CSJ was churning out a series of reports which diagnosed Britain as a 'broken' society. 'Breakthrough Glasgow' had been published in February 2008. Duncan Smith and the CSJ identified 'Shettleston man' as personifying Glasgow's social ills: he lived in social housing and was terminally unemployed; stress, drink and bad food was killing him. He would be dead by sixty-three. Cameron used the Gallowgate event to set out his stall as a prospective government in waiting: 'This is the Broken Society by-election … as we see a society that is in danger of losing its sense of personal responsibility, common decency and yes, even public morality.' 'Broken Britain' would become a catchphrase during the 2010 general election.

The media pack descended on Glasgow East looking for Shettleston man in his grim habitat and reporting from the front line in overwhelmingly negative terms. Jeremy Paxman's supercilious remark – that it was the kind of place where you could stick a red rosette on a Christmas pudding and it would get elected – was typical. Simon Heffer in the *Telegraph* commented: 'If you seek Labour's monument, look at this hellhole of a constituency.' A relentlessly stigmatising picture was painted of the 'horrendous social experiment' which had created a sink estate of welfare junkies – a place variously likened to Gaza, a Kenyan shanty town, North Korea, Albania and Bangladesh. Politicians and pundits of all stripes were happy to parrot the CSJ diagnosis that the area's poverty and crime was largely down to the inadequacies and deviant behaviours of its inhabitants. Few dug deeper into the long-term structural causes of its ills.

Deborah Orr, from a similar background in Motherwell, did. Among the residents she spoke to, a youth worker recalled that when he was a boy everyone had an expectation of work. He never saw trouble and never saw the police. The women ran the social side of life, and the men went to work. 'He is awed still at how quickly and recklessly it was all dismantled – the mills, the steelworks, the shipbuilding, the car-making. And he remains appalled [that Thatcherism] swept in to take its place.'

Curran was critical of coverage depicting a bleak wasteland overrun with drug dealers and criminals. She promised – with *Taggart* star John Michie alongside – to be tough on crime, but her campaign was beset by blunders and accusations of arrogance. Organised from London, it used software which could not recognise tenement addresses and out-of-date maps. Dispirited activists wasted hundreds of hours. Curran told an insider she had never read her personal message in her leaflet. Labour canvassers told one paper that disenchanted former supporters had been throwing old furniture at them over the balconies of tower blocks. A blogger gave regular gaffe updates while *Scotland on Sunday* derided the party's 'slapstick politics' and the London media gleefully contrasted the strange absence of Gordon Brown with the ever-present Alex Salmond.

Riding the momentum, and with celebrity backers including Sean Connery, Elaine C. Smith and Jimmy Reid, the respected ex-Communist trade union leader, Salmond claimed that voters were comparing a popular and successful SNP government with a deeply disliked Labour administration. Elaine lived in the constituency and recalls:

> A lot of entitlement, complacency and laziness had set in. The need to realign and capture that disaffected Labour vote was obvious. One night, walking to a match at Parkhead, I heard some middle-aged guys talking about voting SNP – they were going to give it a shot. I turned to my husband and said, 'Did you hear that? I never thought I would hear those words uttered in the East End, far less at solid Labour Celtic Park.' A few weeks later I met an old Labour comrade out campaigning. He was chastising me for being out on the stump with Salmond. I replied, 'You've had fifty years to make this place better and look at it. People have had enough – they deserve better.'

New Labour's 2007 'workfare' reform of the social security system, making benefits conditional on employment-seeking and introducing sanctions, was a key issue. So was the cost of living. Brown's government was accused of crass attempts to bribe voters when mid-campaign it announced postponement of a rise in fuel duty and then of a scheduled parliamentary debate on the controversial Human Fertilisation and

Embryo Bill. On 13 July, Bishop Joe Devine wrote to all Scottish parliamentarians criticising the Bill and claiming the government had lost its ethical credibility. In a constituency with a large Catholic population, this intervention may have been a factor for some. Mason, who wanted the time limit for abortions reduced and opposed embryo research, thought so. But it was bread-and-butter issues that really mattered.

By polling day, it was clear that a major upset was on the cards. The SNP with its large and motivated team of activists had run an impressive campaign of the kind which would turn them into an election-winning machine for the next decade. By contrast, Labour's was shambolic and lacked local volunteers on the ground. Elaine C. Smith had been in Easterhouse holding street rallies with Salmond. 'An old man invited us in,' she recalls. 'He was a widower with holy pictures displayed round the house. He shook Alex's hand and said, "Time for a change, eh?" And that's when I knew something seismic was happening.'

The declaration came at 2.20 a.m., after Labour demanded a recount. The SNP had won by 365 votes, with a 22.5 per cent swing. It was a sensational result, making the SNP and Salmond look unstoppable. Mason called it a victory off the Richter scale. One Scottish columnist in full apocalyptic mode predicted that it could presage the end of Labour as a party of British government.

The tectonic plates of Scottish politics had certainly shifted. John Curtice extrapolated the result to a general election, showing that a similar swing would win the SNP fifty seats. That didn't happen in 2010 when Curran duly won Glasgow East back for Labour, but an SNP landslide gave them fifty-six MPs in 2015. The party had become a formidable political force. John Mason was elected as MSP for Shettleston in 2011. Over the years, he has been something of an SNP outsider, at odds with the progressive social policies of his party and with a reputation for foot-in-mouth comments. In October 2024, he was finally expelled for social media posts disputing that Israel was committing genocide in Gaza.

The Glasgow East result intensified pressure on the government and on Brown, although the Westminster bubble's obsession with his future was not generally shared by local voters. A clever spoof YouTube video, 'Gordon Brown's Downfall', riffed on the 2005 film about Hitler but also leaned into all the stigmatising stereotypes of a Glasgow underclass. Disgruntled Labour Party members accused the PLP of being out of touch if it thought that having taken a beating, the solution was simply to change leader. During a TV debate about the future of Brown and Labour in government, some participants warned Labour to reconnect urgently with its traditional constituency, to be bolder on taxation, redistribution and state intervention in response to the financial crisis; voters were rejecting their policies, not the leader. Curran herself urged the party to heed the message that people were angry and would not be placated with clichés. Brown clung on, but the end of the New Labour era was fast approaching. The elections of the coalition government in 2010 and of a majority SNP government at Holyrood in 2011 widened the fissure between political terrains in Scotland and England. Broken austerity Britain was compelled to reorientate around the constitutional question of independence.

Lesley Orr is a historian, activist and writer from Edinburgh. She is currently writing a biography of suffragette, Red Clydeside leader and internationalist Helen Crawfurd (Edinburgh University Press, forthcoming).

75

CLACTON

9 OCTOBER 2014
UKIP GAIN FROM CONSERVATIVES

TIM SHIPMAN

Result: Douglas Carswell (UKIP), 21,113, 59.7 per cent; Giles Watling (Conservative), 8,709, 24.6 per cent; Tim Young (Labour), 3,957, 11.2 per cent; Chris Southall (Green), 688, 1.9 per cent; Andy Graham (Liberal Democrats), 483, 1.4 per cent; Bruce Sizer (Independent), 205, 0.6 per cent; Alan 'Howling Laud' Hope (Monster Raving Loony), 127, 0.4 per cent; Charlotte Rose (Independent), 56, 0.2 per cent
Size of majority: 12,404
Swing: 44.1 per cent from Conservative to UKIP
Name of previous MP and party: Douglas Carswell (Conservative)
Reason for by-election: Resignation following defection to UKIP
Result at previous general election: Douglas Carswell (Conservative), 22,867, 53.0 per cent; Ivan Henderson (Labour), 10,799, 25.0 per cent; Michael Freen (Liberal Democrats), 5,577, 12.9 per cent; Jim Taylor (BNP), 1,975, 6.0 per cent; Terry Allen (Tendring First), 1,078, 2.5 per cent; Chris Southall (Green), 535, 1.2 per cent; Chris Humphrey (Independent), 292, 0.7 per cent
Date by-election called: 2 September 2014
Date by-election took place: 9 October 2014
Size of total electorate: 69,118
Total number of votes cast: 35,338
Turnout: 51.1 per cent

The Clacton by-election of 2014 was a key waypoint on the road to the Leave campaign's victory in the EU referendum twenty months later – and may have even affected the result. It was called because the sitting MP, Douglas Carswell, wanted Britain to leave the European Union.

The drama began on 28 August 2014 at the Edwardian splendour of One Great George Street, the grandest event space in Westminster. The press had gathered for what they believed was the unveiling of a new donor for the UK Independence Party (UKIP), led by Nigel Farage. Instead, Carswell, who had been a Conservative MP since 2005 (first for Harwich then, since 2010, for the renamed seat of Clacton) walked out and announced that he was defecting to UKIP.

It was that rare thing, a moment the media claimed had 'electrified Westminster' which actually did so. Even more explosively, Carswell announced that he would resign and fight a by-election to give his constituents the opportunity to endorse or reject his approach. He was not, in fact, UKIP's first MP. That distinction belonged to Bob Spink, the Tory MP for Castle Point who defected in 2008, but he lost his seat in 2010. The prize Carswell sought was to be the party's first ever elected MP – and to transform British politics.

Clacton-on-Sea, a seaside resort on the Essex coast of around 50,000 people, was a decaying and neglected place whose main purpose had been rendered obsolete by the advent of cheap flights and affordable family holidays in Europe's summer hotspots. Pushing two hours from London at the end of a slow railway line, it was the sort of town where young people escaped in search of work. Those who remained were typical of those who voted for Brexit – the impoverished and disillusioned, failed for decades by all stripes of the London political class, who remembered better days and were willing participants in a very British revolution.

Carswell was from altogether more exotic stock than most of his constituents. He had been born and brought up in Africa, where his doctor father, Wilson Carswell, had diagnosed the first cases of HIV/Aids in Uganda. Wilson's experiences under the regime of Idi Amin became the model for the lead character in Giles Foden's novel *The Last King of Scotland*.

After a history degree at the University of East Anglia, Carswell got a job as a parliamentary researcher, in which role he became friends with Daniel Hannan, who was then running the first iteration of the European Research Group, set up to help Tory MPs campaign against the European Union and which later became a key player in the Brexit wars in Parliament. In 2003, Hannan persuaded Carswell that the campaign for an in/out referendum should be the goal of Eurosceptics.

In December 2009, Carswell tabled a Bill in the Commons calling for such a referendum. He was named *The Spectator* magazine's parliamentarian of the year for his troubles. It was a factor in ramping up the pressure on David Cameron, Tory leader since 2005, announcing in January 2013 that he would seek to renegotiate Britain's relationship with the EU and then put the deal to the people in a referendum.

Carswell's decision to trigger the Clacton by-election a year and a half later emerged from polling data on the role Nigel Farage and UKIP should play in a future referendum. Summarised by the *New Statesman* in April 2014 as 'the Farage Paradox', the numbers showed that the more media exposure the charismatic populist got, the higher UKIP's national standing rose but at the same time support for leaving the EU fell. Support for Leave had a sixteen-point lead over Remain in 2013, according to YouGov, but by the spring of 2014, UKIP were becoming a national force and the two sides were tied. When Farage ran rings around Nick Clegg in a televised debate on Europe hosted by LBC, the Remain team had a six-point lead in YouGov's next poll.

Carswell concluded that Farage was an impediment to winning the referendum because UKIP's image as a merry band of eccentrics would allow the political establishment to paint the cause of Brexit as a fringe pursuit of fruitcakes and extremists. With Hannan's knowledge, he began secret talks with Farage about defecting. But what he didn't tell Farage was that his plan was to jump ship and detoxify UKIP:

> We wanted to put men in their trench, and to do that, we had to go over the top. Nigel did a superb job in making sure we got the referendum. One of the reasons I joined UKIP was because I thought I could detoxify this brand that was ruining our chances of winning the referendum. If it became a choice between being rude about Romanian immigrants versus the economy, we would lose 60–40.

In April 2014, Farage had said he would be 'concerned' if Romanian men moved in next door.

In his defection speech, Carswell adopted a very different tone to his new leader, who had spent two decades equating the causes of Euroscepticism and immigration control. 'I am not against immigration,' Carswell declared to the still shell-shocked press pack as he condemned 'angry nativism', adding: 'We must welcome those who come here to contribute.' He even praised political correctness as 'straightforward good manners'.

Carswell, with his jutting jawline and contrarian manner, had a reputation as an independent-minded libertarian, a bit of a loner and if Farage smelled a cuckoo in the nest, he did not at this point say so, praising Carswell's bravery for defecting and putting his decision to the people. But the somewhat awkward but principled Carswell and the pugnacious Farage would soon become mortal enemies.

Following Carswell's resignation, Roger Lord, UKIP's candidate for the 2015 general election in Clacton, declared that he still wanted to stand. The party's National Executive Committee voted to select Carswell instead. UKIP had not even stood a candidate against Carswell in 2010 because of his cast-iron Eurosceptic credentials.

Despite a brief media campaign, led by the *Telegraph* journalist Peter Oborne, for Cameron to 'beg' Boris Johnson, the Mayor of London, to stand for the Tories, the Conservative candidate was Giles Watling, a Tendring district councillor and former actor, best known for playing the role of the vicar Oswald in the TV sitcom *Bread*. He was chosen in an open primary on 11 September, a contest which attracted a paltry 240 votes from local residents. The omens were not good for the Tories. Watling's prospects were not improved when, two days before the by-election, Johnson forgot his name in an interview with LBC's Nick Ferrari. 'He's a superb man,' Johnson blustered. 'Stirling? Girling? Something like that.'

Two early opinion polls showed Carswell with a substantial lead. He defected on a Friday. That weekend's *Mail on Sunday* carried a Survation survey which put him on 64 per cent of the vote, a staggering forty-four points ahead of the Tories, with Labour on 13 per cent and the Lib Dems on just 2 per cent. In the same survey, Tory voters declared Carswell a 'hero' rather than a 'traitor' by a margin of 49 per cent to 17 per cent. Those surveyed wanted to leave the EU by a margin of more than two to one and half said immigration was their top issue, with Europe second. Asked why they were supporting Carswell, 57 per cent of UKIP voters said they liked the party and 34 per cent said because of Carswell, an unusually high personal vote which captured the scale of Tory voters switching with their man. Just 9 per cent said it was a protest vote, often the main motivation in by-elections.

Tory high command sent out Michael Fallon, the Defence Secretary who was Cameron's best media fireman, to try to douse the flames and peddle the Tory attack line that UKIP would let in the pro-EU Ed Miliband, the Labour leader: 'The only prospect of delivering an in/out referendum is a clear Conservative majority at the next election. Anything else and you will end up with a Miliband government which wants no change at all in Europe.' The Survation poll found that for every voter who stuck with the Tories as a result of this argument, slightly more were even more determined to vote UKIP.

The Tories tried to direct the campaign away from Carswell, sending out a leaflet called 'The Big Clacton Survey', focused on issues such as 'local train and tube services'. Gleeful UKIP activists pointed out that the nearest Tube station was more than fifty miles away.

Carswell campaigned in part on local issues regarding planning and the overcrowding of GP surgeries, which he called 'a factor in my decision to resign'. Freed of loyalty to the government, he was able to criticise the provision of public services in neglected towns like Clacton – an argument which played back into the debate about whether leaving the EU would direct more resources to British communities which needed it. But in truth, there was really only one issue on the ballot paper. The by-election was a referendum on Carswell's decision.

On the ground, a huge public meeting took place at Clacton Coastal Academy on 24 September, where Farage and Carswell addressed around 700 people.

Carswell was always confident of victory – and for good reason. He knew his patch backwards and was one of those MPs who made a virtue of studying the data. He had canvassed every house in the constituency multiple times over the years and it was quickly clear that his vote was holding up after the defection once the by-election door knocking began. Journalists who flocked to Clacton found him greeting constituents by name in the street, where he attracted a mostly warm welcome. He was bolstered by what his campaign claimed were 150 local Conservative Party members who joined his canvassing team. Two Tory councillors also defected, citing an article by *The Times* columnist Matthew Parris that 'Clacton-on-Sea is going nowhere' and should be disregarded by the Conservatives. Carswell declared Parris's views 'reflective of what so many in the upper echelons of the Tory party really think'.

Carswell's data operation was run by Chris Bruni-Lowe, one of the most talented numbers men outside the main parties, who defected from the Tories at the same time and later became a key component in the messaging and polling successes of UKIP and its cousin-successors, the Brexit Party and Reform UK.

With the result barely in doubt, the most significant event of the campaign was the announcement that there would be another by-election. On 27 September, at the UKIP annual conference in Doncaster, perfectly timed for maximum political damage on the eve of the Conservative Party conference, Tory MP Mark Reckless announced that he was defecting to UKIP as well. Reckless, who represented Rochester & Strood in Kent, had previously masterminded the first successful backbench defeat of the Tory–Lib Dem coalition government, in which fifty-three Conservative MPs rebelled over the EU Budget. Shortly afterwards, Tory donor Arron Banks announced that he was giving UKIP £1 million.

On 2 October, Cameron – who had called Carswell's defection 'bizarre' and 'counterproductive' – visited Clacton and donned a hi-vis jacket for a meeting on the beach with Watling, admitting that his party were 'underdogs'.

A week after that, on 9 October, the people of Clacton went to the polls, symbolically on Cameron's forty-eighth birthday, and returned Carswell to Parliament. He slightly increased his majority to 12,404, with a 44 per cent swing from the Tories to UKIP. In his acceptance speech, he continued the detox plan: 'We must be a party for all Britain and all Britons, first and second generation as much as every other.'

In his first interview after winning, with the *Sunday Times*, Carswell declared that the role he now wanted was 'chief leaflet distributor in the most marginal ward in Rochester'. Reckless held his Rochester & Strood seat in the subsequent by-election on 20 November but was to lose it to the Tories at the general election six months later.

Shortly after the second by-election, with Westminster abuzz about further defections, Cameron announced that he would legislate to hold a referendum within the first hundred days of a Tory government being elected. 'That closed off the possibility of anyone else coming over,' Carswell said later.

His mission was on the way to becoming accomplished, however. When the Tories won the 2015 election and could govern without the Lib Dems, Cameron attempted a new negotiation with Brussels, though the results fell short of what he wanted or could sell to the electorate.

Throughout 2015 and early 2016, the Leave campaign was bitterly split into two factions. Farage and Banks joined forces to set up Leave.EU to fight for the right to run the official campaign chosen by the Electoral Commission. Carswell sided instead with Matthew Elliott and his Vote Leave campaign director Dominic Cummings, lending vital UKIP cover to their cause and helping them secure the designation. In so doing, he prevented the Farage-led campaign he had feared.

The split campaign probably helped the Leave cause. Vote Leave, harnessing the political power of Boris Johnson and Michael Gove, gave Eurosceptic Tories cover to oppose a Conservative Prime Minister. Farage, appealing to white working-class voters in the north, some of whom usually voted Labour or did not vote at all, had a different appeal. Together they secured 52 per cent of the vote.

The Clacton by-election of 2014 was not a huge upset. From early on in the campaign, it seemed like a foregone conclusion. But it was one of the most seismic. In a world where shock victories against the ruling party are often undone at the ensuing general election, there is a plausible case that it had the most far-reaching political implications of any by-election in the first quarter of the twenty-first century.

Carswell resigned from UKIP in March 2017 and did not stand at the subsequent general election that year, allowing Watling to finally become an MP. When he left Parliament, the commentator Alex

Massie observed that 'by any reasonable measure, Carswell has been one of the most influential backbenchers in recent memory. Possibly, even, the most influential of all … He is that rarity: an actual radical who actually achieved something significant.' Most political careers end in failure. Carswell's was a rare success.

This was not Clacton's last moment at the heart of the British political drama. A decade later, after he had resigned and returned to UKIP, set up the Brexit Party and then taken over its successor, Reform UK, Farage stood himself as the candidate in the 2024 general election. Carswell, now living in the US, said he was 'thrilled Nigel Farage is standing in my old seat'. In his eighth attempt to become an MP, Farage was finally victorious, defeating Watling by more than 8,000 votes. The Brexit he and Carswell fought for having been delivered, inadequately, as Farage saw it, he was back fighting for a new revolution. Proof, perhaps, that most political wins are fleeting.

Tim Shipman is political editor of The Spectator, *having spent many years as political editor and chief political commentator of the* Sunday Times. *His quartet of books on the EU referendum and its aftermath –* All Out War, Fall Out, No Way Out *and* Out *– are recognised as the definitive first draft of history. He has won three British press awards for his political reporting and commentary. The London Press Club named him print journalist of the year in 2017 and political journalist of the year in 2024.*

76

BATLEY & SPEN

20 OCTOBER 2016
LABOUR HOLD

MATHEW HULBERT

Result: Tracy Brabin (Labour), 17,506, 85.8 per cent; Therese Hirst (English Democrat), 969, 4.8 per cent; David Furness (BNP), 548, 2.7 per cent; Garry Kitchin (Independent), 517, 2.5 per cent; Corbyn Anti (English Independence), 241, 1.2 per cent; Jack Buckby (Liberty GB), 220, 1.1 per cent; Henry Mayhew (Independent), 153, 0.8 per cent; Waqas Ali Khan (Independent), 118, 0.6 per cent; Richard Edmonds (National Front), 87, 0.4 per cent; Ankit Love (One Love), 34, 0.2 per cent
Size of majority: 16,537
Swing: N/A
Name of previous MP and party: Jo Cox (Labour)
Reason for by-election: Murder of incumbent
Result at previous general election: Jo Cox (Labour), 21,826, 43.2 per cent; Imtiaz Ameen (Conservative), 15,769, 31.2 per cent; Aleks Lukic (UKIP), 9,080, 18.0 per cent; John Lawson (Liberal Democrats), 2,396, 4.7 per cent; Ian Bullock (Green), 1,232, 2.4 per cent; Dawn Wheelhouse (TUSC), 123, 0.2 per cent; Karl Varley (Patriotic Socialist), 53, 0.1 per cent
Date by-election called: 13 September 2016
Date by-election took place: 20 October 2016
Size of total electorate: 79,781
Total number of votes cast: 20,393
Turnout: 25.6 per cent

This by-election was called in the most tragic of circumstances. The murder of Jo Cox on 16 June 2016 shocked the nation and sent shockwaves through the British body politic.

Cox, who was elected in the May 2015 general election and who was already seen as a rising star in the Parliamentary Labour Party, was heading to hold a surgery in her constituency, to meet and listen to her constituents and to seek to help them. Cox, who previously worked for Oxfam, was shot twice in the head, once in the chest and was then stabbed fifteen times, on Market Street in Birstall.

This was the first murder of a sitting MP since the provisional IRA killed the senior Conservative MP Ian Gow in 1990 by means of a car bomb at his home. White supremacist Thomas Alexander Mair, fifty-three, was found guilty of her murder and other offences in November 2016.

Inevitably, the by-election for Batley & Spen's new MP was very different to the usual. It coincided with a by-election taking place in Witney, Oxfordshire, and they were the fifth and sixth by-elections to have taken place in the fifty-sixth UK parliament.

It came just a matter of months after the Brexit referendum and all of the divisions, in government, in parties, in businesses and in families, that had caused. The by-election was also just months into the premiership of Theresa May and around a year into Jeremy Corbyn's controversial leadership of the Labour Party. Indeed, the murder of Jo Cox happened exactly a week before polling day in the EU referendum.

Batley & Spen is in the Pennines of West Yorkshire. The constituency was created in 1983 and is made up of parts of the old parliamentary constituencies of Batley & Morley, Brighouse & Spenborough and Dewsbury; it includes within its boundaries Batley, Birkenshaw, Birstall, Cleckheaton, East Bierley, Gomersal, Hunsworth and Liversedge. Though held by Labour ever since the Blair landslide of 1997, it was first held by the Conservative Elizabeth Peacock.

The nature of the reason behind the calling of this by-election meant it was far from politics as usual. Despite the many divisions in the politics of the day, in an unusual show of unity, the Conservatives, Lib Dems, Greens and UKIP didn't contest the by-election, making a Labour victory all but inevitable.

Nine other smaller parties/independents did take on Labour, including a host of hard-right outfits such as the BNP, Liberty GB and the National Front. The English Democrats stood Therese Hirst as their candidate. Hirst, when Therese Muchewicz, previously led Veritas, the political vehicle launched by the perma-tanned former TV host and East Midlands MEP Robert Kilroy-Silk when he left UKIP, launched in January 2005 at a golf club in Hinckley, Leicestershire.

There was a showbiz connection with Labour's candidate too. Before entering politics, Tracy Brabin was an actress in a host of popular TV soaps, including *EastEnders*, *Emmerdale*, *Casualty* and *Doctors*. She was arguably best known for playing the role of Tricia Armstrong in *Coronation Street*, a hard-up single mum who had regular interactions with busybody with a heart of gold Vera Duckworth, played by national treasure and fellow Labour supporter Liz Dawn. Brabin defeated Jane Thomas, a local campaigner from Keighley, for the Labour nomination on 23 September. Brendan Cox, husband of Jo, had earlier ruled himself out of the running.

Earlier in 2016, the British National Party's candidate David Furness had stood in the London mayoral contest, getting 0.5 per cent of the vote. Meanwhile, former BNP member Jack Buckby stood for Liberty GB, which stood under the banner 'no to terrorism, yes to Britain'. The party's Facebook page described it as a 'patriotic counter-jihad party for Christian civilisation, Western rights and freedoms, British culture, animal welfare and capitalism'.

Independent Waqas Ali had been the UKIP candidate for Shipley at the 2015 general election, coming third. Neil Humphrey stood for the English Independence Party and appeared on the ballot paper as 'Anti Corbyn'. Independent Garry Kitchin had previously stood in local elections for the Green Party. Ankit Love stood for the One Love Party, campaigning for better air quality.

On a visit to the constituency during the campaign, Jeremy Corbyn told a gathering of residents and some journalists:

> I have to say this is the worst and saddest circumstances one would ever want for a by-election. Nobody ever wanted this by-election. The tragedy of the loss of Jo is something that is going to live with us for the rest

of our lives. And, in her memory, we are going to win. In her memory we're going to fight for our National Health Service. In her memory we're going to fight for good, strong communities all over the country.

Other big Labour names visited Batley & Spen during the campaign, including then former Cabinet minister Yvette Cooper, who was asked by one resident, when being filmed for TV, if she was Ed Balls's wife.

In the same Channel 4 News piece, a member of Jo Cox's staff noted a dreadful irony which wouldn't have been lost by many. He said, 'It's such an awful irony that, in the by-election to find somebody to re-place Jo, if that's even possible, we end up being inundated with the hatred (by hard-right elements) that caused this by-election. There's a terrible irony in that, I think.'

In an interview with *The Guardian* published on 30 September 2016, Brabin said she hoped, if successful, to build on Jo Cox's legacy. It had been Cox herself who had originally told Brabin that she should con-sider standing for Parliament herself when Brabin had campaigned for her in the lead-up to the 2015 general election.

Brabin told *The Guardian*: 'While we were going door knocking, she said, "Tracey you should think about being an MP." The irony is horrid, isn't it?'

Referencing her hard-right opponents, she said, 'Here in Batley & Spen people saw what happened as a tragedy, but there are people out there who see it as an opportunity. It's really heartbreaking actually.'

Brabin said her campaign would focus on community cohesion, stopping the downgrading of Dewsbury hospital and improving trans-port links to Bradford and Leeds.

Another tragic irony, noted in the piece, is that as a child Brabin regularly frequented the library outside which Cox was killed and had campaigned with Cox to save it.

She said:

That library was a place I used to love when I was a kid because I used to go there to do my homework, for the peace and quiet because of having a chaotic family life. That library is where everything started for me, and for this to be its legacy is just so hard.

Perhaps concerned about only being seen by some voters as a former soap actor, Brabin also stressed her campaigning credentials, telling reporter Frances Perraudin:

> People just think I've been an actor, but I've been a campaigner and trade unionist for 30 years, from Greenham Common through to the miners. I've worked with refugees, victims of torture, I've run after-school clubs in film-making, I've spoken at the European Parliament at the request of Equity, on gender.

Much of the campaigns of the smaller parties contesting the election centred on the divisive issue of immigration, possibly hoping to ratchet up tensions and benefit from the fissures caused by the Brexit referendum held just months earlier, with some making highly questionable claims about how they could reduce it to zero. This led to at least one verbal confrontation between Labour activists and supporters of the hard-right parties. But no amount of, putting it at its politest, very unhelpful rhetoric was going to change the result.

Announced at 1.45 a.m. at Cathedral House in Huddersfield, Labour and Brabin were victorious with 85.8 per cent of the vote (17,506) albeit on one of the lowest turnouts since the Second World War, at just 25.8 per cent. None of the other candidates reached the 5 per cent of the vote needed to retain their deposits.

Some of the other candidates/their supporters heckled Brabin as she gave her victory speech. She said, 'Tonight is a bittersweet occasion for me. That this by-election had to take place at all is a tragedy. Whether you voted for me, voted for other candidates, or didn't vote, I give you my word, I will be equally strong for each and every one of you.'

While her victory was, of course, welcome news for Corbyn and the wider Labour leadership, it was hardly a surprise and didn't do much to dampen down the criticism of him from the Labour right and much of the mainstream media.

Brabin made her maiden speech in the Commons on 2 November, describing Cox as 'inspirational' as she paid tribute to her late predecessor.

After retaining the seat with an almost 9,000 majority in the surprise

2017 general election called by Prime Minister Theresa May, Brabin was promoted to the role of shadow Secretary of State for Digital, Culture, Media and Sport (DCMS) having previously been shadow Early Years Minister.

When Keir Starmer won the Labour leadership after Corbyn stood down following the party's disastrous showing in the 2019 election, he replaced Brabin as shadow DCMS Secretary but kept her on the front bench in the more junior role of shadow Minister for Cultural Industries.

Brabin would hold the seat until May 2021, upon contesting and winning the fight to become the first elected Mayor of West Yorkshire, winning 43 per cent of the first-round vote in the proportional contest and 59.8 per cent of transfer second-round votes. The role includes powers over local transport and planning matters. Brabin won a second term as mayor of the region in 2024.

The 2021 by-election would be won by Jo Cox's sister Kim Leadbeater, who would go on to introduce a Private Members' Bill on assisted dying that would be debated in November 2024.

In the wake of her death and in her memory, the Jo Cox Foundation was set up to make meaningful change on issues that she was passionate about: nurturing strong communities, championing respect in politics and advocating for a fairer world.

One of its main initiatives is the Jo Cox Civility Commission which, the organisation says, has 'identified a range of practical recommendations across different sectors – from central government, to policing, and social media' and is now 'campaigning for the adoption of these recommendations so that urgent progress can be made on this issue'.

It warned starkly: 'If action is not taken, we risk seeing more politicians stepping down due to abuse and intimidation, fewer people putting themselves forward as candidates and less diversity and representation in UK politics.'

It has recommendations on behaviour, political literacy, social media, police and security, parliaments, local government and elections. These include modelling behaviour – the idea that if people see elected representatives behaving badly, they're less likely to treat them with respect in return. It also aims to ensure that MPs and other elected politicians implement and demonstrate the Nolan principles of behaviour in public life which include selflessness, integrity, objectivity and accountability.

Speaking in January 2024 when chair of the foundation, the former Home Secretary Jacqui Smith said, 'Abuse and intimidation of elected politicians is a genuine threat to democracy in this country and now is the time to act if we want to prevent elected representatives from stepping down and ensure a diverse and talented future pipeline of politicians.'

In her maiden speech in Parliament, Jo had focused on what brings us together. She said, 'We are far more united and have far more in common than that which divides us.'

Mathew Hulbert is a Lib Dem activist and a former borough and parish councillor in Leicestershire. He is a regular commentator on TV and radio and is co-host of the Political Frenemies *podcast.*

77

RICHMOND PARK

1 DECEMBER 2016
LIBERAL DEMOCRAT GAIN
FROM CONSERVATIVES

AGGIE CHAMBRÉ

Result: Sarah Olney (Liberal Democrats), 20,510, 49.68 per cent; Zac Goldsmith (Independent), 18,638, 45.15 per cent; Christian Wolmar (Labour), 1,515, 3.67 per cent; Howling Laud Hope (Monster Raving Loony), 184, 0.45 per cent; Fiona Syms (Independent), 173, 0.42 per cent; Dominic Stockford (CPA), 164, 0.40 per cent; Maharaja Jammu and Kashmir (One Love), 67, 0.16 per cent; David Powell (No description), 32, 0.08 per cent
Size of majority: 1,872
Swing: N/A
Name of previous MP and party: Zac Goldsmith (Conservative)
Reason for by-election: Resignation following government decision to back a third runway at Heathrow
Result at previous general election: Zac Goldsmith (Conservative), 34,404, 58.21 per cent; Robin Meltzer (Liberal Democrats), 11,389, 19.27 per cent; Sachin Patel (Labour), 7,296, 12.34 per cent; Andrée Frieze (Green), 3,548, 6.00 per cent; Sam Naz (UKIP), 2,464, 4.17 per cent
Date by-election called: 26 October 2016
Date by-election took place: 1 December 2016
Size of total electorate: 77,243
Total number of votes cast: 41,283
Turnout: 53.44 per cent

I t was over a chicken korma and a Cobra beer that the accountant was convinced that she should run.

It was 2015 and Sarah Olney had been invited to a Kingston Lib Dems' curry night. She'd only joined the party months before – having been radicalised during the EU referendum campaign – and so was surprised to discover that she had been sat between the leader and the former Energy Secretary.

'I was kind of, oh, gosh, I'm sitting between Tim Farron and Ed Davey. Look at me, celebrities either side of me. I was very naive back then.'

Halfway through the dinner, the penny dropped.

'I realised that Ed had engineered it because he wanted to butter me up to think about standing as the parliamentary candidate.'

She quickly capitulated, assuming that the general election would not be for four years. But just a few months later, a by-election was triggered that would thrust Olney into the national limelight.

In many ways, the resignation of Zac Goldsmith – now Lord Goldsmith – was not a surprise. He'd been saying since 2010 that if the Conservatives went ahead with a third Heathrow runway, he would resign:

There were many times I regretted having made that promise, but I felt very strongly about Heathrow, and I wanted people to know that I was serious about it. And in 2010 – I believed the government. I believed that this was a strong commitment that David Cameron had made. So I just took him at his word. And I said to Richmond Park, if he breaks that promise, I will trigger a by-election. So that's your insurance.

Had he not made that promise – he says – he's sure he would have failed to gain the seat from the Lib Dems in 2010.

Theresa May, too, when she became Prime Minister, promised not to expand Heathrow. But in 2016, Goldsmith went to see her and it was clear she'd changed her mind:

I could tell from her body language. She wouldn't look me in the eye. And so I went away and just began to consider how I would trigger the by-election. What the process involved, and whether or not I wanted to stand in it, which I didn't really because I was kind of done with politics.

Days later, the then Prime Minister announced her plans to build a third runway at the site. And Goldsmith kept his word – calling it the 'most polluting, most disruptive, most expensive option' – and promptly quit.

His resignation fired the starting gun on what would be a seismic and bitterly fought contest. Goldsmith decided to stand as an Independent, 'because I thought it would allow me to just make a lot of noise for a couple of months about a stupid decision the government was making'.

Although this seat had been Conservative held for six years, the Lib Dems had three major advantages.

The first was Brexit. The referendum had been held just six months previously and was still at the forefront of the public's mind. Political parties were split over whether Britain should seek a 'soft' or 'hard' Brexit, meaning remaining in or leaving the single market and customs union, and when to begin the two-year process of leaving the EU by triggering Article 50.

Goldsmith was pro-Brexit. Olney was against. Richmond, it was estimated by the University of East Anglia, had one of the lowest 'Leave' votes in the country, with around 72 per cent voting to Remain.

So far, so good for Olney.

The second thing working in the party's favour was the Conservatives' decision not to field a candidate, for the first time since 1963.

'I sort of wish they had,' Goldsmith lamented.

The party had, in part, made the decision because many officials in the local party had said they wanted to campaign for Goldsmith, with the majority supporting his Heathrow stance. Had they campaigned with him and not the local Conservative candidate, they'd have been sacked.

'The party buckled.'

The Conservative candidate would have had to stand on a platform of pro-Heathrow expansion. But instead, as Goldsmith noted, 'I was up against someone who shared my view on Heathrow expansion, [so] they were able to move the goalposts. It meant that it became 100 per cent a campaign about Brexit.'

Olney told me: 'He was fighting on quite weak ground. So we made the by-election about sending a message to the government about Article 50. And my personal pledge was that I wouldn't vote to trigger Article 50.'

There were some calls – like from top Labour politicians Lisa Nandy, Clive Lewis and Jonathan Reynolds – for Labour not to field a candidate, so as to help the Liberal Democrats defeat Goldsmith. But Labour ploughed on – choosing Christian Wolmar. His most notable intervention came when a recent blog post revealed he doesn't use loo paper, wants to ban it and was desperate to bring in 'automatic bidets' or 'butt cleaners'.

The Greens and UKIP didn't put forward candidates, backing the Lib Dems and Goldsmith, respectively.

The third advantage to the Liberal Democrats was that Zac Goldsmith had just had an unsuccessful run at becoming the Mayor of London. He had not only lost the election but had also lost the support and respect of many of his constituents. His team had been accused of running a 'divisive' and 'racist' campaign – due to attempts to paint his rival Sadiq Khan as a 'closet extremist'. Goldsmith denies this. Olney told me: 'He'd run what people really perceived to be a very racist campaign, and Labour voters in Richmond Park were absolutely furious about that.' They wanted to 'teach him a lesson'.

Despite these reasons for Lib Dem cheer, Goldsmith was the bookies' clear favourite, with good reason. He was defending a majority of 23,015. The Lib Dems had not won a parliamentary by-election since 2006 – and had not won a parliamentary seat from the Conservatives at a by-election since 2000. The party had been trounced at the 2015 general election and left with just eight MPs.

Sarah Olney had never been a candidate in any election and had no local reputation.

But as Olney pounded the pavements through the campaign, the seasoned activists by her side could sense a shift in the public mood:

> We had canvassers with big smiles on their faces saying we haven't had reception like this for years and years, people are pleased to see us! For these old timers who've been through the coalition and everything else, this was a novel experience. But I didn't have much of a feel, the campaign team weren't telling me anything.

For Goldsmith, however, as soon as the campaign began in earnest, he felt hopeless. Within a day, he knew he was going to lose:

> There were moments where I walked with my four or five closest volunteers, people I've worked with, we'd go into a pub and the entire pub would be filled with people with orange stickers, and they just sort of stopped what they were doing, and they'd gaze. I'd have to sit at one of the tables. It was absolutely awful. It felt like that sort of scene in *Zulu*, you know, tens of thousands of people coming over the horizon, and just sort of like ten people left standing.

Just weeks earlier, the Lib Dems had test-run a new, post-Brexit style of campaigning, in another by-election. After David Cameron's surprise resignation as an MP, the Conservatives were forced to hold a by-election for the former Prime Minister's seat of Witney. The Lib Dems threw the 'kitchen sink' at the campaign. They lost – but managed to reduce the Conservative majority by 20,000 votes. And it was there that the Liberal Democrats tested out a lot of new campaign tactics.

'It gave us a lot of confidence. We went almost directly from the Witney by-election to the Richmond Park by-election, and activists poured in, and I mean, poured in from all over the country,' Olney said. 'People came from Manchester, from Scotland, from Birmingham, they came from all over the country.'

Goldsmith noticed this. He said it really 'felt like they were busing people in'. Whereas he was at a major campaigning disadvantage. It would have been illegal for him to use any of the infrastructure available to Conservative candidates, like the office and their data.

'So it basically was just literally putting papers together and putting them through every single door. And because I could, there was no national party above me, which meant that my budget was probably about ten times, maybe twenty times smaller than the budget of the Lib Dems.'

After the election, Olney was interviewed by police under caution for allegedly breaking official spending limits, but the Crown Prosecution Service ruled that there was no evidence and closed the case.

Goldsmith and Olney both spent those by-election weeks canvassing night and day. Goldsmith increasingly felt isolated and unlucky. Especially when a volunteer hit him with his own car while he was out canvassing. Other than a temporary limp, he was unharmed.

Olney, on the other hand, was buoyed by her crowds of supporters. Like when Boomtown Rats rocker Bob Geldof joined the campaign supporting Olney – and started a chant of 'Zac is crap' on the high street.

The day before the election, the Liberal Democrats Central Office shared their internal polling with *The Guardian*, which predicted Olney would win 47.2 per cent of the vote to Goldsmith's 45.8 per cent. The story was intended to create a sense of optimism among anti-Goldsmith voters that he could be defeated. It worked.

Some 20,510 Richmond constituents woke up on 1 December and cast their vote for Sarah Olney.

At 11.30 p.m., ninety minutes after the polls had closed, Olney realised for the first time that she had won while watching the BBC. Journalist Chris Mason was speaking and just behind him was her campaign manager, James Lillis.

'James had the biggest smile on his face,' she recalls.

And I hadn't seen him smiling at all in all that time. And that was the moment when I was kind of like, well, James can only be smiling if it's going well. He wouldn't be smiling if we weren't winning.

And then I got a phone call probably about an hour later, an hour and a half later, saying, yes, you've won. You need to get down to the count.

Olney became the Liberal Democrat's ninth MP with a majority of 1,872, a swing from the Conservatives of 30.4 per cent. Labour's Christian Wolmar received so few votes that he lost his deposit.

Olney credits Brexit, Heathrow and the shadow of Donald Trump's first win in the States. That, and a really good campaign.

The result foreshadowed new voting coalitions in British politics, initially of pro-Leave and pro-Remain parties, which have made huge upsets like Richmond more common. These coalitions haven't required formal agreements between politicians – as the Labour MPs calling for a 'Progressive Alliance' were suggesting. But they have relied on a weakening of voters' tribal loyalty and a greater number simply voting for the party in the best position to defeat the candidate they dislike most, as many Labour voters did in Richmond.

Goldsmith said:

> It wasn't the worst political experience I've had. I've had many, many worse.
>
> I wish I hadn't had to do it, because it was a pain in the arse fighting a campaign [that] you know you can't win. But I just had to do it. If I hadn't done it, I would have just become the kind of caricature politician. It wasn't worth becoming that caricature.

Six months later, Theresa May called a snap general election. Goldsmith, who hadn't ruled out standing again for the Conservatives during the by-election campaign, decided to run again.

'I remained very close to the party. [There] didn't seem to be any resentment at all that I'd lost the seat through my own stupid pledge. They adopted me pretty much unanimously for the next round, and I just crept over the line.'

He won by forty-five votes.

Olney stayed close to politics – becoming chief of staff to the then Liberal Democrat leader Vince Cable. She ran again against Goldsmith in 2019 – and won.

That same year, Goldsmith was elevated to the Lords. He says he has no regrets – his period in politics between 2017 and 2019 was the best he had. He had a 'dream job' as a minister and got more done than he 'ever dreamed possible'.

And what of the Liberal Democrats? Many in the party see this by-election as critical to their most recent election success. The honing of their campaigning strategy in Witney and Richmond has helped them go on to win four more by-elections, and they currently hold more seats in Parliament than ever before.

Aggie Chambré is the political correspondent at LBC. Previously, she hosted the Westminster Insider *podcast at Politico. She won Multimedia Journalist of the Year at the Press Awards in 2024.*

78

COPELAND

23 FEBRUARY 2017
CONSERVATIVE GAIN FROM LABOUR

CHRISTOPHER WHITESIDE

Result: Trudy Harrison (Conservative), 13,748, 44.2 per cent; Gillian Troughton (Labour), 11,601, 37.3 per cent; Rebecca Hanson (Liberal Democrats), 2,252, 7.2 per cent; Fiona Mills (UKIP), 2,025, 6.5 per cent; Michael Guest (Independent), 811, 2.6 per cent; Jack Lennox (Green), 515, 1.7 per cent; Roy Ivinson (Independent), 116, 0.4 per cent

Size of majority: 2,147

Swing: 6.7 per cent from Labour to Conservative

Name of previous MP and party: Jamie Reed (Labour)

Reason for by-election: Resignation of incumbent

Result at previous general election: Jamie Reed (Labour), 16,750, 42.3 per cent; Stephen Haraldsen (Conservative), 14,186, 35.8 per cent; Michael Pye (UKIP), 6,148, 15.5 per cent; Danny Gallagher (Liberal Democrats), 1,368, 3.5 per cent; Allan Todd (Green), 1,179, 3.0 per cent

Date by-election called: 23 January 2017

Date by-election took place: 23 February 2017

Size of total electorate: 60,602

Total number of votes cast: 31,068

Turnout: 51.3 per cent

The first portent of an extraordinary by-election came within seconds of the re-election of Jeremy Corbyn as Labour Party leader. Before Corbyn had finished his acceptance speech, the MP for Copeland, Jamie Reed, tweeted his letter of resignation as a shadow Health Minister.

Among various reasons for Jamie Reed's antipathy to Jeremy Corbyn, one of the most important, and the reason Labour had difficulty in the Copeland constituency throughout Corbyn's leadership, was his long-standing hostility to nuclear power. Jeremy Corbyn had spoken at a 'Vigil for Fukushima' on 20 March 2011 and uttered the words which were to become the centrepiece of the Conservative campaign in Copeland: 'I say no nuclear power, decommission the stations we've got.'

Reed's resignation letter told the Labour leader his opposition to nuclear power was 'poorly informed and fundamentally wrong'.

The Copeland constituency in Cumbria was typical in many ways of northern Labour constituencies which became known two years later as 'red wall' seats. It already showed signs of abandoning Labour, just as a swathe of such seats would flip in 2019. The area had for centuries been linked to energy industries, first mining, then when Britain's first atomic power station opened at Calder Hall, nuclear power, and later wind power. West Cumbria calls itself the 'Energy Coast'.

A quarter of the working population of West Cumbria work in the civil nuclear industry, at the Sellafield reprocessing plant, the National Nuclear Laboratory, the Low Level Waste Repository near Drigg, other nuclear facilities or their supply chains.

So many people in Copeland were connected to nuclear organisations that Copeland Council's frequent discussions of nuclear issues had evolved a unique tradition of declaring interests en masse. At the start of such items, debate paused for five minutes to go round the Chamber while nearly every councillor declared an interest. Those who were not employed in the industry themselves almost all had family or friends who were: political candidates in every party had people delivering their leaflets who worked at nuclear facilities. (Even the Greens, though they had fewer!)

At the southern end of the constituency lived a significant number of voters who commuted to work at the BAE nuclear submarine yards in Barrow. Corbyn's opposition to nuclear weapons went down as badly with them as his opposition to nuclear power did with those connected to that industry.

Various conspiracy theories were put forward about why Jamie Reed and another Labour MP, Tristram Hunt, resigned and precipitated simultaneous by-elections in Copeland and Stoke-on-Trent Central, respectively. I personally accept the reason Reed himself gave, that he could do more for his constituency in a senior position at Sellafield than as an MP. He never added 'in Jeremy Corbyn's Labour Party', but many people in Copeland suspected that's what he meant.

In late 2016, the new Prime Minister Theresa May was enjoying a honeymoon with positive net approval ratings, up to 35 per cent, for which most Prime Ministers would have given their right arm, and a consistent lead in voting intention polls. By contrast, Jeremy Corbyn had negative net opinion ratings, often below -30 per cent, and had been challenged for re-election after losing a vote of no confidence among Labour MPs by 172 votes to forty.

When rumours began to circulate that Jamie Reed had been offered a job at Sellafield which would mean a by-election, the Conservatives didn't wait for confirmation to start campaigning, trying to get as much done as possible before the poll was called and spending limits kicked in.

The first of many Conservative leaflets attacking the Labour leader's anti-nuclear stance and featuring Corbyn's words quoted earlier had already started to go through letterboxes when Jamie Reed announced his resignation on 21 December 2016, to take effect on 23 January.

Neither the Christmas holidays nor Storm Barbara prevented campaigning from intensifying almost immediately and it continued unabated until polling day, 23 February 2017, which coincided with another named storm, Doris.

Weather and geography made the campaign challenging for the thousands of volunteers who poured in from all over the country to help both Labour and Conservative campaigns, many travelling hundreds of miles. The constituency was enormous, had poor connectivity and a lot of housing on steep hillsides. There were jokes that much of the seat wasn't 'Zimmer-frame accessible' and about 'the Copeland by-election cardiovascular workout' from people delivering or canvassing where there was a steep climb to get to most doorsteps. None of this dented the enthusiasm of volunteers.

Both main parties faced tensions between national HQ and their constituency organisation over their respective candidate selections. Both parties wanted someone local: in both cases, the national leadership settled on a fresh face who had recently joined the party and was seen as reflecting the future. They went about it rather differently.

Media outlets such as the *New Statesman* and *The Guardian* suggested it was 'understood' that the Labour leader's office was backing Cumbria's 'woman of the year 2015', local businesswoman and charity organiser Rachel Holliday, who had joined the party two years before. Local Labour members preferred instead local councillor Gillian Troughton, who had trained as a doctor but now worked as a volunteer ambulance driver. This generated headlines like 'Corbyn's choice to fight Copeland by-election rejected by local party'.

The Conservative leadership was determined not to allow any such upset: the party's by-election rules allowed the national party to put forward to the local association a shortlist with one name on it.

Conservative HQ decided that the candidate with the best chance of winning the by-election was Trudy Harrison, a campaigner for local schools and services who had worked at Sellafield and for Copeland Council. Harrison had joined the party even more recently than Holliday, having been inspired by Theresa May's speech on becoming Prime Minister, but she did have one or two influential backers within the local association.

The national party put forward a shortlist with just Trudy Harrison's name and asked the most prominent alternative candidates to propose and second her. Presented with a fait accompli, and as the person they were being asked to back was a strong local candidate rather than some outsider parachuted in, the association did as they were told and unanimously adopted Harrison as their candidate.

The Lib Dems selected Cockermouth town councillor Rebecca Hanson; UKIP picked their Cumbria county chairman, Fiona Mills. The Greens selected a software engineer from Keswick, Jack Lenox. There were two independent candidates: Michael Guest, who had been Mayor of Whitehaven Town Council the previous year, and Roy Ivinson.

There was a debate on local radio between the candidates and three public hustings at Millom, Keswick and Whitehaven. All were well attended and produced robust debate. Several local issues came up, including the state of local roads and schools, and at Millom proposals by the national grid to build pylons nearby on some of the most beautiful areas of the country. But the same two subjects dominated the hustings and the by-election as a whole: the nuclear issue and the NHS.

The most memorable line of the hustings came from UKIP candidate Fiona Mills, an NHS accountant, referring to private finance initiative (PFI) funding for hospital building, which she called: 'Get one hospital, pay for six.'

Cumberland Infirmary in Carlisle had been the first hospital built with PFI money and the long-term costs affected the finances of the NHS in Cumbria for years.

Both main parties campaigned ruthlessly with total focus on the single issue they thought favourable to them. Those running both campaigns were convinced that if votes were cast based on the nuclear issues, the Conservatives would win, and if people voted on the NHS, Labour would win.

The by-election essentially became a contest between efforts by the Conservatives to persuade the electorate that voting for a party led by Jeremy Corbyn was a vote to shut down the nuclear industry and Labour attempts to persuade them that a vote for anyone else was a vote to shut down the local NHS.

Both main parties ran tightly disciplined campaigns with few mistakes – indeed, the main mistake on one side resulted from keeping too tight a grip.

Channel 4 sent Michael Crick to cover the by-election. He has a deserved reputation for finding chinks in the armour of politicians of all parties, and Labour was not the only party which warned its candidate and activists to be careful what they said to him. However, only the Labour campaign didn't arrange for their candidate to meet him when Channel 4 asked them all for interviews.

Crick's response was an ambush with cameras running outside one of Gillian Troughton's campaign stops, asking why she wouldn't meet him. Channel 4's broadcast included interviews with all other party candidates and footage of Troughton walking past Crick and not replying. It went viral on social media and didn't help Labour's campaign.

On the Conservative side, the biggest problem with unfortunate word choices came from a letter written a few months before the by-election was called, from the Prime Minister to outgoing MP Jamie Reed. He had asked her about deeply unpopular proposals on which Cumbria's NHS trusts were consulting, to downgrade the local West Cumberland Hospital (WCH), including removing consultant-led maternity care. Some of these proposals from NHS managers had been around for a decade; indeed, Reed himself had been slow-handclapped at a march against plans to downgrade maternity when they first came out while Labour was in power.

All candidates opposed plans to downgrade the hospital.

Theresa May's reply to Jamie Reed did not quite commit to supporting the proposed maternity downgrade, and she disavowed the interpretation Labour subsequently put on her words. However, her letter did describe the position of local NHS leaders in terms which could easily be read as an endorsement and which could plausibly be quoted by Labour's Copeland campaign to suggest the government backed the proposals. Extracts from the Prime Minister's letter to Reed were deployed by the Labour campaign in Copeland as extensively as the Conservatives used Jeremy Corbyn's anti-nuclear quote.

As both Conservative and Labour efforts intensified, the tone of some campaign literature became stronger, particularly Labour's NHS material. They described whichever option would do most damage to local services as Tory policy regardless of whether the Conservatives or anyone else supported it. For example, the trust was really proposing to *increase* the number of beds at Mary Hewetson Community Hospital in Keswick. Conservatives had supported this increase, and it subsequently happened, but there was an option in the consultation document to scrap all the beds there, which Labour leaflets represented as Tory policy.

Labour leaflets used language like: 'Mothers will die. Babies will die. Babies will be brain damaged.'

There was debate in the Conservative campaign about whether to respond to these Labour attacks. Such leaflets infuriated Conservative activists who had campaigned to keep the maternity unit. Campaign professionals from Conservative Campaign Headquarters (CCHQ) said Labour's extreme language was a sign of desperation, warning that dignifying such material by replying to it would only give it more credibility and divert attention from the focus on nuclear issues which was winning the Conservatives the election.

The CCHQ professionals got their way, and the outcome suggests they were right. After the by-election, some Labour activists told Business Insider their own side's darker NHS material had backfired. One Labour source was quoted saying, 'Leaflets and newspaper ads in which the core message boils down to "vote Labour or babies will die" is pretty ugly, even by the standards of by-elections. That can be off-putting.'

Local Conservative resentment at Labour's NHS campaign was mirrored by local Labour resentment of the relentless Conservative onslaught against their national leader's anti-nuclear past. Their candidate, and their party's formal position, were pro-nuclear. But while Corbyn was leader, nothing Labour could say would convince local residents they could be trusted to support the nuclear industry.

On election day, Storm Doris brought vile weather but failed to discourage more than half Copeland's electors from casting ballots. A 6.7 per cent Labour to Conservative swing gave Trudy Harrison victory with a majority of 2,147. It was the first by-election gain for a governing party since Mitcham & Morden during the Falklands War. The commentator Matt Singh of Number Cruncher Politics suggested it was the first by-election gain for a governing party in directly comparable circumstances since 1878.

The by-election vote was seen as excellent for the Conservatives and dire for Labour and triggered fresh calls for Jeremy Corbyn to stand down as Labour leader.

Trudy Harrison was re-elected twice, remaining MP for the Copeland constituency for the rest of its existence, stepping down when it was split up in 2024 after boundary changes. She was parliamentary private secretary to Boris Johnson for part of his premiership, then served as a Transport and later an Environment Minister.

The future of maternity care at West Cumberland Hospital, which had been an issue in the campaign, was finally resolved two years later, with success for the all-party campaign to keep consultant-led maternity services at WCH. Harrison also secured tens of millions of pounds of investment in the hospital, with the last of several major developments opening in 2024.

Many MPs who visited the seat to campaign became aware of how long it took to get round it and how much needed doing to improve roads like the A595 and local hospitals and schools. Trudy Harrison and local campaigners called in a number of promises made during the campaign by ministers, securing long-awaited rebuilding programmes at several schools in the constituency as well as at WCH.

The extent to which the Copeland by-election triggered events which up-ended British politics will remain difficult to assess unless Theresa May discloses how much it contributed to reversing her previous emphatic insistence that she would not call an early election.

On 18 April, seven weeks after victory in Copeland, May gave in to the temptation to take advantage of her lead in the polls and asked Parliament to call a general election. But instead of increasing her majority, the election eliminated it; instead of giving her a mandate, it severely wounded her authority and set the scene for the extraordinary political psychodrama which was to follow.

Had there been no Conservative gain in the Copeland by-election, I suspect there would have been no 2017 general election.

Parliamentary arithmetic in the 2015 House of Commons was not enormously different to that in the 2017–19 parliament which produced two years of deadlock over Brexit. It is certain that bruising battles over Britain's departure from the EU and the terms of that exit would still have happened.

However, Theresa May would have gone into those battles with her authority vastly stronger, with a parliamentary majority, albeit a small one, and without having lost the time taken by the election and rebuilding her government afterwards. It is eminently possible that the eventual form Brexit took, and British history after 2019, might have looked quite different.

Christopher Whiteside MBE *is an economist. He was Conservative parliamentary candidate for Copeland in 2005 and 2010 and for Leeds North East in 2024 and Conservative Copeland mayoral candidate in 2015. He participated in the Conservative campaign in the Copeland by-election.*

79

HARTLEPOOL

6 MAY 2021
CONSERVATIVE GAIN FROM LABOUR

ALIA MIDDLETON

Result: Jill Mortimer (Conservative), 15,529, 51.9 per cent; Paul Williams (Labour), 8,589, 28.7 per cent; Sam Lee (Independent), 2,904, 9.7 per cent; Claire Martin (Heritage), 468, 1.6 per cent; John Prescott (Reform UK), 368, 1.2 per cent; Rachel Featherstone (Green), 358, 1.2 per cent; Andrew Hagan (Liberal Democrats), 349, 1.2 per cent; Thelma Walker (Independent), 250, 0.8 per cent; Chris Killick (Independent), 248, 0.8 per cent; Hilton Dawson (North East), 163, 0.5 per cent; W. Ralph Ward-Jackson (Independent), 157, 0.5 per cent; Gemma Evans (Women's Equality), 140, 0.5 per cent; Adam Gaines (Independent), 126, 0.4 per cent; The Incredible Flying Brick (Monster Raving Loony), 108, 0.4 per cent; David Bettney (Social Democratic), 104, 0.3 per cent; Steve Jack (Freedom Alliance), 72, 0.2 per cent

Size of majority: 6,940

Swing: 16.0 per cent from Labour to Conservative

Name of previous MP and party: Mike Hill (Labour)

Reason for by-election: Resignation of incumbent

Result at previous general election: Mike Hill (Labour), 15,464, 37.7 per cent; Stefan Houghton (Conservative), 11,869, 28.9 per cent; Richard Tice (Brexit), 10,603, 25.8 per cent; Andy Hagon (Liberal Democrats), 1,696, 4.1 per cent; Joe Bousfield (Independent), 911, 2.2 per cent; Kevin Cranney (Socialist Labour), 494, 1.2 per cent

Date by-election called: 16 March 2021

Date by-election took place: 6 May 2021

Size of total electorate: 70,768

Total number of votes cast: 29,933

Turnout: 42.3 per cent

The constituency of Hartlepool, centred on the town itself, was created in 1974, succeeding the earlier seat of The Hartlepools. The formerly vital local industry of shipbuilding had petered out in the area after the Second World War, ending entirely in 1961. Manufacturing in the town was also in massive decline; a series of steelwork closures in 1977 and 1983 caused a substantial increase in unemployment and poverty in the area. A programme of regeneration was initiated in the 1990s, but in 2015, Hartlepool had an income deprivation level which was the second highest in the north-east and more than one and a half times the English average. Voters in the constituency voted 69.6 per cent Leave in the 2016 Brexit referendum, and in September 2019, ten independent borough councillors joined the Brexit Party.

On the national stage, the Conservatives had been in government for eleven years, and Boris Johnson was their third Prime Minister in this time. He had won the 2019 general election, gaining a majority for the party for the first time since 2015, largely by capturing former Labour heartland seats in the north of England, campaigning with the slogan 'Get Brexit Done'. These seats were predominantly those which had voted for Brexit and were exactly the same type of constituencies as Hartlepool, although the seat had remained Labour-held. Nationally, Labour had suffered a historic defeat in the 2019 general election, and the party's new leader, Sir Keir Starmer, had been in place since April 2020.

Since its creation in 1974, Hartlepool had been held by a succession of Labour MPs: the long-serving Ted Leadbitter, the former Labour director of communications and Cabinet minister Peter Mandelson and latterly Iain Wright, who had won the seat at a by-election in 2004 triggered by Mandelson's resignation. Wright, the chair of the Business, Innovation and Skills Select Committee, announced on 19 April 2017 that he would not be standing in the snap election called for 8 June. His successor was Mike Hill, who defended the seat, increasing his majority from 7.7 per cent to 18.3 per cent. Hill had previously unsuccessfully contested the Richmond (Yorkshire) seat at the 2015 general election, which was won by future Prime Minister Rishi Sunak. A long-term Hartlepool resident and former UNISON employee, Hill once again defended the seat at the 2019 general election, although his majority was cut to 8.8 per cent as future Reform Party leader Richard

Tice stood for the Brexit Party in the constituency, likely preventing a Conservative victory.

By the time of his second victory, however, Hill had been suspended by Labour between September and October 2019 amid allegations of sexual harassment, until the claim was dropped. Yet by June 2020, Hill was under investigation by an Independent Expert Panel for sexual misconduct. Hill quit Parliament on 16 March 2021; Starmer had been urging him to resign for some time. His resignation came amid the ongoing investigation into his conduct, which finally concluded on 20 May that year. Its findings indicated that had Hill not resigned, he would have been subject to a 'significant sanction'. A further employment tribunal later in the year, at which Hill's request to remain anonymous was denied, also concluded that Hill had sexually assaulted and harassed a member of parliamentary staff, including climbing into her bed. She had refused his advances and subsequently been victimised by Hill, who eventually made her redundant.

With the by-election called for 6 May 2021 (the same date as elections to English councils, the Scottish Parliament, the Welsh Senedd and the London Assembly – so-called Super Thursday), the parties began to assemble their candidates. It was the first by-election of the parliament, and the last by-election contest, held in August 2019, had seen the ultra-safe Brecon & Radnorshire lost by the Conservatives. Indeed, the government had not won a by-election seat from another party since Copeland in 2017. However, the Conservatives saw a glimmer of hope in Hartlepool; the party had led Labour in opinion polls since February 2021, and the day before polls opened in Hartlepool saw the Conservatives sitting on a ten-point lead nationally. The by-election was also seen as the first electoral test not only of how the government had handled the COVID pandemic, including the vaccine rollout, but also how well the new Labour leader Sir Keir Starmer was reconnecting with Labour voters. To defend Hill's majority in the now marginal seat, Labour chose Paul Williams, who had been Stockton South's MP between 2017 and 2019 before losing his seat to the Conservative Matt Vickers. Williams, a GP and chief executive of the Hartlepool and Stockton Health GP Federation, was then currently in the running for the Cleveland Police and Crime Commissioner role but stepped down to contest the Hartlepool by-election. A vocal Remainer, his selection came amid substantial controversy; potential Labour candidates were given just one day to apply, and the selection process resulted in Williams being the only name on the shortlist, essentially appointed by the National Executive Committee. The speed of the process was defended by Labour as enabling their campaign to begin quickly. This was the first time since 1999 that a former MP had been selected to fight a by-election, and some expressed consternation why an MP rejected by one group of voters already would be the best choice for them. Shortly after his selection, Williams had to apologise for inappropriate historical tweets.

Despite initial speculation that the 2019 Conservative candidate Stefan Houghton would run again, Jill Mortimer was selected from a three-strong shortlist to contest the by-election. Mortimer was a farmer and district councillor in Hambleton, North Yorkshire, and her selection in Hartlepool also caused some controversy. She was seen to have tenuous ties to the local area, did not live in the seat and admitted she didn't spend much time in the constituency. The Conservative Tees Valley metro mayor Ben Houchen was slow to congratulate her, and there were concerns from local Conservative voters that her selection may have handed victory to Labour. In total, sixteen candidates contested the by-election, including another two former Labour MPs; Thelma Walker, MP for Colne Valley 2017 to 2019 was an Independent endorsed by the Northern Independence Party, whereas Hilton Dawson, MP for Lancaster & Wyre 1997–2005 stood for the North East Party. Ralph Ward-Jackson, a Kensington property entrepreneur, also contested the seat, hoping to follow in the footsteps of his ancestor who founded West Hartlepool and became its first MP in 1868.

The campaign itself was largely uneventful. The Conservatives minimised the presence of Mortimer in the campaign, assisted by her lack of social media presence. The party instead chose to run the campaign by emphasising Ben Houchen's track record in regional initiatives alongside the national leadership of Boris Johnson. Johnson himself visited the constituency several times, canvassing with Mortimer, playing football and visiting local businesses. The Labour campaign, run by the shadow Transport Secretary Jim McMahon, attempted to appeal to Brexit voters by asking activists to hand out St George's flag leaflets, urging voters to place them in their windows. McMahon was criticised by some in the party for not understanding the local area, instead focusing on gimmicks. Williams suffered on the doorsteps despite visits by Starmer and much of the shadow Cabinet, not only because of his Remainer views, at odds with the overall constituency profile, but also because he had formerly been part of a clinical commissioning group that had sought to remove critical care from Hartlepool's hospital.

Mortimer won the seat with 51.9 per cent of the vote, overturning Hill's 8.8 percentage point majority on a swing of 16 per cent from Labour to the Conservatives, with a turnout of 42.3 per cent. The size of the swing was the largest towards a governing party since 1945. This was the first Conservative victory since the seat's creation in 1974 and Mortimer became its first female MP. In her victory speech, she praised the 'historic result' and said Labour had taken Hartlepool for granted. The victory was seen as an indication of the party being able to consolidate its gains from the 2019 election and was only the second time in forty years that the governing party had taken a seat from the opposition. There was also a strong showing from a local Independent candidate Sam Lee, fighting on a ticket of being local, urging voters to move away from two-party politics. She gained 9.7 per cent of the vote. The Brexit Party's successor, the Reform Party, received just 1.2 per cent of the vote – a massive 24.6 per cent decrease, which was arguably the key contributor to Mortimer's victory. In all, thirteen candidates, including the Liberal Democrat, failed to attract enough seats to retain their deposit.

The defeat saw Williams leave the count by the back door, refusing to answer questions, and came as a blow to Sir Keir Starmer in his first electoral test as party leader; he was bitterly disappointed and took full responsibility for trying to turn the party's fortunes around. Figures from the left of the party, including Diane Abbott, criticised his leadership, and UNITE chairman Len McCluskey urged Starmer to change his approach, indicating in a radio interview that he did not trust the Labour leader. However, other centrist figures in Labour, such as the seat's former MP Peter Mandelson, blamed the legacy of Corbyn and that the pandemic had not allowed the impact of Starmer's new direction for the Labour Party to be understood by voters. Later reports suggested Starmer had considered resigning over the result but was persuaded to stay. By 4.30 a.m., a giant inflatable Boris Johnson was erected outside the leisure centre where the count was taking place. The victorious Mortimer was treated to a visit by Prime Minister Boris Johnson himself on the morning of her victory, accompanied by the inflatable version.

The defeat was seen to be not only the result of the contest itself but symptomatic of a wider ebbing away for support for Labour in the constituency, which had attributed cuts to the local hospital, including the removal of its emergency and maternity departments, the closure of the custody suites in the town's police station as well as job losses in the steel industry to the party. Hartlepool was exactly the type of constituency in the red wall that fell to the Conservatives at the 2019 election, although at that time, it had remained Labour largely due to the Brexit Party's splitting of the vote.

Jill Mortimer entered Parliament and was staunch in her support for Boris Johnson amid the tumult of July 2022. She was briefly a parliamentary private secretary in September of that same year but resigned after just two weeks to concentrate on her constituency. She contested the seat again at the 2024 general election, seeing her majority of 23.2 per cent overturned, with the seat returning once again to Labour, this time with a 21.7 per cent majority. The reinvigorated Reform UK came second, beating Mortimer into third place.

The Hartlepool result seems to have been a brief high point in the by-election fortunes of the Conservative government of the time; in the subsequent three years of the parliament, this was the last by-election seat they gained from any other party, and eleven of their seats were lost to other parties. Despite the prominence of Johnson in the Hartlepool campaign and victory, just a little over a year later, Johnson had resigned as Prime Minister.

Alia Middleton *is a senior lecturer at the University of Surrey. Her research interests include political leadership, voting behaviour and campaigning strategies, and her publications include* Communicating and Strategising Leadership in British Elections *(Palgrave Macmillan, 2021).*

80

CHESHAM & AMERSHAM

---

17 JUNE 2021
LIBERAL DEMOCRAT GAIN FROM CONSERVATIVES

ROSIE CAMPBELL

Result: Sarah Green (Liberal Democrats), 21,517, 56.7 per cent; Peter Fleet (Conservative), 13,489, 35.5 per cent; Carolyne Culver (Green), 1,480, 3.9 per cent; Natasa Pantelic (Labour), 622, 1.6 per cent; Alex Wilson (Reform UK), 414, 1.1 per cent; Carla Gregory (Breakthrough), 197, 0.5 per cent; Adrian Oliver (Freedom Alliance), 134, 0.4 per cent; Brendan Donnelly (Rejoin EU), 101, 0.3 per cent
Size of majority: 8,028
Swing: 25.2 per cent from Conservative to Liberal Democrats
Name of previous MP and party: Cheryl Gillan (Conservative)
Reason for by-election: Death of incumbent
Result at previous general election: Cheryl Gillan (Conservative), 30,850, 55.4 per cent; Dan Gallagher (Liberal Democrats), 14,627, 26.3 per cent; Matt Turmaine (Labour), 7,166, 12.9 per cent; Alan Booth (Green), 3,042, 5.5 per cent
Date by-election called: 21 May 2021
Date by-election took place: 17 June 2021
Size of total electorate: 72,828
Total number of votes cast: 37,954
Turnout: 52.1 per cent

The Chesham & Amersham by-election, held on 17 June 2021, was triggered by the death of Conservative MP Dame Cheryl Gillan. First elected to represent the constituency in 1992, Gillan served as a junior minister for Education and Employment (1995–97) and as Secretary of State for Wales (2010–12), the first woman to hold the position. Her vocal criticism of HS2 (high-speed rail), which would cross the constituency, perhaps explains the lack of subsequent Cabinet posts. The sale of her constituency home, and her move out of the constituency to Epsom, prior to the announcement that HS2 would go ahead was a source of some controversy. She was a committed advocate for people with autism; she chaired the All-Party Parliamentary Group on Autism and was the architect of the Autism Act of 2009.

From its formation in 1974 until 2021, Chesham & Amersham was held continuously by the Conservative Party, always with more than half of the vote. It was a typical safe Conservative seat in the prosperous and, in parts, picturesque Home Counties situated in Buckingham-shire in the commuter belt to the north-west of London. When Gillan was first elected, her majority was a sizeable 22,220. This fell to 16,223 by 2019, but nonetheless the seat was 166 out of 367 of Conservative seats ranked by size of vote majority.

When the by-election was announced, there was relatively little media interest in a by-election in a safe Conservative seat, at a time when the party had secured a majority of eighty in the general election two years prior and was ahead of Labour in the polls by seven to ten percentage points. More attention was directed at the first by-election of the 2019–24 parliament in Hartlepool (see Chapter 79), held on 6 May, the first also for Sir Keir Starmer as the leader of the Labour Party, which was expected to be a tight race. Labour lost the seat to the Conservatives with a swing of 16 per cent. This was an astounding result that received con-siderable press attention and, at the time, did not bode well for Labour's hopes of regaining support in its historic heartlands. Another surprise result was not expected in Chesham & Amersham.

In 2019, the Conservative vote share in Chesham & Amersham was 55.4 per cent, more than double that of the second-placed party, the Liberal Democrats, who secured 26.3 per cent of the vote. Although the Lib Dems have a history of doing well in by-elections, a victory here looked highly unlikely. However, a closer look at election data over the period shows a steady and sustained increase in support for the Lib Dems. A critical turning point was the 2016 EU referendum:

estimates show that 55 per cent of voters in the constituency supported Remain. In the 2015 general election, the Lib Dems came fourth with 9 per cent of the vote; after the referendum, the Lib Dem share increased to 13 per cent in 2017 and then doubled to 26 per cent in 2019. The topline story of the May 2021 local elections was Conservative gains in Labour heartlands, but a less noticed byline were losses in middle-class commuter areas; one such loss was Amersham Council, which fell to the Lib Dems. Even with this trajectory of growth in Lib Dem support, overturning a 16,000-plus majority was against the odds (twenty-eight to one at one point during the campaign and four to one on polling day itself).

At the outset, the campaign was not set to be intensive. No hustings were organised, as the result was considered a foregone conclusion. The Lib Dems, however, threw everything at this by-election. The party leader, Sir Ed Davey, was in the constituency nearly every day of the campaign, visiting sixteen times. They ran a traditional Lib Dem local campaign, focusing on a tsunami of leaflets and street signs with an emphasis on feet on the ground, going door to door. The reason for all this effort was that the seat typified the 'blue wall' of historic Conservative seats that had voted Remain and had a higher-than-average concentration of degree holders in the population, which the Lib Dems hoped to capture. Being seen to be in contention in places like Chesham & Amersham was a critical opportunity to start to improve the Lib Dems' electoral fortunes after the catastrophic result in the 2015 general election, when the party lost forty-nine seats leaving them with just eight MPs in total and had barely improved its position in the following two elections.

Chesham & Amersham was an attractive target for the Lib Dems not just because the majority voted Remain, and the demographics were aligned with Lib Dem constituencies elsewhere, but also because it gave the party the opportunity to leverage local issues, a Lib Dem speciality. Two significant local factors were at play: HS2 and the Conservative government's proposed reform of planning laws that would limit local communities' ability to reject planning applications. The Liberal Democrats navigated a gap between their national position, support for HS2 and a local campaign led by the candidate

Sarah Green, a marketing and communications professional, who was strongly opposed to HS2. She also campaigned hard on protection of the green belt and against planning reform.

As internal party polling showed the gap between the Conservatives and the Liberal Democrats shrinking, and the betting odds narrowed, attention became more focused on Chesham & Amersham. Several senior Conservatives visited the constituency during the campaign, including the party co-chair Amanda Milling and the Prime Minister himself. Boris Johnson extolled the virtues of the Conservative candidate, Peter Fleet, an automotive industry executive, emphasising his local credentials and attempting to reassure voters about changes to planning laws. Johnson highlighted Fleet's aspiration to designate the Chilterns as a national park and his focus on building on brownfield sites, not green belt land, in an attempt to reassure voters.

The by-election result was a seismic shock to politicians and journalists alike. Liberal Democrat Sarah Green won the seat with 56.7 per cent of the vote, with a swing from the Conservatives of 25.2 per cent. The Conservative vote fell from 30,850 to 13,489, giving them 35.5 per cent of the vote. At the time, some commentators said that the result was due to dissatisfied Conservative voters staying at home rather than switching their allegiance, pointing to the fact that turnout was down to 52.1 per cent of the electorate compared with 76.8 per cent in the 2019 general election.

However, observing the change in the Labour vote suggests that tactical voting, not just low turnout, was a significant feature of the result; the Labour candidate, Natasa Pantelic, received just 622 votes compared with 7,166 votes secured by the Labour candidate in 2019. Sir Keir Starmer had conceded that Labour would not win in Chesham & Amersham, sending a signal that likely promoted tactical voting. The Chesham & Amersham by-election was perhaps the first moment where it became apparent that the divisions on the left that helped the Conservatives win in many constituencies in England could melt away in an era of partisan dealignment.

After the astonishing result, the Conservatives and the Liberal Democrats, unsurprisingly, leaned on different explanations for the Lib Dem victory and the Tory loss. For Sir Ed Davey and the Lib Dems, this was the first chip in the Conservative blue wall and evidence that the party's strategy of focusing on Conservative-held seats in the south was working. Several Conservative commentators, on the other hand, focused on the idiosyncratic local features of the campaign. In a BBC interview, Peter Fleet, the Conservative candidate, argued that the result was driven by 'very local circumstances' and Boris Johnson said that 'particular circumstances' were at play.

But there were Conservatives who were alarmed by the result. Damian Green, the Conservative MP for Ashford in Kent, warned that the party could become 'disconnected' if it failed to listen to the voters. The twin by-elections of Hartlepool and Chesham & Amersham, one a resounding success and the other a historic loss for the party, illustrated the tensions that the Conservatives faced in holding together the electoral coalition that saw them return a substantial majority in 2019 and inflicted the worst result for Labour since 1935. While traditional Labour voters in post-industrial parts of the country were disaffected and drawn to the Conservatives promises of levelling up and traditional values, a parallel shift was taking place in swathes of the Conservatives' home turf. The cost of living in London had pushed younger, liberal graduates and more members of ethnic minority communities into the commuter belt, gradually replacing older generations of Conservative supporters. The Chesham & Amersham by-election result was the first hard evidence that breaking through Labour's red wall potentially might come at a price in Conservative heartlands. The former Conservative MP for South West Hertfordshire David Gauke, expelled from the party by Johnson over Brexit, said that in 'very prosperous, middle-class commuter areas … the current trajectory of the Conservative party is not particularly sympathetic to those areas, and the local residents are not particularly sympathetic to what the Conservative party has become'.

Sir Ed Davey celebrated the by-election victory by smashing down a blue wall with an orange mallet, by no means the most spectacular of his visual publicity stunts but perhaps the first. In a post on Twitter, he said: 'Congratulations to @SarahGreenLD who has just sent a shockwave through British politics. If @libdems can beat the Tories here, we can beat them anywhere. The blue wall can be smashed by @libdems.'

'Anywhere' was perhaps a stretch, but the result did prove portentous. The Liberal Democrats won seventy-two seats in the 2024 general election, nearly fivefold more than the fifteen sitting Lib Dem MPs when the election was called; they made astonishing gains from the Conservatives, taking four seats from sitting Cabinet ministers and three seats formerly held by Conservative Prime Ministers. The exit poll suggested that the Conservatives would regain Chesham & Amersham, but many polls indicated that the Lib Dems would hold on, and indeed Sarah Green held the seat with 45 per cent of the vote.

Commenting after the by-election result was declared, polling expert Professor Sir John Curtice said, 'In remain-voting middle class seats in the south of England, the Conservative coalition has been weakened to some degree in the wake of Brexit – the Liberal Democrats are best placed to profit from that.' With hindsight, this weakening was the start of what turned out to be a momentous collapse for the Conservatives in the south of England in the 2024 general election. It is now evident that the Chesham & Amersham by-election was a critical turning point for the party. One rule of thumb that Liberal Democrat strategists used when identifying target seats for the 2024 general election was 'does it have a Gail's?' Gail's is an upmarket bakery commonly found near a Waitrose supermarket (another higher price bracket retailer associated with the middle class). Gerrards Cross, in the constituency of Chesham & Amersham, has both a Gail's bakery and a Waitrose.

Rosie Campbell *is a professor of politics in the Department of Political Economy, King's College London. Her publications cover the subjects of voting behaviour, public opinion and political recruitment. Rosie has presented eight episodes of Radio Four's* Analysis, *most recently on 'Does it matter who our MPs are?'*

81

BATLEY & SPEN

1 JULY 2021
LABOUR HOLD

EMMA BURNELL

Result: Kim Leadbeater (Labour), 13,296, 35.3 per cent; Ryan Stephenson (Conservative), 12,973, 34.4 per cent; George Galloway (Workers), 8,264, 21.9 per cent; Tom Gordon (Liberal Democrats), 1,254, 3.3 per cent; Corey Robinson (Yorkshire), 816, 2.2 per cent; Thérèse Hirst (English Democrat), 207, 0.5 per cent; Jack Thompson (UKIP), 151, 0.4 per cent; Howling Laud Hope (Monster Raving Loony), 107, 0.3 per cent; Mike Davies (Alliance for Green Socialism), 104, 0.3 per cent; Paul Bickerdike (CPA), 102, 0.3 per cent; Jonathan Tilt (Freedom Alliance), 100, 0.3 per cent; Anne Marie Waters (For Britain Movement), 97, 0.3 per cent; Andrew Smith (Rejoin EU), 75, 0.2 per cent; Oliver Purser (SDP), 66, 0.2 per cent; Jayda Fransen (Independent), 50, 0.1 per cent; Susan Laird (Heritage), 33, 0.1 per cent
Size of majority: 323
Swing: 2.9 per cent from Labour to Conservative
Name of previous MP and party: Tracy Brabin (Labour/Co-operative)
Reason for by-election: Resignation following being elected West Yorkshire mayor
Result at previous general election: Tracy Brabin (Labour/Co-operative), 22,594, 42.7 per cent; Mark Brooks (Conservative), 19,069, 36.0 per cent; Paul Halloran (Heavy Woollen District Independents), 6,432, 12.2 per cent; John Lawson (Liberal Democrats), 2,462, 4.7 per cent; Clive Minihan (Brexit), 1,678, 3.2 per cent; Ty Akram (Green), 692, 1.3 per cent

Date by-election called: 27 May 2021
Date by-election took place: 1 July 2021
Size of total electorate: 79,373
Total number of votes cast: 37,695
Turnout: 47.5 per cent

All by-elections happen under what can feel like portentous circumstances. The death or resignation of a sitting MP midway through a parliament (a time when governments traditionally struggle in the polls) make these events feel like major political flashpoints – a way of measuring how well a government is doing and a chance for voters to give them a kicking if the answer is negative.

But, all that said, few by-elections of recent years have felt more consequential than the one in Batley & Spen that took place on 1 July 2021. It was a by-election that came at a time when politics, Britain and the world were all in a very unusual state.

In December 2019, Labour went down to their biggest general election defeat of the modern era, while Boris Johnson's government was re-elected with the largest Conservative Party majority since Margaret Thatcher's victory in 1987. That same month, the first case of a new virus was reported in Wuhan, China.

It may be hard to remember with all that we know now, but for most of 2020 and 2021, Johnson's government polled well on their response to the virus. There were loud voices on both sides calling either for stricter restrictions or none at all, but in general, the government largely had the support of the populace as they pursued measures such as lockdowns and went hell-for-leather in search of a vaccine. A vaccine was found and successfully rolled out, starting in December 2020, and a huge number of people were jabbed in early 2021, creating a sense of relief and gratitude in the population as a whole that the COVID nightmare was finally coming to an end. This led to a spike in Johnson's personal polling and that of his government that has since become known as the 'vaccine bounce' (this was somewhat tempered as news broke during the by-election campaign that the Health Secretary Matt Hancock had been caught breaking lockdown rules and was forced to resign before election day).

Meanwhile, however, the Labour Party were still at a very low ebb, with voters continuing to shun them and internal strife continuing to tear the party apart.

In October 2020, the party had been put in special measures by the equalities watchdog the Equalities and Human Rights Commission (EHRC) over their handling of antisemitism complaints. Infighting was rife after former leader Jeremy Corbyn had been suspended from the Parliamentary Labour Party for his response to the EHRC report in which he claimed that the problem had been 'dramatically overstated for political reasons'.

In May 2021, Labour lost eight councils as the Conservatives gained thirteen. On the same day, a 16 per cent swing saw Labour lose the Hartlepool by-election. We now know that Keir Starmer considered resigning at that point. Had the Batley & Spen by-election gone the same way, there is considerable doubt as to whether he would have survived an almost inevitable leadership challenge.

The by-election itself had come about because the MP Tracy Brabin had stepped down to run for (and ultimately win) the role of West Yorkshire mayor. Within Labour circles, there was some muttering about Starmer's party management skills in relaxedly allowing this to happen (a somewhat ironic charge given later accusations of too heavy-handed party management from Starmer and his team).

Brabin herself had replaced the MP Jo Cox, who was murdered by a far-right terrorist days before the Brexit referendum of 2016. Brabin was re-elected in 2017, with a majority of 8,961, then again in 2019, this time with a reduced majority of only 3,525 – a pretty slim margin, especially when looked at next to the almost identical 2019 Labour majority of 3,595 that was overturned in Hartlepool.

Labour selected Kim Leadbeater as their candidate. Despite having previously been a party member, Leadbeater had not been one for the requisite twelve months prior to the selection, as she had been running the cross-party Jo Cox Foundation. Given this, she had to be given special dispensation to run by Labour's National Executive Committee. However, as the sister of Cox and a resident of the constituency, this was not much more than a formality and she went on to be selected with the support of more than 80 per cent of the constituency party.

Labour's campaign for the by-election was almost entirely focused on Leadbeater. Their 'only Kim can win' strategy for the selection was carried through into their campaign which one of her key staffers described to me as 'very Kim-centric'. Labour made a big deal of Leadbeater's local connections – she was the only candidate who could vote for herself in the constituency. Her campaign was focused on speaking to people on the doorsteps of the villages and towns around the constituency – being the most visible, most local candidate.

The Liberal Democrats initially selected television producer Jo Conchie who then had to withdraw for health reasons, being replaced by the leader of Wakefield Council Liberal Democrats, Tom Gordon.

The Green Party selected international Rugby League player Ross Peltier as their candidate. However, just before the deadline for nominations, historic homophobic tweets of Peltier's were discovered and the party withdrew his candidacy without replacing him, meaning they did not run in the by-election.

Meanwhile, Reform UK also decided not to run a candidate, in their case in order to leave the way clear for a Conservative victory. Their then leader Richard Tice said that he hoped this would lead to a snap general election and that this would be the 'final nail in Labour's coffin'.

On the other hand, the Conservative selection was relatively smooth, with Leeds councillor and chairman of the West Yorkshire Conservatives Ryan Stephenson being chosen to fight the seat.

The final high-profile candidate to join the race was George Galloway, standing for the Workers Party of Britain. It was, in part, his entry into the race that guaranteed the level of national coverage the contest was given and arguably also ensured what the tone of the race would come to be.

The traditional – and expected – fight was to be between Labour and the Conservatives.

Reading the national coverage at the time, you might have been forgiven for thinking that it was a contest between Leadbeater and Galloway. From much of Galloway's rhetoric, you might even have thought it was a fight between him and Starmer, as he announced at the start of his campaign: 'I'm standing against Keir Starmer. If Keir Starmer loses this by-election, it's curtains for Keir Starmer.'

It is fair to say that Galloway has been a serial candidate over the years, with varying levels of success. The expelled former Labour MP won for Respect in Bethnal Green & Bow in 2005 (losing the seat in 2010), for Respect in Bradford West in 2012 (losing the seat in 2015) and for the Workers Party in Rochdale in 2024 (which will be covered later in this book). He also stood unsuccessfully as the Respect candidate for London mayor in 2016, to be MP for Manchester Gorton in 2017 and for West Bromwich East in 2019 (both times as an Independent). At each contest, he has brought with him his iconoclastic, bombastic style, attention from the national press and accusations of a campaigning style from his supporters — and occasionally from himself — that tends to the aggressive.

Galloway's entrance into the campaign changed the atmosphere of the by-election but did not ultimately shift the traditional dynamic. The vast majority of the campaign was conducted through doorstep conversations, leaflets, targeted local social media and hustings, just as with any by-election campaign.

But those leaflets and conversations happened in a significantly more charged atmosphere which many put down to the entrance of Galloway.

Batley & Spen was considered a classic 'red wall' seat — though this nomenclature slightly belies its more marginal status. While it had returned Labour MPs consistently since 1997, their majorities were rarely over 6,000 (with the exception of Brabin's first election in 2016 when — out of a mark of respect for Cox — the other main political parties did not stand), so not a completely 'safe seat'. Batley & Spen voted 60 per cent to leave the EU, another factor making the Labour majority more fragile as this played a major part in fracturing the pro-Remain party from much of its traditional non-urban base.

Largely working class, the seat was comprised of its largest town, Batley, which has a significant population of South Asian heritage and Muslim identity, and a series of other towns and villages including Birkinshaw, Birstall and Cleckheaton, which do not have a significant non-white population, and Heckmondwike, which does.

By-elections are, by their nature, higher profile than being one of 650 simultaneous general election contests. As such, they attract numerous fringe and controversial candidates and extremely high levels of media scrutiny at the best of times. Given the heightened circumstances, this was always going to be a high-profile by-election, and the fragility of Starmer's leadership and the entry of Galloway onto the scene guaranteed this contest would receive high levels of national scrutiny. Though many of those I spoke to from the constituency and from both the Labour and Conservative campaigns (I messaged George Galloway through his website to ask for his recollections of the campaign but received no response) argued that the issues the national press focused on were not always – or even often – the same as those raised by voters on the doorsteps, there is no doubt that this atmosphere led to violence and intimidation at times.

One sour note in Labour's campaign came in a leaflet that led with a picture of Boris Johnson shaking hands with Narendra Modi and a heading warning voters not to risk a 'Tory MP who is not on your side', which was widely seen as a sectarian appeal to Muslim voters. Both Stephenson and Leadbeater raised – without prompting – their discomfort with this leaflet. But it was far from the only – or worst – sectarian issue of the campaign.

The murder of Cox still cast a shadow over the constituency five years on. More so, because the candidate selected by Labour was Jo's sister and her family and team had real concerns about both her safety and what toll the campaign might take on her. Leadbeater had to be given police protection as the campaign deteriorated into incidents of threats and intimidation.

On one occasion, a retired local GP and former chair of the local mosque – who was supporting Leadbeater – was pelted with eggs, and a campaigner he was with was knocked to the ground and kicked while on the floor.

One particular incident earlier in 2021 got local and national attention and stoked much of the divisiveness that would come to dominate memories of the by-election. In March, a teacher at Batley Grammar School was suspended (he was later cleared of any wrongdoing) after showing a satirical image of the Prophet Muhammad (which is interpreted by some readings of the Koran as blasphemous) in school, triggering protests and leading the teacher to go into hiding fearing for their safety and in considerable distress.

A week before the election, there was a rally that was initially billed as about free speech in defence of the teacher and was attended by the right-wing politicians Laurence Fox and Martin Daubney as well as Galloway. The day before, there had been an altercation (at which Galloway was present but claimed to have had no involvement) between Leadbeater and a Muslim activist, who aggressively berated her over her stance on LGBT rights (Leadbeater happens to be a lesbian) and their teaching in schools.

This became a theme at this rally, where Galloway found the common ground of the right-wing anti-Muslim protesters and the Muslim counter protesters and focused on his belief in the right for parents to control what children are taught in school about sexuality.

Talking to both the Labour and Tory candidates, what struck me was that they were telling essentially the same story about the campaign details but from slightly different perspectives.

Stephenson – who struck me (a lifelong Labour supporter and admirer of Leadbeater) as a decent and committed councillor and candidate – was at odds to say that he was deeply uncomfortable with the perception that he was standing back and hoping that Galloway would split the Labour vote. As it turned out, it may be that a combination of Leadbeater's local roots and a 'stop Galloway' mood helped her in the more traditionally Tory-voting wards. But the sense that the Tory campaign was hoping to gain from these splits in Labour's vote was there from the Labour camp and wider coverage.

On election night, neither Labour nor the Conservatives were confident of victory. Mobile phones were banned from the count and so most of the news the candidates were receiving was through television coverage. At one point, Sky's Jon Craig declared that the Tories had won and it was just a case of by how much. However, Stephenson delights in telling the story of his entering the count later (now aware of how the night had gone) to overhear Craig announcing to the nation: 'The loser, Mr Stephenson, has now arrived.' Leadbeater, meanwhile, had not prepared her victory speech, convinced as she was that she had lost.

Despite the narrow 323 vote victory – which wasn't announced until 5.25 a.m. – there was no recount. On the night, Galloway blustered and – as is pretty much customary for him when losing – made noises about taking legal action to have the result set aside. When I asked Leadbeater whether he had ever followed through on this, I received the classic Yorkshire response of 'Has he heck!'

Leadbeater now represents the new seat of Spen Valley. But the atmosphere of this by-election was reportedly replicated at the 2024 general election in the new seat of Dewsbury & Batley where an Independent was elected amid now familiar accusations of intimidation. Stephenson did not contest either seat and Galloway had moved on, across the Pennines to Rochdale where in 2024 he first won, then lost, the constituency. But the atmosphere that followed him to an already scarred Batley & Spen remains. Galloway is famously litigious, so it is just the opinion of this author that if asked whether he cares about that, my response would echo Kim's – 'does he heck'.

Emma Burnell was a freelance journalist and playwright at the time of writing this essay. She has since taken up the post of editor of LabourList.

82

NORTH SHROPSHIRE

16 DECEMBER 2021
LIBERAL DEMOCRAT GAIN FROM
CONSERVATIVES

COREY FROGGATT

Result: Helen Morgan (Liberal Democrats), 17,957, 47.2 per cent; Neil Shastri-Hurst (Conservative), 12,032, 31.6 per cent; Ben Wood (Labour), 3,686, 9.7 per cent; Duncan Kerr (Green), 1,738, 4.6 per cent; Kirsty Walmsley (Reform UK), 1,427, 3.8 per cent; Andrea Allen (UKIP), 378, 1.0 per cent; Martin Daubney (Reclaim), 375, 1.0 per cent; Alan 'Howling Laud' Hope (Monster Raving Loony), 118, 0.3 per cent; Suzie Akers-Smith (Independent), 95, 0.2 per cent; James Elliot (Heritage), 79, 0.2 per cent; Boris Been-Bunged (Rejoin EU), 58, 0.2 per cent; Earl Jesse (Freedom Alliance), 57, 0.1 per cent; Russell Dean (Party), 19, 0.1 per cent; Yolande Kenward (Independent), 3, 0.0 per cent
Size of majority: 5,925
Swing: 34.2 per cent from Conservative to Liberal Democrat
Name of previous MP and party: Owen Paterson (Conservative)
Reason for by-election: Resignation of incumbent
Result at previous general election: Owen Paterson (Conservative), 35,444, 62.7 per cent; Graeme Currie (Labour), 12,495, 22.1 per cent; Helen Morgan (Liberal Democrats), 5,643, 10.0 per cent; John Adams (Green), 1,790, 3.2 per cent; Robert James (Shropshire), 1,141, 2.0 per cent
Date by-election called: 9 November 2021
Date by-election took place: 16 December 2021
Size of total electorate: 82,314
Total number of votes cast: 38,022
Turnout: 46.2 per cent

'Contritionem praecedit superbia et ante ruinam exaltatur spiritus.'
'Pride goeth before destruction, and an haughty spirit before a fall.'
– PROVERBS 16:18

*'Empty pots and pans reach high temperatures very quickly, and when heated
accidentally over 348 °C (660 °F) the coating can begin to deteriorate.'*
– TEFLON

Boris Johnson's popularity soared during the pandemic, reaching heights that nearly rivalled his hero Winston Churchill. He had delivered Brexit, survived a particularly rough bout of COVID-19 and turned the red stronghold of Hartlepool blue in a by-election. Since 2019, he'd sustained a polling lead for most of his premiership – and that was no small feat. Scandals came and went, from the cost of refurbishing his flat above No. 11 Downing Street to controversies over PPE contracts and his relationship with US businesswoman Jennifer Arcuri, to name but three. Yet Johnson had brushed them aside with his signature nonchalance: a ruffle of the hair, a joke, some mumbling. He was the 'non-stick' Prime Minister. But one scandal, and his response to it, broke this pattern. It marked a turning point in the fortunes of this supposedly indestructible premier. It marked the beginning of the end for Boris Johnson.

Owen Paterson had been North Shropshire's MP for twenty-four years. On 4 November 2021, he announced his resignation, saying he wanted to escape the 'cruel world of politics'. Nine days before, the parliamentary commissioner for standards Kathryn Stone, along with the Standards Committee, had published a damning report. It concluded Paterson had breached paid advocacy rules by lobbying on behalf of two companies that employed him as a paid consultant. Those nine days, and Johnson's handling of them, arguably set the Prime Minister on a course that would lead to his eventual downfall.

Paterson's connection to Randox, a healthcare diagnostics company based in Northern Ireland, began during his time as shadow Northern Ireland Secretary. After stints as Secretary of State for Northern Ireland (2010–12) and then at DEFRA (2012–14), Paterson returned to the back benches and formally took on a consultancy role with Randox.

He reportedly earned £100,000 annually advising on rural and public health issues, which he argued aligned with his interests and expertise. However, in 2019, *The Guardian* accused Paterson of improperly lobbying on behalf of Randox and another company, Lynn Country Foods, sparking a formal investigation.

The Standards Committee's ensuing report upheld allegations of fourteen breaches of lobbying rules. Among the most serious were Paterson's communications with Health Secretary Matt Hancock, advocating for government contracts for Randox during the pandemic, and his interventions with the Food Standards Agency which might have ended up benefiting Lynn Country Foods. The committee ruled that Paterson's actions violated the parliamentary codes of transparency and impartiality. Paterson has always denied any wrongdoing. (In a 2024 documentary *Justice? The Owen Paterson Story*, he sets out his case and says he sought avenues to challenge the findings. However, due to parliamentary privilege, he has been unable to bring the case before a UK court. His hope for the European Court of Human Rights to hear the case was extinguished when the court ruled it 'inadmissible'. (Paterson has since called on Prime Minister Keir Starmer, a former human rights lawyer, to waive parliamentary privilege and allow him his day in court.)

Despite his protests of innocence, the committee recommended a thirty-day suspension. That may not sound like much, but it was well above the threshold for triggering a recall petition – and, with enough votes from disgruntled constituents, a by-election.

Johnson, meanwhile, was on the move, attending the G20 in Rome and COP26 in Glasgow. He later admitted in his book *Unleashed* that 'by the Tuesday evening I had not properly read [the commissioner's] report'. Upon returning to Westminster, he relied on advice from Chief Whip Mark Spencer and Leader of the House Jacob Rees-Mogg, who considered the process a stitch-up. They argued that Paterson hadn't been able to properly defend himself and that Kathryn Stone had been the 'judge and jury in her own cause'. Johnson, convinced the process was unfair, decided to intervene.

Another factor in his decision was undoubtedly the tragic fact that Owen Paterson's wife, Rose, had taken her own life in June 2020.

Paterson said that the investigation 'played a massive role in creating the extreme anxiety which led to her suicide'. Paterson spoke movingly of his wife: 'She was quite tremendous. We met at Cambridge 45 years ago, we were married for 41 years. She was highly intelligent, extremely well-read.' He urged others to seek help for mental health struggles: 'Please talk! Please talk to other members of your family. Please go and talk to your doctor – don't be embarrassed … and please look out for people.'

On 3 November, just after Prime Minister's Questions (PMQs), the motion proposing Paterson's thirty-day suspension was due to be debated in the House of Commons. But the government had other plans. Instead of letting the suspension pass, it supported an amendment tabled by senior backbencher Andrea Leadsom to delay the suspension and establish a cross-party committee of MPs to re-examine the case. This move, seen by many as an attempt to shield Paterson, would effectively quash the suspension – at least for the time being.

By Boris Johnson's own account, he was still skimming through the Standards Committee report ninety minutes before PMQs and began to have doubts. 'Hmmm,' he recalled thinking, 'as some of Owen's emails leaped out at me. I don't like the look of this … He had definitely been interceding on behalf of these companies – and in quite an assertive way.' Despite his doubts, Johnson felt bound by promises made to Paterson's allies, including Charles Moore, and had already reassured colleagues that he would defend Paterson. By then, the wheels were in motion, and reversing course was not an option.

The government issued a three-line whip to Conservative MPs, ensuring the amendment had the full weight of party discipline behind it. When it passed, cries of 'shame' erupted from the opposition benches – a foretaste of the coming backlash. Discontent brewed within the Prime Minister's own ranks and across the media. Even Johnson later admitted the optics were terrible: 'It looked as though I had tyrannically used my eighty-seat majority to crush the findings of the independent parliamentary commissioner for standards to protect a Tory colleague.'

The government's plan to create a new cross-party panel to review the case was a non-starter. Labour MPs categorically refused to participate.

Nevertheless, ministers were sent out to defend the decision on the evening media rounds, an increasingly futile exercise given the growing outrage.

He marched them up to the top of the hill... and he marched them down again.

The next day, the government performed a humiliating U-turn. It restaged the motion, abandoned the amendment and voted through Paterson's suspension. In the aftermath, Paterson resigned to 'escape the cruel world of politics', as he put it in his statement. The by-election was set in motion from 9 November. By then, though, the damage had been done. Labour leader Keir Starmer accused Johnson of 'trashing our democracy', while the Liberal Democrats dismissed the entire episode as a 'farce'. Whether seen as malign or simply incompetent, neither narrative reflected well on the Conservatives — and both would shape the campaign that followed.

Discussions had taken place between the Lib Dems, Labour and the Greens about standing aside in favour of a cross-party independent to maximise the chance of taking North Shropshire from the Conservatives. Ultimately, no formal agreement was reached, and each party fielded its own candidate. That said, not all parties campaigned with equal vigour. Labour, whose 2019 candidate Graeme Currie came second, might have been expected to mount the strongest challenge. But the Liberal Democrats were hungrier. Their strategy of targeting rural and affluent Tory heartlands had already borne fruit earlier in the year with a stunning victory in Chesham & Amersham.

Labour pulled back its campaign effort, with shadow International Development Minister Yasmin Qureshi openly admitting to Times Radio: 'Let's face it, Labour are never going to win North Shropshire. The Lib Dems do have an opportunity to do so.' This sentiment did not go down well with local Labour canvassers, who felt their efforts were being undermined by the national party. Frustration among some of them deepened when Labour's NEC blocked Graeme Currie from standing again after he shared posts on social media relating to Jeremy Corbyn and Palestine. Furious, Currie accused the party of 'Stalinist' behaviour and quit. Labour selected 27-year-old Ben Wood, who was born and raised in the area and 'started working life in a local hardware shop'. Despite limited resources from Labour HQ, Wood remained optimistic, boldly claiming in an interview: 'We've spoken to around a thousand people, and one person is thinking about voting Lib Dem. It's a two-horse race between the Labour and the Tories, and it always has been around here.' His campaign focused on public transport and creating good quality, high-skilled jobs – both areas he said were sorely lacking in North Shropshire.

The Liberal Democrats, meanwhile, initially approached Martin Bell – he of the white suit – to stand as their candidate. Lib Dem leader Ed Davey, ever eager for a stunt, saw an opportunity for Bell to once again seize a Tory stronghold rocked by scandal, just as he had against Neil Hamilton in Tatton during the cash-for-questions row in 1997. But this time, Bell declined, citing his age and, more importantly, his belief that no party could overturn the Conservatives' 23,000 majority in North Shropshire. In the end, the Lib Dems stuck with their 2019 candidate, Helen Morgan. A relative newcomer to politics, Morgan had worked as a chartered accountant for companies such as KPMG and British Gas and only joined the Lib Dems in 2016. Popular locally and within the party – one source later called her 'the funniest MP we have' – Morgan campaigned heavily on ambulance delays, a key issue in the constituency. 'You'd find someone on almost every canvass round who'd had an appalling experience waiting for an ambulance,' she said. Another central theme of her campaign was the sense that local people felt left behind and taken for granted – a frustration she said was palpable on the doorstep. But Morgan faced a daunting challenge. Martin Bell had a point: this was a Brexit-loving rural constituency that had been Tory for 187 of the last 189 years. Morgan's 2019 result, just 10 per cent of the vote, suggested she had a considerable mountain to climb.

The Conservatives selected Neil Shastri-Hurst, a barrister based in Birmingham, a former British Army medical officer and an honorary NHS consultant. Despite his impressive credentials, his candidacy stirred controversy. Critics labelled him a 'parachute' candidate, a charge his opponents eagerly exploited. Shastri-Hurst defended his ties to the area, pointing out that he had obtained medical training locally and was stationed at a nearby barracks during his time in the army. However, for some local Conservatives, this wasn't good enough. Mark

Whittle, the deputy mayor of Market Drayton, quit the party in protest after taking Shastri-Hurst on a tour of the town and concluding that 'he knew absolutely zilch about the area'. Shastri-Hurst's campaign emphasised improving ambulance response times, as well as increasing support for farmers. He also made sure to mention that, in his view, Brexit freedoms would allow him to 'put North Shropshire first', in an attempt to tap into the sentiment which led to roughly 57 per cent of Shropshire's vote going to 'leave'. Still, the criticism over his outsider status fed into the Lib Dems' narrative that the Conservatives were taking the seat for granted.

Various smaller parties ran their own candidates, including the Greens and Reform UK. But an honourable mention must go to yacht broker Russell Dean who ran for the Party Party, a name he hoped would help him go about 'attracting young people into politics and encouraging them to engage'. (Spoiler: he secured just nineteen votes.)

With election day two weeks away, polling suggested the Liberal Democrats had overtaken Labour for second place. For the Conservatives, the by-election was shaping up to be a referendum not only on Boris Johnson's handling of the Paterson scandal but on the broader perception of sleaze in his government. To steady the ship, the Conservatives needed to hold on in North Shropshire – but the Lib Dems were clearly on the march. Then, on 30 November, *Daily Mirror* political editor Pippa Crerar burst onto the scene and opened a monumental can of worms. Suddenly, the idea of the Tories losing this safe seat wasn't just possible – it was plausible.

Crerar revealed that three parties had taken place in Downing Street during Tier 3 COVID restrictions in 2020. In his book, Boris Johnson recalled hearing the reports and thinking they 'sounded like a load of old cobblers'. No. 10 insisted that COVID rules were followed at all times. But the next day, Keir Starmer used the revelations to skewer Johnson at PMQs: 'Does the Prime Minister really expect the country to believe that while people were banned from seeing their loved ones at Christmas last year, it was fine for him and his friends to throw a boozy party in Downing Street?' Johnson stressed in response that 'all guidance was followed completely'.

The revelations didn't stop there. On 7 December, ITV News

aired a leaked video showing press secretary Allegra Stratton during a mock press conference in December 2020 joking about a Downing Street Christmas party. The next day, Johnson declared at PMQs that he was 'sickened and furious' when he saw the clip. Later that day, Stratton tearfully resigned. In the following days, stories of other lockdown-breaking events, from a Treasury drinks party to a Christmas quiz, piled on.

Back in North Shropshire, as the campaign wore on, the Conservatives' campaign was faltering. Shastri-Hurst was accused of avoiding media interviews. 'He's a nice bloke and will no doubt be a quick learner if he's elected, but it's embarrassing that a Tory in North Shropshire is essentially hiding away,' lamented one local party member. Labour's Ben Wood quipped: 'They should at least have the decency not to lock him up for the duration of the campaign.' The Conservatives' regional press officer for the West Midlands, Matthew Follows, dismissed such claims as 'absolute rubbish' and pointed to the multiple hustings their candidate was signed up for. But you could see why Shastri-Hurst might have wanted to steer clear of the spotlight.

Not only was Partygate bubbling away in Westminster but there were local headaches too. Two sitting Conservative councillors defected – one to the Reclaim Party and the other to Reform UK. Then, the *Mirror* unearthed a 2015 ConservativeHome op-ed in which Shastri-Hurst questioned if the NHS was 'worth fighting for', arguing it 'cannot be a bottomless pit of resources and money' and should be cut back. He had also written that clapping for carers during the pandemic was 'slightly embarrassing'.

Meanwhile, Lib Dem candidate Helen Morgan made a gaffe of her own. In a Twitter clash over Channel migrants, she told Home Secretary Priti Patel to 'tear up her copy of Goebbels' manual'. It wasn't her first controversy involving Nazi comparisons – she had already apologised for social media posts which appeared to liken the plight of Channel migrants to Jewish prisoners at Auschwitz. She had also invoked the Nazi analogy in 2019 when describing Boris Johnson's proroguing of Parliament, suggesting 'it's what Hitler did in 1933 … a shameless power grab'. But none of this came close to matching the damage inflicted by the ongoing Partygate saga, which dominated headlines.

As polling day drew near, bookmakers began tipping the Lib Dems to win. Ed Davey called it a 'coin toss', claiming that even lifelong Conservative voters were defecting, 'tired of being taken for granted by Boris Johnson'. The Prime Minister had gone from being an enormous asset in 2019 to being a liability in North Shropshire. Even Neil Shastri-Hurst conceded there was 'a real mix' of reactions to Boris Johnson after the tumultuous couple of months.

The results were extraordinary: a huge 34.2 per cent swing from the Conservatives to the Liberal Democrats, surpassing the Chesham & Amersham by-election earlier that year and smashing all expectations. Helen Morgan summed up her surprise: 'I thought we could give them a scare and get into a good second place, but it was so overwhelming to win.'

In this, the sixth by-election of the 2019 parliament, voters had sent a very clear message to the government – and it sent shockwaves through the Conservative Party. MPs who had watched the mishandling of the Paterson case and the Partygate fallout now faced a stark warning: if North Shropshire could fall, no seat was safe.

Five months later, the Conservatives lost hundreds of council seats in local elections. By July, following the Chris Pincher scandal, Boris Johnson announced his resignation.

Johnson could have been one of the great Prime Ministers. He was an early and steadfast supporter of Ukraine in the war against Russia, his government rolled out the COVID vaccines with remarkable speed and his wit and charisma endeared him to many. But he lost it all when he lost the trust of his colleagues. That collapse began in North Shropshire. This wasn't just a loss; it was the opening chapter in the unravelling of Johnson's premiership and, in time, the Conservatives' fourteen-year grip on power.

Corey Froggatt *is a journalist and producer for LBC.*

83

SOUTHEND WEST

24 FEBRUARY 2022
CONSERVATIVE HOLD

IAIN DALE

Result: Anna Firth (Conservative), 12,782, 86.1 per cent; Jason Pilley (Psychedelic Movement), 512, 3.4 per cent; Steve Laws (UKIP), 400, 2.7 per cent; Catherine Blaiklock (English Democrat), 320, 2.2 per cent; Jayda Fransen (Independent), 299, 2.0 per cent; Ben Downton (Heritage), 236, 1.6 per cent; Christopher Anderson (Freedom Alliance), 161, 1.1 per cent; Graham Moore (English Constitution), 86, 0.6 per cent; Olga Childs (Independent), 52, 0.3 per cent
Size of majority: 12,280
Swing: 26.9 per cent for Conservative
Name of previous MP and Party: David Amess (Conservative)
Reason for by-election: Murder of incumbent
Result at previous general election: David Amess (Conservative), 27,555, 59.2 per cent; Aston Line (Labour), 13,096, 28.1 per cent; Nina Stimson (Liberal Democrats), 5,312, 11.4 per cent; 77 Joseph (Independent), 574, 1.2 per cent
Date by-election called: 5 January 2022
Date by-election took place: 3 February 2022
Size of total electorate: 66,354
Total number of votes cast: 15,942
Turnout: 24.0 per cent

The morning of Friday 15 October 2022 seemed just like any other, as local Conservative MP Sir David Amess readied himself to meet constituents at his regular advice surgery at Belfairs Methodist Church in Leigh-on-Sea. The morning was to end in tragedy. Just before midday, Sir David entered the church hall, accompanied by two female staff members. He started chatting to constituents who had arrived before him, when a man approached him and stabbed him multiple times. Amid the horrific scene, emergency services were called. Paramedics treated Sir David for more than an hour but were unable to save him. He was pronounced dead at 1.13 p.m. The attacker, British Somalian Ali Harbi Ali, a Daesh sympathiser, made no attempt to escape and was arrested by police at the scene. He was found guilty of Sir David's murder and of the preparation of terrorist acts in April 2023 and sentenced to a life term.

The murder of Sir David Amess was not the first time an MP had become a victim of terrorist murder. Airey Neave, Sir Anthony Berry, Ian Gow and Jo Cox had all lost their lives in the service of Parliament.

MPs of all parties, Sir David's constituents and the whole country were united in their grief and condemnation of what had happened. Prime Minister Boris Johnson and opposition leader Sir Keir Starmer paid a joint visit to Leigh-on-Sea the following day to pay tribute to their fallen colleague, and Parliament spent some of its proceedings the following Monday allowing MPs from all sides to do the same.

Southend West was once known as 'Guinness by the Sea', as it had been represented for sixty-two years by a member of the Guinness family, from 1935 until 1997 – Sir Henry 'Chips' Channon, more renowned for his gossipy diaries than for any political achievements, and then, following his death in 1958, his son Paul won the ensuing by-election in January 1959. The very opposite of his father in flamboyance and temperament, Paul Channon eventually rose to being a Cabinet minister in the later stages of Margaret Thatcher's government. In 1997, David Amess was selected to succeed him, his Basildon seat having had its boundaries drastically redrawn.

Even in the Blair landslide of 1997, Amess achieved a majority of 2,615. Since then, including 2019, majorities had varied between 7,000 and nearly 15,000. As in Basildon, Amess quickly established a reputation for being a fine constituency MP. If anyone was ever to compile a Top Ten List of Most Assiduous Constituency MPs, David Amess would have been near the top. He WAS Mr Southend. His relentless campaign for Southend to achieve city status was only realised when, sadly, he wasn't alive to witness it, but it was the perfect tribute to his memory.

It was some time before anyone wished to turn their attention to the required by-election. Southend West Conservatives were utterly grief-stricken and it was to be some weeks before they could face thinking about selecting a candidate to fight the by-election.

The day after the murder, both Labour and the Liberal Democrats announced they would not field a candidate in the by-election. The Green Party later followed suit. The same had happened after the murder of Jo Cox but not in 1990, when the IRA murdered senior Conservative MP Ian Gow in a car bomb at his Eastbourne home. The Lib Dems won the seat in the ensuing by-election.

The Conservatives opened their selection process on 25 November, three days after Sir David's funeral. In the circumstances, it was understandable that it was said that the local Conservative association wanted a candidate with clear local links. Paul Channon's daughter Katie was one of the initial applicants, along with Andrew Sheldon, leader of Castle Point Borough Council, and Tamkeen Shaikh, who had previously stood for Southend Borough Council and was the candidate in Barking at the 2019 general election. In the end, Julia Jeapes, a Chelmsford city councillor, competed with Andrew Sheldon and Anna Firth to be the new candidate.

It was Anna Firth who emerged triumphant in the final selection meeting on 11 December. Firth was born in Leigh-on-Sea and had fought two losing general election campaigns previously, in 2015 in Erith & Thamesmead and in 2019 when she lost to Labour's Rosie Duffield in Canterbury, a seat she had been expected to win back. A barrister by profession, she was also a councillor on Sevenoaks Borough Council in Kent. Firth won on the second ballot runoff with Andrew Sheldon. After the chairman of the association, John Lamb, read out the result, he pulled out a letter from his jacket pocket and started to read it out, his voice cracking as he did so. It was from Lady Amess, who wanted to wish the new candidate well. There wasn't a dry eye in the room, as Anna Firth stood up to make her acceptance speech.

Politically, it was a difficult time for any Conservative candidate on the doorstep. Partygate was in full swing and the Conservatives had recently lost the safe seat of North Shropshire to the Liberal Democrats. Had Labour put up a candidate, they might well have given the Conservatives a run for their money, given that they won the seat at the 2024 general election, although this was in large part due to the number of Conservatives who switched to Reform UK. *The Times* reported on 15 January that someone they called a 'veteran activist' said that doorstep canvassers had been 'met with a wall of disapproval such that [they] have never had before in 25 years of doing this'.

Anna Firth maintains this is a fiction. She immediately realised it wouldn't be a normal election. Instead of the usual mass canvass, she concentrated on visiting local businesses and charities. Door knocking and canvassing was not partisan. Voters were invited to share their memories of Sir David Amess, rather than talk about politics.

She recounts meeting countless Labour and Lib Dem voters who wanted to shake her hand and wish her well. She remembers hundreds of houses who were still burning candles of remembrance for Sir David Amess in their windows. She says everyone had a tale to tell of meeting him, including one gentleman whose door David had knocked on, while he was building a new conservatory. 'Let me know when you've finished it,' said the MP, 'and I will come and officially open it.' Which he duly did. Firth was also struck by the number of people whose weddings or christenings he had attended.

Some locals grumbled about the lack of real choice in the by-election, complaining the other main parties had stood down. Local retiree Ray Pallett told *The Times*: 'There wasn't much choice this time. It [is] just the Conservative candidate and a bunch of oddballs.'

He wasn't wrong. Among the other eight candidates were a motley crew of five representatives of fringe right-wing parties. Jason Pilley proved to be the most successful of the fringe candidates, representing the Psychedelic Movement, coming in second place with 512 votes. Unsurprisingly, he wished to end the 'war on drugs'. During the campaign, Hope Not Hate reported that Pilley's manifesto included a proposal to put far-right EDL leader Tommy Robinson into the House of Lords. Graham Moore had the bright idea of making Southend a freeport, despite it not, er, actually being a port. Several of the other candidates based their campaigns on being anti-immigration and anti-COVID lockdowns.

Even UKIP managed only 400 votes, a mere 2.7 per cent of the total. Olga Childs pulled out of the campaign two weeks before polling day due to ill health. She asked people to vote for other candidates. Only fifty-two people ignored her plea, and she duly came bottom of the poll.

It came as no surprise that Anna Firth won a massive 86.1 per cent of the vote. Equally unsurprising was the paltry turnout of 24 per cent, low by even by-election standards. In her victory speech, Firth referenced how proud she was to represent the town of her birth and acknowledged it was a sad day for the Amess family. She declared: 'For Sir David's family and his friends tonight will be a sad and painful day and I would like to pay tribute to Lady Amess and their children. We are thinking of you tonight.'

There were protests, though. The PA News Agency reported having seen many spoiled ballot papers, with voters voicing protests at the conduct of the Prime Minister, Boris Johnson. This explains why party managers refused to let the Prime Minister anywhere near the constituency during the campaign.

There was a total of 1,084 spoiled ballot papers, four times as many compared to the 2019 general election.

Anna Firth wasted no time in taking her seat in the House of Commons and was introduced on the Monday following the by-election by her constituency neighbours Mark Francois and Sir James Duddridge. She made her maiden speech three months later on 10 May. She hadn't been able to do so before then because of the trial of Ali Harbi Ali. Anna Firth soon made up for lost time, becoming one of the House of Commons Chamber's most regular contributors. She was only in Parliament for fifteen months, but she left a legacy, amending the Offensive Weapons Bill to outlaw Zombie knives, securing £100 million for the local hospital, helping to save the local football club and managing to get her Pet Abduction Bill onto the Statute Book just as Rishi Sunak called a general election at the end of May.

Jason Pilley returned to the electoral fight in the 2024 general election in Southend West and contrived to lose 80 per cent of his votes, scoring a measly ninety-nine. Catherine Blaiklock took her brand of English nationalism back to her home seat of Great Yarmouth – a seat which Reform UK won – gaining a paltry 171 votes. Steve Laws went on to defect from UKIP to the English Democrats and stood for them in Dover & Deal in 2024, coming eighth with only 185 votes. In June 2022, Jayda Fransen forsook the delights of Southend to stand in the Wakefield by-election, in which she finished the last of fifteen candidates, with a grand total of twenty-three votes. This came as little surprise to those who received one of her leaflets in Southend which appeared to encourage voters to spoil their ballot papers.

Anna Firth is expected to run again in Southend West & Leigh (as the constituency is now called) at the next election to attempt to win back the seat from David Burton-Sampson who ousted her for Labour in July 2024.

Iain Dale is a radio presenter on LBC Radio. He is a broadcaster, writer and newspaper columnist and a visiting professor of politics and broadcasting at the University of East Anglia. He has written or edited more than sixty books.

84

SELBY & AINSTY

20 JULY 2023
LABOUR GAIN FROM CONSERVATIVES

EDWARD YOUNG

Result: Keir Mather (Labour), 16,456, 46.0 per cent; Claire Holmes (Conservative), 12,295, 34.3 per cent; Arnold Warneken (Green), 1,838, 5.1 per cent; Mike Jordan (Independent), 1,503, 4.2 per cent; Dave Kent (Reform UK), 1,332, 3.7 per cent; Matt Walker (Liberal Democrats), 1,188, 3.3 per cent; Nick Palmer (Independent), 342, 1.0 per cent; John Waterston (Social Democratic), 314, 0.9 per cent; Sir Archibald Stanton (Monster Raving Loony), 172, 0.5 per cent; Guy Phoenix (Heritage), 162, 0.5 per cent; Andrew Gray (Independent), 99, 0.3 per cent; Tyler Wilson-Kerr (Independent), 67, 0.2 per cent; Luke Wellock (Climate), 39, 0.1 per cent
Size of majority: 4,161
Swing: 23.7 per cent from Conservative to Labour
Name of previous MP and party: Nigel Adams (Conservative)
Reason for by-election: Resignation of incumbent
Result at previous general election: Nigel Adams (Conservative), 33,995, 60.3 per cent; Malik Rofidi (Labour), 13,858, 24.6 per cent; Katharine Macy (Liberal Democrats), 4,842, 8.6 per cent; Mike Jordan (Yorkshire), 1,900, 3.4 per cent; Arnold Warneken (Green), 1,823, 3.2 per cent
Date by-election called: 10 June 2023
Date by-election took place: 20 July 2023
Size of total electorate: 80,150
Total number of votes cast: 35,876
Turnout: 44.7 per cent

The summer sunshine gave no hint of the thunderstorms to come. At the end of a narrow lane, on the outskirts of a North Yorkshire village, in a hot, airless regeneration centre, in a hall which looked like a school classroom longing for a quiet weekend, Selby Conservatives were meeting to select a parliamentary candidate.

For thirteen years, Selby & Ainsty had been held by a popular local Conservative, Nigel Adams. Nigel was a mirror of the constituency: down to earth, gregarious, a self-made businessman who had grown up and lived most of his life in Selby. My mother, who for many years worked in Marks & Spencer in York, always remembered that at local recruitment fairs Nigel would stay for hours afterwards talking to the different teams.

Since 2010, the local Conservatives had steadily increased their majority in Selby & Ainsty. At the 2019 general election, Nigel Adams had beaten the Labour candidate by over 20,000 votes. But four years on, the world had changed. In the spring of 2022, Nigel had announced he would not be standing at the next general election. One year later, the selection process for a new parliamentary candidate was in its final stages. The purpose of the meeting in Riccall on Friday 9 June was to select one candidate from the final three.

Nothing about the night seemed rushed or extraordinary. There was plenty of time before a general election in 2024. But as the meeting went on, the mood in the room began to shift. Shortly after 8 p.m., a wave of noise rippled through the audience. Boris Johnson had announced his intention to resign as an MP. The details were unclear, but there were rumours of a row with the new Prime Minister, Rishi Sunak, over peerages for some of Johnson's closest allies.

The focus fell back onto Selby & Ainsty. Some of the candidates had been asked during the interview whether they would be prepared to fight a by-election if selected. This was because of the growing speculation that if Boris Johnson resigned, so would several of his supporters – including Nigel Adams. Earlier that same day, Nadine Dorries, another close follower of Boris Johnson, had said she was standing down immediately. In political terms, the moves were lethal: three resignations meant three by-elections, with the Tories some fifteen points behind Labour in the polls.

The meeting in Riccall gained fresh urgency. At 9 p.m., a winner emerged. Michael Naughton had stood in a number of elections previously. He won the membership vote by a healthy majority. The next day, Nigel Adams announced his decision on social media: 'Yesterday, Selby Conservatives selected an excellent new parliamentary candidate. I've today informed the chief whip that I will be standing down as a Member of Parliament with immediate effect.'

During the thirteen years the constituency existed, Selby & Ainsty was marked by the calmness and beauty which can be found across the Vale of York. Acres of arable farmland stretch out flat between two large towns. Tadcaster in the north remains a brewing capital. John Smith's factory stands firm alongside the River Wharfe and the busy A64 dual carriageway. Selby in the south was once a mining centre, although the mine only opened in the 1970s. Today, Selby is better known for its ancient abbey and a large retail community. For many years, my father sold cars in the car park of the large Morrisons in town. Meanwhile, in the south, the old grey cooling towers of Drax power station can be seen for miles through the constituency, industrial giants against an arable landscape.

The prevailing attitude was conservative but not political. These were farmers, small business owners and retirees. The constituency also brought together an array of different and sometimes conflicting beliefs. Selebians themselves remain proud of their heritage as an old mining community and there is a robust Labour voter base in the town. To the south, the future of Drax and its employees was a priority, not just for those people and their families but also for the wider local economy. Meanwhile, dozens of small, ancient villages cherished their own history and identity, including as battlegrounds and way stations during the Civil War. What united the constituency, therefore, was not so much any one set of issues but rather a strong respect for institutions and a firm belief in high standards of service.

Meanwhile, the Conservatives faced a technical challenge. The selection meeting on 9 June had been to choose a candidate for the next general election. That election would be fought on new boundaries – with most of the north and west breaking off to form a new constituency, and in its place, Selby gaining two wards from the outskirts of

Leeds. The impact of these changes threw the Riccall result into confusion. In effect, the Conservatives had selected a candidate but for a different constituency.

Party bosses dusted down the Conservative constitution. As one local official explained: 'I knew the rules. If your Association makes up more of a previous Association and there is a by-election on old boundaries, your candidate is the candidate. But admittedly that wasn't clear to most people.' The confusion culminated in a Tadcaster meeting on Thursday 15 June. Michael Naughton introduced himself to the members of the wider Selby & Ainsty Association. He came through that meeting but within hours found himself at the centre of a family medical crisis. He had little choice but to pull out. The Conservatives, having emerged fastest from the traps, were now back at the starting line.

Meanwhile, a new protagonist emerged. Keir Mather had grown up in East Yorkshire. After studying history and politics at Oxford, he had gone on to work in Westminster politics, including for the shadow Health Secretary, Wes Streeting. But he had kept his hand in with the local Labour Party and was one of a group of activists who had maintained Labour's campaigning presence in the constituency. At the time of Nigel Adams's resignation, Keir Mather was twenty-five years old.

Normally, the process for selecting Labour parliamentary candidates resembles a long-winded American primary, with candidates producing flashy websites filled with endorsements designed to prove how working class they are, followed by a hard slog of local canvassing before a final selection meeting. None of this was feasible now. Candidates for Selby were instead invited to apply directly. A dozen or so local councillors and Labour activists duly submitted applications; within five days, the list had been whittled down to two.

The final selection took place almost exactly at the same time as the Conservatives were meeting in Tadcaster. Around seventy Labour members gathered in Selby Town Hall, an old Methodist chapel which had later served as a tyre depot. Keir Mather's local links and track record of campaigning had earned him a place on the shortlist. His pitch to the members was personal as well as political. If elected, he would be the first Labour MP who had been born after Tony Blair's victory in 1997. In many ways, he argued, his life was a reflection of Labour's legacy. He was also local to Selby in a way that other candidates were not – his family home in East Yorkshire shared many of the same characteristics as Selby. In the end, the result was not even close. The next morning, Keir Mather headed into the media maelstrom.

The main campaign commenced that weekend. The Conservatives were still short of a candidate, but within forty-eight hours the team at Conservative Campaign Headquarters had drawn up a new shortlist. On Sunday, local Conservatives gathered once again in the Riccall Regeneration Centre. The victor this time was a barrister from East Yorkshire. Claire Holmes came from a family of miners and had grown up in Castleford, just south of the constituency. As well as serving as a local councillor, Claire Holmes was the mother of two young children and a Beaver Scout leader. The weekend of the selection she was meant to be at Scout camp, but she told her colleagues she had to go to a job interview. By the time she arrived in Riccall on Sunday morning, she wasn't nervous. 'It just felt right … It felt like the stars had aligned and I just needed to do this.'

The frantic start to the by-election now gave way to a more traditional campaign. In an essay of this length, there is not space to pay tribute to the broad and eccentric range of candidates who threw themselves forward. In the end, some thirteen candidates offered their services, covering a baffling range of political perspectives, from the Monster Raving Loony Party through to the SDP.

Two things defined the next four weeks. The first was the weather. Anyone who spent time campaigning during June and July 2023 will remember the strange climate, with baking heat followed by epic bursts of rain. Even many weeks later, after the three by-elections in Selby & Ainsty, Somerset & Frome and Uxbridge were long over, the winning MPs were marked out by their farmers' tans.

The second aspect was political. For Claire Holmes, it was hard to imagine a weaker reason to ask people to vote Conservative. This was a by-election which had been called in the middle of a row about MPs not receiving peerages, against a backdrop of sky-high inflation and with the Conservative Party having almost completely lost the discipline which had seen it outperform Labour at four successive general elections. It is telling that both Claire Holmes and Keir Mather had a similar impression of the mood on doorsteps. Thus, in Claire Holmes's words: 'It's not you. I like you. But I can't vote Conservative. Not after all this.' Similarly, Labour campaigners described conversations which began: 'I can't believe we're having this election. I've voted Conservative all my life, but not this time.'

The question was whether Labour could capitalise or if the result would simply be a reduced Conservative majority. From his family home in Brough, Keir Mather threw himself into the contest, canvassing for three or four sessions each day, starting at 10 a.m. and finishing in the early evening. As many candidates find, after the early media scrutiny, being able to focus on door-to-door campaigning was peaceful and calming. However, in Keir's case, these interactions were affected by injury: he had broken his hand playing rugby a few weeks previously and was unable to shake anyone's hand.

The Labour campaign faced three big challenges. The first was data. A decade of Conservative success in Selby & Ainsty had taken its toll on Labour's campaigning efforts in the area and the party's voting intention data was thin. But what Labour lacked in insight they made up for in people power. Almost every member of the Parliamentary Labour Party came to campaign for Keir Mather. According to one figure at the centre of the campaign, 'it felt that the entire Labour Party were out on polling day'.

A second question was Keir Mather's age and experience. 'I can't count the number of times we got jip about it on the doorstep,' one campaigner admitted. In response, Labour made the point that voters would be getting someone with new energy and ideas to represent them. But being young also created other challenges, not least that Keir had not learned to drive. At the start of the campaign, Keir also only owned one blazer – a large, oversized, grey jacket. This coat became his campaign uniform, so much so that when he took it off and went into Labour's campaign HQ, some of the Labour activists did not recognise their candidate and he was asked if he had turned up to volunteer.

But the biggest challenge for Labour was convincing people to switch. It was not enough just to tell people not to vote Conservative. They had to unite people behind a vote for change. On the doorstep,

Keir's argument was simple: I am a local young person who has felt the same pressures as you; I haven't felt any improvement over the past decade, and we're now in a situation where the local and national party seems to be taking you for granted, so isn't it time for a fresh start?

Meanwhile, the Conservative campaign moved through the gears. With two young children at school, Claire Holmes tried to keep things as normal as possible. 'I would get up in the morning and take the kids to school. Then I'd have a morning meeting on Teams and then set off for Selby.' Like Labour, the Conservatives ran several campaign sessions each day, although with less focus on canvassing and more on delivering literature, much of which centred on campaigns to defend the green belt. Claire herself also faced a scheduling challenge. Although she had cleared her diary for most of the campaign, she was unable to withdraw from a fraud case she was duty bound to prosecute. So from 3 July, she lost the best part of another five days, spending her days in court in Bradford before driving back to Selby for evening campaign sessions with visiting ministers and activists. It was far from ideal but at least gave her the opportunity to utter one of the best excuses when leaving a courtroom: 'I'm sorry, but I have a meeting with the Attorney General.'

A range of local issues came up during the campaign, from flooding around Tadcaster through to infrastructure in Sherburn in Elmet. But the overriding feeling was detachment. Many people were more interested in the Ashes, where England were starting to fight back after losing the first two Tests.

Two weeks out from polling day, it became clear that Labour could win. One opinion poll had Labour twelve points ahead. On the final weekend of the campaign, I spent a day campaigning in Whixley with three fellow Conservatives and a dalmatian called Hugo. That day can be taken as a proxy for the entire by-election. Tropical downpours were followed by hours of sunshine.

Whixley itself qualifies as one of the most beautiful villages in Britain. Thanks to a quirk of local transport services, any villager who chose to travel by bus to nearby Knaresborough, a town seven miles away, would first have to take a detour north to Ripon and only arrive in Knaresborough having spent over two hours driving through various North Yorkshire lanes. The four of us, meanwhile, spent several rainy hours campaigning, searching for hidden voters in the various homes and cottages scattered through the village. Eventually, we found a local shop and decided to stock up on sweets and fizzy drinks. The shop, it turned out, only opened for a few hours each week and sold just one newspaper: not the *Yorkshire Post* but the *Daily Telegraph*. As we paid for our supplies, a girl came in from Queen Ethelburga's boarding school, having spent the morning horse-riding. She told us that this would be the first time she voted. She hadn't decided who to vote for yet, but she thought she would probably be voting Green.

As polling day arrived on 20 July, the experiences of the two main candidates diverged for ever. Perhaps knowing they were set for victory, the Labour campaign bosses encouraged Keir Mather to relax ahead of the count that evening. Meanwhile, Claire Holmes ploughed on valiantly. At one point, she came across a man walking two dogs. One had a blue lead, the other a red.

'There goes a gentleman with a bit of political balance,' Claire commented.

'The only way I can tell them apart is the colour of their leads,' he replied.

'I just thought that sums up people's views really,' Claire said later. 'They just think that politicians are all the same.'

After the polls closed, Keir Mather tried but failed to gain a few hours of sleep. To distract himself, he switched between watching the Tour de France and waiting for the result in Uxbridge. Despite the Tories only defending a majority of just over 7,000 in Middlesex, thanks to the fierce opposition to the ULEZ charge imposed by the Labour Mayor of London, the Conservatives had held the seat.

Meanwhile, in Selby Leisure Centre, the counting finished. Keir Mather, Claire Holmes and the other candidates assembled. As with all by-elections, an official from the House of Commons was in attendance, clutching an envelope which would be presented to the winner containing vital details about how to get set up in Parliament. The result was announced at 4 a.m. Labour gained 16,456 votes, compared to 12,295 for the Conservatives. The Greens, Yorkshire Party, Reform UK and the Liberal Democrats gained almost 6,000 votes between them. Most electors had not voted at all.

There are two ways of looking at the outcome. On the one hand, it remains one of the biggest majorities overturned in British by-election history. On the other, Labour had only gained 2,600 more votes than they had in 2019, and 2,700 fewer votes than they had received in 2017. In other words, they had mobilised Labour voters more successfully than they had encouraged former Tories to switch. The Conservative vote had simply collapsed. Alex Tant-Brown, the deputy chair of Selby Conservatives, offered a glimpse of what had happened: 'My own family didn't vote Conservative and they are true Blues. They voted Monster Raving Loony.'

After results such as this, it is always easy to point fingers. Claire Holmes was a strong candidate, and she worked hard during the campaign. Her campaign team were resilient in the face of major obstacles, not least the lack of time. One common complaint was the literature, which focused on Claire's local connections without telling a strong personal or political story. 'It was a big lesson for me,' she said later. 'If we had had a longer run up, we could have got across more of a message about me.' But it was a minor factor set against the scale of the defeat.

Campaigners from all sides paid tribute to the way Labour ran its campaign. Keir Mather was himself shrewdly advised by another by-election victor, Simon Lightwood, the MP for Wakefield. The campaign was led by Keir's agent, Scott Hardy, who, in the words of one colleague, 'combines likeability with ruthless efficiency'. The Labour team also gave themselves an optical advantage by setting up a prominent campaign office next to W. H. Smith in the middle of Selby.

The real moral of the Selby story, however, is different. Three by-elections took place on 20 July 2023: Uxbridge, Selby & Ainsty and Somerton & Frome. Of the three, Uxbridge had by far the smallest Conservative majority – but it was the only one the Conservatives held. The reason for this was not resources, candidates or strategy. It was that in Uxbridge there was a clear reason to vote Conservative: to stop the Mayor of London's anti-car crusade. In any election, and particularly a by-election, it is not enough to be local, to have a strong candidate or to have huge resources and manage the campaign well. You also need to give people a genuine reason to vote *for* you. For Conservatives in Selby & Ainsty that summer, that reason was missing.

After the count, Claire Holmes went to bed for a few hours then drove to her parents' house to pick up her children. 'It was back to normal,' she said. 'So I wanted to take them to school.' The following year, Claire and her husband Matt welcomed their third child in the same month Rishi Sunak called a general election.

Meanwhile, long-suffering Labour supporters celebrated. The following morning, the Labour leader, Keir Starmer, joined Keir Mather at a rally at Selby Town Football Club. Because of the timings of the election just before the summer recess, it was many weeks before Keir could take his seat in Parliament. When he finally gave his maiden speech, he drew on his history degree to tell the story of another by-election in Selby. In 1905, a local Conservative candidate had been defeated against the odds by a Liberal opponent, Joseph Andrews. But the victory was short-lived. Three months later, Joseph Andrews lost at the subsequent general election, having never had chance to take his seat in Parliament. He died three years later from appendicitis. By contrast, at the time of writing, Keir Mather remains in good health and is still very much the Member of Parliament for Selby.

In the days that followed the by-election, people across Selby & Ainsty carried on with their lives as if nothing had happened. Many focused on the cricket, with the fourth Ashes Test taking place. As is often the case, the battle that weekend was not just against Australia but also with the weather. Across Yorkshire, it poured with rain.

Edward Young is a partner at Headland Consultancy and the co-author with Doulgas Hurd of Disraeli: or, The Two Lives *(Orion, 2013). In 2017, Ed stood as the Conservative candidate for York Central.*

85

RUTHERGLEN & HAMILTON WEST

5 OCTOBER 2023
LABOUR GAIN FROM SNP

MARK McGEOGHEGAN

Result: Michael Shanks (Labour), 17,845, 58.6 per cent; Katy Loudon (SNP), 8,399, 27.6 per cent; Thomas Jordan Kerr (Conservative), 1,192, 3.9 per cent; Gloria Adebo (Liberal Democrats), 895, 2.9 per cent; Cameron Eadie (Scottish Green), 601, 2.0 per cent; David Stark (Reform UK), 403, 1.3 per cent; Niall Fraser (Scottish Family), 319, 1.0 per cent; Bill Bonnar (Scottish Socialist), 271, 0.9 per cent; Colette Walker (Independence for Scotland), 207, 0.7 per cent; Christopher Anthony Sermanni (Trade Unionist and Socialist Coalition), 178, 0.6 per cent; Andrew Vincent Daly (Independent), 81, 0.3 per cent; Ewan Hoyle (Volt UK), 46, 0.2 per cent; Prince Ankit, Love Emperor of India (Independent), 34, 0.1 per cent; Garry Patrick Cooke (Independent), 6, 0.0 per cent

Size of majority: 9,446

Swing: 20.4 per cent from SNP to Labour

Name of previous MP and party: Margaret Ferrier (SNP)

Reason for by-election: Recall of incumbent

Result at previous general election: Margaret Ferrier (SNP), 23,775, 44.2 per cent; Ged Killen (Labour), 18,545, 34.5 per cent; Lynne Nailon (Conservative), 8,054, 15.0 per cent; Mark McGeever (Liberal Democrats), 2,791, 5.2 per cent; Janice MacKay (UKIP), 629, 1.2 per cent

Date by-election called: 1 August 2023

Date by-election took place: 5 October 2023

Size of total electorate: 82,104

Total number of votes cast: 30,477
Turnout: 37.1 per cent

On 28 September 2020, Margaret Ferrier, then the SNP MP for Rutherglen & Hamilton West, took a train from Scotland to London and spoke in a House of Commons debate before returning to Scotland the following morning. She had first noted COVID-19 symptoms two days prior, travelled anyway and returned to Scotland despite receiving a positive COVID-19 test on the day she appeared in the Commons.

Ferrier apologised for breaching COVID-19 rules on 1 October 2020, and over the next thirty-two months, she was suspended from the SNP; was arrested and charged by Police Scotland with 'culpable and reckless conduct', to which she pled guilty; was found by the parliamentary commissioner for standards to have breached the MPs' Code of Conduct; and was suspended from the House of Commons for thirty days.

Ferrier's suspension triggered a recall petition under the Recall of MPs Act of 2015, the first held in Scotland. Overall, 14.7 per cent of eligible registered voters in Rutherglen & Hamilton West signed the recall petition against Ferrier, rendering the seat vacant on 1 August 2023. The SNP's Chief Whip, Owen Thompson MP, moved the writ to hold a by-election on 4 September, setting the by-election for 5 October. Ferrier declined to contest the by-election.

In the three years between Ferrier's breaching of COVID-19 rules and the Rutherglen & Hamilton West by-election, her actions and their consequences formed just one thread in a tapestry telling the story of the SNP's decline from hegemonic dominance of Scottish electoral politics.

Throughout September and October 2020, the SNP polled an average of 53 per cent in Westminster voting intention in Scotland, leading Labour by 34.3 points, and support for independence averaged 53.6 per cent against 46.4 per cent opposed, amid a string of twenty polls putting support for independence ahead. Nicola Sturgeon, First Minister of Scotland and the SNP's talismanic leader, was at the height of her powers with a net approval rating of +48, just one point below her high of +49 in January 2015, and 70 per cent of Scots believed that she was handling the pandemic well.

The SNP would win the 2021 Scottish Parliament election with the second-largest number of votes recorded by any party in any election in the history of Scottish democracy (second only to their tally in the 2015 UK general election). In the 2022 Scottish local elections, they would win the largest proportion of first preferences of any party since the change to using the Single Transferable Vote in 2007 and win 37 per cent of Scotland's councillors, the party's best-ever local election result.

By October 2023, that dominance had ended. Nicola Sturgeon resigned as Scotland's First Minister in February 2023, followed by twin blows against the SNP's reputation. The first was a bloodletting of a leadership race that saw Humza Yousaf narrowly elected as party leader and First Minister.

The second was the dramatic escalation of Operation Branchform, Police Scotland's investigation into allegations of fraud and embezzlement by figures in the SNP. In April 2023, Nicola Sturgeon's husband and the SNP's recently resigned chief executive, Peter Murrell, and the party's treasurer and MSP for Midlothian North & Musselburgh, Colin Beattie, were both arrested (and released without charge) in connection with Branchform. Police erected tents in the back and front gardens of Sturgeon's home for several days as they searched for evidence, and they seized documents from the SNP's headquarters in Edinburgh. Sturgeon was arrested and released without charge in June 2023. Her husband was later charged with embezzlement in 2024, and his case is ongoing.

At that exact moment, Scottish Labour recorded their first Westminster voting intention lead over the SNP since June 2014. The SNP's gargantuan 34.3-point lead when Ferrier first breached COVID-19 rules had evaporated. The SNP's national polling had recovered somewhat by early October 2023, leading Labour by an average of 36.3 per cent to 29 per cent in the month before the by-election. But this reflected a swing of 9.6 points from the SNP to Labour, which – if replicated precisely in the by-election – would have resulted in a Labour win by 44.1 per cent to 34.6 per cent, almost a complete reversal of the result in the 2019 UK general election. At the time, political analysts further speculated that lower turnout, dissatisfaction with the SNP Scottish government and the lingering anger at Ferrier could mean an even bigger Labour win on the day.

The by-election was the first and only parliamentary electoral test of Humza Yousaf's leadership of the SNP. The somewhat naive hope on the SNP's part was that they could prove the polls wrong or at least put up a better fight than expected. Scottish Labour, on the other hand, correctly saw the by-election as a golden opportunity to show that, as Scottish Labour leader Anas Sarwar put it, 'Scotland is going to lead the way in delivering a UK Labour government', generating momentum going into the 2024 general election.

Campaigning began before the by-election was called, a by-product of the new recall petition system. In anticipation of the recall petition, Labour selected Michael Shanks as their candidate in May amid some controversy. He saw off three other candidates – but only after claims of a stitch-up when the panel shortlisting candidates ruled out some local favourites. Local constituency Labour parties wrote to Sarwar and UK Labour leader, Sir Keir Starmer, to complain about the process and communicate concerns about its 'integrity'. Shanks had unsuccessfully run as a Labour candidate for Glasgow City Council in 2012, the Scottish Parliament in 2016 and the House of Commons in 2017 before resigning from the party in 2019 – citing Brexit and antisemitism under Jeremy Corbyn – and rejoining under Sir Keir's leadership.

While the SNP's selection process began before the House voted to suspend Ferrier, their candidate, Katy Loudon, was not confirmed until three days after that vote. Her selection was not uncontroversial either, as it emerged Yousaf had personally rejected several local candidates. Loudon had represented South Lanarkshire Council's Cambuslang East ward in the constituency since 2017.

Labour and the SNP formally registered as campaigners in favour of the petition, but the SNP's support appeared to be a tokenistic attempt to project confidence. Labour spent £8,091 on campaigning for constituents to sign the recall petition, eight times the SNP's spend, and assigned their Scottish deputy leader, Dame Jackie Baillie, to lead the campaign.

The by-election campaign drew out a strategic chasm between Labour and the SNP. The Scottish Labour leader, Anas Sarwar, had already alighted on a powerful narrative hook: Labour was the answer not just to a despised Conservative government in London but also to an SNP Scottish government that Scotland was increasingly disillusioned with. Labour focused heavily on their historic record of tackling poverty and proposed reforms to strengthen employment rights, with messaging tailored to land with the electorate of this deindustrialised, central belt constituency that had voted Labour from 1964 until the independence referendum.

In contrast, the SNP were still struggling to come to terms with the end of their hegemonic dominance of Scottish politics and Labour's resurgence in the polls. Having relied on pro-independence and anti-Brexit messaging in the context of Conservative dominance of British politics, under Humza Yousaf they found themselves narratively rudderless. The salience of both issues had collapsed, and the competence of the Scottish government was in question. The by-election served as a testing ground for messaging that the SNP felt might be effective against Labour, which in practice led to the party erratically casting around for a message.

Where they landed proved unfruitful. The SNP attempted to paint Labour as a party of Brexit, which was unimportant to voters, and of austerity, which was difficult to land for a party that had presided over substantial cuts to Scottish public services. They attempted to elevate Labour's commitment to retain the two-child benefit cap and contrast it with the Scottish Family Payment, despite retaining the cap being supported by the majority of Scots and Shanks publicly opposing the policy.

Local issues played a muted role in the overall campaign. The prospect of rising council taxes was controversial – in the wake of defeat, Humza Yousaf announced a council tax freeze – and the Labour leader of South Lanarkshire Council, Joe Fagan, narrowly survived a confidence vote in late August after leaking a confidential list of facilities reportedly at risk of closure under the previous SNP administration. Late in the campaign, the SNP was attacked for allegedly keeping quiet about plans to close a series of Lanarkshire police stations.

However, it is unclear whether local issues significantly affected the outcome of the by-election. The vote was essentially decided by national issues, from the cost of living and dissatisfaction with the NHS to scandal in the SNP and a deep desire to get rid of the Conservative government in London. It was just as nationalised in media coverage as a bellwether or, as BBC Scotland's political correspondent David Lockhart put it a couple of days before the vote, the 'barometer of the nation'.

The importance of the vote, not just locally but also for setting political narratives nationally, meant a frenzied campaign. Scarcely a day passed between the success of the recall petition and the by-election itself without the leading candidates and their teams pounding the pavements and knocking on doors. While Loudon cannot be faulted for her energy and quality as a candidate, the intensity of the campaign further exposed growing weaknesses in the SNP's ground game as they were caught hiring leafleters on the very zero-hours contracts that the party has vociferously opposed and used as one example of why employment law should be devolved. The *Scottish Sun* reported that one such leafleter told a local resident, 'I don't support the SNP – I'm just getting paid to hand this shite out.'

As polling day approached, the intensity of the campaign only grew. On the Labour side, Sir Keir Starmer and Anas Sarwar repeatedly campaigned in the constituency. Senior shadow Cabinet ministers, including Angela Rayner, Rachel Reeves and Wes Streeting, knocked on doors for Shanks, as did many more junior Labour MPs.

Humza Yousaf was a regular fixture, as were the majority of the Scottish Cabinet and other senior figures like Stephen Flynn, the Westminster leader, and Mhairi Black, then his deputy. But Nicola Sturgeon was conspicuous by her absence, and *The Economist* noted unease among voters about her resignation and the circumstances surrounding it.

In the days before the by-election, analysts warned against over-interpreting the result. As I wrote in *The Herald*, 'Rutherglen and Hamilton West is among the lowest hanging of the low-hanging fruit for Labour.' Labour were expected to win by around five to ten percentage points, but in a general election, we would have expected them to win by fifteen points if they were to overtake the SNP.

The eventual winning margin of 31 points, with a 20.4-point swing from the SNP to Labour, dwarfed those expectations. The swing was the fourth largest of any Scottish parliamentary by-election since the Second World War, and Labour's majority of 9,446 votes was larger than the SNP's 8,399 total votes.

Rutherglen & Hamilton West immediately became part of the pantheon of iconic Scottish by-elections. The result not only confirmed polling that told us that the SNP might be in trouble, but it was the first indication that a freight train of deep unhappiness with government and hunger for change was hurtling towards them – and that they had no idea how to address that. Moreover, the result did what Labour had hoped, establishing a narrative that Labour could beat the Conservatives in England and Wales and the SNP in Scotland. Labour was, once again, a truly national party in the sense that it could win anywhere in Great Britain.

Scottish Labour went into the 2024 UK general election making the exact arguments they had first road-tested in Rutherglen & Hamilton West – that they were the answer to unpopular governments in both London and Edinburgh. The SNP were similarly incapable of countering them, recycling many of the same unsuccessful arguments they deployed in Rutherglen & Hamilton West.

Scottish Labour won 35.3 per cent of the vote and thirty-seven of Scotland's fifty-seven MPs, to the SNP's 30 per cent and nine MPs. The notional swing from the SNP to Labour was disproportionately high in central belt seats like Rutherglen & Hamilton West, peaking at 26.1 points in Alloa & Grangemouth.

The month after the by-election, I was asked to speak to SNP MPs and staffers at Westminster and was repeatedly told that their problem was turnout and that if they could find a workable independence message, they would get 'their' vote out. One MP told me that the SNP had had their worst year ever and that things would improve. I quipped that they had had their worst year *so far*, and they laughed and asked what I knew. I suppose I knew what everyone else in Scotland did – that the freight train was hurtling towards them, and they had no answer to it but to bury their heads in the sand.

Loudon and Shanks contested the new seat of Rutherglen at the

2024 UK general election, with Shanks winning with 21,460 votes (50.5 per cent) to Loudon's 12,693 votes (29.9 per cent), a notional swing since 2019 from the SNP to Labour of 16.3 points. In the aftermath of Labour's victory in that election, Shanks was appointed Parliamentary Under-Secretary of State for Energy.

In the short run, the Rutherglen & Hamilton West by-election proved a harbinger of a much broader resurgence for Labour in Scotland and established that Labour could beat the SNP in the central belt once again. It is a critical staging post in that story. However, its significance in the long term has yet to become apparent.

Scottish Labour hope that they can build on their achievements in the past couple of years to oust the SNP in the Scottish Parliament elections in 2026, but the reality is that Labour got off to a rocky start in power, and the SNP have a new, relatively popular leadership team in the form of John Swinney and his Deputy First Minister, Kate Forbes.

Post-election polling showed that Sir Keir Starmer experienced the fastest post-election collapse in Prime Ministerial approval and favourability ratings on record, except for the historical outlier of Liz Truss. Favourability towards Anas Sarwar and Scottish Labour also declined significantly, as did the proportions of Scots who felt a Labour-led Scottish government could do a better job than the SNP.

The Rutherglen & Hamilton West by-election's place in history is yet to be determined. It may prove the harbinger of a Labour resurgence in Scotland that stands the tests of the coming years, or it may merely be a reflection of the intense dissatisfaction with politics and politicians that ultimately fuels the kind of outsider politics the SNP best represent north of the border, a bump in the road to Scottish independence. We are cursed to live in interesting times, and I am infinitely interested in how this story ends.

Mark McGeoghegan *is a Glasgow University researcher of nationalism, secessionism and contentious politics, a columnist on Scottish politics for* The Herald *and an associate member of the Centre on Constitutional Change.*

86

MID BEDFORDSHIRE

19 OCTOBER 2023
LABOUR GAIN FROM CONSERVATIVES

HENRY RILEY

Result: Alistair Strathern (Labour), 13,872, 34.1 per cent; Festus Akinbusoye (Conservative), 12,680, 31.1 per cent; Emma Holland-Lindsay (Liberal Democrats), 9,420, 23.1 per cent; Gareth Mackey (Independent), 1,865, 4.6 per cent; Dave Holland (Reform UK), 1,487, 3.7 per cent; Cade Sibley (Green), 732, 1.8 per cent; Ann Kelly (Monster Raving Loony), 249, 0.6 per cent; Antonio Vitiello (English Democrat), 107, 0.3 per cent; Sid Cordle (CPA), 101, 0.2 per cent; Alan Victor (True and Fair), 93, 0.2 per cent; Alberto Thomas (Heritage), 63, 0.2 per cent; Prince Ankit Love, Emperor of India (No description), 27, 0.1 per cent; Chris Rooney (Mainstream), 24, 0.1 per cent
Size of majority: 1,192
Swing: 20.5 per cent from Conservative to Labour
Name of previous MP and party: Nadine Dorries (Conservative)
Reason for by-election: Resignation of incumbent
Result at previous general election: Nadine Dorries (Conservative), 38,692, 59.8 per cent; Rhiannon Meades (Labour), 14,028, 21.7 per cent; Rachel McGann (Liberal Democrats), 8,171, 12.6 per cent; Gareth Ellis (Green), 2,478, 3.8 per cent; Alan Victor (Independent), 812, 1.3 per cent; Ann Kelly (Monster Raving Loony), 536, 0.8 per cent
Date by-election called: 12 September 2023
Date by-election took place: 19 October 2023
Size of total electorate: 92,578
Total number of votes cast: 40,720
Turnout: 44.0 per cent

Mid Bedfordshire had never been a politically volatile seat. With consistently healthy Conservative majorities, the constituency had been Tory since the 1930s, until a drizzly Thursday night in October 2023 which concluded a bizarre, bitter and bad-tempered three-way election battle. A by-election described by a senior Labour MP as 'reminiscent of the campaign they [the Liberal Democrats] ran against Peter Tatchell in the 1980s'.

Located in one of the smallest counties in the UK, Mid Bedfordshire boasts outstanding countryside beauty and has — in its various guises — been represented by Whig, Liberal and Conservative MPs. From Lord Boyd, a leading advocate for decolonisation who served in the post-war Conservative Cabinet of Winston Churchill, to one of the longest-serving government law officers Lord (Nicholas) Lyell — indeed part of the constituency was at one point represented by Samuel Whitbread, who founded the brewery turned multinational company of the same name.

The county also played host to one of the most anticipated, protracted by-election contests in modern history.

The incumbent had announced that she would stand down with 'immediate effect' at 3.50 p.m. on Friday 9 June, yet the election for her successor occurred a staggering 132 days later. Why? Two words: Nadine Dorries.

First elected in the constituency in 2005, Nadine Dorries said in her maiden speech 'during my time as the MP for Mid-Bedfordshire, I will use the House to highlight the concerns of my constituents. I promise to do my best and base everything that I do on integrity.' But the MP had already attracted controversy, especially when she entered the Australian jungle for the 2012 series of *I'm A Celebrity… Get Me Out of Here!*

A former Cabinet minister at the Department of Culture, Media and Sport, Dorries was synonymous with the Boris Johnson administration; indeed her resignation post on Twitter was made just hours before the former Prime Minister announced he, too, would be immediately departing the House of Commons.

The slew of resignations (with former minister Nigel Adams following less than twenty-four hours later) occurred just over seven months into Rishi Sunak's administration, bequeathing yet more challenges for the then Prime Minister. Electoral tests at a time where the government was grappling with the fallout of the Liz Truss administration, sky-high interest rates and an impending 'Partygate' report left the Conservatives significantly trailing Labour in national opinion polls.

Just days later the mundane parliamentary procedures were enacted, the writ moved and two by-elections were declared – one in Johnson's seat of Uxbridge & South Ruislip and another in Adams's Selby & Ainsty constituency. Yet, curiously, no such contest materialised in Mid Bedfordshire.

Nonetheless, a by-election campaign began in earnest with Police and Crime Commissioner Festus Akinbusoye being selected as the Conservative candidate, former maths teacher turned Bank of England climate expert Alistair Strathern selected for Labour and the Liberal Democrats choosing local councillor and charity campaigner Emma Holland-Lindsay.

Reform UK, still relatively in its infancy, formed an electoral alliance with Laurence Fox's vaccine-sceptic Reclaim Party – who had recently welcomed expelled Conservative MP Andrew Bridgen to their ranks. Dave Holland would stand for Reform in Mid Bedfordshire, in exchange for Nigel Farage's party (then led by Richard Tice) standing aside for Laurence Fox in the Uxbridge by-election.

The Greens selected social care worker Cade Sibley, while three-time previous Mayor of Flitwick Gareth Mackey stood as an Independent.

Nadine Dorries had last spoken in Parliament some fourteen months before she formally decided to stand aside – the last time she uttered a single word in the House of Commons was while serving as Culture Secretary on 7 July 2022 – the same day as Boris Johnson resigned as Prime Minister from the steps of Downing Street.

An electorate eager to select their next representative, the candidates were raring to go, parties on an election footing and activists pounded the streets. Months passed, scrutiny intensified – but a by-election date did not come. Indeed, the Labour candidate Alistair Strathern found himself on the front page of *The Sun* in that time dressed as a zombie during a Greenpeace demonstration and was dubbed 'Keir's Eco Zealot'. Strathern later quipped that he would have put better makeup on, had he known the endeavour was to end up on the front page of a national newspaper.

In an unexpected move, Rishi Sunak even launched a blistering attack against Nadine Dorries, a former Cabinet colleague. He told LBC's Nick Ferrari that Mid Bedfordshire residents 'deserve to have an MP that represents them' and conceded that 'people aren't being properly represented'. A senior Tory source had started referring to Dorries to journalists as the 'Mid Beds blocker'. Indeed, local activists also tried to force the MP out, with both Flitwick and Shefford Town Councils writing an open letter calling for her to resign.

Posters were erected across the constituency, including a banner in the town of Flitwick which read 'Dosser Dorries Out' — I was even dispatched as an LBC reporter armed with 'wanted posters' to try to gauge the mood from her constituents.

Nadine Dorries claimed that she could not stand aside as she was conducting an investigation into the 'sinister forces' that blocked her from receiving a peerage as part of Boris Johnson's resignation honours list. She later criticised Rishi Sunak and his political secretary James Forsyth as 'posh boys', who 'duplicitously and cruelly' prevented her elevation to the House of Lords.

Eventually, however, more than two months after pledging to resign and saying it was 'time for another to take the reins', Nadine Dorries stood aside and issued a scathing attack on the Prime Minister. She accused him of 'demeaning his office' and trying to 'whip up a public frenzy' against her. The following month, the motion was moved in Parliament and a date for one of the most eagerly anticipated by-elections was decided: 19 October 2023.

Ordinarily, with a big majority and a relatively well-known candidate serving as the county's Police and Crime Commissioner, the contest should have been plain sailing for the governing party — yet with the media circus the race had attracted, it felt far from certain. Indeed, towering Conservative majorities had evaporated in the weeks previous — with the party losing a near 20,000 majority to the Liberal Democrats in Somerton & Frome, and Nigel Adams's seat of Selby & Ainsty going red against a similar Tory majority.

Nadine Dorries had an even larger majority of nearly 25,000, which meant Labour winning Mid Bedfordshire seemed like a tall order. The party had finished second to the Conservatives in the seat in the 2015, 2017 and 2019 elections. A distant second best, but nevertheless they saw themselves as the natural opponents. But there was one problem – the Liberal Democrats.

Early talk of a non-aggression pact, or informal agreement, was vastly overstated and could not have been further from reality. The astonishing aspect of the race for Mid Bedfordshire was how the election turned into a public, amplified Lib Dem vs Labour spat. Sir Ed Davey's party pounced on the fact that Labour's Alistair Strathern was an elected councillor forty-odd miles from the constituency in London's Waltham Forest, accusing the party of 'parachuting him in'.

The row first erupted after an internal email from the Liberal Democrats to activists. Referencing the Labour candidate, it read 'in a constituency with traditional values, selecting this particular candidate makes your job pretty much impossible'. Liberal Democrat MP Christine Jardine, who was leading the election for her party, claimed that the memo was 'not criticising him, it's criticising the Labour leadership', and accused Labour of attempting to 'make this by-election about an internal email'.

The Liberal Democrats consistently claimed in campaign leaflets that Labour 'couldn't win' in the seat – indeed Caron Lindsay, the editor of Liberal Democrat Voice, wrote a post just weeks before the result with the headline 'Peter Kyle knows fine Labour can't win in Mid Beds', saying it was based on 'solid evidence' and that 'Labour won't win but they probably won't lose their deposit and could stop us from winning'.

But the Lib Dem tactics led to an incandescent response from Peter Kyle, the Labour MP and then shadow Cabinet minister who led the local campaign for Labour. In an interview with *The News Agents* podcast, he described the Lib Dem campaign as 'deeply personal' and 'aimed at the candidate', likening what he had witnessed as being 'reminiscent of the campaign they [the Lib Dems] ran against Peter Tatchell in the 1980s' (a campaign which Tatchell described as the 'most homophobic UK election ever').

Kyle asserted that his liberal opponents were 'so desperate to make an impact in Mid Bedfordshire that if our candidate was gay, they would be doing a family values campaign'. It was also reported that Labour had sent a 'cease and desist' demanding Lib Dem leaflets were destroyed and accusing their political rivals of going 'feral' and 'misleading' voters.

The mud-slinging between the two opposition parties did give Conservative Festus Akinbusoye a possible route to victory. His campaign was run by former Conservative Party chairman Dame Amanda Milling and sought to focus on law and order given his elected role. Indeed, he faced calls to stand down from his post from the Bedfordshire Police and Crime Panel citing concern that the campaign would affect his commitment to the role.

Conservative activists were extremely concerned, yet unsurprised, at how often Nadine Dorries's name came up on the doorstep. One Conservative canvasser told me: 'It's Dorries wot lost it,' alleging that their candidate was routinely lambasted for the actions, or lack thereof, of his predecessor.

Despite arguably suffering from 'long Dorries', there were other key themes of the campaign — agreed by canvassers I spoke with from all political persuasions. These boiled down to affordable housing provision and the availability of healthcare.

One key issue was a long-running campaign for a new GP surgery in the town of Wixams — a new town which started being built in 2007 and is due to have over 20,000 people, and yet to date has no GP surgery.

On housing, Mid Bedfordshire had also seen population growth in the constituency above the national average, leading to calls for more houses but familiar debates about where to build them.

Each party felt they had a chance of winning during the campaign and sent heavy hitters. Lib Dem leader Ed Davey stood with his wellies in the River Flit talking about sewage, Rishi Sunak visited the prestigious Cranfield University, Conservative Cabinet ministers Dame Priti Patel, Kemi Badenoch and James Cleverly all travelled up the M1 to lend a hand, while Sir Keir Starmer and Angela Rayner were joined by a steady stream of Labour shadow Cabinet ministers to pound the streets.

I covered the by-election 'count' and 'declaration' on the night for LBC. To say it was tense at Central Bedfordshire Council's office would be a vast understatement. Labour activists ignoring Liberal Democrat members; Conservative campaigners isolated and resigned to a difficult night but praying a split opposition vote might be enough. The only brief moment of levity was when veteran by-election reporter-in-chief Jon Craig of Sky News was presented with a cake by the High Sheriff of Bedfordshire, Russell Beard, to celebrate his fortieth by-election.

Also noteworthy was Ann Kelly, a former Mayor of Flitwick and the only candidate to have fought the seat previously – this was her fourth occasion standing for the Official Monster Raving Loony Party, on a platform which included auctioning out honours, including peerages and knighthoods.

In the early hours of Friday 20 October came a not unexpected but nonetheless remarkable result for Labour. After the votes had been counted from across the forty-eight towns and villages of Mid Bedfordshire, Alistair Strathern was elected as the first and, to date, only Labour MP for the area. A 20.5-point swing was enough to put it in the top ten of by-election swings from Conservative to Labour in history. Against a tough backdrop of an acrimonious relationship with the local Lib Dems, Labour squeaked home with a majority of 1,192 and twelve other candidates vying for the seat.

The election saw the largest numeric Tory majority ever overturned by Labour at a by-election since 1945, and later that morning the Labour leader headed to the countryside to visit the Forest of Marston Vale in Bedford to bask in the glory of a resounding victory. Speaking with a picturesque backdrop, Sir Keir Starmer hailed the victory as 'incredible', boasting that a 'fantastic candidate' had 'made history in a three-way fight'. Sir Keir proudly exclaimed that 'voters here have turned their back on a failed Tory government and are crying out for change'.

His sentiment was echoed by the sleep-deprived by-election victor Alistair Strathern, who had swapped his formal suit from a few hours previous and was now donning a more casual Labour-red cardigan. He praised his party leader for 'taking this seriously from day one' and boasted that there were no longer any 'no-go areas' electorally for Labour.

In his maiden speech just weeks later, Strathern referenced the bad blood with the Lib Dems. He told the House of Commons that 'there are perhaps one or two memories of slightly scarring use of statistics in leaflets, but the maths teacher in me hopes that I will be able to forget those'. He also quipped to Rishi Sunak that he would continue Nadine Dorries's 'proud tradition of robust opposition to this government' – a remark which even tickled the then Prime Minister.

But Strathern's time as Mid Bedfordshire's first Labour MP was short. The seat was taken back by the Conservatives with a wafer-thin majority of 1,321 less than nine months later at the 2024 general election, though Alistair Strathern remained in the House of Commons representing a different seat.

The fresh-faced MP decided to stand in the neighbouring constituency of Hitchin. Boundary changes meant his home in Shefford was now in that constituency rather than Mid Bedfordshire – plus the seat seemed a much safer endeavour for his party. He defeated Conservative Treasury Minister Bim Afolami with a majority of more than 8,000 votes.

Festus Akinbusoye, on the other hand, tried and failed to be readopted as the Conservative candidate for Mid Bedfordshire at the 2024 general election. He would also lose his position to Labour that same year as Bedfordshire's Police and Crime Commissioner.

The Mid Bedfordshire result undoubtedly soured relations between the Liberal Democrats and Labour. On election night, the Lib Dems were claiming that they had helped Labour win by taking votes from the Conservatives.

Surprisingly, however, the war of words continued after the result. Speaking a day later, Labour's Peter Kyle continued to air his frustration. Despite his party's success, he accused the Liberal Democrats of 'dumb politics' and said he was 'wondering what the hell the purpose of the Lib Dems is now'. His comments were met with an official Lib Dem response of 'Peter, go and have a long hot bath, an early night, and then hopefully you can enjoy your result'.

Despite a somewhat fraught, prolonged campaign – just a week after the result – there was a moment of light relief. A chance meeting in Parliament where the new MP Alistair Strathern and his Conservative opponent Festus Akinbusoye bumped into each other and shared a warm embrace.

Henry Riley *is a reporter and presenter at LBC. In his work as a reporter, he often focuses on politics and has been sent to various by-election counts, including the 2023 Mid Bedfordshire contest.*

87

ROCHDALE

29 FEBRUARY 2024
WORKERS GAIN FROM LABOUR

SUNDER KATWALA

Result: George Galloway (Workers), 12,335, 39.7 per cent; David Tully (Independent), 6,638, 21.3 per cent; Paul Ellison (Conservative), 3,731, 12.0 per cent; Azhar Ali (Labour), 2,402, 7.7 per cent; Iain Donaldson (Liberal Democrats), 2,164, 7.0 per cent; Simon Danczuk (Reform UK), 1,968, 6.3 per cent; William Howarth (Independent), 523, 1.7 per cent; Mark Coleman (Independent), 455, 1.5 per cent; Guy Otten (Green), 436, 1.4 per cent; Michael Howarth (Independent), 246, 0.8 per cent; Ravin Rodent Subortna (Monster Raving Loony), 209, 0.7 per cent
Size of majority: 5,697
Swing: 41.8 per cent from Labour to Workers
Name of previous MP and party: Tony Lloyd (Labour)
Reason for by-election: Death of incumbent
Result at previous general election: Tony Lloyd (Labour), 24,475, 51.6 per cent; Atifa Shah (Conservative), 14,807, 31.2 per cent; Chris Green (Brexit), 3,867, 8.2 per cent; Andy Kelly (Liberal Democrats), 3,312, 7.0 per cent; Sarah Croke (Green), 986, 2.1 per cent
Date by-election called: 29 January 2024
Date by-election took place: 29 February 2024
Size of total electorate: Approx. 78,350
Total number of votes cast: 31,107
Turnout: 39.7 per cent

George Galloway declared that his victory in the Rochdale by-election on the leap year day of 29 February 2024 would produce a 'tornado to tear through British, Israeli and global politics'. The Lancashire town's votes lacked that geopolitical impact, but it was a dramatic, record-breaking by-election in British electoral history.

The fall in the Labour vote from 51.6 per cent to 7.7 per cent was Labour's largest ever collapse in vote share – and the biggest drop for any incumbent party in any Westminster constituency contest since universal suffrage, albeit in a context where the party had suspended its candidate.

Galloway was the first MP elected to represent a fourth different Westminster constituency since Winston Churchill. He became the only MP since party politics began to win in three different constituencies from outside the governing or official opposition party. That hat-trick of electoral upsets gives Galloway a fair claim to have been the most recurringly successful populist underdog in our political history – though Rochdale soon became the third constituency in a row not to re-elect him.

So while Prime Minister Rishi Sunak declared the result 'beyond shocking', George Galloway's prize for his Rochdale victory proved much more ephemeral than the electoral tsunami he prophesied. He had just 150 days representing Rochdale as the town's MP before losing the seat in the July 2024 general election to Labour candidate Paul Waugh.

Would Rochdale be remembered as a by-election that shook politics – or rather more of a footnote, as the final by-election of the 2019–24 parliament? It may yet depend on what happens next. The by-election illuminated fissures and cracks in the electoral demographics of an increasingly diverse Britain, which formed a significant sub-plot of the 2024 general election. They may reverberate more in the by-elections and general elections to come in the second half of this decade.

Labour intended the Rochdale by-election of 2024 to be a rapid and routine contest that nobody would have reason to remember.

Veteran MP Tony Lloyd had represented Rochdale since 2017, his final act in over thirty years in elected politics as an MP and Police and Crime Commissioner. Lloyd had been undergoing cancer treatment for a year, making a public announcement that he had incurable leukaemia and was leaving hospital to spend his remaining time with his family, the week before his death in January 2024.

Labour moved the by-election writ before the funeral of the late MP, with his family's consent. The party had selected its by-election candidate Azhar Ali, a Lancashire county councillor, just eleven days after Lloyd's death. Yet Ali had already been suspended by Labour by the time mourners gathered for Lloyd's requiem mass and funeral on 16 February, leaving Labour's by-election campaign in tatters.

Incumbent parties often hold by-elections with haste to minimise the opportunity for rivals to organise. A more specific motive for haste in Rochdale was to contain the potential electoral fallout of the Middle Eastern conflict. Yet this was to prove the cause of Ali's downfall too.

After the Hamas terrorist attack of 7 October 2023 and Israel's military response in Gaza, Labour leader Keir Starmer had come under more political pressure than Prime Minister Rishi Sunak. Fifty-six Labour MPs had voted for a ceasefire motion, with eight resigning from the front bench to do so.

Ali had been recorded voicing the conspiracy theory that Israel had deliberately allowed Hamas to attack on 7 October as a pretext to retaliate. 'They deliberately took the security off, they allowed ... that massacre that gives them the green light to do whatever they bloody want,' Ali had said. He described his own comments as 'deeply offensive, ignorant, and false' once these appeared in the press.

Labour wavered for a couple of days before deciding to suspend Ali. The leadership of the Jewish Labour Movement expressed surprise at these revelations about a man with a track record as an ally who had opposed antisemitism in the party. Some wondered if supporting a contrite candidate could be the 'lesser evil' if the alternative was to risk a George Galloway victory. Some circumstantial evidence suggests that the veteran Lancashire councillor may have voiced this antisemitic conspiracy theory without believing it himself – with the motive of hoping it might help him connect with disaffected councillors who he sought to dissuade from leaving the party. Yet, if that is what happened, such a cynical deployment and reinforcement of conspiratorial prejudice could be as or more corrosive as a sincere belief in that narrative.

Ultimately, the Labour leadership could not surmount the difficulty of calling Ali's comments 'inexcusable' while asking Rochdale's voters to excuse them sufficiently to send him to Parliament as their MP. Keir

Starmer had given a high priority to a message of zero tolerance for antisemitism – after the Corbyn-era party had been found in breach of its legal obligations by the Equalities and Human Rights Commission. Keeping Ali as a candidate would have given Labour's opponents ammunition to argue that the pledge had been sacrificed to political expediency – putting Starmer's broader claim to have changed the Labour Party in doubt.

So Labour withdrew from the by-election. With a general election due before the end of the year, the risk of facilitating a Galloway victory was ultimately the 'lesser evil'.

Palestine was an issue of particular – but not exclusive – concern to Muslim voters. Most media coverage of the Rochdale by-election focused on the battle for local Muslim voters. Around 30 per cent of those eligible to vote were Muslim – so Rochdale ranks twenty-second on the list of the fifty Westminster constituencies where Muslim voters make up over a fifth of the electorate. The 48,000 votes cast in the constituency in the 2019 general election would have included approximately 14,000 Muslim voters alongside over 30,000 who were white British.

Yet however strongly such a significant minority group coalesced around one voter or candidate, Rochdale was unlikely to be a constituency which could be won – in theory or practice – by minority votes. One significant difference between House of Commons constituencies compared to US congressional constituencies is that there are many fewer British parliamentary constituencies which can be won with the votes of a minority community. There are just three Westminster constituencies where Muslim voters make up a majority of the electorate. This is also a difference, in British politics, between local council wards – where there are several hundred with a majority-minority group – and parliamentary elections.

Nor are Muslim voters a monolithic bloc. National polling found that Palestine was a top issue for a quarter of Muslim voters – compared to 2 or 3 per cent of the general public – but behind the NHS and the cost of living.

George Galloway directed much of his campaign at Muslim voters. His open letter to 'voters of the Muslim faith' in Rochdale stated that

'I, George Galloway, have fought for Muslims at home and abroad all of my life and I have paid a heavy price for it'.

The letter declared that 'the political class have failed Rochdale, failed Britain and failed Gaza' with a central emphasis on what Galloway called 'Labour's support for Israel's genocide in Gaza'. 'If Labour lose this by-election, Sir Keir Starmer — a top supporter of Israel — could well be forced out as Labour leader' was Galloway's pitch for the impact the by-election might have.

Galloway's response to the cross-community challenge was to run two parallel campaigns — adapting Donald Trump's slogan to Lancashire with his 'Make Rochdale Great Again' pitch when appealing to voters outside Rochdale's Muslim communities. This Galloway campaign emphasised the closure of the maternity ward at Rochdale infirmary and protecting the open-air market and local football club. A shared theme of these parallel campaigns was Galloway's social conservatism — telling voters that he 'knew what a woman was' and arguing against treating homosexuality as a norm in education. On asylum and Channel crossings, Galloway used language about an invasion by 'men of fighting age' more associated with the populist right.

The Workers Party rejected charges that this segmented targeting was divisive or sectarian. 'Our election slogan is "For Gaza. For Rochdale." It is that message which resonates across Rochdale: young and old, white and black,' his campaign team told the media.

Galloway's political opponents were keen to highlight the endorsement of his campaign by former BNP leader Nick Griffin, which Galloway called 'unwelcome'.

The bookmaker Ladbrokes initially quoted odds for a Labour victory of one to thirty-three on — an implied probability of around 97 per cent — as the campaign began, prior to Ali's suspension. A secondary market for second place initially envisaged a close contest between George Galloway and the Conservative Party.

With the Labour suspension taking place after nominations closed, it was unclear what proportion of the electorate would hear about it — and which candidates would now challenge for the seat.

Eleven candidates stood in the by-election — with, unusually, an all-male line-up.

Rochdale had a chequered political history – in its party affiliations and in the conduct of some of its representatives. Liberal MP Cyril Smith had represented the town for two decades from 1972 to 1992. After his death in 2010, warm obituary tributes to him as a larger-than-life figure soon gave way to evidence that he had been a serial paedophile and child sex abuser. Smith's notorious history still casts some shadow over modern Liberal Democrat prospects in the town. The party had won the seat again in 2005 – before losing it in the national post-coalition collapse of 2015. The MP Paul Rowen, who had been the local council leader, was among those criticised by the inquiry into Smith's historic abuse – for taking insufficient action to pursue historic allegations while Smith was alive.

Reform chose the town's former MP Simon Danczuk – elected for Labour in 2010 and 2015. Yet Danczuk had been suspended by Labour over inappropriate sexual texts to a teenager and lost his deposit with just 1.8 per cent of the vote as the incumbent MP, standing as an Independent, in 2017. Reform responded to Labour's withdrawal with leaflets declaring the by-election to now be a 'two-horse race' between their candidate and George Galloway – but Reform was to finish in sixth place.

The Greens had formally withdrawn support from their candidate over past social media posts that he had described as 'regrettable' expressing prejudiced views about Muslims.

Conservative Paul Ellison was known and respected locally for championing the Rochdale in Bloom horticultural displays, for which he had been awarded an OBE, but faced the handicap of representing an unpopular governing party.

Independent candidate David Tully's campaign resonated with voters keen to see more priority given to Rochdale's local issues in the by-election. Focus groups conducted by More in Common found that this theme was voiced by both white British and British Asian residents.

George Galloway won the by-election with 39.7 per cent of the vote and a majority of over 5,000. Galloway's 12,335 votes outnumbered the combined total for the national parties – with Labour, the Conservatives, the Liberal Democrats and Reform winning only just over 10,000 votes between them.

Independent candidate David Tully finished second with an impressive 6,638 votes, almost double the vote of the Conservatives in third. The short campaign curtailed Tully's effort to convey to voters how he was emerging as a popular choice among those hoping to coalesce around an alternative to George Galloway.

Reform finished sixth on just 6.3 per cent, behind Labour's suspended candidate and the Liberal Democrats. This was the only one of the quartet of 2024 by-elections when Reform did not reach double digits. That Reform won 17 per cent of the vote in Rochdale, finishing third, four months later in the general election shows that running a former MP with a history of personal scandal damaged Reform's local credibility rather than bolstering it.

Reform leader Richard Tice and Nigel Farage claimed the election had not been 'free or fair' – complaining about both candidate intimidation and alleging corrupt practices with postal votes. 'There is no doubt that Galloway won on the postal vote. We need to know: What methods were used to collect them?' said Farage.

Tice claimed on election night that 23,000 postal votes had been cast and said the party was considering an official complaint. Yet that was based on rumour and misunderstandings. Council data showed that 13,000 of the 21,000 people who had registered for a postal vote did cast their vote – and another 18,000 people voted on the day. It had been Labour which tried to encourage postal vote registrations, anticipating the by-election. Galloway simply began his campaign too late to have a significant opportunity. Reform's inaccurate claims went beyond the legitimate scrutiny of election integrity to promote tropes and stereotypes about ethnic minority and Muslim voters.

Winning 39.7 per cent of the vote on a 39.7 per cent turnout meant that around one in six of Galloway's 80,000 new Rochdale constituents voted to send him to Westminster.

A national YouGov poll immediately after the result found that 11 per cent of the public held a favourable view of George Galloway and 46 per cent an unfavourable one, with 28 per cent very unfavourable. In Rochdale, 16 per cent of those on the electoral register had voted for Galloway – while 24 per cent had split their votes between the other ten candidates and 60 per cent had not voted in the by-election.

There were no constituency polls with detailed demographic breakdowns of the vote. Politics-watchers across the local parties concurred that Galloway's pitch had secured him a clear majority of the 10,000 or so Muslim votes cast in the by-election. His vote share would be consistent with a winning electoral coalition combining over two-thirds of the votes cast by Muslim voters in the by-election with a significant minority share of a fifth to a quarter of non-Muslim voters. Those supporters included those who also agreed with Galloway on foreign policy, others responding to his 'Rochdale First' pitch and others again casting a protest vote for a candidate able to bring attention to the town.

'This is going to spark a movement, a landslide, a shifting of the tectonic plates in scores of parliamentary constituencies,' George Galloway declared in his victory speech. Galloway's by-election victory dominated a political news cycle but did not endure beyond that.

Prime Minister Rishi Sunak declared it 'beyond alarming' that the Rochdale by-election had returned Galloway, arguing 'he dismisses the horror of what happened on 7 October, who glorifies Hezbollah and is endorsed by Nick Griffin, the racist former leader of the BNP'. 'There are forces here at home trying to tear us apart,' Sunak claimed. The Board of Deputies of British Jews, labelling Galloway as a conspiracy theorist, called his victory as 'a dark day for the Jewish community in this country and for British politics in general'.

Galloway said that he would use his new platform as an MP to create a 'Grand Alliance' to remove Labour from controlling Rochdale Council. It proved a damp squib. Galloway's invitation to local independent David Tully was rejected. The Workers Party gained two of the twenty seats up for election in May 2024. Labour held fourteen of the fifteen council seats it was defending, maintaining a dominant position on the council with forty-four of the sixty seats.

Labour won Rochdale back in the 2024 general election, with former journalist Paul Waugh winning 33 per cent of the vote to Galloway's 29 per cent – a narrow majority of 1,440 votes, in the different context of a general election, where voters were thinking too about the choice of governments and Prime Ministers.

Had Galloway simply been an accidental MP – the lucky beneficiary of the Labour shambles – or could he have sprung a by-election shock in an election which Labour had campaigned and contested? The narrow general election defeat suggests he would have been competitive in a contested by-election.

Galloway's Workers Party stood 152 candidates in the general election, but 123 lost their deposits. The party came second in three constituencies – including Rochdale and two in Birmingham – but Galloway said they had been underprepared for a summer rather than autumn election, when they may have fielded 500 candidates, he claimed. Galloway's party, overall, underperformed other independent candidates running on a pro-Gaza ticket – four of whom won surprise election victories in Labour-held seats, including in Blackburn, Birmingham Perry Barr, Leicester South and Dewsbury & Batley.

The 2024 general election was the first when a majority of British Asian voters did not vote Labour – losing many Muslim voters to Independents and Greens on the left, and Indian Hindu voters to the right. Yet winning Rochdale back meant that Labour did hold on to forty-six of the fifty constituencies with the most Muslim voters – despite losing up to a third of the party's Muslim voters – giving Labour MPs an opportunity to rebuild links.

Winning a fourth Westminster constituency in Rochdale put George Galloway in elevated company. Only Winston Churchill, Ramsay MacDonald and Arthur Henderson – two Prime Ministers and an opposition leader – achieved that in the twentieth century. Yet Rochdale has now joined Bethnal Green in 2005 and Bradford West in 2012 as places where voters gave Galloway a shock victory – but were not ready to vote for him twice.

George Galloway, at seventy, has said that he may not stand at the next general election. Another by-election may bring him back to the fray. But if Rochdale does prove his political swansong, it will demonstrate that Galloway was a populist left-wing underdog, able to generate electoral tremors without quite being able to convert them into a political earthquake.

Sunder Katwala *is the director of British Future and author of* How to Be a Patriot *(HarperNorth, 2023).*

88

RUNCORN & HELSBY

1 MAY 2025
REFORM GAIN

HARRY HORTON

Result: Sarah Pochin (Reform UK), 12,645, 38.72 per cent; Karen Shore (Labour), 12,639, 38.70 per cent; Sean Houlston (Conservative), 2,341, 7.17 per cent; Chris Copeman (Green), 2,314, 7.09 per cent; Paul Duffy (Liberal Democrats), 942, 2.88 per cent; Dan Clarke (Liberal), 454, 1.39 per cent; Michael Williams (Independent), 363, 1.11 per cent; Alan McKie (Independent), 269, 0.82 per cent; Peter Ford (Workers), 164, 0.50 per cent; John Stevens (Rejoin EU), 129, 0.40 per cent; Howling Laud Hope (Monster Raving Loony), 128, 0.39 per cent; Catherine Blaiklock (English Democrat), 95, 0.29 per cent; Paul Andrew Murphy (SDP), 68, 0.21 per cent; Jason Philip Hughes (Volt UK), 54, 0.17; Graham Harry Moore (English Constitution), 50, 0.15 per cent
Size of majority: 6
Swing: 17.4 per cent from Labour to Reform UK
Name of previous MP and party: Mike Amesbury (Labour)
Reason for by-election: Resignation following conviction for assaulting a constituent
Result at previous general election: Mike Amesbury (Labour), 22,358, 52.94 per cent; Jason Moorcroft (Reform UK), 7,662, 18.14 per cent; Jade Marsden (Conservative), 6,756, 16.00 per cent; Chris Copeman (Green), 2,715, 6.43 per cent; Chris Rowe (Liberal Democrats), 2,149, 5.09 per cent; Danny Clarke (Liberal), 479, 1.13 per cent; Paul Murphy (SDP), 116, 0.27 per cent
Date by-election called: 17 March 2025
Date by-election took place: 1 May 2025

Size of total electorate: 70,666
Total number of votes cast: 32,655
Turnout: 46.21 per cent

It started with a punch – and ended with the closest by-election result in modern history.

'You won't threaten your MP again, will you?' shouted Mike Amesbury just after 2 a.m. on 26 October 2024. The Labour MP for Runcorn & Helsby was yelling at a constituent who he'd just knocked to the ground on the high street of the Cheshire market town of Frodsham.

Lying on the floor was 45-year-old Paul Fellows, a local quantity surveyor. After being floored by Amesbury's left hook, he was punched at least four more times. Three people had to pull Amesbury away.

The MP had been drinking at three pubs on an empty stomach. Fellows had confronted him about 'a local bridge', recalled Amesbury.

'I did feel personally threatened at that time and I made an instantaneous judgement call which was wrong,' he told ITV's *Good Morning Britain*.

Only months earlier Amesbury had been re-elected for the second time with an increased majority as part of Labour's 2024 landslide. The 55-year-old, born in Cheshire, was popular locally and with his fellow Labour MPs in Westminster. He'd worked for both Angela Rayner and Andy Burnham and had served on Manchester City Council.

But his long political career was about to come to a sudden end – as an insurgent Reform UK party sprang into action.

Within hours of the drunken assault, footage appeared on social media of Amesbury pushing and punching his constituent. By the afternoon, he had reported himself to police. By the end of the weekend, Labour had suspended the whip. And within a few days, the party began preparing for what it felt was an inevitable by-election – the first under the new Labour government.

Mike Amesbury pleaded guilty to assault when he appeared at Chester Magistrates' Court in February. He was sentenced to ten weeks in prison but was released early after an appeal. The judge described Amesbury's behaviour as 'simply disgraceful'. He challenged the notion Amesbury had felt threatened before the assault and said the MP had told police a 'pack of lies'.

On 17 March, Mike Amesbury resigned as an MP. He had spent three nights in prison and admitted in a letter to the Chancellor, Rachel Reeves, that he 'should have walked away' from the punch confrontation that sent him there. The long-awaited by-election campaign was now officially underway.

But Reform UK's campaign was already up and running – and had been ever since the end of October. Activists had begun collecting constituents' data in the form of a petition calling on Mike Amesbury to resign. Ad vans had been driving round the area carrying Reform's national campaign messaging around stopping illegal immigration. And Reform had a strong presence in local Facebook groups – even managing to take control of some. Labour's campaign was almost non-existent. The party had to catch up – and fast.

Runcorn & Helsby, a constituency redrawn in 2023, covers two council areas: Cheshire West & Chester Council and Halton Borough Council. The two authorities quickly agreed the by-election would take place on 1 May, the same day as local elections in England.

The constituency sits just south of the Mersey estuary and is split between the commuter town of Runcorn and the more rural market town of Frodsham as well as many smaller Cheshire villages including Helsby.

The town of Runcorn, like many others in northern England, had suffered the effects of de-industrialisation. British chemical giant Imperial Chemical Industries (ICI) had been one of the town's main employers for much of the twentieth century. In the '60s, Labour's Harold Wilson government designated Runcorn a 'new town', more than doubling its population. It brought new housing estates and a new town centre with a brutalist, American-style shopping mall at its heart, unimaginatively named 'Shopping City'.

But by the turn of the millennium, many of ICI's operations had begun to wind down and Runcorn's manufacturing industry was on its knees. After the 2008 financial crash, Shopping City saw an exodus of retailers, leaving many of its outlets empty. Young people left to find jobs and entertainment in the nearby cities of Liverpool and Manchester. Cuts to public services left much of Runcorn's new town looking tired, shabby and unloved.

Just a ten-minute drive away, the small market town of Frodsham and surrounding villages could not feel more different. This is where the *James Bond* actor Daniel Craig spent much of his youth and where Take That's lead singer Gary Barlow was born and raised. The hearty pub lunch menus, weekly high-street market stalls and well-attended church services ooze Cheshire wealth.

When the by-election was called in March 2025, Reform UK was leading national opinion polls. Nigel Farage's latest political party had secured more than 4 million votes at the 2024 general election, finishing in third place on that metric. But it had gained only five MPs – and one, Rupert Lowe, had quit the party in a predictable falling out with Farage. Reform had proven its support was real – but it was still building the political operation and ground game to turn that support into winning elections.

Reform's Runcorn & Helsby candidate had barely campaigned in the 2024 general election but managed to finish in second place, beating the Conservatives but lagging more than 14,000 votes behind Labour. Nigel Farage sensed an opportunity at the by-election and threw everything at it.

For Farage, it was win-win. The Conservatives were still licking their wounds after an electoral drubbing and fourteen bruising years in government. The Liberal Democrats and Green Party didn't have the resources to mount a serious campaign. If Reform could close the gap with Labour and test out its new ground campaign in a safe Labour seat, it would keep up the party's momentum. If Reform could actually win the seat, it would prove that Nigel Farage's movement was a threat not just in Conservative territories – but in Labour heartlands too.

The Labour Party was less than a year into government. It had been a rocky start. Just weeks into power, the Chancellor, Rachel Reeves, had decided to cut winter fuel payments for all but the poorest pensioners. It had proven deeply unpopular and quickly became the number one topic brought up with Labour MPs by their constituents.

Illegal immigration – which saw thousands of people arriving across the English Channel on small boats – was an issue that the previous Prime Minister, Rishi Sunak, had tried and failed to control. His successor, Keir Starmer, had promised to 'smash the criminal gangs' running the people-smuggling industry, but his plans had so far had no impact on reducing the crossings.

There were other difficulties too: ministers accepting freebie tickets, controversial welfare reforms, pressure to hold a national inquiry into grooming gangs. All of it used by voters to berate Labour during the campaign.

Labour selected its candidate before Mike Amesbury officially resigned as an MP. Karen Shore was a former teacher and local councillor, serving as deputy leader of Cheshire West & Chester Council. She was seen as someone with strong local links and a track record of delivery. Shore was calm and quiet – but Labour's team felt she came across as human and empathetic and would win people over on the doorstep.

Reform picked a former Conservative councillor, Sarah Pochin. She had served on Cheshire East Council for eight years until 2023 – and even served as mayor. She was the Conservative candidate for Bolton South East in the 2017 general election, finishing in second place behind Labour. She'd also worked in the chemicals industry and served as a magistrate. Pochin was a shire Tory from leafy Cheshire turned anti-establishment Reform firebrand. 'We're looking to send a shockwave through Westminster,' she declared.

Nigel Farage hailed his new candidate as someone with political and business experience. But she also helped address a growing criticism that his Reform UK Party was a boys' club. The overwhelming majority of Reform's staff were young men and all its four MPs were men. If elected, Farage hoped that Sarah Pochin could blunt those attacks and help soften Reform's image.

The Conservatives, who had for decades been Labour's challengers in the area, ran a skeleton campaign. Their candidate, Sean Houlston, was realistic about his chances of winning. 'I think we're going to do OK,' was the best he could muster to reporters.

Reform centred its campaign on the issue of illegal immigration, hoping to appeal to working-class voters who felt let down by the new government. Early on in the by-election, a national newspaper had highlighted the Labour candidate Karen Shore's past remarks about her council 'warmly welcoming' asylum seekers. Reform seized on the comments. 'Labour's candidate welcomes the boats,' claimed one Reform flyer with a picture of young men crowded on a dinghy.

A local hotel used to house asylum seekers quickly became a flashpoint. The Daresbury Park was once a plush hotel, spa and wedding venue – but had been closed for years and for many was a symbol of decline in the area.

The Labour campaign didn't want to be caught on the back foot and knew it had to respond. Within days, Karen Shore posted a statement saying: 'I'll campaign to close the local asylum hotel.' Some on the left of the Labour Party branded it 'callous and indefensible' and local trade unions used it as an excuse to boycott the campaign. But in truth, Labour's 2024 election manifesto had proposed closing all asylum hotels and Shore's statement helped neutralise Reform's attacks. For the rest of the campaign, Reform switched their anti-immigration messaging to be about Turkish barbers and overcrowded housing.

Nigel Farage visited the seat three times during the campaign and spent all of election day in the constituency. His face was plastered all over Reform's election literature and its campaign office. He was the face of the campaign, with the candidate Sarah Pochin often appearing behind him. The Prime Minister, Keir Starmer, did not visit once and his name was barely visible on Labour leaflets.

Dozens of Labour Cabinet ministers were dispatched to help. Wes Streeting, the Health Secretary, was sent to hammer home a claim that Reform wanted to privatise the NHS. Labour strategists knew that Nigel Farage was a great recruiter – but also a hugely polarising figure. A huge part of Labour's campaign was trying to tap into this, with canvassers sent out to find and win over anti-Farage voters. But traditional Labour voters – underwhelmed at the new government's first nine months in power – felt depressed, demotivated and even angry.

When Northern Ireland Secretary Hilary Benn came to knock doors with Shore, ITV's cameras were invited along to film. These scenes are usually heavily choreographed by the party and only the houses with the most reliable voters are knocked on. But on this occasion, one voter hadn't read the script. Karen Shore had barely found time to introduce herself when the Runcorn resident unleashed a barrage of criticism of the Labour government and Prime Minister. 'I can't stand the man, I wouldn't vote for the man. I'm going Green. Bye bye!' She slammed the door in the Labour candidate's face. It was an embarrassing but telling sign of how unpopular the Labour Party was. And it was now playing out on national TV and being shared across social media.

The bookies expected Labour to lose and Reform to win. But as the campaign progressed, Labour MPs, staff and activists felt they were closing the gap. A poor performance by Sarah Pochin in a BBC TV hustings boosted Labour morale. Reform's campaign was nervous. The party knew it was close to victory but couldn't match Labour's vastly more experienced campaign machine. In the days before the vote, Reform's script was all about managing expectations.

Election day was sunny and warm. Turnout was – for a modern by-election – relatively high. Labour's get-the-vote-out operation was in full flow, with hundreds of activists knocking on doors across the constituency. Reform's campaign was stretched – the party was also hoping to win hundreds of council seats and mayoral authorities in elections on the same day – but most senior staff were dispatched to Runcorn.

With voting over, Nigel Farage and Sarah Pochin were stationed at a house a short drive from the count, while Zia Yusuf, Reform's chair, and other campaign staff watched the ballots pile up in person.

As the night turned to morning, Labour staff looked more and more anxious. Reform's team appeared nervous. At one point, a Reform aide instructed photographers to assemble at the door for the arrival of Nigel Farage. One broadcaster claimed he'd seen the Reform's leader circling the car park outside but had driven off when it appeared Labour might sneak a win. Farage later denied anything of the sort had ever happened.

Just before 4 a.m., all fifteen candidates were summoned by the returning officer. Disputed ballot papers were argued over. 'I've never seen so many drawn penises,' quipped one Labour official. With all the votes counted, Reform was ahead by four votes. The candidates were stunned. Zia Yusuf told reporters his party had won but Labour wouldn't accept the result. Labour demanded a recount – desperate to find a handful of votes that could overturn the result.

An hour and a half later, the recount was complete and Reform had increased their lead to six votes. Labour's exhausted campaign team formed a huddle and phoned party leaders in London. It was almost 6 a.m. The spring sunshine had appeared outside. The returning officer was about to order the hundreds of council staff, journalists and politicians to go home for a few hours of rest before resuming the count later that day. At the last second, Labour concluded there was no viable path to victory and conceded the by-election.

After almost twenty-four hours of campaigning and waiting, Sarah Pochin had gone to sleep. She was awoken by a Reform aide who told her she had won the by-election and that a car was waiting outside to take her and Nigel Farage to the count.

As the result was officially announced, a grinning Nigel Farage held up six fingers in celebration of the closest by-election victory in modern times. It was a stunning result. The months of preparation for the by-election, the visits to Runcorn, the all-day effort to get people to vote had all paid off. Reform had its first female Member of Parliament.

The win was huge for Farage and his party. It proved that Reform's lead in the national opinion polls should be taken seriously. And it showed Reform was ready to take on Labour.

'The narrative around everything I've ever done in politics is that somehow I'm sort of a splinter of a fringe off the Conservative Party,' said Nigel Farage to a huge huddle of journalists. 'That's been disproved tonight in a very, very big way.'

A few hours later on Frodsham high street, just across the road from where Mike Amesbury had assaulted a constituent six months earlier, an elderly man was cheering Reform's victory.

'I'm a pensioner. I've lost two hundred pounds of winter fuel allowance, and I see these people come across the Channel, uninvited to this country, being put up in hotels,' he said. 'I used to be a staunch Labour voter, but they don't represent people like me anymore, the working class. You go in that pub over there and you tell them you vote Labour? Forget it. You wouldn't get out alive.'

Weeks later, Keir Starmer would announce a U-turn on his cuts to the winter fuel allowance, widely seen as a response to the by-election result.

In the hours after winning in Runcorn, Reform UK went on to win more than 600 council seats, two mayoral authorities and take control of ten English councils. The results far exceeded the expectations of Nigel Farage. Anyone who hadn't already considered the prospect of Prime Minister Nigel Farage certainly was now. The century-old two-party domination of Westminster politics was on the verge of being blown up for good.

Harry Horton is a political correspondent at ITV News. Before that he was a correspondent in Washington DC.

BY-ELECTION STATISTICS SINCE 1945

Twenty Largest Swings in Percentage Share of Votes

Election	Swing (per cent)	From	To
1983 Bermondsey by-election	44.2	Labour	Liberal
2014 Clacton by-election	44.1	Conservative	UKIP
1973 Lincoln by-election	43	Labour	Democratic Labour
2024 Rochdale by-election	41.8	Labour	Workers Party
1967 Hamilton by-election	37.9	Labour	SNP
2012 Bradford West by-election	36.6	Labour	Respect
1993 Christchurch by-election	35.4	Conservative	Liberal Democrats
2021 North Shropshire by-election	34.2	Conservative	Liberal Democrats
1988 Glasgow Govan by-election	33.1	Labour	SNP
1976 Newcastle-upon-Tyne Central by-election	32.8	Labour	Liberal
1972 Sutton & Cheam by-election	32.6	Conservative	Liberal
1979 Liverpool Edge Hill by-election	30.2	Labour	Liberal
2022 Tiverton & Honiton by-election	29.9	Conservative	Liberal Democrats
1994 Dudley West by-election	29.2	Conservative	Labour
2023 Somerton & Frome by-election	29	Conservative	Liberal Democrats
2003 Brent East by-election	28.9	Labour	Liberal Democrats
2024 Wellingborough by-election	28.5	Conservative	Labour
1993 Newbury by-election	28.4	Conservative	Liberal Democrats
2014 Rochester & Strood by-election	28.3	Conservative	UKIP
2004 Birmingham Hodge Hill by-election	26.7	Labour	Liberal Democrats
1962 Orpington by-election	26.3	Conservative	Liberal
2024 Blackpool South by-election	26.3	Conservative	Labour
1973 Ripon by-election	25.3	Conservative	Liberal
2021 Chesham & Amersham by-election	25.1	Conservative	Liberal Democrats

Ten Largest Swings to an Incumbent Governing Party

Election	Swing (per cent)	From	To
2021 Hartlepool by-election	16	Labour	Conservative
1945 Bournemouth by-election	10.3	Conservative	Labour
1982 Mitcham & Morden by-election	10.2	Labour	Conservative
1878 Worcester by-election	9.9	Liberal	
2017 Copeland by-election	6.7	Labour	
1978 Hamilton by-election	4.5	SNP	Labour
1945 Smethwick by-election	2.9	Conservative	
1997 Beckenham by-election	2.6		
1945 Edinburgh East by-election	2.0		
1978 Berwick & East Lothian by-election	0.8		

Twenty-Five Largest Falls in Percentage Share of Votes

Election	Fall (per cent)	Party	Result
1948 Glasgow Camlachie by-election	51.3	Independent Labour Party	Unionist gain
2024 Rochdale by-election	43.9	Labour	Workers Party gain
2024 Wellingborough by-election	37.6	Conservative	Labour gain
1983 Bermondsey by-election	37.5	Labour	Liberal gain
1969 Birmingham Ladywood by-election	33.4	Labour	Liberal gain
1993 Christchurch by-election	32.5	Conservative	Liberal Democrats gain
2024 Blackpool South by-election	32.2	Conservative	Labour gain
1946 Glasgow Bridgeton by-election	32.1	Independent Labour Party	Independent Labour Party hold
1958 Rochdale by-election	31.7	Conservative	Labour gain
2021 North Shropshire by-election	31.1	Conservative	Liberal Democrats gain
1994 Dudley West by-election	30.2	Conservative	Labour gain
1995 North Down by-election	29.9	Northern Ireland Conservatives	UK Unionist gain from Popular Unionist
1967 Hamilton by-election	29.7	Labour	SNP gain
2004 Birmingham Hodge Hill by-election	29.6	Labour	Labour hold
1961 Paisley by-election	29.5	Unionist	Labour hold

Election	Fall (per cent)	Party	Result
2003 Brent East by-election	29.4	Labour	Liberal Democrats gain
1993 Newbury by-election	29	Conservative	Liberal Democrats gain
1968 Caerphilly by-election	28.7	Labour	Labour hold
1999 Hamilton South by-election	28.7	Labour	Labour hold
2023 Mid Bedfordshire by-election	28.6	Conservative	Labour gain
2014 Clacton by-election	28.4	Conservative	UKIP gain
1962 West Lothian by-election	28.3	Unionist	Labour hold
1979 Liverpool Edge Hill by-election	28.1	Labour	Liberal gain
1958 Torrington by-election	27.7	Conservative	Liberal gain
1968 Oldham West by-election	27.6	Labour	Conservative gain

Thirty Largest Increases in Percentage Share of Votes

Election	Increase in Share (per cent)	Party	Result
1986 East Londonderry by-election	56	UUP	UUP hold
2012 Bradford West by-election	52.8	Respect	Respect gain
1983 Bermondsey by-election	50.9	Liberal	Liberal gain
1986 South Antrim by-election	48.4	UUP	UUP hold
1986 East Antrim by-election	47.5	UUP	UUP hold
1986 North Antrim by-election	43.2	DUP	DUP hold
2016 Batley & Spen by-election	42.6	Labour	Labour hold
1972 Sutton & Cheam by-election	39	Liberal	Liberal gain
1993 Christchurch by-election	38.6	Liberal Democrats	Liberal Democrats gain
1988 Glasgow Govan by-election	38.4	SNP	SNP gain
2022 Tiverton & Honiton by-election	38.1	Liberal Democrats	Liberal Democrats gain
2021 North Shropshire by-election	37.1	Liberal Democrats	Liberal Democrats gain

Election	Increase in Share (per cent)	Party	Result
1979 Liverpool Edge Hill by-election	36.8	Liberal	Liberal gain
2014 Heywood & Middleton by-election	36.1	UKIP	Labour hold
1986 Belfast East by-election	35.7	DUP	DUP hold
1986 Belfast North by-election	35.3	UUP	UUP hold
1973 Glasgow Govan by-election	31.6	SNP	SNP gain
1986 Lagan Valley by-election	31.5	UUP	UUP hold
2021 Chesham & Amersham by-election	30.4	Liberal Democrats	Liberal Democrats gain
1973 Ripon by-election	30.4	Liberal	Liberal gain
2016 Richmond Park by-election	30.3	Liberal Democrats	Liberal Democrats gain
1981 Croydon North West by-election	29.5	Liberal	Liberal gain
1968 Caerphilly by-election	29.3	Plaid Cymru	Labour hold
2003 Brent East by-election	28.5	Liberal Democrats	Liberal Democrats gain
1994 Dudley West by-election	28	Labour	Labour gain
1987 Greenwich by-election	27.9	SDP	SDP gain
1972 Merthyr Tydfil by-election	27.4	Plaid Cymru	Labour gain
1966 Carmarthen by-election	27.4	Plaid Cymru	Plaid Cymru gain
1991 Ribble Valley by-election	27.1	Liberal Democrats	Liberal Democrats gain
1994 Monklands East by-election	26.9	SNP	Labour hold

Ten Largest Winning Shares of the Vote

Candidate	Party	Election	Votes	Share (per cent)
Ernest Gates	Conservative	1940 Middleton & Prestwich by-election	32,036	98.7
Ian Paisley	DUP	1986 North Antrim by-election	33,937	97.4
John Craik-Henderson	Conservative	1940 Leeds North East by-election	23,882	97.1
Charles Key	Labour	1940 Bow & Bromley by-election	11,594	95.8
John Taylor	UUP	1986 Strangford by-election	32,627	94.2
Clifford Forsythe	UUP	1986 South Antrim by-election	30,087	94.1

Candidate	Party	Election	Votes	Share (per cent)
William Ross	UUP	1986 East Londonderry by-election	30,922	93.9
Arthur Woodburn	Labour	1939 Clackmannanshire & East Stirlingshire by-election	15,645	93.7
Spencer Summers	Conservative	1940 Northampton by-election	16,587	93.4
Harry Thorneycroft	Labour	1942 Manchester Clayton by-election	8,892	93.3

Ten Largest Numerical Majorities Overturned

Candidate	Party	Election	Majority Overturned	New Majority
Alistair Strathern	Labour	2023 Mid Bedfordshire by-election	24,664	1,192
Richard Foord	Liberal Democrats	2022 Tiverton & Honiton by-election	24,239	6,144
Sarah Olney	Liberal Democrats	2016 Richmond Park by-election	23,015	1,872
Diana Maddock	Liberal Democrats	1993 Christchurch by-election	23,015	16,427
Helen Morgan	Liberal Democrats	2021 North Shropshire by-election	22,949	5,925
Tim Smith	Conservative	1977 Ashfield by-election	22,915	264
Keir Mather	Labour	2023 Selby & Ainsty by-election	20,137	4,161
Sarah Edwards	Labour	2023 Tamworth by-election	19,634	1,316
Michael Carr	Liberal Democrats	1991 Ribble Valley by-election	19,528	4,601
Jim Sillars	SNP	1988 Glasgow Govan by-election	19,509	3,554

Ten Lowest Winning Shares of the Vote

Candidate	Party	Election	Votes	Share (per cent)
Henry Strauss	Conservative	1946 Combined English Universities by-election	5,483	30
Lisa Forbes	Labour	2019 Peterborough by-election	10,484	30.9
Mike Thornton	Liberal Democrats	2013 Eastleigh by-election	13,342	32.1
Edward Campbell	Conservative	1930 Bromley by-election	12,782	32.4
George Machin	Labour	1973 Dundee East by-election	14,411	32.7

Candidate	Party	Election	Votes	Share (per cent)
Roy Jenkins	SDP	1982 Glasgow Hillhead by-election	10,106	33.4
Guy Barnett	Labour	1962 South Dorset by-election	13,783	33.5
Alistair Strathern	Labour	2023 Mid Bedfordshire by-election	13,872	34.1
James Carmichael	Independent Labour Party	1946 Glasgow Bridgeton by-election	6,351	34.3
Leah Manning	Labour	1931 Islington East by-election	10,591	34.7

Ten Lowest Shares of the Vote for a Major Party

Candidate	Party	Election	Votes	Share (per cent)
Geoff Juby	Liberal Democrats	2014 Rochester & Strood by-election	349	0.9
Lee Dargue	Liberal Democrats	2022 Birmingham Erdington by-election	173	1
Stephen Arrundale	Liberal Democrats	2021 Airdrie & Shotts by-election	220	1
Andrew Hagon	Liberal Democrats	2021 Hartlepool by-election	349	1.2
Roger Goodfellow	Liberal	1948 Glasgow Camlachie by-election	312	1.2
James Scott Duckers	Liberal	1924 Westminster Abbey by-election	291	1.3
Andrew Graham	Liberal Democrats	2014 Clacton by-election	483	1.3
Hugh Annand	Liberal Democrats	2013 South Shields by-election	352	1.4
Robert McCreadie	Liberal Democrats	1989 Glasgow Central by-election	411	1.5
Sunny Virk	Liberal Democrats	2023 Tamworth by-election	417	1.6

Candidates Winning Fewer Than Ten Votes

Votes	Candidate	Party	Election
3	Yolande Kenward	No description	2021 North Shropshire by-election
5	Bill Boaks	Public Safety Democratic Monarchist White Resident	1982 Glasgow Hillhead by-election
5	Smiley Smilie	Independent	2016 Tooting by-election
5	Bobby Smith	No description	2019 Peterborough by-election
5	Kailash Trivedi	Independent Janata Party	1988 Kensington by-election
6	Gary Cooke	No description	2023 Rutherglen & Hamilton West by-election

Votes	Candidate	Party	Election
7	John Connell	Peace – Stop ITN Manipulation	1984 Chesterfield by-election
8	David Bishop	Church of the Militant Elvis Party	2022 Birmingham Erdington by-election
8	Esmond Bevan	Systems Designer	1983 Bermondsey by-election
8	Tony Farnon	Independent	2008 Haltemprice & Howden by-election
8	77 Joseph	Independent	2023 Uxbridge & South Ruislip by-election
8	Norman Scarth	Independent	2008 Haltemprice & Howden by-election
9	Bobby Smith	Bring Back Elmo	2016 Tooting by-election

Twenty Smallest By-Election Majorities Since 1945

Votes	Election	Result
6	2025 Runcorn & Helsby by-election	Reform UK gain
57	1973 Berwick-upon-Tweed by-election	Liberal gain
62	1967 Walthamstow West by-election	Conservative gain
100	1986 West Derbyshire by-election	Conservative hold
205	1965 Leyton by-election	Conservative gain
219	1958 Torrington by-election	Liberal gain
220	1962 Central Norfolk by-election	Conservative hold
264	1977 Ashfield by-election	Conservative gain
289	1982 Birmingham Northfield by-election	Labour gain
293	1950 Dunbartonshire West by-election	Labour hold
323	2021 Batley & Spen by-election	Labour hold
359	1946 Combined English Universities by-election	Conservative gain
365	2008 Glasgow East by-election	SNP gain
395	1948 Glasgow Camlachie by-election	Unionist gain
430	1980 Southend East by-election	Conservative hold
437	1950 Brighouse & Spenborough by-election	Labour hold
452	1946 Heywood & Radcliffe by-election	Labour hold
460	2004 Birmingham Hodge Hill by-election	Labour hold
478	1969 Swindon by-election	Conservative gain
495	2023 Uxbridge & South Ruislip by-election	Conservative hold

Highest Turnouts Since 1918

Election	Turnout (per cent)
1969 Mid Ulster by-election	91.5
1955 Mid Ulster by-election	89.7

Election	Turnout (per cent)
1928 Ashton-under-Lyne by-election	89.1
1981 (August) Fermanagh & South Tyrone by-election	88.6
1956 Mid Ulster by-election	88.4
1923 Tiverton by-election	88.1
1926 Darlington by-election	87.6
1957 Carmarthen by-election	87.4
1981 (April) Fermanagh & South Tyrone by-election	86.9
1925 Stockport by-election	85.7
1950 Brighouse & Spenborough by-election	85.4

Lowest Turnouts Since 1918

Election	Turnout (per cent)
2012 Manchester Central by-election	18.2
1999 Leeds Central by-election	19.6
2022 Southend West by-election	24
1958 Shoreditch & Finsbury by-election	24.9
1999 Wigan by-election	25
2000 Tottenham by-election	25.4
2012 Cardiff South & Penarth by-election	25.7
2016 Batley & Spen by-election	25.8
2022 Stretford & Urmston by-election	25.8
1974 Newham South by-election	25.9
2012 Middlesbrough by-election	26
2012 Croydon North by-election	26.5
2022 Birmingham Erdington by-election	27
2000 West Bromwich West by-election	27.6
2011 Feltham & Heston by-election	28.8
2000 Preston by-election	29.6
1999 Kensington & Chelsea by-election	29.7

By-Elections Featuring Fifteen or More Candidates

Year	Number of Candidates	By-Election
2008	26	Haltemprice & Howden
1993	19	Newbury
1999	18	Kensington & Chelsea
2023	17	Uxbridge & South Ruislip
1984		Chesterfield
2021	16	Batley & Spen
1983		Bermondsey
2003		Brent East
2021		Hartlepool

Year	Number of Candidates	By-Election
1988		Kensington
2019	15	Peterborough
2025		Runcorn & Helsby
2022		Wakefield

Shortest-Serving By-Election Victors Since 1945

Member of Parliament	Election	Party	Duration (days)
Bobby Sands	1981 (April) Fermanagh & South Tyrone by-election	Anti H-Block	25
Michael Carr	1990 (May) Bootle by-election	Labour	57
Oswald O'Brien	1983 Darlington by-election	Labour	77
George Galloway	2024 Rochdale by-election	Workers Party	91
Margo MacDonald	1973 Glasgow Govan by-election	SNP	92
Jane Dodds	2019 Brecon & Radnorshire by-election	Liberal Democrats	97
Charles Beattie	1955 Mid Ulster by-election	UUP	123
Mark Reckless	2014 Rochester & Strood by-election	UKIP	130
Lisa Forbes	2019 Peterborough by-election	Labour	153
Sarah Olney	2016 Richmond Park by-election	Liberal Democrats	153
Nicol Stephen	1991 Kincardine & Deeside by-election	Liberal Democrats	154
Ashok Kumar	1991 Langbaurgh by-election	Liberal Democrats	154
Helen McElhone	1982 Glasgow Queen's Park by-election	Labour	189
David Austick	1973 Ripon by-election	Liberal	217
John Spellar	1982 Birmingham Northfield by-election	Labour	224
Christopher Ward	1969 Swindon by-election	Conservative	231
William McCrea	2000 South Antrim by-election	DUP	259
Parmjit Singh Gill	2004 Leicester South by-election	Liberal Democrats	294
David Colville Anderson	1963 Dumfriesshire by-election	Unionist	309
Steve Tuckwell	2023 Uxbridge & South Ruislip by-election	Conservative	316

Longest Period Without a By-Election

From	To	Period (days)
1 August 2019	6 May 2021	645
20 November 1997	10 June 1999	567
7 November 1991	6 May 1993	546

From	To	Period (days)
12 March 1987	14 July 1988	489
14 February 2002	18 June 2003	483
23 February 2017	3 May 2018	434
12 November 2009	13 January 2011	427
23 May 1974	26 June 1975	399
18 June 2003	15 July 2004	393
29 June 2006	19 July 2007	385

By-Elections Prompted by Assassination

Date of assassination	Member	Detail	By-Election	By-Election Date	Defending Party	Winning Party
15 October 2021	Sir David Amess	Stabbed during a surgery by an Islamic extremist	2022 Southend West by-election	3 February 2022	Conservative	Conservative
16 June 2016	Jo Cox	Killed by a white nationalist	2016 Batley & Spen by-election	20 October 2016	Labour	Labour
30 July 1990	Ian Gow	Killed by Provisional IRA bomb under his car	1990 Eastbourne by-election	18 October 1990	Conservative	Liberal Democrats
12 October 1984	Sir Anthony Berry	Killed by Provisional IRA bombing of Brighton	1984 Enfield Southgate by-election	13 December 1984	Conservative	Conservative
14 November 1981	Rev. Robert Bradford	Shot by Provisional IRA	1982 Belfast South by-election	4 March 1982	UUP	UUP
22 June 1922	Field Marshal Sir Henry Wilson, 1st Baronet	Shot outside his home by IRA gunmen	July 1922 North Down by-election	21 July 1922	UUP	UUP

By-Elections Prompted by Suicide

Member	By-Election	By-Election date	Defending Party	Winning Party
Gordon McMaster	1997 Paisley South by-election	6 November 1997	Labour	Labour
John Heddle	1990 Mid Staffordshire by-election	22 March 1990	Conservative	Labour
Jocelyn Cadbury	1982 Birmingham Northfield by-election	28 October 1982	Conservative	Labour
Bernard Floud	1968 Acton by-election	28 March 1968	Labour	Conservative
Sir Albert Braithwaite	1960 Harrow West by-election	17 March 1960	Conservative	Conservative
Thomas Stamford	1949 Leeds West by-election	21 July 1949	Labour	Labour
John Whittaker	1946 Heywood & Radcliffe by-election	21 February 1946	Labour	Labour
Sir Charles Cayzer	1940 City of Chester by-election	7 March 1940	Conservative	Conservative
Anthony Muirhead	1939 Wells by-election	13 December 1939	Conservative	Conservative
Edward Marjoribanks	1932 Eastbourne by-election	28 April 1932	Conservative	Conservative

By-Elections Prompted by Accidental Death

Date of Death	Member	Detail	By-Election	By-Election date	Defending Party	Winning Party
6 September 2014	Jim Dobbin	Died of alcohol poisoning	2014 Heywood & Middleton by-election	9 October 2014	Labour	Labour
24 February 2000	Michael Colvin	Killed by a house fire	2000 Romsey by-election	4 May 2000	Conservative	Liberal Democrats
7 February 1994	Stephen Milligan	Accidentally choked himself while attempting autoerotic asphyxia	1994 Eastleigh by-election	9 June 1994	Conservative	Liberal Democrats
12 April 1994	Bob Cryer	Killed in a car crash	1994 Bradford South by-election	9 June 1994	Labour	Labour

Date of Death	Member	Detail	By-Election	By-Election date	Defending Party	Winning Party
22 December 1986	David Penhaligon	Killed in a car crash	1987 Truro by-election	12 March 1987	Liberal	Liberal
30 April 1980	Thomas McMillan	Died from injuries received in falling from a bus	1980 Glasgow Central by-election	26 June 1980	Labour	Labour
31 October 1962	Jack Jones	Killed in a car crash	1963 Rotherham by-election	28 March 1963	Labour	Labour
9 December 1958	Sidney Dye	Killed in a car crash	1959 South West Norfolk by-election	25 March 1959	Labour	Labour
3 February 1958	Wilfred Fienburgh	Killed in a car crash	1958 Islington North by-election	15 May 1958	Labour	Labour
3 August 1957	Richard Stokes	Died from injuries received in a car crash	1957 Ipswich by-election	24 October 1957	Labour	Labour
31 January 1953	Sir Walter Smiles	Killed in the MV *Princess Victoria* disaster during the storm surge	1953 North Down by-election	15 April 1953	UUP	UUP
31 May 1952	Thomas Cook	Killed in a car crash	1952 Dundee East by-election	17 July 1952	Labour	Labour
3 September 1948	Evan Durbin	Drowned while swimming	1948 Edmonton by-election	13 November 1948	Labour	Labour
7 October 1947	Joseph Westwood	Killed in a car crash	1948 Stirling & Falkirk by-election	7 October 1948	Labour	Labour
20 December 1947	Sir William Allen	Died from injuries received in a road accident	1948 Armagh by-election	5 March 1948	UUP	UUP

Date of Death	Member	Detail	By-Election	By-Election date	Defending Party	Winning Party
3 June 1947	Dr Richard Clitherow	Died due to an overdose of barbiturates after he had been 'run down and jaded'	1947 Liverpool Edge Hill by-election	11 September 1947	Labour	Labour
6 February 1947	Ellen Wilkinson	Killed by an accidental overdose of medication	1947 Jarrow by-election	7 May 1947	Labour	Labour
28 December 1945	Francis Beattie	Killed in a car crash	1946 Glasgow Cathcart by-election	12 February 1946	Unionist	Unionist
27 July 1945	Alfred Dobbs	Killed in a car crash	1945 Smethwick by-election	1 October 1945	Labour	Labour
5 January 1945	James Walker	Killed in a road accident	1945 Motherwell by-election	12 April 1945	Labour	SNP
16 January 1944	Lieutenant-Colonel Frank Heilgers	Killed in the 1944 Ilford rail crash	1944 Bury St Edmunds by-election	29 February 1944	Conservative	Conservative
9 July 1942	John Jagger	Killed in a motorcycle accident	1942 Manchester Clayton by-election	17 October 1942	Labour	Labour
15 August 1939	Anthony Crossley	Killed in a plane crash	1939 Stretford by-election	8 December 1939	Conservative	Conservative
1 May 1933	Viscount Knebworth	Killed in a plane crash	1933 Hitchin by-election	8 June 1933	Conservative	Conservative

Occasions When an Incumbent Government has Gained a Seat

Party	By-Election	Losing Party
Conservative	2021 Hartlepool by-election	Labour
	2017 Copeland by-election	
	1982 Mitcham & Morden by-election	
	1961 Bristol South-East by-election	
	1960 Brighouse & Spenborough by-election	
	1953 Sunderland South by-election	
	1926 Combined English Universities by-election	Liberal
	1923 Berwick-upon-Tweed by-election	National Liberal
	1922 Hackney South by-election	Independent
	1921 Woolwich East by-election	Labour
	1920 Stockport by-election	Coalition Labour
Labour	1929 Liverpool Scotland by-election	Irish Nationalist
	1929 Preston by-election	Liberal
	1924 Liverpool West Toxteth by-election	Conservative
Liberal	1913 Chesterfield by-election	Labour
	1913 Londonderry City by-election	Irish Unionist
	1912 Hanley by-election	Labour
	1912 Hackney South by-election	Independent